YBM
전략토익
RC

**YBM
전략 토익
RC**

발행인	허문호
발행처	YBM
편집	최정현, Steve Homer, Marilyn Hook
감수	황상길
디자인	DOTS
마케팅	정연철, 박천산, 고영노, 박찬경, 김동진, 김윤하

초판발행 2018년 1월 5일
14쇄발행 2024년 10월 1일

신고일자	1964년 3월 28일
신고번호	제 1964-000003호
주소	서울시 종로구 종로 104
전화	(02) 2000-0515 [구입문의] / (02) 2000-0563 [내용문의]
팩스	(02) 2285-1523
홈페이지	www.ybmbooks.com

ISBN 978-89-17-22876-2

저작권자 © 2018 YBM
이 책의 저작권, 책의 제호 및 디자인에 대한 모든 권리는 출판사인 YBM에게 있습니다.
서면에 의한 저자와 출판사의 허락 없이 내용의 일부 혹은 전부를 인용 및 복제하거나 발췌하는 것을 금합니다.

낙장 및 파본은 교환해 드립니다.
구입 철회는 구매처 규정에 따라 교환 및 환불 처리됩니다.

토익 주관사가 제시하는 토익비법

YBM 전략토익 RC
이렇게 다릅니다!

토익 주관사의 사명감으로 개발했습니다

YBM은 1982년부터 한국의 토익시험을 운영해온 토익 주관사로, 지난 30여 년간 400권이 넘는 토익 교재를 출간, 토익 수험자들의 영어 능력 향상에 이바지했습니다. 이제 YBM이 한 세대 넘게 쌓아 온 전문성을 바탕으로 〈YBM 전략토익 RC〉를 선보입니다.

시험에 나오는 정보들만 실었습니다

쏟아지는 토익 정보들 중에서 토익 고득점을 위해 꼭 알고 있어야 하는 핵심 전략들과 정답 패턴, 빈출 표현들을 엄선해 수록했습니다. 정기시험에 실제 출제되는 표현과 문제 유형들로 각 토익 문항들을 개발, 수험자들이 신토익 환경에 빠르게 적응할 수 있도록 설계했습니다.

ETS 교재 출간 노하우를 고스란히 담았습니다

출제기관 ETS의 토익 교재를 독점 출간하는 YBM이 그동안 쌓아온 노하우를 바탕으로 개발하였습니다. 본 책에 실린 모든 문항과 설명은 출제자의 의도를 정확히 반영하고 분석했기 때문에 타사의 어떤 토익 교재와도 비교할 수 없는 퀄리티를 자랑합니다.

YBM의 모든 노하우가 집대성된 〈YBM 전략토익 RC〉는 최단 시간에 최고의 점수를 토익 수험자 여러분께 약속드립니다.

YBM 토익연구소

CONTENTS

PART 5&6

UNIT 1 문장 구조 ·· 18
- 공식 1   주어나 목적어 자리에는 명사가 답이다.
- 공식 2   There is 뒤에는 명사가 답
- 공식 3   절이 한 개면 동사도 한 개
- 공식 4   빈칸 뒤에 목적어 없으면 자동사 vs. 목적어 있으면 타동사
- 공식 5   be동사 뒤에는 형용사가 답이다.
- 공식 6   「keep+명사」 뒤는 형용사가 답이다.
- PART 6   공식 7   문장 고르기 문제 1 - 대명사를 활용한다.

UNIT 2 명사 ·· 30
- 공식 8   주목보는 명사 자리이다.
- 공식 9   관형명 소형명
- 공식 10   estimate은 명사도 된다.
- 공식 11   복합명사는 통째로 외운다.
- 공식 12   주어와 동사는 수를 일치시킨다.
- 공식 13   불가산명사는 뒤에 (e)s가 붙지 않는다.
- 공식 14   빈칸 앞에 a/the/소유격이 없으면 가산 단수명사는 답이 아니다.
- 공식 15   보기에 명사가 여러 개이면 문맥에 맞는 명사를 고른다.
- PART 6   공식 16   문장 고르기 문제 2 - 지시어를 활용한다.

UNIT 3 대명사 ·· 44
- 공식 17   동사 앞은 주격, 동사/전치사 뒤는 목적격이 답이다.
- 공식 18   명사 앞은 소유격이 답이다.
- 공식 19   주어와 목적어가 같을 때 목적어로 재귀대명사를 쓴다.
- 공식 20   주어 뒤, 목적어 뒤는 재귀대명사가 답이다.
- 공식 21   by 뒤에는 재귀대명사가 1순위이다.
- 공식 22   「------+who/p.p./전치사」는 those가 답이다.
- 공식 23   부정대명사 자리라면 수도 파악한다.
- 공식 24   부정대명사 중에는 짝지어 다니는 표현들이 있다.
- PART 6   공식 25   문장 고르기 문제 3 - 접속부사를 활용한다.

UNIT 4 동사 ·· 58
- 공식 26   동사 문제는 주어의 수부터 확인한다.
- 공식 27   「all of the 명사」가 주어일 때는 명사의 수에 동사의 수를 일치시킨다.
- 공식 28   빈칸 뒤에 목적어 있으면 능동 vs. 목적어 없으면 수동
- 공식 29   수동태가 되어도 빈칸 뒤에 목적어가 있는 동사가 있다.
- 공식 30   명령문이나 조동사 뒤에는 동사원형이 온다.
- 공식 31   yesterday가 보이면 과거시제가 답이다.
- 공식 32   over the past five years가 보이면 have p.p.가 답이다.
- 공식 33   next가 보이면 will이 답이다.
- 공식 34   「If+주어+___, 주어+will」에는 현재시제가 답이다.
- 공식 35   「by the time+주어+과거시제, 주어+___」에는 had p.p.가 답이다.
- PART 6   공식 36   문장 고르기 문제 4 - 빈칸 주변의 동사와 명사를 활용한다.

UNIT 5 To부정사 & 동명사 ······ 74

- **공식 37** 완전한 절 앞/뒤에는 부사 역할의 to부정사가 1순위이다.
- **공식 38** 「allow+목적어」 뒤는 to부정사가 답이다.
- **공식 39** 「명사/형용사+to부정사」 관용 표현을 익혀 두자.
- **공식 40** 전치사 to로 끝나는 관용표현은 ing를 붙여 외운다.
- **공식 41** plan 뒤는 to부정사가 답이다.
- **공식 42** consider 뒤는 동명사가 답이다.
- **공식 43** 빈칸 뒤에 목적어 없으면 명사 vs. 목적어 있으면 동명사
- **공식 44** 전치사 뒤는 동명사가 1순위이다.
- **PART 6 공식 45** 시제 문제 1 - 앞뒤 문장 동사의 시제를 확인한다.

UNIT 6 분사 ······ 88

- **공식 46** 명사 앞 분사는 '명사가 ~하면' ing vs. '명사가 ~되면' p.p.
- **공식 47** 의미가 헷갈리는 분사가 있다.
- **공식 48** 분사가 명사를 뒤에서 수식할 때는 분사 뒤 목적어 유무를 확인한다.
- **공식 49** 명사가 감정을 느끼면 p.p. vs. 못 느끼면 ing
- **공식 50** 절의 앞이나 뒤에 콤마로 연결되는 수식어구가 있으면 분사구문을 떠올리자.
- **공식 51** 부사절 접속사 뒤에 주어가 없으면 분사가 답이다.
- **PART 6 공식 52** 시제 문제 2 - 문서 작성일도 단서가 된다.

UNIT 7 형용사 & 부사 ······ 100

- **공식 53** 관부형명 관형형명
- **공식 54** timely는 형용사다.
- **공식 55** 보기에 형용사/ing/p.p.가 섞여 있으면 형용사를 1순위로 고려한다.
- **공식 56** 「every+단수명사」 vs. 「all+복수명사」
- **공식 57** 「be ___ p.p./ing/형」는 부사가 답이다.
- **공식 58** 완전한 절 앞이나 뒤에는 부사가 붙는다.
- **공식 59** late는 늦게 vs. lately는 최근에
- **공식 60** afterwards는 접속사가 아니라 부사다.
- **PART 6 공식 61** 접속부사 문제는 앞뒤 문장의 관계를 따진다.

UNIT 8 전치사 ······ 114

- **공식 62** 「완전한 절+___」 뒤에 명사구만 남아 있으면 전치사가 1순위이다.
- **공식 63** 「within+기간」 vs. 「before+시점」
- **공식 64** 동사 짝꿍을 보고 고르는 전치사
- **공식 65** 빈칸 뒤에 힌트가 있는 전치사
- **공식 66** regardless of도 전치사이다.
- **공식 67** regarding/given도 전치사이다.
- **공식 68** 움직이면 to/from vs. 고정이면 in/near
- **공식 69** '대상/목적/이유/용도'에는 for가 답이다.
- **PART 6 공식 70** 대명사 문제는 빈칸의 앞 문장에서 명사를 찾는다.

UNIT 9 접속사 ······ 128

- **공식 71** 완전한 절+부사절 접속사+완전한 절
- **공식 72** after는 전치사도 되고, 부사절 접속사도 된다.
- **공식 73** 보기에 부사절 접속사가 여럿일 때는 해석으로 고른다.
- **공식 74** so that도 부사절 접속사이다.
- **공식 75** 빈칸이 명사 자리인데 뒤에 절이 있으면 명사절 접속사가 답이다.

	공식 76	「that+완전한 절」 vs. 「what+불완전한 절」
	공식 77	의문사+ever는 명사절 접속사 또는 부사절 접속사로 쓰인다.
	공식 78	「사람명사+____+주어가 빠진 절」에는 관계사 who가 답이다.
	공식 79	「명사+____+명사+동사」는 관계사 whose가 답이다.
	공식 80	「명사, most of +____+동사」는 관계사 whom/which가 답이다.
	PART 6 공식 81	어휘 문제는 빈칸의 앞뒤 문장에 정답과 유의어가 있다.

UNIT 10 특수구문 ·········· 144

	공식 82	and는 앞뒤로 대등한 품사를 연결한다.
	공식 83	not only가 보이면 but also가 답이다.
	공식 84	「as+___+as」는 원급이 정답이다.
	공식 85	원급 비교는 다양한 관용 표현을 함께 기억한다.
	공식 86	than 앞은 비교급이 답이다.
	공식 87	빈칸 앞에 the가 보이면 비교급보다는 최상급이 답이다.
	공식 88	「If+주어+had p.p., 주어+_____」에는 would have p.p.가 답이다.
	공식 89	「_____+주어+동사원형, 명령문」에는 should가 답이다.
	PART 6 공식 90	문법 문제는 한 문장 안에서 해결한다.

UNIT 11 어휘 1 ·········· 158

	공식 91	제안/요구 동사 뒤에 오는 that절에는 동사원형이 답이다.
	공식 92	「자동사+전치사」는 짝꿍으로 고른다.
	공식 93	inform의 목적어는 '~을/를'이 아니고 '~에게'
	공식 94	address와 issue는 짝꿍이다.
	공식 95	동사를 고를 때는 빈칸 뒤 전치사를 확인한다.
	공식 96	시험에 자주 보이는 전치사 덩어리 표현
	공식 97	「목적어+to부정사」 앞은 require가 답
	공식 98	빈칸 뒤 to부정사는 단서가 될 수 있다.

UNIT 12 어휘 2 ·········· 170

	공식 99	닮은꼴 형용사를 주의한다.
	공식 100	빈칸 뒤 전치사가 단서가 되는 형용사
	공식 101	extensive와 experience는 짝꿍이다.
	공식 102	빈칸 뒤 전치사가 단서가 되는 명사
	공식 103	현재 시제에는 빈도부사부터 넣어본다.
	공식 104	짝꿍을 보고 고르는 부사

PART 7   CHAPTER 1 문제 유형별

UNIT 1 주제/목적 문제 ·········· 182

	공식 105	주제·목적은 지문의 전반부를 주목하라.
	공식 106	주제문의 단서가 되는 빈출 표현을 알아두자.

UNIT 2 세부사항 문제 ·········· 184

	공식 107	문제 키워드와 관련된 대문자, 숫자, 기호부터 찾는다.
	공식 108	요청사항이나 연락 방법을 묻는 문제는 후반부에서 답을 찾는다.

UNIT 3	의도 파악 문제		186
	공식 109	해당 메시지의 바로 앞뒤 메시지에 단서가 있다.	

UNIT 4	Not/True 문제		188
	공식 110	특정 정보를 묻는 문제는 곧바로 지문에서 문제 키워드를 찾는다.	
	공식 111	전반적인 정보를 묻는 문제는 보기를 활용한다.	

UNIT 5	동의어 문제		190
	공식 112	동의어 문제는 반드시 단어 앞뒤를 해석해 본다.	
	공식 113	다의어를 미리 알아 두자.	

UNIT 6	추론 문제		192
	공식 114	추론 문제의 단서는 간접적으로 제시된다.	
	공식 115	대상·출처 문제는 주로 광고문이나 정보문에서 출제된다.	

UNIT 7	문장 삽입 문제		194
	공식 116	문장이 들어갈 위치를 찾을 때는 연결어를 활용한다.	
	공식 117	연결어가 없을 때는 앞뒤 문맥을 활용한다.	

UNIT 8	연계 문제		196
	공식 118	두 지문에 공통적으로 보이는 단어는 반드시 연계된다.	
	공식 119	문제의 키워드가 양식에 보이면 그 주변 단어를 연계 단서로 삼는다.	

Chapter 2 지문 유형별

UNIT 1	편지/이메일		200
	공식 120	편지/이메일은 「목적 → 세부사항 → 요청」 순이다.	
	공식 121	문제에 사람 이름이 있으면 수/발신인부터 확인한다.	

UNIT 2	공지/회람/광고		212
	공식 122	구조가 거의 정해져 있다.	
	공식 123	구인 광고는 자격 요건에 대한 문제가 빈출 유형이다.	

UNIT 3	문자 메시지/온라인 채팅		222
	공식 124	온라인 채팅은 인물 간 관계 파악에 주의한다.	
	공식 125	구어체 표현이 나온다.	

UNIT 4	웹 페이지/안내문		232
	공식 126	정보를 제공하고 설명하는 글로서, 지문 흐름이 정해져 있다.	
	공식 127	웹 페이지/안내문에 자주 나오는 표현들이 있다.	

UNIT 5	기사/발표문		244
	공식 128	단락별 주제를 파악해 둔다.	
	공식 129	인용문에 주목해라.	

UNIT 6	기타 양식		256
	공식 130	*(별표)와 Note(주의 사항) 주변에 답이 있다.	
	공식 131	양식 지문의 종류별로 빈출 항목들이 있다.	

지문별 공략 어휘 268

FINAL TEST

이 책의 구성과 특징

[일목요연한 토익 전략]

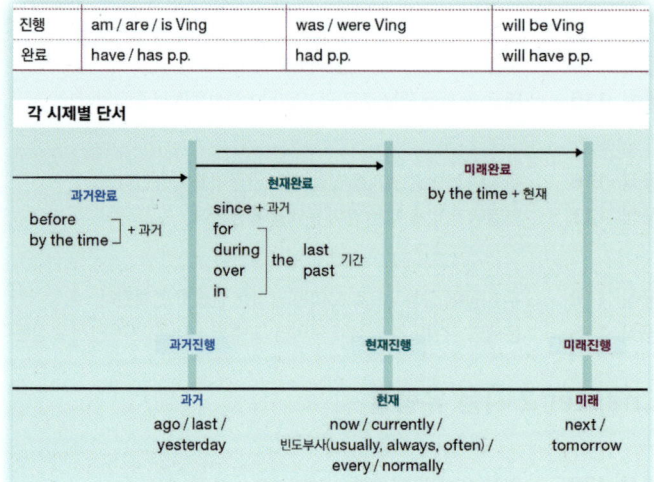

각 Part별 빈출 유형을 분류,
토익 기술 습득을 위한 기본 개념을
단순 명료하게 제시했습니다.

[신토익 데이터 반영]

신토익을 포함한 최근 수년간 기출
데이터를 분석하여, 최빈출 포인트를
빈도 순으로 정리했습니다.

[출제되는 핵심 정보만 집중공략]

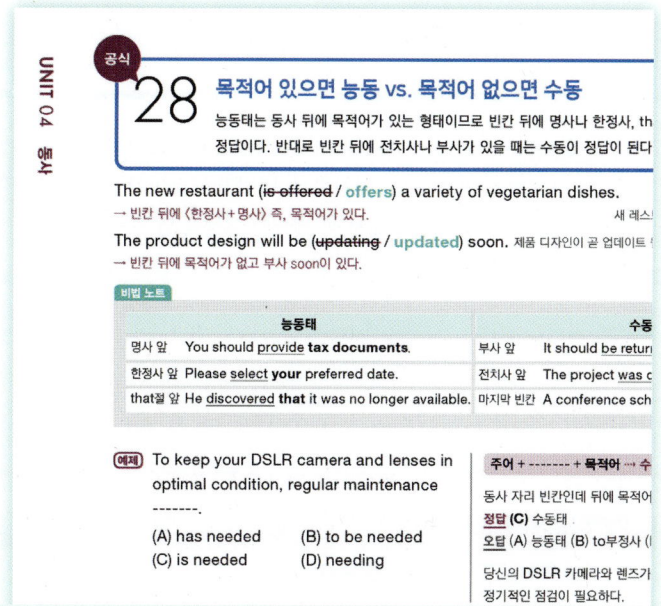

최근 시험에 출제되는 지식들만 콤팩트하게 정리했습니다.

[방대한 실전문제]

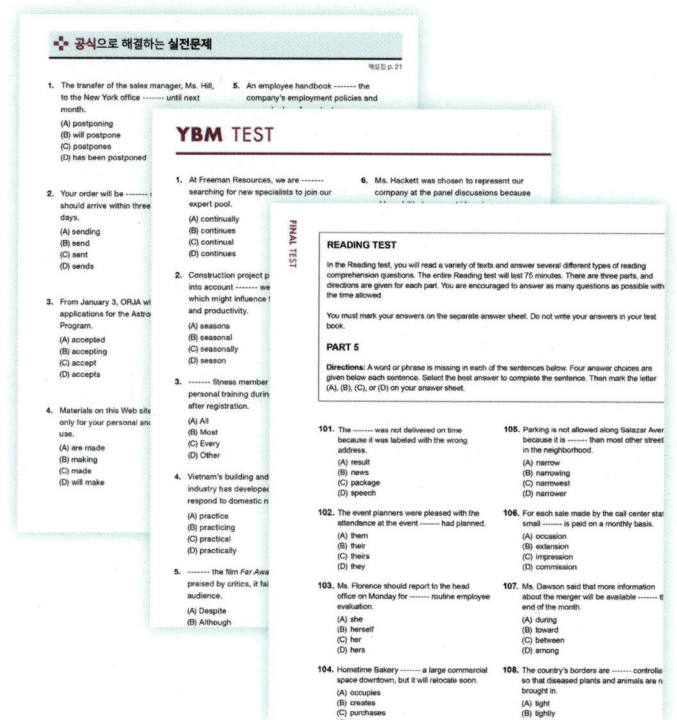

각 공식 학습 후 바로 풀어보는 **공식으로 해결하는 실전문제**, 단원 평가 문제 **YBM TEST**, 시험 직전 점검을 위한 **FINAL TEST**로 구성했습니다.

토익의 구성과 수험 정보

TOEIC은 어떤 시험인가요?

Test of English for International Communication(국제적 의사소통을 위한 영어 시험)의 약자로서, 영어가 모국어가 아닌 사람들이 일상생활 또는 비즈니스 현장에서 꼭 필요한 실용적 영어 구사 능력을 갖추었는가를 평가하는 시험이다.

시험 구성

구성	Part	내용		문항수	시간	배점
듣기 (L/C)	1	사진 묘사		6	45분	495점
	2	질의 & 응답		25		
	3	짧은 대화		39		
	4	짧은 담화		30		
읽기 (R/C)	5	단문 빈칸 채우기(문법/어휘)		30	75분	495점
	6	장문 빈칸 채우기		16		
	7	독해	단일 지문	29		
			이중 지문	10		
			삼중 지문	15		
Total	7 Parts			200문항	120분	990점

TOEIC 접수는 어떻게 하나요?

TOEIC 접수는 한국 토익 위원회 사이트(www.toeic.co.kr)에서 온라인 상으로만 접수가 가능하다. 사이트에서 매월 자세한 접수 일정과 시험 일정 등의 구체적 정보 확인이 가능하니, 미리 일정을 확인하여 접수하도록 한다.

시험장에 반드시 가져가야 할 준비물은요?

신분증   규정 신분증만 가능
(주민등록증, 운전면허증, 기간 만료 전의 여권, 공무원증 등)

필기구   연필, 지우개 (볼펜이나 사인펜은 사용 금지)

시험은 어떻게 진행되나요?

09:20	입실 (09:50 이후는 입실 불가)
09:30 - 09:45	답안지 작성에 관한 오리엔테이션
09:45 - 09:50	휴식
09:50 - 10:05	신분증 확인
10:05 - 10:10	문제지 배부 및 파본 확인
10:10 - 10:55	듣기 평가 (Listening Test)
10:55 - 12:10	독해 평가 (Reading Test)

TOEIC 성적 확인은 어떻게 하죠?

시험일로부터 약 9~11일 후, 인터넷 홈페이지와 어플리케이션을 통해 성적을 확인할 수 있다. TOEIC 성적표는 우편이나 온라인으로 발급받을 수 있다(시험 접수 시 양자택일). 우편으로 발급받을 경우는 성적 발표 후 대략 일주일이 소요되며, 온라인 발급을 선택하면 유효기간 내에 홈페이지에서 본인이 직접 1회에 한해 무료 출력할 수 있다. TOEIC 성적은 시험일로부터 2년간 유효하다.

TOEIC은 몇 점 만점인가요?

TOEIC 점수는 듣기 영역(LC) 점수, 읽기 영역(RC) 점수, 그리고 이 두 영역을 합계한 전체 점수 세 부분으로 구성된다. 각 부분의 점수는 5점 단위이며, 5점에서 495점에 걸쳐 주어지고, 전체 점수는 10점에서 990점까지이며, 만점은 990점이다. TOEIC 성적은 각 문제 유형의 난이도에 따른 점수 환산표에 의해 결정된다.

신토익 경향 분석

PART 5

어휘 문제
동사, 명사, 형용사, 부사와 관련된 어휘 문제가 각각 2~3개씩 골고루 나온다.

품사 문제
명사와 부사와 관련된 품사 문제가 2~3개씩 나오며, 형용사와 관련된 품사 문제가 상대적으로 적은 편이다.

문법 문제
시제와 대명사와 관련된 문법 문제가 2개씩, 한정사와 분사와 관련된 문법 문제가 1개씩 나온다. 시제 문제의 경우 능동태/수동태나 수의 일치와 연계되기도 한다. 그 밖에 한정사, 원급/비교급/최상급, 능동태/수동태, 부정사, 동명사 등과 관련된 문법 문제가 나온다.

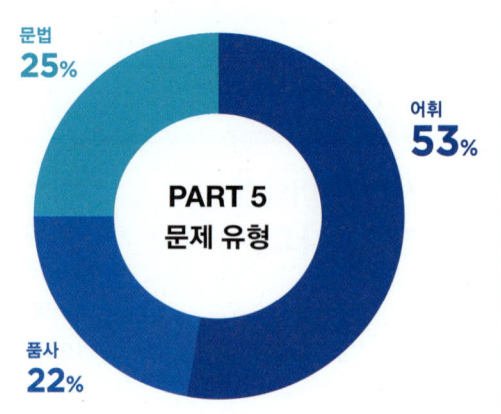

PART 5 문제 유형
- 어휘 53%
- 문법 25%
- 품사 22%

PART 6

4문제로 이루어져 있는 한 지문에 평균적으로 어휘 문제가 2개, 품사나 문법 문제가 1개, 문맥에 맞는 문장 고르기 문제가 1개 들어간다.

어휘 문제
동사, 명사, 부사, 어구와 관련된 어휘 문제는 매번 1~2개씩 나오며, 부사 어휘 문제의 경우 therefore(그러므로)나 however(하지만)처럼 문맥의 흐름을 자연스럽게 연결해 주는 부사가 자주 나온다.

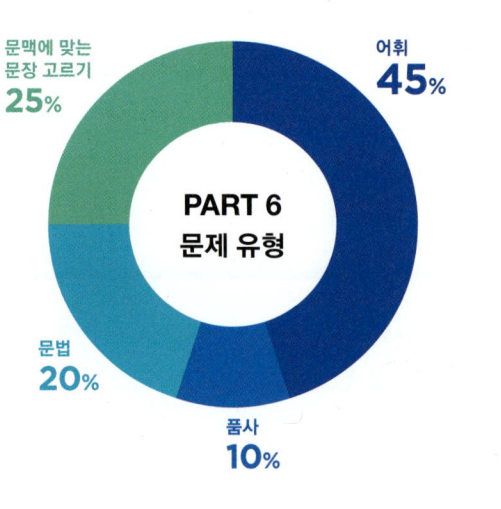

PART 6 문제 유형
- 어휘 45%
- 문맥에 맞는 문장 고르기 25%
- 문법 20%
- 품사 10%

PART 7

- 동의어 문제는 주로 이중 지문이나 삼중 지문에 나온다.
- 연계 문제는 일반적으로 이중 지문에서 한두 문제씩, 삼중 지문에서 두세 문제씩 나온다.
- 의도 파악 문제는 일반적으로 2문항짜리 단일 지문과, 4문항짜리 단일 지문에 각각 한 문제씩 나온다. 지문 유형은 문자 메시지(text-message chain)나 온라인 채팅(online chat discussion)이다.
- 문장 삽입 문제는 일반적으로 3문항짜리 단일 지문과, 4문항짜리 단일 지문에 각각 한 문제씩 나온다. 지문 유형은 주로 기사, 이메일/편지이다.

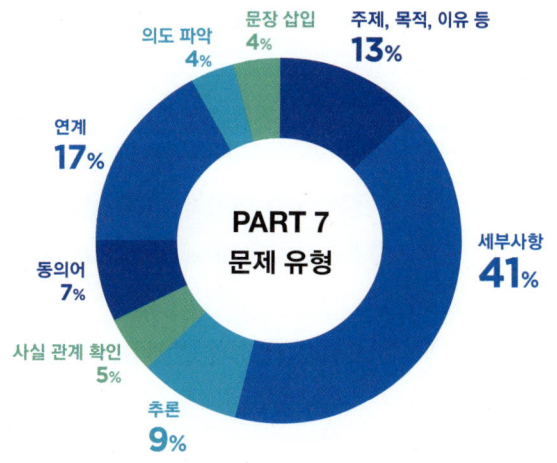

- 이메일/편지, 기사 유형 지문은 거의 항상 나오는 편이며 많은 경우 합해서 전체의 50~60%에 이르기도 한다.
- 기타 지문 유형으로 agenda, brochure, comment card, coupon, flyer, instructions, invitation, invoice, job-fair posting, list, menu, policy statement, program, receipt, report, schedule, sign, survey, voucher 등 다양한 자료가 골고루 나온다.

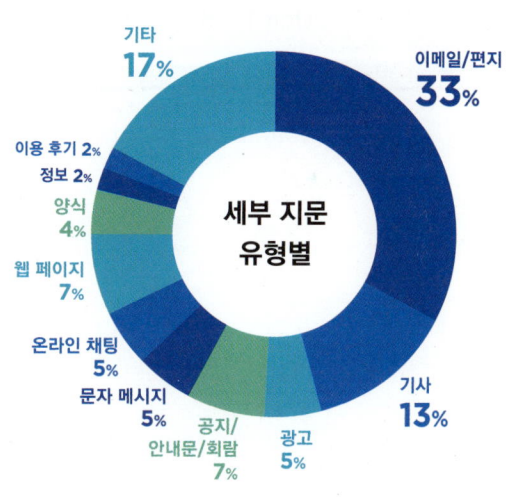

(이중 지문과 삼중 지문 속의 지문들을 모두 낱개로 계산함 – 총 23지문)

STUDY PLAN

2주 완성 플랜
단기간에 토익을 마스터하고자 중고급 학습자를 위한 2주 완성 플랜

	DAY 1 월	DAY 2 화	DAY 3 수	DAY 4 목	DAY 5 금
WEEK 1	PART 5 & 6 Unit 1, 2	PART 5 & 6 Unit 3, 4	PART 5 & 6 Unit 5, 6	PART 5 & 6 Unit 7 ~ 9	PART 5 & 6 Unit 10 ~ 12
	DAY 6 월	DAY 7 화	DAY 8 수	DAY 9 목	DAY 10 금
WEEK 2	PART 7 CHAPTER 1 Unit 1 ~ 8	PART 7 CHAPTER 2 Unit 1, 2	PART 7 CHAPTER 2 Unit 3, 4	PART 7 CHAPTER 2 Unit 5, 6	Final Test

4주 완성 플랜

토익을 차근차근 정복하고 싶은 초중급 학습자를 위한 4주 완성 플랜

	DAY 1 월	DAY 2 화	DAY 3 수	DAY 4 목	DAY 5 금
WEEK 1	PART 5 & 6 Unit 1	PART 5 & 6 Unit 2	PART 5 & 6 Unit 3	PART 5 & 6 Unit 4	PART 5 & 6 Unit 5
	DAY 6 월	DAY 7 화	DAY 8 수	DAY 9 목	DAY 10 금
WEEK 2	PART 5 & 6 Unit 6	PART 5 & 6 Unit 7	PART 5 & 6 Unit 8	PART 5 & 6 Unit 9	PART 5 & 6 Unit 10
	DAY 11 월	DAY 12 화	DAY 13 수	DAY 14 목	DAY 15 금
WEEK 3	PART 5 & 6 Unit 11	PART 5 & 6 Unit 12	PART 7 CHAPTER 1 Unit 1 ~ 8	PART 7 CHAPTER 2 Unit 1	PART 7 CHAPTER 2 Unit 2
	DAY 16 월	DAY 17 화	DAY 18 수	DAY 19 목	DAY 20 금
WEEK 4	PART 7 CHAPTER 2 Unit 3	PART 7 CHAPTER 2 Unit 4	PART 7 CHAPTER 2 Unit 5	PART 7 CHAPTER 2 Unit 6	Final Test

UNIT
01-12

UNIT 01 문장 구조

기본 학습

문장을 볼 때 한눈에 주어와 동사를 찾을 수 있어야 한다. 주어와 동사를 기준으로 목적어, 보어, 수식어 등의 문장 구조를 파악해, 각 자리에 들어갈 적절한 품사를 고르는 것이 파트 5, 6 문제의 핵심이다.

주어 ⓢ

'누가[무엇이] ~한다/~이다'에서 '누가[무엇이]'에 해당하는 말로, 주로 문장 맨 앞에 온다. 주어 자리에는 명사 혹은 명사처럼 쓸 수 있는 말(대명사, 동명사구, 명사절)이 들어간다.

명사(구)	**Wisdom Books** values the security of our customers' information. 위즈덤 북스는 고객 정보 보호를 중요하게 여긴다
대명사	**You** are invited to the upcoming event. 귀하를 곧 있을 행사에 초대합니다.
동명사구	**Travelling abroad** is a great way to learn about other cultures. 해외 여행은 다른 문화에 대해 배울 수 있는 훌륭한 방법이다.
명사절	**Whoever comes first** will be served first. 먼저 오는 사람이 누구든지 간에 먼저 서비스를 받을 것이다.

동사 ⓥ

행위나 상태를 나타내는 말로 우리말 '~이다/~하다'에 해당한다. 모든 문장에는 동사가 반드시 들어가야 하고, 주어 뒤에 온다. 동사 자리에는 동사 혹은 「조동사+동사원형」이 들어가며, to부정사, 동명사, 분사는 동사 자리에 들어갈 수 없다.

동사의 종류 동사의 종류에 따라 뒤에 무엇이 어떤 순서로 오는지 결정된다.

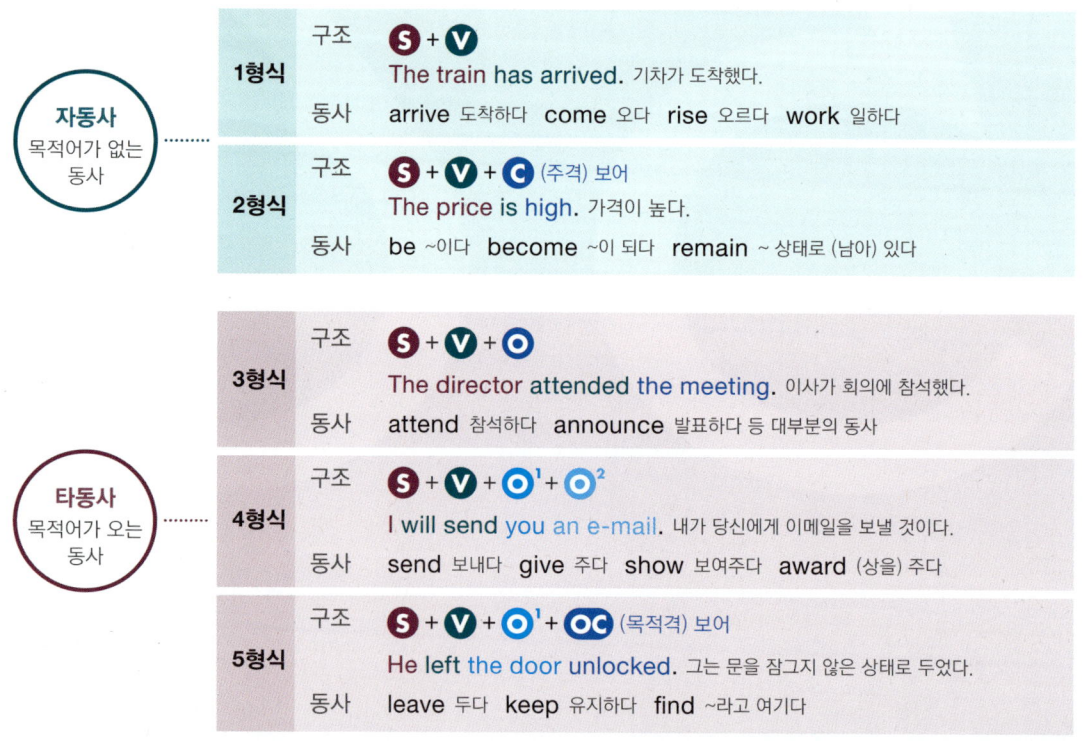

자동사 목적어가 없는 동사

- **1형식**
  - 구조: Ⓢ + Ⓥ
  - The train has arrived. 기차가 도착했다.
  - 동사: arrive 도착하다 come 오다 rise 오르다 work 일하다

- **2형식**
  - 구조: Ⓢ + Ⓥ + Ⓒ (주격) 보어
  - The price is high. 가격이 높다.
  - 동사: be ~이다 become ~이 되다 remain ~ 상태로 (남아) 있다

타동사 목적어가 오는 동사

- **3형식**
  - 구조: Ⓢ + Ⓥ + Ⓞ
  - The director attended the meeting. 이사가 회의에 참석했다.
  - 동사: attend 참석하다 announce 발표하다 등 대부분의 동사

- **4형식**
  - 구조: Ⓢ + Ⓥ + Ⓞ¹ + Ⓞ²
  - I will send you an e-mail. 내가 당신에게 이메일을 보낼 것이다.
  - 동사: send 보내다 give 주다 show 보여주다 award (상을) 주다

- **5형식**
  - 구조: Ⓢ + Ⓥ + Ⓞ¹ + ⓄⒸ (목적격) 보어
  - He left the door unlocked. 그는 문을 잠그지 않은 상태로 두었다.
  - 동사: leave 두다 keep 유지하다 find ~라고 여기다

목적어 ◎

동사의 대상이 되는 말로 우리말 '~을[를]'에 해당하며, 타동사 뒤나 전치사 뒤에 온다. 목적어 자리에는 명사 혹은 명사처럼 쓸 수 있는 말(대명사, 동명사구, to부정사구, 명사절)이 들어간다.

명사(구)	Please complete **the application form**. 신청서를 작성하시오.
대명사	Some of **you** own small businesses. 여러분 중 일부는 작은 사업체를 소유하고 있다.
동명사구	YelloSage Catering is considering **opening its third restaurant** in the city. 옐로우세이지 케이터링은 도시에 세 번째 식당을 여는 것을 고려하고 있다.
to부정사구	Fantek has decided **to discontinue production** of the Fantom 4. 팬텍 사는 팬텀 4의 생산을 중단하기로 했다.
명사절	Mr. Kay announced **that the company is preparing** to launch a new line of products. 회사가 신제품 출시를 준비 중이라고 케이 씨가 발표했다.

보어 ◉

말 그대로 의미를 보충해 주는 말이다. 주격 보어는 주어를 보충 설명하는 말로서 2형식 동사 뒤에 오고, 목적어를 보충 설명하는 목적격 보어는 「5형식 동사 + 목적어」 뒤에 온다. 보어 자리에는 주로 형용사(상태나 성질을 나타낼 때)나 명사(동격일 때)가 들어가지만, 동사의 종류에 따라 to부정사, 분사, 동사원형 등이 들어가기도 한다.

주격 보어	Mr. Williams may be **late** due to traffic congestion. 윌리엄즈 씨는 교통 혼잡 때문에 늦을 수도 있다.
	The building became **a museum** two years ago. 그 건물은 2년 전에 박물관이 되었다.
목적격 보어	The management found the sales results **disappointing**. 경영진은 판매 결과가 실망스럽다고 생각했다.
	The manager asked his team members **to work** overtime. 매니저가 팀원들에게 추가 근무를 하라고 요청했다.

➕ 가주어와 가목적어

- **가주어 it**: to부정사구, that절 같은 긴 주어는 뒤로 보내고 주어 자리에 가주어 it을 대신 쓴다.

  (It) is important **to comply** with the company regulations. 회사 규정을 준수하는 것은 중요하다.
         진주어

  (It) is essential **that** new employees go through the training sessions. 신입사원들은 훈련받는 것이 필수적이다.
     진주어

- **가목적어 it**: 5형식 동사 뒤 it은 주로 가목적어로, 뒤에 진짜 목적어(to부정사구, that절)가 온다.

  You will find (it) easy **to learn** the new software program.
       목적 보어 목적어
  당신은 새로운 소프트웨어 프로그램이 배우기 쉽다는 것을 알게 될 것이다.

  The marketing director considers (it) frustrating **that** there might be a budget cut.
            목적 보어   목적어
  마케팅 이사가 예산 삭감이 있을 수 있다는 것을 불만스럽게 생각한다.

UNIT 01 문장 구조

공식 1 주어나 목적어 자리에는 명사가 답이다.

주어와 목적어는 주로 명사가 들어가는 자리이다. 문장 맨 앞이나 동사 앞쪽에 빈칸이 있으면 주어 자리, 타동사나 전치사 뒤에 빈칸이 있으면 목적어 자리를 묻는 문제이므로 명사를 고른다.

(**Interest** / ~~Interested~~) in Sherwood Park remains strong after an early burst of enthusiasm.
→ 문장 앞 주어 자리
초기 열광적이었던 반응 이후에도 셔우드 파크에 대한 관심이 여전히 높다.

A number of passengers are expressing (~~irritated~~ / **irritation**) with the noise of other commuters.
→ 동사 are expressing의 목적어 자리
많은 승객들이 다른 출퇴근자들의 소음에 불만을 표하고 있다.

비법 노트 빈출 명사 자리

- **형용사 뒤** The current **schedule** is valid until tomorrow. 현재 스케줄은 내일까지 유효합니다.
  관사 형용사   명사
- **소유격 뒤** Please submit your **reports** by March 9. 보고서를 3월 9일까지 제출하세요.
  소유격 명사
- **접속사 뒤** Please note that **products** are delivered within five days. 제품은 5일 이내로 배송됨을 유념해주세요.
  접속사 명사

[예제] ------- to Churton Street will be permanently closed, effective from February 12.

(A) Access   (B) Accessed
(C) Accessibly   (D) Accessible

------- + (수식어구) + 동사 → 주어 자리

문장 맨 앞, 동사(will be) 앞 빈칸이므로 주어 자리

정답 (A) 명사

2월 12일 이후로 처튼 가 통행이 영구적으로 통제될 것이다.

공식 2 There is 뒤에는 명사가 답

「There+be동사 ~(~가 있다)」 구문에서는 be동사 뒤가 주어 자리이므로, There is/are 뒤 빈칸에는 명사가 들어간다. 이때 is 뒤에는 단수명사, are 뒤에는 복수명사가 온다.

Some investors are concerned that there is a (**possibility** / ~~possible~~) of substantial losses.
일부 투자자들이 상당한 손실 가능성이 있을 수 있다는 점을 우려하고 있다.

There were some (~~error~~ / **errors**) on the server while it was processing the request.
요청을 처리하는 동안 서버에 오류가 있었다.

비법 노트

- **There remain** ~이 남아 있다
  There **remains** only one **option**. 한 개의 선택권만이 남아있다.
- **There exist** ~이 존재하다
  There **exist** several **differences** between them. 그들 사이엔 몇 가지 차이점이 존재한다.

[예제] There are increasingly many ------- thrown out only after a single use.

(A) producing   (B) product
(C) products   (D) produced

there are + ------- → 복수명사 자리

정답 (C)

점점 더 많은 제품들이 한 번만 쓰고 버려지고 있다.

공식으로 해결하는 실전문제

1. ------- are advised to leave home earlier than usual this morning as heavy traffic is expected.
   (A) Commuters
   (B) Commute
   (C) Commutable
   (D) Commuting

2. All employees are eligible for ------- if they consistently achieve their sales targets.
   (A) promote
   (B) promotes
   (C) promotion
   (D) promotional

3. Livewell Group, an international health insurance -------, continues to satisfy an increasing need for access to healthcare.
   (A) providing
   (B) provider
   (C) provided
   (D) provides

4. Weizen Food Industries' ------- for the first-quarter are expected to beat the market's expectations.
   (A) earnings
   (B) earned
   (C) earn
   (D) earns

5. Because our shopping center is located in the heart of the city, there is easy ------- to public transportation.
   (A) access
   (B) accessing
   (C) accessible
   (D) accessed

6. The study identifies the possible ------- of on-demand business aviation as compared with scheduled airline transportation.
   (A) beneficial
   (B) benefits
   (C) beneficially
   (D) benefited

7. Researchers admit that there are ------- to the data, due mainly to incomplete knowledge of the marine ecosystem.
   (A) limitation
   (B) limitless
   (C) limited
   (D) limitations

8. ------- of Black Hills Institute will be recognized for their years of service and dedication during the annual Employee Awards Reception.
   (A) Employs
   (B) Employed
   (C) Employment
   (D) Employees

공식 3. 절이 한 개면 동사도 한 개

절에는 반드시 하나의 동사가 필요하다. 따라서 빈칸이 소속된 절 하나에 동사가 따로 보이지 않으면 빈칸은 동사 자리이다. 접속사로 두 개의 절이 연결된 문장은 동사도 두 개가 있어야 한다.

SolaWorld (**has implemented** / ~~to implement~~) cost-cutting measures to reduce operating expenses.
→ 문장에 동사가 없으므로 빈칸은 동사 자리
솔라월드는 운영비를 줄이기 위해 비용 절감 조치를 실시했다.

Please call customer service <u>if</u> you (~~encountering~~ / **encounter**) any problems.
→ if로 연결된 절에 동사가 없으므로 빈칸은 동사 자리
어떠한 문제라도 접하게 될 경우 고객 서비스 부서로 전화하세요.

비법 노트
- **동사가 될 수 있는 형태**
  ① 동사   ② 조동사+동사원형   ③ be동사+-ing/p.p.   ④ have+p.p.
- **동사가 될 수 없는 오답 형태**
  ① to+동사원형   ② 분사(-ing/p.p.)   ③ 동명사(-ing)

[예제] ABS's streaming service ------- a variety of movies and popular TV shows.
(A) including   (B) to include
(C) includes   (D) inclusion

문장에 동사가 없다 ⋯ 동사 자리
주어 뒤에 동사가 없으므로 빈칸은 동사 자리
정답 (C)
ABS의 스트리밍 서비스는 다양한 영화와 인기 TV 쇼를 포함한다.

공식 4. 빈칸 뒤에 목적어 없으면 자동사 vs. 목적어 있으면 타동사

자동사는 뒤에 목적어가 붙지 않고, 타동사는 목적어가 와야 한다. 따라서 동사가 능동형인데 빈칸 뒤에 부사나 전치사만 있으면 자동사, 목적어가 있으면 타동사가 답이다.

Mystagram Stories has (~~appointed~~ / **emerged**) as a clear favorite for marketers.
→ 빈칸 뒤에 전치사 as가 있으므로 자동사 자리
미스타그램 스토리즈가 마케터들의 총아로 부상했다.

Naomi (**entered** / ~~came~~) the annual Flower Arranging Competition. 나오미가 연례 꽃꽂이 대회에 출전했다.
→ 빈칸 뒤에 목적어 the ~ Competition이 있으므로 자동사 came은 오답

비법 노트
- **빈출 자동사**

rise 오르다	fall 떨어지다	arrive 도착하다	function 기능하다
work 일하다	emerge 부상하다	commence 시작되다	proceed 진행하다, 나아가다
expire 만료되다	occur 발생하다	happen 일어나다	take place 일어나다

[예제] The annual Outstanding Staff Awards Ceremony will ------- promptly at 6 P.M.
(A) hold   (B) commence
(C) give   (D) honor

빈칸 뒤에 목적어가 없다 ⋯ 자동사
빈칸 뒤에 목적어 없이 부사가 바로 왔다.
정답 (B) 자동사(시작하다)   **오답** (A), (C), (D) 타동사
연례 우수 직원 시상식이 오후 6시 정각에 열릴 것이다.

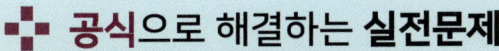

1. Upon request, we ------- black and green olives in various types of packaging.
   (A) provision
   (B) providing
   (C) provider
   (D) provide

2. Pet foods offered by Flatev ------- in a variety of flavors and can be customized to suit your pets' preferences.
   (A) make
   (B) buy
   (C) come
   (D) find

3. If you ------- any difficulties installing the software, please visit the Tech4U Support FAQ pages.
   (A) experiencing
   (B) to experience
   (C) having experienced
   (D) experience

4. Alex Vitello has been ------- hard as a risk consultant at Keid Auditing Co. for five years.
   (A) working
   (B) visiting
   (C) attending
   (D) hiring

5. The London Marathon will ------- according to the plan, despite the storm threat.
   (A) cancel
   (B) proceed
   (C) delay
   (D) complete

6. The maintenance staff in Kona Toy's factory ensures that the production systems ------- properly.
   (A) functional
   (B) functioning
   (C) are functioning
   (D) functionally

7. According to *Business Weekly*, increased capacity and intense competition ------- airlines from raising their rates.
   (A) prevent
   (B) prevention
   (C) preventable
   (D) preventably

8. The Ho-Ran Art Museum ------- several temporary exhibitions every year in collaboration with emerging artists.
   (A) expires
   (B) holds
   (C) occurs
   (D) arrives

공식 5. be동사 뒤에는 형용사가 답이다.

be동사 같은 2형식 동사 뒤에는 주어를 보충 설명해 주는 말인 보어가 온다. 보어가 주어와 동격 관계일 때는 명사가 오기도 하지만, 토익 문제에서는 주어의 상태나 성질을 나타내는 형용사가 주로 정답이다.

Mr. Milton was (~~reluctantly~~ / **reluctant**) to take on new responsibilities at work.
→ 부사는 be동사 was의 보어가 될 수 없다.   밀턴 씨는 회사에서 새로운 업무를 맡기를 주저했다.

The results were completely (**different** / ~~differently~~) from what we had expected.
결과가 우리가 예상했던 것과 완전히 달랐다.

비법 노트

- **2형식 동사**
  - be (상태가) ~하다
  - feel ~하게 느끼다
  - become/turn ~하게 되다
  - prove ~라고 판명되다
  - remain/stay ~한 상태로 있다
  - look/seem/appear ~해 보이다

[예제] Funds from the sale of personal assets are ------- if the appropriate documentation is available.

(A) accepts (B) accepting
(C) acceptable (D) acceptance

be동사 뒤 빈칸 ⋯→ 형용사 자리

be동사 뒤 보어 자리로, 주어인 Funds의 상태나 성질을 나타내는 말인 형용사가 적절하다.
정답 (C) 형용사
적절한 서류가 구비될 수 있다면 개인 자산의 판매로부터 나온 자금도 수용할 수 있다.

공식 6. 「keep + 명사」 뒤는 형용사가 답이다.

5형식 문장 「주어 + 동사 + 목적어 + 목적격 보어」에서 목적격 보어 자리에는 명사나 형용사가 올 수 있는데, 주로 형용사가 정답이다.

It is important that we keep customer records (**private** / ~~privately~~). 고객 정보를 비공개로 유지하는 것은 중요하다
→ 빈칸은 주어 we가 아니라 목적어 customer records의 상태를 나타내는 목적격 보어 자리

Many users found the instructions for the Z-phone 8 (**confusing** / ~~confuse~~).
많은 사용자들이 Z-phone 8의 사용 설명서가 헷갈린다고 생각했다.

비법 노트

- **5형식 동사**
  - keep ⋯를 ~하게 유지하다
  - make ⋯를 ~하게 만들다
  - find ⋯를 ~라고 알게 되다
  - leave ⋯를 ~하게 두다
  - consider/deem ⋯를 ~하다고 여기다

[예제] According to the employment contract, our employees should keep company information -------.

(A) confidential (B) confidence
(C) confidentially (D) confide

keep + 명사 + ------- ⋯→ 형용사 자리

목적격 보어 자리인데, 빈칸이 company information의 성질을 나타낸다.
정답 (A) 형용사 **오답** (B) 명사 (D) 동사
고용 계약에 따르면, 우리 직원들은 회사 정보를 기밀로 해야 한다.

공식으로 해결하는 실전문제

1. Strong skills and extensive knowledge are ------- to attain long-term financial success.
   (A) necessitate
   (B) necessary
   (C) necessarily
   (D) necessitating

2. Many of the employees at Jupitor Corporation consider the leadership training programs quite -------.
   (A) use
   (B) usefulness
   (C) uses
   (D) useful

3. You will find the experience of working on a volunteer project in South Africa truly -------.
   (A) to reward
   (B) rewarding
   (C) rewardingly
   (D) reward

4. A marketing expert, Ronda Eagers stated that companies should remain politically ------- on social media.
   (A) neutral
   (B) neutrally
   (C) neutralizing
   (D) neutralization

5. After pretesting of the data collection tools and processes, the research team deemed some revisions -------.
   (A) essence
   (B) essentialize
   (C) essentially
   (D) essential

6. The changes to the company's policies on the use and maintenance of equipment will become ------- starting next Monday.
   (A) effective
   (B) effect
   (C) effectively
   (D) effecting

7. The study on the diets of the region's children found that consumption of fresh foods was surprisingly -------.
   (A) lowest
   (B) lowly
   (C) low
   (D) lows

8. By subscribing to our Infographic service, you can ------- the payment process easy for your online customers.
   (A) build
   (B) acquire
   (C) make
   (D) offer

YBM TEST

1. Mr. Shulda's ------- for water skiing has led to his second consecutive Wisconsin Water Skiing Championship.

   (A) enthused
   (B) enthusiastic
   (C) enthusiastically
   (D) enthusiasm

2. Satisfaction with the National Health Care Service has ------- significantly, according to an analysis of the influential Spanish Social Attitudes survey.

   (A) expected
   (B) evaluated
   (C) risen
   (D) provided

3. Humphrey Penn, the mayor of Philadelphia stated that massive ------- would be made to bring new investment into in the city.

   (A) effortless
   (B) effortlessly
   (C) effortful
   (D) efforts

4. Security personnel must make sure that all visitors to the building ------- to reception.

   (A) to report
   (B) reporter
   (C) report
   (D) reporting

5. Since its ------- in 1925, Green Dairy Products, Inc. has been a leading manufacturer of butter and dairy products.

   (A) establishes
   (B) established
   (C) establish
   (D) establishment

6. In preparation for the workshop, it is ------- to carefully match instructors with workshop attendees.

   (A) importance
   (B) important
   (C) importantly
   (D) more importantly

7. The ------- of the graphic designer include developing designs and producing materials for online promotions.

   (A) responsible
   (B) responsibilities
   (C) responsive
   (D) responsibly

8. It is unfortunate ------- we cannot provide an approximate delivery time for your shipment.

   (A) there
   (B) this
   (C) that
   (D) to

9. Saga Carman has made its digital music player more ------- by adding up-to-date features.

   (A) attracting
   (B) attracts
   (C) attractively
   (D) attractive

10. Our database system indicates that your subscription to *Office Always* will ------- on August 31.

    (A) expire
    (B) cover
    (C) install
    (D) guarantee

11. Franco Guller watches are instantly ------- for their unique and beautiful design.

    (A) recognizable
    (B) recognizing
    (C) recognizably
    (D) recognizes

12. *GardenDeco* magazine publishes four ------- per year, plus one special edition once every few years.

    (A) issuing
    (B) to issue
    (C) issues
    (D) issued

13. There are positive ------- that the world economy will finally see the pace of growth improve after a long recession.

    (A) signs
    (B) sign
    (C) signed
    (D) to sign

14. It is not easy to keep wireless Internet connections fast and ------- on subways.

    (A) stability
    (B) stabilize
    (C) stable
    (D) stably

15. Child safety car seats became increasingly ------- and are now legally required for children under six.

    (A) commonly
    (B) common
    (C) commons
    (D) commonest

16. Advances in data storage have made it difficult ------- the personal privacy.

    (A) to violate
    (B) violation
    (C) violate
    (D) violates

17. It is not ------- for companies to develop error-free software because doing so is too costly.

    (A) feasibly
    (B) feasibleness
    (C) feasibility
    (D) feasible

18. FunPlay can ------- the Chinese market by partnering with a Chinese gaming giant.

    (A) access
    (B) proceed
    (C) work
    (D) emerge

19. After a mixed reaction, the architect behind the city's tallest tower ------- the revised design.

    (A) explanation
    (B) explained
    (C) explainable
    (D) to explain

20. Ms. Green ------- to open another vegetarian restaurant after the success of her first one.

    (A) deciding
    (B) decision
    (C) decidedly
    (D) decided

PART 6

> **공식 7** 문장 고르기 문제 1 – 대명사를 활용한다.
>
> 파트 6에는 문장으로 구성된 보기가 주어지고, 문맥상 적절한 문장을 고르는 문제가 출제된다.
> 대명사는 앞에 나온 명사를 대신하는 말이므로, 문장 고르기 문제에서 중요한 단서로 활용할 수 있다.

만점 전략

1. 보기 문장에 대명사가 보일 경우 ➜ 빈칸의 앞 문장에 있는 명사를 대신한 말인지 확인한다.

   [앞 문장] a blender ⋯→ [보기] **it** is powerful
   [앞 문장] a user manual ⋯→ [보기] download **one**

2. 빈칸 뒤 문장에 대명사가 보일 경우 ➜ 보기 문장에 있는 명사를 대신한 말인지 확인한다.

   [뒤 문장] <u>Both</u> are famous ~ ⋯→ [보기] **ABC company and XYZ company** ~

예제 해설집 p.6

Doris of Houston, TX
Comments written on Aug. 19

I wanted to upgrade my phone so I bought EZ Smart. Compared with my old phone, this phone has more interesting applications to use and it has a better camera. I'm not a technical person but I've had no difficulty learning how to use it. Overall, ❶**I've had a very pleasant experience with this EZ Smart.** -------.

(A) My subscription will expire next year.
(B) I'd be happy to complete the survey.
(C) I don't use my smartphone that much.
(D) I'd definitely recommend ❷**it** to my friends.

대명사를 활용하여 문장 고르기

❶ 빈칸 앞: EZ 스마트폰에 만족했다.
❷ 보기 문장의 대명사: it이 EZ 스마트폰을 대신하는 대명사
⋯→ 스마트폰을 긍정적으로 평가하고 나서, 다른 사람들에게 그것을 추천하겠다고 하는 흐름이 자연스럽다.

정답 (D) 친구들에게 그것을 틀림없이 추천할 거예요.

YBM TEST

Questions 1-4 refer to the following article.

Alma Travel and Diversity Travel Management to Merge

Cupertino, CA, Aug. 4 – Alma Travel and Diversity Travel Management announced this week that they are to merge effective September 1. -------. With combined gross annual sales of ------- $70 million, the new company is expected to create the sixth ------- travel management company in the country. Pat Hoeke, the current chief executive of Alma Travel, will lead the merger of the two businesses, which will be headquartered in Alma's existing building on Miller Avenue in Cupertino.

"This merger allows us to put together the best talent and experience from both companies. We will have exciting ------- to create something that is truly market leading with increased buying power, expertise, and a broader customer base," said Mr. Hoeke.

1. (A) Both are leading players in the travel management industry.
   (B) Diversity Travel Management has been in business for over 30 years.
   (C) The firm has suffered from financial difficulties.
   (D) Offers from other companies have been rejected.

2. (A) over
   (B) beneath
   (C) even
   (D) between

3. (A) larger
   (B) large
   (C) largest
   (D) largely

4. (A) substitutes
   (B) exaggerations
   (C) conveniences
   (D) opportunities

UNIT 02 명사

기본 학습

사람, 사물, 혹은 추상적인 개념에 붙여진 이름을 뜻한다.

형태

주로 -tion, -sion, -ment, -ance, -ness, -ty 등으로 끝난다.

| regula**tion** 규정 | improve**ment** 개선 | assist**ance** 도움 | willing**ness** 의향 | securi**ty** 보안 |

역할

명사는 문장에서 주어, 목적어, 보어로 쓰인다.

주어		**The museum building** in Glasgow is currently under renovation. 글래스고에 있는 박물관 건물은 현재 보수 공사 중이다.
목적어	타동사 뒤	The company will hire more **employees** over next 6 months. 회사는 향후 6개월 동안 더 많은 직원들을 고용할 것이다.
	전치사 뒤	We offer a special price for **students**. 우리는 학생들을 위해 특별한 가격을 제공한다.
보어		Ibrand Company is a leading **manufacturer** of sunglasses. 아이브랜드 컴퍼니는 선도적인 선글라스 제조업체이다.

명사의 수

명사는 가산명사(셀 수 있는 명사)와 불가산명사(셀 수 없는 명사)로 구분할 수 있다.

가산 단수명사	가산 복수명사	불가산 명사
앞에 반드시 한정사가 온다.	뒤에 (e)s가 붙는다.	뒤에 (e)s가 붙을 수 없고, 단수 취급한다.
a customer the couch my report	customer**s** couch**es** report**s**	information equipment merchandise

한정사

명사 앞에 붙어서 '하나의 ~, 그 ~, 나의 ~'처럼 명사의 범위를 한정시켜 주는 말을 뜻한다. 한정사는 뒤에 오는 명사의 종류가 정해져 있으므로 중요한 단서가 된다.

구분	종류	단수 앞	복수 앞	불가산 앞
관사	a / an 하나의	O		
	the 그	O	O	O
소유격	my 나의 your 너의 its 그것의 Kimora's 키모라의	O	O	O
지시형용사	this 이 that 저	O		O
	these 이 those 저		O	
부정형용사	any 어떤 no 없는	O	O	O
	all 모든 most 대부분의 more 더 많은 some 약간의 other 다른		O	O
	many 많은 few 거의 없는 both 둘 다 several 몇몇의		O	
	much 많은 little 거의 없는			O
	each 각각의 every 모든 another 다른 하나의 either 둘 중 하나의	O		

Ms. Smith is **an** active **member** of the local council. 스미스 씨는 지역 의회에서 활동 중인 의원이다.
Matt lost some of **his** **files** when **his** **computer** crashed. 매트는 컴퓨터가 고장 났을 때, 일부 파일을 날렸다.
All **employees** should attend the meeting. 전 직원들은 회의에 참석해야 한다.

주의해야 할 명사

생김새 때문에 다른 품사와 혼동하기 쉬운 명사들이 있으므로 주의해야 한다.

형용사처럼 생긴 명사

approval 승인   arrival 도착   proposal 제안   renewal 갱신   removal 제거
appraisal 평가   referral 소개, 추천   withdrawal 인출   critic 평론가   initiative 계획, 주도권
perspective 관점   incentive 장려금   complaint 불만   recipient 수령인   detergent 세제

명사로도 쓰는 동사

request 명 요청 동 요청하다   report 명 보고(서) 동 보고하다   help 명 도움 동 돕다
change 명 변화, 거스름돈 동 변하다   plan 명 계획 동 계획하다   visit 명 방문 동 방문하다
schedule 명 일정 동 일정을 잡다   interview 명 면접 동 면접을 보다   aim 명 목표 동 목표하다

명사로도 쓰는 형용사

potential 명 잠재력 형 잠재적인   official 명 공무원 형 공식적인   individual 명 개인 형 개인의
editorial 명 사설 형 편집의   disposable 명 일회용품 형 처분할 수 있는   specific 명 명세 형 구체적인
characteristic 명 특징 형 특유의   executive 명 임원 형 행정의   alternative 명 대안 형 대안이 되는
objective 명 목표 형 객관적인   representative 명 대표, 직원 형 대표하는   professional 명 전문가 형 전문적인

공식 8 주목보는 명사 자리이다.
명사는 문장 속에서 주목보 즉 주어, 목적어, 보어 자리에 들어간다.

(**Payment** / ~~Payable~~) should be made within 30 days from the invoice date.
→ 동사 앞 주어 자리
송장 발행일로부터 30일 이내에 지급이 이루어져야 한다.

Upon (~~receive~~ / **receipt**) of each rent payment, a confirmation e-mail will be sent to you.
→ 전치사 뒤 목적어 자리
매번 임대료를 지불 받자마자, 확인 이메일이 당신에게 발송될 것이다.

[예제] The ------- of the national economy will last longer than two years, according to recent economic research.

(A) expandable   (B) expansion
(C) expanded   (D) expand

------- + (수식어구) + 동사 ⋯ 주어 자리

정답 **(B)** 명사 오답 **(D)** 동사

최근 경제 조사에 따르면, 국가 경제의 확장이 2년 이상 지속될 것이다.

공식 9 관형명 소형명
관사(a/an/the)나 소유격(your, its 등)은 뒤에 반드시 명사가 와야 한다. 그리고 관사[소유격]와 명사 사이에는 명사를 수식하는 형용사가 붙기도 하므로 '관형명', '소형명' 순서로 기억하자.

David Kasai announced his (**resignation** / ~~resign~~) from the position of NIDE President.
→ 소유격(his)의 수식을 받는 명사 자리
데이빗 카사이가 NIDE 사장직에서 사퇴한다고 발표했다.

The packaging design requires a considerable (**modification** / ~~modify~~).
→ 관사(a)와 형용사(considerable) 뒤 빈칸이므로 명사 자리
포장 디자인에 상당한 수정이 필요하다.

비법 노트

- **관사[소유격] 뒤**   Chloe is the **manager** of the sales team. 클로이는 영업팀의 매니저이다.
  관 명

  Please send the item to my new **location** in Calgary. 그 물품을 캘거리의 새 주소로 보내주세요.
  소 형 명

  The order contains an especially large **item**. 매우 큰 물품이 주문에 포함되어 있다.
  관 부 형 명

SKILL UP ① 명사 앞에는 관사나 소유격 대신 다른 한정사(all, any, many, no, this 등)가 붙기도 한다.
  Mr. Jones has worked in many different **countries**. 존스 씨는 여러 나라에서 일해오고 있다.
② 정관사 the와 전치사 of 사이 빈칸은 명사가 1순위이다.
  The exhibition featured the **work** of several artists. 그 전시회는 여러 화가들의 작품을 다뤘다.

[예제] Ahmed Hunter has a worldwide ------- as an expert in business journalism.

(A) reputes   (B) reputation
(C) reputable   (D) reputably

관 + 형 + ------- ⋯ 명사 자리

정답 **(B)**

아메드 헌터 씨는 비즈니스 저널리즘 전문가로서 세계적인 명성을 갖고 있다.

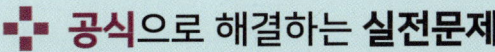
공식으로 해결하는 실전문제

1. The ------- from the devastating financial crisis has been unusually lengthy due to poor government policies.
   (A) recover
   (B) recovers
   (C) recovered
   (D) recovery

2. We decided to include some tests to see how well our prospective interns would follow -------.
   (A) instructions
   (B) instruct
   (C) instructive
   (D) instructively

3. Applicants for the research position should provide at least three ------- from previous employers.
   (A) referred
   (B) refer
   (C) references
   (D) referring

4. Kornell received the Entrepreneurial Institution Award for ------- in entrepreneurship.
   (A) excellent
   (B) excel
   (C) excellence
   (D) excelled

5. The corporation claims that it has no ------- to peaceful protest.
   (A) objection
   (B) object
   (C) objected
   (D) objectify

6. The personnel director offered his sincere ------- to Ms. Ellis on winning the company's Most Outstanding Employee Award.
   (A) congratulate
   (B) congratulations
   (C) congratulated
   (D) congratulatory

7. Following the ------- of a yearlong project to establish a new management process, all team members will receive a paid holiday.
   (A) completion
   (B) completed
   (C) complete
   (D) completely

8. Sham Associates issued an official ------- for the behavior of its field representative at the recent trade fair.
   (A) apologize
   (B) apology
   (C) apologizes
   (D) apologizing

공식 10 estimate은 명사도 된다.

estimate처럼 명사(견적), 동사(추산하다)로 모두 쓰이는 단어들이 있다. 동사와 명사의 형태가 동일한 빈출 어휘를 암기해 두자.

Three companies have submitted (~~estimating~~ / **estimates**) for our renovation project.
세 회사가 보수공사 프로젝트에 대한 견적서를 제출했다.

Officeking has been a leading manufacturer of office (**supplies** / ~~supplier~~) for more than a decade.
오피스킹은 10년 이상 동안 선도적인 사무용품 제조업체였다.

비법 노트 | 명사와 동사 형태가 같은 어휘

advance 진보; 진보하다	**supply** 공급, 물품(supplies); 공급하다	**recruit** 신입사원; 채용하다
project 프로젝트; 예상하다	**support** 지원; 지원하다	**function** 기능; 기능하다
delay 지연; 연기하다	**use** 이용; 이용하다	**study** 연구; 공부하다
limit 제한, 경계(limits); 제한하다	**charge** 요금; 청구하다	**demand** 수요; 요구하다
benefit 혜택; 혜택을 보다	**request** 요청(서); 요청하다	**purchase** 구매(품); 구매하다
monitor 화면; 감시하다	**access / approach** 접근; 접근하다	**proceed** 수익금(proceeds); 진행하다

예제 According to the bonus program, new ------- must stay with the company for two years to receive a bonus.

(A) recruiting (B) recruits
(C) recruitment (D) recruited

명사 빈칸 ⋯ recruit 명사, 동사

빈칸은 동사 must stay 앞 주어 자리
정답 (B) recruits 신입사원
오답 recruiting 채용 활동 recruitment 모집

보너스 프로그램에 따르면, 신입사원들은 2년간 회사에서 근무해야 보너스를 받을 수 있다.

공식 11 복합명사는 통째로 외운다.

두 개의 명사가 모여 하나의 명사처럼 쓰이는 것을 복합명사라고 한다. 복합명사의 경우, 명사 바로 앞/뒤 빈칸에 또 명사가 들어간다는 점에 주의한다.

(~~Safe~~ / **Safety**) inspections are strongly recommended to minimize hazards at the work place.
안전 점검이 작업장에서의 위험을 최소화하기 위해 강력하게 권고된다.

비법 노트 | 빈출 복합명사

safety inspection 안전 점검	**safety procedure** 안전 절차	**staff evaluation** 직원 평가
job performance 직무 수행	**product information** 제품 정보	**recommendation letter** 추천서
business proposal 사업 제안서	**cost reduction** 비용 절감	**employee productivity** 직원 생산성
admission fee 입장료, 입회금	**working environment** 근무 환경	**survey result** 설문조사 결과
improvement project 개선 사업	**information distribution** 정보 배포	**expiration date** 만기일

SKILL UP ① 복합명사 문제에서 명사 앞 빈칸에 명사 수식어인 형용사나 분사를 고르지 않도록 주의한다.
② 복합명사 문제에서 명사 뒤 빈칸에 부사를 고르지 않도록 주의한다.

예제 An employee ------- is an excellent tool to measure job performance.

(A) evaluate   (B) evaluation
(C) is evaluated (D) evaluated

명사 + ------- + 동사 ⋯ 복합명사

복합명사 employee evaluation(직원 평가)
정답 (B)

직원 평가는 업무 수행을 평가하기 위한 훌륭한 도구이다.

공식으로 해결하는 실전문제

1. As a ZED member, you'll have ------- to a large collection of knowledge and career resources.
   (A) access
   (B) accessed
   (C) accessing
   (D) accessible

2. Six entries will be spotlighted as "Best Creation" winners in this open international ------- competition.
   (A) to design
   (B) designed
   (C) design
   (D) designing

3. The ------- of a camera flash is strictly prohibited at all times in Memorial Museum.
   (A) used
   (B) uses
   (C) use
   (D) useless

4. Staff job ------- is one of the most important factors for maintaining and increasing productivity.
   (A) performance
   (B) performer
   (C) perfomed
   (D) perfoms

5. If payment is not received within 30 days of the invoice date, an extra ------- will be incurred.
   (A) charges
   (B) charging
   (C) charged
   (D) charge

6. According to the analysis report, further cost ------- are needed to keep the business profitable.
   (A) reduce
   (B) reductions
   (C) reducing
   (D) reduces

7. Antivirus software firms are expected to provide continuous ------- to the Internet users.
   (A) supported
   (B) supportive
   (C) supportively
   (D) support

8. The board of directors will get together next Thursday to discuss ways to increase employee -------.
   (A) productive
   (B) productivity
   (C) product
   (D) productively

UNIT 02 명사

공식 12 주어와 동사는 수를 일치시킨다.

빈칸이 주어 자리인데 보기에 단수명사와 복수명사가 섞여 있으면, 동사가 단수인지 복수인지부터 확인한다. 단수동사에는 단수/불가산명사, 복수동사에는 복수명사로 수를 일치시킨다.

(**Advertising** / ~~Advertisements~~) contributes to wider economic growth. 광고는 더 폭넓은 경제 성장에 기여한다.
→ 동사가 단수(contributes)이므로 복수명사는 주어가 될 수 없다.

According to a study by a job match site, job (**openings** / ~~opening~~) are generally not made public.
구인구직 사이트의 연구에 따르면, 일자리가 대개 일반인에 공고되지 않고 있다.

비법 노트
- **수식어 주의** 동사 앞 명사가 항상 주어는 아니다. 수식어와 상관없이 주어와 동사의 수를 일치시킨다.
  Our **reputation** among customers **is** well established. 고객들 사이에서 우리 평판이 좋다.
  Students majoring in marketing management **are** preferred. 마케팅 관리를 전공한 학생을 선호합니다.

[예제] The ------- from the market research firm are being analyzed by Mr. Wilson.

(A) reporter   (B) reports
(C) report   (D) reporting

------- + (수식어구) + are ⋯ 복수명사

정답 (B)

월슨 씨가 시장 조사 회사의 보고서를 분석 중이다.

공식 13 불가산명사는 뒤에 (e)s가 붙지 않는다.

불가산명사는 셀 수 없는 명사이므로 복수를 나타내는 -(e)s를 붙일 수 없다. 따라서 불가산명사 뒤에 (e)s가 붙어 있으면 오답이다. 또한 빈칸 앞에 a(n), many처럼 하나 혹은 여럿 등의 수를 나타내는 표현이 있으면 불가산명사는 답이 될 수 없고, much, little처럼 양과 관련된 표현이 있으면 불가산명사가 답이다.

Alib Holdings and Marot Inc. announced the (**establishment** / ~~establishments~~) of a joint venture.
알립 홀딩스와 매럿 사가 합작 회사의 설립을 발표했다.

Mr. Nguyen has submitted a design for (**approval** / ~~approvals~~). 응우옌 씨가 승인을 받기 위해 디자인을 제출했다.

비법 노트 대표적인 불가산명사

access 접근	equipment 장비	information 정보	baggage/luggage 수하물
approval 승인	advice 충고	knowledge 지식	consent 동의
research 연구	work 일	merchandise 상품	interest 관심, 흥미
permission 허가	machinery 기계류	furniture 가구	money/cash 돈

[예제] Public ------- to the beach near Half Moon Bay was closed after a change in its ownership.

(A) accessing   (B) accesses
(C) access   (D) accessible

access ⋯ 불가산명사

동사 was 앞 주어 자리

정답 (C)

소유권이 이전된 후 하프 문 베이 근처 해안에 대한 일반인 출입이 통제되었다.

공식으로 해결하는 실전문제

해설집 p.9

1. Over the years, ------- has enjoyed steady growth and become one of the fastest growing economic sectors in the world.
   (A) tourism
   (B) tours
   (C) tourists
   (D) toured

2. If you have any questions about your -------, you will find contact information on your receipt.
   (A) merchandise
   (B) merchandises
   (C) merchandised
   (D) merchandising

3. Our ------- give you guidance on all aspects of your project from designs to costs.
   (A) architecture
   (B) architectural
   (C) architect
   (D) architects

4. In general, ------- from our online store are shipped for delivery within 3 business days of purchase.
   (A) ordering
   (B) order
   (C) orders
   (D) ordered

5. MingCentral Inc. has attracted ------- from several cloud-based software providers after its revenue rose significantly.
   (A) interested
   (B) interests
   (C) interesting
   (D) interest

6. After months' of hard -------, Dr. Ahn and his team managed to launch a new smartphone application successfully.
   (A) work
   (B) workable
   (C) works
   (D) worked

7. The ------- are developed by multidisciplinary working groups through a vast global consultative process.
   (A) guideline
   (B) guide
   (C) guidelines
   (D) guided

8. You can download a detailed ------- of any of our appliances at www.lcappliances.com.
   (A) information
   (B) description
   (C) recipe
   (D) instruction

37

UNIT 02 명사

공식 14. 빈칸 앞에 a / the / 소유격이 없으면 가산 단수명사는 답이 아니다.

가산 단수명사 앞에는 관사(a / an / the)나 소유격 같은 한정사가 반드시 필요하다. 따라서 명사 자리인 빈칸 앞에 한정사가 없으면 가산 단수명사는 답이 될 수 없다. 한정사가 없을 경우, 가산명사는 반드시 복수 형태로 와야 한다.

Through outsourcing, companies can reduce (**costs** / ~~cost~~). 외주제작을 통해, 회사들은 비용을 줄일 수 있다.

비법 노트 셀 수 없는 것처럼 보이는 가산명사

price 가격	rate 요금, 속도	fee 수수료, 요금	expense 경비
cost 비용	fund 자금, 기금	discount 할인	order 주문(품)
load 짐, 화물	estimate 견적(서)	account 계정, 계좌	permit 허가증
certificate 증명서	document 서류, 문서	task 일, 과제	approach 접근(법)

[예제] The state-run telecom operator DFL has decided to offer its services at discounted -------.

(A) rates (B) rate
(C) rated (D) rating

전치사 + 형용사 + ------- → 단수명사 불가

빈칸 앞에 한정사가 없을 때는 복수나 불가산명사 중에서 선택
정답 (A) 오답 rate(요금) / rating(등급)은 가산 단수명사

국영 통신사인 DFL은 할인된 요금으로 서비스를 제공하기로 결정했다.

공식 15. 보기에 명사가 여러 개이면 문맥에 맞는 명사를 고른다.

생김새가 비슷한 사람명사와 사물 / 추상명사 중에서 문맥에 맞는 답을 고르는 문제가 출제되므로, 생김새와 뜻을 구분할 수 있어야 한다.

If used properly, technology can increase (~~producer~~ / **productivity**).
적절히 활용될 경우, 기술은 생산성을 증가시킬 수 있다.

비법 노트

사람명사	사물 / 추상명사	사람명사	사물 / 추상명사	사람명사	사물 / 추상명사
advisor 고문	advice 충고, 조언	architect 건축가	architecture 건축	inspector 조사관	inspection 점검, 검사
applicant 지원자	application 지원	assistant 비서	assistance 도움	technician 기술자	technicality 전문적 사항
competitor 경쟁자	competition 경쟁	resident 거주자	residence 거주, 주택	instructor 강사	instruction 지시, 설명
employee 직원 / employer 고용주	employment 고용	entrant 출전자	entrance 입구	authority 권위자	authorization 허가
guide 안내인	guideline 지침	recipient 수령인	receipt 수령, 영수증	manufacturer 제조업자	manufacture 제조
supplier 공급자	supplies 물품	specialist 전문가	specialty 전문	operator 작동자	operation 작동, 운영
participant 참가자	participation 참여	investor 투자자	investment 투자	correspondent 기자	correspondence 서신

- 사람명사는 주로 -er / -or / -ee / -ant / -ent / -ist 등으로 끝난다.
- 빈칸 앞에 한정사가 없으면 단수 형태의 사람명사는 답이 되기 어렵다.

[예제] Consumers want food authorities to conduct a thorough ------- of all meat products.

(A) inspects (B) inspection
(C) inspector (D) inspected

사람명사 vs. 사물 / 추상명사 → 문맥

'철저한 ___를 실시키길 원한다'에는 '검사'가 적절
정답 (B) 오답 inspector(조사관)는 문맥상 탈락

소비자들은 식품 관리처가 모든 육류 제품에 대해 철저한 검사를 실시하길 원한다.

공식으로 해결하는 실전문제

해설집 p.10

1. Those who received training were able to focus their attention on individual ------- for longer.
   (A) tasking
   (B) tasks
   (C) tasked
   (D) task

2. While the government has already cut taxes, more needs to be done to encourage -------.
   (A) invested
   (B) investor
   (C) invest
   (D) investment

3. To confirm your ------- at the training session, you are required to sign a form.
   (A) attendee
   (B) attendance
   (C) attend
   (D) attended

4. Miriad Materials is currently looking for a skilled excavator ------- to work on civil projects.
   (A) operator
   (B) operation
   (C) operate
   (D) operational

5. Job seekers should not expect ------- to look at their résumés and immediately guide them in the job search.
   (A) recruiting
   (B) recruiters
   (C) recruit
   (D) recruited

6. In the event that you have lost your receipt, you can provide a bank statement as proof of -------.
   (A) purchase
   (B) purchased
   (C) purchaser
   (D) is purchased

7. Though we do not provide free shipping, ------- can be offered for bulk orders over 200 units.
   (A) discount
   (B) discounted
   (C) discounts
   (D) discounting

8. ------- at the KeepLearn Systems are provided with continuing education courses on leadership development.
   (A) Employing
   (B) Employees
   (C) Employment
   (D) Employ

YBM TEST

1. Interested ------- should visit our Web site for more detailed information on membership benefits.

    (A) individually
    (B) individual
    (C) individuals
    (D) individuality

2. No agreement has yet been reached and the ------- are still ongoing.

    (A) negotiated
    (B) negotiations
    (C) negotiate
    (D) negotiators

3. Researchers must obtain approval from the department head before they begin any research -------.

    (A) active
    (B) activate
    (C) activity
    (D) activation

4. Our offers are subject to ------- with the hotels, in terms of price and availability.

    (A) confirmed
    (B) confirms
    (C) confirmative
    (D) confirmation

5. All anticipated ------- for your business trip need to be included in the travel approval request form.

    (A) expensive
    (B) expense
    (C) expenses
    (D) expensively

6. There were some changes to our bank policy and a small ------- of $4.00 will now be charged for incoming transfers.

    (A) money
    (B) fee
    (C) interest
    (D) cash

7. All ------- letters must be submitted electronically along with the online application.

    (A) recommendation
    (B) recommendable
    (C) recommend
    (D) recommending

8. As ticket availability for the War Memorial Museum is limited, visitors are strongly advised to make ------- well in advance.

    (A) reserved
    (B) reservations
    (C) reserves
    (D) reserve

9. More than 100 companies sent ------- to the Job Fair held in Madrid in order to interview and hire talented students.

    (A) representative
    (B) representing
    (C) representatives
    (D) represent

10. With regard to shipments, we will not be liable for ------- caused by events beyond our control.

    (A) delayed
    (B) delayable
    (C) delayer
    (D) delays

11. Lummer Financial Group president Sarah Cury will discuss comprehensive financial ------- applicable to small business owners.

(A) strategies
(B) strategically
(C) strategic
(D) strategize

12. The editors of *Monthly Trends* always welcome topical ------- from our readers on any subject.

(A) correspond
(B) correspondent
(C) corresponding
(D) correspondence

13. The fundraiser last Saturday was a fantastic -------, and we raised more than a million dollars.

(A) succeed
(B) success
(C) successes
(D) successfully

14. PreKo Corp. is a leading company that manufactures a comprehensive range of sports ------- to fit every athlete's needs.

(A) equipments
(B) equipped
(C) equips
(D) equipment

15. We provide our members with personalized gardening ------- so that they can learn what grows best in their garden.

(A) advisor
(B) advice
(C) advisory
(D) advise

16. The production manager has recently led a ------- of the food processing factory for loyal clients.

(A) tourist
(B) tour
(C) tourism
(D) tours

17. All ------- from the event will be donated to the Child Foundation.

(A) procedure
(B) proceed
(C) proceeds
(D) proceeded

18. Before these ------- are released to the public, they will be examined by the senior accountants.

(A) document
(B) documentation
(C) documents
(D) documented

19. At Upex Logistics, our goal is to provide excellent logistics services at a reasonable -------.

(A) price
(B) priced
(C) pricing
(D) prices

20. Any local residents or groups wishing to publicize their events in the *City Tribune* are advised to submit the request form in -------.

(A) advanced
(B) advancing
(C) advancement
(D) advance

PART 6

> **공식**
> ## 16 문장 고르기 문제 2 – 지시어를 활용한다.
>
> 앞서 언급된 대상을 지칭하는 말인 지시어도 문장 고르기 문제에서 중요한 단서가 된다. 지시어를 활용한 문제는 출제 빈도가 매우 높으므로, 보기 문장이나 빈칸의 앞뒤 문장에서 지시어가 보인다면 이 지시어가 앞문장의 무언가를 가리키는 것은 아닌지 먼저 확인하는 것이 유리하다.

만점 전략

1. 보기 문장에 지시어가 보일 경우 ➡ 빈칸의 앞 문장에 있는 단어나 내용을 지칭한 말인지 확인한다.
2. 빈칸 뒤 문장에 지시어가 보일 경우 ➡ 보기 문장에 있는 단어나 내용을 지칭한 말인지 확인한다.

- **한정사:** this/these 이 ~   that/those 저 ~   such 그러한
  20,000 visitors ⋯ **such a number** ~   delay ⋯ apologize for **this inconvenience**
- **장소, 시간을 지칭하는 부사:** there 거기에(서)   then 그때   at that time 그 때에
  attend the conference ⋯ meet you **there**
- **앞에 나온 명사를 구체적으로 다시 언급할 때:** 「the+명사」 그 ~
  a training session ⋯ **the session** includes ~
- **사건, 상황 등을 지칭하는 대명사:** this 이는, 이러한 점은
  we won a contract ⋯ **this** was made possible ~

예제   해설집 p. 13

We are sorry to announce that the management decided to close our office permanently by the end of this financial year. ❶Some employees will be selected and transferred to the head office.
-------. A generous compensation package will be given to those whose employment with us will end, … 중략

(A) We wish you the best of success in your new business.
(B) If you are on ❷this list, you will be notified shortly.
(C) We were unable to maintain the business any longer.
(D) The site selection for the head office was postponed.

지시어를 활용하여 문장 고르기

❶ 빈칸 앞: 직원 일부가 선택되어 본사로 가게 될 것이다.
❷ 보기 문장의 지시어: this list가 선택된 직원 명단을 지칭
➝ 본사로 가게 되는 직원들이 있을 예정임을 발표했으므로, 그 명단에 오른 사람들에게는 통지하겠다는 말이 이어지는 게 자연스럽다.

정답 (B) 만약 당신이 이 명단에 들어간다면 곧 통지가 갈 것입니다.

YBM TEST

Questions 1-4 refer to the following letter.

January 18
Carla Hollerman
440 Montgomery St.
San Francisco, CA 94103

To the income tax officer,

I am writing this letter to request a reimbursement for an overpayment of income tax for the tax year 2016-2017. Due to a miscalculation by my previous employer, Mouser Electronics, my taxes were overpaid. ------- my calculations, I have paid $2,300 in excess. I paid a total amount of $8,200 whereas I was obliged to pay only $5,900.

For your reference, I have enclosed all the ------- documents, which will provide a ------- work history at Mouser Electronics and proof of tax payment. -------. If you have any further questions, please feel free to contact me any time at chollerman@yahoo.net.

Yours faithfully,

Carla Hollerman

1. (A) Based on
    (B) Likewise
    (C) Instead of
    (D) As well as

2. (A) numerous
    (B) diverse
    (C) relevant
    (D) qualified

3. (A) completion
    (B) completing
    (C) completely
    (D) complete

4. (A) The income tax returns were filed by my accountant.
    (B) I believe this is enough information for you to process my claim.
    (C) It has been 6 months since I claimed the tax refund.
    (D) Please note I have no intention to return to work for a while.

UNIT 03 대명사

기본 학습

명사를 반복적으로 언급하는 것을 피하기 위해 명사 대신 쓰는 말로, 명사와 마찬가지로 주어, 목적어, 보어 역할을 한다.

1. 인칭대명사

인칭	수	성	주격 -은/는/이/가	소유격 -의	목적격 -을/를/에게	재귀대명사 스스로, 직접	소유대명사 -의 것
1인칭	단수(나)		I	my	me	myself	mine
	복수(우리)		we	our	us	ourselves	ours
2인칭	단수(너)		you	your	you	yourself	yours
	복수(너희들)		you	your	you	yourselves	yours
3인칭	단수	남성(그)	he	his	him	himself	his
		여성(그녀)	she	her	her	herself	hers
		사물(그것)	it	its	it	itself	-
	복수(그들, 그것들)		they	their	them	themselves	theirs

▶ **주격, 소유격, 목적격**

주격	At Danomart, **we** pride ourselves on our excellent customer service. 우리 다노마트에서는 뛰어난 고객 서비스를 자랑합니다.
소유격	Before articles are published online, they go through **our** production process. 기사는 온라인으로 발표되기 전에, 우리의 제작 공정을 거친다.
목적격	If you decide to cancel your reservation, please call **us** at 555-1234. 만약 예약을 취소하기로 결정하셨다면 555-1234로 전화 주세요.

▶ **재귀대명사**

① **목적어로 쓰일 때(재귀 용법):** 동사의 주체(주어)와 대상(목적어)이 같을 때 목적어 자리에 쓴다.

Daniel proved **himself** qualified for the managerial position.
다니엘은 스스로가 관리자 직급에 자격이 있음을 증명했다.

② **강조할 때(강조 용법):** 명사를 강조할 때 쓴다. 보통 강조하는 말 바로 뒤나 문장 끝에 온다.

Daniel himself wrote the business proposal. 다니엘이 직접 사업 제안서를 작성했다.
= **Daniel** wrote the business proposal **himself**.

▶ **소유대명사:** 「소유격+명사」를 대신한 말로, 주어, 목적어, 보어로 쓰인다.

Karen said that the packages delivered to the reception desk were **hers**.
캐런은 접수처로 배송된 소포들이 자기의 것이라고 말했다.   = her packages

A colleague of **mine** will contact you sometime next week.
제 동료 중 한 명이 다음 주 언제고 당신께 연락할 겁니다.

2. 지시대명사

특정한 사람이나 사물을 가리키는 말

① **단수:** this 이것 / that 저것
This is an e-mail to confirm your appointment with Dr. Hanson on Feb 12.
이것은 2월 12일, 핸슨 박사와의 진료 예약을 확인하기 위한 이메일입니다.

② **복수:** these 이것들 / those 저것들
You should discard clothes in the designated bins. **These** are located in room B3.
의류는 지정된 수거함에 넣으셔야 합니다. 이 수거함들은 B3실에 있습니다.

③ **that / those:** 문장 내에서 먼저 나온 명사를 대신할 때 쓰기도 한다. 이때는 뒤에 수식어가 오는 게 일반적이다.
Rent prices in Hong Kong are much higher than **those** in Seoul. 홍콩의 집세가 서울의 집세보다 훨씬 높다.
= rent prices

④ **형용사 역할:** 명사 앞에서 지시형용사로도 쓰인다. this / that은 단수명사 앞, these / those는 복수명사 앞에 온다.

3. 부정대명사

'하나, 일부, 대부분'과 같이 분명하게 정해지지 않은 대상을 지칭하는 말로, another, some, each, several, many 등이 대표적인 부정대명사이다.

* another / the other(s) / others

one	(정해지지 않은) 하나	○●○○○	My laptop is too slow, so I need to buy a new **one**. 내 노트북 컴퓨터가 너무 느려서 새로 하나 사야겠다.
another	또 다른 하나	●●○○○	If the item is defective, we will replace it with **another**. 제품에 결함이 있을 경우, 다른 제품과 교환해 드립니다.
the other	나머지 하나	●●	We only have two tables left, one near the entrance and **the other** on the balcony. 두 테이블만 남았는데, 하나는 입구 근처에 있고 나머지 하나는 발코니에 있다.
the others	나머지 전부	●●●●●	Mr. Shin is doing better than **the others** on the team. 신 씨가 나머지 팀원 전부보다 잘 하고 있다.
some	몇 개 / 몇 명	●●○○○	**Some** of the applicants are willing to work abroad. 지원자 중 일부는 해외에서 근무할 의향이 있다.
others	다른 것들 (남는 게 있을 때)	●●●●○	Some items are much cheaper than **others**. 일부 제품들은 다른 것들보다 훨씬 쌉니다.

UNIT 03 대명사

공식 17 동사 앞은 주격, 동사/전치사 뒤는 목적격이 답이다.

보기가 모두 대명사로 구성된 문제는 빈칸이 무슨 자리인지 파악해 알맞은 '격'을 고르면 된다. 주어 자리(동사 앞)는 주격, 목적어 자리(동사 뒤, 전치사 뒤)는 목적격이 답이다.

Noel Fenlon from MSC, stated that (**they** / ~~them~~) had a very successful fundraiser last week.
MSC의 노엘 펜런이 지난주에 매우 성공적인 모금행사를 했다고 말했다.

If you get any news about the event, please update (**me** / ~~my~~) right away.
그 행사에 대해 어떤 소식이라도 듣게 되면 제게 즉시 알려주세요.

[예제] Ms. Brown indicated that ------- used to work as a marketing consultant at a sports gear company.

(A) herself   (B) hers
(C) she   (D) her

접속사 + ------- + 동사 ⋯ 주격 자리

정답 (C)
오답 (A) 재귀대명사 (B) 소유대명사 (D) 소유격/목적격

브라운 씨는 자신이 스포츠 장비 회사에서 마케팅 고문으로 근무했다고 말했다.

공식 18 명사 앞은 소유격이 답이다.

동사 앞뒤나 전치사 뒤에 있는 빈칸이라도 빈칸 뒤로 명사가 보이면 소유격이 답이다. 빈칸과 명사 사이에는 형용사가 잘 끼므로 '소형명'을 기억하자.

Mr. Lamond said that (~~he~~ / **his**) visit to the Shanghai office has been canceled.
→ that절의 주어인 명사 visit을 수식하는 소유격 자리
래먼드 씨가 그의 상하이 사무소 방문 일정이 취소되었다고 말했다.

These jobs are open to students in (~~them~~ / **their**) final year. 이 일자리들은 졸업반 학생들에게 열려 있습니다.
→ 전치사의 목적어인 명사 year를 수식하는 소유격 자리

[비법 노트]

■ **소유격+own+명사**   소유격을 강조하는 own(자신의)
Mr. Peng will be opening **his own restaurant** this summer. 펭 씨가 올 여름 자신의 식당을 열 것이다.
= his restaurant

[예제] Our research suggests that a company's reputation is essential to ------- survival.

(A) they   (B) itself
(C) its   (D) them

------- + 명사 ⋯ 소유격 자리

빈칸 뒤에 명사가 있으므로 소유격 자리
정답 (C)

본 연구는 회사의 평판이 생존에 필수적임을 보여준다.

공식으로 해결하는 실전문제

1. Kelley Stephenson said that ------- needs more volunteers to help complete the work at the Community House.
   (A) her own
   (B) she
   (C) herself
   (D) her

2. If you want to receive a more detailed itinerary, I will send ------- electronically.
   (A) you
   (B) them
   (C) it
   (D) there

3. As the senior UX designer, Ms. Hills works closely with ------- engineering and product teams.
   (A) she
   (B) hers
   (C) herself
   (D) her

4. Over the next few weeks, some of ------- will be out of the office on a business trip to Chicago.
   (A) our
   (B) ourselves
   (C) we
   (D) us

5. Greg Patterson will talk about ------- new book Kid Eccentric, which he wrote with Nadia Witman.
   (A) whose
   (B) his
   (C) who
   (D) himself

6. The workshop participants can check our Web site to see if ------- are already registered.
   (A) they
   (B) them
   (C) theirs
   (D) themselves

7. All members of the global architectural organization, GCA, are accomplished professionals in ------- fields.
   (A) their own
   (B) them
   (C) they
   (D) theirs

8. After submitting ------- application form, you cannot make any further changes to it.
   (A) you
   (B) your
   (C) yourself
   (D) yours

UNIT 03 대명사

공식 19 주어와 목적어가 같을 때 목적어로 재귀대명사를 쓴다.

동작을 행하는 주체(주어)와 그 행위를 당하는 객체(목적어)가 같을 때는 목적어 자리에 인칭대명사의 목적격이 아니라 재귀대명사를 넣는다.

All visitors to our production facility should identify (~~them~~ / **themselves**).
→ them은 방문객들이 아닌 제 3자를 뜻한다
우리의 생산 시설을 방문한 모든 방문객들은 신원을 확인해야 한다.

Mr. Ekuno requested a shuttle service from the airport to the hotel for (**himself** / ~~him~~).
→ him은 Mr. Ekuno가 아닌 다른 남성
에쿠노 씨는 공항에서 호텔까지 자신이 이용할 셔틀 서비스를 요청했다.

비법 노트

- **명령문의 재귀대명사** 명령문은 주어 you가 생략되었으므로 명령문에서 재귀대명사를 골라야 할 때는 yourself가 답.
Please make an effort to familiarize **yourself** with the procedures. 절차에 익숙해지도록 노력하세요.

[예제] Before graduating, Thomas treated ------- to a vacation in Hawaii.
(A) himself   (B) his
(C) its   (D) itself

주어(Thomas) = 목적어(Thomas) ⋯ 재귀대명사
빈칸은 동사 뒤 목적어 자리
정답 **(A)**   오답 (B) 소유격 / 소유대명사
졸업하기 전에, 토마스는 큰맘을 먹고 하와이에서 휴가를 보냈다.

공식 20 주어 뒤, 목적어 뒤는 재귀대명사가 답이다.

재귀대명사는 '직접, 몸소'라는 뜻으로 명사를 강조하기 위해, 명사 바로 뒤나 완전한 문장의 맨 끝에 붙인다. 대개 주어를 강조하기 위해 주어 바로 뒤, 또는 절의 맨 끝(목적어 뒤)에 붙인다.

Ms. Lama analyzed the data from the earlier survey (**herself** / ~~her~~).
→ 빈칸 없이도 문장이 완전하면 재귀대명사가 답
라마 씨는 이전 설문조사에서 나온 자료를 직접 분석했다.

The president (~~him~~ / **himself**) announced his intent to resign at the board meeting.
사장이 은퇴할 의사를 이사회에서 직접 발표했다.

[예제] Ms. Gilmore put together all the data ------- before she produced the sales analysis report.
(A) she   (B) her
(C) her own   (D) herself

주어 + 동사 + 목적어 + ------- ⋯ 재귀대명사
빈칸은 완전한 절의 끝에서 '직접'이란 뜻으로 주어를 강조하는 역할
정답 **(D)**
길모어 씨는 판매 분석 보고서를 작성하기 전에 직접 모든 자료를 종합했다.

공식으로 해결하는 실전문제

해설집 p.15

1. Ms. Duckworth designed the company logo ------- even though she is not a designer.
   (A) she
   (B) herself
   (C) her
   (D) hers

2. Nonprofit organizations are prohibited from distributing money among -------.
   (A) theirs
   (B) themselves
   (C) their
   (D) they

3. Although Ms. Rowller is the author of three best-selling cookbooks, she does not consider ------- to be a professional cook.
   (A) themselves
   (B) her
   (C) them
   (D) herself

4. Don't forget to introduce ------- in a brief and clear manner before starting the presentation.
   (A) your
   (B) yourself
   (C) you
   (D) yours

5. Dr. Long ------- will demonstrate new firewall, which protects cellphones from security threats.
   (A) he
   (B) his
   (C) himself
   (D) his own

6. You are advised to ask for assistance from our technical experts rather than replacing the car engine -------.
   (A) himself
   (B) themselves
   (C) ourselves
   (D) yourself

7. Director Anna Lopez always makes reservations for transportation and accommodation for her business trips -------.
   (A) she
   (B) herself
   (C) her
   (D) hers

8. TechRecruit has earned ------- a reputation for providing professional talent with the skills and expertise your business needs to thrive.
   (A) them
   (B) it
   (C) itself
   (D) its

공식 21 by 뒤에는 재귀대명사가 1순위이다.

재귀대명사는 전치사와 함께 특정한 뜻을 나타내는 관용 표현으로 쓰인다. 「전치사+재귀대명사」 표현 중 by oneself(혼자서)가 가장 자주 출제된다.

Ms. Desai planned the company picnic by (**herself** / ~~her~~). 데사이 씨는 혼자서 회사 야유회를 계획했다.
→ her는 Ms. Desai가 아닌 제3자인 여성을 지칭

비법 노트 재귀대명사의 관용 표현

| by oneself 혼자서(=on one's own) | for oneself 스스로, 자신을 위해 | in itself 그 자체가, 본질적으로 |

예제 Ms. Harrison had to work on the project by ------- until Mr. Farrow came back from his business trip.

(A) her (B) she
(C) herself (D) hers

by + -------: 혼자서 → 재귀대명사

정답 (C)

해리슨 씨는 패로 씨가 출장에서 돌아올 때까지 혼자서 프로젝트 관련 업무를 해야 했다.

공식 22 「-------+who / p.p. / 전치사」는 those가 답이다.

those는 관계대명사 who로 시작하는 관계사절이나, 분사, 전치사구 등의 수식을 받아 '~한 사람들' 이라는 뜻으로 쓰인다. 다른 인칭대명사(they, them, we 등)나 지시대명사(this, that 등)는 이와 같은 용도로 쓰지 않으므로 주의한다.

Information was collected on (~~them~~ / **those**) who attended the movie premiere.
→ those는 who ~ premiere의 수식을 받으면서 '~한 사람들'을 의미 영화 시사회에 참석했던 사람들에 대한 정보가 수집되었다.

There are online courses for (**those** / ~~which~~) interested in leadership training.
리더십 훈련에 관심 있는 사람들을 위한 온라인 강좌가 있다.

This room is accessible only to (~~us~~ / **those**) with authorization. 이 방은 허가받은 사람들만 들어갈 수 있다.

비법 노트

- **anyone who+단수동사** ~하는 누구라도
  <u>Anyone</u> who **registers** after May 15 will have to pay additional fees.
  Those(X) 5월 15일 이후에 등록하는 사람은 누구든지 추가 요금을 지불해야 할 것이다.

예제 ------- who have purchased a festival pass are automatically entered to win a special prize.

(A) Those (B) Whoever
(C) Which (D) Our

------- + who: ~한 사람들 → those

빈칸은 동사 are 앞의 주어 자리로, 관계사절 「who have ~ pass」의 수식을 받는다.

정답 (A)

축제 입장권을 구매한 사람들은 특별 상품에 당첨될 수 있도록 자동으로 응모된다.

공식으로 해결하는 실전문제

1. Mr. Louis will attend the sales conference by ------- because other team members are busy preparing the training seminar.
   (A) his
   (B) he
   (C) him
   (D) himself

2. ------- with nut allergies should notify us at least 48 hours prior to the flight's departure.
   (A) We
   (B) Those
   (C) That
   (D) Them

3. ------- who would like to participate in the writing competition should submit their entry form as early as possible.
   (A) Whichever
   (B) Other
   (C) They
   (D) Anyone

4. Edward Duran expressed deep appreciation to ------- involved in supporting his Sports Foundation.
   (A) those
   (B) this
   (C) them
   (D) they

5. After Linda Hosaki left the apparel retailer, Lululand, she started a business on -------.
   (A) her
   (B) her own
   (C) hers
   (D) herself

6. Bowers offers counseling services for job seekers and ------- unsatisfied with their jobs.
   (A) these
   (B) whomever
   (C) those
   (D) you

7. Until you see for -------, it may be hard to believe our new air conditioning system can lower your bills by so much.
   (A) you
   (B) yourself
   (C) yours
   (D) your

8. Please make sure that all the proposals are reviewed by ------- department head prior to submission to the sponsor.
   (A) you
   (B) yours
   (C) your
   (D) yourself

UNIT 03 대명사

공식 23 부정대명사 자리라면 수도 파악한다.

부정대명사 문제는 형용사, 의문사, 부사 등이 보기에 섞여 나오므로 빈칸에 들어갈 품사가 무엇인지 자리부터 파악한다. 그리고 나서 빈칸이 어떤 명사를 대신하는지 파악하여 수를 일치시킨다.

Mr. Rowland returned (~~very~~ / **everything**) that he rented from CampingGeek.
→ 빈칸은 동사 return의 목적어 자리   롤랜드 씨는 캠핑긱에서 대여한 모든 것을 반환했다.

We carry a variety of home appliances, (~~much~~ / **most**) with the Energy Star label.
→ 복수명사(appliances)의 일부분도 복수 취급   우리는 다양한 가전제품을 취급하며, 대부분이 에너지 스타 인증을 받은 것들이다.

비법 노트 수량을 나타내는 부정대명사

단수 취급	one 하나 each 각각 either 둘 중 어느 하나 another 다른 것[사람]
복수 취급	(a) few 소수 both 둘 다 several 여럿 many 많은 사람들[것들]
불가산(단수 취급)	(a) little 소량 much 다량
복수 혹은 불가산	all 전부 most 대부분 half 절반 any 어느 것[누구든] some 약간

* every(모든)와 other(다른)는 형용사이므로 명사 자리에 들어갈 수 없다.

[예제] ------- of our products goes through a thorough examination to ensure its quality.

(A) Every   (B) Each
(C) Their own   (D) All

------- + 수식어구 + 단수동사 ⋯→ 단수주어

빈칸은 단수동사 goes 앞 주어 자리
정답 (B)   오답 (A) 형용사

각각의 우리 제품들은 품질을 보장하기 위해 철저한 검사를 통과한다.

공식 24 부정대명사 중에는 짝지어 다니는 표현들이 있다.

one은 뒤에 another, some은 뒤에 others가 자주 온다. 또한 one은 앞에 주로 「관사 + 형용사」가 붙어 '~한 것'이란 의미로도 출제된다.

You can move all your e-mails from one Qmail account to (~~either~~ / **another**).
→ one account에서 another account로 이동   당신은 큐메일의 한 계정에서 다른 한 계정으로 모든 이메일을 옮길 수 있다.

Bring your old laptop and get 10% off a new (**one** / ~~any~~).
                                          낡은 노트북 컴퓨터를 가져오셔서 새 상품에 대해 10% 할인 받으세요.

비법 노트

- **주어 불가**   '서로'를 의미하는 each other과 one another는 주어 자리에 들어갈 수 없다.

[예제] Some products are more vulnerable to damage than -------.

(A) them   (B) everyone
(C) others   (D) one another

some ~ ------- ⋯→ others

Some products(일부 제품들)의 비교 대상인 '다른 제품들 (others=other products)'을 지칭
정답 (C)   오답 (A) 그것들 (B) 모두 (D) 서로

어떤 제품들은 다른 제품들보다 손상에 좀 더 취약하다.

공식으로 해결하는 실전문제

1. ------- will be available to take your calls tomorrow since it is a holiday for our company.
   (A) Anything
   (B) All other
   (C) No one
   (D) Whoever

2. Mr. Cameron was informed that ------- from the London office would be waiting at the airport to pick him up.
   (A) us
   (B) they
   (C) someone
   (D) each other

3. Researchers at King's College are working on creating robots that communicate with -------.
   (A) another
   (B) this
   (C) each other
   (D) much

4. Mr. Kaminsky is researching why some insurance policies are much more expensive than -------.
   (A) other
   (B) other one
   (C) each other
   (D) others

5. While the sales representatives had relatively modest targets, ------- managed to reach them.
   (A) us
   (B) anyone
   (C) either
   (D) few

6. If a check is lost, you must have the bank put a stop payment on that check and issue a new -------.
   (A) that
   (B) any
   (C) one
   (D) almost

7. In large assembly projects, it is useful to be able to replace one interchangeable part with ------- in the same family.
   (A) every
   (B) it
   (C) nearly
   (D) another

8. Harold came up with a marketing plan that was agreeable to ------- involved in the launch of the new product.
   (A) everyone
   (B) whatever
   (C) anything
   (D) mostly

YBM TEST

1. Luke Kapoor, a food truck owner, values professional critics' writings because many of ------- have spent years developing their tastes.

   (A) themselves
   (B) their own
   (C) them
   (D) theirs

2. The research shows that some people do their best work as part of a group, while others prefer working by -------.

   (A) itself
   (B) themselves
   (C) yourself
   (D) ourselves

3. Bobson College will hold an open house at the National Energy Center for ------- interested in energy careers.

   (A) which
   (B) those
   (C) either
   (D) them

4. Please send an e-mail to Mr. Bauers to let ------- know about some changes to the seminar schedule.

   (A) him
   (B) he
   (C) his own
   (D) his

5. Maum communications offers a tool for migrating data from one account to ------- all at once.

   (A) another
   (B) ones
   (C) other
   (D) it

6. CEO Greg Foran regularly visits every office across the country ------- to get to know the employees.

   (A) he
   (B) his
   (C) him
   (D) himself

7. Kow Inc. has successfully rebuilt ------- as an innovative company with a major focus on customer service.

   (A) itself
   (B) it
   (C) their
   (D) them

8. The board of Edoire Furniture decided to recall all the furniture that ------- sold in Japan last year.

   (A) it
   (B) itself
   (C) them
   (D) themselves

9. Child care providers help young children become independent by encouraging them to learn things for -------.

   (A) themselves
   (B) theirs
   (C) them
   (D) they

10. ------- who has experienced our catering service will vouch for the quality of our service.

    (A) Those
    (B) That
    (C) Anyone
    (D) Every

11. The government announced ------- plan to give more students the opportunity to learn to code in schools.

(A) its
(B) which
(C) these
(D) there

12. The research shows that some businesses are more vulnerable to changes in the business cycle than -------.

(A) that
(B) other
(C) others
(D) them

13. Lisa Krizio was scheduled to leave Tokyo on March 19 but ------- will return earlier to join the board meeting.

(A) her
(B) herself
(C) her own
(D) she

14. The project manager asked us to work together as a team rather than doing the work on -------.

(A) ours
(B) our own
(C) us
(D) ourselves

15. As an independent event planner, Amelia Ortega handles most aspects of her business ------- while relying on freelancers for help on some issues.

(A) her
(B) she
(C) herself
(D) hers

16. ------- applying for part-time positions will not receive benefits such as paid vacations, medical insurance and bonuses.

(A) We
(B) Them
(C) Whomever
(D) Those

17. At the beginning of the workshop, the participants will be given a chance to introduce themselves to -------.

(A) mostly
(B) one another
(C) no one
(D) any other

18. The president of Nara Apparel is very proud of ------- for creating a highly successful company in the retail apparel industry.

(A) himself
(B) any
(C) who
(D) he

19. We will implement ------- new food safety inspections in all our outlets starting Monday, June 7.

(A) us
(B) our own
(C) we
(D) ourselves

20. Tiver Fitness Center is equipped with a full range of exercise machines, and ------- are state of the art.

(A) much
(B) most
(C) it
(D) nearly

55

PART 6

> **공식 25** 문장 고르기 문제 3 – 접속부사를 활용한다.
>
> 접속부사는 앞 문장과 뒤 문장이 어떤 관계로 연결되었는지를 보여주는 실마리가 된다. 보기나 빈칸 뒤 문장에 접속부사가 있다면, 이 접속부사를 기준으로 양쪽 문장이 어떻게 연결되었는지를 파악한다.

만점 전략

다음 단서들을 지문과 보기 문장에서 찾아 빈칸에 적절한 문장을 고른다.

■ 인과	원인+결과	therefore 그러므로 consequently 그 결과	thus 따라서 as a result 결과적으로	hence 그런 이유로
■ 역접	내용+반대되는 내용	however 하지만 to the contrary 반대로	even so 그렇더라도 nevertheless, nonetheless 그럼에도 불구하고	in contrast 그에 반해서
■ 시간	사건+이후 발생 사건	then 그 다음에, 그때 subsequently 그 뒤에	afterwards 그 후에 finally 마침내	
	사건+동시 발생 사건	meanwhile 그동안	in the meantime 그동안	
■ 추가	내용+비슷한 내용	furthermore 게다가 plus 게다가 additionally, in addition 추가로	moreover 게다가 also 또한	besides 게다가 likewise 마찬가지로
■ 조건	조건+수반되는 결과	if so 만일 그렇다면 in this case 이 경우	if not = otherwise 그렇지 않으면 accordingly 그에 따라	
■ 기타	예시, 대안 등	in fact 사실 unfortunately 불행히도 for example, for instance 예를 들면	alternatively 대안으로 regrettably 유감스럽게	instead 대신에 after all 결국

예제 해설집 p.19

FAMILY NIGHT FUNDRAISER

Everybody has right to be safe in their own home. ❶**The Lotus Women's Shelter is pleased to invite you to a Family Night Fundraiser on February 15** at the Gibbs Recreation and Wellness Center. -------. ❷**Additionally, the event includes a build-your-own-taco bar.** Admission is $5.00 at the door.

(A) Finally, we offer education opportunities.
(B) A local band, The Young Family Band will entertain.
(C) Check our Web site at www.lotus.org.
(D) Please note that entry is free for all.

접속부사를 활용하여 문장 고르기

❶ 빈칸 앞: 2월 15일 모금행사에 귀하를 초대합니다.
❷ 빈칸 뒤: 추가로, 타코를 직접 만들어 먹는 행사도 있습니다.
⋯▶ 빈칸 뒤에 앞 문장과 비슷한 내용이 이어짐을 알려주는 단서 additionally가 있다. 모금행사 초대 → 이벤트 행사 안내 → 추가 행사를 소개하는 흐름이 자연스럽다.

정답 (B) 지역 밴드인 영 패밀리 밴드가 공연할 예정입니다.

Questions 1-4 refer to the following notice.

Health and Safety Policy
Mobile Devices on Worksites

The purpose of this policy is to establish a procedure to reduce injuries related to operating mobile devices on worksites. There are many hazards associated with operating mobile devices on worksites. It can distract employees from their work tasks and surroundings that require full attention. -------.
                                                                                 1.

Restricting the operation of mobile devices on worksites will ------- increase the level of
                                                                2.
concentration of employees. -------, the quality of their work performance will improve and
                              3.
the number of accidents related to the distractions caused by ------- mobile devices will
                                                                4.
decrease.

This policy applies to all workers and visitors except those individuals authorized by Project Management.

---

1. (A) Supervisors should be at one of the designated safe areas.
   (B) Therefore, the use of mobile devices is not permitted while working.
   (C) Approved safety hats should be worn on the job by all personnel.
   (D) Accidents and injuries should be promptly reported to supervisors.

2. (A) intimately
   (B) permissibly
   (C) exclusively
   (D) significantly

3. (A) As a result
   (B) In detail
   (C) Nevertheless
   (D) Even so

4. (A) use
   (B) usage
   (C) using
   (D) used

UNIT 04 동사

기본 학습

동사는 동작이나 상태를 나타내는 말이다. 모든 문장에는 반드시 동사가 있어야 하며, 주어 뒤에 온다.

수일치

3인칭 단수주어
- be동사 — is — The employee **is** motivated. 그 직원은 의욕적이다.
- do동사 — does — Ryan **does** his best. 라이언은 최선을 다한다.
- have동사 — has — She **has** a lot of experience. 그녀는 경험이 많다.
- 일반동사 — V-(e)s — The exhibit **attracts** many visitors. 그 전시회가 많은 방문객들을 끌어들인다.

복수주어 (2인칭 단수 포함)
- be동사 — are — The employees **are** motivated. 직원들이 의욕적이다.
- do동사 — do — We **do** our best. 우리는 최선을 다한다.
- have동사 — have — They **have** a lot of experience. 그들은 경험이 많다.
- 일반동사 — 동사원형 — The exhibits **attract** many visitors. 그 전시회들이 많은 방문객들을 끌어들인다.

※ be동사는 과거 시제일 때도 주어와 수를 일치시킨다. → 단수주어+was / 복수주어+were

주의해야 할 수일치

1. 수식어는 수일치에 영향을 주지 않는다.
<u>All instructors</u> working at Sun Gym **are** highly qualified. 선 짐에서 일하는 모든 강사들은 충분한 자격을 갖췄다.

2. 관계대명사절의 동사는 선행사의 수에 일치시킨다.
<u>Those</u> who **are** familiar with the program should help their coworkers.
그 프로그램에 익숙한 사람들은 동료들을 도와야 한다.

수량 표현의 수일치

1. of 뒤 명사에 수일치

many / few / a few / both / several	of the	복수명사	복수동사
much / little / a little	of the	불가산명사(복수가 없으므로 항상 단수 형태)	단수동사
all / most / some / any	of the	복수명사	복수동사
		불가산명사	단수동사

All of the <u>programs</u> **are** listed on the Web site. 모든 프로그램이 웹 사이트에 열거되어 있다.
All of the <u>information</u> **is** listed on the Web site. 모든 정보가 웹 사이트에 열거되어 있다.

2. 항상 단수동사

one / each / either / neither	of the	복수명사	단수동사

<u>One</u> of the files **is** missing from the server. 파일 중 하나가 서버에서 빠져 있다.

능동태와 수동태

능동태는 주어가 동사 행위를 직접 하는 것, 즉 <주어가 …를 ~한다>를 의미하며 타동사 뒤에 목적어가 온다. 수동태는 주어가 행위를 당하거나 받는 것, 즉 <주어가 ~되다 / 받다 / 당하다>를 뜻하고 동사 뒤에 목적어가 오지 않는다.

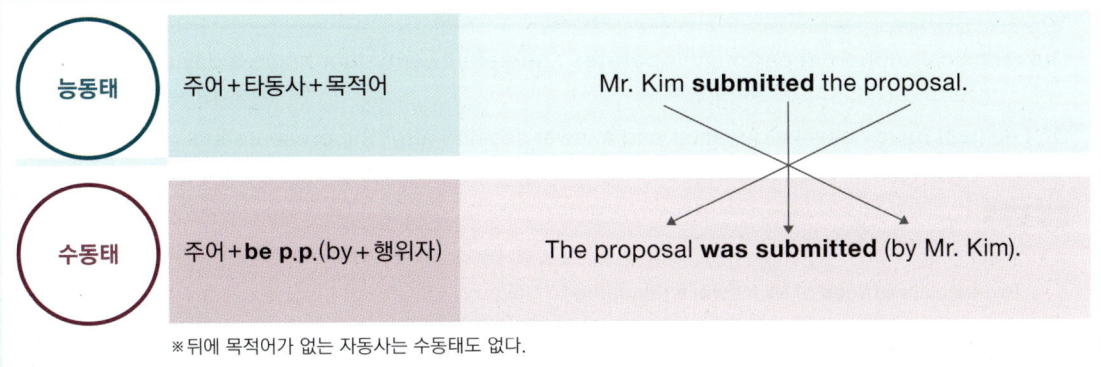

※ 뒤에 목적어가 없는 자동사는 수동태도 없다.

시제

문장의 내용이 현재에 관한 것인지, 혹은 과거에 일어났던 것인지 등에 따라 동사의 형태를 맞춰 주어야 한다. 주로 문장에 주어진 시제 관련 단서(yesterday, next Monday 등)를 통해 시제를 파악할 수 있다.

	현재	과거	미래
단순	am / are / is 동사원형 / 동사원형(e)s	was / were 동사원형(e)d / 불규칙 과거동사	will 동사원형
진행	am / are / is Ving	was / were Ving	will be Ving
완료	have / has p.p.	had p.p.	will have p.p.

➕ 각 시제별 단서

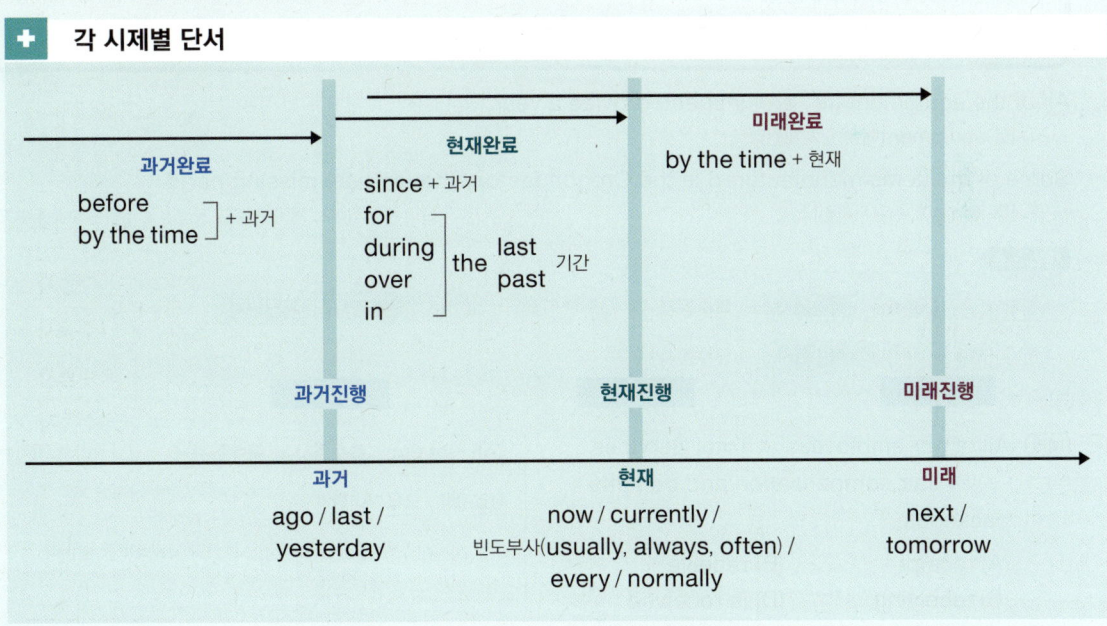

UNIT 04 동사

공식 26 동사 문제는 주어의 수부터 확인한다.

동사 자리가 빈칸이면 주어와의 수일치부터 확인하여 오답을 소거한다. 현재 시제인 경우 3인칭 단수 주어나 불가산명사 주어 뒤의 동사는 반드시 -(e)s로 끝나야 한다.

Our technical support department (**operates** / ~~operate~~) twenty-four hours a day.
→ 주어 department가 단수이므로 동사도 단수 우리 기술 지원부서는 24시간 운영한다.

Dr. Lee (**will have** / ~~have~~) a question and answer session after the presentation.
→ 단수주어이므로 복수동사 have는 오답 이 박사가 발표 후에 질의 응답 시간을 가질 것이다.

비법 노트

- **수식어 주의!** 주어와 동사 사이에 수식어가 올 수 있으므로 주어를 정확히 파악한다.
  Two satellite **offices** of MUO **were** relocated to Calgary. MUO의 위성 사무실 두 개가 캘거리로 이전되었다.
- **-s로 끝나는 고유명사** 회사 이름 등의 고유명사는 복수명사처럼 끝에 s가 붙더라도, 단수 취급한다.
  Leptom Electronics **was** founded 25 years ago. 렙톰 일렉트로닉스는 25년 전에 설립되었다.

[예제] East Capital Partners ------- an experienced construction manager to join our team.

(A) seeking (B) have sought
(C) seek (D) is seeking

3인칭 단수 주어 + ------- → 단수동사

주어가 회사 이름이므로 3인칭 단수이다.

정답 (D) 오답 (A) 동명사/분사

이스트 캐피탈 파트너스가 우리 팀에 합류할 경력 있는 건설 관리자를 구하고 있다.

공식 27 「all of the 명사」가 주어일 때는 명사의 수에 동사의 수를 일치시킨다.

전부나 일부를 뜻하는 부정대명사(all / most / some / many 등)가 「부정대명사 + of the + 명사」 형태로 주어 자리에 올 경우, of 뒤 명사에 동사를 수일치시킨다. 단, 부정대명사 주어가 단수(one, each 등)를 뜻할 경우에는 동사도 단수가 와야 한다.

All of the equipment (**is** / ~~are~~) inspected twice a year. 장비 전부가 일 년에 두 번 점검받는다.
→ 동사를 equipment에 수일치시킨다.

Some of the items manufactured in the Oregon factory (**have** / ~~has~~) missing parts.
→ 동사를 items에 수일치시킨다. 오리건 공장에서 제조된 일부 제품들에 누락된 부품들이 있다.

비법 노트

전부/일부	of the	복수명사	→ 복수동사
전부/일부	of the	단수명사/불가산명사	→ 단수동사
하나/단수	of the	복수명사	→ 단수동사

[예제] All of our employees at Total Services ------- fair compensation and benefits packages.

(A) receipt (B) receive
(C) receiving (D) is received

All + of our + 복수명사 → 복수동사

정답 (B) 오답 (A) 명사

토탈 서비시즈의 전 직원은 정당한 보상과 복지혜택을 받는다.

공식으로 해결하는 실전문제

해설집 p.20

1. Business expert Dr. Kelley ------- on the Today Show to discuss the current market trends in India.
   (A) appearance
   (B) has appeared
   (C) appear
   (D) appearing

2. Mr. Park has noticed that some of the information on his medical charts ------- incorrect.
   (A) are
   (B) have been
   (C) being
   (D) is

3. Most of the banks ------- loans to those who cannot provide suitable guarantees.
   (A) refuse
   (B) refusing
   (C) refusal
   (D) is refusing

4. Flexible workspace in Brisbane ------- high prices from customers because of strong demand.
   (A) commanding
   (B) commands
   (C) have commanded
   (D) commandment

5. Martin's work regularly ------- the expectations of his supervisors at the company.
   (A) surpasses
   (B) having surpassed
   (C) are surpassed
   (D) to surpass

6. A recent study by Financial Research Corporation found that more than 70% of credit reports ------- errors.
   (A) containing
   (B) container
   (C) contains
   (D) contain

7. According to company policy, all interviewees ------- exactly the same questions to ensure fairness.
   (A) has asked
   (B) to ask
   (C) are asked
   (D) has been asked

8. At Central Hotel, all guests ------- a complimentary welcome drink and light refreshments upon check-in.
   (A) to receive
   (B) receivable
   (C) receive
   (D) has received

UNIT 04 동사

공식 28 빈칸 뒤에 목적어 있으면 능동 vs. 목적어 없으면 수동

타동사의 능동태는 동사 뒤에 목적어가 있는 형태이므로 빈칸 뒤에 명사나 한정사, that절 등이 있으면 능동이 정답이다. 반대로 빈칸 뒤에 전치사나 부사가 있을 때는 수동이 정답이 된다.

The new restaurant (is offered / **offers**) a variety of vegetarian dishes.
→ 빈칸 뒤에 〈한정사+명사〉 즉, 목적어가 있다. 새 레스토랑은 다양한 채식 메뉴를 제공한다.

The product design will be (updating / **updated**) soon. 제품 디자인이 곧 업데이트 될 것이다.
→ 빈칸 뒤에 목적어가 없고 부사 soon이 있다.

비법 노트

	능동태		수동태
명사 앞	You should <u>provide</u> **tax documents**.	부사 앞	It should <u>be returned</u> **directly** to the shop.
한정사 앞	Please <u>select</u> **your** preferred date.	전치사 앞	The project <u>was completed</u> **on** time.
that절 앞	He <u>discovered</u> **that** it was no longer available.	마지막 빈칸	A conference schedule <u>was approved</u>.

[예제] To keep your DSLR camera and lenses in optimal condition, regular maintenance -------.

(A) has needed (B) to be needed
(C) is needed   (D) needing

주어 + ------- + 목적어 ⋯ 수동태

동사 자리 빈칸인데 뒤에 목적어가 없고, '요구된다'로 해석된다.
정답 (C) 수동태 **오답 (A)** 능동태

당신의 DSLR 카메라와 렌즈가 최적의 상태를 유지하려면, 정기적인 점검이 필요하다.

공식 29 수동태가 되어도 빈칸 뒤에 목적어가 있는 동사가 있다.

4형식 동사(수여동사)는 목적어가 2개이므로 수동태가 되어도 동사 뒤에 목적어(명사)가 하나 남고, 5형식 동사는 수동태가 되면 동사 뒤에 목적보어(명사나 형용사)가 남아 있다.

Residents will be (**given** / received) access to complimentary Internet.
→ 빈칸 뒤에 목적어 access(명사)가 있으므로 3형식 동사의 수동태는 오답 거주자들은 무료로 인터넷을 쓰게 될 것이다.

IGOX is (**considered** / regarded) a leader in the pharmaceutical industry.
→ 5형식 동사인 consider는 수동태일 때 목적보어(명사나 형용사)가 뒤에 남는다. IGOX는 제약업계에서 선도 업체로 간주된다.

비법 노트 5형식 동사의 수동태

be made possible 가능해지다
be deemed sound 타당하다고 여겨지다
be held responsible 책임이 있다
be made available 이용할 수 있게 되다
be considered appropriate 적절하다고 여겨지다
be named Best Film 최우수 영화로 선정되다

[예제] Software updates are scheduled to occur every three months unless they are ------- necessary.

(A) deemed   (B) conducted
(C) accessed (D) installed

주어 + be p.p. + 형용사 ⋯ 5형식 동사의 수동태

정답 (A)
오답 (B), (C), (D)는 뒤에 목적보어가 올 수 없다.

소프트웨어 업데이트는 필요하다고 간주되지 않는 한 3개월 주기로 예정되어 있다.

공식으로 해결하는 실전문제

해설집 p.21

1. The transfer of the sales manager, Ms. Hill, to the New York office ------- until next month.
   (A) postponing
   (B) will postpone
   (C) postpones
   (D) has been postponed

2. Your order will be ------- out tomorrow and should arrive within three to five business days.
   (A) sending
   (B) send
   (C) sent
   (D) sends

3. From January 3, ORJA will be ------- applications for the Astronaut Candidate Program.
   (A) accepted
   (B) accepting
   (C) accept
   (D) accepts

4. Materials on this Web site ------- available only for your personal and non-commercial use.
   (A) are made
   (B) making
   (C) made
   (D) will make

5. An employee handbook ------- the company's employment policies and general rules of conduct.
   (A) is outlined
   (B) outlining
   (C) outlines
   (D) to outline

6. The second edition of the *Encyclopedia of Housing* may not ------- by the original publisher.
   (A) be published
   (B) published
   (C) be publishing
   (D) have published

7. The national bank ------- a strong 8% growth rate for the domestic economy this year.
   (A) project
   (B) is projected
   (C) has projected
   (D) projection

8. Salt Water in Nottingham has been ------- the best restaurant in the U.K. by the *Bon Appétit* magazine.
   (A) praised
   (B) named
   (C) selected
   (D) recognized

UNIT 04 동사

공식 30 명령문이나 조동사 뒤에는 동사원형이 온다.

명령문은 주어인 you가 생략되고 동사원형으로 시작하는 문장이다. 토익에서는 please 뒤 빈칸이나, 주어 없이 동사자리에 빈칸이 있으면 동사원형이 정답이다. 또한 조동사 뒤에는 반드시 동사원형이 와야 하므로 조동사 뒤 빈칸도 동사원형 자리이다.

Please (**include** / ~~includes~~) all the relevant details when writing up the report.
보고서를 작성할 때 모든 관련 사항을 포함시키세요.

The full survey results will (**be announced** / ~~announces~~) next week. 조사 결과 전체가 다음 주에 공개될 것이다.

비법 노트

- **부사절+명령문** If절/When절+명령문: ~하면/~할 때 …해라
  When you make a purchase, simply enter a promotional code. 구매하실 때 단지 할인코드만 입력하시면 됩니다.
- **조동사+부사+동사원형** 조동사와 동사원형 사이에는 not, no longer, probably 등 부사가 올 수 있다.
  Mr. Huber will **finally** be joining our team. 후버 씨가 마침내 우리 팀에 합류할 것이다.

[예제] ------ your personal information online by changing your passwords frequently.

(A) Protects (B) To protect
(C) Protecting (D) Protect

주어 없이 동사로 시작하는 문장 ⋯ 명령문

문장에 동사가 없으므로 빈칸은 동사 자리.
정답 (D) 오답 (A) 단수동사

비밀번호를 자주 바꿔서 당신의 온라인 개인 정보를 보호하십시오.

공식 31 yesterday가 보이면 과거 시제가 답이다.

명확한 과거 시점을 알려주는 단서인 ago, last, yesterday 등을 보고 과거동사(동사+ed)를 고를 수 있는 문제가 출제된다.

At yesterday's meeting, a new Internet usage policy (**was introduced** / ~~is introduced~~).
어제 회의에서, 새로운 인터넷 사용 방침이 소개되었다.

Mr. Matthewson (~~will purchase~~ / **purchased**) a small farm land near the river last summer.
매튜슨 씨는 지난여름에 강 옆에 있는 작은 농장 부지를 매입했다.

비법 노트 과거 시제 단서

| ago 전에 | last 지난 | yesterday 어제 | in+과거 연도 ~년에 |
| previously, formerly 이전에 | originally 원래 | initially 처음에 | recently 최근에(현재완료 시제도 가능) |

SKILL UP **현재 시제** 현재의 상태, 일반적인 사실, 반복적으로 일어나는 일을 나타낸다.
Ms. Yi **currently** serves as the chair of our foundation. 이 씨가 현재 우리 재단의 회장을 맡고 있다.
Magazine One releases a new issue **every month**. 〈매거진 원〉은 매달 새 잡지를 출간한다.

[예제] The Finnish mobile phone maker, Makia Telefon ------ the Indian market three years ago.

(A) enters (B) enter
(C) entered (D) has entered

three years ago ⋯ 과거 시제 단서 표현

명확한 과거 시점은 과거 시제의 단서이다.
정답 (C)

핀란드의 휴대폰 제조업체인 마키아 텔레폰은 3년 전에 인도 시장에 진출했다.

공식으로 해결하는 실전문제

1. Please take a moment to fill out the comment card and ------- it on the bed table.
   (A) leave
   (B) leaving
   (C) left
   (D) leaves

2. Researchers assured participants that their personal information would ------- strictly confidential.
   (A) remain
   (B) remains
   (C) remaining
   (D) to remain

3. At Fav Dancewear, we normally ------- returns for any items that show signs of being worn or washed.
   (A) had rejected
   (B) rejecting
   (C) reject
   (D) rejects

4. Business Networking Groups ------- the first offline gathering of its members in 2012.
   (A) hold
   (B) to be held
   (C) is holding
   (D) held

5. ------- the instructions below carefully to set up and test basic wireless connectivity.
   (A) Following
   (B) Followed
   (C) Follow
   (D) Follows

6. With our Open Save Files tool, you can check what files ------- recently on your computer.
   (A) will be opened
   (B) is opened
   (C) open
   (D) were opened

7. Poor customer service and unhappy employees can badly ------- any company's reputation.
   (A) damaging
   (B) damage
   (C) damaged
   (D) damages

8. Charles Johnson, the newly appointed vice president at Atlanta Bank, previously ------- as a director in the investment counseling department.
   (A) server
   (B) served
   (C) serves
   (D) serving

공식 32 · over the past five years가 보이면 have p.p.가 답이다.

현재완료(have p.p.)는 과거에 시작된 일이 현재까지 계속되거나 현재에 완료된 상태를 나타내는 시제이다. 현재완료 시제와 같이 다니는 「over the past + 기간」과 「since + 과거」를 단서로 해서 현재완료를 고를 수 있는 문제가 출제된다.

Global oil prices (**have fallen** / ~~are falling~~) sharply over the past nine months.
→ 「over the past + 기간(nine months)」이 있으므로 현재완료 시제   국제 유가가 지난 9개월간 급격히 하락했다.

Our customer base (**has grown** / ~~grew~~) since last year. 우리 고객층이 작년 이래로 늘었다.
→ 「since + 과거(last year)」가 있으므로 현재완료 시제

비법 노트 현재완료 시제 단서

- **지난 ~ 동안**   for/during/over/in the last[past] + 기간
  He has been my supervisor **for the last three years**. 그는 지난 3년간 내 상관이었다.

- **~ 이래로 쭉**   since + 과거
  Sales have increased **since** we **renovated** the showroom. 전시장을 보수한 뒤부터 판매가 늘고 있다.

예제 Cnocs ------- a very popular brand over the past few years.

(A) has become   (B) to become
(C) is becoming   (D) becomes

over the past + 기간 ⋯ 현재완료

정답 (A) 오답 (C) 현재진행 (D) 현재 시제

크녹스는 지난 몇 년간 매우 인기 있는 브랜드가 되었다.

공식 33 · next가 보이면 will이 답이다.

미래 시제를 알려주는 단서인 next, tomorrow 등을 보고 「will + 동사원형」을 고르는 문제가 출제된다.

Next year, we (**will start** / ~~have started~~) to sell our products at ten more retail outlets.
내년에 우리는 추가로 열 군데의 소매점에서 제품을 판매하기 시작할 것이다.

The budget proposal (~~was submitted~~ / **will be submitted**) to the board for approval tomorrow.
예산안이 내일 이사회의 승인을 위해 제출될 것이다.

비법 노트 미래 시제 단서

next 다음의   tomorrow 내일   soon 곧   until further notice 추후 통지 때까지
as of/effective/starting/beginning + 미래 시점 ~부터 (시행[시작]해서)

SKILL UP 미래를 의미하는 현재진행 시제   현재진행 시제가 가까운 미래에 잡혀 있는 일정을 나타내기도 한다.
We are launching a new product **next week**. 우리는 다음 주에 신제품을 출시할 것이다.

예제 Starting next Friday, the Kindle edition of the popular novel *Miracle* ------- for free on Emarket.

(A) had offered   (B) was offered
(C) offer   (D) will be offered

starting next ~ ⋯ 미래 시제

정답 (D) 오답 (A) 과거완료 (B) 과거 시제 (C) 현재 시제

다음 주 금요일부터 시작해, 인기 소설 〈미라클〉의 킨들용 판이 이마켓에서 무료로 제공될 것이다.

공식으로 해결하는 실전문제

1. With only three films, Kevin Anderson ------- to become a globally acclaimed director over the last seven years.
   (A) rising
   (B) has risen
   (C) will rise
   (D) rise

2. Our new product launch event ------- in the ball room of the Churchill Hotel next Tuesday.
   (A) has held
   (B) holds
   (C) will have been holding
   (D) will be held

3. At the next meeting, the committee ------- who will lead the Rogersville community park design project.
   (A) deciding
   (B) has decided
   (C) had decided
   (D) will decide

4. The price of the main material used in most of our products ------- significantly since last year.
   (A) has increased
   (B) increases
   (C) increase
   (D) will be increased

5. Our gas piping ------- several times since it was installed two years ago.
   (A) has been inspected
   (B) to inspect
   (C) is inspected
   (D) was inspecting

6. Stockholm-Wikes ------- significant growth in manufacturing over the past 15 years.
   (A) experience
   (B) is experiencing
   (C) has experienced
   (D) experiences

7. The Land of Birds ------- to the public until further notice due to the risk of a bacterial infection.
   (A) will be closed
   (B) close
   (C) closing
   (D) closure

8. As of January 2, Hove Village ------- extensive remodeling in order to offer guests even greater style and comfort.
   (A) is undergone
   (B) undergone
   (C) to undergo
   (D) will undergo

UNIT 04 동사

공식 34 「If + 주어 + ___, 주어 + will」에는 현재 시제가 답이다.

시간/조건 부사절에서는 미래의 일을 이야기하더라도 미래 시제가 아닌 현재 시제를 쓴다. 따라서 미래에 대한 내용일 때 「If/When + 주어 + 현재 시제, 주어 + will」로 써야 한다.

If it (~~will rain~~ / **rains**) on the event day, the outdoor activities will be canceled.
→ 조건 부사절에는 현재 시제, 주절(접속사가 없는 절)에는 미래 시제를 쓴다.   행사 당일에 비가 내릴 경우, 야외 활동은 취소될 것이다.

비법 노트

- **시간 접속사** when ~할 때   before ~ 전에   after ~ 후에   while ~하는 동안
               until ~할 때까지   as soon as ~하자마자

- **조건 접속사** if 만약 ~라면   unless ~이 아니라면   in case (that) ~인 경우에
               providing (that), provided (that) ~라면

[예제] If entries for the competition ------- after the deadline, they will not be judged.

(A) are received   (B) received
(C) will receive   (D) will be received

If + 주어 + -------, 주어 + will ⋯ 현재 시제

정답 (A)

마감일까지 수령되지 않을 경우, 대회 출품작들은 심사 받지 못할 것이다.

공식 35 「by the time + 주어 + 과거 시제, 주어 + ___」에는 had p.p.가 답이다.

과거완료(had p.p.)는 과거의 사건보다 더 전에 일어난 일을 나타내는 시제이다. 그러므로 「by the time/before + 주어 + 과거동사」와 짝을 이루는 주절에는 과거완료가 정답이 된다.

By the time the presentation began, Mr. Tanaka (~~will install~~ / **had installed**) the projector.
발표가 시작할 때쯤, 다나카 씨가 영사기를 설치했다.

Before we arrived at the airport, the flight to Dublin (**had left** / ~~leaves~~).
우리가 공항에 도착하기 전에, 더블린행 비행기가 떠났다.

비법 노트

- **과거완료 단서**   by the time/before + 주어 + 과거 시제, 주어 + had p.p.
                 after + 주어 + had p.p., 주어 + 과거 시제
                 After they **had finished** the work, the client arrived. 그들이 일을 끝내고 난 뒤 고객이 도착했다.

- **미래완료 단서**   by the time + 주어 + 현재 시제, 주어 + will have p.p.
                 By the time Mr. Torres retires, he **will have worked** for 25 years.
                 토레스 씨가 은퇴할 때쯤 그는 25년간 근무한 것이 될 것이다.

[예제] Ms. O'Brian ------- the report before she left for the leadership workshop.

(A) finishes   (B) will finish
(C) had finished (D) having

주어 + -------, before + 주어 + 과거 시제 ⋯ 과거완료

정답 (C)

오브라이언 씨는 리더십 워크숍으로 떠나기 전에 보고서를 완료했다.

공식으로 해결하는 실전문제

1. Before the regional manager visited the store, the store staff ------- merchandise neatly on shelves.
   (A) had arranged
   (B) will arrange
   (C) arranges
   (D) arrangement

2. The human resources team ------- interview questions by the time they were ready to recruit new interns.
   (A) will develop
   (B) develop
   (C) had developed
   (D) developers

3. We will replace or refund items if they ------- to be defective or damaged.
   (A) found
   (B) have found
   (C) will be found
   (D) are found

4. A registration confirmation message will be e-mailed to you as soon as you ------- your details.
   (A) will submit
   (B) submit
   (C) were submitted
   (D) to submit

5. While the sales director is in California to attend the annual conference, he ------- the offices in the area.
   (A) visit
   (B) visiting
   (C) will visit
   (D) has visited

6. Ms. Graham ------- a senior financial position at GT Group before joining our team last year.
   (A) will be held
   (B) had held
   (C) has held
   (D) holding

7. Payment in full will be required when you ------- your order on our Web site.
   (A) places
   (B) be placed
   (C) place
   (D) will have placed

8. Before her novel was published, Ms. Nolan ------- her manuscript professionally copyedited.
   (A) has
   (B) will have
   (C) having
   (D) had had

YBM TEST

1. As a first-time visitor to this facility, you ------- to present your identification card to the security staff upon request.
   (A) requiring
   (B) are required
   (C) being required
   (D) has been required

2. In the business management article, Dr. Wright ------- advice on implementing new business systems in organizations.
   (A) providing
   (B) were provided
   (C) provides
   (D) provision

3. The machine does not give change so please ------- the exact amount when buying a new OKTravelCard.
   (A) inserting
   (B) to insert
   (C) insert
   (D) in inserting

4. Effective next year, the company ------- eligible employees with four full weeks of paid family vacation.
   (A) will be provided
   (B) will be providing
   (C) has provided
   (D) was providing

5. The red biohazard bags filled with waste must ------- into the designated receptacles.
   (A) be placed
   (B) placed
   (C) placing
   (D) places

6. At Midas Auto Service, we ------- our operating license every year to comply with government regulations.
   (A) renew
   (B) are renewed
   (C) had renewed
   (D) renewing

7. After Farmers Ltd. ------- operational issues in its production facilities, it partnered with Control Assemblies.
   (A) experiencing
   (B) experiences
   (C) had experienced
   (D) was experienced

8. All of the attendees ------- asked to select the sessions they want to attend.
   (A) been
   (B) are
   (C) has been
   (D) being

9. By the time Mr. Wilson meets the financial director next week, he ------- the budget proposal.
   (A) completes
   (B) had completed
   (C) will have completed
   (D) has completed

10. Two weeks ago, WB Software ------- the 8.1.2 update for its Premiere ProQ messaging application.
    (A) will release
    (B) releases
    (C) released
    (D) has released

11. In the past few years, many charity organizations ------- financial difficulties and been forced to close.

(A) are facing
(B) will be faced
(C) have faced
(D) were faced

12. Any updates to the schedule, such as flight delays and, gate changes, will be ------- immediately on the information screens at the airport.

(A) posting
(B) post
(C) posts
(D) posted

13. You will receive a 15% discount on parking at Garden Square if you ------- for our fitness center membership.

(A) registering
(B) register
(C) will be registered
(D) to register

14. Ms. Hackett ------- from a news program before she hosted a local talk show at a Baltimore TV station.

(A) has fired
(B) fired
(C) will be fired
(D) had been fired

15. Foreign Minister Kang says that the government ------- reforms to cultivate cultural diversity in society.

(A) is implemented
(B) to implement
(C) to be implemented
(D) is implementing

16. Each of the submitted proposals ------- and discussed by the Property Appraisal Committee.

(A) has been reviewed
(B) reviewing
(C) are reviewed
(D) review

17. Tom Collins ------- to become like the legendary sales agent Dave Brown since he joined GoodLife Insurance.

(A) aspiring
(B) has aspired
(C) aspire
(D) is aspiring

18. If you exceed the baggage allowance, you ------- to pay an additional fee for excess checked bags.

(A) will be required
(B) are requiring
(C) have been required
(D) require

19. Beginning next Monday, the online order deadline for Telecom Cube mobile phones ------- to 5 P.M. before your desired pick-up date.

(A) has been extended
(B) will be extended
(C) extending
(D) extended

20. The director ------- every team member to contribute equally to the upcoming construction project.

(A) expects
(B) is expected
(C) expecting
(D) expect

PART 6

공식 36 문장 고르기 문제 4 – 빈칸 주변의 동사와 명사를 활용한다.

대명사, 지시어, 접속부사 등 활용할 만한 단서가 눈에 띄지 않는 경우에는 독해를 통해 문맥을 파악한다. 빈칸 앞뒤 문장에서 동사와 명사 위주로 키워드를 파악한 다음, 선택지 넷 중에서 이 키워드와 가장 관련성이 깊어 보이는 구문이나 동의어가 많이 보이는 선택지 위주로 빈칸에 대입해서 정답을 찾는다.

만점 전략

앞문장 키워드	뒷문장 키워드	⋯➔ 정답 문장 키워드
confirm / flight booking 확인 / 항공권 예약	if / not received / confirmation 만약 / 못 받는다 / 확인	⋯➔ flight details / will be e-mailed 항공편 정보 / 이메일로 발송된다
trial period / try out 체험 기간 / 체험해 보라	it's free 무료	⋯➔ during the trial / pay nothing 체험 기간 동안 / 돈 안 낸다
store / clothes 보관한다 / 옷	availability 이용 가능성	⋯➔ lockers / be provided 보관함 / 제공된다

예제

해설집 p.26

Bluwing Airlines FAQ

❶ What if my flight is cancelled or delayed?

-------. ❷ Refunds are permitted for flight delays of 90 minutes or more for domestic tickets. If the flight delay is caused by inclement weather conditions, labor strikes, security shutdowns, or any other factors beyond our control, we are only obliged to refund the ticket and are not required to provide accommodations or other compensation.

(A) Your flight information will be e-mailed to you.
(B) Your seat will be assigned after you check in for a flight.
(C) You will be asked for your credit card to secure your reservation.
(D) In case of flight cancellation, you may request a refund.

키워드 활용하여 문장 고르기

❶ 빈칸 앞: 비행편이 취소되거나 지연된다면?
❷ 빈칸 뒤: 국내선은 90분 이상 지연되면 환불된다.
⋯➔ 비행편 취소나 지연의 경우에 취해지는 조치가 안내되고 있는데, 빈칸 뒤에서 환불 방식을 설명하고 있으므로 빈칸에는 환불 관련 내용이 들어가는 것이 자연스럽다.

정답 (D) 항공편이 취소된 경우, 환불을 요청할 수 있습니다.

YBM TEST

해설집 p.27

Questions 1-4 refer to the following letter.

October 21
Ms. Aisha Chen
59 Hamilton Road Teaneck, NJ 07648

Dear Ms. Chen

Thank you for your recent ------- from Bora's Premium BBQ.
        1.

I am pleased to ------- you that your order was shipped on October 20 via BHL Express. For
                2.
your reference, the tracking number is 3873173242.

All our meat products are packed fresh and shipped by refrigerated airfreight to ensure the
best possible final product. -------. If there is any problem with your order, please let us know
                             3.
about it. We will refund your money or credit you on your next order.

It has been a pleasure to serve you. Please do not hesitate to contact us ------- we be able to
                                                                         4.
assist you again in the future.

Sincerely,

Yuri Ellerson
Lead Customer Service Representative

---

1. (A) survey
   (B) interest
   (C) order
   (D) subscription

2. (A) inform
   (B) suggest
   (C) explain
   (D) respond

3. (A) Regrettably, your order will be delayed by one week.
   (B) Our reputation is built on premium meat delivered fresh.
   (C) However, the item is out of stock and we are unable to process our order.
   (D) We value and appreciate your feedback as we work to improve.

4. (A) as well as
   (B) whenever
   (C) if
   (D) should

UNIT 05 To부정사

기본 학습

동사원형 앞에 to를 붙여 명사, 형용사, 부사처럼 활용하는 말이다.

형태

기본형	to + 동사원형	We are waiting for him **to reply** to the message. → for + 목적격: to부정사의 의미상의 주어 우리는 그가 메시지에 응답하기를 기다리고 있다.
부정형	not to부정사	Ms. Leonard chose **not to participate** in the design competition. 레너드 씨는 디자인 대회에 참가하지 않기로 결정했다.
수동형	to be p.p.	Quarterly sales reports need **to be reviewed** by the financial director. 분기별 매출 보고서는 재무 이사에 의해 검토되어야 한다.
완료형	to have p.p.	We are happy **to have achieved** certification of the ISO standard. → 문장의 시제보다 이전 시점일 때 우리는 ISO 표준 인증을 받게 되어 기쁘다.

역할

명사, 형용사, 부사 역할을 하며, 동사 자리에 들어갈 수 없다.

명사 역할	~하는 것	Mr. Thain has agreed **to accept** the position of Chief Financial Officer. 동사 목적어 테인 씨는 재무 담당 최고 책임자 직위를 수락하기로 동의했다.
형용사 역할	~하는, ~할	Citizens of the United States have a right **to own** guns. 미국 시민들은 총기를 소유할 권리가 있다.
부사 역할	~하기 위해서	Everyday Mart is offering discounts **to attract** new customers. 에브리데이 마트는 신규 고객을 끌어들이기 위해 할인을 제공하고 있다.

성질

동사 역할은 할 수 없지만 동사의 성질을 그대로 지닌다.

목적어 수반	We ask you **to review** the application form before submission. → 타동사의 to부정사형은 뒤에 목적어가 와야 한다. 제출하기 전에 당신이 지원서를 검토할 것을 요청한다.
보어 수반	It is expected **to be** sunny tomorrow. 내일 맑을 것으로 예상된다. → 2형식 동사의 to부정사형은 뒤에 보어가 와야 한다.
부사가 수식	We should be able **to respond** quickly to changes in the market. 우리는 시장의 변화에 빠르게 대응할 수 있어야 한다.

동명사

기본 학습

동사원형 뒤에 ing를 붙여 동사를 명사처럼 활용하는 말이다.

형태

기본형	V+ing	Avoid **wiping** this sculpture with a damp cloth. 젖은 천으로 이 조각상을 닦지 마세요.
부정형	not V+ing	Marcus apologized for **not replying** earlier. 마커스는 더 일찍 답변하지 못한 것에 대해 사과했다.
수동형	being p.p.	Some items are prohibited from **being taken** into the airplane. 일부 품목들은 기내로 반입되는 것이 허용되지 않는다.
완료형	having p.p.	Ms. Lopez was recognized for **having made** a major contribution. → 문장의 시제보다 이전 시점일 때 로페즈 씨는 크게 기여한 것에 대해 인정받았다.

역할

명사 역할을 하고, 동사 자리에 들어갈 수 없다.

주어 자리	**Using** multiple antivirus programs is not a good idea. 여러 개의 바이러스 예방 프로그램을 사용하는 것은 바람직하지 않다.
목적어 자리	Samuel enjoys **making** short films with his smartphone. 새뮤얼은 스마트폰을 이용해 단편 영화를 만드는 것을 즐긴다. Mamas Bistro is known for **serving** only locally produced food. 마마스 비스트로는 오직 현지에서 생산된 음식만을 제공하는 것으로 유명하다.
보어 자리	The key to success in business is **understanding** your customers. 사업에서 성공하기 위한 열쇠는 고객을 이해하는 것이다.

성질

동사 역할은 할 수 없지만 동사의 성질을 그대로 지닌다.

목적어 수반	Mr. Cummings is being investigated for **receiving** bribes. 커밍스 씨는 뇌물 수수 혐의로 조사 받는 중이다. → 타동사의 동명사형은 뒤에 목적어가 와야 한다.
보어 수반	Yuki is worried about **being** late for the meeting. 유키는 회의에 늦을까 봐 걱정한다. → 2형식 동사의 동명사형은 뒤에 보어가 와야 한다.
부사가 수식	We look forward to **working** more closely with you. 당신과 더욱 긴밀하게 일하기를 기대합니다. → 명사는 형용사가 수식하고, 동명사는 부사가 수식한다.

UNIT 05 To부정사 & 동명사

공식 37. 완전한 절 앞/뒤에는 부사 역할의 to부정사가 1순위이다.

to부정사는 완전한 절에 덤으로 붙어 부사처럼 수식하는 역할을 하며, 주로 목적(~하기 위해서)을 뜻한다. 완전한 절 뒤에 빈칸이 오거나, 문장 맨 앞에 빈칸이 있으면서 '~하기 위해서'로 해석되면 (in order) to부정사가 답이다.

The museum will hold a reception (**to celebrate** / ~~celebration~~) its reopening.
→ 완전한 절 뒤에 빈칸이 있고 '축하하기 위해서'라는 목적을 의미　　박물관은 재개관을 축하하기 위해 연회를 열 것이다.

(**In order to** / ~~after all~~) meet the deadline, Karen has to work overtime tonight.
→ 빈칸 뒤의 meet과 어울려 부사구를 만들 수 있는 표현 자리　　마감일을 맞추기 위해, 카렌은 오늘 밤 초과 근무를 해야 한다.

비법 노트 목적을 나타내는 표현

- in order to do = so as to do ~하기 위해서[~할 수 있도록]
  Bring travel-sized toiletries **so as to reduce** the weight of luggage.
  여행 가방의 무게를 줄이기 위해서 여행용 사이즈의 세면도구를 가져와라.

[예제] IDEE conducts market research on a regular basis ------- a competitive edge.

(A) will maintain　　(B) maintaining
(C) maintains　　　(D) to maintain

완전한 절 + 수식어구 + ------- ⋯ to부정사
완전한 절 뒤에 빈칸이 있고, '유지하기 위해서'로 해석된다.

정답 (D)

IDEE는 경쟁력 우위를 유지하기 위해 정기적으로 시장 조사를 한다.

공식 38. 「allow + 목적어」 뒤는 to부정사가 답이다.

「allow + 목적어 + to부정사」처럼 목적어 뒤 목적격 보어 자리에 to부정사가 오는 동사들이 있다. 동사 자리나 to부정사 자리가 빈칸으로 출제되며, 수동형도 빈출 유형이므로 능동형과 수동형 둘 다 암기한다.

Gina is expecting the package (**to arrive** / ~~arrived~~) by this afternoon.
→ 빈칸은 목적어 package를 보충 설명하는 목적격 보어 자리　　지나는 오늘 오후까지 소포가 도착하기를 기대하고 있다.

On flights, passengers are asked (~~turning~~ / **to turn**) off all electronic devices.
→ 「ask A to do」의 수동형은 「A be asked to do」　　기내에서 승객들은 모든 전자 장치의 전원을 꺼 줄 것을 요청받는다.

비법 노트 빈출 표현

allow A to do A가 ~하는 것을 허락하다	ask A to do A에게 ~할 것을 요청하다	advise A to do A에게 ~하라고 충고하다
expect A to do A가 ~하리라 기대하다	enable A to do A가 ~할 수 있게 하다	require A to do A에게 ~하라고 요구하다
urge A to do A에게 ~할 것을 촉구하다	invite A to do A가 ~하도록 청하다	encourage A to do A가 ~하도록 격려하다
be allowed to do ~하도록 허락되다	be asked to do ~하도록 요청받다	be advised to do ~하도록 권고받다
be expected to do ~할 것으로 예상되다	be enabled to do ~하는 것이 가능해지다	be required to do ~하는 것이 필수적이다
be urged to do ~하도록 촉구되다	be invited to do ~하라고 요청받다	be encouraged to do ~하라고 권장받다
be instructed to do ~하라고 지시받다	be requested to do ~하라고 요청받다	be reminded to do ~하라고 상기받다

[예제] Our new camera lens allows you ------- clear photos even in low light conditions.

(A) capturing　　(B) capture
(C) to capture　　(D) captured

allow + 목적어 + ------- ⋯ to부정사

정답 (C)

우리의 새 카메라 렌즈는 당신이 낮은 조도에서조차 선명한 사진을 찍도록 해 준다.

공식으로 해결하는 실전문제

해설집 p.27

1. To ------- the right decision, the board of directors needed more detailed information.
   (A) make
   (B) making
   (C) be made
   (D) made

2. All employees at Zonax Inc. are now required to ------- timesheets electronically, not manually.
   (A) completion
   (B) complete
   (C) completing
   (D) completes

3. SpeedyJet allows passengers ------- their own seats for free at the time of booking.
   (A) choose
   (B) to choose
   (C) choices
   (D) chosen

4. Rani Catering needs to know the expected guest count in advance ------- provide enough food and beverages for them.
   (A) so that
   (B) for
   (C) in order to
   (D) causing

5. You must pay the parking tickets by the due date ------- late fees and collection fees.
   (A) avoided
   (B) to avoid
   (C) avoiding
   (D) avoidably

6. All employees are instructed ------- an instructor-led discussion on the recently revised handbook.
   (A) attendance
   (B) attendant
   (C) attending
   (D) to attend

7. Payment service providers need to modify their security procedures in order to ------- with the new regulation.
   (A) complying
   (B) compliance
   (C) complies
   (D) comply

8. Ms. Smith believes that the prize draw event will encourage customers ------- products.
   (A) purchase
   (B) purchasing
   (C) to purchase
   (D) purchases

77

공식 39 「명사 / 형용사 + to부정사」 관용 표현을 익혀 두자.

to부정사는 명사 뒤에 붙어서 명사를 수식하며, '~할, ~하기 위한'으로 해석된다. 또한 특정 형용사와 짝을 이뤄 「be+형용사+to do」의 구문을 이루기도 한다.

At Mostcom, we reserve the right (**to search** / ~~searching~~) customers' bags.
→ 빈칸이 앞 명사 right를 수식하는 자리
모스트컴에서, 우리는 고객들의 가방을 살펴볼 권리를 가진다.

The maintenance crew was able (**to identify** / ~~identifies~~) the cause of water leaks.
→ 빈칸은 앞 be able과 결합해 '~할 수 있다'를 의미
그 정비 요원은 누수의 원인을 규명할 수 있었다.

비법 노트

■ 명사+to부정사

ability to do ~할 수 있는 능력	plan to do ~할 계획	attempt to do ~하려는 시도
decision to do ~하려는 결정	effort to do ~하기 위한 노력	chance to do ~할 기회
opportunity to do ~할 기회	offer to do ~하자는 제안	proposal to do ~하자는 제안
right to do ~할 권리	way to do ~하기 위한 방법	obligation to do ~할 의무

■ be+형용사+to부정사

be (un)able to do ~할 수 있다[없다]	be bound to do 반드시 ~하다	be eager to do ~하기를 간절히 원하다
be eligible to do ~할 자격이 되다	be willing to do 기꺼이 ~하다	be ready to do ~할 준비가 되다
be likely[prone] to do ~할 것 같다	be sure to do 반드시 ~해라	be scheduled[set] to do ~할 예정이다
be pleased[delighted / happy] to do ~하게 되어 기쁘다		be reluctant[hesitant] to do ~하길 망설이다

[예제] Sharon Gilbert is eager ------- on her new role as a plant manager in Halifax.

(A) take (B) to take
(C) taking (D) will take

be eager + ------- ⋯→ to부정사

빈칸 앞 is eager가 to부정사와 짝을 이뤄 '~하기를 간절히 원하다'란 의미를 갖는다.   정답 **(B)**

샤론 길버트는 핼리팩스 공장 관리인으로서 새 역할을 맡길 원한다.

공식 40 전치사 to로 끝나는 관용 표현은 ing를 붙여 외운다.

to 뒤에 빈칸이 올 경우, to부정사의 to 뒤에는 동사원형, 전치사 to 뒤에는 명사나 동명사(V-ing)가 온다. 전치사 to를 to부정사로 헷갈리지 않도록 전치사 to로 끝나는 관용 표현은 ing를 붙여 외우면 편하다.

We look forward to (**meeting** / ~~meet~~) you at the interview. 면접 때 당신을 만나기를 기대한다.
→ look forward 뒤에 오는 to는 전치사이다.

비법 노트 전치사 to+V-ing

be committed to ing ~에 헌신[전념]하다	be dedicated to ing ~에 전념하다	be devoted to ing ~에 전념하다
be accustomed to ing ~에 익숙하다	be subject to ing ~의 대상이다	look forward to ing ~을 고대하다
be comparable to ing ~에 필적할 만하다	contribute to ing ~에 기여하다	in addition to ing ~에 추가로

[예제] In addition to ------- free consultations, we also provide quotes at no cost.

(A) offer (B) offering
(C) offers (D) be offered

전치사 + ------- ⋯→ 동명사

빈칸 앞 to가 전치사이므로 동사원형은 오답이며, 빈칸 뒤에 명사구가 있으므로 명사도 오답

정답 **(B)** 동명사   오답 (A) 동사 / 명사 (C) 동사 / 명사 (D) 동사

무료 상담을 제공할 뿐 아니라, 우리는 또한 무료로 견적서를 제공한다.

공식으로 해결하는 실전문제

해설집 p.28

1. Ms. Lynne's leadership has contributed greatly to ------- strong relationships with local business partners.
   (A) building
   (B) builder
   (C) build
   (D) have built

2. Atlantis travel agency is dedicated to ------- travelers with the best holiday experience.
   (A) provide
   (B) have provided
   (C) providing
   (D) provider

3. Increasingly variable precipitation is likely ------- the water supply across the country.
   (A) to affect
   (B) affect
   (C) affecting
   (D) affected

4. In an effort ------- on operating expenses, BNC Corp. is striving to become paperless.
   (A) save
   (B) saving
   (C) will save
   (D) to save

5. The study shows that exceptional leaders are more willing ------- the risks and move an organization forward.
   (A) taker
   (B) taking
   (C) will take
   (D) to take

6. Chris Crumb, Curator of D-Gallery, is committed to ------- together art regardless of genre classification.
   (A) pulls
   (B) pulling
   (C) pulled
   (D) be pulled

7. The contest winners will receive an opportunity ------- a presentation at the BIO Business Forum.
   (A) giving
   (B) to give
   (C) to giving
   (D) gave

8. The Chief Financial Officer of Sunray Power is looking forward to ------- his company's remarkable achievements at the shareholder meeting.
   (A) presenting
   (B) presentation
   (C) presenter
   (D) present

UNIT 05 to부정사 & 동명사

공식 41 plan 뒤는 to부정사가 답이다.

to부정사를 목적어로 취하는 동사들이 있다. 동사 뒤에 빈칸이 있으면 빈칸 앞 동사를 보고 to부정사를 바로 고를 수 있도록 암기해 두자.

The hiring committee plans (~~hold~~ / **to hold**) a job fair in May. 고용 위원회는 5월에 채용 박람회를 개최할 계획이다.
→ 목적어 자리이므로 명사 역할을 하는 to부정사가 정답

We would like (**to invite** / ~~inviting~~) you to the Award Ceremony. 우리는 당신을 시상식에 초대하고 싶습니다.
→ would like는 to부정사를 목적어로 취한다.

비법 노트 to부정사를 목적어로 취하는 동사

would like to do ~하고 싶다	want to do ~하길 원하다	wish to do ~하길 바라다	hope to do ~하길 희망하다
plan to do ~할 계획이다	need to do ~할 필요가 있다	strive to do ~하도록 노력하다	fail to do ~하지 못하다
offer to do ~할 것을 제안하다	ask to do ~할 것을 부탁하다	decide to do ~하기로 결정하다	tend to do ~하는 경향이 있다

예제 The factory hopes ------- labor productivity and efficiency by replacing old machinery.

(A) to increase   (B) increasing
(C) increasingly (D) increases

hope + ------- ⋯→ to부정사

정답 **(A)**   오답 (B) 동명사 / 분사 (C) 부사 (D) 동사 / 명사

공장은 낡은 기계를 교체해 노동 생산성 및 효율성을 제고하기를 희망한다.

공식 42 consider 뒤는 동명사가 답이다.

목적어 자리에 동명사(V-ing)가 오는 동사들도 정해져 있다. 빈칸 앞 동사를 보고 동명사를 바로 고를 수 있도록 암기해 두자.

George is considering (**changing** / ~~to change~~) his career. 조지는 직업을 바꿀 것을 고려 중이다.
→ consider는 목적어로 to부정사를 취하지 않는다.

We hope that our new subscribers will enjoy (~~reads~~ / **reading**) our articles.
우리는 새로운 구독자들이 우리 글을 읽는 것을 즐기기를 바란다.

비법 노트 동명사를 목적어로 취하는 동사

avoid -ing ~을 피하다	consider -ing ~을 고려하다	recommend -ing ~을 추천하다
discontinue -ing ~을 중단하다	suggest -ing ~을 제안하다	enjoy -ing ~을 즐기다
keep -ing ~을 유지하다	mind -ing ~을 꺼리다	finish -ing ~을 끝내다

SKILL UP to부정사와 동명사 둘 다 목적어로 갖는 동사들도 있다.
like ~을 좋아하다   start[begin] ~을 시작하다   continue ~을 계속하다   intend ~을 의도하다

예제 To keep your computer safe, avoid ------- anything from an unfamiliar Web site.

(A) installed   (B) to install
(C) installs   (D) installing

avoid + ------- ⋯→ 동명사

정답 **(D)**

컴퓨터를 안전하게 유지하기 위해, 생소한 웹 사이트로부터 어떤 것도 설치하지 마세요.

공식으로 해결하는 실전문제

해설집 p.29

1. We recommend ------- tickets in advance through the Web site because the park can get very crowded.
   (A) purchasing
   (B) purchase
   (C) purchased
   (D) to purchase

2. Dr. Remington suggests ------- the amount of time that you spend on social media.
   (A) limits
   (B) limit
   (C) limited
   (D) limiting

3. After serious consideration, the management has decided ------- the contract with Nexus Travel to cut costs.
   (A) is terminating
   (B) has terminated
   (C) to terminate
   (D) termination

4. Although Jeff Clark is the CEO of FlyAsia Airways, he does not mind ------- in economy class.
   (A) to fly
   (B) flying
   (C) flew
   (D) flies

5. GemPro provides free trial options for those who wish ------- our product before making a purchase decision.
   (A) is using
   (B) used
   (C) using
   (D) to use

6. Digitalway always strives ------- fast and reliable Internet connections for all customers in the region.
   (A) to provide
   (B) having provided
   (C) provider
   (D) provided

7. AP Publishing plans ------- résumés until next week and then hold interviews the week after.
   (A) accept
   (B) acceptable
   (C) accepting
   (D) to accept

8. Waimat Vineyards keeps ------- the goal of becoming the leading producer of top quality wines in South America.
   (A) to pursue
   (B) pursued
   (C) pursuing
   (D) pursues

UNIT 05 To부정사 & 동명사

공식 43 빈칸 뒤에 목적어 없으면 명사 vs. 목적어 있으면 동명사

동명사는 명사처럼 주어, 목적어, 보어로 쓰이지만, 명사와는 달리 뒤에 목적어가 올 수 있다. 빈칸 뒤에 목적어가 없으면 명사, 목적어가 있으면 동명사를 선택한다.

DIO Health specializes in (~~analyzing~~ / **analysis**) of health care data.
→ 빈칸은 전치사 in의 목적어 자리인데, 빈칸 뒤에 목적어가 없다.   DIO 헬스는 건강 관리 자료의 분석을 전문으로 한다.

(**Delivering** / ~~Delivery~~) large packages to other departments is not Liam Perry's duty.
다른 부서에 대형 소포를 배달하는 것은 리암 페리의 업무가 아니다.

비법 노트

- **자동사로 만든 동명사** 뒤에 목적어가 없다.

  Mr. Uemura was interested in **participating in** the workshop. 우에무라 씨는 워크숍 참석에 관심이 있었다.

〔예제〕 Applicants are advised to review what they have entered before ------- the form.

(A) submitting   (B) submit
(C) submission   (D) submits

전치사 + ------- + 명사 ⋯ 동명사

정답 **(A)**   오답 (B) 동사 (C) 명사 (D) 동사

지원자들은 서류를 제출하기 전에, 입력한 것을 검토할 것을 권고받는다.

공식 44 전치사 뒤는 동명사가 1순위이다.

동명사 문제는 전치사 뒤 목적어 자리에 동명사를 넣는 문제가 가장 많이 출제된다. 전치사 뒤에 빈칸이 있고 빈칸 뒤에 명사구가 있으면, 즉 전치사와 명사구 사이의 빈칸은 동명사가 1순위이다.

Patrons must check out all books before (~~left~~ / **leaving**) the library.
→ 빈칸은 명사 역할을 하면서 the library를 목적어로 취하는 동명사 자리   고객들은 도서관을 나가기 전에 모든 책을 대출해야 한다.

PayMoby lets you pay online without (**registering** / ~~registers~~) your account.
페이모비는 계좌 등록 없이 온라인 계산이 가능하게 해 준다.

비법 노트

전치사+**동명사**+명사구	전치사+**형용사**+명사구
빈칸 뒤의 명사구가 빈칸의 목적어일 때는 동명사	빈칸이 뒤의 명사를 수식하는 자리라면 형용사
without (**registering** / ~~registers~~) your account → your account가 registering의 목적어 계좌 등록 없이	without (~~registering~~ / **registered**) nurses → 분사 형용사 registered가 명사를 수식하는 역할 공인된 간호사들 없이

〔예제〕 World Bank plans to expand its business by ------- overseas branch offices.

(A) opened   (B) opens
(C) opening   (D) open

전치사 + ------- + 명사구 ⋯ 동명사

빈칸은 전치사 뒤 목적어 자리

정답 **(C)**

월드 은행은 해외 지점을 개설함으로써 사업을 확장할 계획이다.

공식으로 해결하는 실전문제

1. Upon ------- a delivery containing damaged goods, you have up to 15 days to return them for a full refund.
   (A) receipt
   (B) receive
   (C) receives
   (D) receiving

2. Install-Ban is the perfect solution to prevent employees from ------- software on company computers.
   (A) installing
   (B) installs
   (C) install
   (D) installed

3. The manual explains how you can back up the database management system without -------.
   (A) interrupting
   (B) interrupt
   (C) interrupts
   (D) interruption

4. The board members expressed reservation about ------- the retail price as it might lead to lower demand.
   (A) increases
   (B) increasing
   (C) increased
   (D) increasingly

5. The president of Ulett-Milton stated that ------- the company into two different companies would help streamline operations.
   (A) division
   (B) divides
   (C) dividing
   (D) divisible

6. Our online courses are ideal for those who are interested in ------- their basic computer skills.
   (A) improvement
   (B) improving
   (C) improves
   (D) improved

7. Before ------- for a job, you are advised to prepare a list of professional references such as former colleagues, supervisors or clients.
   (A) apply
   (B) applying
   (C) applies
   (D) application

8. Thanks to ------- investments in manufacturing equipment, the factory achieved a high level of productivity growth.
   (A) consider
   (B) considering
   (C) considerable
   (D) considers

YBM TEST

1. To ------- online sales, it is vital that our customers leave positive reviews and feedback.
   (A) increases
   (B) increased
   (C) increasing
   (D) increase

2. Job seekers are advised ------- good communication and problem solving skills instead of relying on certificates they have acquired.
   (A) to develop
   (B) developing
   (C) developed
   (D) development

3. The board members decided ------- a reward at each meeting to the member who had shown the most commitment.
   (A) give
   (B) to give
   (C) giving
   (D) having given

4. Our subscribers can enjoy ------- all of *I-Money* magazine's contents on their tablet with access to our digital edition.
   (A) reading
   (B) reader
   (C) to read
   (D) to have read

5. Unlike its rival chain Best Shop Co., Al-Mart Stores will discontinue ------- free unlimited shipping starting next month.
   (A) offer
   (B) offering
   (C) offered
   (D) to offer

6. ------- two hours before a flight is not always necessary if you are flying domestically.
   (A) Arrive
   (B) Arrives
   (C) Arrived
   (D) Arriving

7. A lot of small business owners are concerned about ------- the minimum wage because it will increase the costs of hiring workers.
   (A) to raise
   (B) raised
   (C) raising
   (D) raiser

8. NetCloud, the software firm, has announced its decision ------- Nerby, the online advertising company.
   (A) acquisition
   (B) to acquire
   (C) acquires
   (D) acquired

9. Any claims must be reported within 15 days of the invoice date for customers ------- a full refund.
   (A) receipt
   (B) receive
   (C) receiving
   (D) to receive

10. Cybersecurity experts urge users ------- a good anti-virus program and keep their computers up-to-date.
    (A) install
    (B) installing
    (C) to install
    (D) have installed

11. All prices and menu items are subject to ------- based on market or seasonal availability.

    (A) changing
    (B) change
    (C) changed
    (D) changer

12. Zenna Jennings noted in her blog that she had finished ------- the first draft of her upcoming novel *Silver Age*.

    (A) writing
    (B) wrote
    (C) writer
    (D) written

13. LingFong Agency, a public relations firm based in Singapore, is planning ------- its first international branch in Seoul next month.

    (A) opening
    (B) openings
    (C) opens
    (D) to open

14. After successful ------- of the defensive driving course, you may be eligible for insurance discounts.

    (A) complete
    (B) completion
    (C) completing
    (D) completed

15. Dr. Sanchez is scheduled ------- an opening speech for the 12th International Conference on Alzheimer's disease.

    (A) give
    (B) giver
    (C) to give
    (D) gives

16. Certain groups of people who meet specific criteria will be exempt from ------- income taxes.

    (A) pay
    (B) payment
    (C) pays
    (D) paying

17. ------- maintain our food safety standards, we do not allow any leftover food to be taken out of the restaurant.

    (A) In order to
    (B) As a result of
    (C) So that
    (D) Considerably

18. The proposal ------- a waterfront stadium requires approval of the state government.

    (A) to build
    (B) building
    (C) builder
    (D) built

19. Green Breeze is committed to ------- renewable energy sources, particularly wind energy.

    (A) develops
    (B) developing
    (C) developer
    (D) development

20. Elizabeth Dayton will be recognized at the annual Employee Awards for ------- consistently excellent customer service.

    (A) delivery
    (B) delivers
    (C) deliverer
    (D) delivering

PART 6

공식 45 — 시제 문제 1 — 앞뒤 문장 동사의 시제를 확인한다.

파트 6의 시제 문제는 빈칸이 있는 문장만으로는 답을 고를 수 없고 주변 문맥을 통해 답을 찾을 수 있는 문제가 출제되고 있다. 빈칸의 앞뒤 문장에서 동사의 시제를 확인한 후 시간의 흐름을 파악한다.

만점 전략

1. 시간의 흐름으로 파악하는 경우

답장을 쓰고 있다 →	귀하께서 요청했다 요청할 것이다 →	요청대로 ~했다
절차를 개선하고 있다 개선해야 한다 →	다음 달부터 바뀔 것이다 →	효율성이 높아질 것이다
근로자가 더 필요하다 →	일자리가 증가해 왔다 →	정부는 경제 호전의 징후로 여긴다 여겼었다

2. 광고: 정보 전달을 목적으로 하기 때문에 주로 현재 시제로 표현된다.

우리 아파트는 전망이 좋다 → 냉방 시설이 구비되어 있다 → 공간도 넓다
좋았다

3. 공지/회람: 앞으로 있을 계획 및 변경 사항을 알리는 글이 많기 때문에 주로 미래 시제로 표현된다.

새 장비가 설치되었음을 알린다 → 업무 흐름이 향상될 것이다 → ~또한 기대한다
향상되었다

예제
해설집 p.33

To: All Boa Beverage Employees
From: Nora Parmetti

At yesterday's meeting, **❶the board of directors** of the Boa Beverage Company unanimously **approved the recommendation of current chairman** and chief executive officer **Hugh Gilbert** for the firm's senior leadership structure. Under the new structure, **❷Michael Parkinson**, chief operating officer, **will succeed Mr. Gilbert** as CEO, effective next month. Mr. Gilbert ------- to serve as chairman of the board of directors.

(A) will continue   (B) had continued
(C) was continuing (D) will have continued

문맥으로 시제 찾기

❶ 첫 문장: 이사회가 길버트 씨를 승인했다.
❷ 빈칸 앞: 파킨슨 씨가 그의 후임이 될 것이다.
⋯ 길버트 씨는 의장으로서의 임무를 '지속할 것이다'가 문맥상 적절하다

정답 (A) 미래 시제

YBM TEST

해설집 p.33

Questions 1-4 refer to the following letter.

Patrick Louis
215 Orchard Lane,
San Francisco, CA 92010

Dear Mr. Louis,

We are writing to inform you about a delayed rent payment. According to the Rental Agreement, you are supposed to pay the rent by the 5th day of ------- calendar month. However, our records show that your rent ------- much later than that on a regular basis, which is a breach of the terms of our agreement. -------. From now on, if the rent is not received in time, we will assume that you are no longer interested in staying in our apartment.

We request that you pay the rent by the due date. Thank you in advance for your -------.

Regards,
Nancy Bower
Property Manager

---

1. (A) all
   (B) each
   (C) another
   (D) most

2. (A) has been paid
   (B) will be paid
   (C) should be paid
   (D) pays

3. (A) Payment will be accepted in cash only.
   (B) Due to rising housing costs, it is necessary to increase your rent.
   (C) Since you are a new tenant, we will waive the first month's rent.
   (D) We cannot accept such repeated delays in payment.

4. (A) cooperation
   (B) renewal
   (C) information
   (D) solution

UNIT 06 분사

기본 학습

분사는 동사원형에 ing나 ed를 붙여 형용사로 활용하는 말이다.

역할

형용사와 마찬가지로 명사 앞이나 뒤에서 명사를 직접 수식하거나 명사에 대해 보충 설명하는 보어 역할을 한다.

명사 수식	Recently **revised** <u>policies</u> have been posted on the company intranet. 최근에 개정된 규정이 회사 인트라넷에 게시되었다. <u>Entries</u> **received** after the deadline will not be considered. 마감일 이후에 접수된 출품작은 고려되지 않을 것이다.
주격 보어	The flight <u>has been</u> **canceled** due to the inclement weather conditions. 악천후로 인해 비행이 취소되었다. The recent data shows that an economic recession <u>is</u> **coming**. 최근 자료는 경기 침체가 가까워오고 있음을 보여준다.
목적격 보어	Dr. Choi will talk about how to <u>keep</u> employees **motivated** at work. 최 박사는 직장에서 직원들에게 계속 동기가 부여될 수 있도록 하는 방법에 대해 강연할 것이다.

성질

동사 역할은 할 수 없지만 동사의 성질을 가지고 있어서 능동/수동의 성질을 띤다. 현재분사(V-ing)는 '~한/하고 있는'으로 능동 및 진행의 의미를 가지고, 과거분사(V-ed)는 '~된/해진'으로 수동의 의미를 가진다. 또한 명사를 뒤에서 수식할 때 현재분사(V-ing)는 동사처럼 뒤에 목적어가 있고, 과거분사(V-ed)는 목적어가 없다.

명사 앞	현재분사	Let's take the **moving** staircase to go up to the next floor. 움직이는 계단(에스컬레이터)을 타고 위 층으로 갑시다.
	과거분사	Please refer to the **attached** file for more details. 추가 정보를 원한다면 첨부된 파일을 참고하세요.
명사 뒤	현재분사	You can find a list of the companies **attending** <u>the event</u> on our Web site. 　　　　　　　　　　　　　　　　　　　　　　　　　　　목적어 우리 웹 사이트에서 행사에 참석하는 회사들의 명단을 확인할 수 있다.
	과거분사	All employees **involved** <u>in the project</u> should report directly to Ms. Tartt. 　　　　　　　　　　　　전치사구 그 프로젝트에 관련된 모든 직원들은 타트 씨에게 직접 보고해야 한다.

분사구문

「접속사+주어+동사」의 형태에서 접속사와 주어를 생략하고, 동사를 분사(동사원형+-ing)로 바꿔서 문장 내에서 부사처럼 쓰는 수식어구이다. 주로 분사로 시작하며, 완전한 절 앞이나 뒤에 붙어 시간, 이유, 결과 등에 대해 부연 설명을 해 준다.

시간	**While Mr. Yamaguchi reviewed** the document, he found several spelling mistakes. = **Reviewing** the document, 서류를 검토하면서, 야마구치 씨가 철자 오류를 몇 개 발견했다.
	Every security officer should wear their uniforms **while they are** on duty. 모든 경비 담당자는 근무 중에 유니폼을 입어야 한다. = **while*** on duty. → 명확한 의미 전달을 위해 접속사가 필요한 경우에는 생략하지 않는다. → be동사의 분사인 being은 생략될 수 있으므로 접속사 뒤에 전치사구만 남을 수 있다.
이유	**Because the banquet hall was constructed** 40 years ago, it needs to be renovated. = **Constructed** 40 years ago, 그 연회장은 40년 전에 건설되었으므로 수리될 필요가 있다.
	As the employees had achieved the sales goals, they received a bonus. = **Having achieved** the sales goals, 직원들이 매출 목표를 달성했기 때문에 보너스를 받았다. → 문장의 시제보다 앞선 시제일 때는 완료형 분사 having p.p.를 쓴다.
결과	Ms. Claude self-published her essay as an e-book, **and she sold** over 50,000 copies. 클로드 씨는 전자 책으로 에세이를 직접 출판하여, 5만 부 이상을 판매했다. = **selling** over 50,000 copies.
동시	As summer approaches, heat stress is becoming an issue. **With summer approaching**, 여름이 다가오면서 더위 스트레스가 문제가 되고 있다. → 동시에 일어나는 상황은 주로 「with+명사+분사」의 형태로 나타낸다.

공식 46. 명사 앞 분사는 '명사가 ~하면' ing vs. '명사가 ~되면' p.p.

분사가 명사 앞에서 수식할 때, 분사가 수식 받는 명사와 능동 관계이면 현재분사, 수동 관계이면 과거분사를 쓴다. 즉, 분사가 '~하는'으로 해석되면 ing, '~된'으로 해석되면 p.p.를 고른다.

This renovation project will be a (**refreshing** / ~~refreshed~~) change for our customers.
→ change(변화)가 활력을 '불어넣는' 주체
이번 수리 작업이 우리 고객들에게 신선한 변화를 선사할 것이다.

You can select your (~~preferring~~ / **preferred**) payment method in our EasyPay app.
→ method(방식)는 사람에 의해 '선호되는' 대상
당신은 우리의 이지페이 앱에서 당신이 선호하는 지불 방식을 선택할 수 있다.

[예제] The ------- delivery date will vary, depending on the shipping service you select.

(A) estimates   (B) estimated
(C) estimating   (D) estimation

배송일은 '추정되는' 것이므로 ⋯ p.p.
빈칸은 명사 delivery date(배송일)를 수식하는 자리
정답 (B) 추정된   **오답** (A) 동사 / 명사 (D) 명사
예상 배송일은 당신이 선택한 배송 서비스에 따라 다를 수 있다.

공식 47. 의미가 헷갈리는 분사가 있다.

~ing / ~ed로 끝나는 단어 중에는 대부분의 분사가 지니는 능동 ing(~한) / 수동 ed(~된)의 의미와 다른 것들이 있는데, 이런 표현들은 생김새와 뜻 있는 그대로 외워 둔다.

Mr. Boman played a (**leading** / ~~led~~) role in the recent project. 보면 씨는 최근 프로젝트에서 주도적인 역할을 했다.
Due to an (~~unexpecting~~ / **unexpected**) flight delay, Mr. Long had to reschedule the meeting.
예상치 못한 항공편 지연 때문에, 롱 씨는 회의 일정을 다시 잡아야 했다.

비법 노트

ing형		p.p.형	
rising 오르는	leading 선두의	limited 제한[한정]된	used 중고의
increasing 증가하는	outstanding 뛰어난	detailed 상세한	damaged 손상된
growing 커지는	contributing 기여[기고]하는	updated 최신의	skilled 숙련된
existing 기존의	upcoming 곧 있을	revised 수정된	experienced 경험[경력]이 많은
remaining 남아 있는	approaching 다가오는	extended 길어진, 연장된	qualified 자격을 갖춘
lasting 지속적인	promising 유망한	complicated 복잡한	accomplished 뛰어난
challenging 어려운, 힘든	inviting 매력[유혹]적인	scheduled 예정된	authorized 공인된
demanding 까다로운	surrounding 주변의	designated 지정된	unexpected 예상치 못한
missing 분실된, 빠진	pending 미결[미정]인, 곧 있을	enclosed 동봉된	unprecedented 전례 없는
preceding 이전의	rewarding 보람 있는	written 서면으로 된	valued 소중한

[예제] In Hard Rock Stadium, smoking is only permitted in ------- areas.

(A) designation   (B) designates
(C) designated   (D) designating

명사를 수식하는 빈칸 ⋯ 형용사 자리
'지정된 구역에'라는 의미가 자연스럽다.
정답 (C)
하드록 경기장에서, 흡연은 지정된 장소에서만 허용된다.

공식으로 해결하는 실전문제

1. After Oxgem reviews the ------- costs for the system upgrade, a final decision will be made on whether to proceed.
   (A) proposed
   (B) propose
   (C) proposals
   (D) proposing

2. A ------- unemployment rate is usually regarded as a sign of a weakening economy.
   (A) rises
   (B) rise
   (C) rising
   (D) rose

3. Last Saturday, a ------- number of Mike's Brand sneakers went on sale at stores nationwide.
   (A) limited
   (B) limiting
   (C) limits
   (D) limitation

4. Wizer Pharmaceuticals provides assistance with the ------- visa application process for foreign employees.
   (A) complicate
   (B) complicating
   (C) complication
   (D) complicated

5. The observatory in the Highfields Park is known for its fantastic view of the ------- landscape.
   (A) surround
   (B) surrounding
   (C) surrounds
   (D) surrounded

6. TDF members get special access to ------- tickets for a variety of Broadway performances.
   (A) discounts
   (B) discounted
   (C) discounting
   (D) discounter

7. The article addresses several ------- changes to the government's new housing policy.
   (A) expecting
   (B) expectation
   (C) expectantly
   (D) expected

8. Buñol is a small but ------- town where the Spanish festival, La Tomatina is held every year.
   (A) invitation
   (B) invited
   (C) inviting
   (D) invite

공식 48 분사가 명사를 뒤에서 수식할 때는 분사 뒤 목적어 유무를 확인한다.

분사가 혼자서 명사를 수식할 때는 명사 앞에 위치하고, 분사 뒤에 다른 성분이 딸려와 수식어가 길어질 때는 명사의 뒤에서 수식한다. 빈칸이 명사를 뒤에서 수식하는 분사 자리일 때, 빈칸 뒤에 목적어가 있으면 V-ing, 목적어가 없으면 p.p.가 답이다.

Construction is underway on the bridge (**connecting** / ~~connected~~) the two buildings.
→ 빈칸 뒤에 목적어 the two buildings가 있다. 두 건물을 이어 주는 다리가 건설되는 중이다.

Handling fees will apply for concert tickets (**reserved** / ~~reserving~~) online.
→ 빈칸 뒤에 목적어가 없고 부사 online만 있으므로 수동 분사 온라인으로 예약된 콘서트 티켓에는 취급 수수료가 적용된다.

비법 노트
- **자동사로 만든 분사** 뒤에 목적어가 없어도 ing가 답이 된다.
  Employees **applying** for a maternity leave are required ~. 출산 휴가를 신청하는 직원들은 ~해야 한다.
  전치사

[예제] This offer is valid only for orders ------- through our Web site.

(A) placed (B) placing
(C) places (D) are placed

명사 + ------- + 전치사 → p.p.

빈칸은 명사 orders(주문)를 뒤에서 수식하는 분사 자리이고, 뒤에 목적어가 없다. **정답 (A)** 과거분사

이 할인가는 우리 웹 사이트를 통해 이루어진 주문에만 해당된다.

공식 49 명사가 감정을 느끼면 p.p. vs. 못 느끼면 ing

감정을 표현하는 분사는 감정을 느끼는 대상을 수식할 때는 과거분사를 쓰고, 감정을 일으키는 원인이 되는 명사를 수식할 때는 현재분사를 쓴다.

We would be (~~pleasing~~ / **pleased**) if you accepted our invitation. 당신이 우리의 초청을 받아준다면 기쁘겠습니다.
Frank found his job (**overwhelming** / ~~overwhelmed~~) at first. 프랭크는 처음에 그의 일이 벅차다고 생각했다.

비법 노트

감정을 일으키는 쪽이면 ing	감정을 느끼는 쪽이면 p.p.	감정을 일으키는 쪽이면 ing	감정을 느끼는 쪽이면 p.p.
amazing 놀라운	amazed 놀란	gratifying 만족스러운	gratified 만족한, 기뻐하는
encouraging 고무적인	encouraged 고무된	surprising 놀라운	surprised 놀란
startling 놀라운	startled 놀란	fascinating 매혹적인	fascinated 매료된
exciting 신나는	excited 신이 난, 흥분한	confusing 혼란스러운	confused 혼란스러워하는
interesting 흥미로운	interested 흥미를 느낀	disappointing 실망스러운	disappointed 실망한
pleasing/delighting 기분 좋게 하는	pleased/delighted 기쁜	frustrating 좌절감을 주는	frustrated 좌절한
satisfying/satisfactory 만족스러운	satisfied 만족한	overwhelming 압도적인	overwhelmed 압도당한

* 명사를 수식하는 자리인데 의미가 비슷한 일반 형용사와 분사 중에서 정답을 골라야 한다면 일반 형용사를 선택한다.
We enjoyed a (**delightful**/~~delighting~~) lunch buffet at the restaurant. 레스토랑에서 기분 좋은 점심 뷔페를 즐겼다.

[예제] John Magnani is famous for his ------- skills as a presenter and public speaker.

(A) amazed (B) amaze
(C) amazement (D) amazing

skills는 감정을 못 느낌 → ing

빈칸의 수식을 받는 skills(기술)는 '놀라움을 유발하는' 원인

정답 (D) 현재분사

존 매그나니는 진행자 및 연설가로서의 놀라운 능력으로 유명하다.

공식으로 해결하는 실전문제

1. Investors were ------- to learn that the coffee giant, Coffibox will close its online business.
   (A) surprise
   (B) surprising
   (C) surprises
   (D) surprised

2. During the second week of June, the number of parking spaces ------- for visitors will be limited due to construction work.
   (A) reserving
   (B) reserve
   (C) reservation
   (D) reserved

3. The city council has released documents ------- its plans to build a new community center.
   (A) outline
   (B) outlines
   (C) outlining
   (D) outlined

4. We are ------- to announce the launch of our new SweetHome Web site, which will cover the latest information on home decorating trends.
   (A) excite
   (B) excited
   (C) excitedly
   (D) exciting

5. In his statement ------- Monday morning, Space Airways CEO Mira Nunez apologized to the passenger mistreated by the crew members.
   (A) released
   (B) releasing
   (C) releases
   (D) releasable

6. The developers of the new XYZ video game are hoping to attract new players by offering ------- new features.
   (A) impression
   (B) impressive
   (C) impressed
   (D) impresses

7. This year's winner of the WorldChic Design Award is Fanali Louis, ------- for her creative thinking and practical designs.
   (A) knowing
   (B) know
   (C) known
   (D) knew

8. Anyone ------- an online application for a passport must provide personal information such as name, date of birth and home address.
   (A) submitting
   (B) submits
   (C) submitted
   (D) submit

공식 50 절의 앞이나 뒤에 콤마로 연결되는 수식어구가 있으면 분사구문을 떠올리자.

분사구문은 완전한 절 앞이나 뒤에서 콤마(,)로 연결되는 수식어구이다. 주로 분사나 접속사로 시작하며, 명사나 동사로는 시작할 수 없다는 점을 기억한다.

(**Working** / ~~Work~~) as a marketing director, David made many positive contributions.
마케팅 이사로 일하면서, 데이빗은 많은 긍정적인 기여를 했다.

Sejin Law Office recently installed CCTV systems, (**saving** / ~~saved~~) money on security.
세진 법률 사무소는 최근 CCTV 시스템을 설치하고, 보안에 드는 비용을 절감했다.

[예제] ------- with last year, our SUV sales increased 6.3% this year.
(A) Compare (B) Compares
(C) Compared (D) Comparison

------- [수식구], 완전한 절 ⋯ 분사

「___ with last year」는 완전한 절 앞에 붙은 수식어구이므로 동사나 명사는 정답이 될 수 없다.

정답 (C) 분사 **오답** (A) 동사 (B) 동사 (D) 명사

우리의 SUV 차량 판매는 작년과 비교해 올해 6.3% 증가했다.

공식 51 부사절 접속사 뒤에 주어가 없으면 분사가 답이다.

분사구문에서 부사절 접속사가 생략되지 않으면 「접속사+분사~」 형태가 된다. 따라서 빈칸 앞에 부사절 접속사만 있고 주어가 없으면, 동사가 아닌 분사(-ing, p.p.)를 골라야 한다.

Employees should wear safety equipment while (**working** / ~~works~~) at the construction site.
→ while 뒤에 주어와 동사가 없으므로 빈칸은 분사 자리
직원들은 공사장에서 작업하는 동안 안전 장비를 착용해야 한다.

The design project is proceeding smoothly as (**planned** / ~~planning~~).
→ 부사절 접속사 as 뒤에 주어 없이 빈칸으로 끝났으므로 수동형 분사가 필요
디자인 프로젝트는 계획된 대로 순조롭게 진행 중이다.

비법 노트 분사구문 빈출 표현

when -ing ~할 때	when revising a report 보고서를 수정할 때
when p.p. ~될 때	when assembled properly 적절하게 조립됐을 때
as p.p. ~된 대로	as discussed 논의된 대로 as originally scheduled 원래 예정된 대로
unless otherwise p.p. 달리 ~되지 않으면	unless otherwise noted[stated] 달리 명시되지 않으면

[예제] When ------- a video conference meeting in different time zones, you should use the firm's meeting planner.
(A) scheduled (B) schedules
(C) scheduling (D) are scheduling

부사절 접속사 + ------- + 목적어 ⋯ 분사

부사절 접속사(When) 뒤에 주어와 동사가 없으므로 빈칸에 분사가 와야 하고, 빈칸 뒤로 목적어가 있으므로 능동.

정답 (C)

시간대가 다른 지역의 화상 회의 일정을 잡을 때에는 회사의 회의 계획표를 이용해야 한다.

공식으로 해결하는 **실전문제**

해설집 p.35

1. When ------- potential customers, make sure you are dressed well and turn up on time.
   (A) meeting
   (B) met
   (C) meets
   (D) meet

2. The Lany group will open a new shopping center, ------- to attract younger customers.
   (A) hope
   (B) hopes
   (C) hoped
   (D) hoping

3. While ------- the seminar at the Swiss Bel Hotel, you can enjoy free WiFi service.
   (A) attending
   (B) attends
   (C) attendance
   (D) attend

4. For your safety, read the manual thoroughly and operate the machine as -------.
   (A) instructed
   (B) instruction
   (C) instructor
   (D) instruct

5. Mr. Shaw has won 17 Net Music Awards, ------- him the most-awarded musician in the award's history.
   (A) makes
   (B) made
   (C) making
   (D) make

6. When ------- about the resignation rumors, TG Energy CEO Rex Miller declined to comment.
   (A) asking
   (B) asks
   (C) ask
   (D) asked

7. Ms. Cox declined a job offer from *Mobio Journal*, ------- to work as a freelance reporter.
   (A) prefer
   (B) preferred
   (C) preferring
   (D) preference

8. Every laboratory worker should inspect equipment thoroughly, ------- that safeguards are in place.
   (A) ensure
   (B) ensures
   (C) ensuring
   (D) ensured

YBM TEST

1. On our Web site, you will find ------- information on our tools and services as well as shipping options.

    (A) detailing
    (B) detailed
    (C) details
    (D) detail

2. Should you be ------- in extra shifts over the busy season, please contact Donna in the Personnel Department.

    (A) interested
    (B) interests
    (C) interesting
    (D) interest

3. In today's seminar, Dr. Kwan will discuss techniques for effectively dealing with ------- customers.

    (A) demanding
    (B) demands
    (C) demand
    (D) demanded

4. We at OfficeFinder lease or purchase office space, ------- with air conditioning and Internet access.

    (A) equipped
    (B) equipment
    (C) equips
    (D) equipping

5. You need to determine your purpose and identify the key issues related to the topic when ------- the presentation.

    (A) prepared
    (B) prepares
    (C) preparing
    (D) prepare

6. Nearly half of all meat and meat products ------- domestically are imported from foreign countries.

    (A) consume
    (B) consumed
    (C) consumer
    (D) consuming

7. We would be ------- to create a menu to your taste and budget for your wedding ceremony.

    (A) delights
    (B) delightful
    (C) delighted
    (D) delight

8. The smartphone giant, Benysoft relocated its production base to Vietnam, ------- factories in other parts of the world.

    (A) closed
    (B) closure
    (C) closing
    (D) close

9. Many highly ------- applicants are rejected simply because they failed to follow the application instructions precisely.

    (A) qualified
    (B) qualify
    (C) qualification
    (D) qualifying

10. ------- a contract to supply 500 trucks to a Japanese logistics firm, Ms. Song was rewarded with a substantial bonus.

    (A) Having won
    (B) Won
    (C) Had won
    (D) To win

11. At Macy Jewelry, we are constantly working on new designs to keep our customers -------.

(A) satisfies
(B) satisfactorily
(C) satisfying
(D) satisfied

12. WE Network president Steve Simon, ------- by chief financial officer Matt Furlong, met Fan Game CEO Michael Thompson to discuss the merger.

(A) accompanying
(B) accompanied
(C) accompany
(D) will accompany

13. When ------- a job application via e-mail, don't forget to attach your résumé and cover letter to an e-mail message.

(A) send
(B) sending
(C) sent
(D) sends

14. There is concern over soaring health care costs resulting from the ------- elderly population.

(A) grow
(B) growing
(C) grown
(D) grows

15. The payroll department will help you prepare all the income information ------- to file a tax return.

(A) requiring
(B) requires
(C) required
(D) is required

16. Employees at the insurance company found it ------- when profits increased as a result of their hard work.

(A) gratify
(B) gratified
(C) gratifyingly
(D) gratifying

17. The number of Chinese tourists ------- South Korea has plummeted due to the political tension between the two countries.

(A) visitors
(B) visit
(C) visiting
(D) visited

18. ------- rising operating costs, BNDC decided to close all its retail stores in South America.

(A) Face
(B) Faces
(C) Faced
(D) Facing

19. The firm will decide on whether they should adopt flexible working, ------- on the employee survey results.

(A) base
(B) basis
(C) basing
(D) based

20. Once ------- by the city's building committee, work on the Highway 91 expansion will begin immediately.

(A) approves
(B) approved
(C) approving
(D) approval

PART 6

공식 52 — 시제 문제 2 — 문서 작성일도 단서가 된다.

동사의 시제를 묻는 문제에서 빈칸 주변에 날짜가 보이면, 지문의 상단에 문서 작성일이 있는지부터 확인한다. 문서 작성일이 표시된 경우, 빈칸 주변에서 언급된 날짜와 전후 관계만 따져도 쉽게 시제를 파악할 수 있다.

만점 전략

① 문서 작성일을 활용한 문제는 주로 이메일, 편지, 메모에서 출제된다.
② 문서 작성일은 보통 지문의 왼쪽 상단에 표시되어 있다.
③ 확실하게 정해진 미래 일정은 미래 시제 대신에 현재 시제로 표현할 수 있다.

[이메일] 작성일: **2월 15일** – 3월 1일에 본사에 도착하면, 앤더슨 씨가 _____ → (안내할 것이다 / 안내했다)

[편지] 작성일: **5월 11일** – 6월 30일에 당신의 멤버십이 _____ → (종료될 것이다 / 종료되었다)

[메모] 작성일: **9월 21일** – 10월 1일부터, 새 규정이 _____ → (적용된다 / 적용되었다)

예제
해설집 p.38

To: Monique Claude <claude@bluesky.co.uk>
From: Bernard Ashton <ashton@agym.co.uk>
Subject: Membership Renewal
Date: ❶ 5 April

Dear Monique,

This is a friendly reminder to let you know your gym membership ------- on ❷ 31 March. Your membership is invaluable to us, and we would like to take this opportunity to extend our appreciation by offering you a 15% discount on your membership renewal. We look forward to seeing you again soon.

Bernard Ashton

(A) will expire
(B) would have expired
(C) to expire
(D) expired

문서 작성일을 단서로 시제 찾기

❶ 이메일 작성일: 4월 5일
❷ 빈칸: 3월 31일에 대해 언급
⇢ 과거에 일어난 일

정답 (D) 과거 시제
오답 (B) 가정법 과거완료로, 과거 사실의 반대나 추측(~했었을 텐데)을 의미하는 시제

YBM TEST

해설집 p.38

Questions 1-4 refer to the following e-mail.

To: smiller@fyimail.com
From: bsmith@anachems.co.uk
Date: 15 October
Subject: Your first day at Ana Chemical Corporation

Dear Mr. Miller,

We want to tell you that our whole department is so excited about your decision to ------- our offer of employment. As we agreed, you ------- the new job on Monday, November 21. You are expected to get here by 9 A.M.

We offer staff flexible working hours, and we can talk about your normal hours on Monday when you come in. -------, you will meet your new employee mentor, Robert Gore. He will help you get to know the company and your new department.

We aim to orient you regarding both your new job and the company during your first week, and we are putting together a schedule accordingly. -------.

If you have questions, please feel free to e-mail me. We really look forward to working with you.

Sincerely,

Brandon Smith,
Administrative Manager

1. (A) discuss
   (B) receive
   (C) accept
   (D) request

2. (A) starts
   (B) will start
   (C) have started
   (D) did start

3. (A) In addition
   (B) Now that
   (C) If so
   (D) Nevertheless

4. (A) You will also share an office with Mr. Gore.
   (B) We have set up a meeting schedule with the laboratory assistants.
   (C) You will obtain your employment badge.
   (D) You will be sent the finalized schedule this week.

UNIT 07 형용사

기본 학습

명사의 상태나 성질을 나타내는 말로 명사를 수식해 준다.

형태

일반 형용사	-ive, -ous, -ful, -al, -ic, -able 등으로 끝나는 말
	competit**ive** 경쟁이 있는 care**ful** 주의 깊은 centr**al** 중심적인 reli**able** 믿을 수 있는
	Ms. Wescon is working in the **central** area of the city. 웨스컨 씨는 도시의 중심부에서 근무하고 있다.
분사 형용사	동사에 -ing나 -ed를 붙여 형용사로 쓰는 말
	exist**ing** 기존의 last**ing** 지속적인 qualifi**ed** 자격을 갖춘 detail**ed** 상세한
	Only **existing** employees are entitled to apply for the managerial position. 오직 기존 직원들만이 관리직에 지원할 자격이 된다.
명사+ly	「형용사+ly」는 부사, 「명사+ly」는 형용사
	time**ly** 시기적절한 cost**ly** 비용이 드는 like**ly** ~할 것 같은 order**ly** 질서 있는
	Any further delays in the construction project could be very **costly**. 건설 프로젝트에 있어 추가적인 지연은 많은 비용을 유발할 수 있다.

역할

형용사는 주로 명사 바로 앞이나 뒤에 붙어서 명사를 직접 수식하거나 보어 자리에서 명사에 대해 보충 설명해 준다.

명사 수식	Each of our team members played an **important** role. 우리 팀 멤버들 각자가 중요한 역할을 했다.
	Applicants should provide all the details **relevant** to their previous employment. 지원자들은 이전 고용과 관련된 모든 정보를 제공해야 한다.
주격 보어	Fluency in English is **necessary**. 유창한 영어 구사력이 필수적이다.
목적격 보어	Employers try to keep employees **productive**. 고용주들은 직원들을 생산성 있게 하려고 노력한다.

부사

기본 학습

부사도 형용사처럼 다른 말을 꾸며 주는 수식어이다. 단, 형용사는 명사를 수식하고, 명사를 제외한 나머지는 모두 부사가 수식한다.

형태

주로 「형용사 + ly」 형태이지만 ly가 붙지 않는 부사들도 있다.

형용사 + ly	currently 현재 carefully 주의 깊게 promptly 즉시 conveniently 편리하게 usually 보통
	Kobilum is **currently** seeking a visual artist. 코빌럼은 현재 디자이너를 구하는 중입니다.
기타	very 매우 well 잘 ago 전에 ever 언제든 yet 아직 still 여전히 already 이미 once 한 번, 한때
	They are **very** excited about the renovations to the office.
	그들은 사무실 보수에 대해 매우 기대하고 있다.

역할

부사는 (대)명사를 제외한 나머지 즉, 동사, 형용사, 부사, 구, 문장을 수식한다.

동사 수식	Ms. White **regularly** checks her e-mail. 화이트 씨는 이메일을 정기적으로 확인한다.
	= Ms. White checks her e-mail **regularly**.
형용사 수식	The training session was **very** informative. 그 교육 과정은 매우 유익했다.
부사 수식	We select our materials **very** carefully. 우리는 매우 신중하게 재료를 선택한다.
구 수식	The meeting began **promptly** at 2 P.M. 회의는 오후 2시 정각에 시작했다.
문장 수식	**Generally**, employers prefer to hire from within the company.
	일반적으로, 고용주들은 사내 고용을 선호한다.

UNIT 07 형용사 & 부사

공식 53 관부형명 관형형명

형용사는 명사를 수식하거나 보어로 쓰인다. 특히 명사 앞에 형용사가 올 때는 「관사/소유격+(부사)+형용사+명사」 또는 「관사/소유격+(형용사)+형용사+명사」 순서로 잘 온다.

The media plays an (**important** / ~~importance~~) role in society. 그 미디어는 사회에서 중대한 역할을 한다.
→ 빈칸이 뒤에 있는 명사 role을 수식하는 역할

The AP Q1201 laser printer is (~~capably~~ / **capable**) of printing 50 bar codes per minute.
→ 빈칸은 be동사의 보어 자리
AP Q1201 레이저 프린터는 분당 바코드 50개를 인쇄할 수 있다.

비법 노트

- **명사 앞 빈칸**

1. 빈칸이 명사를 수식할 때

관사/소유격	형용사	명사

their **financial** advisor 그들의 재정 고문

관사/소유격	형용사	형용사	명사

the **famous** financial advisor 유명한 재정 고문

2. 빈칸이 형용사를 수식할 때

관사/소유격	부사	형용사	명사

an **environmentally** conscious consumer
환경 문제에 관심 있는 소비자

예제 The Liang Group is expecting to start work on a very ------- number of new building projects.

(A) large   (B) largely
(C) enlarge (D) largeness

관+부+-------+명 → 형용사 자리
빈칸은 명사(number) 앞에서 명사를 수식하는 형용사 자리
정답 (A) 형용사   **오답 (C)** 동사
리앙 그룹은 다수의 신규 건설 프로젝트에 착수할 것을 기대하고 있다.

공식 54 timely는 형용사다.

timely는 ly로 끝나서 부사처럼 생겼지만 '시기적절한'이란 뜻의 형용사이다. 'ly'로 끝나는 형용사를 미리 암기해 부사로 혼동하지 않도록 주의한다.

Customers expect a (**timely** / ~~timing~~) response to their requests.
고객들은 자신들의 요구에 대한 시기 적절한 대응을 기대한다.

비법 노트 빈출 표현

timely 시기적절한	likely 할 것 같은	costly 비용이 드는	orderly 질서 있는	friendly 친절한	lively 활발한
in a timely manner 시기적절하게	be likely to 부정사/that절 ~할 것 같다			in an orderly fashion 질서 있게	

예제 The passengers were asked to leave the ferry in an ------- fashion.

(A) order   (B) orders
(C) ordering (D) orderly

관+-------+명 → 형용사 자리
빈칸은 명사(fashion) 앞에서 명사를 수식하는 형용사 자리
정답 (D) 질서 있는
승객들은 질서 있는 방식으로 배에서 내릴 것을 요청받았다.

공식으로 해결하는 실전문제

해설집 p.39

1. Classico Pizzeria is always crowded with local diners because it offers fairly reasonable prices and an ------- menu.
   (A) extensive
   (B) extend
   (C) extensively
   (D) extension

2. PMC's new internship program provides ------- insight into its business and culture.
   (A) valuable
   (B) value
   (C) valuably
   (D) values

3. Excellent ------- skills are crucial for business owners who need to balance many different duties.
   (A) organizes
   (B) organizationally
   (C) organizational
   (D) organize

4. Management has decided to give up advertising on TV because doing so is too -------.
   (A) cost
   (B) costed
   (C) costs
   (D) costly

5. Flexible leadership is essential to thrive in the ------- competitive business environment.
   (A) increased
   (B) increasingly
   (C) increase
   (D) increasing

6. It is important to ensure that employees work in a comfortable and ------- environment.
   (A) friends
   (B) friend
   (C) friendliness
   (D) friendly

7. Consumers are ------- to provide personal information to online companies because of privacy concerns.
   (A) most reluctantly
   (B) reluctant
   (C) reluctance
   (D) reluctantly

8. A new study finds that global climate change is ------- to have an adverse effect on economic growth.
   (A) likes
   (B) liking
   (C) likely
   (D) likeness

UNIT 07 형용사 & 부사

공식 55 보기에 형용사/ing/p.p.가 섞여 있으면 형용사를 1순위로 고려한다.

형용사 문제의 보기에는 형용사와 성질이 비슷한 분사(ing / p.p.)가 자주 섞여 나오는데, 이럴 경우 일반 형용사를 우선 선택하여 해석상 적절한지 확인한다.

Basic computer skills are (~~necessitating~~ / **necessary**) for an administrative position.
→ 타동사에서 파생된 necessitating 뒤에는 목적어가 와야 한다.   기본적인 컴퓨터 활용 능력은 행정직에 필수적이다.

[예제] SupremeBox offers reliable and ------- storage containers in Detroit and surrounding areas.

(A) affording (B) afford
(C) affordably (D) affordable

~ing 보다는 형용사 ⋯ affordable

명사 storage containers를 수식하는 형용사 자리로 '가격이 적당한 보관 공간'으로 해석된다.

정답 (D) 형용사

슈프림박스는 디트로이트와 주변 지역에 믿을 만하고 가격이 적당한 보관 공간을 제공한다.

공식 56 「every + 단수명사」 vs. 「all + 복수명사」

수량 형용사를 고르는 문제는 빈칸 뒤 명사와의 수일치가 핵심이다. every와 all은 뜻(모든)이 같지만 every는 단수명사, all은 복수 혹은 불가산명사를 수식하므로 빈칸 뒤 명사의 수에 따라 답이 달라진다.

(~~Every~~ / **All**) files should be registered and maintained in a filing system.
→ 빈칸 뒤에 복수명사 files가 있다.   모든 파일들은 파일 시스템에 등록되고 보관되어야 한다.

비법 노트 수량 형용사의 수일치

each 각각의 every 모든 another 또 하나의	가산 단수명사
many(=a number of, numerous) 많은 (a) few 적은 several (몇)몇의 both 둘 다 a variety of(=various) 다양한 a series of 일련의 a range of 다양한 an array of 다수의	복수명사
much 많은 (a) little 적은 a large amount of 많은 a great deal of 많은	불가산명사
some 약간의 most 대부분 all 모든 other 다른 a lot of 많은	복수/불가산명사
no 어떤 ~도 아닌[없는] any 어떤	모든 명사 (가산, 불가산 모두)

* 「every + 숫자 + 복수명사」는 '~마다', 「another + 숫자 + 복수명사」는 '추가적인'이라는 뜻이다.

[예제] According to the survey, ------- employees are in favor of flexible working arrangements.

(A) every (B) little
(C) many (D) each

------- + 복수명사 ⋯ many

정답 (C) 많은 **오답** (A), (D) 가산 단수 (B) 불가산

설문 조사에 따르면, 많은 직원들이 탄력 근무 시간제를 선호한다.

공식으로 해결하는 실전문제

해설집 p. 40

1. Many workplace accidents and injuries are ------- if safety guidelines and regulations are followed carefully.
   (A) preventing
   (B) preventable
   (C) prevention
   (D) prevents

2. The Inverness Community Center has received a ------- donation from Scotia Bank.
   (A) sizeable
   (B) size
   (C) sized
   (D) sizing

3. Although technical training sessions are intended for the new staff, ------- interested employees are welcome to attend.
   (A) each
   (B) every
   (C) any
   (D) much

4. Benn Incorporated offers ------- career development opportunities including certificates and online courses.
   (A) a lot
   (B) each
   (C) every
   (D) many

5. The panel of judges will review ------- entry in the contest and select the winners.
   (A) all
   (B) each
   (C) most
   (D) whole

6. If you would like ------- information about postgraduate admissions, please complete and submit the request form.
   (A) further
   (B) furthering
   (C) furthered
   (D) furthers

7. The most ------- feature of Sportec's first Manchester shirt is its red mosaic pattern.
   (A) notes
   (B) noting
   (C) notable
   (D) notably

8. The accounting team pays ------- attention to the accuracy of the information posted on the corporate Web site.
   (A) many
   (B) few
   (C) every
   (D) much

UNIT 07 형용사 & 부사

공식 57 「be ___ p.p. / ing / 형」는 부사가 답이다.

부사가 동사를 수식할 때는 동사 앞이나 사이에 들어가며, 형용사를 수식할 때는 형용사 앞에 온다.

The files could be recovered after they were (~~accident~~ / **accidentally**) deleted.
그 파일들은 실수로 삭제된 후에 복구될 수 있었다.

비법 노트 빈출 부사 자리

- **동사 앞**   This café **usually** opens before noon. 이 카페는 보통 12시 전에 연다.
- **동사 사이**   The show will **officially** resume production next year. 그 쇼는 공식적으로 내년에 제작을 재개한다.
  I have **already** submitted the report. 난 이미 보고서를 제출했다.
  Ms. Parker is **still** working at the office. 파커 씨는 여전히 사무실에서 근무 중이다.
- **형용사 앞**   The museum is **really** close to the station. 그 박물관은 역과 정말 가깝다.

예제 A system upgrade was ------- completed by the technical support team last night.

(A) succeed   (B) successfully
(C) successful   (D) succeeded

be + ------- + p.p. ⇢ 부사

be동사와 p.p. 사이에서 completed를 수식한다.

정답 (B) 부사   **오답** (A) 동사 (C) 형용사

시스템 업그레이드는 어젯밤에 기술 지원 팀에 의해 성공적으로 마무리되었다.

공식 58 완전한 절 앞이나 뒤에는 부사가 붙는다.

부사는 완전한 절에 덤으로 붙어, 명사를 제외한 다른 말을 꾸미는 수식어이다. 따라서, 부족한 성분이 없는 완전한 절인데도 빈칸이 있으면 부사가 정답일 확률이 제일 높다.

The special offer is available (~~excluding~~ / **exclusively**) to our loyal customers.
→ 빈칸이 완전한 절 뒤에 있고, 그 뒤의 전치사구를 수식한다.   특가 판매는 오로지 단골 고객만이 이용 가능하다.

(**Generally** / ~~General~~), hotels allow guests to check in from 3 P.M.
일반적으로, 호텔들은 오후 3시부터 투숙객들이 체크인하도록 허용한다.

비법 노트

- **주어 + be p.p. + 부사** | **주어 + 자동사 + 부사**
  수동태는 목적어가 없는 게 일반적이므로 「주어 + be p.p.」만으로도 완전한 절이 될 수 있으며, 자동사도 마찬가지이다. 따라서 수동태나 자동사 뒤 빈칸에는 주로 부사나 전치사가 들어간다.
- **SKILL UP** **부사 + 명사(구)**   only / just / even / quite은 부사이지만, 명사나 명사구를 강조하기도 한다.
  even the technician 그 기술자조차도

예제 If your order is sent in multiple shipments, you will be charged ------- for each shipment.

(A) separation   (B) separately
(C) separate   (D) separable

완전한 절 + ------- ⇢ 부사

완전한 절 뒤에 덤으로 빈칸이 왔다.

정답 (B) 부사   **오답** (A) 명사 (C) 형용사/동사 (D) 형용사

당신의 주문품이 복수 배송될 경우, 당신은 각 배송에 대해 따로 요금이 부과될 것이다.

공식으로 해결하는 실전문제

해설집 p.41

1. Gusto Restaurant is ------- located within walking distance of Churchill Square.
   (A) convenience
   (B) conveniently
   (C) convenient
   (D) conveniences

2. Happy Meal franchisees have responded ------- to the new menu options, much to the relief of the company's executives.
   (A) favor
   (B) favorably
   (C) favors
   (D) favorable

3. The Uphone scheduler will ------- send a message at a chosen time even if your phone is switched off.
   (A) automated
   (B) automatic
   (C) automation
   (D) automatically

4. Every machine in the production facility requires regular maintenance in order to function -------.
   (A) proper
   (B) properness
   (C) properly
   (D) more proper

5. Mr. Brown always double-checks whether the information has been entered ------- when writing a report.
   (A) correct
   (B) correctly
   (C) correcting
   (D) correction

6. New traffic lights at the intersection outside the Jarriot Hotel will not be ------- operational until next week.
   (A) fully
   (B) fullest
   (C) full
   (D) fullness

7. The number of visitors has ------- increased since the opening of the new sculpture exhibition.
   (A) noticeable
   (B) noticeably
   (C) notices
   (D) noticed

8. Due to the high volume of applicants, ------- successful candidates will be contacted.
   (A) if
   (B) though
   (C) once
   (D) only

107

UNIT 07 형용사 & 부사

공식 59 late는 늦게 vs. lately는 최근에

lately는 '늦게'가 아니라 '최근에'를 뜻한다. '늦게'를 뜻하는 부사는 late로 형용사 late(늦은)와 형태가 같다. 이와 같이, 형용사에 ly가 붙으면 뜻이 달라지는 부사들은 혼동하기 쉬우므로 주의해야 한다.

The vice president arrived (**late** / ~~lately~~) at the company banquet. 부사장이 회사 연회에 늦게 도착했다.
Ms. Fumora's previous experience is (**closely** / ~~close~~) related to the job requirements.
뮤모라 씨의 예전 경력은 본 직무 요구조건에 밀접하게 연관되어 있다.

비법 노트 ly가 붙어 뜻이 달라지는 부사

close 휑 가까운 휫 가까이	closely 자세히, 밀접하게	near 휑 가까운 휫 가까이	nearly 거의
high 휑 높은 휫 높게	highly 매우, 대단히	large 휑 큰 휫 크게	largely 주로
late 휑 늦은 휫 늦게	lately 최근에	short 휑 짧은 휫 짧게	shortly 곧
low 휑 낮은 휫 낮게	lowly 초라하게, 하찮게	hard 휑 단단한, 어려운 휫 열심히	hardly 거의 ~아니다 / 없다

예제 In a ------- competitive market, strategic pricing is an important factor in generating profits.

(A) high (B) highly
(C) higher (D) highest

매우 경쟁이 심한 → highly

competitive(경쟁이 있는)를 꾸미는 부사 자리이므로, 문맥상 highly(매우)가 잘 어울린다.

정답 (B) 매우

매우 경쟁이 심한 시장에서, 전략적인 가격 책정은 수익을 내는 데 있어 중요한 요소이다.

공식 60 afterwards는 접속사가 아니라 부사다.

afterwards(그 후에)와 같은 접속부사는 접속사와 비슷한 뜻을 가진 부사이므로 절과 절을 연결하는 접속사 자리에 들어갈 수 없다.

(**After** / ~~Afterwards~~) Ms. Downey left the agency, she opened her travel business.
→ 절이 두 개인 문장이므로 빈칸은 접속사 자리
다우니 씨는 대행사를 떠난 이후, 자신의 여행사를 설립했다.

The shipment arrived late, and (~~when~~ / **moreover**) some items were missing.
→ 접속사 and가 있으므로 빈칸은 접속사 자리가 아니다.
배송물이 늦게 도착했고, 게다가 일부 품목들은 빠져 있었다.

비법 노트 접속부사 vs. 접속사

	접속부사	접속사
인과	therefore/thus 그러므로, 따라서	because/since ~ 때문에
역접	however 그러나 nevertheless/nonetheless 그럼에도 불구하고	but 그러나 although/even though 그럼에도 불구하고
시간	then 그때에 afterwards 후에, 나중에	when ~할 때 after ~ 후에
추가	moreover/furthermore/in addition 게다가	and 그리고

예제 The board meeting has been delayed ------- the sales analysis is not ready yet.

(A) because (B) therefore
(C) in addition (D) moreover

절 + ------- + 절 → 접속사

빈칸은 절[The board~delayed]과 절[the sales ~ yet] 사이에서 두 절을 연결하는 접속사 자리

정답 (A) 접속사 오답 (B), (C), (D) 접속부사

매출 분석이 아직 준비되지 않아서 중역 회의가 연기되었다.

공식으로 해결하는 실전문제

해설집 p. 41

1. The leadership training sessions have been suspended ------- in preparation for the new employee orientation.
   (A) late
   (B) lately
   (C) latest
   (D) later

2. Koratek staff will ------- monitor the loading process and ensure proper handling of the cargo.
   (A) close
   (B) closed
   (C) closing
   (D) closely

3. Despite initial enthusiasm for the electric bike, the sales ------- turned out to be poor.
   (A) moreover
   (B) neither
   (C) nevertheless
   (D) except

4. ------- the Bangkok office is currently short-staffed, it is running well because of the dedication of its employees.
   (A) Although
   (B) Despite
   (C) Furthermore
   (D) In addition

5. Mia Motors' sales have surged, ------- because of its successful launch of the new Max-3 SUV.
   (A) largely
   (B) larger
   (C) large
   (D) largest

6. Carla works part time and ------- is ineligible for paid vacations according to our store policy.
   (A) instead
   (B) even though
   (C) therefore
   (D) except

7. ------- Mr. Juntana joined our company's Vancouver office last spring, he worked as a sales representative.
   (A) After all
   (B) When
   (C) Furthermore
   (D) Prior to

8. Nexun released a software update that is ------- recommended for all users.
   (A) high
   (B) higher
   (C) highly
   (D) height

YBM TEST

1. At Freeman Resources, we are ------- searching for new specialists to join our expert pool.

   (A) continually
   (B) continues
   (C) continual
   (D) continues

2. Construction project planning should take into account ------- weather conditions which might influence the work schedule and productivity.

   (A) seasons
   (B) seasonal
   (C) seasonally
   (D) season

3. ------- fitness member is eligible for free personal training during the first month after registration.

   (A) All
   (B) Most
   (C) Every
   (D) Other

4. Vietnam's building and construction industry has developed a ------- plan to respond to domestic needs.

   (A) practice
   (B) practicing
   (C) practical
   (D) practically

5. ------- the film *Far Away* was highly praised by critics, it failed to attract a large audience.

   (A) Nonetheless
   (B) Although
   (C) However
   (D) Consequently

6. Ms. Hackett was chosen to represent our company at the panel discussions because of her ability to present ideas in an ------- fashion.

   (A) orderly
   (B) ordering
   (C) orders
   (D) order

7. Research from Moomberg Energy indicates that falling battery costs will make electric cars more ------- within a decade.

   (A) afford
   (B) affordably
   (C) affording
   (D) affordable

8. The Animi logo has ------- changed since it was designed more than sixty years ago.

   (A) hard
   (B) harder
   (C) hardly
   (D) harden

9. Argon Corp. was the only company to present a ------- acceptable bid for Highway 12.

   (A) reason
   (B) reasonable
   (C) reasonably
   (D) reasoning

10. To apply for a student grant, you should mail the application form along with all the ------- documents to the Financial Aid Office.

    (A) relevance
    (B) relevant
    (C) relevantly
    (D) relevancy

11. Your tax refund will be transferred ------- to your desired bank account in one month.

    (A) director
    (B) directing
    (C) directed
    (D) directly

12. After deliveries are fully checked, ------- discrepancy in the quantity should be reported immediately to the supplier.

    (A) many
    (B) any
    (C) others
    (D) several

13. All subscribers to *Huffington Daily Post* ------- receive updates from COL media group.

    (A) regularly
    (B) regular
    (C) regularity
    (D) regularized

14. Mr. Park ordered his team members to work ------- together to organize the conference.

    (A) closely
    (B) close
    (C) closed
    (D) closing

15. Once your order has been shipped, your tracking number will be sent to your e-mail address -------.

    (A) immediacy
    (B) immediate
    (C) immediateness
    (D) immediately

16. Please read the instructions ------- before attempting to assemble and install your bookshelf.

    (A) care
    (B) careful
    (C) carefully
    (D) cares

17. Failure to respond to customer inquiries in a ------- manner will have a negative impact on any type of business.

    (A) timing
    (B) timely
    (C) timeliness
    (D) times

18. Chief Public Relations Officer of National Rail Jeremy Valtez said that the repair work had started and that service would resume -------.

    (A) shortly
    (B) shorter
    (C) short
    (D) shortest

19. Ms. Kaminsky missed her flight to Moscow and ------- could not make it on time for her business meeting.

    (A) if
    (B) why
    (C) therefore
    (D) because of

20. Stanford Medical Center strictly requires all the medical staff to keep patients' medical records -------.

    (A) confide
    (B) confiding
    (C) confidentiality
    (D) confidential

PART 6

공식 61 접속부사 문제는 앞뒤 문장의 관계를 따진다.

파트 6에서 접속부사는 문장의 맨 앞에 붙어 그보다 앞에 위치한 문장과의 의미상 연결 관계를 보여준다. 빈칸 앞뒤 문장을 해석해 둘의 관계가 원인과 결과(인과), 시간의 흐름, 앞 문장에 대한 추가 내용이나 예시 등인지를 따져 본다.

만점 전략

주어 + 동사~. -------, 주어 + 동사~. → 접속부사 자리

■ 인과	therefore 그러므로 consequently 그 결과	thus 따라서 as a result 결과적으로	hence 그런 이유로
■ 역접	however 그러나 to the contrary 그와는 반대로	nevertheless 그럼에도 불구하고 even so 그렇더라도	nonetheless 그럼에도 불구하고 in contrast 그에 반해서
■ 시간	then 그 다음에, 그때 in the meantime 그동안	afterwards 그 후에 subsequently 그 뒤에	meanwhile 그동안 finally 마침내
■ 추가	furthermore 게다가 additionally 추가로 plus 게다가	moreover 게다가 in addition 추가로 likewise 마찬가지로	besides 게다가 also 또한
■ 조건	if so 만일 그렇다면 if not 그렇지 않으면	in this case 이 경우	otherwise 그렇지 않으면
■ 기타	for example 예를 들면 instead 대신에 unfortunately 불행히도	for instance 예를 들면 accordingly 그에 따라 regrettably 유감스럽게도	in fact 사실 alternatively 그 대신에 after all 결국

예제
해설집 p.44

Summer Course BREAK

We regret to announce that ❶we will not run a summer session of our popular Cook Together program due to renovation of the kitchen area. -------, ❷we look forward to welcoming you back in the fall. Registration for the fall will commence at the beginning of July. Please check back with us then, or sign up for our e-mail list for updates and notifications concerning fall registration.

(A) Unfortunately (B) Specifically
(C) However (D) For example

문맥으로 접속부사 고르기

❶ 빈칸 앞: 여름 강좌를 운영하지 않을 겁니다.
❷ 빈칸 뒤: 가을에 다시 보길 기대합니다.
→ 서로 상반되는 내용을 이야기하고 있다.

정답 (C) 그러나
오답 (A) 불행히도 (B) 구체적으로 (D) 예를 들어

YBM TEST

Questions 1-4 refer to the following instructions.

Order Cancellation Policy

To cancel an order you have placed with E-Traders.com, you must contact our customer support division via e-mail at cancel@etraders.com or by phone at 1-800-1259-4577. We will make every effort ------- the cancellation of your order as long as it has not shipped yet.
1.
When you contact customer support to cancel an order, please be ready to provide the order number ------- your name and contact information. Please note that if the item has already
2.
shipped, the order cannot be canceled. -------, you can request to return the item for a
3.
refund. -------.
4.

1. (A) accommodating
   (B) to accommodate
   (C) that accommodate
   (D) in the accommodation

2. (A) as well as
   (B) additionally
   (C) as well
   (D) also

3. (A) In contrast
   (B) Furthermore
   (C) Finally
   (D) In this case

4. (A) Our inventory can fluctuate throughout the day.
   (B) The instructions will describe how to cancel the order.
   (C) The cost of return shipping will be charged.
   (D) The cost of shipping is not the only issue.

UNIT 08 전치사

기본 학습

전치사는 명사와 결합해 「전치사+명사」 형태로 구를 이루어 형용사나 부사 같은 수식어 역할을 한다.

역할

1. 전치사: 문장에 명사를 연결해 준다.
   [문장] The train arrived. + [명사] 7 P.M. → The train arrived at 7 P.M. 기차가 저녁 7시에 도착했다.

2. 전치사구: 수식어 역할을 한다. 즉, 형용사처럼 명사를 수식하거나, 부사처럼 명사를 제외한 나머지를 수식한다.

형용사 역할	명사 뒤	The meeting room **on the 3rd floor** is not available today. 3층에 있는 회의실은 오늘 이용할 수 없다.
	보어 자리	The meeting room is **on the 3rd floor**. 회의실은 3층에 있다. ▶ be동사(~에 있다)를 보충
부사 역할	동사 수식	Mr. Khan works **for the government**. 칸 씨는 정부를 위해 일한다.
	형용사 수식	New Novics shoes are now available **for purchase**. 노빅스의 새 신발은 현재 구매 가능하다.
	문장 수식	**As a result,** Mr. Keins will receive a €10,000 prize. 그 결과, 카인즈 씨는 10,000 유로의 상금을 받을 것이다.

전치사구

전치사 뒤에는 명사나 명사를 대신할 수 있는 대명사 혹은 동명사가 온다.

전치사+명사	The international film festival is held every year **in Busan**. 국제 영화제가 부산에서 매년 열린다.
전치사+대명사	Linda will make copies of the meeting agenda **for everyone**. 린다가 모두를 위해 회의 안건을 복사해 놓을 것이다.
전치사+동명사	**Before shutting** down your computer, make sure to save all your work. 컴퓨터를 종료하기 전에, 반드시 모든 작업을 저장하세요.

빈출 전치사

시간	at (시각) ~에 on (요일, 날짜) ~에 in (월, 계절, 연도) ~에
시점	by (동작의 완료) ~까지 until (상태의 지속) ~까지 before ~ 전에 after ~ 후에 as of / effective / beginning / starting ~부터
기간	for ~ 동안 during ~ 동안 within ~ 이내에 throughout ~ 내내 over ~에 걸쳐서 in ~ 후에, ~ 만에
장소	at (특정 지점) ~에 on (표면) ~위에 in (장소, 영역, 공간 내부) ~에 throughout ~ 전역에, ~ 도처에
위치	between 둘 사이에 among (셋 이상) 사이에 beside / next to / by ~의 옆에 in front of ~의 앞에 behind ~의 뒤에
방향	to ~로 from ~로부터 toward(s) ~ 쪽으로 into ~ 안으로 onto ~ 위로 out of ~ 밖으로 across from ~의 맞은편에 opposite ~의 맞은편에 past ~을 지나서 along ~을 따라서
이유	because of / due to / owing to / on account of ~ 때문에 thanks to ~ 덕분에
양보	despite ~에도 불구하고 in spite of ~에도 불구하고 notwithstanding ~에도 불구하고
제외	without ~ 없이 except (for) ~을 제외하고 excluding ~을 제외하고 aside from ~을 제외하고 apart from ~을 제외하고, ~ 이외에
수단	by ~을 통해, ~에 의해 through ~을 통해 with ~을 가지고, ~와 함께
추가	in addition to ~에 더하여 besides ~ 외에도 plus ~뿐만 아니라 including ~을 포함하여
대체	instead of ~ 대신에 in place of ~을 대신해
비교	like ~처럼 unlike ~와 달리 such as ~와 같은
반대	against ~에 반대하여 contrary to ~와 달리
주제	about / on / over ~에 관하여 regarding / concerning ~에 관하여 as to / as for ~에 관하여 pertaining to ~에 관계된 with regard to / in regard to ~에 관하여

The library is open **until** 10 o'clock. 도서관은 10시까지 문을 연다.

There is a print shop **at** the corner of the street. 길 모퉁이에 인쇄소가 있다.

The shipment **from** our Vietnam factory has arrived. 베트남 공장에서 온 물품이 도착했다.

The factory was closed **due to** the strike. 파업으로 인해 공장이 문을 닫았다.

Despite all efforts, the government failed to turn around the economy.
모든 노력에도 불구하고, 정부는 경기를 호전시키는 데 실패했다.

The hotel room was spacious and comfortable **apart from** the bathroom.
욕실을 제외하고는, 호텔 방은 넓고 편안했다.

Besides the CEO Mike Jeffries, the financial director John Lee will speak at the company dinner.
최고경영자 마이크 제프리스 외에도 재무 이사 존 리가 회사 만찬에서 담화를 할 것이다.

I took the subway to work this morning **instead of** driving a car.
나는 오늘 아침에 운전하는 대신 지하철을 타고 출근했다.

Unlike other online banks, Cash Click doesn't offer live chat services.
다른 온라인 은행들과 달리, 캐시 클릭은 실시간 채팅 서비스를 제공하지 않는다.

More than half of the board members voted **against** the new proposal.
이사회의 절반 이상이 새 제안에 반대 투표를 했다.

For more information **about** our winery and wines, please visit the Web site.
우리 와인 양조장과 와인에 대한 추가 정보를 원하시면, 웹 사이트를 방문하세요.

UNIT 08 전치사

공식 62 「완전한 절 + ___」 뒤에 명사구만 남아 있으면 전치사가 1순위이다.

전치사는 명사와 결합해 「전치사 + 명사」의 형태로 절의 앞뒤에 붙어 수식어 역할을 한다. 따라서 완전한 절 앞이나 뒤에 빈칸이 오고, 빈칸 뒤에 명사구만 남아 있으면 전치사를 선택한다.

If someone sends a booking request, we will respond (**within** / ~~while~~) 24 hours.
→ 빈칸 뒤에 명사구가 있다.
누군가 예약 요청문을 보내면 우리는 24시간 이내로 답변한다.

Please check the size limits for carry-ons (~~as if~~ / **before**) checking in.
→ 빈칸 뒤에 동사가 없으므로 접속사는 오답
체크인하시기 전에 기내용 수하물에 대한 사이즈 한도를 확인하세요.

비법 노트
- 접속사와 부사는 명사를 연결하지 못한다. 전치사 문제는 보기에 접속사/부사가 자주 섞여 나오므로 품사 구별에 주의한다.

[예제] ------- the global recession, economic growth in India remained strong.
(A) Despite   (B) Even if
(C) Now that   (D) Recently

------- + 명사구, 완전한 절 ⋯▶ 전치사 자리

빈칸은 절(economic ~ strong)에 명사구 the global recession을 연결하는 자리
정답 (A) 전치사   **오답** (B), (C) 접속사 (D) 부사

전 세계적인 불황에도 불구하고, 인도의 경제 성장은 강세를 유지했다.

공식 63 「within + 기간」 vs. 「before + 시점」

시간을 나타내는 전치사는 시점과 짝을 이루는 전치사, 기간과 짝을 이루는 전치사로 분류된다. 따라서 시간 표현 전치사를 고를 때는 반드시 빈칸 뒤 명사가 시점인지 기간인지를 파악해 짝을 맞춰야 한다.

Customers can return unopened products (~~before~~ / **within**) 30 days of purchase for a refund.
고객들은 환불을 받기 위해 구매일로부터 30일 이내에 개봉하지 않은 제품을 반품할 수 있다.

비법 노트
- ------- + 기간   for/during ~ 동안   throughout ~ 내내   within ~ 이내에   over ~ 동안   in ~ 후에, ~ 만에
- ------- + 시점   before/prior to ~ 전에   after/following ~ 후에   by/until ~까지   from ~부터   since ~ 이래로

[예제] All reimbursement request forms must be received ------- the deadline.
(A) throughout   (B) soon
(C) when   (D) by

------- + 시점 명사 ⋯▶ 시점 전치사

정답 (D) ~ 까지   **오답** (A) 기간 전치사 (B) 부사 (C) 접속사

모든 상환 청구 서류는 마감일까지 접수되어야 한다.

공식으로 해결하는 실전문제

1. The Jefferson Bridge over the Amur River will be closed for repairs ------- further notice.
   (A) while
   (B) until
   (C) instead
   (D) both

2. All staff members who work extra hours ------- the peak season will receive a paid holiday.
   (A) during
   (B) when
   (C) once
   (D) since

3. Our smart phone sales have increased dramatically because of the promotion ------- the last two months.
   (A) about
   (B) until
   (C) over
   (D) up

4. Overnight parking is not allowed ------- prior authorization from the Parking Office.
   (A) unless
   (B) only
   (C) though
   (D) without

5. Juices and other non-alcoholic beverages will be available for free ------- the fundraising event.
   (A) by
   (B) because
   (C) as
   (D) throughout

6. ------- interviewing the top four candidates, the president decided to hire Mr. Richardson as a branch manager.
   (A) Next
   (B) It
   (C) After
   (D) Above

7. While Ms. Nguyen is away on a business trip ------- two weeks, Mr. Kim will take over her responsibilities.
   (A) as
   (B) for
   (C) again
   (D) until

8. Economists are expecting no significant change ------- the jobless figures to be released by the government next week.
   (A) also
   (B) in
   (C) employees
   (D) ultimately

UNIT 08 전치사

공식 64 동사 짝꿍을 보고 고르는 전치사

어떤 전치사가 오는지는 동사에 의해 결정되는 경우가 많다. 예를 들어, send는 '~에/에게' 보내므로 전치사 to, replace는 '~와' 교체하므로 전치사 with가 온다. 이처럼 동사는 전치사를 고를 때 중요한 단서가 된다.

We collect old cell phones and donate them (**to** / ~~on~~) those in need.
우리는 오래된 휴대폰을 모아 도움이 필요한 사람들에게 기부한다.

비법 노트 동사 + 목적어 + 전치사

move[relocate] A to B A를 B로 이동[이전]하다
distribute A to B A를 B에게 나누어 주다
transfer A to B A를 B로 이전[전근]시키다
direct A to B A를 B에게 보내주다[향하게 하다]
congratulate A on B B에 대해 A를 축하하다
choose[select] A from B B에서 A를 고르다

offer A to B A를 B에게 제공하다
ship A to B A를 B에게 배송하다
forward A to B A를 B에게 전달하다
provide A with B A에게 B를 제공하다
discourage/keep A from B A가 B하는 것을 막다[말리다]
assist[help] A with[in] B A가 B하는 것을 돕다

submit A to B A를 B에게 제출하다
deliver A to B A를 B에 배달하다
match A to B A를 B에 맞추다
donate A to B A를 B에 기부하다

SKILL UP replace A with B → A be replaced with B
동사와 짝꿍 전치사는 능동뿐 아니라 수동 형태로도 자주 출제되므로 둘 다 기억한다.

(예제) Mugec CEO Bill Cox has been replaced ------- Casey Hale, former Gericsson Chairman.

(A) with   (B) from
(C) between (D) of

be replaced + ------- ⋯→ with

정답 **(A)**

뮤젝의 CEO 빌 콕스는 전 게릭슨의 의장 캐시 헤일로 교체되었다.

공식 65 빈칸 뒤에 힌트가 있는 전치사

전치사는 그 쓰임새나 의미에 따라 특정 명사와 짝을 이루어 관용표현처럼 쓰이는데, 이런 「전치사 + 명사」 짝꿍 표현을 암기해 두면 빈칸 뒤 명사만 봐도 쉽게 답을 고를 수 있다.

House prices in Bordeaux have risen by 10 percent (**since** / ~~on~~) last year.
보르도의 주택 가격이 작년 이래로 10퍼센트까지 상승했다.

비법 노트

since + 과거 시점 ~ 이래로
along + 긴 장소 ~을 따라
by + 작가/제작자 ~가 쓴/만든

between + A and B A, B 사이에
aboard + 비행기/배 ~에 탑승해
on + 서류/종이 서류에

as + 직함 ~로서
across + 지역 ~ 전역에
under + 감독/통제 감독/통제 하에

SKILL UP ___ + -ing : 동명사와 자주 짝을 이루는 전치사도 암기해 두자.
before[after] -ing ~하기 전[후]에   upon[on] -ing ~하자마자   by -ing ~함으로써   in -ing ~하는 데 있어

(예제) Dublin Museum will undergo extensive reconstruction ------- the direction of project supervisor Ellen Ramsey.

(A) among   (B) beneath
(C) both   (D) under

------- + the direction of ⋯→ under

under the direction of: ~의 감독 하에
정답 **(D)**   오답 (A) ~ 사이에 (B) ~ 아래

더블린 박물관은 프로젝트 총괄 엘렌 램지의 감독 하에 대규모로 재건될 것이다.

공식으로 해결하는 실전문제

해설집 p. 46

1. ------- submitting your order, you will receive a confirmation e-mail from us including your order number.
   (A) Near
   (B) Upon
   (C) Since
   (D) During

2. Applications for food vendor licenses should be submitted directly ------- the City Health Department.
   (A) around
   (B) after
   (C) to
   (D) with

3. Hourly ferry service from Battery Park is available ------- 9 A.M. and 3 P.M. during the winter months.
   (A) on
   (B) among
   (C) between
   (D) above

4. This summer, Ursula Biden will be traveling to 16 cities ------- the country to promote her new book.
   (A) along
   (B) wide
   (C) across
   (D) far

5. The new wireless connection utility has been forwarded ------- the technical support team for a diagnostic test.
   (A) to
   (B) at
   (C) behind
   (D) inside

6. Mr. Timmins will be working ------- a general manager at the new branch office opening in Amsterdam.
   (A) among
   (B) to
   (C) as
   (D) instead

7. We at Minsk Grocery Chain provide our members ------- quality goods at competitive prices.
   (A) to
   (B) from
   (C) into
   (D) with

8. Effective February 1, you will be able to choose any items ------- our online product catalog.
   (A) between
   (B) from
   (C) to
   (D) apart

119

66 regardless of도 전치사이다.

전치사 중에는 regardless of와 같이 두 개 이상의 단어로 이루어진 구전치사가 있다. 구전치사를 활용해 짝을 고르는 문제가 출제되기도 하므로 통으로 암기해 둔다.

All refunds will be assessed a $50 cancellation fee (**regardless of** / regardless) the reason.
→ regardless는 형용사이므로 명사구를 연결할 수 없다.
모든 환불금은 이유를 불문하고 50달러의 취소 수수료가 부과될 것이다.

The Air Show has been cancelled for this weekend (**because** / due) of the wet weather.
→ due는 to와 짝을 이루고, because는 of와 짝을 이룬다.
우천으로 인해 이번 주말에 있을 에어쇼가 취소되었다.

비법 노트 구전치사

regardless of ~에 상관없이	because of ~ 때문에	instead of ~ 대신에
ahead of ~보다 앞서	in spite of ~에도 불구하고	in front of ~ 앞에
as of ~부터, ~ 일자로	next to ~ 옆에	prior to ~ 전에
thanks to ~ 덕분에	pertaining to ~와 관련된	due[owing] to ~ 때문에
according to ~에 따르면	along with ~와 더불어	based on ~을 근거로
rather than ~보다는	aside[apart] from ~ 외에도	across from ~ 맞은편에
except for ~을 제외하고	as for[as to] ~에 관하여	adjacent to ~ 근처에

(예제) ------- the current renovation project in the airport, fewer gates than usual are available at Terminal 3.

(A) Across from   (B) In spite
(C) In addition   (D) Because of

because of … ~ 때문에

빈칸은 전치사 자리인데, 전치사 (A)와 (D) 중 문맥상 because of가 적절하다.
정답 (D) ~ 때문에 **오답** (A) ~ 맞은편에 (B), (C) 부사

현재 진행 중인 공항 보수 공사 때문에 3번 터미널은 평소보다 적은 수의 게이트가 운영될 것이다.

67 regarding / given도 전치사이다.

전치사 중에는 regarding(~에 관하여), given(~을 고려해 볼 때)과 같은 분사형 전치사들이 있다.

Complaints (**regarding** / to) noise have increased over the past few weeks.
지난 몇 주간 소음에 대한 불만이 증가했다.

(**Given** / Follow) the time constraints, we need to shorten our work process.
시간 제약을 고려해 볼 때, 우리는 업무 절차를 간소화해야 한다.

비법 노트 분사형 전치사

regarding ~에 관하여	including ~을 포함하여	excluding ~을 제외하고	notwithstanding ~에도 불구하고
considering ~을 고려하면	following ~ 후에	concerning ~에 관한	given ~을 고려해 볼 때

(예제) ------- some technical issues, the first Mobile Games Forum was a great success.

(A) Throughout   (B) As a result of
(C) Eventually   (D) Notwithstanding

notwithstanding … 전치사

정답 (D) ~에도 불구하고
오답 (A) ~내내 (B) ~의 결과로 (C) 부사

일부 기술상의 문제에도 불구하고, 첫 모바일 게임 포럼은 대성공이었다.

공식으로 해결하는 실전문제

해설집 p.47

1. ------- a new WMA study, the number of mobile cellular subscribers around the world will surpass 5 billion shortly.
   (A) According to
   (B) Provided that
   (C) Instead
   (D) As

2. The Iowa Occupational Handbook includes information ------- the number of people working in the state.
   (A) regarding
   (B) among
   (C) during
   (D) throughout

3. TravelWithUs can handle your visa application ------- all your flight and hotel reservations.
   (A) even though
   (B) due to
   (C) along with
   (D) rather than

4. ------- the tight deadline, more staff will be assigned to the team to help complete the project on time.
   (A) Giver
   (B) Giving
   (C) Given
   (D) Gives

5. At Top Enterprise, you will acquire highly practical skills and experience ------- to every aspect of running a successful business.
   (A) pertain
   (B) pertaining
   (C) pertains
   (D) pertinently

6. You will have a chance to taste some of our most popular wines ------- a guided tour of our winery.
   (A) only
   (B) which
   (C) following
   (D) since

7. At Sunnyhills Stores, the prices of local produce are determined ------- the condition of the goods.
   (A) adjacent to
   (B) in spite of
   (C) based on
   (D) such as

8. BluRibbon Airways' Web site lists all flight schedules and baggage fees, ------- fees for additional and overweight baggage.
   (A) including
   (B) following
   (C) during
   (D) pending

121

공식 68. 움직이면 to/from vs. 고정이면 in/near

장소 앞에 오는 전치사는 어떤 방향으로 움직이는 것을 의미하는 방향 전치사, 고정된 장소를 의미하는 위치 전치사로 나뉜다. '움직이면 to' vs. '고정이면 in'을 기억하자.

Hilltop Restaurant has recently relocated (in̶ / **to**) Bath, Somerset.
→ Bath 방향으로 움직이는 것이므로 방향 전치사 자리
힐탑 레스토랑은 최근 서머싯의 배스로 이전했다.

The duty free pick up point is (**near** / into̶) Gate 28. 면세품 인도장은 28번 게이트 근처에 있다.
→ gate 28은 고정된 장소

비법 노트 방향 전치사 vs. 위치 전치사

- **방향 전치사** to ~로/에 into ~ 안으로 onto ~ 위로 toward ~ 쪽으로
  from ~로부터/에서 through ~을 통해 along ~을 따라서
- **위치 전치사** in/on/at ~에 near ~ 근처에 next to/beside/by ~ 옆에 above/over ~ 위에
  behind ~ 뒤에 below/under ~ 아래에 across ~ 전역에 throughout ~ 전역에

[예제] Any items left behind ------- the room by hotel guests will be kept for a month.

(A) into (B) in
(C) from (D) through

left behind는 고정된 상태 ⋯ 위치 전치사
정답 **(B)** 위치 전치사 오답 (A), (C), (D) 방향 전치사
호텔 숙박객이 방에 남기고 간 물건은 한 달 동안 보관될 것이다.

공식 69. 대상/목적/이유/용도에는 for가 답이다.

전치사 for는 두 달에 한 번 이상 나올 정도로 자주 출제되므로 따로 정리해 두자. 빈칸 뒤 명사가 앞 문장 내용의 대상(~를 대상으로 한), 목적(~을 위한), 이유(~ 때문에), 용도(~용)를 나타낼 때는 for가 답이다.

Requests (**for** / in̶) cancellations must be received in writing by November 27.
취소 요청은 11월 27일까지 서면으로 접수되어야 한다.

Ms. Avlon will be recognized (as̶ / **for**) her leadership in corporate social responsibility.
애블론 씨는 기업의 사회적 책임 분야에서 보여준 그녀의 리더십에 대해 인정받을 것이다.

비법 노트

- **대상** guidelines for applicants 지원자들을 위한 지침   a job opening for designers 디자이너 구인
- **목적** preparation for peak season 성수기 준비   submission for approval 승인을 위한 제출
- **이유** an award for excellence 우수함에 대한 상   gratitude for attendance 참석에 대한 감사
- **용도** an office for meetings 회의를 위한 사무실   a ticket for admission 입장을 위한 티켓

[예제] SamBi carries a variety of goods specially designed ------- left-handed people.

(A) at (B) to
(C) for (D) until

left-handed people은 디자인의 대상 ⋯ for
정답 **(C)** ~을 위해
샘비는 왼손잡이를 위해 특별히 설계된 다양한 상품을 취급한다.

공식으로 해결하는 실전문제

해설집 p.48

1. Online giant Globezon operates more than 100 retail outlets ------- the country.
   (A) throughout
   (B) toward
   (C) away
   (D) into

2. Anna Fonghong has decided to close her restaurant ------- Shrewsbury Street when the lease expires next month.
   (A) from
   (B) to
   (C) on
   (D) between

3. Nuri Bank offers attractive loan rates and terms ------- first-time home buyers with good credit.
   (A) so
   (B) either
   (C) for
   (D) from

4. The Honor Hall in the Corex Convention Center is perfect ------- large events with hundreds of guests.
   (A) at
   (B) to
   (C) in
   (D) for

5. Ms. Dalhart goes jogging ------- the Han River in Seoul every morning to enjoy the fresh air.
   (A) along
   (B) below
   (C) between
   (D) off

6. J-Kitchen was voted the best restaurant in Sidney ------- its truly innovative and delicious dishes.
   (A) apart
   (B) for
   (C) often
   (D) according to

7. Requests ------- assitance in booking international business travel should be submitted five weeks prior to the departure date.
   (A) with
   (B) by
   (C) for
   (D) from

8. All visitors to the JH Center should park their vehicles ------- designated visitor parking areas.
   (A) down
   (B) in
   (C) among
   (D) onto

YBM TEST

1. Ms. Pearson will explain how your employees will benefit ------- the implementation of our new HR software.

   (A) from
   (B) while
   (C) them
   (D) beside

2. If you are interested in opportunities to volunteer at the Sierra Music Festival, please fill out our Contact Us page ------- June 9.

   (A) below
   (B) with
   (C) before
   (D) within

3. A new cook book by Susan Ramsey includes a diverse range of simple recipes ------- beginners.

   (A) for
   (B) to
   (C) and
   (D) in

4. All employees at Veracity are eligible for the retirement plan ------- part-time employees working less than 20 hours per week.

   (A) exclusively
   (B) excluding
   (C) exclusion
   (D) excludes

5. Questionnaire forms will be distributed ------- every participant before the training session begins.

   (A) by
   (B) to
   (C) on
   (D) of

6. Residents of Peshawar suffered an unexpected power outage last night ------- a malfunction in the power supply.

   (A) as a result
   (B) so that
   (C) because of
   (D) in order to

7. The winner of the competition will be announced ------- 8 P.M. right after the speech of our president, Bob Staten.

   (A) in
   (B) under
   (C) among
   (D) at

8. ------- the company, we plan to replace old office equipment with new, energy-efficient models.

   (A) Additionally
   (B) Throughout
   (C) Altogether
   (D) In advance

9. ------- just a few years, smartphone games have become a really common sight everywhere.

   (A) By
   (B) In
   (C) Between
   (D) Only

10. The train passing ------- the longest rail tunnel in the world departs from Zurich every morning.

    (A) except
    (B) between
    (C) over
    (D) through

11. Queenfisher, America's largest home improvement retailer, has reported a fall in sales ------- the second quarter.

    (A) again
    (B) without
    (C) by
    (D) during

12. ScuWeather's analytics show that over half a million businesses ------- the southern area will be impacted by Hurricane Marvey.

    (A) many
    (B) in
    (C) until
    (D) onto

13. At the year-end meeting held last Tuesday, the president personally congratulated Ms. Larson ------- her remarkable achievements.

    (A) on
    (B) such as
    (C) overall
    (D) along

14. ------- limiting scholarship grants, the foundation board has decided to seek financial support from individual donors.

    (A) Due to
    (B) Instead of
    (C) Through
    (D) Which

15. ------- Bill's substantial contribution to sales growth, his rapid promotion to the regional manager position is not surprising.

    (A) Considering
    (B) Except for
    (C) Because
    (D) Even

16. Sharp Crack Studios is ------- the leading advertising agencies in Germany.

    (A) toward
    (B) along
    (C) into
    (D) among

17. Since the renovation has been completed ------- schedule, we are able to reopen the store next week.

    (A) along
    (B) even if
    (C) almost
    (D) ahead of

18. The president expressed deep appreciation ------- the hard work and dedication of the project members.

    (A) for
    (B) up
    (C) as
    (D) to

19. If an e-mail contains sensitive or confidential information, make sure to check the address ------- clicking the send button.

    (A) before
    (B) among
    (C) than
    (D) to

20. Berkeley Research indicates that companies benefit when they discourage employees ------- working extra hours or taking work home.

    (A) for
    (B) notwithstanding
    (C) from
    (D) out of

PART 6

> **공식 70** 대명사 문제는 빈칸의 앞 문장에서 명사를 찾는다.
>
> 파트 6에서 대명사 문제는 보기가 모두 대명사로 구성되는 편이다. 대명사 문제는 빈칸의 앞 문장에서 빈칸이 대신하는 명사를 찾아내 이를 대신하기에 적절한 대명사를 고르는데, 이때 수일치(단수/복수)에 주의한다.

만점 전략

빈칸이 대신하는 명사를 명확하게 찾을 수 없는 경우

1. **쓴 사람(본인)**을 지칭할 때 → I / my / me / mine   **읽는 사람**을 지칭할 때 → you / your / yours
   편지 / 이메일 / 메모에서는 주로 글을 쓴 사람이 본인의 상황을 설명하거나, 편지를 읽는 상대에게 요청 혹은 지시하는 내용을 다룬다.

2. **'(우리) 회사'**를 지칭할 때 → we / our / us
   경영진이 전 직원을 대상으로 쓴 글에서 회사에 관한 정보를 알리거나 회사가 앞으로 나아가야 할 방향을 제시할 때, 회사(경영진 및 전 직원)를 '우리'라고 지칭한다.

3. 광고문이나 명령문에서 글을 읽는 **대상**을 지칭할 때 → you
   광고문이나 명령문은 읽는 사람인 'you'를 상대로 쓴 글이므로, 달리 언급된 명사가 없다면 you가 답이다.

4. 앞 문장에서 언급된 **내용 전체**를 대신해 '이러한 점[것]'을 지칭할 때 → this

예제   해설집 p.51

Instructions regarding the Travel Expense Reimbursement Form

You need to download the Travel Expense Reimbursement Form that corresponds with the dates of your business trip from the company intranet site. The form is an Excel file, and thus, you do not need to do any calculations yourself. It is a "read only" file, so ❶**you will have to save it to your computer before filling out the form.**
❷**If you have trouble saving ------- to your computer,** please call the technical support team at extension 4175.

(A) them   (B) those
(C) mine   (D) it

앞 문장에서 빈칸이 의미하는 명사 찾기

❶ 빈칸 앞: 양식을 작성하기 전에 저장해라
❷ 빈칸 문장: 컴퓨터에 ____를 저장하는 데 곤란을 겪는다면 전화해라
→ 빈칸이 the form(양식)을 의미하므로 단수인 사물을 대신할 수 있는 대명사 자리

정답 (D) 그것
오답 (C) the form은 '내 것' 즉, 글쓴이의 것이 될 수 없다.

YBM TEST

해설집 p.51

Questions 1-4 refer to the following advertisement.

For the best self-storage facility in San Rafael, CA, look no further than Easy Self Storage. Our state-of-the-art facility combines security and convenience to provide ------- with a
                                                                                                              1.
comfortable space for storage. -------.
                               2.
At Easy Self Storage, we are ------- to keeping customers satisfied with our storage services.
                             3.
All of the storage units are equipped with air-conditioning and ventilation systems managed by expert staff. We are here to help you with everything from storage rental to move-in or out. Do you need assistance selecting a storage unit? Please feel free to contact us, and we will be delighted to assess your belongings so that you can make an ------- choice.
                                                                                      4.

1. (A) them
   (B) you
   (C) us
   (D) both

2. (A) We also sell packing materials onsite to make your move-in process quick and easy.
   (B) Use our online inventory to get your goods back whenever you need them.
   (C) You should hire a pest control service to keep the storage units free from pests and rodents.
   (D) We may require you to submit your personal information due to the nature of our services.

3. (A) commitments
   (B) commits
   (C) committing
   (D) committed

4. (A) exclusive
   (B) evident
   (C) informed
   (D) additional

UNIT 09 접속사

기본 학습

접속사는 단어와 단어, 구와 구, 절과 절을 이어 주는 연결어이다.

부사절 접속사

이미 완전한 절에 추가로 붙어 부사 역할을 하는 절을 부사절이라 하고, 부사절 접속사가 부사절을 연결한다. 대표적인 부사절 접속사로는 because(~ 때문에), as soon as(~하자마자), if(만약 ~라면) even though(~에도 불구하고), while(~하는 동안) 등이 있다.

> Mr. Ichiguro may be late for the meeting **because** his train has been delayed.
> 이치구로 씨는 기차가 지연되는 바람에 회의에 늦을지도 모른다.
>
> **As soon as** the orders are shipped, you will receive a notification.
> 제품이 선적되자마자, 알림 메시지를 받게 될 것이다.

명사절 접속사

절 전체가 명사 역할을 하는 것을 명사절이라 하고, 명사절 접속사는 명사절을 문장에 연결하는 역할을 한다. that(~하는 것), if/whether(~인지 아닌지), 의문사(what, who, how 등)가 명사절 접속사에 속한다.

주어	**Whether** the price of our new product line will be adjusted depends on the survey results. 신제품 라인의 가격이 조정될 여부는 설문조사 결과에 달려 있다.
동사의 목적어	The manager requests **that** all team members attend the weekly meeting. 매니저는 모든 팀 멤버들이 주간 회의에 참석할 것을 요청한다.
전치사의 목적어	A prize will be awarded to **whoever** solves the quiz first. 퀴즈를 처음으로 해결한 사람에게 누구든 상금이 수여될 것이다.
보어	The problem is **that** we don't have enough money for the project. 문제는 프로젝트를 위한 자금이 충분하지 못하다는 것이다.

관계사(형용사절 접속사)

명사 뒤에서 명사를 수식하는 형용사 역할을 하는 절을 형용사절 혹은 관계사절이라고 한다. 이때 형용사절을 연결해 주는 접속사를 관계사, 형용사절 앞에서 수식을 받는 명사를 선행사라고 한다.

The report which Sophia submitted to the production manager contains several errors.
선행사
소피아가 생산 관리자에게 제출한 보고서는 몇 가지 오류를 포함하고 있다.

Robert couldn't open **the file** that was attached to the e-mail from his supervisor.
선행사
로버트는 그의 상관이 이메일에 첨부한 파일을 열 수 없었다.

1. 관계대명사

「접속사+대명사」의 역할을 하며, 뒤에 불완전한 절이 온다.

선행사 / 격	주격	목적격	소유격
사람	who / that	whom(= who) / that	whose
사물, 동물	which / that	which / that	whose

① **주격**   Ms. Kim is the candidate **who** meets our requirements.
→ 관계절에 주어가 없다.   김 씨는 우리 요구조건을 충족시키는 후보자이다.

② **목적격**   Mr. Brown contacted the candidate **that** he interviewed yesterday.
→ 관계절에 목적어가 없다.   브라운 씨는 그가 어제 면접을 본 후보자에게 연락했다.

          The candidate to **whom** I sent an e-mail is Ms. Kim.
→ 전치사 뒤에도 목적격이 오는데, that은 전치사 뒤에 올 수 없다.   내가 이메일을 보냈던 후보자는 김 씨이다.

③ **소유격**   Ms. Kim is the candidate **whose** résumé is the most impressive.
김 씨는 이력서가 가장 인상 깊은 후보이다.

2. 관계부사

① 「전치사+관계대명사」의 역할을 하며, 뒤에 완전한 절이 온다.

Nellie Chen relocated to the city **and** she was born in it[the city].
→ Nellie Chen relocated to the city **which** she was born in.
= Nellie Chen relocated to the city **in which** she was born.
= Nellie Chen relocated to the city **where** she was born.   넬리 첸은 그녀가 태어난 도시로 이사했다.

② when, where, why, how가 있으며, 선행사의 종류에 따라 달라진다.

The summer holiday season is <u>the period</u> **when** the museum offers extended hours.
                                 시간 명사   여름 휴가 시즌은 박물관이 연장 운영하는 기간이다.

<u>The banquet hall</u> **where** we had the retirement party was small.   우리가 은퇴식을 했던 연회장은 작았다.
    장소 명사

Ms. Pandit will report <u>the reason</u> **why** our sales declined.   판디트 씨가 판매량이 하락한 원인을 보고할 것이다.
                         이유

I have no <u>idea</u> **how** I should drive a motorcycle.   나는 모터사이클을 어떻게 운전하는지 모른다.
          ~~the way how~~

UNIT 09 접속사

공식 71 완전한 절 + 부사절 접속사 + 완전한 절

문장에 동사가 두 개 있는데 접속사는 없다면 빈칸이 접속사 자리이다. 빈칸 없이도 완전한 절이 두 개라면 부사절 접속사를 넣는다.

We will be closed tomorrow (**as** / ~~due to~~) it is a national holiday. 내일은 국경일이기 때문에 휴점합니다.
→ 빈칸 앞뒤로 완전한 절이 있으므로 부사절 접속사 자리이다.

(~~Within~~ / **Before**) the flight takes off, all passengers must be seated.
→ within은 전치사이므로 절을 연결할 수 없다. 비행기가 이륙하기 전에 모든 승객들은 착석해야 한다.

비법 노트

- **오답 주의!** 접속사 문제는 보기에 전치사나 부사가 자주 섞여 나오므로 해석에 의존하지 말고, 동사의 개수부터 확인한다.

[예제] ------- the payment has been received, we will start to process your order.

(A) As soon as   (B) Compared to
(C) Not only   (D) According to

------- + 완전한 절, 완전한 절 → 부사절 접속사 자리

정답 **(A)** ~하자마자
오답 **(B)** 전치사(~와 비교하여) **(D)** 전치사(~에 따르면)

지불액이 납입되자마자 당신의 주문을 처리하기 시작할 것입니다.

공식 72 after는 전치사도 되고, 부사절 접속사도 된다.

after, before, as 등은 부사절 접속사이면서 전치사이기도 하다. 이들은 「절+절」은 물론 「절+명사(구)」를 연결하는 자리에도 들어갈 수 있다.

No applications will be accepted (~~from~~ / **after**) the deadline has passed.
마감일이 지난 후에는 신청서를 받지 않는다.

No applications will be accepted (~~later~~ / **after**) the deadline. 마감일 이후에는 신청서를 받지 않는다.

비법 노트 접속사 겸 전치사

as 접 ~할 때/~ 때문에/~ 대로 전 ~로서/처럼	before 접 전 ~ 전에	after 접 전 ~ 후에
since 접 ~ 이래로/때문에 전 ~ 이래로	than 접 전 ~보다	until 접 전 ~까지
considering 접 전 ~을 감안하면	given 접 전 ~을 고려해 볼 때	

[예제] ------- you are a valued customer, you are eligible for this special offer.

(A) Since   (B) In case of
(C) Besides   (D) Due to

since → 접속사 겸 전치사

since와 due to는 의미(~ 때문에)가 비슷하지만 빈칸은 접속사 자리
정답 **(A)** ~ 때문에   오답 **(B), (C), (D)** 전치사

귀하는 소중한 고객이므로 이 특가 판매에 대한 자격이 되십니다.

공식으로 해결하는 실전문제

1. Ms. Eiffel knows how to deal with demanding clients ------- she has worked as a customer service representative.
   (A) because
   (B) rather
   (C) not only
   (D) after all

2. ------- you have registered for the Anyjob Club, you will have access to the largest jobs database in the country.
   (A) Already
   (B) Once
   (C) As well
   (D) So

3. ------- the city introduced the congestion charge, the traffic volume has decreased in the central area.
   (A) But
   (B) Within
   (C) Since
   (D) Due to

4. It is important that you have the property inspected ------- you finalize your purchase.
   (A) despite
   (B) during
   (C) before
   (D) besides

5. ------- roads are closed for the marathon, many city buses will run on alternative routes.
   (A) Throughout
   (B) During
   (C) Over
   (D) While

6. ------- we have tickets left, we might sell them at the door on the day of the event.
   (A) If
   (B) Yet
   (C) Nor
   (D) Despite

7. ------- the initial sales of our new hair-care line were strong, they have gradually declined over the past six months.
   (A) Moreover
   (B) In addition
   (C) In spite of
   (D) Even though

8. Please note that players will be unable to connect to WinnerZ servers ------- maintenance is complete.
   (A) next
   (B) until
   (C) within
   (D) because of

UNIT 09 접속사

공식 73 보기에 부사절 접속사가 여럿일 때는 해석으로 고른다.

부사절 접속사 문제의 보기에는 전치사나 부사가 자주 섞여 나온다. 빈칸이 부사절 접속사 자리이고 보기 중에 부사절 접속사가 여럿 있으면 해석상 가장 적절한 접속사를 고른다.

(**As** / ~~Though~~) our 10th anniversary is approaching, we are planning a gala dinner.
10주년 기념식이 다가오고 있기 때문에 우리는 만찬을 계획하고 있다.

(~~Even if~~ / **Because**) HCS Group is opening multiple new branches, they need more bank tellers.
HCS 그룹은 여러 지점을 열 예정이기 때문에 더 많은 은행원을 필요로 한다.

비법 노트 빈출 부사절 접속사

- 보기 네 개가 모두 부사절 접속사라면 자리 파악할 필요 없이 바로 해석상 적절한 답을 고른다.

| when ~할 때 | while ~하는 동안 | once 일단 ~하면 | as soon as ~하자마자 | as long as ~하는 한 |
| if 만약 ~라면 | unless ~하지 않으면 | whereas ~인 반면에 | so+형용사/부사+that 매우 ~해서 …하다 |
| although/though/even though/even if 비록 ~일지라도 |

예제 You don't need to submit references ------- they are requested.

(A) as (B) whereas
(C) although (D) unless

보기가 모두 부사절 접속사 → 해석
'제출할 필요 없다 + 요청되지 않으면'이 자연스럽다.
정답 (D) ~하지 않으면
오답 (A) ~하기 때문에, ~할 때 (B) ~인 반면 (C) 비록 ~일지라도
추천서는 요구되지 않으면 제출할 필요가 없다.

공식 74 so that도 부사절 접속사이다.

so that과 같이 부사절 접속사처럼 생기지 않은 접속사들은 따로 암기해 둔다.

Easywing works hard (~~although~~ / **so that**) our passengers feel safe and comfortable.
이지윙은 승객들이 안전하고 편안할 수 있도록 열심히 일한다.

(**In the event** / ~~In addition~~) a customer complains about prices, let the floor manager handle it.
고객이 가격에 대해 불평할 경우, 매장 관리자가 처리하도록 하세요.

비법 노트 우리도 부사절 접속사

now that ~이므로	in order that ~하기 위해	in case (that) ~인 경우에 대비해
so (that) ~할 수 있도록	providing (that) 만약 ~라면	provided (that) 만약 ~라면
assuming (that) 만약 ~라면	in the event (that) ~인 경우에	at the time ~할 때
given (that) ~을 고려해 볼 때	considering (that) ~을 감안하면	

예제 Significant increases in productivity are expected ------- the factory is fully automated.

(A) what (B) neither
(C) now that (D) in anticipation of

완전한 절 + ------- + 완전한 절 → 부사절 접속사
정답 (C) ~이므로
오답 (A) 명사절 접속사 (B) 대명사, 부사 (D) 전치사
공장이 완전 자동화되었기 때문에 생산성에 있어 상당한 증가가 예상된다.

132

공식으로 해결하는 실전문제

해설집 p.52

1. ------- the team consists of only four staff, their achievement in securing the contracts is amazing.
   (A) Considerably
   (B) Considering
   (C) Consider
   (D) Considers

2. You can easily sign up for Urail membership ------- you purchase your tickets either at ticketing booths or online.
   (A) because
   (B) when
   (C) as if
   (D) whereas

3. We need to increase the international travel budget ------- we are looking to expand into overseas markets.
   (A) assuming
   (B) whereas
   (C) unless
   (D) even though

4. ------- the time allocated for presentations is limited, you should keep yours to no longer than 15 minutes.
   (A) Therefore
   (B) After
   (C) So
   (D) Because

5. ------- Jeremy Corbyn resigns from his post as IBC chairman in May, Mr. Shaub will take his place.
   (A) As soon as
   (B) Resulting from
   (C) Whereas
   (D) Nearly

6. It was surprising Ms. Potter was appointed marketing director ------- she was a design expert.
   (A) so that
   (B) in case
   (C) given that
   (D) additionally

7. ------- the project goes according to schedule, we can expect a substantial bonus this year.
   (A) As a result
   (B) In place of
   (C) Provided that
   (D) Either

8. ------- the organizing committee took into consideration the potential impact of Hurricane Gemma, they have decided to cancel the Leadership Seminar.
   (A) Even if
   (B) In case
   (C) As a result
   (D) After

133

공식 75 빈칸이 명사 자리인데 뒤에 절이 있으면 명사절 접속사가 답이다.

문장에 동사가 두 개 있는데, 접속사가 없고 명사 자리(주어, 목적어, 보어)에 빈칸이 있다면 명사절 접속사 자리이다.

The company announced (**that** / ~~upon~~) it had agreed to merge with Softmart.
→ 동사 뒤 목적어 자리인데 동사가 두 개(announced, had agreed) 있다.   회사가 소프트마트와의 합병에 동의했다고 발표했다.

The management will decide (**if** / ~~about~~) the firm will adopt a casual dress policy.
경영진은 회사가 평상복 착용 정책을 채택할지에 대해 결정할 것이다.

비법 노트

- **명사절 접속사 + to부정사**
「명사절 접속사 + 주어 + 동사」에서 주어를 생략하여 「명사절 접속사 + to부정사」로 축약할 수 있다.
what to make 무엇을 만들지   how to improve 어떻게 개선하는지   whether to accept 수락할지 말지

(예제) Mr. Tilley called the hotel to ask ------- he could make changes to his reservation.

(A) although   (B) nor
(C) should   (D) whether

동사1 + to ask 목적어 자리 + 동사2 ⋯ 명사절 접속사
정답 **(D)** ~인지 아닌지   오답 (A) 부사절 접속사
틸리 씨는 호텔에 전화해 예약을 변경할 수 있는지에 대해 물었다.

공식 76 「that + 완전한 절」 vs. 「what + 불완전한 절」

that과 what은 '~하는 것'으로 의미는 같지만 뒤에 오는 절의 형태가 다르다. 이처럼 명사절 접속사는 뒤에 완전한 절이 오는 것과, 명사가 하나 빠진 불완전한 절이 오는 것으로 나뉘므로 빈칸 뒤 절이 완전한지 아닌지 확인한다.

The test results were not (~~that~~ / **what**) Ms. Fender had expected. 시험 결과는 펜더 씨가 예상했던 것이 아니었다.
→ 빈칸 뒤에 목적어가 빠진 불완전한 절이 왔다.

The supervisor said (**that** / ~~which~~) all volunteers would receive a lunch ticket.
모든 자원봉사자가 점심 식사권을 받게 될 것이라고 관리자가 말했다.

비법 노트

- **that / if / whether / when / where / how / why** + 완전한 절
- **who / what / which** + 불완전한 절

TIP 900+ **what / which + 명사**   what / which가 형용사로 쓰이면 「what / which + 명사 + 불완전한 절」의 형태가 된다.
The test will show **which colors** suit your personality.
그 검사는 어떤 색이 네 성격과 잘 맞는지 보여줄 것이다.

(예제) The mayor believes ------- the new transportation system is a major improvement.

(A) that   (B) like
(C) what   (D) despite

주어 + 타동사 + 목적어 자리 + 완전한 절 ⋯ that
정답 **(A)**
시장은 새 교통 시스템이 현저히 개선된 것이라고 믿는다.

공식으로 해결하는 실전문제

1. The personnel director asked ------- Mr. Jones was still interested in the position before making a hiring decision.
   (A) whether
   (B) even though
   (C) either
   (D) which

2. As a result of gamers' feedback, the management has decided ------- they will not release a new game this year.
   (A) what
   (B) that
   (C) each
   (D) about

3. ------- will give the keynote speech at the Amsterdam Urban Forum has not been decided yet.
   (A) Every
   (B) Someone
   (C) Each
   (D) Who

4. Our licensed agents can tell you exactly ------- insurance plans are most suitable for your personal medical needs.
   (A) which
   (B) each
   (C) most
   (D) although

5. The government will decide ------- to raise the minimum wage to boost the domestic economy.
   (A) so
   (B) try
   (C) whether
   (D) upon

6. This Web page describes ------- the basic requirements are for eligibility for the city's unemployment allowance.
   (A) about
   (B) what
   (C) how
   (D) if

7. The maintenance work on the state parks will proceed regardless of ------- there is a budget agreement.
   (A) what
   (B) another
   (C) with
   (D) whether

8. During the job opportunity seminar, Dr. Morales explained ------- participating in competitions can benefit one's career.
   (A) regarding
   (B) this
   (C) how
   (D) for

공식 77. 의문사+ever는 명사절 접속사 또는 부사절 접속사로 쓰인다.

〈의문대명사(who/what/which)+ever〉는 뒤에 불완전한 절이 오고 명사절 접속사/부사절 접속사의 두 가지 역할로 쓰이는 반면, 〈의문부사(when/where/how)+ever〉는 뒤에 완전한 절이 오고 부사절 접속사로만 쓰인다.

For dinner, you can choose (**whatever** / ~~them~~) you like from our menu.
저녁 식사로, 우리 메뉴에서 마음에 드는 것은 무엇이든 선택할 수 있다.

Alerts will be sent to you (~~somehow~~ / **whenever**) transactions occur on your credit card.
신용카드로 거래가 이루어질 때는 언제든지 알림 메시지가 발송될 것이다.

비법 노트

- **명사절 접속사** whoever(누가 ~하든)/whatever(무엇이[을] ~하든)/whichever(어떤 것이[을] ~하든) +불완전한 절
- **부사절 접속사** whoever(~하는 누구든)/whatever(~하는 무엇이든)/whichever(~하는 어떤 것이든) +불완전한 절
  whenever(언제 ~하든)/wherever(어디에 ~하든)/however(아무리 ~해도) +완전한 절

SKILL UP 빈칸이 접속사 자리인데 빈칸 바로 뒤에 형용사나 부사가 있다면 how나 however가 답이다.
The problem will be solved **however** difficult it is. 아무리 어렵더라도 그 문제는 해결될 것이다.

(예제) You can change your username to ------- you'd like, but you can not use special characters.

(A) most   (B) them
(C) whatever (D) this

전치사 + + 절 ⋯ 명사절 접속사

정답 (C)

당신이 원하는 무엇으로든지 사용자 명을 변경할 수 있지만, 특수 기호는 사용할 수 없습니다.

공식 78. 「사람 명사+ ___ +주어가 빠진 절」에는 관계사 who가 답이다.

빈칸 앞에 명사가 있고 빈칸 뒤로 수식절[(주어)+동사]이 보이면, 빈칸은 관계사 자리이다. 관계사절(빈칸 뒤 절)에 주어가 빠져 있으면 주격, 목적어가 빠져 있으면 목적격 관계사가 답이다.

Employees (**who** / ~~they~~) are interested in a transfer should consult with their supervisor.
→ 동사가 두 개(are, should consult)이므로 빈칸은 접속사 자리   전근에 관심 있는 직원들은 관리자와 상담해야 한다.

Fragile stickers must be put on the boxes (**that** / ~~if~~) contain easily breakable items.
→ 빈칸 앞에 명사가 있고 빈칸 뒤에 주어가 빠진 절이 있다.   쉽게 깨지는 제품이 들어 있는 상자에는 취급 주의 스티커가 부착되어야 한다.

(예제) Preference will be given to candidates ------- have completed our internship program.

(A) whoever   (B) who
(C) they   (D) themselves

사람 명사 + ------- + 주어가 빠진 절 ⋯ who

빈칸 뒤는 candidates를 수식하는 관계절이므로 사람 명사 뒤에 오는 주격 관계대명사가 정답이다.

정답 (B)

인턴직을 완료한 후보자들에게 우선권이 주어질 것이다.

공식으로 해결하는 실전문제

해설집 p.54

1. The warehouse staff should be able to take the inventory ------- the supervisor deems it necessary.
   (A) themselves
   (B) whenever
   (C) in addition
   (D) furthermore

2. We at WidU24 Stores are looking for someone ------- is able to work on evenings and weekends.
   (A) who
   (B) they
   (C) them
   (D) so that

3. We need to create a budget plan ------- includes the travel expenses of the project team.
   (A) where
   (B) while
   (C) that
   (D) then

4. Myrat Hotel will offer a special Christmas package for free to ------- downloads its reservation app first.
   (A) any
   (B) whoever
   (C) another
   (D) those

5. Durability and reliability are two things ------- distinguish our laptop computers from those of our competitors.
   (A) where
   (B) then
   (C) those
   (D) that

6. ------- carefully the costs are calculated, the actual project costs may differ from the estimates.
   (A) Hardly
   (B) Nearly
   (C) However
   (D) But

7. The Tourism Bureau has been holding an annual lantern festival, ------- attracts both domestic and international tourists.
   (A) who
   (B) whoever
   (C) whatever
   (D) which

8. We can provide assistance ------- you need to find a house for rent in San Jose and surrounding areas.
   (A) whenever
   (B) in consequence
   (C) somewhere
   (D) compared to

137

공식 79 「명사+____+명사+동사」는 관계사 whose가 답이다.

명사 뒤로 빈칸이 있고, 빈칸 뒤에 명사로 시작하면서 주어나 목적어가 빠지지 않은 절이 있으면 whose가 답이다. 단, whose는 소유격이므로 빈칸과 두 번째 명사 사이에 관사나 소유격이 있다면 정답이 될 수 없다.

There are many applicants (**whose** / ~~those~~) qualifications match our needs.
자격 조건이 우리의 요구에 부합하는 지원자들이 많다.

Passengers (~~who~~ / **whose**) flights are cancelled will receive a full refund.
항공편이 취소된 승객들은 전액 환불을 받을 것이다.

비법 노트

- 명사1+____+명사2+동사 〈'명사1'의 '명사2'가 '동사'하다〉라는 해석이 자연스러우면 whose 자리.
  I purchase clothes **whose** prices have fallen. 나는 가격이 떨어진 옷을 구매한다.
  → '옷(clothes)의 가격(prices)이 내려갔다(have fallen)'라는 해석이 자연스럽다.

[예제] The EW Award honors the writers ------- articles have demonstrated excellence in medical writing.

(A) whose　　(B) these
(C) which　　(D) such

명사 + ------- + 명사 + 동사 ⋯ whose

'작가의 글이 우수성을 증명했다'라는 해석이 자연스럽다.
정답 **(A)** 소유격 관계사
EW 상은 의료 저술 분야에서 우수함을 보여 준 글을 쓴 저자를 기념한다.

공식 80 「명사, most of +____+ 동사」는 관계사 whom/which가 답이다.

관계사절이 앞 명사의 일부를 수식할 때는 「명사, 부정대명사 + of + 관계대명사 +동사」의 구조가 된다. 이때 관계대명사는 앞에서 수식 받는 명사(선행사)가 사람이면 whom, 사물이면 which가 답이다.

Yorkshire enjoyed an influx of tourists, most of (**whom** / ~~them~~) were foreign tourists.
→ 동사가 두 개(enjoyed, were)이므로 접속사 자리　　요크셔는 관광객의 유입을 누렸는데, 그들 대부분이 외국인 관광객이었다.

Gardenhill showcases a variety of plants, all of (~~whom~~ / **which**) are available for purchase.
→ 전치사 뒤 빈칸이므로 목적격 자리인데 선행사 plants가 사물　　가든힐은 다양한 식물을 진열하고 있는데, 이들은 모두 구매 가능합니다.

비법 노트

- 사람 명사, 부정대명사+of+____+V → whom
- 사물 명사, 부정대명사+of+____+V → which

SKILL UP 전치사 + whom[which] + 완전한 절
Ms. Kaminsky is the designer **with whom** I would like to work.
카민스키 씨는 내가 같이 일하고 싶은 디자이너이다.

[예제] The town hall meeting was attended by many residents, none of ------- were late.

(A) them　　(B) those
(C) each　　(D) whom

사람 명사, none of + ------- + 동사 ⋯ whom

none은 '아무(것)도 ~않다'를 의미하는 부정대명사
정답 **(D)** 목적격 관계사
많은 거주자들이 마을회관 회의에 참석했고, 그들 중 누구도 늦지 않았다.

공식으로 해결하는 실전문제

해설집 p.55

1. Any bag ------- total dimensions exceed 158 centimeters will be treated as oversized.
   (A) another
   (B) whose
   (C) which
   (D) what

2. The number of applicants for British citizenship is more than 150,000, many of ------- are from China.
   (A) whom
   (B) where
   (C) them
   (D) these

3. A student ------- request for an extension is refused must submit the work by the course deadline.
   (A) what
   (B) when
   (C) who
   (D) whose

4. Several employees expressed interest in the position at the Vietnam branch, none of ------- are married.
   (A) whose
   (B) them
   (C) themselves
   (D) whom

5. ELL Institute is seeking an experienced language instructor ------- native language is English.
   (A) whose
   (B) when
   (C) where
   (D) which

6. India's startup ecosystem has been attracting many companies, ------- are in the technology sector.
   (A) thanks to them
   (B) inasmuch as
   (C) resulting in
   (D) most of which

7. Local farmers supply our restaurant with fresh organic produce, with ------- all of our meals are prepared.
   (A) that
   (B) this
   (C) which
   (D) one

8. Innel Electronics Group works with a local software vendor called NEZ, ------- anti-virus software is widely used in Asia.
   (A) where
   (B) such
   (C) whose
   (D) every

YBM TEST

1. Please have your serial number ready ------- you call for technical assistance.
   (A) even
   (B) why
   (C) when
   (D) otherwise

2. The Korea Trade Agency offers practical advice to businesses ------- are seeking opportunities in overseas markets.
   (A) if
   (B) where
   (C) then
   (D) that

3. ------- public funds should be used to build a sports facility will be discussed at tonight's council meeting.
   (A) Whether
   (B) While
   (C) Regardless of
   (D) Because

4. ------- smartphone sales have picked up, Monia Display will operate all of its next-generation OLED display production lines at full capacity.
   (A) For
   (B) So
   (C) Often
   (D) As

5. The new hotel by the YZ group will cater mainly to business travelers, ------- most of the other properties owned by the group are targeted toward tourists.
   (A) because
   (B) whereas
   (C) as though
   (D) once

6. ------- volunteers at the film festival will enjoy free tickets and lunch.
   (A) Every
   (B) Anyone
   (C) Another
   (D) Whoever

7. Artists ------- entries have been selected for the competition will be informed by the end of August via e-mail.
   (A) each
   (B) whose
   (C) which
   (D) what

8. Mr. Blair invested a considerable amount of money in multiple startup companies, all of ------- are considered promising.
   (A) them
   (B) what
   (C) those
   (D) which

9. ------- the city encouraged cycling by making public bicycles available, most people continued using their cars to get around town.
   (A) Whenever
   (B) Although
   (C) Nevertheless
   (D) In order that

10. The company will provide Mr. Rajeeve with temporary accommodations ------- his long-term housing can be arranged.
    (A) until
    (B) throughout
    (C) in
    (D) above all

11. Any student ------- plans an event on campus must submit a request form to the administration two weeks in advance.

(A) whoever
(B) every
(C) who
(D) with

12. The survey indicates ------- nearly a third of consumers are willing to spend more for products from socially responsible companies.

(A) but
(B) from
(C) what
(D) that

13. The market survey on ------- the company based its pricing policy was conducted by a third-party research firm.

(A) which
(B) somehow
(C) it
(D) neither

14. Investments in foreign currencies involve a high risk of substantial losses, ------- thoroughly they are planned.

(A) rather
(B) however
(C) even
(D) regardless

15. Those interested in the conference are advised to purchase tickets in advance ------- they are expected to sell out quickly.

(A) in order
(B) as
(C) but
(D) resulting from

16. Sophia Fowler, ------- contributed significantly to developing the new payroll system, has been promoted to head accountant.

(A) her
(B) when
(C) who
(D) herself

17. We are short of time ------- solutions for slow sales have to be found before the board meeting on Thursday.

(A) consider
(B) consideration
(C) considered
(D) considering

18. Individuals ------- incomes are higher than $200,000 will enter a new tax bracket of 35% under the revised tax system.

(A) what
(B) who
(C) themselves
(D) whose

19. You may make sound recordings during a check-up with your physician, ------- you notify us in advance.

(A) provided that
(B) together with
(C) according to
(D) regardless of

20. When developing the product, you need to define ------- your target consumers are.

(A) whether
(B) that
(C) who
(D) but

PART 6

공식 81. 어휘 문제는 빈칸의 앞뒤 문장에 정답과 유의어가 있다.

파트 6에서 어휘 문제는 빈칸의 주변 문장에 단서가 숨어 있다. 빈칸 앞뒤 문장에 나열된 단어 및 구문과 관련성이 깊은 단어 혹은 의미가 비슷한 단어가 보기에 보인다면, 그 단어가 바로 정답이다.

만점 전략

앞 문장에서 단서 찾기

no longer want 더 이상 원하지 않는다	→ cancel 취소하다
sick leave 병가	→ for health reasons 건강상의 이유로
welcome to the company 입사를 환영하다	→ accept the job 일자리를 수락하다
expect to increase 증가할 것을 예상하다	→ this forecast 이 예측은
quickly 빨리	→ fast 빠른
new buildings 새 건물들	→ additional units 추가 구성물

뒷 문장에서 단서 찾기

expire 만기가 되다	← change[renew] ~ as soon as possible 가능한 빨리 변경[갱신]하다
launch a company 회사를 설립하다	← the new firm 새 회사
final phase 최종 단계	← evaluation process 평가 절차
accept the job 일자리를 수락하다	← look forward to working with you 당신과 함께 일하기를 기대하다
space for residents' clothing 거주자들의 옷을 위한 공간	← laundry area 세탁실

예제 해설집 p.58

Register for our trial print subscription and ❶get two free copies of our monthly magazine. ❷We will mail you our current ------- right away, and also the one after that. After two months, we'll send you an invoice, at which time you can either cancel or start your paid subscription. … 중략

(A) itinerary
(B) registration
(C) issue
(D) content

빈칸 앞 문장에서 관련 있는 어휘 찾기

❶ 빈칸 앞: 저희 월간지 두 부를 무료로 받아 보세요.
❷ 빈칸: 저희가 당월 ____를 즉시 보내 드리겠습니다.
→ copies와 magazine을 뜻하는 단어가 답이다.

정답 (C) 호
오답 (A) 여행 일정표 (B) 등록 (서류) (D) 내용물

YBM TEST

해설집 p.58

Questions 1-4 refer to the following letter.

April 9

Ralph Furley
9602 Santa Monica Blvd.
Beverly Hills, CA, 90210

Dear Ms. Furley,

On 31 March, I ------- you if you failed to take care of the broken window in 123 Homeward
                 1.
Place Apt. 3B within a week, I myself would arrange for the ------- to be made and seek
                                                          2.
reimbursement for the cost. Since my request was ignored, I called a glass repair service,
Glass Doctor, and had the problem fixed on 8 April.

------- is a copy of the invoice for the cost of materials and labor involved in the repair work,
3.
in the amount of $180. -------.
                      4.

Respectfully,

John Kurkela

1. (A) have notified
   (B) notified
   (C) will notify
   (D) notify

2. (A) purchases
   (B) reservations
   (C) repairs
   (D) gifts

3. (A) Enclosing
   (B) Enclosure
   (C) Enclose
   (D) Enclosed

4. (A) I will deduct that amount from my next rent payment.
   (B) Please arrange a time for the repair work to be done.
   (C) It is important that you fix it quickly.
   (D) You are required to give me a written receipt for the amount paid.

UNIT 10 특수구문

기본 학습

등위접속사

등위접속사는 단어와 단어, 구와 구, 절과 절을 대등하게 연결하는 역할을 한다.

and 그리고	Roots Ltd. plans to open offices in <u>Dublin</u> **and** <u>Glasgow</u>. 루츠 사는 더블린과 글래스고에 사무실을 열 계획이다.
or 또는	If you have trouble <u>sending</u> **or** <u>receiving</u> e-mails, please let me know. 이메일을 보내거나 받는 데 문제가 있다면, 저한테 알려주세요.
but, yet 그러나	The advertisement of Berry's new phone was <u>simple</u> **but** <u>effective</u>. 베리 사의 새 전화기 광고는 간단하지만 효과적이었다.
so 그래서	Kate is on a limited budget, ***so** she avoids travelling during the peak season. 케이트는 예산이 한정적이어서 성수기 동안 여행하는 것을 피한다. *so는 절과 절만 연결할 수 있고, 단어나 구는 연결하지 못한다.

상관접속사

상관접속사는 둘 이상의 단어가 짝을 이루어 접속사 역할을 한다.

both A and B A와 B 둘 다	For this job, you will need to be able to speak **both** English **and** Chinese. 이 직업에 지원하려면 영어와 중국어 둘 다 할 수 있어야 한다.
either A or B A, B 둘 중 하나	Due to a scheduling conflict, I have to **either** delay the meeting **or** cancel it. 일정상의 문제로, 나는 회의를 연기하거나 취소해야 한다.
neither A nor B A도 B도 아닌	**Neither** Ms. Smith **nor** Mr. Ashton attended the workshop. 스미스 씨와 애시턴 씨 둘 중 누구도 워크숍에 참석하지 않았다.
not A but B = B, (but) not A A가 아니라 B	Mr. Song is **not** a lawyer **but** a banker. 송 씨는 변호사가 아니라 은행가이다. = Mr. Song is a banker, **(but) not** a lawyer.
not only A but (also) B = B as well as A A뿐만 아니라 B도	Defective products damage **not only** sales **but also** consumer confidence. = Defective products damage consumer confidence as well as sales. 결함이 있는 제품은 판매뿐 아니라 고객 신뢰에 악영향을 미친다.

비교

원급은 원래 형용사와 부사를 그대로 활용하고, 비교급과 최상급은 단어의 길이에 따라 형태를 변형시켜 표현한다.

- **원급**: 'A는 B만큼 …하다'는 뜻으로, 비슷한 두 개의 대상을 비교할 때 쓴다. (as + 원급 + as)
  The weather this summer is **as** hot **as** last year. 올 여름 날씨는 작년만큼 덥다.
- **비교급**: 'A는 B보다 더 …하다'는 뜻으로, 두 대상의 우열을 비교할 때 쓴다. (원급 + er / more + 원급)
  The convention hall was **more spacious than** we expected. 회의장은 우리가 예상했던 것보다 넓었다.
- **최상급**: 비교 대상이 셋 이상일 경우, '가장 …하다'는 뜻으로 비교할 때 쓴다. (the + 원급 + est / the most + 원급)
  This is **the tallest** building in New York. 이것이 뉴욕에서 가장 높은 빌딩이다.

가정법

실제로 일어나지 않은 일 혹은 사실과 반대되는 상황을 가정할 때 쓰는 표현이다.

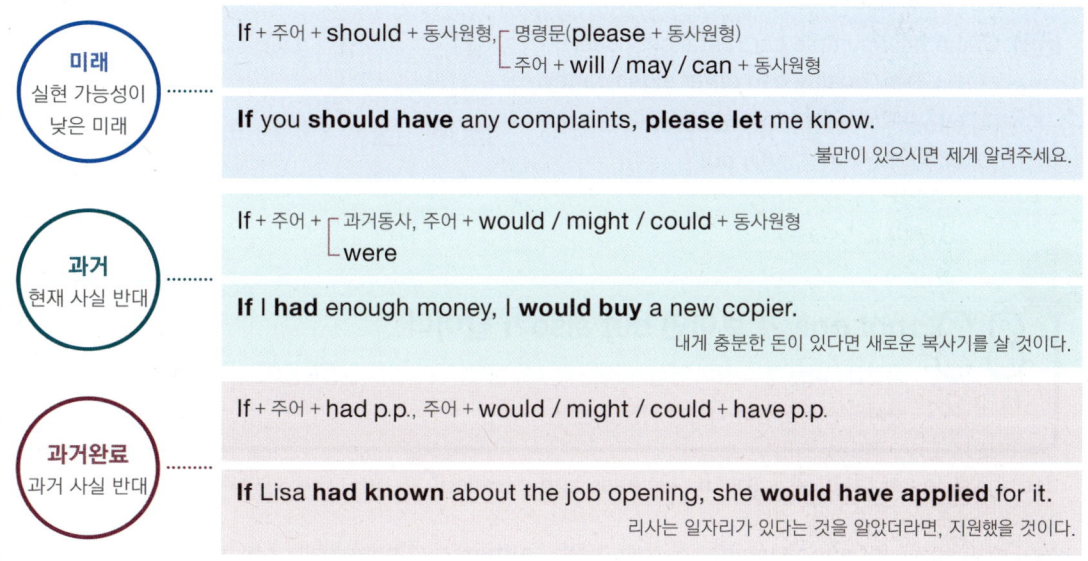

도치

특정한 말을 문장 맨 앞으로 보내고 뒤에 있는 주어와 동사를 의문문처럼 「(조)동사 + 주어」 순서로 바꾸는 것이다.

1. **부정어 도치:** never(절대 ~하지 않다), hardly(거의 ~않다), seldom(좀처럼 ~않다) 등의 부정어가 맨 앞으로 올 때
   Never has the company **experienced** such substantial growth as this year.
   회사는 올해 같은 높은 성장을 경험해 본 적이 없다.
2. **only 도치:** only가 이끄는 부사, 부사구, 부사절이 맨 앞으로 올 때
   Only occasionally **do** we **outsource** the recruitment process. 우리는 가끔씩만 고용 업무를 외부에 위탁한다.
3. **보어 도치:** 보어가 맨 앞으로 올 때
   Enclosed is a report on environmental assessment. 환경 평가에 대한 보고서가 동봉되어 있다.
4. **가정법 도치:** if가 생략되고 동사가 맨 앞으로 올 때
   Had Lisa **known** about the job opening, she **would have applied** for it.
   리사는 일자리가 있다는 것을 알았더라면, 지원했을 것이다.

UNIT 10 특수구문

공식 82 and는 앞뒤로 대등한 품사를 연결한다.

등위접속사는 대등한 성분을 연결하므로, 등위접속사를 기준으로 좌우가 대칭 구조를 이룬다. 적절한 등위접속사를 고르는 문제는 물론, 등위접속사 좌우에 대등한 품사를 넣는 문제도 출제된다.

Marcel Chang is responsible for recruiting and (**training** / ~~train~~) new employees.
→ for의 목적어인 동명사 recruiting과 training을 and가 연결   마르셀 장은 신입 직원들의 채용 및 훈련을 책임지고 있다.

Roots UK Ltd. has recently opened its flagship stores in Seoul (**and** / ~~so~~) Shanghai.
루츠 UK 사는 최근 서울과 상하이에 주력 상점을 개점했다.

비법 노트

- **등위접속사 자리**   ① 단어 ____ 단어   ② 구 ____ 구   ③ 절 ____ 절
  * 등위접속사는 문장 맨 앞에는 쓰지 않는다.

- **같은 품사가 답!**   ① 명사 and ____ → 명사   ② ____ or 형용사 → 형용사   ③ 부사 but ____ → 부사
  * 등위접속사가 연결하는 성분이 무엇인지 정확히 판단해야 한다.

예제) Guam has multiple car rental services, ------- their quality can differ significantly.

(A) either   (B) according to
(C) or   (D) but

절 + ------- + 절 → 등위접속사

문맥상 '하지만'이 어울린다.
정답 (D)   오답 (A) 둘 중 하나 (B) ~에 따르면 (C) 또는

괌에는 다수의 자동차 대여 업체가 있지만, 업체 수준에는 상당한 차이가 있을 수 있다.

공식 83 not only가 보이면 but also가 답이다.

상관접속사는 둘 이상의 단어가 짝을 이루어 단어나 구, 절을 연결하는데, 빈칸 주변에 있는 상관접속사 한쪽을 단서로 삼아 나머지 짝을 고른다.

Jessica's dessert recipe is (**both** / ~~or~~) easy and practical. 제시카의 디저트 조리법은 쉽고 실용적이다.
→ 빈칸 뒤에 A and B가 있다.

You may apply for a food vendor permit (~~both~~ / **either**) by phone call or by e-mail.
→ 빈칸 뒤에 A or B가 있다.   전화나 이메일로 식품 판매상 허가증을 신청하실 수 있습니다.

비법 노트

| both A ____ B → and   A B 둘 다 | not only A ____ B → but (also)   A뿐만 아니라 B도 |
| ____ A or B → either   A B 둘 중 하나 | neither A ____ B → nor   A도 B도 아닌 |

예제) We are developing cars that are not only cost-effective ------- eco-friendly.

(A) neither   (B) but also
(C) so   (D) both

not only ------- → but also

정답 (B)

우리는 비용 효율적일 뿐 아니라 환경 친화적인 차를 개발하고 있다.

공식으로 해결하는 실전문제

해설집 p.59

1. When we recruit new employees, we consider both internal ------- external candidates.
   (A) or
   (B) and
   (C) nor
   (D) just as

2. To become a successful presenter, you need to learn how to speak with ------- and passion.
   (A) confident
   (B) confidence
   (C) confidential
   (D) confidently

3. Unless otherwise stated, IT training sessions will take place on ------- Thursday or Friday.
   (A) in case
   (B) not only
   (C) either
   (D) both

4. The airline may require passengers to present a photo ID at the boarding gate ------- at the check-in counter.
   (A) but
   (B) both
   (C) between
   (D) and

5. If you attend less than 70% of the workshop, you will receive neither a certificate ------- reimbursement for expenses from the company.
   (A) nor
   (B) or
   (C) and
   (D) like

6. Dragon Rider is ------- the biggest mobile game, but also the most popular one in Europe.
   (A) either
   (B) or
   (C) as well as
   (D) not only

7. Our aim is to help our customers look and ------- better, with our extensive range of health and beauty products.
   (A) feel
   (B) feeling
   (C) feels
   (D) felt

8. At InnoTech, we choose our products carefully ------- offer our customers the best price.
   (A) both
   (B) so
   (C) and
   (D) as

UNIT 10 특수구문

공식 84 「as+___+as」는 원급이 정답이다.

「as+____+as ~」는 '~만큼 ___하다'라는 뜻으로, as와 as 사이에 형용사와 부사의 원급이 들어간다. as와 as 사이의 품사를 고를 때는 빈칸 앞 as와 빈칸 뒤를 모두 지우고 남은 성분만 따지면 쉽다. 빈칸이 보어 자리이면 형용사, 동사를 수식하면 부사를 고른다.

The sales at AZ Sports doubled as (**soon** / ~~sooner~~) as Market Mall closed nearby.
근처에 있던 마켓 몰이 문을 닫자마자 AZ 스포츠의 판매량이 두 배가 되었다.

This year's workshop format should be kept as (**simple** / simply) as the last one.
→ as와 빈칸 뒤를 지우면 5형식의 수동태 「be kept+형용사」 구문이 남는다. 올해 워크숍 구성은 지난번처럼 간소하게 유지되어야 한다.

(예제) T-Bus's new app will make airport bus booking as ------- as flight booking.
(A) conveniently   (B) convenience
(C) more convenient (D) convenient

5형식 동사 + 목적어 + as ------ as ⋯ 원급 형용사
as와 수식어구를 지우면 빈칸은 목적격 보어 자리.
정답 (D) 오답 (C) 비교급
T-Bus의 새 앱은 공항 버스 예약을 비행기 예약만큼 편리하게 만들 것이다.

공식 85 원급 비교는 다양한 관용 표현을 함께 기억한다.

「as+원급+as possible」은 '가능한 한 ~하게'라는 표현으로 대표적인 빈출 유형이다. 또한 원급 비교 앞에 배수가 붙으면 '몇 배 더 ~하다'라는 의미가 되며, as 앞에 the same이 붙으면 '~와 똑같은'이라는 의미가 된다.

When talking with customers on the phone, speak as (~~clear~~ / **clearly**) as possible.
→ as ~ as possible을 지우고 나면 빈칸이 동사 speak를 수식하는 자리임을 알 수 있다.
고객과 통화할 때는 가능한 한 명료하게 말하세요.

비법 노트 관용 표현

as _____ as possible 가능한 한 ~한[하게]	Please be as detailed as possible. 가능한 한 상세하게 해주세요.
배수 + as _____ as ~ ~의 몇 배만큼 ~한	twice as fast as the previous model 지난 모델보다 두 배 더 빠른
the same(+ 명사) + **as ~** ~와 똑같은	the same revenue as in the first quarter 1/4분기와 똑같은 수익
as many + 복수명사[**much** + 불가산명사] **as ~** ~만큼 많은	Fill out the form with as much information as possible. 가능한 한 많은 정보를 서류에 기입하세요.
*as ~ as 사이에 명사가 단독으로 들어갈 수 없다.	as many cameras as we sold in 2012 우리가 2012년에 팔았던 만큼의 카메라

(예제) Ms. Lim ordered her team to finish the budget proposal as ------- as possible.
(A) quicker   (B) quickly
(C) quickest   (D) more quickly

as ------- as possible ⋯ 원급
정답 (B) (가능한 한) 신속히
림 씨는 가능한 한 신속히 예산안을 마무리하라고 팀에 지시했다.

공식으로 해결하는 실전문제

1. Leina is as ------- for the vacant position as any other member of the team.
   (A) more qualified
   (B) qualifies
   (C) qualified
   (D) most qualified

2. Today, Bell introduced an all-new 10.5-inch B-Pad for the same price ------- the previous model.
   (A) than
   (B) as
   (C) just
   (D) as well

3. Explore the world with Easy Car Rentals and get a fantastic rate as ------- as $16 per day.
   (A) low
   (B) lowest
   (C) lower
   (D) lowly

4. Retaining talented employees can be as ------- as recruiting them in the first place.
   (A) more challenging
   (B) challenges
   (C) most challenging
   (D) challenging

5. Moyoda claims that fuel-cell vehicles are about twice as ------- as gas-powered cars in terms of fuel consumption.
   (A) efficiency
   (B) efficient
   (C) more efficient
   (D) efficiently

6. Dr. Song tried to answer ------- questions as possible after the seminar on Clinical Medicine and Surgery.
   (A) as much
   (B) so many
   (C) so much
   (D) as many

7. In order to store chemicals as ------- as possible, clutter should be kept to a minimum in the laboratory.
   (A) safely
   (B) safest
   (C) safer
   (D) safe

8. The company aimed to make its customer service as ------- to its customers' needs as possible.
   (A) responsively
   (B) responsive
   (C) responds
   (D) respond

공식 86 than 앞은 비교급이 답이다.

「비교급+than ~」은 '~보다 더 ___하다'는 뜻으로 두 대상의 우열을 비교할 때 쓰므로, 빈칸 뒤에 than이 보이면 비교급이 정답이다. 또한 비교급을 강조하는 부사를 고르는 문제도 출제되므로 함께 기억한다.

Rumix office software is (~~simple~~ / **simpler**) than its alternatives.
→ 빈칸 뒤에 than이 있으므로 비교급 자리
루믹스 사무용 소프트웨어는 다른 제품들보다 더 간단하다.

Simple Pay makes it (**much** / ~~very~~) easier to make payments using your mobile device.
심플 페이는 모바일 장치를 이용한 지불을 훨씬 더 쉽게 해 준다.

비법 노트 비교급 강조 부사

much/far/even 훨씬 considerably/significantly/substantially 상당히 noticeably 눈에 띄게

SKILL UP ① 굳이 비교 대상을 밝힐 필요가 없을 때는 「than+비교 대상」을 생략한다.
The new model, A-30, is more durable. 신모델인 A-30이 내구성이 더 좋다.
② less 덜 ~한 less expensive 덜 비싼 less often 덜 자주

[예제] One-way airfares are often ------- than round-trip tickets.
(A) expensive   (B) more expensive
(C) expensively   (D) most expensive

------- + than + 비교 대상 ⋯ 비교급

정답 (B)
편도 항공 요금은 종종 왕복 요금보다 더 비싸다.

공식 87 빈칸 앞에 the가 보이면 비교급보다는 최상급이 답이다.

「the/소유격+최상급」은 비교 대상이 셋 이상일 때 '가장 ___하다'를 뜻한다. 빈칸 앞에 the/소유격이 있고, 문장에 최상급과 잘 어울리는 표현이 있으면 원급이나 비교급이 아닌 최상급을 넣는다.

The CEO stressed that safety is the (**most important** / ~~more important~~) value in the company.
최고 경영자는 안전이 회사에서 가장 중요한 가치라고 강조했다.

비법 노트 관용 표현

the + 최상급 +	**in** + 장소 ~에서	the highest building in New York 뉴욕에서 가장 높은 빌딩
	of / among + 복수명사 ~ 중에서	the cheapest among these computers 이 컴퓨터들 중 가장 싼
	yet / to date 지금까지	the most difficult test to date 지금까지 중 가장 어려운 시험
	have ever p.p. ~한 중에서	the best that I have ever seen 내가 본 것 중 최고
	possible / available 가능한 가장 ~한	to book the cheapest flights possible 가능한 가장 싼 비행편 예약하기
one of the 최상급 + 복수명사 가장 ___한 것 중 하나		one of the most respected scientists 가장 존경받는 과학자들 중 한 명
the + 서수 + 최상급 ~ 번째로 ___한		the second largest city 두 번째로 큰 도시

[예제] The Sagrada Familia is considered one of the ------- landmarks in Barcelona.
(A) most popular   (B) popularly
(C) popularity   (D) more popularly

the + ------- + in + 장소 ⋯ 최상급

정답 (A) 오답 (C) 명사 (D) 비교급 부사

사그라다 파밀리아는 바르셀로나에서 가장 인기 있는 명소 중 하나로 간주된다.

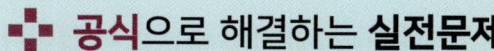 공식으로 해결하는 **실전문제**

1. Our new Enterprise Solutions is ------- than virtually any other resource planning system.
   (A) flexible
   (B) flexibly
   (C) more flexible
   (D) more flexibly

2. As the membership fee has increased, watching movies on Netfilms has become ------- more expensive.
   (A) much
   (B) very
   (C) that
   (D) many

3. English is by far the ------- studied foreign language in the world, according to a study by Edu Research.
   (A) common
   (B) more common
   (C) more commonly
   (D) most commonly

4. At Best Appliances, we provide you with the best prices and the ------- selection available.
   (A) widely
   (B) wider
   (C) widen
   (D) widest

5. OfficeWorld is planning to lower its prices in order to make its products even ------- to buyers.
   (A) attractive
   (B) more attractive
   (C) most attractive
   (D) attractively

6. Electric cars run ------- than those with petrol engines, so pedestrians find it hard to hear them coming.
   (A) quietly
   (B) most quietly
   (C) more quietly
   (D) quiet

7. Chairmaster is proud to be ranked as the third ------- furniture brand by *DecoDaily*.
   (A) most popular
   (B) popularity
   (C) more popular
   (D) popularly

8. Last Fighter VII is the most ------- game that Yaho Online Games has ever developed.
   (A) success
   (B) successful
   (C) successfully
   (D) succeed

UNIT 10 특수구문

공식 88 「If + 주어 + had p.p., 주어 + _____」에는 would have p.p.가 답이다.

If가 보이는 가정법 문장에 동사가 빈칸으로 나오면, 상대절의 동사를 보고 시제를 맞춰 준다. 가정법, 미래(if ~ should 동사원형, ~ will / 명령문), 과거(if ~ 과거동사, ~ would), 과거완료(if ~ had p.p., ~ would have p.p.)를 외운다.

If there had been online courses, Nora (**might have registered** / ~~has registered~~).
온라인 강좌가 있었더라면, 노라는 등록했을 수도 있다.

If you should see Mr. Smith, (**tell** / ~~told~~) him to come to the meeting room.
스미스 씨를 보게 되면, 회의실로 오라고 전해 주세요.

비법 노트

- 가정법 미래 If S should 동사원형, S will[may/can] 동사원형
   If S should 동사원형, 명령문
- 가정법 과거 If S 과거동사(be동사는 were), S would[might/could] 동사원형
- 가정법 과거완료 If S had p.p., S would[might/could] have p.p.

[예제] If the flight ------ on time, we wouldn't have missed Ms. Calloway's presentation.

(A) departing (B) departed
(C) had departed (D) will depart

If ------, wouldn't have p.p. → had p.p.

정답 **(C)**

비행기가 제때 출발했다면, 우리는 캘러웨이 씨의 발표를 놓치지 않았을 것이다.

공식 89 「_____ + 주어 + 동사원형, 명령문」에는 should가 답이다.

가정법 문장에서는 if를 생략할 수 있는데 이때, if 바로 뒤의 어순이 「동사 + 주어」로 도치된다. 주로 미래와 과거완료 가정법이 도치 문제로 출제되므로, 미래(Should + 주어 + 동사원형), 과거완료(Had + 주어 + p.p.)를 기억하자.

(**Should** / ~~How~~) you have any questions, please let me know. 질문이 있으시면 제게 알려주세요.
→ 'If you should have any questions ~'에서 if가 생략되면서 도치

(**Had** / ~~Have~~) the shipment arrived on time, we would have finished work earlier.
→ 'If the shipment had arrived ~'에서 if가 생략되면서 도치 배송물이 제때 도착했더라면 작업을 더 일찍 끝냈을 것이다.

비법 노트

- 가정법 미래 Should 주어 동사원형, S will[may/can] 동사원형
   Should 주어 동사원형, 명령문
- 가정법 과거완료 Had 주어 p.p., 주어 would[might/could] have p.p.

 ------ you wish to modify your shipping details, please contact our customer service.

(A) Why (B) Although
(C) Should (D) Nevertheless

------ + 주어 + 동사원형, 명령문 ⋯▸ Should

가정법 미래 문장 'If you should wish~'에서 if가 생략되면서 도치가 일어난 형태

정답 **(C)**

배송 정보를 수정하길 원하시면 고객 서비스 부서로 연락 주세요.

공식으로 해결하는 실전문제

해설집 p.61

1. If the Black Socks ------- one more game, they would have qualified for the Champions League semifinals.
   (A) have won
   (B) won
   (C) is winning
   (D) had won

2. ------- you take a defensive driving course, you will qualify for a five percent discount off your car insurance rates.
   (A) Unless
   (B) Even
   (C) As well as
   (D) Should

3. If you had purchased your tickets three weeks prior to the departure, you ------- a ten percent discount.
   (A) would have received
   (B) will receive
   (C) were received
   (D) would have been received

4. ------- the board approved the design of the new car model, production would have already begun.
   (A) Have
   (B) Had
   (C) Would
   (D) If

5. ------- you require any further assistance, please do not hesitate to contact us at any time.
   (A) Should
   (B) Elsewhere
   (C) Because
   (D) Also

6. If safety precautions had been strictly followed, the devastating accident -------.
   (A) could have avoided
   (B) is avoided
   (C) could have been avoided
   (D) has avoided

7. Should the error message ------- again, please phone our contact center to investigate further.
   (A) is appeared
   (B) appeared
   (C) appear
   (D) appearing

8. If you should encounter any difficulties while browsing, please ------- us by submitting the contact form.
   (A) notification
   (B) notify
   (C) notifying
   (D) notifies

YBM TEST

1. Members of the BI Network receive a monthly business newsletter ------- opportunities to connect with local business.

   (A) likewise
   (B) moreover
   (C) as well as
   (D) as a result

2. The personnel director found Daniel Louis's career ------- more impressive than Bill Rotack's.

   (A) very
   (B) far
   (C) yet
   (D) like

3. According to the Net Times, the World College Rankings are the ------- used rankings among international students.

   (A) wide
   (B) widen
   (C) most widely
   (D) more widely

4. Staff evaluations should be as ------- as possible, covering all the areas essential to rating performance.

   (A) comprehensively
   (B) comprehension
   (C) comprehensive
   (D) comprehend

5. Hayaas has decided to reduce the size of its nuclear energy business ------- not to stop working in the industry completely.

   (A) but
   (B) with
   (C) either
   (D) both

6. Should anyone ------- problems in downloading the forms, we will have to send them via e-mail.

   (A) experiences
   (B) experience
   (C) experienced
   (D) experiencing

7. Greentable is allocating ------- resources as possible into building up its new blog to drive more organic traffic.

   (A) as many
   (B) as much
   (C) so much
   (D) so many

8. Register before September 30 and ------- the early bird discount for the career development conference.

   (A) receive
   (B) receipt
   (C) received
   (D) receiving

9. The study by M2 Business suggests that today's office workers are nearly twice as ------- as their counterparts in the 1970s.

   (A) produce
   (B) productively
   (C) produced
   (D) productive

10. Had Mr. Long ------- that road work was underway on Highway 16, he wouldn't have driven to work.

    (A) know
    (B) knew
    (C) knowing
    (D) known

154

11. Only by using our Rail Reservation app, ------- to see our last minute discounts.

    (A) your ability
    (B) are you able
    (C) you
    (D) able

12. If the office had not upgraded the computers' firewall settings, the scale of damage caused by the malware attacks ------- enormous.

    (A) could have been
    (B) will be
    (C) were
    (D) has been

13. We offer a specialized pet transportation service that helps your pets travel as ------- as possible.

    (A) comfortably
    (B) more comfortable
    (C) most comfortably
    (D) comfortable

14. Our airline will let you either cancel the reservation entirely ------- change it, at no extra cost within 24 hours of booking.

    (A) both
    (B) or
    (C) and
    (D) as well as

15. ------- Ms. Rowhead attended the trade fair two months ago, she would have had a chance to meet Romeo Musk, the founder of Nesla.

    (A) Should
    (B) Were
    (C) Would
    (D) Had

16. In general, large companies can afford to offer ------- employee-benefits packages than small ones.

    (A) generous
    (B) generously
    (C) most generous
    (D) more generous

17. All new staff members are required to visit the reception area ------- provide their contact details on their first day.

    (A) so
    (B) nor
    (C) not only
    (D) and

18. The Korean online game industry has rapidly emerged as one of the ------- in the world.

    (A) most dynamic
    (B) more dynamism
    (C) dynamics
    (D) dynamically

19. ------- you wish to cancel your subscription to HDN Cable, please complete the cancellation form and return it to us.

    (A) Would
    (B) Had
    (C) Should
    (D) Have

20. If the airport ------- regular maintenance on its software, the baggage system failure could have been prevented.

    (A) performs
    (B) performing
    (C) had performed
    (D) has performed

PART 6

문법 문제는 한 문장 안에서 해결한다.

파트 6는 파트 7의 독해 지문에 파트 5의 문제를 결합시킨 형태이다. 파트 6의 문법 문제는 기본적으로 파트 5와 같은 방식으로, 빈칸에 들어가기에 알맞은 품사를 고르는 문제이다. 따라서 문법 문제는 파트 5에서와 마찬가지로 빈칸이 들어 있는 문장 안에서만 구조를 파악하면 된다.

만점 전략

▪ 명사	「관사+형용사+명사」을 기억한다. **동사나 전치사 뒤** 목적어 자리에도 명사가 답이다.
▪ 동사	동사 자리를 파악해 주어와 **수일치**시키고 능동/수동을 구분한다. 빈칸 뒤에 **목적어가 있으면 능동, 없으면 수동**을 넣는다.
▪ to부정사	완전한 절 앞뒤에 붙어 '~하기 위해서'라고 해석된다.
▪ 분사/형용사	명사를 수식한다. **be동사 뒤** 혹은 **관사와 명사 사이 자리**가 자주 출제된다.
▪ 부사	형용사와 동사를 수식한다. 「be+___+형용사/분사」와 「주어+___+동사」에서 빈칸은 부사 자리이다.
▪ 전치사	빈칸 뒤로 남아 있는 **명사**를 절에 연결하는 자리는 전치사가 1순위이다.
▪ 관계사	**주격 관계대명사**가 자주 출제된다. 접속사 자리인데 명사와 동사 사이 빈칸이면 주격 관계대명사가 정답일 가능성이 높다.

예제   해설집 p.64

Dear Mr. Taylor,

Thank you for agreeing to speak at our company workshop. I am writing this letter ------- some basic information about the workshop. Enclosed is a tentative agenda. You are scheduled to speak on June 12th at 3 P.M. about Communication Strategies.

We are looking forward to your presentation.

Sincerely,
Jane W. McEwen
HR Director of Metropolitan Ltd.

완전한 절 + ------- + 명사구 ⋯ to부정사

완전한 절 뒤에 추가로 붙어 뒤에 있는 명사구(some basic information)를 연결하는 자리

정답 (B) (기본 정보를) 제공하기 위해서

(A) provided
(B) to provide
(C) provide
(D) provision of

YBM TEST

해설집 p. 64

Questions 1-4 refer to the following article.

By Samuel Lewis (December 26) – *The Boston Times* announced Wednesday that it was promoting its design director, Amy Brown, to deputy editor. A native of Boston City ------- **1.** Massachusetts University, Ms. Brown began her career as a ------- for the BBS Broadcast **2.** Group and served as an art director at *Fine Arts* magazine. She joined *The Boston Times* 6 years ago as an art director of the Home section. -------. She will continue to oversee **3.** a team of 65 art directors, graphic artists, web designers, and others responsible for the appearance of the paper and its Web site. The promotion is ------- from January 1. **4.**

1. (A) who attended
   (B) attending those
   (C) that attend
   (D) whose attendance

2. (A) design
   (B) designs
   (C) designer
   (D) designing

3. (A) Two years later, she was appointed as a design director.
   (B) The editorial board welcomes her to the newspaper.
   (C) She felt she needed to take some time off from work.
   (D) She stepped down as chief editor last month.

4. (A) available
   (B) promising
   (C) undecided
   (D) effective

UNIT 11 어휘 1

공식 91 제안/요구 동사 뒤에 오는 that절에는 동사원형이 답이다.

제안/요구/의무를 뜻하는 동사나 형용사 뒤에 오는 that절에는 주어 뒤에 동사원형이 온다. 따라서 that절에 3인칭 단수주어가 와도 동사와 수일치되지 않으며, be동사도 원형 그대로 쓴다.

The factory manager suggested that the old equipment (**be replaced** / ~~was replaced~~).
→ 제안하다(suggest)라는 동사 뒤에 오는 that절에는 동사원형이 온다. 공장 관리자는 노후한 장비가 교체되어야 한다고 제안했다.

비법 노트 뒤따르는 that절에 동사원형이 오는 동사와 형용사

demand 요구하다	ask 요청하다	insist 주장하다	propose 제안하다	urge 촉구[권고]하다
request 요청하다	require 요구하다	suggest 제안하다	order 명령하다	recommend 권고[추천]하다
necessary 필요한	important 중요한	critical 중요한	essential/vital/imperative 필수적인

[예제] We ------- that newly painted walls be allowed to completely dry for at least three days.

(A) recommend   (B) mention
(C) assume   (D) believe

------- + that + 주어 + 동사원형 … 제안 동사

정답 **(A)** 권고하다
오답 (B) 언급하다 (C) 추정하다, 떠맡다 (D) 믿다

새로 페인트칠한 벽이 완전히 마르도록 최소한 3일 동안 둘 것을 권고드립니다.

공식 92 「자동사 + 전치사」는 짝꿍으로 고른다.

자동사는 목적어를 취하지 못하므로, 뒤에 명사가 올 경우 전치사가 연결해 준다. 자주 짝지어 다니는 「자동사 + 전치사」를 외워두면 빈칸 앞뒤 짝꿍만 봐도 바로 답을 고를 수 있다.

Zarka Pastry (**specializes** / ~~deals~~) in making desserts and cupcakes.
→ deal은 뒤에 with가 온다. 자카 페이스트리는 디저트와 컵케익을 만드는 것을 전문으로 한다.

비법 노트 자동사 + 전치사

serve(= work) as ~로 근무하다	lead to ~로 이어지다	result in (결과를) 낳다
result from ~로 인해 발생하다	apply for ~에 지원하다	comply with ~을 준수하다
conform to ~을 따르다	enroll in = register for ~에 등록하다	participate in ~에 참석하다
deal with ~을 다루다	specialize in ~을 전문으로 하다	proceed with ~를 진행하다
concentrate(= focus) on ~에 집중하다	subscribe to ~을 구독하다	consist of ~로 구성되다
benefit from ~로부터 이익을 얻다	contribute to ~에 기여하다	refer to ~을 참고하다
communicate with ~와 소통(연락)하다	rely(= depend) on ~에 의지하다	account for ~을 설명하다, 차지하다
qualify for ~에 자격을 얻다	object to ~에 반대하다	refrain from ~을 삼가다

[예제] The stone bridge spanning the small stream ------- to Brighton Museum & Art Gallery.

(A) directs   (B) places
(C) takes   (D) leads

동사 빈칸 뒤 전치사 to … 자동사 자리

lead to + 명사: ~로 이어지다
정답 **(D)**

작은 개울을 가로지르는 돌다리는 브라이튼 박물관으로 이어진다.

공식으로 해결하는 실전문제

해설집 p.65

1. Bluejet Airlines requests that passengers ------- their own food on board for the flight.
   (A) brought
   (B) bring
   (C) brings
   (D) are bringing

2. Kelly McKaig has ------- as an investment adviser since she joined our team in 2009.
   (A) experienced
   (B) hired
   (C) served
   (D) promoted

3. Ms. Watanabe, the chief administrator, suggested that the current notification procedure -------.
   (A) is simplifying
   (B) has simplified
   (C) simplify
   (D) be simplified

4. It is ------- that every member of the marketing team be present at the annual International Marketing Trends Conference.
   (A) important
   (B) surprising
   (C) persuasive
   (D) insightful

5. If you wish to ------- for a special reservation for a free session, complete a registration card.
   (A) apply
   (B) submit
   (C) attend
   (D) request

6. By opening a liaison office in New York, the firm can better ------- with branch offices in the U.S.
   (A) separate
   (B) inform
   (C) communicate
   (D) focus

7. We ask that all information in the application ------- carefully prior to submission.
   (A) reviews
   (B) reviewed
   (C) be reviewed
   (D) has reviewed

8. Every employee in the accounting department is required to ------- in the training session for the new accounting software.
   (A) attend
   (B) qualify
   (C) register
   (D) participate

UNIT 11 어휘 1

공식 93 inform의 목적어는 '~을/를'이 아니고 '~에게'

inform 뒤에는 목적어로 행위의 대상(사람/회사)이 온다. announce처럼 뜻은 비슷하지만 뒤에 대상이 오려면 전치사가 필요한 동사들과 함께 출제되곤 하는데, 목적어를 따져서 오답부터 걸러낸다.

We are pleased to (**inform** / ~~announce~~) you that your proposal has been accepted.
→ announce의 뒤에 발표 대상이 오려면 「to+사람」의 형태로 온다.   당신의 제안서가 통과되었음을 알리게 되어 기쁩니다.

비법 노트

- **동사 + 사람**
  - inform ~에게 알리다
  - remind ~에게 상기시키다
  - notify ~에게 알리다
  - advise ~에게 충고하다
  - assure ~에게 장담하다
  - warn ~에게 경고하다
  - convince ~에게 확신시키다
  - tell ~에게 말하다

- **동사 + (to + 사람)**
  - announce ~을 알리다
  - say ~을 말하다
  - mention ~을 언급하다
  - suggest ~을 제안하다
  - explain ~을 설명하다
  - propose ~을 제안하다
  - describe ~을 묘사하다
  - recommend ~을 권고[추천]하다

- **동사 + 사람 + of + 명사**
  - inform / notify / assure / convince / remind / warn + 사람 + of + 명사

[예제] The company will ------- all applicants of the results when the hiring decision is made.

(A) announce (B) persuade
(C) inform (D) require

------- + 사람 + of + 알리는 내용 ⋯ inform

정답 (C)

고용이 결정되면 회사는 모든 지원자들에게 결과를 통보할 것이다.

공식 94 address와 issue는 짝꿍이다.

address issues(문제를 다루다), conduct a study(연구를 하다), make a reservation(예약을 하다)처럼 자주 짝지어 다니는 「동사+명사」 표현은 암기해두면, 서로를 단서 삼아 쉽게 답을 고를 수 있다.

A task force has been set up to (**address** / ~~install~~) the mobile application's compatibility issues.
모바일 앱의 호환성 문제를 다루기 위해 대책 위원회가 구성되었다.

비법 노트

- take measures 조치를 취하다
- complete the form 서류를 작성하다
- enter the data 자료를 입력하다
- implement a policy 정책을 실시하다
- make profits 수익을 내다
- submit a request 요청서를 제출하다
- take precautions 대비를 하다
- express + 감정명사 감정을 표현하다
- attract[draw] customers 손님을 끌다
- earn[build] a reputation 명성을 얻다[쌓다]
- present an award 상을 수여하다
- improve productivity 생산성을 향상시키다
- take a course 수업을 듣다
- attend + 행사 행사에 참석하다
- accept an offer 제안을 받아들이다
- make an attempt 시도하다
- make a decision 결정하다
- extend ~ hours ~ 시간을 연장하다

[예제] The marketing team is ------- a study to determine whether to change the company's logo.

(A) conducting (B) writing
(C) investigating (D) placing

------- + a study ⋯ conduct

정답 (A) 실시하다, 행하다
오답 (B) 쓰다 (C) 조사하다 (D) 배치하다

마케팅 팀이 회사의 로고를 바꿀지를 결정하기 위한 조사를 수행하고 있다.

공식으로 해결하는 실전문제

1. The organizers of Pictagram photo contest will ------- winning contestants that they will be receiving awards.
   (A) recommend
   (B) explain
   (C) send
   (D) notify

2. The City Metro will ------- its nighttime operating hours by 90 minutes during major national holidays.
   (A) consider
   (B) extend
   (C) magnify
   (D) obtain

3. Arecka's, a sports retailer, today ------- its plan to close 80 stores beginning in August.
   (A) informed
   (B) announced
   (C) reminded
   (D) solved

4. Mayor William Everett expressed his ------- for the volunteers' willingness to participate in the public health project.
   (A) appreciation
   (B) proposal
   (C) attendance
   (D) abundance

5. Big Technologies priced its new computer at about $380 in an effort to ------- new customers.
   (A) inform
   (B) refer to
   (C) promote
   (D) attract

6. During the seminar tomorrow, Dr. Matthew Lee will address the topic of how to ------- investors on hi-tech stocks.
   (A) advise
   (B) mention
   (C) order
   (D) argue

7. The Application Developers of the Year Award will be ------- to the winners selected from over 2,000 entrants from all over the world.
   (A) dedicated
   (B) demonstrated
   (C) presented
   (D) related

8. Cruise America ------- passengers that the tours are meticulously prepared and fully insured.
   (A) explains
   (B) attract
   (C) assures
   (D) provide

UNIT 11 어휘 1

공식 95 동사를 고를 때는 빈칸 뒤 전치사를 확인한다.

특정 전치사와 어울려 다니는 동사의 경우 미리 짝꿍 전치사를 암기했다가, 동사 어휘를 고를 때 빈칸 뒤 전치사를 참고하면 쉽게 답을 고를 수 있다.

Mr. Anderson (**submitted** / ~~deleted~~) the sales analysis report to the manager.
앤더슨 씨는 매니저에게 판매 분석 보고서를 제출했다.

비법 노트

submit A to B A를 B에 제출하다	forward[direct] A to B A를 B에게 보내다
attribute A to B A를 B 덕(탓)으로 돌리다	prohibit[forbid] A from B A를 B로부터 금지시키다
prevent[keep] A from B A를 B로부터 막다	delete[remove] A from B A를 B로부터 제거하다
expand A into B A를 B로 확장(진출)시키다	divide[separate] A into B A를 B로 나누다
compensate A for B A에게 B에 대해 보상하다	reward A for B A에게 B에 대해 보답하다
reimburse A for B A에게 B에 대해 환급해 주다	present A with B A에게 B를 주다(수여하다)
replace A with B A를 B와 교체하다	provide A with B(= provide B to A) A에게 B를 공급하다
equip A with B A에게 B를 갖추다	match A to B A를 B에 맞추다

[예제] A network problem is ------- the printers on the 3rd floor from responding to the request.

(A) presenting (B) arranging
(C) preventing (D) notifying

------- + A + from + B ⇢ **prevent**

정답 (C) 막다, 방지하다
오답 (A) 수여[제시]하다 (B) 정리하다 (D) 알리다

네트워크 문제가 3층에 있는 인쇄기가 요청에 응하는 것을 막고 있다.

공식 96 시험에 자주 보이는 전치사 덩어리 표현

토익에는 until further notice(추후 통지 때까지), behind schedule(일정보다 늦게) 등 전치사로 시작하는 덩어리 표현이 자주 출제되므로 정리해 두자.

Due to a lack of funding, the road repairs have fallen (**behind** / ~~toward~~) schedule.
자금 부족 때문에, 도로 정비 작업이 일정보다 뒤쳐졌다.

비법 노트

on schedule 일정대로	ahead of schedule 일정보다 앞서	at all times 항상
at a later time 나중에	in advance 사전에	on a regular basis 정기적으로
within walking distance 도보 거리 이내에	upon[on] receipt 수령 즉시	in writing 서면으로
for your convenience 편의를 위해	for your reference 참고할 수 있도록	under construction 공사 중인
without prior notice 사전 통보 없이	for further information[details] 추가 정보를 원하시면	
in the near[foreseeable] future 가까운 미래에	for[during/over/in] the next[past/last] + 기간 향후[지난] ~ 동안	

[예제] Gina Devei's new book has appeared repeatedly on the best seller list ------- the last three months.

(A) around (B) over
(C) until (D) among

------- + the last + 기간 ⇢ **over**

「over the last + 기간」은 현재완료시제(have p.p.)와 잘 어울린다.
정답 (B) ~에 걸쳐 **오답** (A) ~ 주위에 (C) ~까지 (D) ~ 사이에

지나 드베이 씨의 새 책이 지난 3개월 동안 베스트셀러 리스트에 반복적으로 올랐다.

공식으로 해결하는 실전문제

해설집 p.66

1. Mr. Crawford ------- the successful launch of the new product line to his hardworking team.
   (A) created
   (B) earned
   (C) finalized
   (D) attributed

2. Royal Lima Resort is conveniently located ------- walking distance of Pearson Airport.
   (A) within
   (B) near
   (C) even
   (D) from

3. At Jobsupporter, our consultants help job seekers ------- their résumés and cover letters to the requirements of each job.
   (A) provide
   (B) include
   (C) match
   (D) separate

4. Michael Rosella was ------- with the appreciation plaque by DPC President Charles Dayton in recognition of his 20 years of service.
   (A) committed
   (B) presented
   (C) related
   (D) selected

5. All businesses that prepare and serve food must be inspected by the public food safety organization on a regular -------.
   (A) assortment
   (B) basis
   (C) base
   (D) overhaul

6. Xprints' chief executive said he expected a deal involving the Japanese smartphone company to be announced in the ------- future.
   (A) around
   (B) surrounding
   (C) near
   (D) nearby

7. Complaints regarding staff members and their service must be ------- to their immediate supervisors.
   (A) directed
   (B) treated
   (C) considered
   (D) organized

8. For your -------, we have added a feature that allows your mobile phone to run multiple programs concurrently.
   (A) occurrence
   (B) elevation
   (C) combination
   (D) convenience

UNIT 11 어휘 1

공식 97 「목적어+to부정사」 앞은 require가 답

「require+목적어+to부정사」처럼 목적어 다음의 목적격 보어 자리에 to부정사가 오는 동사를 암기해 두면, 빈칸 뒤 「목적어+to부정사」만 봐도 답이 보인다. 이 동사들은 수동태(be required to부정사)로도 출제되므로 「be p.p. to부정사」 형태를 숙어처럼 암기하면 편하다.

All participants are (~~interviewed~~ / **asked**) to complete a survey. 모든 참석자들은 설문조사 작성을 요청 받는다.

비법 노트

■ 능동
- allow A to do A에게 ~을 허가하다
- invite A to do A에게 ~을 초대하다
- remind A to do A에게 ~을 상기시키다
- require A to do A에게 ~을 요구하다
- enable A to do A에게 ~을 가능하게 하다
- want A to do A에게 ~을 원하다
- force A to do A에게 ~을 강요하다
- encourage A to do A에게 ~을 장려하다
- ask A to do A에게 ~을 요청하다
- permit A to do A에게 ~을 허가하다
- request A to do A에게 ~을 요청하다
- cause A to do A에게 ~을 야기하다

■ 수동
- be allowed to do ~하는 것이 허락되다
- be invited to do ~하도록 초대받다
- be scheduled to do ~하기로 예정되다
- be enabled to do ~하는 것이 가능해지다
- be expected to do ~할 것으로 예상되다
- be requested to do ~할 것이 요청되다
- be asked to do ~하도록 요청받다
- be urged to do ~하도록 촉구되다
- be forced to do ~하도록 강요받다

[예제] The recently revised construction policy ------- new buildings to include solar panels on their rooftops.

(A) records (B) guides
(C) covers (D) requires

------- + 목적어 + to부정사 ⋯ require

정답 (D) 오답 (A) 기록하다 (B) 안내하다 (C) 씌우다

최근에 개정된 건설 정책은 새 건물 옥상에 태양 전지판을 설치할 것을 요구한다.

공식 98 빈칸 뒤 to부정사는 정답 단서가 될 수 있다

유독 to부정사의 수식을 자주 받는 명사와 형용사들이 있다. 이들은 뒤에 따라 붙는 to부정사와 함께 숙어처럼 외워두면, 빈칸 뒤 to부정사를 결정적 단서로 활용해 답을 고를 수 있다.

The recent (**attempts** / ~~experiences~~) to raise the minimum wage have failed.
최저 임금을 인상하려던 최근 시도가 실패로 돌아갔다.

비법 노트

■ 명사+to부정사
- ability to ~할 능력
- effort to ~하기 위한 노력
- opportunity to ~할 기회
- attempt to ~하기 위한 시도
- authority to ~할 권한
- time to ~할 시간

■ 형용사+to부정사
- be (un)able to ~할 수 있다[없다]
- be reluctant to ~하길 망설이다
- be hesitant to ~하길 망설이다
- be ready to ~할 준비가 되다
- be bound to 반드시 ~하다
- be likely to ~할 것 같다

 You are ------- to check the delivery status of your order with this tracking number.

(A) valuable (B) possible
(C) skillful (D) able

be + ------- + to부정사 ⋯ able

정답 (D) 오답 (A) 소중한 (B) 가능한 (C) 능숙한

이 추적 번호로 주문품의 배송 상태를 확인하실 수 있습니다.

공식으로 해결하는 실전문제

해설집 p.67

1. The Japanese A-level course is ------- to be cancelled due to the low registration number.
   (A) usual
   (B) available
   (C) typical
   (D) likely

2. The orders we placed last week from the Paper Mill Store are ------- to arrive by tomorrow afternoon.
   (A) related
   (B) expected
   (C) expressed
   (D) recorded

3. Mr. Cordell, the founder of Houston Business Institute, is ------- to deliver a talk on how to minimize financial losses during uncertain times in the stock market.
   (A) visited
   (B) found
   (C) reached
   (D) scheduled

4. Small Earth, a social networking service, offers great ------- for small business owners to connect with each other online.
   (A) recruiters
   (B) opportunities
   (C) industries
   (D) entrances

5. In an ------- to increase employee productivity, the company is considering an incentive program.
   (A) effort
   (B) operation
   (C) opinion
   (D) achievement

6. Ms. Kasai is ------- to take on a new project because she is planning a vacation for next month.
   (A) responsive
   (B) aware
   (C) knowledgeable
   (D) reluctant

7. Flexible working hours have ------- employees to achieve a better work-life balance.
   (A) enabled
   (B) emerged
   (C) improved
   (D) preferred

8. Narazon, a giant online retailer, ------- shoppers to spend more by offering them free shipping.
   (A) features
   (B) decides
   (C) encourages
   (D) acquires

YBM TEST

1. It is ------- that regular safety and performance inspections be done on all production equipment.

    (A) probable
    (B) automated
    (C) disrupted
    (D) essential

2. Our new 15-minute webinar ------- the benefits of X-ray inspection to food and pharmaceutical manufacturers.

    (A) inserts
    (B) explains
    (C) decides
    (D) convinces

3. All department managers are responsible for ensuring that employees ------- with the company policy.

    (A) observe
    (B) dedicate
    (C) comply
    (D) respond

4. An internationally renowned architect, Daniel Craig is praised for his ------- to evoke positive emotions in buildings.

    (A) position
    (B) belief
    (C) ability
    (D) issue

5. If you require any assistance with the CEPT product, please ------- your request to our online Help Center.

    (A) submit
    (B) detach
    (C) apply
    (D) vacate

6. The government has yet to make a ------- on whether to cancel the construction of the nuclear power plants.

    (A) precaution
    (B) preference
    (C) strategy
    (D) decision

7. The Boston Shipping Corporation plans to ------- its ferry service into new destinations, including nearby coastal cities.

    (A) choose
    (B) cooperate
    (C) reserve
    (D) expand

8. The presenter ------- participants to complete the evaluation form at the end of the workshop.

    (A) agreed
    (B) declared
    (C) reminded
    (D) specified

9. Please note that the town council meeting has been postponed ------- further notice due to unforeseen scheduling conflicts.

    (A) onto
    (B) until
    (C) every
    (D) since

10. You should ------- safety concerns first with your immediate supervisor even if you have a company safety director.

    (A) talk
    (B) address
    (C) result
    (D) inquire

11. The senior researcher at STC Laboratories will ------- the research objectives into three different categories.

    (A) give
    (B) divide
    (C) consider
    (D) notify

12. Construction workers are ------- to take extra precautions and breaks as temperatures soar in the region.

    (A) urged
    (B) concerned
    (C) regarded
    (D) remained

13. Bayat Bank has no plans to open more branches and will ------- on developing its online banking services.

    (A) operate
    (B) focus
    (C) benefit
    (D) propose

14. We are pleased to ------- participants that all the projects from the last workshop have been uploaded on our Web site.

    (A) create
    (B) announce
    (C) inform
    (D) recommend

15. To be ------- for any travel expenses, employees must submit a travel expense report along with all original receipts.

    (A) reimbursed
    (B) returned
    (C) entitled
    (D) obtained

16. Upon ------- of any alert, our trained security systems operators will take actions in accordance with your corporate security policy.

    (A) receipt
    (B) request
    (C) entry
    (D) appeal

17. As space is limited at the wine certification seminar, we will ------- our members to register before offering spots to the public.

    (A) cooperate
    (B) reflect
    (C) include
    (D) allow

18. The manager of the sales team ------- that accommodations and transportation be arranged prior to his departure for the conference.

    (A) expected
    (B) requested
    (C) indicated
    (D) reserved

19. Due to the high volume of visitors to our botanical garden, we strongly recommend that you make reservations in -------.

    (A) guide
    (B) series
    (C) advance
    (D) agency

20. Given that the population in the region is declining, property prices are ------- to fall over time.

    (A) covered
    (B) limited
    (C) bound
    (D) profitable

Questions 21-24 refer to the following press release.

"The Museum Explorer" is a talk radio show that showcases the ongoing events occurring at Birmingham's many museums. One museum will ------- per week, allowing for each museum to be covered ------- once every two months. Each week, a guest from that week's featured museum will join us to discuss a ------- such as a theme in museum exhibitions or a specific event. The guest may be a member of the museum staff or an exhibitor at the museum.
21.   **22.**   **23.**

The program will be broadcasted weekly for 90 minutes. -------. Our DJ Becky Anderson will encourage listeners to call in and ask questions and to find out about exhibits or events they may be interested in. "The Museum Explorer" intends to provide its listeners with a more direct connection to the cultural life of Birmingham.
                                            24.

21. (A) be featuring
    (B) be featured
    (C) feature
    (D) featuring

22. (A) approximation
    (B) approximated
    (C) approximate
    (D) approximately

23. (A) topic
    (B) benefit
    (C) composition
    (D) article

24. (A) It may be re-broadcasted once during the same week.
    (B) The show will be partly produced by museum patrons.
    (C) "The Museum Explorer" targets two main groups of listeners.
    (D) Listeners might be too busy to actually go to the museum.

Questions 25-28 refer to the following memo.

To: All Durant Energy Corp. Managers
From: Kevin Durant
Date: April 6
Subject: A Special Meeting

There have been a lot of developments in the economic and financial situation ------- might
25.
have a significant impact on the operations of our company. We need to take immediate
measures to deal with these changing circumstances. -------.
26.
The meeting will be held on 11th April at 11 A.M. in conference room C. If there is any
information that could contribute significantly to our discussion, don't hesitate to bring it
to the meeting. Please find the enclosed attachment for the agenda of the meeting. It is
mandatory for all managerial staff to be present at the meeting. -------, if you are unable to
27.
attend the meeting because of a scheduling ------- or for any other reason, please inform me
28.
beforehand.

25. (A) then
    (B) that
    (C) how
    (D) where

26. (A) Therefore, we have decided to call a special meeting.
    (B) The company will recover from the current situation soon.
    (C) This is because we are confident the situation will improve.
    (D) We assure you that this is only a temporary measure.

27. (A) Moreover
    (B) Similarly
    (C) For example
    (D) However

28. (A) suggestion
    (B) conflict
    (C) request
    (D) claim

UNIT 12 어휘 2

공식 99 닮은꼴 형용사를 주의한다.

considerable(상당한)과 considerate(사려 깊은)은 철자가 비슷하지만 전혀 다른 의미의 형용사들이다. 비슷한 생김새 때문에 의미를 혼동하는 함정에 빠지지 않도록 주의해야 한다.

SafeWallet helps you store (**confidential** / ~~confident~~) data securely on your PC.
세이프월릿은 컴퓨터에 기밀 정보를 안전하게 저장할 수 있도록 해 준다.

비법 노트 빈출 표현

confident 자신 있는 – confidential 기밀의	competent 능숙한 – competitive 경쟁력 있는, 경쟁을 하는
comparable 비슷한 – compatible 호환이 되는	complimentary 무료의 – complementary 상호보완적인
variable 변동이 심한 – various 다양한	reliable(dependable) 믿을 만한 – reliant(dependent) 의지하는
favorite 매우 좋아하는 – favorable 좋은, 유리한	successful 성공한 – successive 연속적인
impressed 감명 받은 – impressive 인상적인	considerate 사려 깊은 – considerable 상당한

예제
Please note that Workingbee thermostats are not ------- with high voltage systems.

(A) comparable (B) compatible
(C) competitive (D) cooperative

호환이 되다 → **be compatible**

정답 **(B)** 오답 (A) 비슷한 (C) 경쟁을 하는 (D) 협동하는

워킹비 온도 조절 장치는 고압 시스템과 호환이 되지 않는다는 것을 명심하세요.

공식 100 빈칸 뒤 전치사가 단서가 되는 형용사

be available for(~로 이용 가능하다)와 같이 시험에 자주 출제되는 「be동사 + 형용사 + 전치사」 구문을 암기했다가, 형용사나 전치사 자리가 빈칸으로 나왔을 때 서로 짝을 맞춰 보면 쉽게 답을 찾을 수 있다.

All the goods on display are (**available** / ~~capable~~) for purchase. 진열되어 있는 모든 제품은 구매 가능합니다.
→ be capable 뒤에는 of가 온다.

비법 노트

be aware of ~을 알다	be responsible for ~을 책임지다	be compatible with ~와 호환이 되다
be exempt from ~를 면제받다	be eligible for ~에 자격이 되다	be responsive to ~에 대응하다
be pleased[delighted] with ~에 기뻐하다	be satisfied with ~에 만족하다	be capable of ~을 할 수 있다
be dependent[reliant] on ~에 의존하다	be similar to ~와 비슷하다	be accessible to ~에 접근하기 쉽다
be adequate[suitable] for ~에 적합하다	be full of ~로 가득하다	be indicative of ~을 나타내다
be subject to ~될 수 있다, ~의 영향을 받다	be relevant to ~에 관련되다	be familiar with ~에 익숙하다

예제
The CEO of Netplus said that he was ------- of the rumors about a possible merger with Mattel.

(A) known (B) informative
(C) serious (D) aware

be + ------- + of → **aware**

be aware of ~을 알고 있다

정답 **(D)** 오답 (A) 알려진 (B) 유익한 (C) 심각한

넷플러스의 최고 경영자는 마텔과의 합병 가능성에 대한 소문을 알고 있다고 했다.

공식으로 해결하는 실전문제

해설집 p.71

1. Both DLC Contractors, Inc. and Yuma Associates, Inc. offer ------- benefits so Ms. Long is still undecided between the two job offers.
   (A) comparable
   (B) reflected
   (C) satisfied
   (D) considerate

2. All goods produced in Mikel Textile's Cambodian factory are ------- to a thorough inspection before they are shipped.
   (A) fragile
   (B) subjective
   (C) cautious
   (D) subject

3. Customers who place an online order with a minimum value of $50 are ------- for free standard shipping.
   (A) convenient
   (B) eligible
   (C) verified
   (D) valuable

4. AT Enterprise's plan to streamline its operations is a part of an effort to make the firm more ------- to a changing industry.
   (A) impressed
   (B) observant
   (C) forceful
   (D) responsive

5. Witopia provides customers with ------- Internet connections, so they never have to worry about service interruptions.
   (A) reliable
   (B) considerable
   (C) courteous
   (D) reliant

6. The smartphone market is becoming increasingly -------, with new companies trying to lure customers away from established brands.
   (A) domestic
   (B) competitive
   (C) steady
   (D) frequent

7. The company's management has been ------- with the results of the vigorous advertising program for the new OLED TV sets.
   (A) impressive
   (B) pleased
   (C) reflected
   (D) enjoyable

8. To be eligible for a ------- one-week membership, you must be a first-time user of our fitness center.
   (A) variable
   (B) subsequent
   (C) complimentary
   (D) promising

UNIT 12 어휘 2

공식 101 extensive와 experience는 짝꿍이다.

extensive experience(폭넓은 경험), detailed information(자세한 정보) 등과 같이 자주 짝지어 다니는 「형용사+명사」 표현을 통째로 암기해 두면, 서로를 단서 삼아 쉽게 답을 찾을 수 있다.

Mr. Blodgett has (**extensive** / ~~punctual~~) experience in concerts and musical performances.
블로젯 씨는 콘서트와 음악 공연 분야에 폭넓은 경력이 있다.

비법 노트

key factor 주요한 요인
sufficient space 충분한 공간
vacant position 공석
sizable demand 상당한 수요
a detailed[specific] description 자세한[구체적인] 설명(서)
reasonable[competitive/affordable] prices 합리적인[경쟁력 있는/적당한] 가격
thorough inspection 철저한 검사
strict regulations 엄격한 규정
surrounding area 인근 지역
collaborative effort 공동의 노력
sensible solution 합리적인 해결책
leading manufacturer 선도적인 제조업체
outstanding performance 뛰어난 업적
revised policy 수정된 정책

예제

To make deliveries efficiently, shipping companies need ------- information about traffic on its routes.

(A) indicative (B) deliberate
(C) detailed   (D) vacant

------- + information ···→ detailed

정답 (C) 오답 (A) ~을 나타내는 (B) 고의의 (D) 비어 있는

효율적인 배송을 위해, 배송 회사는 배송 경로에 대한 자세한 교통 정보가 필요하다.

공식 102 빈칸 뒤 전치사가 단서가 되는 명사

시험에 자주 나오는 「in+명사+전치사」 표현을 미리 암기해 두면, 명사 문제에서 빈칸 앞 in과 빈칸 뒤의 전치사를 단서 삼아 쉽게 답을 고를 수 있다.

City Bus Company has hired advisers in (**preparation** / ~~operation~~) for an annual audit.
시티 버스 컴퍼니는 연례 감사를 준비하기 위해 자문위원들을 고용했다.

비법 노트

in addition to ~에 더하여
in favor of ~에 찬성하여
in response to ~에 응하여
in charge of ~을 담당하는
in advance of ~보다 앞에
in exchange for ~대신에
in honor for ~을 기념하여
in cooperation with ~와 협력하여
in accordance with ~에 따라서
in preparation for ~에 대한 준비로
in observance of ~을 기념하여
in recognition of ~을 인정하여
in appreciation of ~에 감사하여
in place of ~을 대신하여
in the vicinity[proximity] of ~의 근처에
in case of(=in the event of) ~의 경우에
in celebration of ~을 축하하여
in light of(=in view of) ~을 고려하여
in conjunction with ~와 함께
in compliance with ~을 준수하여
in anticipation of ~을 예상하여

예제

Original Brewing Company introduces unique dishes in ------- to craft beers at its German franchises.

(A) addition   (B) outcome
(C) promotion   (D) selection

in + ------- + to ···→ addition

in addition to ~에 더하여

정답 (A) 오답 (B) 결과 (C) 홍보 (D) 선택

오리지널 브루잉 컴퍼니는 독일 가맹점에서 수제 맥주와 더불어 참신한 요리를 판매한다.

공식으로 해결하는 실전문제

해설집 p.72

1. Mobia's smartwatch is now available at a discounted price at its online store for a ------- time only.
   (A) favorite
   (B) covered
   (C) limited
   (D) prominent

2. In ------- of your loyal patronage, we are pleased to offer you gift certificates worth £75.
   (A) result
   (B) recognition
   (C) assistance
   (D) replacement

3. Macon Technology's commitment to innovation has made the company one of the ------- manufacturers of advanced computer chips.
   (A) selective
   (B) leading
   (C) rigorous
   (D) delicate

4. Birmingham City Schools plans to adopt the education program that was designed in ------- with the Lindberg School of Education.
   (A) cooperation
   (B) placement
   (C) institution
   (D) reputation

5. Katy Ferris became the youngest recipient of a Hana Foundation grant for demonstrating her potential to produce ------- poetry.
   (A) relative
   (B) outstanding
   (C) numerous
   (D) transitional

6. Located in the ------- of Malahide's beautiful golden beach, Evergreen Hotel offers a great deal of comfort.
   (A) vicinity
   (B) majority
   (C) direction
   (D) immediacy

7. Guidelines have been established to ensure farm owners are in ------- with their water usage regulations.
   (A) activation
   (B) achievement
   (C) permission
   (D) compliance

8. Everizon Wireless is offering up to 2 GB of free data to customers in Chatham and the ------- areas hit by Hurricane Erma.
   (A) compatible
   (B) supplementary
   (C) consequential
   (D) surrounding

173

공식 103 현재 시제에는 빈도부사부터 넣어본다.

현재 시제는 반복적으로 일어나는 일을 묘사할 때 주로 쓰는 시제이므로 반복되는 횟수나 빈도를 나타내는 빈도부사와 종종 함께 쓰인다. 현재 시제 문장은 빈도부사가 답인지부터 확인한다.

The vice president, Rick Harrington, (**routinely** / ~~tightly~~) attends the shareholder meeting.
부사장 릭 해링턴 씨는 주주 회의에 일상적으로 참석한다.

비법 노트 현재 시제와 잘 어울리는 부사

frequently/often 자주	usually/normally 보통	commonly 보통, 흔히	occasionally 가끔
typically 전형적으로	periodically 주기적으로	regularly 정기적으로	routinely 일상적으로
generally 일반적으로	customarily 관례상		

예제 Part-time workers ------- do not receive benefits such as medical insurance or sick leave.

(A) previously (B) usually
(C) well (D) mutually

------- + 현재 시제 ⟶ 빈도부사

정답 (B) 오답 (A) 이전에 (C) 잘 (D) 상호간에

시간제 근로자들은 보통 의료 보험이나 병가와 같은 복지 혜택을 받지 못한다.

공식 104 짝꿍을 보고 고르는 부사

숫자 앞 빈칸에는 '거의'를 뜻하는 nearly, approximately와 같은 부사가 빈출 정답이며, unless otherwise p.p.(달리 ~되지 않으면)처럼 특정 구문에 자주 등장하는 부사들도 있으니 통으로 암기한다.

SG Bank branches are (**conveniently** / ~~consistently~~) located across the country.
→ conveniently located는 '입지가 좋은'이라는 의미이다.
SG 은행 지점들은 전국에 걸쳐 편리한 곳에 위치하고 있다.

비법 노트

nearly/approximately/almost 거의 over/more than ~ 이상 at least 최소 up to 최대 ~까지	+	숫자
immediately/shortly/soon/directly/right 곧, 바로	+	before/after 직전에/직후에
conveniently 편리하게 ideally 이상적으로 centrally 중심부에	+	located 입지가 좋은
considerably/significantly/substantially 상당히 sharply 급격히 noticeably/remarkably/markedly 두드러지게 rapidly 빠르게	+	증가 동사 increase, rise, grow, soar, boost
gradually 서서히 steadily 꾸준히 slightly 약간	+	감소 동사 decrease, drop, fall, reduce, decline

예제 The Airport Railroad Express will take you directly to Seoul Station in ------- 40 minutes.

(A) approximately (B) truly
(C) immediately (D) shortly

숫자 앞 빈칸 ⟶ approximately

정답 (A) 거의, 대략 오답 (B) 정말로 (C) 즉시 (D) 곧

공항 고속 철도는 당신을 약 40분 후에 서울역으로 곧장 데려다 줄 것이다.

공식으로 해결하는 실전문제

해설집 p.73

1. Ms. Wright has arranged to meet the property owner ------- after the inspection is completed.
   (A) slightly
   (B) immediately
   (C) closely
   (D) recently

2. The average price of raw cotton fell ------- affected because of sluggish demand.
   (A) slightly
   (B) carefully
   (C) simultaneously
   (D) availably

3. Routine aircraft maintenance takes more than 5 hours and is ------- performed during the night.
   (A) formerly
   (B) loosely
   (C) typically
   (D) previously

4. Fintek's quarterly performance review allows managers to ------- assess employee performance.
   (A) regularly
   (B) recently
   (C) similarly
   (D) inconclusively

5. Linden Power is a leading supplier of industrial gases that are ------- used for chemical processing.
   (A) obediently
   (B) persistently
   (C) considerately
   (D) generally

6. Unless stated -------, all times shown on the itinerary represent the local time.
   (A) once
   (B) occasionally
   (C) otherwise
   (D) around

7. WoW Accounting ------- outsources complex IT projects to reduce operating expenses.
   (A) lately
   (B) occasionally
   (C) interestingly
   (D) somewhat

8. Hugh Herman is looking for a venue that can accommodate ------- 50 guests for the retirement party for Ms. Finley.
   (A) so that
   (B) with
   (C) at least
   (D) even so

YBM TEST

1. In ------- of a surge in deliveries, Fastwheels will hire about 300 temporary workers to help deliver packages during the holiday season.

   (A) estimate
   (B) strategy
   (C) anticipation
   (D) receipt

2. The trip from the ferry terminal to the resort takes ------- 25 minutes when there is little traffic on the highway.

   (A) nearly
   (B) nearby
   (C) near
   (D) nearing

3. Mu Furnishing ------- sends out e-mail newsletters to customers, highlighting new items and the latest furniture trends.

   (A) totally
   (B) previously
   (C) briefly
   (D) periodically

4. The City Council announced that local artisans with an annual income of up to $5,000 are ------- from registration under the new tax plans.

   (A) skillful
   (B) respective
   (C) exempt
   (D) separate

5. Paper copies of the ------- store policy should be printed and distributed to all Olite employees within a week.

   (A) revised
   (B) pure
   (C) obliged
   (D) slight

6. Victoria Station is ------- located in London, so it provides easy access to most locations in the city.

   (A) exactly
   (B) formerly
   (C) centrally
   (D) intentionally

7. Z-Mobile offers regular customers ------- advantages such as a 15% discount on additional plans.

   (A) variable
   (B) variety
   (C) various
   (D) vary

8. If you suspect your log-in information was stolen, you should change your password ------- to prevent unauthorized access to your account.

   (A) as soon as
   (B) immediately
   (C) exactly
   (D) prominently

9. Because of a very successful advertising campaign, Zenotek expects its revenues to increase ------- for the current quarter.

   (A) evenly
   (B) exclusively
   (C) significantly
   (D) eagerly

10. We're sorry for the delay in answering your questions, but our head of customer service will get back to you -------.

    (A) cooperatively
    (B) permissibly
    (C) abruptly
    (D) shortly

11. Fantasia Department Store announced Monday that it will introduce a robot ------- of holding simple conversations at its main store.

    (A) defective
    (B) capable
    (C) practical
    (D) perceptive

12. The government's commitment to business-friendly tax reform created ------- conditions for foreign investment in the manufacturing industry.

    (A) variable
    (B) considerable
    (C) proposed
    (D) favorable

13. While there seems to be ------- demand for the new K-Phone, the high price point of over $1,000 could be a hindrance.

    (A) sizable
    (B) responsible
    (C) spacious
    (D) ready

14. Dr. White's research reveals that the frequency and intensity of extreme storms have increased ------- in the North Pacific.

    (A) markedly
    (B) dividedly
    (C) intimately
    (D) consequently

15. In ------- with the new visa regulations, only those with an onward ticket will be granted a tourist visa.

    (A) event
    (B) accordance
    (C) benefit
    (D) assurance

16. Development of a new park on Greenhill Road is ------- on financing from our partners in the private sector.

    (A) delayed
    (B) dependent
    (C) dependable
    (D) distinguished

17. Unless ------- notified, all employees are expected to be at the training session at 10 A.M.

    (A) otherwise
    (B) indeed
    (C) accordingly
    (D) briefly

18. With Polaris' All-You-Can-Fly club membership, you will not only receive bonus award miles, but also travel at ------- prices.

    (A) renowned
    (B) loose
    (C) relevant
    (D) reasonable

19. For more detailed ------- of our graduate courses, the online catalogue is available at https://dsf.uni.ac.de.

    (A) journals
    (B) admissions
    (C) questions
    (D) descriptions

20. Please note that this 10% off coupon can only be used individually and not in ------- with any other sales promotions.

    (A) completion
    (B) application
    (C) courtesy
    (D) conjunction

Questions 21-24 refer to the following advertisement.

Your life will be wonderful in this large, stylishly contemporary residence with a stunning ocean view, located ------- walking distance of white sand. The floor plan includes three
21.
spacious bedrooms, two luxurious bathrooms, and a sleek and modern kitchen which flows through to the dining room and private rear patio. The master bedroom comes with a walk-in wardrobe and en suite. -------. Moreover, the sparkling ocean, viewed through the floor-to-
22.
ceiling windows in this room, will let ------- escape from the stress of city life.
23.
This house is ideally situated to allow guests to enjoy the close ------- to beaches and a
24.
selection of cafes and restaurants. It is a perfect choice whether you are planning a family holiday or a private weekend break.

21. (A) until
(B) for
(C) within
(D) on

22. (A) This allows parents to have a private space.
(B) Upstairs are the lavishly decorated bedrooms.
(C) This is truly a dream house for a big family.
(D) You can make arrangements to view the house.

23. (A) them
(B) you
(C) these
(D) her

24. (A) intimacy
(B) locality
(C) majority
(D) proximity

Questions 25-28 refer to the following letter.

June 27

Jessica Perez
7440 Woodland Drive
Indianapolis, IN, 46278

Dear Jessica,

We are pleased to ------- you a transfer to the position of forest programs coordinator at the
                        25.
Dearborn County office with an anticipated start date of August 1. -------. There will be no
                                                                    26.
interruption in either health insurance coverage or pension contributions.

To assist you with the transition to your new position, I ------- performance discussions with
                                                          27.
you through evaluations. The evaluations will be conducted ------- several times during the
                                                            28.
first year. Please contact me at any time if you have questions about your new position or
your performance.

Congratulations on being selected for your new position, and I look forward to working with
you as we serve the people of Indiana!

Best regards,
Louis Hamilton
Personnel Director

25. (A) discuss
    (B) accept
    (C) promote
    (D) offer

26. (A) All employees are eligible to apply for a transfer opportunity.
    (B) You will need to submit at least 3 copies of references.
    (C) Your benefits will remain unchanged with this transfer.
    (D) Your inquiries regarding the posted position will remain confidential.

27. (A) was holding
    (B) holding
    (C) have hold
    (D) will be holding

28. (A) periodicals
    (B) periodically
    (C) periodic
    (D) period

PART 7

UNIT 01 주제/목적 문제

> **공식**
> ## 105 주제·목적은 지문의 전반부를 주목하라.
> 주제·목적을 묻는 문제는 2~3개 지문마다 한 번씩, 지문의 첫 번째 문제로 출제된다. 주제나 목적은 대부분 글의 앞부분에서 거론되는 편이므로 지문의 전반부에서 정답의 단서를 찾는다. 기사나 광고처럼 제목이 있는 지문에서는 제목이 주제를 알려주는 중요한 단서가 되기도 한다.

[예제] 광고 해설집 p.78

Q What is being advertised?
(A) A storage service
(B) A residential building

❶ Are you moving to a smaller home? Do you have excess belongings that you don't want to get rid of? Then Conley Enterprises is the solution. ❷ We offer temperature-controlled units of various sizes to store your furniture, paperwork, electronics, and more. … 중략

STEP 1 질문 유형 파악하기
Q. 무엇이 광고되고 있는가? ⋯▶ 주제를 묻는 문제

STEP 2 전반부에서 단서 찾기
❶ 작은 집으로 이사하시나요?
❷ 저희는 가구 등을 보관할 수 있는 창고를 제공합니다.
⋯▶ 물건을 보관하는 업체임을 알 수 있다.

STEP 3 적절히 패러프레이징한 보기 고르기
저희는 보관용 창고를 제공합니다. ➔ 보관 서비스 광고
정답 (A)

> **공식**
> ## 106 주제문의 단서가 되는 빈출 표현을 알아두자.
> 지문의 전반부에는 주로 글을 쓴 목적, 전하고자 하는 내용, 감사 표현 등의 주제문이 언급된다. 만약 전반부에서 주제가 파악되지 않으면, 후반부에 제안이나 요청사항이 있는지 확인한다.

목적	I'm writing to ... ~하기 위해 글을 씁니다	This is an e-mail to ... 이는 ~하기 위한 이메일입니다
	This is to remind ... 이는 ~를 상기시켜 드리고자 합니다	Please note that ... ~에 유의하세요
	The purpose of this letter is to ... 이 편지의 목적은 ~하기 위함입니다	
통지	I would like to announce ... ~을 알리고자 합니다	
	We regret(pleased) to inform you that ... ~를 알리게 되어 유감입니다(기쁩니다)	
	This is to provide notice to ... 이는 ~하다는 공지를 드리고자 합니다	
요청	We would appreciate if ... ~해 주시면 감사하겠습니다	We would like to ... ~하고 싶습니다
	We hope that you ... 당신이 ~하길 바랍니다	Please let me know ... ~을 저에게 알려주세요
감사	We are grateful for ... ~에 대해 감사드립니다	I really appreciate ... ~해 주셔서 정말 감사합니다

YBM TEST

Questions 1-3 refer to the following e-mail.

E-mail

To: Tia Hester <t_hester@houmafinancial.com>
From: Byungmin Choi <b_choi@houmafinancial.com>
Date: May 18
Subject: Please note

Dear Ms. Hester,

I am writing about the task you were assigned at the quarterly meeting. I would like to offer my sincere thanks for the wonderful job you did on implementing a new policy regarding handling client leads. We tried a Performance-Based Leads (PBL) system last year. One month in, it seemed promising. However, after three months of use, we abandoned the program because it was too competitive, and some staff members even quit because they didn't feel like they were being treated equally.

The system you developed is far superior. Employees feel that potential clients are being distributed fairly. This has helped to improve teamwork as well as overall job satisfaction. It is clear that promoting you to team leader was the right decision.

I know that you would like to get together with Branch Director Trevor Pasco and me to discuss some of your other ideas. I will call him to find out about his schedule and then get back to you. In the meantime, keep up the excellent work!

Sincerely,

Byungmin Choi

---

1. What is the main purpose of the e-mail?
   (A) To welcome an employee
   (B) To show appreciation
   (C) To introduce a policy
   (D) To assign a task

2. For how long was the PBL system used?
   (A) One month
   (B) Two months
   (C) Three months
   (D) Four months

3. Why most likely will Mr. Choi contact Mr. Pasco?
   (A) To set up an in-person meeting
   (B) To discuss funding for a project
   (C) To recommend Ms. Hester for a promotion
   (D) To get approval for an overtime schedule

UNIT 02 세부사항 문제

공식 107   문제 키워드와 관련된 대문자, 숫자, 기호부터 찾는다.

세부사항 문제는 인물이나 장소, 시간 등 지문에 나오는 특정 사항에 대한 구체적인 정보를 묻는다. 문제의 키워드가 대문자나 숫자, 기호 등 찾기 쉬운 정보와 연관되는 경우가 많으므로 이를 활용한다.

예제 메모   해설집 p.78

Q1 Who is Ms. Bevell?
(A) A branch manager
(B) An event planner

> The annual company outing for Kinney Consulting will take place on Friday, July 31, at Salinas Vineyard. **Marie Bevell has made all of the necessary arrangements.** We'll take a shuttle bus from the office … 중략

STEP 1 질문 유형 파악하기
Q1. Ms. Bevell은 누구인가? … 인물에 대한 세부사항 문제

STEP 2 찾기 쉬운 정보 활용하기
사람 이름: 지문에서 대문자 / Ms. / Mr.부터 찾는다.

STEP 3 적절히 패러프레이징한 보기 고르기
베벨 씨가 모든 준비를 끝냈다. ➜ 그녀가 행사를 담당한다.
정답 (B)

공식 108   요청사항이나 연락 방법을 묻는 문제는 후반부에서 답을 찾는다.

지문 후반부에서는 주로 요청이나 제안 사항, 미래의 일정, 추가 지침, 연락처 등이 다뤄진다.

요청이나 제안	문제 – ask, require, recommend, should가 보인다. 단서 – 명령문, please, ask, require, recommend, encourage, should 등을 찾는다.
미래의 일정	문제 – will, next, happen 등이 보인다. 단서 – will, plan, is expected to 또는 날짜를 찾는다.
연락 방법이나 담당자	문제 – who, how, contact, call이 보인다. 단서 – 전화번호(숫자), 이메일(@), 웹 사이트(www.), 이름(대문자, Ms. / Mr.)을 찾는다.

Q2 What will happen on July 25?
(A) An enrollment period will end.
(B) A staff will have a company outing.

> … 중략 We'll take a shuttle bus from the office and have lunch at the vineyard, followed by a walking tour. Please note that **you must sign up for the course no later than July 24.** I hope everyone has a great time!

STEP 1 질문 유형 파악하기
Q2. 7월 25일에 일어날 일은?
… 미래 일정에 대한 세부사항 문제

STEP 2 찾기 쉬운 정보 활용하기
날짜: 지문에서 숫자를 찾는다.

STEP 3 적절히 패러프레이징한 보기 고르기
늦어도 7월 24일까지 등록해야 한다.
➜ 7월 25일에는 등록 기간이 끝날 것이다.   정답 (A)

YBM TEST

Questions 1-4 refer to the following letter.

Lynette Mueller
St. Andrews Lane
Camden, NJ 08102

December 29

Dear Ms. Mueller,

On behalf of the Valentino Free Clinic, I would like to express my sincere appreciation for your donation to our cause. Thanks to the generous support of community members like you, hundreds of low-income families and individuals can receive the medical attention they need. Over the past year, we raised nearly $380,000 from government grants and private donations. Our standard operating budget is $295,000, and this money is spent on treatment programs ($180,000), medical equipment ($65,000), insurance ($30,000), building upkeep ($15,000), and administration and miscellaneous expenses ($5,000).

As we have a surplus in our budget for the first time in the clinic's two-decade history, we are able to fund a project that has been on our wish list for the past five years. We are adding an extension to our building that will allow for more consultation rooms so that our team of volunteer physicians and nurses can see more patients during the clinic's opening hours. The new section of the building will be designed by Cody Farrish from Lancelot Incorporated, a popular architecture design firm. He has worked on a number of public projects and has an exceptional talent for making the best use of limited space. The building project will begin in the spring, and Drayton Hospital has agreed to lend us some space on days when the construction work necessitates the closure of the clinic.

Without your help, this amazing project never would have been possible. Each year, we celebrate the contributions of our staff and donors with a special dinner in the ballroom of Mercado Hall. This year, it is scheduled for Saturday, January 28, at 6:30 P.M. We hope you can be there.

All the best,

Tai Ren

---

1. Why did Mr. Ren write to Ms. Mueller?
   (A) To ask for a financial donation to a charity
   (B) To thank Ms. Mueller for giving him some advice
   (C) To explain how to book a medical appointment
   (D) To provide an update on how some funds were used

2. For how long has Mr. Ren's organization been in operation?
   (A) For five years
   (B) For ten years
   (C) For fifteen years
   (D) For twenty years

3. Where does Mr. Farrish work?
   (A) At a convention center
   (B) At an architectural firm
   (C) At a pharmacy
   (D) At a hospital

4. What is Ms. Mueller asked to do?
   (A) Attend an annual banquet
   (B) Schedule a meeting
   (C) Pledge money to a cause
   (D) Extend an invitation

UNIT 03 의도 파악 문제

빈출 문제
At 2:45 P.M., what does Mr. Pang most likely mean when he writes, "I am off now"?
오후 2시 45분에 팽 씨가 "난 가야겠어"라고 말한 의도는 무엇인가?

At 10:14 A.M., what does Ms. Garzo most likely mean when she writes "I know"?
오전 10시 14분에 가르조 씨가 "알아"라고 말한 의도는 무엇인가?

> **공식 109** 해당 메시지의 바로 앞뒤 메시지에 단서가 있다.
>
> 의도 파악 문제는 매회 2문제씩 출제된다. 대화의 흐름을 통해 화자의 진의를 파악해야 하며, 대부분 바로 앞뒤 사람의 말에서 단서를 찾을 수 있다. 메시지의 사전적 의미만으로 답을 고르지 않도록 주의한다.

예제 문자 메시지 해설집 p.80

Q At 1:27 P.M., what does Ms. Portillo most likely mean when she says, "I wouldn't order from them again"?
   (A) She received the goods late.
   (B) She is disappointed by the quality.

Edgar Lebeau, 1:23 P.M.
Did you get the shipment from Houston Stationery yet?

Kyra Portillo, 1:24 P.M.
Yes, I signed for it this morning. Everything in the order is correct.

Edgar Lebeau, 1:26 P.M.
Great. This is our first time using Houston Stationery. ❶ How is the quality?

Kyra Portillo, 1:27 P.M.
❷ I wouldn't order from them again.

Edgar Lebeau, 1:28 P.M.
❸ I knew the low prices were too good to be true.

STEP 1 메시지 파악하기
Q. 오후 1시 27분에 Ms. Portillo가 "다시는 거기에 주문하지 않을 거예요."라고 말한 의도는 무엇인가?
⋯ 주문한 물건에 문제가 있음을 알 수 있다.

STEP 2 앞뒤 메시지 파악하기
❶ 앞 메시지: 품질이 어떤가?
❷ 해당 메시지: 다시는 주문하지 않겠다.
❸ 뒤 메시지: 가격이 너무 낮아서 이상했다.
⋯ 품질이 만족스럽지 못함을 알 수 있다.

STEP 3 적절히 패러프레이징한 보기 고르기
불만족스러운 품질에 대해 표현한 보기를 고른다.
정답 (B) 그녀는 품질에 실망했다.

YBM TEST

Questions 1-2 refer to the following text-message.

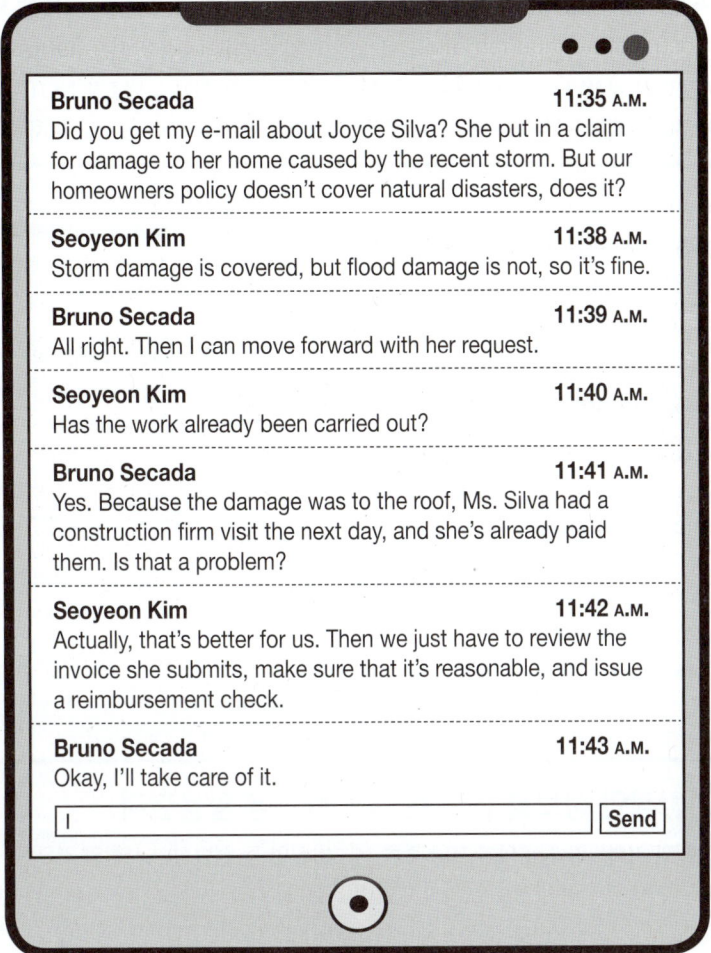

1. Where most likely do the speakers work?
   (A) At an insurance company
   (B) At an interior design firm
   (C) At a weather station
   (D) At a construction company

2. At 11:42 A.M., what does Ms. Kim most likely mean when she says, "that's better for us"?
   (A) Some expenses were cheaper than projected.
   (B) Mr. Secada should encourage Ms. Silva to choose an option.
   (C) A process is expected to be easy to complete.
   (D) A regulation has been set up to protect the company.

UNIT 04 Not / True 문제

공식 110 특정 정보를 묻는 문제는 곧바로 지문에서 문제 키워드를 찾는다

문제에서 파악한 키워드가 특정 정보에 관한 것일 경우, 곧바로 지문부터 보고 해당 키워드를 찾는다. 지문에서 찾아낸 단서의 주변에 나열된 정보와 보기를 하나씩 대조해 NOT/TRUE 여부를 확인한다. 지문에서 키워드를 찾을 때는 주로 문제가 출제된 순서에 따라 단서도 위치한다는 점을 활용한다.

[예제] 광고 해설집 p. 81

Q1 What is indicated about massages?
(A) They must be booked in advance.
(B) They last for different periods of time.

Cliffside Spa

Hours of operation: Mon.–Fri. 8 A.M.–9 P.M.
Services*: Massages, Facial Treatments, Nailcare, Waxing

Massages
Swedish Massage: 1 hour, 1.5 hours
Thai Massage: 30 minutes, 1 hour
Hot Stone Massage: 1 hour … 중략

STEP 1 문제 키워드 파악하기
Q1. 마사지에 관해 사실은? ⋯→ 마사지=특정 정보

STEP 2 지문에서 키워드 찾기
'마사지' 주변: 마사지 종류와 시간 정보가 나열되어 있다.
(A) 미리 예약해야 한다. (X)
(B) 지속 시간이 각기 다르다. (O) **정답** (B)

공식 111 전반적인 정보를 묻는 문제는 보기를 활용한다.

문제의 키워드가 지문의 주제나 종류, 수/발신인 등 전반적인 사항일 경우, 단서가 곳곳에 퍼져 있어 지문 전체를 읽어야 하므로 시간이 많이 걸린다. 따라서 각 보기의 키워드를 먼저 파악한 후 지문을 살피고, 단서를 발견할 때마다 해당 보기와 대조해 NOT/TRUE 여부를 확인한다.

Q2 What is true about Cliffside Spa?
(A) Its staff members are highly qualified.
(B) It is open every day.

Cliffside Spa

Hours of operation: Mon.–Fri. 8 A.M.–9 P.M.
Services*: Massages, Facial Treatments, Nailcare, Waxing
… 중략

*All employees are licensed with the state and have also taken other supplementary certification courses.

STEP 1 문제 키워드 파악하기
Q2. Cliffside Spa에 관해 사실인 것은?
⋯→ 전반적인 정보를 묻는 True 문제

STEP 2 보기의 키워드 파악 → 주변 정보와 보기 대조
(A) 직원 자격 ⋯→ employees are licensed (O)
(B) 매일 영업 ⋯→ Mon-Fri (X)

STEP 3 적절히 패러프레이징한 보기 고르기
직원들이 자격증을 갖고 있고 추가 자격증 과정도 수료했다.
→ 직원들이 충분한 자격을 갖췄다.

YBM TEST

Questions 1-3 refer to the following Web page.

---

www.felosaairlines.com

| HOME | BOOK A FLIGHT | BAGGAGE POLICY | FREQUENT FLYER CLUB | CONTACT US |

Felosa Airlines Baggage Policy

In compliance with the Federal Aviation Association, we are making our baggage policy publicly available. For passengers using paper tickets, these terms are also printed on the back of the ticket. We strongly recommend making payments for excess baggage at the time of booking in order to expedite check-in. Please note that credit cards are the only form of payment accepted at the check-in counter.

Standard Bags: Maximum dimensions (length + width + height) of 62 inches, weighing up to 50 pounds

	First Bag	Second Bag	Third Bag
Economy Passengers	$25	$50	Not available
First-Class Passengers	Free	$25	$50

Please note that Felosa Airlines reserves the right to limit the number of bags during the peak travel season. Passengers will be notified by e-mail at least 48 hours prior to departure if baggage restrictions are in place.

Overweight/Oversized Bags:

	Overweight: 51–90 pounds	Overweight: 91+ pounds	Oversized: 63–100 inches (L+W+H)	Oversized: 101–120 inches (L+W+H)
All Passengers	$75	Not accepted*	$75	$85

*Exception: cellos, guitars, brass horns, etc. in hard-shell cases

For overweight and oversized bags, please check in at least 2 hours before your departure time to ensure that your bag will not be delayed. For inquiries, please contact our customer service department anytime by calling 1-800-555-0147, or click here to submit an online inquiry.

---

1. What is stated about Felosa Airlines' check-in counter?
   (A) It can only process one payment type.
   (B) It has a priority line for frequent flyers.
   (C) It issues paper tickets to all passengers.
   (D) It opens two hours before the departure time.

2. What is true about the weight limit?
   (A) It is regulated by the Federal Aviation Agency.
   (B) It depends on the passenger's ticket.
   (C) It does not apply to musical instruments.
   (D) It is lowered during peak travel times.

3. What is NOT indicated about Felosa Airlines?
   (A) Its first-class passengers do not have to pay for any checked luggage.
   (B) It may restrict the number of bags depending on the time of year.
   (C) It allows economy passengers to check only two bags.
   (D) Its customer service department is available twenty-four hours a day.

UNIT 05 동의어 문제

공식 112 동의어 문제는 반드시 단어 앞뒤를 해석해 본다.

동의어 문제는 매 시험마다 2~3문제씩 출제된다. 다의어가 자주 출제되므로, 잘 알려진 대표적 의미만으로 동의어를 고르다가는 오히려 함정에 빠질 수 있다. 반드시 지문에서 단어 앞뒤를 해석해 보고 문맥을 통해 단어의 정확한 의미를 파악해야 한다.

[예제] 편지 　　　　　　해설집 p.82

Q The phrase "back up" in paragraph 1, line 7, is closest in meaning to
(A) copy
(B) support

Dear Ms. Norton,

I run Blueberry Bakery. ❶I recently applied for a loan for my growing business and ❷was notified this morning that my application was not accepted. This is hardly understandable. ❸My business has had strong revenue, and I was able to back up that claim by providing tax documents for the past two years. … 중략

STEP 1 단어 위치 파악하기
Q. 1번째 단락 7번째 줄에 있는 "back up"

STEP 2 단어 앞뒤 해석하기
❶ 대출 신청을 했다.
❷ 대출 승인이 나지 않았다고 통보받았다.
❸ 높은 수익을 냈고, 납세증명서로 'back up'했었다.
→ '(주장을) 뒷받침하다'라는 의미가 자연스럽다.

STEP 3 동의어 고르기
(A) 복사하다
(B) 뒷받침하다　　　　　　　　정답 (B)

공식 113 다의어를 미리 알아 두자.

동의어 문제에는 한 단어에 여러 의미가 있는 다의어가 자주 출제되므로, Part 7에 자주 등장하는 다의어를 미리 암기해 두자.

acquire the skills 기술을 습득하다	**earn** 얻다 purchase 사다 (×)	It was a tough **call**. 힘든 결정이었다.	**decision** 결정 phone 전화 (×)
address the issue 문제를 다루다	**handle** 다루다 lecture 강연하다 (×)	**refer** any questions to me 질문을 내게 넘기다	**direct** 보내다 consult 참고하다 (×)
draw attention 주의를 끌다	**attract** 끌다 sketch 그리다 (×)	**employ** a different strategy 다른 전략을 사용하다	**use** 사용하다 hire 고용하다 (×)
take a paid **leave** 유급 휴가를 갖다	**vacation** 휴가 departure 출발 (×)	**attend to** business 업무를 처리하다	**take care of** 처리하다 take part in 참석하다 (×)
monitor sales trends 판매 동향을 지켜보다	**observe** 관찰하다 supervise 감독하다 (×)	**sensitive** information 민감한 정보	**confidential** 기밀의 delicate 연약한 (×)
locate missing files 분실된 파일을 찾다	**find** 찾다 position 두다 (×)	**critical** factors 필수적인 요소들	**essential** 필수적인 disapproving 찬성하지 않는 (×)

YBM TEST

Questions 1-4 refer to the following article

Jarvis Designs Steps It Up

January 18—Jarvis Designs, known for its sleek and stylish athletic clothing and footwear, is teaming up with Tate Incorporated to add a technology-enabled running shoe to its line. At first glance, the companies seem like an unlikely pair. Jarvis Designs was founded by Kurt Jarvis, who graduated with a degree from the Wilson School of Design in San Francisco, taking on a paid internship at a fashion house there before raising the funds to open his own business in Chicago. Tate Incorporated, on the other hand, was founded in New York by Kimball Tate. It began as an automotive manufacturing plant but transitioned to the production of GPS equipment about ten years ago.

The two firms are using the best that each has to offer to develop a GPS-enabled athletic shoe. A demo version of the shoe, unnamed at the time, was debuted at the International Health and Beauty Expo in Seattle last month. Company representatives demonstrated how the shoe can track factors such as distance covered, average speed, and calories burned. It can even identify possible issues with the runner's form. The development of the JDT-360, the name given to the product, has cost millions, but the project is expected to turn profitable quickly once it hits the shelves in March. Pre-orders for the JDT-360 are already being accepted on the Jarvis Designs Web site. The shoes will be sold online and in all major department stores.

1. What is the article mainly about?
   (A) A leadership change
   (B) A business partnership
   (C) A market trend
   (D) A fashion show

2. Where did Mr. Jarvis first work in the field of fashion?
   (A) In Chicago
   (B) In New York
   (C) In San Francisco
   (D) In Seattle

3. What is indicated about the JDT-360?
   (A) It underwent several name changes.
   (B) It was designed by Kimball Tate.
   (C) It was first shown at an international expo.
   (D) It is the company's best-selling item.

4. The word "turn" in paragraph 2, line 13, is closest in meaning to
   (A) ensure
   (B) curve
   (C) resolve
   (D) become

UNIT 06 추론 문제

공식 114 추론 문제의 단서는 간접적으로 제시된다.

추론 문제를 푸는 방식은 세부사항 문제나 Not / True 문제와 유사하지만, 단서가 간접적으로 제시되기 때문에 난이도가 높은 편이다. 문제 키워드와 관련된 단서들의 함축적인 의미를 파악한다.

예제 이메일
해설집 p. 83

Q1 What is implied about Ms. Pollard?
(A) She was concerned about a dinner menu.
(B) She asked Mr. Bower for suggestions.

To: Kasandra Pollard
From: Chris Bower

I know ❶you are busy getting ready for the visit from our investors from China. Following our conversation on Monday, I have been trying to think of a place to take them after dinner, since ❷you said you still needed recommendations. How about going to the International Dance Exhibition? … 중략

STEP 1 질문 유형 파악하기
Q1. Ms. Pollard에 대해 암시되는 것은?
⋯→ 수신인에 대한 추론 문제

STEP 2 키워드에 대한 단서 찾기
보통 발신인 단서는 I / we, 수신인 단서는 you로 제시된다. Mr. Pollard는 수신인이므로 you가 나오는 문장 위주로 단서를 찾는다.
❶ 투자자들 방문을 준비하느라 당신이 바쁜 걸 안다.
❷ 당신이 그때 추천해달라고 했었는데, 전시회는 어떤가?

STEP 3 적절히 패러프레이징한 보기 고르기
추천이 필요하다 → 제안을 부탁하다
정답 (B)

공식 115 대상·출처 문제는 주로 광고문이나 정보문에서 출제된다.

글을 읽는 대상이나 글의 출처를 묻는 문제는 보통 지문의 전반부에서 제품 / 서비스의 종류(광고문), 주제 / 목적(안내문), 다루는 정보(정보문)만 파악하면 쉽게 답을 알 수 있지만, 단서가 명확하지 않을 경우에는 마지막에 내용을 종합해서 푼다.

예제 정보문
해설집 p. 83

Q2 Where would the information most likely be found?
(A) In a user manual
(B) In a tourist brochure

❶Thank you for purchasing our product. ❷Please read the following information carefully. It will allow you to make the most of our product's special features.
… 중략

STEP 1 질문 유형 파악하기
Q2. 이 정보는 어디에서 보게 될 것 같은가?
⋯→ 출처에 대한 추론 문제

STEP 2 전반부에서 키워드 찾기
❶ 제품을 구매해 주셔서 감사합니다.
❷ 꼼꼼히 읽으시면 이 제품의 특징을 최대한 활용하실 수 있습니다.

STEP 3 논리적으로 추론하기
정답 (A) 사용 설명서

YBM TEST

Questions 1-4 refer to the following article.

February 18—Elkview city officials have announced an ambitious project aimed at reducing mercury contamination levels at Akron Lake. Researchers from Harrison University have been monitoring the toxicity of the lake annually for the past thirty years, and the latest reports have demonstrated elevated levels of mercury in the water and the surrounding soil. As the land bordering the northern shore of the lake is zoned for industrial use, the water is susceptible to pollutants from nearby factories. A recent court case determined that Melendez Manufacturing, which produces fluorescent light bulbs, was the primary source of the contamination. Taxpayers were relieved to discover that the company will be required to pay for the entire restoration of the site, and work is expected to get underway later this year.

The Elkview City Council has appointed a subcommittee to oversee the Akron Lake Remediation Plan (ALRP), which is projected to cost approximately $100 million. "We are working closely with specialists to ensure that the project is implemented with care," said Joshua Hester, the head of the committee. "There are countless plant and animal species living in and around the lake, and we want to avoid disturbing their habitats any more than necessary."

The project will consist of three phases, and the lake's on-site amenities will be off limits during some parts of the procedure. Phase One is two months of testing soil and water samples from in and around the lake, Phase Two involves four months of dredging the bottom of the lake to remove contaminated sediment and disposing of it according to the regulations regarding hazardous waste, and Phase Three consists of the replanting of submersed aquatic plants to restore the natural balance. The final phase could last as long as three years.

1. What is the purpose of the article?
   (A) To explain a nature education program
   (B) To highlight a cleanup effort
   (C) To promote an investment venture
   (D) To introduce a local fundraiser

2. Who most likely is Mr. Hester?
   (A) A city council member
   (B) A university professor
   (C) A corporate spokesperson
   (D) A research scientist

3. What is implied about the ALRP?
   (A) It will prevent soil erosion.
   (B) It will be privately funded.
   (C) It was developed by a manufacturing company.
   (D) It is expected to last three years in total.

4. What is NOT suggested about Akron Lake?
   (A) It will have temporary facility closures.
   (B) It is the home of a variety of wildlife.
   (C) It has contaminated a drinking water supply.
   (D) It is located near an industrial district.

UNIT 07 문장 삽입 문제

예제 광고

해설집 p. 84

Rivera Carpets

No matter what the size of your project, Rivera Carpets can help you bring style and charm to your home with new wall-to-wall carpeting. —[1]— **Q2**We have a strong reputation for having the most experienced installers in the business, so you can be confident that the work will last for many years. —[2]— **Q2**During the visit, **Q1**one of our employees will calculate the size of your room(s) and provide an estimate. —[3]— **Q1**Once you've made your decision, we can begin the work within three days of signing the contract. We look forward to serving you! —[4]—

공식 116 문장이 들어갈 위치를 찾을 때는 연결어를 활용한다.

문제에 제시된 삽입문을 먼저 읽고, 삽입문과 지문 속 번호 앞뒤 문장에 있는 연결어, 즉 지시어, 대명사, 접속부사, 시간의 전후 관계를 나타내는 부사를 활용해 서로 연결이 잘 되는지 확인한다.

Q1. In which of the positions marked [1], [2], [3], and [4] does the following sentence best belong?

"You can then come into our store at your convenience to see product samples."

(A) [1]   (B) [2]
(C) [3]   (D) [4]

STEP 1 삽입문의 연결어 then 활용하기
"그런 다음, 편한 시간에 저희 매장에 오셔서 제품 샘플을 보세요." → 매장 이외의 장소에서 진행될 일을 언급한 문장 뒤에 들어가는 것이 적절하다.

STEP 2 적절한 위치에 문장 삽입 후 확인
직원이 방문하여 견적을 내드립니다. → 샘플 보러 오세요 → 결정하시면 3일 내로 시작합니다   **정답** (C)

공식 117 연결어가 없을 때는 앞뒤 문맥을 활용한다.

단서로 활용할 연결어가 보이지 않을 때는 앞뒤 문맥만으로 문장이 들어갈 위치를 찾아야 한다. 단, 다른 문제를 풀면서 지문의 흐름이 어색한 부분이 보이면 삽입문을 넣어서 확인해본다.

Q2. In which of the positions marked [1], [2], [3], and [4] does the following sentence best belong?

"Call us at any time to book your free in-home consultation."

(A) [1]   (B) [2]
(C) [3]   (D) [4]

STEP 1 삽입문 파악하기
"언제든지 전화하셔서 무료 가정 방문 상담을 예약하세요."

STEP 2 적절한 위치에 문장 삽입 후 확인
높은 명성+내구성 홍보 → 전화 예약 권유 → 직원 방문 안내
정답 (B)

YBM TEST

Questions 1-3 refer to the following e-mail.

E-Mail message

To:	<tenantlist@creeksideapts.com>
From:	<osborneh@creedsideapts.com>
Date:	August 13
Subject:	Important Information

Dear Creekside Apartments Tenants,

As part of our ongoing upgrades to the building, we have booked an appointment to have a representative from the municipal utility company perform maintenance on the transformers in our building. The work will be carried out on Wednesday, August 20, from 2 P.M. to approximately 4 P.M. For safety reasons, the electricity to the entire building must be shut off during this period. — [1] —. We apologize in advance for any inconvenience this may cause.

We suggest powering down your computer before 2 P.M. on that day so you do not lose any data. — [2] —. You should not have to worry about the effect on the items in your refrigerator and freezer as long as you keep the doors shut. The temperature is able to be maintained for up to four hours, and the working period is expected to last a maximum of two hours. — [3] —.

Future building improvements will be revealed at the next tenants' meeting, which is scheduled for Thursday, August 28, at 7 P.M. in the recreation room. — [4] —. Please see the attached list of topics that are to be discussed at the next meeting and let me know if anything needs to be added.

Sincerely,

Heather Osborne
Property Manager, Creekside Apartments

---

1. What is the purpose of the e-mail?
   (A) To remind tenants about safety regulations
   (B) To announce a redecorating project
   (C) To inform tenants of a planned loss of power
   (D) To explain a new apartment policy

2. What does Ms. Osborne include with her e-mail?
   (A) An inspection schedule
   (B) A list of safety tips
   (C) A consent form
   (D) A meeting agenda

3. In which of the positions marked [1], [2], [3], and [4] does the following sentence best belong?

   "As long as this is the case, there should be no spoilage."

   (A) [1]
   (B) [2]
   (C) [3]
   (D) [4]

UNIT 08 연계 문제

공식 118 두 지문에 공통적으로 보이는 단어는 반드시 연계된다.

똑같은 단어가 두 지문에서 보이면 그 단어를 매개로 정보를 연계시켜 푸는 문제가 반드시 출제된다. 두 지문에 공통적으로 제시된 단어의 주변은 미리 확인해 연결 관계를 파악해 두자.

예제 보고서 & 이메일 해설집 p. 85

Q1. What brand of appliance does Ms. Brunswick own?
(A) Littleton
(B) ADR

Smith Brothers Plumbing
Employee Work Report

Job#	Address	Description of Work
303	428 Pine St.	❷Installation of Littleton washing machine
306	23 Creek Rd.	Install ADR dishwasher

================================
To: Smith Brothers Plumbing
From: Sandra **Brunswick**

I received some plumbing services at ❶**my residence, 428 Pine Street**, yesterday. The technician arrived on time and completed the work in a timely manner.
… 중략 …

STEP 1 지문간 관계 파악하기
[지문1] 배관 설비 직원의 작업 보고서
[지문2] 브런즈윅 씨가 배관 설비 회사에 보낸 이메일

STEP 2 공통으로 나온 단어 주변 파악하기
지문1과 지문2의 공통 단어 → 428 Pine St.

STEP 3 단서를 연계시켜 문제 풀기
Q1. 브런즈윅 씨가 소유한 가전제품의 브랜드는?
❶ 브런즈윅 씨의 거주지 주소: 428 Pine St.
❷ 428 Pine St.에 리틀턴 세탁기를 설치했다.
→ 브런즈윅 씨의 집에 설치한 제품은 리틀턴 세탁기이다.

정답 (A)

> **공식**
> # 119 문제의 키워드가 양식에 보이면 그 주변 단어를 연계 단서로 삼는다.
> 양식(표)이 포함된 복수 지문에서는 양식(표)에 있는 특정 정보를 단서로 다른 지문에 있는 나머지 정보를 찾아 연계시키는 문제가 반드시 출제된다. 특히, 문제의 키워드가 양식(표)에 보일 경우, 양식(표)에서 그 키워드와 관련된 주변의 단어를 새로운 단서로 삼아 다른 지문에서 정보를 찾으면 쉽게 정답을 파악할 수 있다.

[예제] 이메일 & 송장 해설집 p.86

Q2. Why was Ms. Sims charged £113 by Modar Travel?
(A) Ms. Sims extended the duration of her travel.
(B) Ms. Sims traveled to the Seven Sisters attraction.

To: Jena Sims
From: David Silva, Modar Travel

Dear Ms. Sims,

… Please find the enclosed invoice. It has been revised to reflect the ❷**additional expenses incurred during your trip on 9 May to and from Seven Sisters Cliffs.** …
================================
Modar Travel Invoice
Date: 28 May
Bill to: Jena Sims

Description	Quantity	Price
Vacation Package to Southern England	1	£1,270
❶ Additional Trip	1	£113
	Total	£1,383

STEP 1 지문간 관계 **파악하기**
[지문1] 여행사에서 심즈 씨에게 보낸 이메일
[지문2] 심즈 씨에게 청구된 모다르 여행사 송장

STEP 2 양식에 있는 문제 키워드 **파악하기**
Q2. 모다르 여행사는 왜 심즈 씨에게 113파운드를 청구했는가?
❶ 양식(지문 2)에 있는 문제 키워드 → £113
£113과 관련된 주변 정보 → Additional Trip

STEP 3 다른 지문에서 나머지 정보 찾기
❷ 세븐 시스터즈 절벽을 다녀오면서 발생된 추가 비용
→ 심즈 씨가 세븐 시스터즈 명소를 여행했다.   **정답** (B)

YBM TEST

Questions 1-5 refer to the following schedule, comment form, and e-mail.

Port Diaz: Daily Ferry Schedule

At Clearwater Ferries, we endeavor to keep our service on time for the convenience of our passengers. However, please note that delays or cancellations may occur during times of severe weather.

Destination	Departure Time	Fares*: Adult / Child
Granston	8:05 A.M.	€25 / €13
Washburn	11:30 A.M.	€18 / €8
Somerville	1:25 P.M.	€12 / €6
Chelmsford	5:50 P.M.	€20 / €10

*Passengers who frequently travel on the ferry may apply for an EZ-Pass, which allows the holder to travel at a 20% discount.

---

https://www.clearwaterferries.com/feedback

Clearwater Ferries Customer Feedback Form

Customer Name: Natalie Milne   E-mail Address: nataliem@kzservices.com

Type(s) of Feedback: [X] Inquiry   [X] Complaint   [ ] Suggestion   [ ] Other

Comments:

I recently had an issue with my Clearwater Ferries EZ-Pass. While taking a ferry from Port Diaz on June 20, the card scanner at the dock's entrance would not read my pass. After several attempts to get it to work, and some assistance from an employee, I was told I would have to purchase a ticket. Fortunately, I had enough cash to buy the ticket to my destination. I assume I can get a refund for the difference, so I would like to know how to do this. My EZ-Pass number is 38492.

```
=============== E-Mail message ===============
To:       Natalie Milne <nataliem@kzservices.com>
From:     Clearwater Ferries info@clearwaterferries.com
Date:     June 23
Subject:  Clearwater Ferries Customer Feedback
```

Dear Ms. Milne,

On behalf of Clearwater Ferries, I would like to apologize for the recent disappointing experience you had at Port Diaz. Unfortunately, the card-reading machines there are very old and do not always function as required. We are in the process of replacing them. Our records show that the machine did acknowledge the presence of your card at the dock shortly after 1 P.M. on your date of travel, but it did not permit entrance for some reason. Our refund policy is to send refunds by check to the address listed on the EZ-Pass registration for cash purchases and to issue a reimbursement payment to the credit card account for credit card purchases. You can expect a refund for the price difference within ten working days. I hope this resolves the matter to your satisfaction.

Sincerely,

Sebastian Russell

1. What is suggested about Ms. Milne?
   (A) She traveled on a weekday.
   (B) She uses the ferry frequently.
   (C) She lost a transportation card.
   (D) She works in Port Diaz.

2. In the form, the word "assume" in paragraph 1, line 5, is closest in meaning to
   (A) accept
   (B) realize
   (C) confirm
   (D) suppose

3. What most likely was Ms. Milne's travel destination?
   (A) Granston
   (B) Washburn
   (C) Somerville
   (D) Chelmsford

4. What does Mr. Russell mention about Port Diaz?
   (A) Its equipment is outdated.
   (B) Its staff needs more training.
   (C) It is undergoing construction.
   (D) It is crowded during the day.

5. What is true about Ms. Milne's refund?
   (A) It will be issued through a check.
   (B) It will be for the entire ticket price.
   (C) It has already been sent to her.
   (D) It will appear on a credit card statement.

UNIT 01 편지 / 이메일

예제 이메일 해설집 p. 87

> To: Ayumi Negishi <negishiayumi@marquettepost.com> ——— 수신인
> From: Mariana Cavalcanti <m.cavalcanti@benitassolar.com> ——— 발신인
> *이메일 계정으로 인물 간 관계나 회사 업종을 파악
>
> Dear Ms. Negishi,
> **Q1❶** It was a pleasure to meet you during last week's appointment to assess your property for its suitability for installing solar panels. **Q1❷** Due to the size and position of your roof, I believe that a fifteen-panel system would be appropriate.
>
> 주제/목적
> 지난주에 있었던 평가 결과 통지
>
> Based on the energy usage you reported, **Q2❶** you can expect a monthly reduction in your energy bill of approximately 56%. … 중략 **Q2❷** your system will save you even more per month in the future.
>
> 세부사항
> 구체적인 평가 내용
>
> Please let me know if you would like to go forward with the project. ——— 요청/제안
> 피드백 요청
>
> Mariana Cavalcanti
> Consultant, Benitas Solar ——— 발신인의 직책과 소속

공식 120 편지 / 이메일은 「목적 → 세부사항 → 요청」 순이다.

편지와 이메일은 대부분 〈주제/목적 → 세부사항에 대한 구체적인 설명 → 요청/제안 및 첨부/동봉〉 순서로 전개된다. 이를 이용해 각 질문의 단서를 어느 부분에서 찾으면 되는지 쉽게 짐작할 수 있다.

Q1. Why did Ms. Cavalcanti write to Ms. Negishi?
(A) To request a bill payment
(B) To follow up on a visit

주제 / 목적은 전반부에서 단서 찾기
Q1. 편지를 왜 썼는가?
❶ 지난주에 태양 전지판 설치 적합성을 평가
❷ 평가에 따른 적절한 시스템 추천
정답 (B) 방문에 대한 후속 조치

공식 121 문제에 사람 이름이 있으면 수/발신인부터 확인한다.

편지와 이메일에는 사람 관련 문제가 자주 출제되는데, 이 사람이 수신인인지 발신인인지부터 먼저 파악한다. 발신인에 관한 내용은 1인칭(I, we 등), 수신인에 관한 내용은 2인칭(you / your)으로 언급되므로 그 주변에서 단서를 찾는다.

Q2. What is suggested about Ms. Negishi?
(A) She is interested in saving energy.
(B) She was overcharged for her energy use.

수신인에 대한 정보는 you 주변에서 찾기
Q2. 네기시 씨(수신인)에 대해 암시된 것은?
❶ 당신의 월별 전기 요금이 줄 것이다.
❷ 향후에는 더 절약될 것이다.
정답 (A) 네기시 씨는 에너지 절약에 관심이 있다.

YBM TEST

Questions 1-2 refer to the following e-mail.

To:	Staff List <staff@pemberton1.com>
From:	Sherry Flynn <sflynn@pemberton1.com>
Date:	November 23
Subject:	Next round of lessons

Hello Everyone,

I'm pleased to say that Pemberton will open for business on December 10. For those of you who aren't bringing your own skis and poles, be sure to reserve the equipment you need from the on-site shop before the opening day. Based on the online bookings so far, it looks like we will have a lot of large groups with many people who have never tried the sport before. Therefore, you should expect the beginner level to make up about 75% of the business, rather than the 40% we've seen in other years. The first few weeks of the season will be particularly hectic, so we need some of you to pick up extra shifts. If you are interested in doing so, please send an e-mail to Kathleen Clark at kclark@pemberton1.com.

Thanks!

Sherry Flynn

1. Who most likely are the recipients of the e-mail?
   (A) Cooking teachers
   (B) Music tutors
   (C) Ski instructors
   (D) Weight trainers

2. Why should employees e-mail Ms. Clark?
   (A) To volunteer to work additional hours
   (B) To reserve some equipment
   (C) To complete some tax paperwork
   (D) To share suggestions for improvements

Questions 3-5 refer to the following e-mail.

E-Mail message

To:	Jodie Obregon <j.obregon@eastonsales.com>
From:	Huang Lao <h.lao@eastonsales.com>
Date:	February 3
Subject:	Phone update

Dear Ms. Obregon,

I am writing to follow-up on the task you assigned me regarding company cell phones. — [1] —. As requested, I have reviewed the terms and conditions of a number of cell phone packages from various providers to determine which one might best suit our needs. I know you recommended using Formula Communications. Although they offer an attractive monthly rate for unlimited minutes, the package only includes 500 megabytes of data per user. — [2] —. If this limit is exceeded, the cost of data becomes very expensive. Employees could easily exceed the allotted amount, pushing the bill way over budget. — [3] —.

I had considered Tibbs Mobile, which has a much more generous data plan that isn't much more expensive than Formula's package. However, after looking into customer reviews, it doesn't seem worth it. Tibbs Mobile is known for having a lot of dropped calls and out-of-service areas. — [4] —. So, this isn't the right option for us either.

Since we don't need to make a decision until our current contract expires, there is more time to work on this project. I will give you an update again early next week.

Sincerely,
Huang Lao

---

3. What has Mr. Lao been asked to do?
   (A) Distribute phones to employees
   (B) Research phone packages
   (C) Test cell phone features
   (D) Carry out phone repairs

4. Why does Mr. Lao reject Ms. Obregon's suggestion?
   (A) He discovered that it was no longer available.
   (B) He cannot find enough information about it.
   (C) He thinks it could lead to overspending.
   (D) He is concerned that it will take too long to implement.

5. In which of the positions marked [1], [2], [3], and [4] does the following sentence best belong?

   "Above all, we need something reliable so as not to negatively affect our business."

   (A) [1]
   (B) [2]
   (C) [3]
   (D) [4]

Questions 6-9 refer to the following letter.

Christopher Murphy
861 Wilkinson Street
Franklin, MA 02038

March 2

Dear Mr. Murphy,

Our records show that you recently purchased a Lomita Incorporated power-operated recliner from our store. We have been informed by the manufacturer that model L-980 is being removed from the market — effective immediately — due to a potential fire hazard. The casing of the power supply can become easily broken with repeated use, posing a potential risk of electrical shock if users come into contact with exposed wires. This applies to both the leather and the upholstered versions. No injuries have been reported thus far, but the company wants to err on the side of caution for consumers' sake. The items were sold at Boyd Furniture in all five of our stores across the country, as well as at other furniture retailers.

Customers can return the chairs for a full refund. We are offering an in-store drop-off event on March 5 and 6. During this time, you can bring in your item and get the refund processed on-site. Alternatively, from March 10, Lomita Incorporated will provide a residential pick-up service. You can also ship the chair directly to the manufacturer at its main location, the address for which is provided on the enclosed document. No matter which option you choose, your intention to claim a refund must be submitted no later than April 25. Customers should note that a new version of the recliner, with the issue resolved, is expected to go on sale from May 15.

To download a claim form, visit www.boydfurniture.com/documents. If you do not have access to a printer, you may request a form by contacting Lomita Incorporated's hotline at 1-800-555-0184.

Sincerely,

The Boyd Furniture Customer Service Team

Enclosure

6. What is the purpose of the letter?
   (A) To request feedback from a customer
   (B) To introduce a device's features
   (C) To announce a product recall
   (D) To explain some warranty information

7. What is suggested about model L-980?
   (A) It was sold with more than one covering.
   (B) Its design has resulted in injuries.
   (C) It is available exclusively at Boyd Furniture.
   (D) It is sold in five countries.

8. What has been included with the letter?
   (A) A return label
   (B) A mailing address
   (C) A list of stores
   (D) A claim form

9. By when must Mr. Murphy take action?
   (A) March 5
   (B) March 10
   (C) April 25
   (D) May 15

Questions 10-13 refer to the following e-mail.

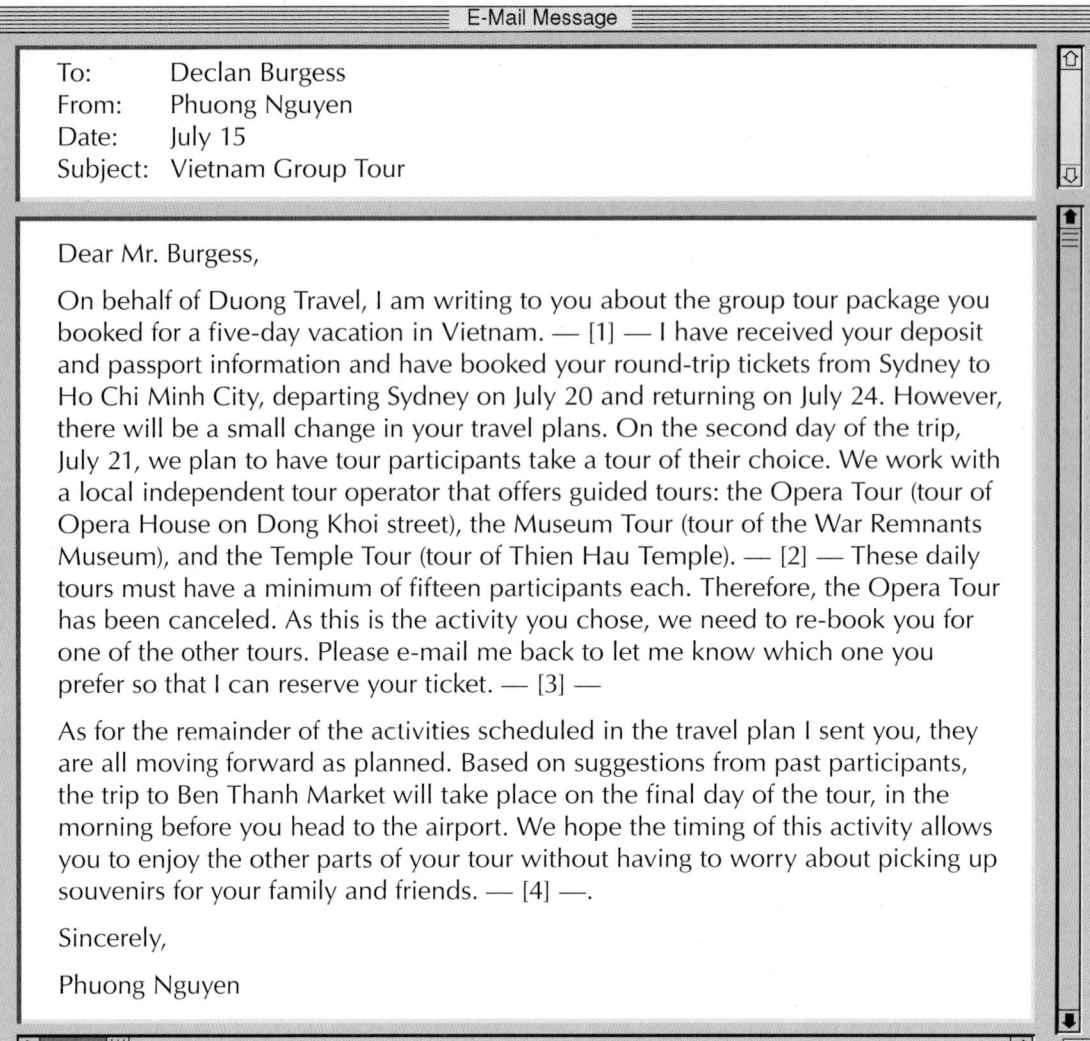

To: Declan Burgess
From: Phuong Nguyen
Date: July 15
Subject: Vietnam Group Tour

Dear Mr. Burgess,

On behalf of Duong Travel, I am writing to you about the group tour package you booked for a five-day vacation in Vietnam. — [1] — I have received your deposit and passport information and have booked your round-trip tickets from Sydney to Ho Chi Minh City, departing Sydney on July 20 and returning on July 24. However, there will be a small change in your travel plans. On the second day of the trip, July 21, we plan to have tour participants take a tour of their choice. We work with a local independent tour operator that offers guided tours: the Opera Tour (tour of Opera House on Dong Khoi street), the Museum Tour (tour of the War Remnants Museum), and the Temple Tour (tour of Thien Hau Temple). — [2] — These daily tours must have a minimum of fifteen participants each. Therefore, the Opera Tour has been canceled. As this is the activity you chose, we need to re-book you for one of the other tours. Please e-mail me back to let me know which one you prefer so that I can reserve your ticket. — [3] —

As for the remainder of the activities scheduled in the travel plan I sent you, they are all moving forward as planned. Based on suggestions from past participants, the trip to Ben Thanh Market will take place on the final day of the tour, in the morning before you head to the airport. We hope the timing of this activity allows you to enjoy the other parts of your tour without having to worry about picking up souvenirs for your family and friends. — [4] —.

Sincerely,

Phuong Nguyen

10. What is the purpose of the e-mail?
(A) To request a payment for services
(B) To revise a travel itinerary
(C) To confirm a passport number
(D) To promote a tour package

11. What is implied about the Opera Tour?
(A) It had too few participants to proceed.
(B) It is operated by Ms. Nguyen's company.
(C) It has been canceled due to bad weather.
(D) It requires an extra fee from Mr. Burgess.

12. On what day will Mr. Burgess visit a market?
(A) July 20
(B) July 21
(C) July 24
(D) July 25

13. In which of the positions marked [1], [2], [3], and [4] does the following sentence best belong?

"I need to do so as soon as possible to guarantee you a spot."

(A) [1]
(B) [2]
(C) [3]
(D) [4]

Questions 14-17 refer to the following letter.

Jwala Nayar
Arbor Advertising
528 Musgrave Street
Oklahoma City, OK 73102

Dear Mr. Nayar,

I am the senior advertising manager at Enderby Incorporated, and I am writing on behalf of Mara Padovesi, a key member of our team. I would like to provide an endorsement for Ms. Padovesi, who has applied for the job opening at your company. — [1] —. I have worked with Ms. Padovesi for the past five years, and I have been continually impressed by her performance. She is the only staff member to have worked her way up from intern to team leader in just two years. Additionally, although she has never received formal managerial training, she has been able to take charge of a team with ease.

The quality of work she has exhibited over the years has been second to none. Enclosed is a flyer that she designed for a local restaurant's grand opening; you can see her creativity for yourself. — [2] —. The client was immensely pleased with the final result and has come back to us regularly with more projects, so we have secured a steady client directly through Ms. Padovesi's efforts, and this is just one case among many. Ms. Padovesi and her team were also responsible for developing a commercial for Metz Athletics. — [3] —. When you do, I think you'll agree that it captures the viewer's attention.

Everyone on the staff believes Ms. Padovesi to be a self-starter with a bright future. We would be disappointed if she were no longer part of the Enderby Incorporated staff, but we understand that her career path is taking her in a new direction.

Should you wish to discuss the matter further, please feel free to contact me at 555-0174, extension 20, according to your availability. — [4] —.

Sincerely,

Chulsoo Jeong

14. What is the letter about?

(A) Promoting a job opening
(B) Applying for a position
(C) Recommending a colleague
(D) Rejecting a job offer

15. What is NOT stated about Ms. Padovesi?

(A) She received promotions more quickly than others.
(B) She is considered to be a motivated individual.
(C) She possesses natural leadership skills.
(D) She is no longer an employee of Enderby Incorporated.

16. What did Mr. Jeong send with the letter?

(A) A promotional leaflet
(B) A schedule of availability
(C) An employment contract
(D) An application form

17. In which of the positions marked [1], [2], [3], and [4] does the following sentence best belong?

"You are sure to catch it at some point."

(A) [1]
(B) [2]
(C) [3]
(D) [4]

Questions 18-22 refer to the following flyer and letter.

Democracy Matters Association
Helping you to make your voice heard

The Democracy Matters Association (DMA) is dedicated to ensuring fair elections at every level, tackling issues with stricter ID regulations, shortening the timeframe for absentee voters, and incorporating more technology into candidate selection. If you are registered to vote in Miller County, DMA members want to hear from you, along with their legal experts, to put forth the best arguments to the election officials. Even at the local level, we don't want people getting used to passively participating in democracy.

The debate will take place at Courtright Hall on Friday, October 3, at 7 P.M. Everyone is welcome to attend, you do not have to be a DMA member, and seating is available on a first come, first served basis. Alternatively, you may send your comments to Robert Klein at r.klein@dmamiller.com. The best ones will be selected by a committee from the DMA, and they will be read aloud at the event by the city's mayor, Daryl Irvine, who will be overseeing the event. We will endeavor to include arguments from a variety of perspectives. The proceedings will be recorded and posted in their entirety as a two-hour video on the DMA Web site the following week.

Sherri Lannon
970 Caldwell Street
Mooreland, OK 73852

Dear Ms. Lannon,

Our committee found your submitted comments on voting procedures to be insightful as well as constructive to our mission of facilitating an open dialog on this topic. We are sorry that you will be unable to attend the October 3 event, but your submission has been selected to be included in the discussion. Because the event will be posted as a video online, we need you to give us official permission to use your remarks. Please fill out the enclosed document and return it using the envelope provided. This should be done no later than September 20. Should you have any questions or concerns, do not hesitate to contact me at 555-0199.

Warmest regards,

Robert Klein
DMA Vice President

Enclosure

18. Who are the intended recipients of the flyer?
    (A) Legal experts
    (B) Political candidates
    (C) Registered voters
    (D) Election workers

19. In the flyer, the word "used" in paragraph 1, line 6, is closest in meaning to
    (A) operated
    (B) recycled
    (C) accustomed
    (D) depleted

20. What is indicated about the October 3 event?
    (A) It is open to members of the DMA only.
    (B) It is expected to conclude at 9 P.M.
    (C) It will be streamed online in real time.
    (D) Its tickets will likely sell out quickly.

21. What is true about Ms. Lannon?
    (A) Her comments will be read by a city official.
    (B) Her submission requires some adjustments.
    (C) Her membership to the DMA has been approved.
    (D) Her ideas will appear in a group's newsletter.

22. What has Mr. Klein included with the letter?
    (A) A voting card
    (B) A pamphlet
    (C) An entry ticket
    (D) A consent form

Questions 23-27 refer to the following schedule and e-mails.

Toledo Square Events
Week of August 17

Sunday, August 17, 9 A.M.–5 P.M.: Square Exercise Day
Get moving and stay active with volleyball, mini golf, a rock climbing wall, and more. All activities are free, but expect long lines due to the high demand.

Tuesday, August 19, 1 P.M.–4 P.M.: Men's Choir Festival
Men's choirs from around the region will be performing a cappella in the square. Outdoor seating will be available on a first come, first served basis.

Friday, August 22, 7 P.M.–9 P.M.: Community Dog Show
Enter the competition through the city's Web site ($5 entry fee). Prizes will be given in various categories such as Funniest Dog, Best Trick, and Best Grooming.

Saturday, August 23, 2 P.M.–3:30 P.M.: Summertime Parade
Celebrate summer with marching musical groups (drum lines, school bands, etc.) as well as floats made by local nonprofit groups. The parade will start at City Hall and end in Toledo Square, where foods stall will be set up.

E-mail

To:	Maya Weismann <wmaya@snappypost.net>
From:	Anish Nayar <nayaranish@valley-mail.com>
Date:	August 11
Subject:	Upcoming event

Hi Maya,

I'm looking forward to preparing our float for the upcoming Summertime Parade. Thanks for purchasing the necessary decorations and supplies. All of our coworkers who signed up to help decorate the float will meet at the Duvall Building this Saturday (August 16) at 2 P.M. We can meet again in the evenings after work next week to put on the finishing touches if necessary. Matheus Ribiero will help on the 16th only and cannot come to the parade. He is going to be a judge in the dog show and will be busy all week. The company is going to carry an article about our efforts in the next newsletter, so we can't forget to take lots of pictures of the float-making process.

See you on Saturday!

Anish

E-mail

To: Anish Nayar <nayaranish@valley-mail.com>
From: Maya Weismann <wmaya@snappypost.net>
Date: August 12
Subject: RE: Upcoming event

Dear Anish,

Great news! I recruited one more person to help us at the parade, Renee Hahn from the publicity department. She won't be able to help with decorating, but she can walk with the float at the parade and pass out candy. She will just meet us at the starting point on the day of the parade.

Maya

---

23. What is indicated about Square Exercise Day?
    (A) Prizes will be distributed to the winners.
    (B) Participants might have to wait a long time.
    (C) It requires advance registration for teams.
    (D) A nominal participation fee will be charged.

24. What is suggested about Mr. Nayar?
    (A) He is a member of a men's choir.
    (B) He will be unable to attend an event.
    (C) He plans to buy some decorations.
    (D) He works for a nonprofit organization.

25. In the first e-mail, the word "carry" in paragraph 1, line 7, is closest in meaning to
    (A) publish
    (B) keep
    (C) bring
    (D) accept

26. When will Mr. Ribiero participate in an event?
    (A) On August 17
    (B) On August 19
    (C) On August 22
    (D) On August 23

27. Where will Ms. Hahn meet Mr. Nayar and Ms. Weismann on August 23?
    (A) At City Hall
    (B) At the Duvall Building
    (C) At Toledo Square
    (D) At her office

UNIT 02 공지 / 회람 / 광고

예제 공지
해설집 p. 95

> **CUSTOMER NOTICE:**
>
> Please take care when walking in the store today, especially near the main entrance, as a lot of water is being tracked in due to the heavy rain. ― 주제/목적: 미끄럼 주의 공지
>
> Customers may find complimentary plastic bags for their umbrellas at the entrance. … 중략 We are working to mop up any damp spots. ― 세부사항: 전달 사항 설명
>
> ○ **If you see one you would like to bring to our attention, please speak to a staff member.** Thank you. ― 요청사항/추가 정보: 고객 협조 요청

공식 122 구조가 거의 정해져 있다.

공지와 회람은 새로운 소식을 전하거나 공지 사항을 알리는 글로서, 구조가 거의 일정해 문제에서 요구하는 정보의 위치를 쉽게 짐작할 수 있다. 주로 〈주제/목적 → 구체적인 정보 → 요청사항〉의 순으로 전개된다.

Q. Why should customers talk to an employee?
(A) To get help finding an item
(B) To report a wet area

요청 문제는 후반부에서 찾기
Q. 고객들이 직원에게 얘기를 해야 하는 이유는?
○ 저희가 닦아야 할 젖은 바닥을 보게 되면 직원에게 말씀해 주세요.
정답 (B) 물기 있는 장소를 알려주려고

공식 123 구인 광고는 자격 요건에 대한 문제가 빈출 유형이다.

구인 광고는 〈채용 직책 → 담당 업무 → 지원 자격이나 혜택 → 지원 방법〉 순으로 구성된다. 특히 지원자가 맡게 될 업무나 자격 조건에 대한 문제가 주로 출제되는데, 이때 필수 자격조건과 우대 조건을 혼동하지 않도록 주의한다.

구인 직책	look for ~을 찾다 recruit 채용하다	seek ~을 구하다 (job) opening 공석	hire 고용하다 available position 지원 가능한 자리
담당 업무	responsibility 책임, 의무	duty 담당 업무	task 업무
필수 조건	requirement 필수조건 must possess 소지해야 한다	be required ~가 요구된다 essential/mandatory/necessary 필수적인	should have 가지고 있어야 한다
우대 조건	preferred 선호되는 advantageous 유리한	preferably 되도록이면 not a must 필수적인 것은 아니다	not mandatory 필수적이지 않은
제출 서류	cover letter 자기소개서	résumé 이력서	reference 추천서

YBM TEST

Questions 1-2 refer to the following notice.

NOTICE OF CONSTRUCTION

Beginning May 17, road construction will be carried out on sections of Hamill Avenue between 12th Street and 34th Street. Workers will be repairing potholes and curbs as well as resurfacing some areas of the roadway. We apologize in advance for disruptions caused by the loud machinery. During construction, traffic will be rerouted to Edsel Road. Parking will not be allowed on Hamill Avenue during the work. Residents in the area should call 555-0156 to ask for a short-term pass to park on other streets in the neighborhood. The work will be completed within approximately fourteen days. Thank you for your patience and cooperation.

Department of Transportation

1. What is NOT mentioned about the project?
   (A) It may result in noise disturbances.
   (B) It will last for about two weeks.
   (C) It will help to widen a road.
   (D) It requires road detours.

2. Why should residents call the number provided?
   (A) To request a temporary parking pass
   (B) To report construction problems
   (C) To share opinions about a project
   (D) To ask about future construction plans

Questions 3-5 refer to the following memo.

TO: All Conway Enterprises Staff
FROM: Deborah Adams
DATE: September 25

On behalf of the administrative department, I would like to report the results of the most recent management meeting. The team brainstormed ideas for motivating employees. The sales director suggested flexible vacation time, the HR director proposed a less strict dress code on Fridays, and the accounting director wanted weekly team lunches.

We may introduce all of these changes over time, but we will start with Kerry Stewart's idea. Therefore, beginning from October 1, employees are welcome to wear casual clothing to the office on Fridays. We will implement the new policy on a trial basis until the end of November. At that time, we will request feedback from employees. Please note that when selecting casual clothing, shorts are permitted if made of linen or other fine material, jeans in good condition are allowed, and skirts and dresses are allowed as usual. Please do not wear sneakers or open-toed shoes.

Thank you for your cooperation. Please direct all questions to your immediate supervisor.

3. In which department does Ms. Stewart work?
   (A) Human Resources
   (B) Sales
   (C) Administration
   (D) Accounting

4. How long will the trial period last?
   (A) About two weeks
   (B) About four weeks
   (C) About six weeks
   (D) About eight weeks

5. What is NOT acceptable clothing on Fridays during the trial?
   (A) Sandals
   (B) Shorts
   (C) Skirts
   (D) Jeans

Questions 6-9 refer to the following memo.

> To: All Staff Members
> From: Adam Lenard, Office Manager
> Date: June 3
> Re: Taking time off
>
> Now that summer is underway, I am expecting a lot of vacation requests for July. Requests for time off should be made in writing in the month prior to your desired vacation days. — [1] —. Usually, you have until the 25th of the month to hand in the Vacation Request Form. However, since I'll be going out of town on the 23rd, I need them one week early this month only.
>
> I will do my best to accommodate all requests. — [2] —. I'm very sorry about this. While I want you all to have enjoyable and relaxing vacations, you must keep in mind that we do not want to be short-staffed in July. My number one goal is to make sure our customer service does not suffer during this time. If your vacation request is shortened or denied, this is the reason. — [3] —. If you have any questions, you should direct them to me or your immediate supervisor. — [4] —.
>
> Sincerely,
>
> *Adam Lenard*

6. What is the main purpose of the memo?
   (A) To apologize for an error
   (B) To explain a procedure
   (C) To confirm a store closure date
   (D) To announce a vacation schedule

7. What is the deadline for handing in a form this month?
   (A) June 18
   (B) June 23
   (C) June 25
   (D) June 30

8. According to the memo, what is Mr. Lenard's top priority?
   (A) Extending staff vacation periods
   (B) Maintaining a desired service level
   (C) Improving employee teamwork
   (D) Attracting new business

9. In which of the positions marked [1], [2], [3], and [4] does the following sentence best belong?

   "However, please understand that this will not be possible in all cases."

   (A) [1]
   (B) [2]
   (C) [3]
   (D) [4]

Questions 10-12 refer to the following advertisement.

Maxie's

Whether you're celebrating an anniversary, birthday, or other special occasion, Maxie's has got you covered. Our flowers and potted plants brighten up the interior of any room, and they're the perfect way to show your loved ones that you're thinking about them. We offer free delivery on all our products, and this service includes evenings and weekends to work with your schedule. And last week, we started a new initiative to better serve more customers. Instead of sending out items only within Blue Springs, we now can deliver them to locations up to 20 miles outside the city limits, which includes all parts of Bellsville. That's not all. Place an order anytime within June, and you'll get free greeting card at no extra cost. Call us today at 555-0169, or stop in to speak with one of our friendly staff members at 4981 Lomita Drive.

10. What kind of business is being advertised?
    (A) A landscaping company
    (B) A florist shop
    (C) An interior design firm
    (D) A party planning service

11. What is mentioned about Maxie's?
    (A) It has extended its business hours.
    (B) It recently opened a branch in Bellsville.
    (C) It has expanded its delivery area.
    (D) It is looking for new staff members.

12. According to the advertisement, what will happen on July 1?
    (A) A special offer will end.
    (B) The cost of products will increase.
    (C) An anniversary will be celebrated.
    (D) An online ordering system will be launched.

Questions 13-16 refer to the following advertisement.

Job opening at Crescent Center!

Crescent Center is currently seeking a part-time physical therapist to work in the Tucson area. You'll be part of a dynamic team that is dedicated to patient care and a multidisciplinary approach to treatment. At Crescent Center, you'll have the autonomy to set your own schedule and arrange appointments as you see fit. We are proud to be the largest provider of physical therapy treatments to senior citizens, who make up the vast majority of our client base. The job requires traveling to private residences, so you must own your own car so you can get consistently get yourself to appointments on time. The duties of the role will vary from patient to patient, but all cases will include diagnostic assessment, documenting progress, and developing a treatment plan.

Benefits include competitive hourly wages and annual bonuses for reaching certain performance targets, corporate retirement plan with Crescent Center matching up to 6% of what you invest, and ample vacation time. Crescent Center employees are also eligible to receive discounts on specialty certification programs through Apperson University and the Cohen Institute.

Successful applicants must have a Master of Physical Therapy degree and a valid license from the Arizona State Board of Physical Therapy, which will be validated prior to the interview. Preference will be given to candidates with at least two years of experience, either in an inpatient or outpatient setting. The ability to easily and confidently converse with patients, as well as follow-up with clear written correspondence, is required.

To apply for the position, visit www.crescentcenter.net/careers and complete the online application form, quoting Job Reference Number T-3049. Applications will be accepted until March 31, and interviews will be scheduled for the following week.

13. What kind of position is being advertised?
    (A) Exercise class instructor
    (B) Hospital manager
    (C) Medical professional
    (D) Relationship therapist

14. What is indicated about Crescent Center?
    (A) It recently opened an office in Tucson.
    (B) Its staff members have won an award.
    (C) It currently has several job openings.
    (D) Its services are mainly used by the elderly.

15. What is mentioned as a benefit of the position?
    (A) Generous paid vacation time
    (B) Reimbursement for certification programs
    (C) Employer retirement contributions
    (D) Quarterly performance bonuses

16. What is NOT a requirement for the job?
    (A) A postgraduate degree
    (B) Excellent communication skills
    (C) Reliable transportation
    (D) At least two years of experience

Questions 17-21 refer to the following memo and report.

To: All Sandpiper Gym Employees
From: Ellen Weiland, Manager
Re: Concession Stand

February 6

Now that Sandpiper Gym has completed its building expansion project, we are looking for ways to make the best use of our space. Therefore, we plan to convert a portion of the lobby area into a concession stand that will sell energy bars, juices, and protein powder. VTX Gym on 17th Street has a similar stand, so we want to make sure that our members have access to equivalent amenities.

I am reviewing the various brands of energy bars on the market to determine which ones we should carry at our gym. Attached you will find a summary of the results. I believe that we should offer four options. In an effort to keep the process of supplying the goods from getting too complicated, I don't think it's a good idea to exceed four. Generally, our members are interested in high-protein snacks, due to their contributions to helping to maintain muscle mass. To begin with, we will only open the concession stand during the peak usage time. If sales are high enough to justify keeping it open longer, we will extend the hours of operation at a later time.

Sandpiper Gym Product Review

Date of Report: February 10   Compiled by: Ellen Weiland

Category: Energy Bars

Brand	Protein*	Sugar*
Ace Bar	12 g	10 g
Iron Zone	18 g	5 g
LL-Pump	10 g	26 g
Nu-Gold	16 g	20 g
Zampton	21 g	8 g

*Calculated per 60-gram serving. The bars range in size from 45 to 85 grams.

We will monitor sales closely to see whether protein bars or juice drinks are more popular to those working out during our peak time of 5:30 A.M. to 7:30 A.M.

17. Why will the business make a change?
    (A) To generate funding for a building project
    (B) To offer the same services as a competitor
    (C) To save money on overhead expenses
    (D) To respond to requests from members

18. In the memo, the word "carry" in paragraph 2, line 2, is closest in meaning to
    (A) approve
    (B) lift
    (C) supply
    (D) transport

19. What does Ms. Weiland imply about the variety of energy bars offered?
    (A) It should be increased steadily over time.
    (B) It is based on the number of items available.
    (C) It should remain limited to simplify ordering.
    (D) It will be determined by the members' preferences.

20. What is suggested about the concession stand?
    (A) It will be located near a locker room.
    (B) It will open in the early morning initially.
    (C) It will provide discounts to full-time members.
    (D) It will be staffed by energy bar company employees.

21. Which brand would probably be most popular with Sandpiper Gym's members?
    (A) Ace Bar
    (B) Iron Zone
    (C) Nu-Gold
    (D) Zampton

Questions 22-26 refer to the following notice, e-mail, and article.

NOTICE OF SCHEDULE CHANGE FOR CAST MEMBERS

November 14

Roger Kinney informed me this morning that more time is needed to complete his work than expected, so we are still unable to use the stage area. I spoke with the director, and we have decided to move the final dress rehearsal to November 16 at 7 P.M. Members of the press will be present. Please visit the costume designer before the rehearsal for a final check that your costume fits correctly and to receive adjustments if necessary.

There will be a short interview session on November 15 for journalists who cannot accommodate the change. Yolanda Byers and some of the other lead performers have volunteered to represent the cast.

–Jenna Frazier, Theater Manager

E-mail

To:	Nora Lysander <n.lysander@brighamtribune.com>
From:	Jenna Frazier <jenna@bradfordtheater.com>
Date:	November 14
Subject:	Performance Change

Dear Ms. Lysander,

I'm very sorry to make a change at the last minute, but we have postponed the dress rehearsal of *Holiday Harmonies* to tomorrow. An electrician is fixing our stage lights, and the project is not yet completed. We hope you can join us at 7 P.M. on November 16 for the performance. You will not have to present an entrance pass to get in, as I have put your name on our guest list. We are also holding a brief interview session at 7 P.M. on November 15, the rehearsal date. This will be the only opportunity to speak with the cast members. You are welcome to attend the interview instead of, or in addition to, the November 16 show.

Sincerely,

Jenna Frazier, Theater Manager

Holiday Harmonies Will Make Your Heart Sing
By Nora Lysander

Holiday Harmonies is a musical comedy set in the 1960s in which Donna Flynn, a young college graduate from a small town in the Midwest, travels to Europe to find adventure. With stunning costume designs and enchanting music, *Holiday Harmonies* is sure to please a wide audience. But what really sets it apart is the gifted singers and dancers in the show. "I love being a part of such a quirky production," said lead actress Rosita Provo in an interview earlier this week. "We just hope the audience is having as much fun as we are." *Holiday Harmonies* opens tonight at the Bradford Theater for a six-week run.

22. Who most likely is Mr. Kinney?
    (A) theater manager
    (B) A lead performer
    (C) An electrician
    (D) A journalist

23. What are all cast members asked to do?
    (A) Confirm a rehearsal time
    (B) Volunteer for an interview
    (C) Get their costumes fitted
    (D) Clean up a stage area

24. What has Ms. Frazier done for Ms. Lysander?
    (A) Prepared some interview questions
    (B) Mailed her an entrance pass
    (C) Sent her directions to a theater
    (D) Added her name to a list

25. What is suggested about Ms. Lysander?
    (A) She prefers musicals to dramas.
    (B) She visited Bradford Theater at least twice.
    (C) She reviews performances weekly.
    (D) She interviewed the *Holiday Harmonies* director.

26. What did Ms. Lysander like most about the show?
    (A) The music
    (B) The cast
    (C) The set design
    (D) The costumes

UNIT 03 문자 메시지 / 온라인 채팅

예제 공지
해설집 p.101

> **Jane Birkin [10:42 A.M.]**
> Hi, everyone. ❶I need help. The projector in the meeting room is not working.
>
> **Peter Parker [10:44 A.M.]**
> Not again.
>
> **Marco Verratti [10:44 A.M.]**
> Everything needs to be in order before lunch.
>
> **Jane Birkin [10:48 A.M.]**
> ❷Peter, could you come by and have a look?
>
> **Peter Parker [10:49 A.M.]**
> ❸On my way.
>
> **Marco Verratti [10:51 A.M.]**
> Apart from Jane, is everyone ready?
>
> **Fiona Lopez [10:53 A.M.]**
> Yes, we are all good.

화두
문제점이나 변경 내용을 고지

세부사항
정보나 의견을 교환하면서 업무 진행 상황을 파악하고 문제점 해결

마무리
요청사항을 전달하거나 향후 계획을 공유

공식 124 온라인 채팅은 인물 간 관계 파악에 주의한다.

온라인 채팅 대화문은 보통 3인 이상이 등장하므로 인물간 관계를 파악하는 것이 중요하다. 여러 화자가 번갈아 가며 대화를 주고 받게 되므로 누가 어떤 내용을 누구에게 말하는 것인지 정확히 파악하는 것이 관건이다

Q. At 10:49 A.M., what does Mr. Parker mean when he writes, "On my way"?
(A) He is coming to help Ms. Birkin.
(B) He will meet Mr. Verratti for lunch.

누구에게 하는 말인지 파악하기
Q. "가는 중이다"라는 말의 의미는?
❶❷ 제인: 영사기에 문제가 있는데 와서 봐주겠어요?
❸ 피터: 가는 중입니다.
정답 (A) 버킨 씨를 도우러 가는 중이다.

공식 125 구어체 표현이 나온다.

문자 메시지나 온라인 채팅 지문은 신속한 업무 처리를 위해서 즉석에서 주고받는 정보나 의견들로 구성되기 때문에 다른 지문 유형과는 달리 구어체 표현이 자주 나온다. 직역만으로는 의미 파악이 어려운 관용적인 표현들은 따로 암기해둔다.

Hang on. 잠시만요.	**I got it** 알겠어요.	**I'm off now.** 전 이제 가야겠어요.
I see. 그렇군요.	**It's on me.** 제가 낼게요.	**I'm on it.** 제가 맡을게요.
No doubt. 당연하죠.	**Will do.** 알겠어요. 좋아요.	**That'll work.** 그러면 될 거예요.

YBM TEST

Questions 1-2 refer to the following text-message chain.

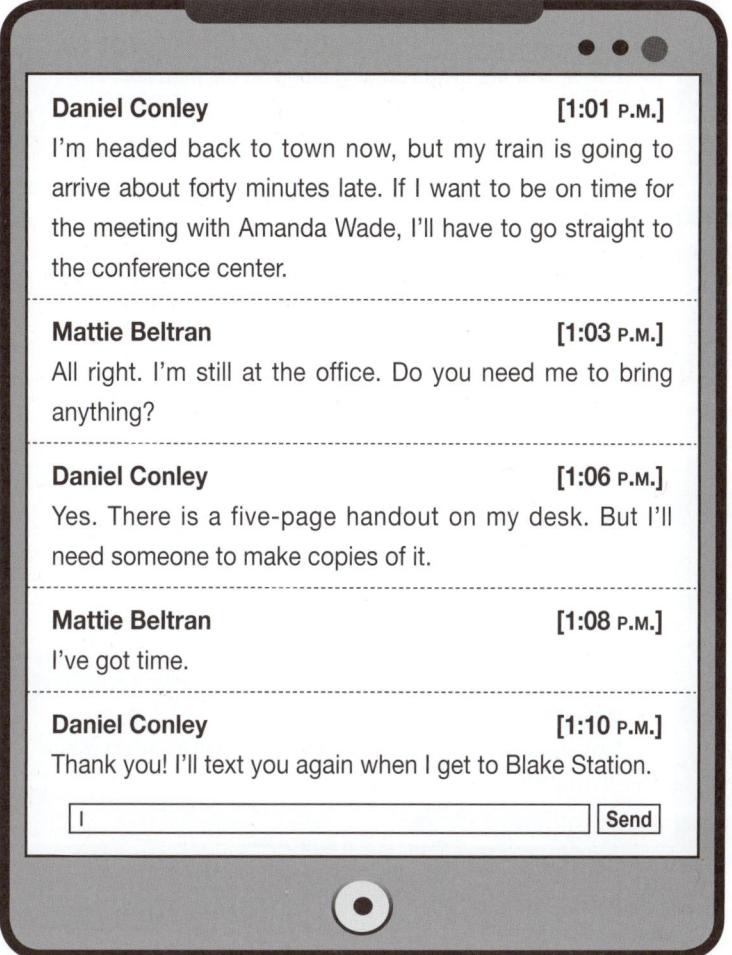

1. From where most likely did Mr. Conley send the message?
   (A) Blake Station
   (B) A train
   (C) A conference center
   (D) An office

2. At 1:08 P.M., what does Ms. Beltran most likely mean when she writes, "I've got time"?
   (A) She will pick up Mr. Conley.
   (B) She will copy some documents.
   (C) She will write a handout.
   (D) She will contact Ms. Wade.

Questions 3-4 refer to the following text-message chain.

Yamal Solanki   12:38 P.M.
Diana, how are things coming along on the third floor?

Diana Bristol   12:40 P.M.
We're on track to have all guest rooms up here cleaned by 2 P.M. as planned. Why?

Yamal Solanki   12:41 P.M.
We've got a tour group from Blakely Tourism coming at 1 P.M., and they'll want to check in at that time.

Diana Bristol   12:42 P.M.
I wish you would have texted sooner. I could have prioritized things differently.

Yamal Solanki   12:43 P.M.
It wouldn't have helped.

Diana Bristol   12:44 P.M.
You just found out yourself?

Yamal Solanki   12:45 P.M.
Exactly. Just do your best and I'll explain the situation when they arrive.

3. Where most likely does Ms. Bristol work?

(A) At a transportation service
(B) At a restaurant
(C) At a tour company
(D) At a hotel

4. At 12:43 P.M., what does Mr. Solanki most likely mean when he writes, "It wouldn't have helped"?

(A) He disagrees with Ms. Bristol's priorities.
(B) He got some information at the last minute.
(C) He does not know how to do a task.
(D) He lost the contact information he needed.

Questions 5-6 refer to the following text-message chain.

Chris Boone, 2:25 P.M.
My car broke down, so I'm going to be about twenty minutes late for my three o'clock tour of the modern painting exhibit. Can you cover for me?

Yuna Lee, 2:27 P.M.
Sorry, but I have my own tour at that time.

Chris Boone, 2:28 P.M.
I guess we can't combine the participants from the two tours because there will be too many people.

Yuna Lee, 2:29 P.M.
Yes, that's the issue. How about setting up the video projector and having your group watch the short film on art history until you arrive?

Chris Boone, 2:30 P.M.
That'll work. I'll ask Phil to get it ready. Thanks!

---

5. At 2:29 P.M., what does Ms. Lee most likely mean when she writes, "that's the issue"?
   (A) She is worried that participants will be late.
   (B) She thinks a group will be too big.
   (C) She is not familiar with an art exhibit.
   (D) She cannot find a video she needs.

6. What will Phil be asked to do?
   (A) Answer participants' questions
   (B) Edit an informational video
   (C) Give a museum tour
   (D) Set up some equipment

Questions 7-10 refer to the following online chat discussion.

Hanita Pandit [1:08 P.M.]
I'm in the process of reviewing the statistics on our airline's performance over the past quarter. The figure for lost luggage seems unusually low. Have you checked it?

Marilyn Kinsman [1:09 P.M.]
Yes, that number is correct. We've seen a sharp decline in the number of bags that did not reach the destination with the passenger who checked them in.

Kakeru Sanwa [1:10 P.M.]
That's wonderful news. We can attribute this positive change to the new handheld scanners used by the baggage team. Employees can check any bag in real time, making it easy to redirect those that have been misplaced.

Leo Ross [1:11 P.M.]
To be honest, I was skeptical at first because the upfront cost was so high, but now I'm completely on board.

Kakeru Sanwa [1:13 P.M.]
Yeah, it was the right decision to buy them.

Marilyn Kinsman [1:14 P.M.]
Thanks. I'm relieved that they are working out as planned.

Hanita Pandit [1:15 P.M.]
With such a low percentage of lost bags, this makes our record the best in the industry.

Leo Ross [1:18 P.M.]
We should use that point in our next ad campaign. Travelers would be interested to know how reliable we are, as this is often more important than the final ticket price.

Hanita Pandit [1:19 P.M.]
That's a valid point. I'll talk to Ms. Nunez to see how she and her team can incorporate this new information.

7. At 1:08 P.M., what does Ms. Pandit most likely mean when she says, "Have you checked it"?
   (A) She is waiting for a package to arrive.
   (B) She encourages others to read a performance report.
   (C) She thinks some data contains an error.
   (D) She wants feedback on a task she completed.

8. What has helped the company to improve its service?
   (A) Giving more power to managers
   (B) Hiring experienced employees
   (C) Using new equipment
   (D) Improving a training program

9. What is suggested about Ms. Kinsman?
   (A) She will present an adjusted plan.
   (B) She resolved a problem quickly.
   (C) She was concerned about expenses.
   (D) She made a purchasing decision.

10. In which department does Ms. Nunez most likely work?
    (A) Human Resources
    (B) Marketing
    (C) Finance
    (D) Sales

Questions 11-14 refer to the following online chat discussion.

Sandeep Ravel [9:12 A.M.] Hi, everyone. I'm here to give you all an update on the upcoming meeting with investors this Friday.

Theresa Moeller [9:13 A.M.] How are things going?

Sandeep Ravel [9:15 A.M.] I wanted to get our finance report printed professionally in nice packets. We can do this, but it's nearly triple what we budgeted for printing. It would be about $30 per packet.

Hannah Archer [9:16 A.M.] I had no idea it was that much.

Sandeep Ravel [9:17 A.M.] Me neither. That's why getting their estimate was a real letdown.

Cyril Lazarev [9:18 A.M.] My friend owns a print shop in Williamsburg. We could get the printing done there and then sent by courier.

Hannah Archer [9:19 A.M.] That sounds promising. Would you call to find out how much it would be for our specific project?

Cyril Lazarev [9:20 A.M.] Of course.

Sandeep Ravel [9:21 A.M.] Theresa, I need the final draft with the updated figures no later than September 18. And remember that you should not make a submission without proofreading it meticulously.

Theresa Moeller [9:22 A.M.] I wouldn't dare. You don't have to worry.

Sandeep Ravel [9:23 A.M.] Thanks! And we'll all meet in the morning on the day of the meeting to make sure everything is in order.

Cyril Lazarev [9:24 A.M.] I'll be recording the meeting since not everyone can be there.

Hannah Archer [9:25 A.M.] Thanks, Cyril. I'll watch it as soon as I get the chance.

11. Why is Mr. Ravel disappointed?
(A) Some printed packets were not delivered.
(B) A service is more expensive than expected.
(C) Some investors have rejected a proposal.
(D) A project may not meet the deadline.

12. What is Mr. Lazarev asked to do?
(A) Assign coworkers to a project
(B) Find a reliable courier
(C) Lead a presentation at a meeting
(D) Get some pricing details

13. At 9:22 A.M., what does Ms. Moeller most likely mean when she writes, "I wouldn't dare"?
(A) She plans to check a document carefully.
(B) She promises not to change a schedule.
(C) She will not disclose confidential information.
(D) She has already sent a final draft.

14. Who will be absent from the meeting on Friday?
(A) Mr. Ravel
(B) Ms. Moeller
(C) Ms. Archer
(D) Mr. Lazarev

Questions 15-18 refer to the following online chat discussion.

Kamal Taneja [10:24 A.M.]
As you know, I've booked Emerald Hotel for your upcoming trip to Singapore for the contract negotiations with Shona Manufacturing. I'm now working on the flights. Do you have any preferences?

Alberto Vaz [10:25 A.M.]
The first meeting is on June 8, so we should arrive the day before, but it doesn't really matter to me what time we arrive.

Nezha Hamed [10:26 A.M.]
We have to keep in mind, though, that there is no airport shuttle service offered by Emerald Hotel. So, I don't want to arrive too late, after the city buses stop running. I think that's around 11 P.M. for that area.

Kamal Taneja [10:27 A.M.]
That's no problem. There's a flight that gets you in by around 6 P.M. That way, you'll have time to relax and have some dinner at a nearby restaurant.

Alberto Vaz [10:29 A.M.]
That shouldn't be on us.

Kamal Taneja [10:30 A.M.]
Don't worry. It's not. All expenses will be covered by our firm.

Nezha Hamed [10:31 A.M.]
That's good to know. We have to keep the receipts from what we spend, right?

Kamal Taneja [10:32 A.M.]
Not for charges to the corporate credit card. But if you pay in cash for some reason, you should retain the receipt for later reimbursement.

Alberto Vaz [10:34 A.M.]
All right. We'll do that.

Kamal Taneja [10:35 A.M.]
I've got your passport details on file for the booking. If you're a member of the Azure Airlines Rewards Program, e-mail me your frequent flyer number so you can earn miles for your flight.

15. Why will Mr. Vaz and Ms. Hamed travel to Singapore?
    (A) To conduct some job interviews
    (B) To negotiate a business arrangement
    (C) To tour a manufacturing site
    (D) To provide training to a partner

16. What is Ms. Hamed concerned about?
    (A) Arriving when public transportation is not operating
    (B) Arriving late after a connecting flight has departed
    (C) Departing from the airport too early in the morning
    (D) Reserving a seat in advance on a hotel's shuttle

17. At 10:29 A.M., what does Mr. Vaz most likely mean when he writes, "That shouldn't be on us"?
    (A) He thinks the company should pay for a meal.
    (B) He wants Shona Manufacturing to book the flight tickets.
    (C) He does not believe there will be time to complete a task.
    (D) He is having trouble deciding which restaurant to visit.

18. What information does Mr. Taneja request?
    (A) An order number
    (B) A passport number
    (C) A membership number
    (D) A credit card number

UNIT 04 웹 페이지 / 안내문

예제 해설집 p.106

---

www.usedsalesforum.com/boats

FOR SALE: USED BOAT WITH TRAILER

Seller: Terrance Wyatt Contact Information: t.wyatt@ilangmail.com
Asking Price: $8,500 Posted: 3 days ago

I'm selling a used 18-foot Kelvey speed boat that is about five years old.

The boat has a gasoline-powered 8-cylinder engine, which recently underwent a mechanic's inspection. … 중략

Conversely, ◎the tires on the trailer are extremely worn and should be switched with new ones at the first opportunity.

주제 / 목적
중고 보트 판매

구체적인 정보
판매 제품에 대한 정보

권고사항
타이어 교체

공식 126 정보를 제공하고 설명하는 글로서, 지문 흐름이 정해져 있다.

웹 페이지 / 안내문은 제품 정보 및 사용 방법, 행사 소개, 회사 정책 안내 등 다양한 소재가 다뤄진다. 주로 〈주제/목적 → 구체적인 정보 → 지침/권고사항/추가정보〉의 순으로 구성된다.

Q. What is recommended for the new owner to do?
(A) Replace the tires as soon as possible
(B) Have the engine inspected

권고사항은 후반부에서 단서 찾기
Q. 새 소유주에게 권고되는 것은?
◎ 트레일러의 타이어가 너무 낡아서 빨리 교체되어야 한다.
정답 (A) 가능한 한 빨리 타이어를 교체하기

공식 127 웹 페이지 / 안내문에 자주 나오는 표현들이 있다.

지침이나 권고 사항, 상품 및 서비스의 이용 방법, 추가 정보에 대한 문의처와 참여 방법 등 안내문에 자주 나오는 표현들을 알아두면 유용하다.

지침 및 권고 사항	please adhere to / abide by / follow the guidelines / instructions 안내/지시 사항을 따르세요 we advise / recommend / urge you to ~할 것을 권고드립니다	
상품 및 서비스 이용	can be used only for ~에만 사용될 수 있다 To keep ~ in good condition ~을 좋은 상태로 유지하려면 as a precaution, power off ~ 예방조치로, ~의 전원을 끄세요 you have access to ~을 이용할 수 있다(~에 접근 권한이 있다)	please consult / refer to ~ ~를 참고하세요 use care when -ing ~할 때 주의하세요 avoid -ing ~를 피하세요
추가 정보 및 참여 방법	to download ~ form ~서류를 다운로드하시려면 available on our Web site 웹 사이트에서 확인할 수 있다 to browse comments / to view testimonials 후기를 보시려면	follow the link 링크를 따라가세요 to sign up for ~ ~에 등록하시려면 click here 여기를 클릭하세요

YBM TEST

Questions 1-2 refer to the following Web page.

---

https//www.maloyappliances/customerfeedback

Kitchen Appliances >> Dishwashers >> **Topeka-80**

Posted by: Sandra Hubert October 4

I cannot recommend the Topeka-80 dishwasher in good conscience. I carried out a great deal of research on various brands and models prior to buying this product, eventually settling on the Topeka-80 due to its Light Cycle, which was promoted as consuming far less electricity than average dishwasher cycles. In reality, its performance did not live up to the claims made by the company. While it's true that the electricity consumption is greatly reduced because of the short running time of the Light Cycle, the dishes do not come out thoroughly cleaned. As a result, they need to be rewashed, which negates any savings that were created.

In addition to this issue, water pools under the device when in operation, and I know it is not an installation error because the setup was performed by a licensed plumber. Fortunately, the dishwasher is still covered by the warranty, so I can get something that better suits my needs.

---

1. Why did Ms. Hubert decide to buy the Topeka-80?
   (A) It comes with a factory warranty.
   (B) It has an energy-efficient setting.
   (C) It has a large storage capacity.
   (D) It is offered at a low price.

2. What is suggested about Ms. Hubert?
   (A) She plans to return a product.
   (B) She will carry out some repairs.
   (C) She installed a machine incorrectly.
   (D) She has contacted customer service.

Questions 3-5 refer to the following information.

Burlington Community Services

The city of Burlington offers a Bulky Collection service so that residents may get rid of old refrigerators, microwaves, ovens, washing machines, and other appliances and pieces of furniture that are too big for the regular garbage service.

To book a collection:
- Visit www.burlington.gov/services31 and complete the form. You must have a minimum of 3 items to collect at a time. Payment is made in advance on the Web site by credit card, and you can select your preferred collection date.

Prior to the collection day:
- Place your items near the curb where your trash and yard waste are usually collected. Be sure they are not blocking the sidewalk.
- Secure the power cord to the side of each appliance with tape
- Print the confirmation page and tape it to one of the items

If city workers did not remove your requested collection on the scheduled day, please call Sanitation Manager Keith Devon at 555-6725, extension 22. To see a complete list of the items that we accept, e-mail Sandra Fox at sfox@burlington.gov.

3. What is the information mainly about?
   (A) Getting belongings inspected
   (B) Recycling yard waste
   (C) Disposing of large items
   (D) Installing kitchen appliances

4. What should residents do before the day of the visit?
   (A) Sweep debris from the sidewalk
   (B) Clean the objects thoroughly
   (C) Call for a confirmation number
   (D) Tape down electrical cords

5. Why should residents contact Mr. Devon?
   (A) To report that a service was not performed
   (B) To change the day of a visit
   (C) To request a more detailed list
   (D) To make arrangements for payment

Questions 6-9 refer to the following Web page.

---

www.concordlandscaping.com [Search]

| HOME | BEFORE & AFTER GALLERY | CUSTOMER REVIEWS | ABOUT US | BOOK AN APPOINTMENT |

Concord Landscaping was established in 1992 by Leonard Concord and his son, Arthur Concord, and the two still oversee operations today. In the early days, the business was no more than a truck and a two-man crew. Since that time, we have grown to become a respected business with locations in Preston City and Anaheim. We have a team of twenty full-time employees, all of whom have been working in the landscaping industry for five years or more, and we also hire seasonal part-time employees.

We can visit your home or business as a one-time project or on an ongoing basis for regular maintenance. We provide services for lawn maintenance, fertilizing, landscape design, tree and bush trimming, excavation, and more. In March of this year, we purchased a cross-cut saw and a stump grinder so that we could start offering tree removal as well.

We aim to serve not only our customers but also our community. We have organized clean-up projects at parks in Preston City and Anaheim, and we have made financial contributions to charities that serve the less fortunate. We are also proud to be a member of the Business Equality Union, which ensures fair hiring practices among private companies.

Whether you are interested in improving the appearance of your yard or getting rid of trees and shrubs that have become overgrown, we can help. You can book an appointment online or call us at 555-0177. If you'd like to browse comments from past and current Concord Landscaping customers, click here.

---

6. What is the purpose of the Web page information?

   (A) To highlight a company's achievements
   (B) To introduce a new service
   (C) To provide a business profile
   (D) To share some landscaping tips

7. Why has Concord Landscaping purchased equipment this year?

   (A) To keep up with the high customer demand
   (B) To comply with safety regulations
   (C) To provide a new service
   (D) To open a second branch

8. What is NOT mentioned about Concord Landscaping?

   (A) It has made donations to nonprofits.
   (B) It is a family-run business.
   (C) It employs experienced full-time workers.
   (D) It sells plants to customers.

9. What can the Web page's visitors do by clicking the link?

   (A) View images of past projects
   (B) Sign up for a monthly newsletter
   (C) Schedule an appointment
   (D) Read opinions from customers

Questions 10-13 refer to the following information.

Blue Planet Guidelines

Last Updated: June 1

Do you have experience taking snapshots of nature reserves, natural phenomena, or native flora and fauna? Then *Blue Planet* magazine needs you! We accept submissions of digital images on an ongoing basis. Contributions from freelancers make up approximately thirty percent of our media content, and we welcome the prospect of incorporating work from a wide range of individuals. Files can be sent to submissions@blueplanetmag.com.

Please adhere to the following guidelines so that we may process the submission efficiently:
- Files must be in the JPEG format only. There are many free online converters available if you have the image saved in another format.
- A minimum of 1800 x 1200 pixels is required.
- Images must be your own work and must not infringe on the copyrights of others. Each image must be accompanied by a signed legal release, a document that gives *Blue Planet* explicit permission to use and reproduce your image.
- We do not accept images that have a watermark. You will be properly credited in a caption beneath the image.
- The image should be in its original condition, so it should not be altered using editing software.

If your work is selected for publication—either in the print version, online, or both—we will contact you via e-mail. Financial compensation is provided at competitive market rates for all submissions. Due to the high volume of submissions we receive, we are unable to reply to all inquiries. Thank you for your understanding.

10. For whom is the information most likely intended?
(A) Internet bloggers
(B) Photographers
(C) Magazine subscribers
(D) Environmental scientists

11. The phrase "make up" in paragraph 1, line 3, is closest in meaning to
(A) offset
(B) invent
(C) prepare
(D) represent

12. What is required with all submissions?
(A) A sample contract
(B) A processing fee
(C) A written caption
(D) A release form

13. What is indicated about Blue Planet?
(A) It is published once a month.
(B) It responds to all inquiries.
(C) It is available in two formats.
(D) It gives advice on national park visits.

Questions 14-17 refer to the following Web page.

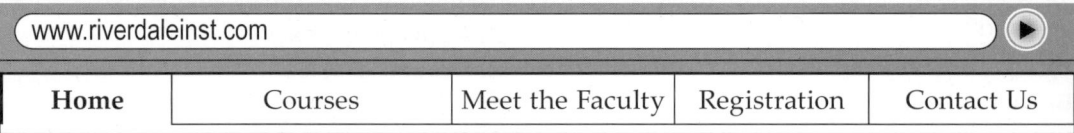

| Home | Courses | Meet the Faculty | Registration | Contact Us |

Riverdale Business Institute

Riverdale Business Institute is a leader in professional education, helping you meet your career goals through high-quality instruction and a comprehensive curriculum that will prepare you for the future. We are fully accredited by the Association of Business Development Education (ABDE), and our renewal by this body has been approved year after year without interruption. We meet all the criteria—both state and federal—for institutions of higher education, and our faculty members are well regarded in their respective fields.

New courses start every semester, covering topics such as economics, finance, corporate responsibility, and marketing. —[1]—. Early registration is recommended, as the most popular classes fill up quickly. If attending classes at our Los Angeles campus isn't right for you, the same material is available through our distance learning program; all you need is a reliable Internet connection.

If you choose Riverdale Business Institute, you can rest assured that you are getting an education that truly opens doors. Our graduates have one of the highest success rates in the industry. —[2]— This compares favorably to the national average of just eighty-two percent.

To find out more about Riverdale Business Institute, e-mail info@riverdaleinst.com to request an information packet that will be mailed to your preferred address. It includes biographies of our faculty, a timetable for the upcoming semester's classes, and details about our fees. —[3]—.

Ready to jump-start your career? Register online now! —[4]—. You can fill out the online application by clicking on the Registration tab above. The form takes approximately twenty minutes to complete, and you will receive e-mail confirmation that we have received it.

14. What is suggested about Riverdale Business Institute?
    (A) It plans to expand the size of its staff.
    (B) It has campuses throughout the country.
    (C) It has passed an official recognition process.
    (D) It was formerly owned by the ABDE.

15. What is mentioned about courses?
    (A) They focus on managing small teams.
    (B) They are offered three times a year.
    (C) They are all taught by business owners.
    (D) They can be taken in two formats.

16. According to the Web page, what is included in the information packet?
    (A) A survey card
    (B) A class schedule
    (C) A campus map
    (D) An application form

17. In which of the positions marked [1], [2], [3], and [4] does the following sentence best belong?

    "In fact, ninety-five percent of our students find work within six months of graduating."

    (A) [1]
    (B) [2]
    (C) [3]
    (D) [4]

Questions 18-22 refer to the following notice and online form.

NOTICE TO SOUTHSIDE SUITES TENANTS

From July 1, Southside Suites will be outsourcing its maintenance work. To use the service, complete the necessary form at www.ortizmaintenance.com/request. When making a request, be sure to list the room where the repairs must be done as well as the brand and serial number of the appliance (if applicable). You should also tell the time you are available during regular business hours and how soon you need the repair completed. If you are unable to be present for the repairs, you must check the box to indicate that you give permission for a technician to enter your home. In this case, Kirby Patricio from the rental office will accompany the technician. The Ortiz Maintenance staff will do their best to keep the appointment times they set. However, if a more pressing matter arises, they may have to postpone your appointment. Questions may be directed to the Ortiz Maintenance manager, John Dumont, at 555-4531. Please note that if you are the one responsible for any damage that needs repairing, our accountant, Clara Krueger, will bill you for the relevant charges. Thank you for your cooperation.

---

www.ortizmaintenance.com/request

| HOME | ABOUT US | **REQUEST** | CONTACT |

Ortiz Maintenance Request Form

Building Name and Unit: Southside Suites, Unit 322
Name: Laurel Tozier   Phone number: (466) 555-0179
Date of Request: July 26   Availability (Weekdays 9 A.M.–6 P.M.): None
  ✓ I consent to an Ortiz Maintenance technician entering my home while I am absent.

Area/Device in Need of Repair: Gargola brand air conditioning unit in the bedroom

Description of the Problem: When I turn on the device, there is a noticeable burning smell. I'm not using the air conditioning unit in that room at all now, which is very inconvenient because of the hot weather. I'm surprised that the device is having this problem because the landlord took out both the old dishwasher and air conditioner and installed new ones last month when I renewed my lease. Tomorrow I am leaving for an overseas vacation for seven days, returning on the 2nd. Therefore, I would like this matter resolved by the morning of August 2, if possible.

18. According to the notice, why might a work appointment be delayed?
    (A) If the work falls on a national holiday
    (B) If components need to be ordered
    (C) If a form is filled out incorrectly
    (D) If more urgent work comes along

19. What is mentioned about the air conditioner?
    (A) It was replaced in June.
    (B) It is the same brand as the dishwasher.
    (C) It is the only one in Ms. Tozier's home.
    (D) It was showing problems for a long time.

20. What is true about Ms. Tozier?
    (A) She plans to contact the business on August 2.
    (B) She frequently works overseas.
    (C) She wants to renew her apartment lease.
    (D) She will take a one-week vacation.

21. What information requested in the notice was NOT provided by Ms. Tozier?
    (A) How soon she needs the work completed
    (B) In which room the maintenance is needed
    (C) How long ago a problem started
    (D) What an appliance's serial number is

22. What is suggested about Mr. Patricio?
    (A) He is the head of the maintenance department.
    (B) He will visit Ms. Tozier's home with a technician.
    (C) He may send a repair bill to Ms. Tozier.
    (D) He will make some repairs in August.

Questions 23-27 refer to the following Web page and e-mails.

www.gusmanmotivation.com/tour

Anthony Gusman National Tour

Motivational speaker Anthony Gusman started out working at Henley Incorporated, but discovered that his true passion was working directly with people. Since founding the Gusman Institute in Los Angeles ten years ago, Anthony has been teaching sold-out classes at that site. Because the demand for his talents has grown, he has decided to take his message on the road with a one-day workshop.

The one-day workshop will build on Gusman's "Fundamental Five," his five points for achieving success that were outlined in his best-selling book of the same name. Audience members should be familiar with these points already in order to make the most of the workshop.

June Tour Dates*

Seattle: June 8 (Shelton Convention Center)
June 11 (Tavares Plaza)
Dallas: June 13 (Pearl Hotel),
Atlanta: June 18 (Whitetail Hall),
June 20 (The Chambers)
Boston: June 25 (Soto Conference Center)

Contact the individual venues for ticketing information.
More dates will be added for July and August, with the tour running until August 31.

E-mail

To:	Anthony Gusman <anthony@gusmanmotivation.com>
From:	Sarah Nagel <s.nagel@snyderincorporated.com>
Date:	July 5
Subject:	Private appearance

Dear Mr. Gusman,

My name is Sarah Nagel, and I am a senior account executive at UBP, an advertising firm that works mainly with clients in the transportation industry. Last month, I had the great privilege of participating in your one-day workshop, the second one of your tour. I found the event to be informative and inspirational, so I would like to invite you to our office for a staff training event. Please let me know whether you make private appearances such as this.

Best regards,

Sarah Nagel

E-mail

To: Sarah Nagel <s.Nagel@snyderincorporated.com>
From: Anthony Gusman <anthony@gusmanmotivation.com>
Date: July 6
Subject: RE: Private appearance

Dear Ms. Nagel,

I'm pleased that you had a positive experience at the workshop, and I hope what you learned there will help you to further your career and give you confidence in the workplace. Your idea for a private appearance at UBP is intriguing. I have not made such activities part of my business plan thus far, but that does not mean it is not a possibility, especially since I have particular insights into your field thanks to my time at Henley Incorporated. I am busy with the tour now, but I will e-mail you again within a few days of its completion so that we may explore the matter further.

Sincerely,

Anthony Gusman

---

23. What is suggested about Mr. Gusman?
    (A) He offers some of the class sessions online.
    (B) He is going on tour for the first time.
    (C) He will visit only four cities during his tour.
    (D) He plans to open a second branch in Los Angeles.

24. What is suggested about the one-day workshop?
    (A) It includes a free best-selling book for attendees.
    (B) Its tickets can be purchased at the Gusman Institute.
    (C) It is designed for corporate executives only.
    (D) Its attendees should learn some concepts in advance.

25. Where did Ms. Nagel attend Mr. Gusman's workshop?
    (A) Seattle
    (B) Dallas
    (C) Atlanta
    (D) Boston

26. What do Ms. Nagel and Mr. Gusman have in common?
    (A) They are both living and working in the same city.
    (B) They have both been employed by Henley Incorporated.
    (C) They both have experience in the marketing field.
    (D) They are both teaching workshops on business success.

27. What will Mr. Gusman most likely do?
    (A) Provide a bulk price on workshop tickets
    (B) Refer Ms. Nagel to a colleague
    (C) Arrange an online class for UBP
    (D) Contact Ms. Nagel in September

UNIT 05 기사/발표문

예제 기사

해설집 p.114

Tarbury Tribune   By Holly Lenz, March 12

Following a poor profits forecast, **Q1❶Tarbury Manufacturing has announced a set of steps aimed at increasing worker output**. The first will be to introduce flexible working hours from the beginning of next month, … 중략

Q1❷The plans also include introducing a bonus scheme in all departments by the end of the summer. … 중략

Observers in the industry disagree as to whether the move will produce the intended results. **Q2❶"Due to the thin profit margin in Tarbury's market sector, a significant increase in output by workers would be needed to offset the costs of keeping the programs running over a prolonged period,"** said Frank Gehry, the market expert.

- 주제: 생산성 제고를 위한 정책 발표
- 세부: 신규 정책의 구체적 내용

- 주제: 추가 정책
- 세부: 정책의 배경

- 주제: 전문가들의 반응
- 세부: 전문가 인터뷰 내용

공식 128 단락별 주제를 파악해 둔다.

기사나 발표문은 난이도가 높은 반면 〈서론-본론-결론〉으로 구조가 논리적이고, 육하원칙의 정보가 명확하게 제시된다. 단락마다 「주제+세부사항」으로 구성되어 있고 각 단락과 그에 연관된 문제가 동일한 순서대로 출제되는 편이므로 단락별로 주제만 파악해도 쉽게 단서를 찾을 수 있다.

Q1. What is the article mainly about?
 (A) Providing flexible payment plans
 (B) Improving worker productivity

단락별 주제 취합하기
Q1. 주로 무엇에 관한 기사인가?
❶ T사가 생산성 향상을 위한 정책을 발표했다.
❷ 보너스를 주는 정책도 포함되어 있다.
정답 (B) 직원 생산성 개선 방안

공식 129 인용문에 주목해라.

기사에는 " "(인용 부호)에 관계자나 전문가 등을 인터뷰한 내용이 삽입되고, 이를 활용한 문제가 자주 출제된다. 특정 인물이 문제에 나올 경우, 대문자 이름과 함께 인용 부호가 있는 부분에서 단서를 찾는다.

Q2. According to the article, what problem does Mr. Gehry mention?
 (A) The performance targets are considered to be unachievable.
 (B) The changes could be too expensive to maintain in the long run.

인용문 내용 파악하기
Q2. Mr. Gehry가 언급한 문제점은 무엇인가?
❶ T사의 수익이 낮다. 장기 운영 비용을 감당하려면 생산성이 상당히 증가되어야 한다.
정답 (B) 변화를 장기간 유지하는 데 비용이 너무 많이 든다.

YBM TEST

Questions 1-3 refer to the following article.

New Changes for Old Property

APPLETON, October 15—The director of the historic home McDougall Manor, Leona Helm, announced plans to make its entrances wheelchair accessible. The spacious building has six entrances for the public. Four of these can currently only be accessed by stairs. Upon completion of the project, all entrances will have ramps. City regulations currently only require one wheelchair ramp per building. However, Helm hopes the change will attract more people to the site, especially those who previously had difficulty exploring the various wings on their own. The entire site must be closed during construction for safety reasons. Helm plans to do this during the slowest month to minimize revenue loss.

The estimated cost of the project is $25,000. After Helm had a failed attempt to get a grant from the city, members of the Appleton Tourism Club volunteered to hold a fundraiser in support of the project. Unfortunately, there was a poor turnout. Helm and her staff reached out to the community for donations from individuals. This was a successful approach, as local businesswoman Cynthia Wilkins made a very generous donation to the cause that accounted for nearly eighty percent of the funds needed. The project will get underway next year, beginning shortly after the first of the year and reaching completion by January 31.

1. According to the article, what is the reason for the renovations?
   (A) To restore a building to its original design
   (B) To reduce waiting times
   (C) To comply with safety regulations
   (D) To attract more visitors

2. Where did McDougal Manor receive most of the funds for the project?
   (A) From a city grant
   (B) From its general budget
   (C) From a private donor
   (D) From a club's fundraiser

3. What is implied about McDougal Manor?
   (A) It is looking for volunteers with construction skills.
   (B) It receives the fewest number of visitors in January.
   (C) It is the meeting place of the Appleton Tourism Club.
   (D) Its annual operating budget is $25,000.

Questions 4-7 refer to the following article.

Graderville Officials to Take Action against Seagulls

May 18—City officials in Graderville have announced an initiative to reduce the seagull population in town, focusing primarily on the Rockwell Beach area. —[1]—. Seagulls have long been a nuisance to beachgoers, and they can potentially be carriers of disease. Visitors to Graderville complained about the problem in record numbers last summer, prompting action from the city.

The initiative will involve using trained dogs to chase the seagulls off the beach, encouraging them to nest and seek food elsewhere. Other seaside communities have seen up to a 97% reduction in seagulls using this method. —[2]—. City workers will also place spikes on windowsills and rooftops near the beach to prevent seagulls from perching.

Scientists at Wayton University have been studying the seagull population in the area and tracking the figures over the years. "According to our calculations," said Wesley Lewis, "there has been an increase of 60% in the seagull population compared to just three years ago. —[3]—. This is partially due to people feeding them, either on purpose or by leaving food waste out, which attracts more birds. That's why they're spending more time in town than ever before."

People who leave food scraps on the ground or those who throw away food in trash cans without a lid will be fined $50 for a first offense and up to $300 for subsequent offenses. Officials hope this will deter people from providing food sources for seagulls in town. —[4]—.

4. What caused the city to launch the initiative?

   (A) New government regulations
   (B) A failed health inspection
   (C) Complaints from tourists
   (D) A budget surplus

5. What is implied about Mr. Lewis?

   (A) He is concerned about animal rights.
   (B) He is a Graderville city official.
   (C) He has published a study.
   (D) He works at a university.

6. According to the article, why will some people in Graderville receive a fine?

   (A) For dumping pollutants in the water
   (B) For disposing of food improperly
   (C) For disrupting the nests of seagulls
   (D) For staying at the beach after hours

7. In which of the positions marked [1], [2], [3], and [4] does the following sentence best belong?

   "It works best when employed during the peak hours of activity."

   (A) [1]
   (B) [2]
   (C) [3]
   (D) [4]

Questions 8-11 refer to the following article.

April 9—A spokesperson for the Bureau of Domestic Affairs on the island of Chilwa has announced the launch of Chilwa in Focus (CIF), a program whose mission is to increase the number of annual visitors to the island by a minimum of twenty-five percent over the next three years. Over $1 million in public funds has been allocated to CIF, which will act as a stimulus for the travel sector by running advertisements around the world that showcase the island's natural beauty and world-class accommodations. —[1]—. Capital will also be provided for participation in prestigious travel exhibitions around the world, which are expected to be highly beneficial. —[2]—. As a relatively unknown island, Chilwa has the chance to make great strides in brand recognition and becoming a "must-see" destination.

"It is imperative that we support this industry," said Geraldine Sampson, who is spearheading the program. "Services to foreign travelers accounted for just five percent of our gross domestic product ten years ago, but that was when we benefited heavily from employment in the industrial goods sector. —[3]—. Because production facilities have slowly closed down over time, we need to shift resources to industries with a positive future outlook and take a proactive approach to creating a stable economy."

In addition to promoting popular seaside attractions, such as the white sand beaches that surround the island, the program will also publicize destinations in the island's predominantly rural interior. —[4]—. The area is considered an untapped market for adventure holiday packages, as younger travelers with disposable income are likely to be interested in visiting sites that are off the beaten path. Chilwa residents are invited to provide feedback about the program by visiting www.chilwaif.org.

8. What is the article about?
   (A) An island's storm recovery plans
   (B) An effort to boost tourism
   (C) A program to reduce pollution
   (D) A new trend in tourist activities

9. According to the article, what has changed about Chilwa?
   (A) Its residents have started to travel more.
   (B) It had a significant growth in population.
   (C) Its laws make it easier for foreigners to visit.
   (D) It used to have more manufacturing jobs.

10. What is suggested about the island's central area?
    (A) It is mainly comprised of countryside.
    (B) It has become a popular destination.
    (C) It is the site of the island's airport.
    (D) It has an excellent view of the seaside.

11. In which of the positions marked [1], [2], [3], and [4] does the following sentence best belong?

    "The one in London is predicted to be particularly advantageous."

    (A) [1]
    (B) [2]
    (C) [3]
    (D) [4]

Questions 12-15 refer to the following announcement.

Owing to a ballot measure passed in the most recent state election, a one percent sales tax will be added to certain purchases in order to fund a development initiative that will upgrade highways and bridges throughout the state. Supporters of the program expect it to create conditions that are attractive to business owners, bringing in start-ups and larger chains. "Under our current situation, companies are reluctant to establish business sites in the state because the poor condition of our roadways makes transportation unreliable. — [1] —. By removing some of these obstacles through this program, we can become better suited for business development and make the most of our resources," said State Senator Maurice Levy, who drafted the ballot measure. "Motorists who use the road network for non-commercial purposes will also enjoy the superior driving surface, wider lanes, and reinforced bridges. — [2] —."

The funds generated by the tax increase will be dispersed at the regional level. Each region will appoint an Infrastructure Action Committee to ascertain the best way to use the funds. Although the state will provide support in the form of planning templates and personnel recommendations, each committee will be responsible for its own region and will not be required to report to another body. — [3] —.

While it is rather unusual for voters to approve of tax increases, the measure passed by an overwhelming majority of eighty-six percent in favor and fourteen percent opposed. — [4] —. "By approving this plan, voters demonstrated that they understand that the change is in their best interest," explained Levy. "Job opportunities in the construction sector will rise in the short-term, and the change could spur long-term growth in other industries and provide greater employment throughout the state."

12. What is the purpose of the announcement?
    (A) To challenge some election results
    (B) To clarify a change in safety regulations
    (C) To outline an improvement plan
    (D) To gather support for an initiative

13. What most likely is true about the regional-level committees?
    (A) They will make decisions independently.
    (B) Their meetings will be open to the public.
    (C) They will be appointed by Mr. Levy.
    (D) Their members will receive a salary from the state.

14. According to Mr. Levy, why did voters support a proposal?
    (A) It will improve environmental conditions.
    (B) It will create more local jobs.
    (C) It will reduce the overall tax burden.
    (D) It will maximize worker productivity.

15. In which of the positions marked [1], [2], [3], and [4] does the following sentence best belong?
    "A poor record for road safety is also discouraging prospective investors."
    (A) [1]
    (B) [2]
    (C) [3]
    (D) [4]

Questions 16-19 refer to the following article.

Joyia Soars to Top Spot in Food Industry Niche

September 30 — Joyia has overtaken Freezeland Snacks as the leader among healthy snack food companies. CEO Camille Klein spoke at the Food Distributors Conference last week about her meteoric rise to success, which she says was fueled by innovation, cooperation, and compassion. With the company contributing five percent of its annual revenue to nonprofit organizations, Joyia certainly lives up to its slogan, "Health and Community." —[1]—.

Klein has been working in the food industry for the fifteen years. She studied business management at Concordia, a highly respected university in New York, graduating at the top of her class. She then took a job at Acres Cuisine, one of the country's largest producers of pre-packaged microwavable meals. —[2]—. After seven years, she left the company to form Joyia.

"I'm grateful for my experience at Acres Cuisine," Klein stated in a recent interview. "It gave me insight into the inner workings of the industry, which has been invaluable in my new venture. I got the idea for Joyia during my days at Concordia, but it wasn't until working at Acres Cuisine that I had the confidence to move forward with it."

Klein created a business plan based on a perceived gap in the market. "As people became more health-conscious, the popularity of healthy snack foods grew significantly. —[3]—. Most contained honey, but studies by nutrition scientists have shown that honey breaks down in the body very similarly to high fructose corn syrup and other sweeteners." In response to this observation, Klein created the granola bar Granogo, and Joyia's technicians have developed numerous varieties tailored specifically to the nutritional requirements of children, adults, athletes, diabetics, and the elderly. —[4]—. Consumers can expect Joyia to be a supermarket staple for years to come.

16. What is indicated about Ms. Klein?
    (A) She donates a portion of her company's profits.
    (B) She has worked as a CEO for fifteen years.
    (C) She purchased a competitor's company.
    (D) She has a degree in nutrition science.

17. When did Ms. Klein first get the idea for her business?
    (A) While participating in a conference
    (B) While working at Acres Cuisine
    (C) While attending university
    (D) While searching for a business partner

18. What is implied about Granogo?
    (A) Its ingredients are supplied domestically.
    (B) It is mainly sold in health food shops.
    (C) Its packaging is made from organic materials.
    (D) It has different formulas for various needs.

19. In which of the positions marked [1], [2], [3], and [4] does the following sentence best belong?

    "Yet there were no truly sugar-free options available."

    (A) [1]
    (B) [2]
    (C) [3]
    (D) [4]

Questions 20-24 refer to the following article and announcement.

Survey Results Bode Well for Vero Incorporated

January 7—An annual survey conducted by the National Hotel Association (NHA) revealed that Vero Incorporated, founded by Renaldo Zito, has attained the coveted top spot in its category for the fifth consecutive year. The survey was given to thousands of hotel guests, who were asked to rate their hotel experience based on factors such as customer service, room quality, overall value, and amenities. Most hotels which are recognized on NHA's list experience notable growth in the following year thanks to increased publicity and an improved public perception. Vero Incorporated performed best among hotels aimed at serving trade and industry professionals. The company has a loyal customer base, as shown by the comments in the survey. "If I can't stay at a Vero property, I reconsider my travel plans," said Adeline Dewitt, a survey respondent and frequent traveler.

"We're extremely pleased with this outcome," said Minu Pandey, Vero Incorporated's CFO. "Our primary focus is on the comfort and convenience of our guests, and NHA's ranking confirms that our hard work is paying off."

Speaking at a press event, Vero Incorporated's president, Keylon Tillman, also expressed satisfaction with the result. "As we've expanded from our headquarters in Boston, to sites all over the country, including our most recently opened branch in Dallas, we have never wavered from providing world-class care for our guests," Tillman said.

Staff Announcement

Retirement Banquet for Jerod Connelly

After over twenty years of serving Vero Incorporated, CEO Jerod Connelly will retire from his duties next month. A banquet to celebrate his contributions will be held at the company headquarters on Friday, October 7. A buffet dinner will be served, and Mr. Connelly will address attendees. All staff members are welcome to attend, but notice of attendance is required so that we can make the proper arrangements for the meal and seating. Call Jia Bai at extension 22 to have a seat set aside for you.

We are thankful for Mr. Connelly's hard work over the years, and we wish him the best as he goes into retirement in order to spend more time with his family. The company's CFO will replace Mr. Connelly, and the two are working together to make the transition as smooth as possible.

20. What is the purpose of the article?
    (A) To report on a business's achievement
    (B) To announce a change in hotel regulations
    (C) To explain a hotel's research efforts
    (D) To recruit members for an industry association

21. What is indicated about Vero Incorporated?
    (A) It caters to business travelers.
    (B) Its staff undergoes regular training.
    (C) It has the lowest prices in its industry.
    (D) It operates a loyalty program.

22. What is indicated about the event on October 7?
    (A) It will feature the distributions of awards.
    (B) It will take place in Boston.
    (C) It will be for full-time employees only.
    (D) It will have live music.

23. Why should employees call Ms. Bai?
    (A) To volunteer for a presentation
    (B) To join a mailing list
    (C) To select an evening meal
    (D) To reserve a spot

24. Who will take over Mr. Connelly's role?
    (A) Ms. Dewitt
    (B) Ms. Pandey
    (C) Mr. Tillman
    (D) Mr. Zito

Questions 25-29 refer to the following article, Web site, and review.

Franklin City Restaurants: Top Picks
By Cecelia Casillas

This weekend, why not upgrade your meal from mundane to memorable? Try one of the sites below for a dining experience you won't forget!

Comida: Comida offers authentic Spanish dishes and live performances of traditional music. The main dining area has a spectacular view of the city.

Benny's Grill: For large portion sizes, fresh seafood, and live music, visit Benny's Grill. Because the restaurant is located right on the shoreline, you can look over beautiful Starfish Bay while you eat.

The Garden: The Garden offers delicious Chinese food served on its rooftop patio, which gives diners a great opportunity to see Franklin City from a unique perspective. Local amateur musicians play at the restaurant frequently.

Wonder Café: Located in the Franklin City Aquarium, Wonder Café has aquarium walls on three sides of the café to give diners a perfect view of the sharks and other wildlife in the tank. A discount admission ticket to the aquarium is given to diners who complete their meal before noon.

---

www.franklincity.gov/tourism/events

Franklin City Events: Week of July 10

Sunday, July 10: Franklin City Farmers Market, Warwick Park [8 A.M.–4 P.M.]
   Purchase fresh, locally grown fruits and vegetables at below supermarket prices.

Tuesday, July 12: Singing Contest, Benny's Grill [7 P.M.–9 P.M.]
   Show off your talent for the chance to win a Benny's Grill T-shirt.

Friday, July 15: Classic Film Series, Montague Theater [7:30 P.M.–9:30 P.M.]
   Screening of director James Faulkner's drama *Twisted Lines*.

Saturday, July 16: Outdoor Arts and Culture Festival, Seneca Park [10:00 A.M.–5 P.M.]
   Watch art demonstrations, purchases paintings, and enjoy a traditional dance performance.

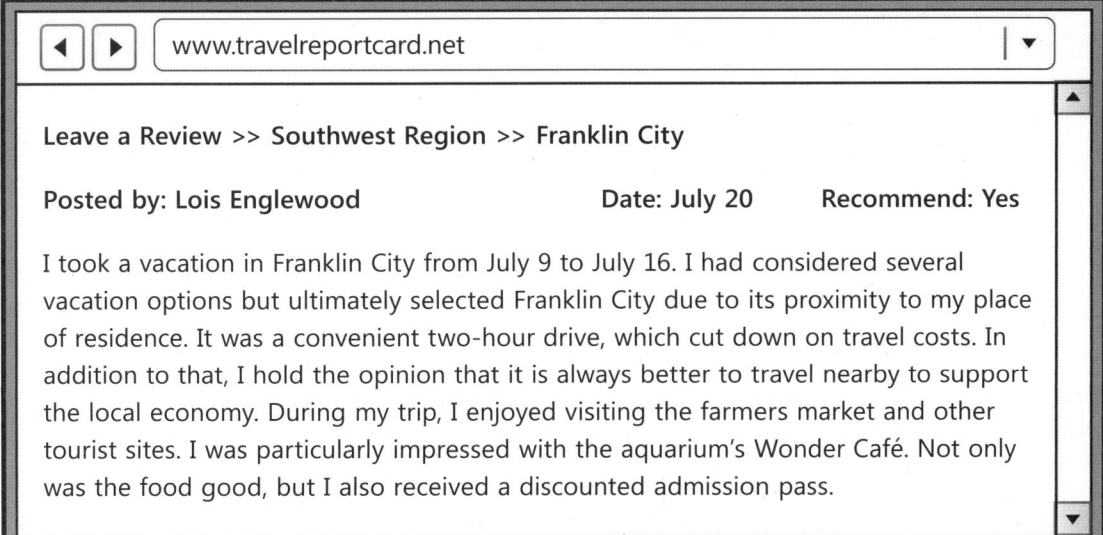

Leave a Review >> Southwest Region >> Franklin City

Posted by: Lois Englewood   **Date: July 20**   **Recommend: Yes**

I took a vacation in Franklin City from July 9 to July 16. I had considered several vacation options but ultimately selected Franklin City due to its proximity to my place of residence. It was a convenient two-hour drive, which cut down on travel costs. In addition to that, I hold the opinion that it is always better to travel nearby to support the local economy. During my trip, I enjoyed visiting the farmers market and other tourist sites. I was particularly impressed with the aquarium's Wonder Café. Not only was the food good, but I also received a discounted admission pass.

25. What feature is included in all of the restaurants?
    (A) An extensive menu
    (B) Live music
    (C) A great view
    (D) Large portions

26. What is true about the singing competition?
    (A) It was held near a coastline.
    (B) It provided vouchers to the winners.
    (C) It is hosted every week.
    (D) It was judged by diners.

27. According to the review, why did Ms. Englewood want to visit Franklin City?
    (A) She had a coupon for a hotel there.
    (B) It was recommended by a friend.
    (C) She did not have to travel far.
    (D) It has cheap flights from her town.

28. In the review, the word "hold" in paragraph 1, line 4, is closest in meaning to
    (A) occupy
    (B) grasp
    (C) own
    (D) maintain

29. What is suggested about Ms. Englewood?
    (A) She decided to extend her vacation.
    (B) She ate at Wonder Café in the morning.
    (C) She made a purchase at the farmers market.
    (D) She visited an aquarium twice.

UNIT 06 기타 양식

[예제] 쿠폰

해설집 p.122

At 8th Street Books, we are celebrating the fact that we have been in business for five years, so we want to offer a special deal to our valued customers. Present this coupon at checkout between April 3 and April 9 to receive the following deal:

❶Buy 2 Hardcover Books, Get a 3rd Book Free*

This coupon can be used for any book, including new releases and textbooks, which rarely go on sale. Thank you for your business!

❷*The two most expensive books will be regular price. Not valid with any other offers.

주제/목적
쿠폰 행사 안내

세부사항
행사 일정, 쿠폰 혜택, 해당 품목 안내

추가 정보
유의 사항

공식 130 *(별표)와 Note(주의 사항) 주변에 답이 있다.

양식 지문은 이름, 주소, 날짜, 가격 등의 단편 정보들이 정답의 단서이므로, 지문의 구성 요소와 정보의 위치를 먼저 간략히 파악한 후 문제를 푼다. 특히, *와 Note, 굵은 문자로 표기된 정보가 정답 단서로 자주 활용되므로 이 부분에 주목한다.

Q. What is indicated on the coupon?
  (A) The coupon will be valid for three days.
  (B) The cheapest item will be free.

*(별표) 주변 확인하고 보기와 대조하기
Q. 쿠폰에 명시된 것은?
❶ 2권 사면 3번째 책은 무료이다.
❷ 가장 비싼 2권은 정가이다.
정답 (B) 가장 저렴한 품목이 무료일 것이다.

공식 131 양식 지문의 종류별로 빈출 항목들이 있다.

송장, 영수증, 할인 쿠폰 등 각종 양식 지문이 출제되는데, 각 지문별로 자주 출제되는 항목들을 미리 알아두면 지문을 파악하는 데 도움이 된다.

flyer(전단지) **coupon(쿠폰)**	• 할인 이유	– clearance sale 창고 정리 판매 anniversary 기념일 relocation 이전
	• 할인 제외 품목	– This offer doesn't apply to leather goods. 이 제안은 가죽 제품에는 적용되지 않습니다.
	• 할인 조건	– Use this coupon code to save $20 off orders over $100. 100달러 이상 구매 시 20달러를 할인 받을 수 있도록 이 쿠폰 코드를 사용하세요.
invoice(송장) **receipt(영수증)**		order from 주문자 customer name 주문자 send to 수령인 ship to 수령인 bill to 결제자 paid by 결제자

Questions 1-2 refer to the following table of contents.

JOURNAL OF SOCIAL PSYCHOLOGY

Vol. 322

Table of Contents

Letter from Editor Monica Conyers	2
Effects of Technology on Human Relationships	3
The Role of Mass Media in Positive Self-Image	16
Interview with Daksha Lodi, Recipient of the Rosebud Prize	28
Strategies for Anxiety Reduction: A University Case Study	41
Cooperative Group Behavior in a Professional Setting	56

Submissions may be sent to editor@journalofsp.com. Only authors considered for publication will be contacted.

1. Who is Mr. Lodi?
   (A) A business journalist
   (B) An award winner
   (C) A job applicant
   (D) A university professor

2. Where can readers find out about working together?
   (A) On page 3
   (B) On page 16
   (C) On page 41
   (D) On page 56

Questions 3-4 refer to the following brochure.

Valley Culinary School

April Session [Updated]: Every Tuesday 6:30 P.M.–8:30 P.M.

Valley Culinary School has split the intermediate level into two sections for April to accommodate the higher registration numbers. We are accepting enrollments until March 16.

Beginner /   Taught by Elizabeth Winstead
Knife Skills, Sanitation, Soups

Lower Intermediate /   Taught by Takahiro Fujimura
Sauces, Choosing Seasonings, Grilling

Upper Intermediate /   Taught by John Boyd
Poaching, Desserts, Handmade Pasta

Advanced /   Taught by Vanessa Sahni
Pastries, Seafood, Menu Creation

3. Why has Valley Culinary School adjusted its schedule?
   (A) Intermediate students did not pass a class.
   (B) Some classrooms are being renovated.
   (C) An instructor could not teach a class.
   (D) Enrollment figures have increased.

4. Who will teach students about selecting herbs?
   (A) Ms. Winstead
   (B) Mr. Fujimura
   (C) Mr. Boyd
   (D) Ms. Sahni

Questions 5-7 refer to the following survey.

Shiny Smile Dental Clinic
Customer Survey

Thank you for taking the time to answer some questions about your experience at Shiny Smile Dental Clinic. Your feedback allows us to improve our services.

Patient Name: Miranda Abner   **Date of Visit:** February 5

Returning Patient: ☑ Yes   ☐ No

Dentist: ☑ Dr. Christopher Medina
☐ Dr. Evelyn Cho
☐ Dr. Janice Brewster

Is the information listed above correct?: ☑ Yes   ☐ No
If no, please write corrections here: _____

Please rate the categories below on a scale of 1 (Poor) to 10 (Excellent)

Ease of making appointment: 5
Parking availability: 9
Waiting time: 9
Dentist: 10
Convenience of hours of operation: 6
Overall cleanliness: 10
Receptionist: 8
Appointment procedure: 9

Comments: Overall, I had a great experience during my appointment. My one complaint was that when I was sent back to the dentist to be examined, I had difficulty finding the room. It would be better if you put large signs above the doors so patients can find the exam rooms more easily.

5. What is indicated about Shiny Smile Dental Clinic?
   (A) It will enter Ms. Abner into a prize drawing.
   (B) It has more than one dental professional on staff.
   (C) It gives discounts to returning patients.
   (D) It has undergone renovations.

6. What is implied about Ms. Abner?
   (A) She had to wait a long time for her appointment.
   (B) She is a new patient at Shiny Smile Dental Clinic.
   (C) She is satisfied with the cleanliness of the facility.
   (D) She had a lot of difficulty finding a parking spot.

7. What change does Ms. Abner suggest making?
   (A) Meeting in the lobby area
   (B) Giving directions to the building
   (C) Expanding the exam rooms
   (D) Marking rooms clearly

Questions 8-10 refer to the following form.

Joanne's Catering
Order Form

Customer/Company Name: Joshua Rico/Mirage Goods **Phone Number:** 555-0193
Date/Time of Event: October 6/11:30 A.M. **Venue:** Redwood Center
Number of Guests: 80 **Servers Needed:** 0

Please indicate the number needed for each type of dish, where applicable.

Lunch Set

Appetizer: Stuffed Mushrooms
Salad: Caesar Salad
Entrée: [72] Chicken Fettuccini Alfredo   [8] Spinach and Ricotta Ravioli*
Dessert: [40] Brownie   [40] Mango Tart

Beverages** (select two): ☑ Coffee ☐ Tea ☑ Iced Lemonade ☐ Soda

*Suitable for vegetarians
**Water with lemon will also be provided.

Delivery Type: ☐ Delivery by Joanne's Catering (surcharge applies)
☑ Customer Pick-up / Provide name if different from above: _____
☐ Pick-up by venue employee
☐ Other (please explain): _____

A half-payment must be made five days before the event. The remainder is due three days after the event.

Customer Notes: <u>This order is for a staff luncheon. One of my coworkers has a peanut allergy, so please confirm that there are no peanuts in the dishes served. I didn't see them listed in the food descriptions, but I just want to double-check.</u>

8. How will Mirage Goods receive the food?
   (A) It will be delivered by the caterer.
   (B) It will be picked up by Mr. Rico.
   (C) It will be transported by the Redwood Center.
   (D) It will be picked up by Mr. Rico's coworker.

9. When should Mr. Rico make his first payment?
   (A) October 1
   (B) October 5
   (C) October 6
   (D) October 9

10. What is true about Mr. Rico?
    (A) He is eligible to receive a bulk discount on his order.
    (B) He wishes for all of the dishes to be suitable for vegetarians.
    (C) He plans to serve only water and hot beverages at the event.
    (D) He wants to make sure that a certain ingredient is excluded.

Questions 11-14 refer to the following schedule.

Irvingville Fair
Weekend Schedule

The town of Irvingville was officially established by charter on August 20, 1878, and it's time once again to commemorate this special occasion! Join in the fun with the activities below:

Saturday, August 19

10 A.M. Floats, bands, and dancers will weave their way through town, starting at City Hall, passing the Sedillo Arena, and ending at Hollyhock Park. A map of the planned route can be downloaded from the city's Web site. Mayor Ashley Martino will give a speech at the end of the parade route at approximately noon. Community groups may call Lydia Voorhees at 555-0133 to be part of the parade.

11 A.M.–7 P.M. Food booths will be operating in Hollyhock Park and the nearby Marquette Park. Sample exotic international cuisine as well as local favorites.

2 P.M. Show off your volleyball skills in this fun 3-on-3 tournament with four age categories. Visit the Irvingville Community Center to sign up.

6 P.M. Irvingville's first-ever Battle of the Bands at Marquette Park. Fill out a form at City Hall to enter your band.

Sunday, August 20

10 A.M. Learn to make your very own acrylic painting with step-by-step instructions from local artist Rosita Beneventi. $15 for materials. Advanced registration is not required.

2 P.M. Bakers across Irvingville will bring in their finest pies and cakes, and the winner will receive a state-of-the-art oven from Fincham Appliances! After the judging is finished, free desserts will be served. E-mail Donald Gilmore at dgilmore@irvingville.gov to join the competition.

4 P.M. Meet the candidates for the upcoming city council election as they're interviewed by local reporter Violet Shaw on stage at Marquette Park.

11. What is suggested about the Irvingville Fair?
    (A) It will raise money for projects in town.
    (B) It is being held for the first time.
    (C) It celebrates a community's founding.
    (D) It is intended to promote tourism.

12. Where does Ms. Martino plan to give a speech?
    (A) At Marquette Park
    (B) At City Hall
    (C) At the Sedillo Arena
    (D) At Hollyhock Park

13. How can musicians sign up for an event?
    (A) By calling a contact number
    (B) By sending an e-mail
    (C) By visiting the Irvingville Community Center
    (D) By completing a form in person

14. What is NOT indicated as an activity at the Irvingville Fair?
    (A) An art lesson
    (B) A sports competition
    (C) A political debate
    (D) A baking contest

Questions 15-19 refer to the following invoice and e-mail.

Mitchell Corporation
Order Confirmation

Customer: Melissa Rinehart
Dispatch Date: October 16
Savings Club Member: Yes
Payment: Paid in full with credit card ending in 5981

Shipping Address: 622 Wheeler Drive, Akron, OH 44304
Delivery Type: Regular (2–3 business days)
Order #: 26505

Item / Brand	Product Description	Price Per Unit	Qty	Total
485 / Horizon	All-purpose surface scrub [11 oz.]	Reg: $12.99 Member: $9.99	2	$19.98
091 / Wapak	Microfiber cloth towels [pack of 24]	Reg: $15.99 Member: $14.99	1	$14.99
337 / Fields	Wooden furniture polish [13.8 oz.]	Reg: $12.99 Member: $9.99	1	$9.99
262 / Schmidt	Bathroom antibacterial spray [30 oz.]	Reg: $16.99 Member: $15.99	3	$47.97
All items will be shipped together. Should you have any issues with your order, please contact us at inquiries@mitchellco1.com.			Shipping	$3.95
			Tax	$5.57
			Total	$102.45

E-mail

To:	inquiries@mitchellco1.com
From:	rinehartm@ciscomail.com
Date:	October 25
Subject:	Order #26505

To Whom It May Concern:

I am following up on a complaint I made about a missing product in my recent order with the Mitchell Corporation (#26505). When I checked the delivery at the time of receipt, Gary Tabor noted the missing item and said he would make a report. However, I haven't heard anything about it since then. I reported the issue to your customer service line, and a representative there suggested sending an e-mail. The missing item is the pack of microfiber cloth towels, and I would like them to be sent as soon as possible. I know you introduced a lot of new products last month, which makes fulfilling orders more complicated, but I still expect the high level of customer service that I've seen from you in the past.

Thank you for your prompt response to the matter,

Melissa Rinehart

15. What kinds of goods does the Mitchell Corporation sell?
    (A) Home electronics
    (B) Casual clothing
    (C) Wooden furniture
    (D) Cleaning supplies

16. What is true about all of the products ordered by Ms. Rinehart?
    (A) They are exempt from tax.
    (B) They were delivered at no charge.
    (C) They arrived on October 16.
    (D) They were eligible for a discount.

17. Which brand was missing from Ms. Rinehart's order?
    (A) Horizon
    (B) Wapak
    (C) Fields
    (D) Schmidt

18. Who most likely is Mr. Tabor?
    (A) A product manufacturer
    (B) A customer service representative
    (C) A delivery person
    (D) A business owner

19. What is NOT mentioned in the e-mail?
    (A) Ms. Rinehart has made a purchase from the Mitchell Corporation before.
    (B) The Mitchell Corporation recently expanded its inventory selection.
    (C) Ms. Rinehart has already reported the problem with her order.
    (D) The Mitchell Corporation should issue a refund for the product.

Questions 20-24 refer to the following article, e-mail, and floor plan.

Community Prepares for Gardening Expo

The Regional Gardening Expo, a showcase of gardening supplies and equipment, is scheduled to take place on Saturday, April 15, at the Zepeda Convention Hall. Last year's debut expo was held at the Cecil Center, but this year required a larger space due to the popularity of the event. Event planners hope to grow the attendance to 20,000 visitors within the next five years, though only a fraction of that is expected this year.

The expo will feature booths in categories divided over four floors: Plants & Flowers (1st floor), Fertilizers & Weed Treatments (2nd floor), Tools & Equipment (3rd Floor), and Accessories & Outdoor Furniture (4th floor). Vendors who rent booths at the expo will have the opportunity to have thousands of gardening enthusiasts encounter their products. They will also have their logo and business description posted on the expo's Web site, which will remain in operation year-round. In addition to the basic benefits, Premium Vendors, who pay an additional fee, will be mentioned by name on the expo's TV commercials and promotional flyers. Banners with their logos will also be posted near the entrance, directing visitors to their booth. Those who register before February 25 may select their own booth placement. After that date, booths will be assigned by the event planners.

Information for both vendors and visitors can be found at www.gardeningex.com.

To:	Jerry Iverson <j_iverson@alvarezincorporated.net>
From:	Tai Xing <t_xing@alvarezincorporated.net>
Date:	February 23
Subject:	Regional Gardening Expo

Hi Jerry,

I've just registered Alvarez Incorporated for the upcoming Regional Gardening Expo, which takes place on April 15. I went for the premium option because I think the benefits are well worth the additional fee. I'll send our logo and company information to the event organizers later this week. Owing to the popularity of the expo, this will be an excellent opportunity for our company to promote our new gas-powered hedge trimmer as well as boost sales for our classic lawn mower.

We need to select the location of our booth. I've attached a map of the available slots. We don't want to be positioned right next to HBR, as it has a very similar product line. Other than that, I think we'd better be as close to the escalators as possible. Let me know what you think.

Sincerely,

Tai

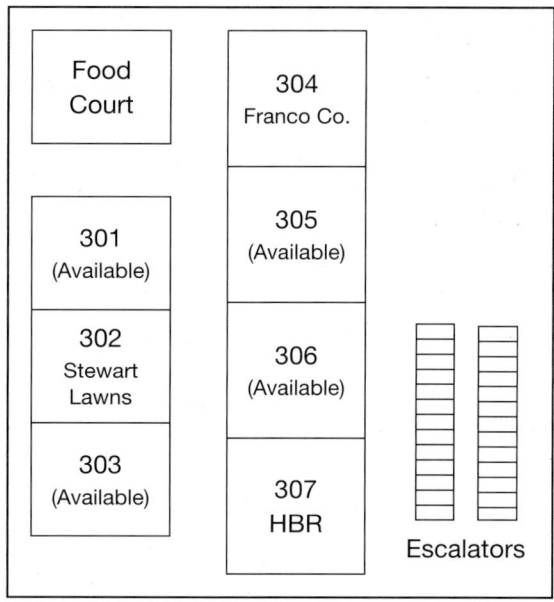

20. What is indicated about the Regional Gardening Expo?
    (A) It is being held for the second time.
    (B) It charges an entrance fee to visitors.
    (C) Its location was changed at that last minute.
    (D) It will provide demonstrations on gardening techniques.

21. According to the article, what benefit can all vendors receive this year?
    (A) A banner featuring their logo
    (B) Access to twenty thousand visitors
    (C) Ongoing publicity on a Web site
    (D) Appearance on a TV commercial

22. In the e-mail, the phrase "went for" in paragraph 1, line 2, is closest in meaning to
    (A) reached
    (B) traveled
    (C) held
    (D) selected

23. What is suggested about Alvarez Incorporated?
    (A) It missed an early registration deadline.
    (B) It is trying to keep its costs down.
    (C) It has participated in the expo before.
    (D) It will have a booth on the third floor.

24. Which booth would Ms. Xing most likely want to reserve?
    (A) 301
    (B) 303
    (C) 305
    (D) 306

PART 7 편지 / 이메일 필수 어휘

주문
account 계좌, 거래처(고객)
bill 청구서
cancel 취소하다
charge 요금; (요금을) 청구하다
confirm 확인하다
fee 수수료
no later than 늦어도 ~까지는
place an order 주문하다
purchase 구매하다; 구매(품)
refund 환불하다
reserve 예약하다
return 반품하다
ship 수송(배송)하다
submit 제출하다
verify 확인하다, 입증하다

감사 / 사과
apologize 사과하다
as a token of appreciation 감사 표시로
be delighted to 기쁘게 ~하다
damaged 손상된
defective 결함이 있는
delay 연기하다 (= postpone)
enclosed 동봉된
grateful 감사하는
in recognition of ~을 인정하여
invaluable 귀중한
on behalf of ~ 대신[대표]하여
patronage 애용, 후원
regretfully 유감스럽게도
voucher 상품권 (= gift certificate)

축하 / 기념
catering 음식 공급
celebrate 축하하다
commemorate 기념하다
in honor of ~을 기념하여
on-site 현장의
organize 조직[준비]하다
participant 참가자
present 수여하다; 참석한
proceedings 행사
reception 환영회
register 등록하다
select 선택하다; 엄선된
take place 일어나다, 개최되다
venue (행사) 장소

구매 / 할인
a variety of 다양한 (= various)
additional 추가의
affordable (가격이) 알맞은
available 구할(이용할) 수 있는
clearance sale 창고 정리 판매
complimentary 무료의 (= free)
consumer 소비자
eligible 자격이 되는
exceed 초과하다
free of charge 무료로 (= at no cost)
in bulk 대량으로
in installments 할부로
including ~을 포함하여
inventory 재고(품)
invoice 송장, 청구서

구매 / 할인
limited 한정된
markdown 가격 할인
office supplies 사무용품
promotional 홍보(판촉)의
redeem 현금(상품)으로 바꾸다
reduced rate 할인 요금
renew 갱신하다
retailer 소매업자
souvenir 기념품
special offer 특가 판매
store credit 가게 포인트
take advantage of ~을 이용하다
vendor 노점상, 판매회사
warranty 품질 보증서

서비스
appointment 약속, 예약
access 접근(권)
accommodation 숙소 (= lodging)
sign up for ~에 가입[신청]하다
assistance 도움
amenity 편의 시설
convenience 편리
dealership 대리점
authorized 인증받은
expire 만료되다
extend 연장하다
maintenance 유지, 보수
reliable 믿을 만한
termination 종결

추천
appropriate 적절한
assign (일을) 맡기다, 배정하다
attentive 배려하는, 신경 쓰는
attitude 태도
certificate 증명서
considerate 신중한, 사려 깊은
cooperation 협력, 협동
demonstrate 입증하다, 보여주다
endeavor 노력
exemplary 모범적인
potential 잠재력; 가능성이 있는
promising 유망한, 조짐이 좋은
qualification 자격, 자질
reference 추천서
referral 소개, 보내기

사업
approval 승인
bid 입찰에 응하다
boost 신장시키다
distribution 유통, 분배
endorsement (공개적인) 지지, 보증[홍보]
expansion 확장
expense 비용 (= cost)
facilitate 가능하게[용이하게] 하다
feasible 실현 가능한
figure 수치 (= number)
license 면허[자격]증
market share 시장 점유율
profitable 수익성이 있는 (= lucrative)
release 공개[출시]하다

자금
allot 할당[배당]하다
approximately 대략
asset 자산
budget 예산
contribution 기부, 공헌
financial 금융의, 재무의
fundraising 모금
immensely 엄청나게
monetary donation 금전적 기부
possess 소유하다
proceeds 수익금
project 프로젝트; 예상[추정]하다
property 재산, 부동산
reimburse 상환하다, 환급하다

공지 / 회람 / 광고 필수 어휘

부동산
- appraisal 평가, 감정
- floor plan 평면도
- furnished 가구가 비치된
- landlord (부동산) 주인 (= owner)
- lease 임대차 계약
- on the premises 건물 내에서
- real estate agency 부동산 중개소
- rent 집세, 임대료
- resident 거주자
- short-term 단기의
- site inspection 부지 점검
- story (건물의) 층
- tenant 세입자
- utility bills 공과금
- within walking distance 도보 거리 이내에

상품 / 서비스
- accommodate 수용하다
- artisan 장인, 기능 보유자
- craft 공예
- customized 주문 제작된
- device 장치, 기구
- durable 내구성이 좋은
- energy efficient 에너지 효율이 좋은
- exclusively 독점적으로
- feature 특징; 특징으로 삼다
- intricate 복잡한 (= complicated)
- replica 복제품 (= duplicate)
- specialize in ~을 전문으로 하다
- testimonial 추천서
- trial 체험판
- versatile 다용도의, 다재다능한

관광
- admission 입장
- arrange 준비(마련)하다
- baggage allowance 수하물 허용치
- carry-on 기내용 수하물
- destination 목적지
- frequent flyer 자주 여행하는 고객
- guided tour 가이드가 있는 여행
- in advance 사전에
- itinerary 여행 일정표
- landmark 주요 지형지물
- landscape 풍경
- peak season 성수기 (= busy season)
- tourist attractions 관광 명소
- transportation 교통 수단

구인 / 구직
- applicant 지원자
- assessment 평가
- benefits (package) 복지 혜택
- candidate 후보자
- degree 학위
- human resources (HR) 인사과
- job openings 공석 (= vacancy)
- preference 우대사항
- qualified 자격을 갖춘
- recruit 채용하다; 신입 사원
- requirement 요건
- shift 교대 근무조
- short-staffed 직원이 부족한
- temporary 임시의 (= short-term)
- vary (각기) 다르다

인사
- administrative 관리의, 운영의
- assume 떠맡다 (= take on)
- be appointed 임명되다 (= be named)
- CEO 최고경영자
- CFO 최고재무이사
- chair 의장; 의장을 맡다
- extension 내선번호
- headquarters 본사 (= main office)
- on duty 근무 중인
- oversee 감독하다
- performance evaluation 업무 평가
- replacement 후임자, 교체
- serve as ~로서 역할을 하다
- task 업무
- transfer 전근 가다(보내다)

정책
- adjust 변경하다 (= modify)
- adopt 채택하다
- allocate 할당하다
- cooperation 협력
- dedicated 전념하는
- effective immediately 즉시 시행하여
- instruction 설명, 지시
- mandatory 의무적인, 필수적인
- policy 정책
- productivity 생산성
- resource 자원
- retain 유지(보유)하다
- revise 개정하다
- violation 위반

회의
- address 다루다, 처리하다
- agenda 의제, 안건
- attendee 참석자
- board of directors 이사회
- brainstorm 묘안을 내다
- committee 위원회
- compile (자료를) 엮다
- minutes 회의록
- nomination 지명, 임명
- outline 약술하다
- performance 성과, 실적
- review 검토; 검토하다
- scheduling conflict 일정이 겹침
- shareholder 주주 (= stockholder)
- unanimous 만장일치의

커뮤니티
- bulletin board 게시판
- city council 시의회
- commuter 통근자
- convert 전환(개조)시키다
- disruption 중단
- grant 승인하다; 보조금
- implement 시행하다
- launch 시작하다
- mayor 시장
- municipal 시의
- overhaul 점검; 점검하다
- renovation 보수, 수리
- resume 재개하다
- waive (세금, 수수료 등을) 면제해 주다
- wing 별관 (= annex)

대회 / 전시
- competition 대회, 경쟁
- content 내용
- critic 비평가
- deadline 마감일
- description 서술, 설명
- draw 추첨, 제비뽑기
- entry 출품(작), 입장
- exhibit 전시하다; 전시품
- judge 심사위원
- material 재료, 자료
- nominee 후보
- notify 통지하다
- on a first-come, first-served basis 선착순으로

PART 7 — 문자 메시지 / 온라인 채팅 필수 어휘

Certainly not. 당치 않아요.
Come up with an idea. 아이디어를 내 주세요.
Could you do me a favor? 좀 도와 주시겠어요?
Could you fill in for me? 제 대신 좀 해 주시겠어요?
Have you checked it? 확인해 보셨나요?
Here we go. 자, 여기요. / 시작합시다.
Keep me posted(informed). 계속 알려 주세요.
Let me find out. 내가 알아볼게요.
Let's give it a go. 한번 해 봅시다.
Never mind. 신경 쓰지 마세요.
No problem. 그럼요.
I bet. 장담해요. 확실해요.
I came across this item. 우연히 이 제품을 발견했어요
I'll catch up. 곧 따라갈게요.
I'll get right to it. 바로 할게요.
I'm heading there. 지금 거기로 향하는 중이에요.
I'm in. 나도 낄게요.
I'm on my way. 가는 중입니다.
I'm working on it. 처리 중입니다.
Is that it? 그게 다인가요?
It makes sense. 일리가 있네요.
It's a lot easier. 그 편이 훨씬 쉬워요.
I'm afraid so. 유감이지만, 그렇습니다.
Absolutely. 물론이죠.
Hold on a minute. 잠깐만 기다려주세요.
I'll figure it out. 제가 알아볼게요.

It's an important source of income. 그것은 중요한 수입원입니다.
It's your call. 그건 당신한테 달렸어요.
I wouldn't dare. 그럴 엄두가 나지 않아요.
Sure thing. 물론이죠.
That explains it. 그래서 그런 거군요.
That happens. 그런 일도 있긴 하죠.
That's a new one. 금시초문이네요.
That's a thought. 괜찮은 생각이네요.
That's fair enough. 좋아요.
That shouldn't be a problem. 문제 될 거 없어요.
That's what I figured. 내 생각도 그래요.
That's the problem. 그게 문제네요.
That's too bad. 그것 참 안됐네요.
That's true. 맞아요.
That will do. 그걸로 족할 겁니다.
That would really help. 그거 정말 도움이 되겠네요.
He turned down the offer. 그가 제안을 거절했어요.
We could learn from each other. 서로 배울 수 있을 겁니다.
We should move in a new direction. 새로운 방향으로 움직여야 합니다.
Why stop now? 왜 지금 멈춰요?
You are in luck. 운이 좋으시네요.
You will come around to my idea. 내 생각에 동조하게 될 겁니다.
I doubt it. 그렇지 않을걸요.

웹 페이지 / 안내문 필수 어휘

제품 정보
portable 휴대하기 쉬운
in good condition 상태가 좋은
worn 닳은
used 중고의 (= second hand)
exterior 외부, 외면
easy to operate 작동하기 쉬운
high performance 고성능
appliance 전자제품
consumption 소비
thoroughly 철저히
install 설치하다
latest 최신의 (= up-to-date)
state-of-the-art 최첨단의
manual 설명서; 수동의

제품 정보
application 응용 프로그램
come with ~이 딸려 나오다
equipment 장비
fragile 깨지기 쉬운
function 기능; 기능을 하다
furnishing 가구
goods 상품
laboratory 실험실
light fixture 조명
merchandise 물품, 상품
part 부품
rechargeable battery 충전용 전지
specification 설명서, 사양
vacuum cleaner 진공 청소기

주문 처리 / 배송
track 추적하다
shipment 수송(품)
a large volume of 다량의
overnight delivery 익일 배송
express 신속한, 급행의
expedite 더 신속히 처리하다
back order 이월 주문
courier 운반원, 택배회사
process 과정; 처리하다
stock 재고(품); (제품을) 갖춰 두다
take long 오래 걸리다
custom order 맞춤제작 주문
customer inquiry 고객 문의
business day 영업일, 평일
distance 거리

행사
extend an invitation 초대장을 보내다
keynote speaker 기조 연설자
conference 학회, 회의
bi-annual 2년마다의
host 주최하다; 주최측
registration 등록
charity 자선 단체
fundraiser 모금 행사
upcoming 다가오는
coordinator 진행자, 조정자
banquet 연회
facility 시설
representative 대표자, 대리인
delegation 대표단

회사 / 업체
consistently 한결같이, 지속적으로
landscaping 조경
establish 설립하다 (= found)
founder 설립자
decade 10년
reputation 명성, 평판
brand awareness 브랜드 인지도
(= brand recognition)
proprietor 소유주 (= owner)
location 위치, 지점
family-run 가족 경영의 (= family-owned)
reinforce 강화하다
overseas 해외의
warehouse 창고

출판
autograph 사인; 사인해 주다
biography 전기
circulation 유통, 판매 부수
edit 편집하다
edition 판, 호
format 구성 방식
freelancer 프리랜서
hardcover 양장본
informative 유익한
issue 문제, (정기간행물의) 호
periodical 정기간행물
publication 출판(물)
submission 제출(물)
subscription 구독(료), 이용
volume 책, 권

청구 / 결제
amount 양, 금액
balance 잔액
billing address 청구 주소
cover (돈을) 대다
deduct 빼다, 공제하다
deposit 보증금; 예금하다
estimate 견적(액); 추정하다
outstanding 미지불된
overdue 기한이 지난
partial payment 부분 지불
preferred 원하는, 선호하는
quote 견적액; 인용하다
reduction 할인, 축소
reimbursement 환급, 상환

여행
botanic garden 식물원
charter bus 전세 버스
conduct a tour 투어를 안내하다
courtesy bus 무료 버스
customs 세관
dining establishment 식당
exotic 이국적인
expedition 탐험
group rate 단체 요금
immigration 출입국 관리소
native 원산의, 토박이의
observatory 전망대
restriction 제한
stopover 경유, 단기 체류

공연
audience 청중
conclusion 결말, 종결
costume (무대) 의상
debut 첫 출연
formal 격식을 차린, 공식적인
intermission 중간 휴식 시간
masterpiece 명작, 걸작
overwhelming 압도적인
refrain from ~을 삼가다
premiere 개봉, 초연
preview 시사회
prohibit 금지하다
sequel 속편
star 주연을 맡다
usher (극장 등의) 안내원

PART 7 기사 / 발표문 필수 어휘

경제
- analysis 분석
- commerce 상업
- debt 빚
- expenditure 지출
- fluctuate 변동을 거듭하다
- generate 발생시키다, 생성하다
- investment 투자
- loan 대출
- offset 상쇄하다
- plummet 급락하다
- recession 불황 (= downturn, depression)
- sector 부문, 분야
- significant 중요한, 상당한
- statistics 통계

경제
- account for (부분·비율을) 차지하다
- audit 회계 감사
- disposable income 가처분 소득
- finance 자금; 자금을 대다
- lack 부족; 부족하다
- noticeable 현저한
- quarter 분기
- revenue 수익 (= profit)
- risk 위험
- sluggish 부진한
- soar 급등하다
- spokesperson 대변인
- stable 안정적인
- struggle 힘겹게 나아가다
- support 지원; 지원하다

경영
- aid 원조, 지원; 돕다
- associate 제휴하다, 결합시키다; 사원
- bring about ~을 야기하다, 초래하다
- commission 위원회, 수수료, 위임(하다)
- competitor 경쟁자
- core 중심부; 핵심적인
- corporation 기업, 법인
- domestic 국내의
- enormous 거대한
- entrepreneur 기업가
- executive 임원; 행정의
- expand 확장하다
- initiative 계획, 주도(권)
- output 생산량

경영
- flexible working hours 탄력 근무 시간제
- merger and acquisition 합병과 인수
- morale 근로 의욕, 사기
- motivate 동기를 부여하다
- obstacle 장애물
- pioneer 개척자
- primary 주된, 주요한, 최초의
- prosperous 번영하는, 번창하는
- rapport 관계
- reward 보상(하다)
- step down 물러나다
- strategy 전략
- take over (기업을) 인수하다; 인수
- workforce 노동력

교통
- alternative 대안; 대안이 되는
- divert 우회[전환]시키다
- fine 벌금, 과태료
- infrastructure 사회 기반 시설
- interrupt 방해하다 (= disturb)
- lane 길, 차선
- parking garage 주차장
- permit 허가증; 허가하다
- public transportation 대중교통
- ramp 경사로
- route 경로, 길
- suburban 시외의
- toll 통행료
- traffic congestion 교통혼잡
- undergo 겪다 (= experience)

건설
- adjacent 인접한
- archaeologist 고고학자
- architect 건축가
- be torn down 철거되다
- capacity 수용력, 용량
- extensive 대규모의
- insulation 단열
- in the vicinity of ~의 부근에
- plant 공장
- proximity 인접, 근접
- refurbish 재단장하다
- restoration 복구, 복원
- transform 변형시키다
- underway 진행 중인

지역사회
- authority 당국, 권한, 인가
- ballot 무기명 투표, 투표용지
- city hall 시청
- city official 시 공무원
- debate 토론
- environment-friendly 환경친화적인
- gathering 모임
- improvement 개선
- measure 조치
- population 인구
- recycle 재활용하다
- region 지역
- the majority of 대다수의
- vote 투표; 투표하다

문화 / 예술
- author 작가
- award-winning 상을 받은
- composer 작곡가
- contemporary 현대의
- contributing writer 기고 작가
- depict 묘사하다
- draft (원고) 초안
- honored 영광스러운
- innovative 혁신적인
- literature 문학
- manuscript 원고
- novel 소설 (= fiction)
- play 연극
- poetry 시
- sculpture 조각

문화 / 예술
- acclaimed 호평을 받는
- archive 기록 보관소
- artifact 인공품, 공예품
- aspiring 장차 ~이 되려는, 포부가 있는
- authentic 진짜인
- collaboration 공동 작업(물)
- collection 소장품, 수집품
- distinguished 유명한, 성공한
- diverse 다양한 (= various)
- inspire 영감을 주다
- patron 후원자, 이용객(고객)
- publicize 알리다, 홍보하다
- renowned 유명한 (= famous)
- respected 존경받는

기타 양식 필수 어휘

양식
- brochure (안내) 책자
- comment 논평, 비판
- complaint 불평
- complete 작성하다 (= fill out)
- content 내용물, 목차
- coupon 쿠폰
- evaluation 평가
- feedback 피드백
- flyer 전단지(= leaflet)
- form 양식, 서식
- receipt 영수증, 수령
- response 반응, 응답
- schedule 일정표 (= timetable)
- survey (설문) 조사
- testimonial 추천서

주문 / 청구서
- ATTN ~귀하
- balance due 미불액
- bill to ~에게 청구
- credit 입금하다
- details 세부사항
- gratuity 봉사료, 팁
- order form 주문서
- payment method 지불 방법
- quantity 수량
- ship to ~에게 배송
- standard 기준, 표준
- subtotal 소계
- tax 세금
- unit 구성단위

주문서
- applicable 해당되는
- beverage 음료
- dimension 크기, 치수
- double check 재확인하다
- due ~하기로 예정된, (돈을) 지불해야 하는
- ingredient 재료(성분)
- measurement 측정, 치수
- per ~당(마다)
- refreshment 다과
- remainder 나머지
- summary 요약
- surcharge 추가요금
- transaction 거래, 매매
- vegetarian 채식주의자

행사
- advanced 상급의
- by courtesy of ~의 호의로
- cuisine 요리(법)
- culinary 요리의
- enrollment 등록
- fair 품평회, 박람회
- forum 포럼, 토론회
- instructor 강사
- intermediate 중급의
- pastry 페이스트리(빵의 일종)
- sanitation 위생 시설(관리)
- occasion 행사, 경우
- parade 퍼레이드, 행진
- serve 제공하다
- stall 가판대, 좌판

평가서
- category 범주
- cleanness 청결
- comfortable 편한
- disappointed 실망한
- indicate 나타내다, 표시하다
- measure 측정(평가)하다
- minor 사소한
- overall 전반적인, 전반적으로
- rate 등급을 매기다
- recommend 추천하다
- responsive 즉각 대응하는
- satisfied 만족하는
- scale 등급, 규모(범위)
- suggestion 제안

신청 / 등록서
- badge 배지
- duration 기간 (= period)
- employer 고용주
- ID(identification) 신분증
- individual 개인; 개인의
- lecture 강의, 강연
- option 선택(할 수 있는 것)
- penalty 벌금, 위약금
- previous 이전의 (= former)
- provide 제공하다
- related 관련된
- request 요청, 신청
- session (특정 활동) 시간, 기간
- signature 서명

신청 / 등록서
- affiliation 소속, 제휴
- cancellation 취소
- credentials 자격
- current 현재의
- expertise 전문 지식
- facilitator 조력자
- field 분야
- guideline 지침
- membership 회원(자격)
- organization 조직, 단체
- post 공고(게시)하다; 우편(물)
- profile 프로필, 개요
- recent 최근의
- subject 주제, 사안
- third-party 제3자

일정표
- accompanying 수반하는
- adjourn 중단하다, 휴회하다
- attendance 참석
- auditorium 강당
- excursion 여행, 소풍
- immediately 즉시
- institute 기관, 협회
- last-minute 막판
- moderate 사회를 보다, 조정하다
- opening remarks 개회사
- preliminary 예비의
- presentation 발표
- press 언론, 기자단
- rear entrance 후문

기타
- alert 경보
- boulevard 도로
- brief 짧은, 간단한
- connecting flight 연결 항공편
- contract renewal 계약 갱신
- curator 큐레이터(전시 책임자)
- fare (교통) 요금
- inclusive 일체의 경비가 포함된
- followed by 뒤이어
- rate 가격, 요금
- scholar 학자
- seating 좌석, 자리
- visiting 객원의
- zip code 우편번호 (= postcode)

FINAL TEST

READING TEST

In the Reading test, you will read a variety of texts and answer several different types of reading comprehension questions. The entire Reading test will last 75 minutes. There are three parts, and directions are given for each part. You are encouraged to answer as many questions as possible within the time allowed.

You must mark your answers on the separate answer sheet. Do not write your answers in your test book.

PART 5

Directions: A word or phrase is missing in each of the sentences below. Four answer choices are given below each sentence. Select the best answer to complete the sentence. Then mark the letter (A), (B), (C), or (D) on your answer sheet.

101. The ------- was not delivered on time because it was labeled with the wrong address.
    (A) result
    (B) news
    (C) package
    (D) speech

102. The event planners were pleased with the attendance at the event ------- had planned.
    (A) them
    (B) their
    (C) theirs
    (D) they

103. Ms. Florence should report to the head office on Monday for ------- routine employee evaluation.
    (A) she
    (B) herself
    (C) her
    (D) hers

104. Hometime Bakery ------- a large commercial space downtown, but it will relocate soon.
    (A) occupies
    (B) creates
    (C) purchases
    (D) orders

105. Parking is not allowed along Salazar Avenue because it is ------- than most other streets in the neighborhood.
    (A) narrow
    (B) narrowing
    (C) narrowest
    (D) narrower

106. For each sale made by the call center staff, a small ------- is paid on a monthly basis.
    (A) occasion
    (B) extension
    (C) impression
    (D) commission

107. Ms. Dawson said that more information about the merger will be available ------- the end of the month.
    (A) during
    (B) toward
    (C) between
    (D) among

108. The country's borders are ------- controlled so that diseased plants and animals are not brought in.
    (A) tight
    (B) tightly
    (C) tightness
    (D) tighten

109. The discount coupon issued to passengers on the delayed flight to Vancouver can only be used -------.
    (A) again
    (B) once
    (C) another
    (D) either

110. Inventory tasks at the warehouse could not be completed ------- an error with the computer system.
    (A) rather than
    (B) due
    (C) because of
    (D) since

111. Mr. Brennan is looking for a ------- apartment to rent, as he doesn't have many belongings of his own.
    (A) furnished
    (B) spacious
    (C) missing
    (D) portable

112. In an effort to improve customer satisfaction, the Shea Corporation ------- new training measures next quarter.
    (A) introducing
    (B) will introduce
    (C) has introduced
    (D) being introduced

113. Taking the airport shuttle from Reimer Station is an ------- alternative to using a private taxi service.
    (A) affordable
    (B) extensive
    (C) expectant
    (D) unreachable

114. In order to make the art contest fair for all participants, it is important to hire ------- judges.
    (A) impartial
    (B) probationary
    (C) impulsive
    (D) mutual

115. The manual given to new employees contains tips on ------- the construction equipment safely.
    (A) operates
    (B) operating
    (C) operation
    (D) operate

116. The store's general manager attended a lecture to learn ways to improve employee -------.
    (A) motivationally
    (B) motivational
    (C) motivation
    (D) motivated

117. Employees will not receive overtime payments for staying late ------- they receive approval from a manager first.
    (A) despite
    (B) while
    (C) once
    (D) unless

118. The hotel does not have its own restaurant, but there are several fine dining establishments -------.
    (A) nearby
    (B) further
    (C) beside
    (D) among

119. ------- noticed on the national level, the factory closure caused a sharp decline in Spring City's local economy.
    (A) Scarcer
    (B) Scarcity
    (C) Scarce
    (D) Scarcely

120. It was difficult to determine ------- the problem was caused by a manufacturing defect or the customer's carelessness.
    (A) whether
    (B) just as
    (C) as if
    (D) whereas

121. ------- donor who contributed to the fundraising campaign is listed on the charity's Web site.
(A) Anyone
(B) Those
(C) Each
(D) Some

122. ------- to its customers such as money-back guarantees and quality assurances make Rymart so popular.
(A) Committing
(B) Commitments
(C) Committed
(D) Commitment

123. VLC Beverages has seen an increase in demand for its caffeinated drinks, ------- its competitors.
(A) unlike
(B) although
(C) throughout
(D) since

124. The CEO of Arellano Software visits the regional offices quarterly to ------- progress at the branches.
(A) get rid of
(B) come up with
(C) run out of
(D) check up on

125. The department heads should ------- their lists of employees to be recommended for the award nomination.
(A) be compiled
(B) have compiled
(C) compiling
(D) compiled

126. Westbury Pharmaceuticals consulted a number of ------- to get opinions on how to improve pain medications.
(A) chemistry
(B) chemists
(C) chemically
(D) chemicals

127. The members of the board voted ------- to appoint Paul Chapman as the interim CEO while the job was being filled.
(A) traditionally
(B) approximately
(C) unanimously
(D) innocently

128. Customers at Treasure Furniture are not allowed to return the ------- pieces because they cannot be resold.
(A) customized
(B) customizing
(C) customizes
(D) customize

129. The management team encouraged both personnel department employees and those ------- linked to hiring to attend the quarterly workshop.
(A) insincerely
(B) inefficiently
(C) indirectly
(D) insecurely

130. During the community softball tournament, Jason Hawthorne ------- his ankle after jumping to catch a ball.
(A) enforced
(B) obstructed
(C) sprained
(D) complied

PART 6

Directions: Read the texts that follow. A word, phrase, or sentence is missing in parts of each text. Four answer choices for each question are given below the text. Select the best answer to complete the text. Then mark the letter (A), (B), (C), or (D) on your answer sheet.

Questions 131-134 refer to the following article.

Automotive Giant Announces Recall

Auto manufacturer JMC has announced the recall of one of its vehicles due to a potential safety risk. This recall ------- the Urbanite model that was released last year, sold in Canada and the U.S.
131.
The company spokesperson reported that the crash sensor in the vehicle may malfunction, causing failure to inflate the airbags in the event of a collision. Gregorio Mendoza, ------- team
132.
designed the airbag system, apologized for the injuries caused by this defect. Anyone who owns one of the affected vehicles should ------- it to the point of purchase. -------.
133. **134.**

131. (A) covering
(B) covers
(C) to cover
(D) is covered

132. (A) that
(B) whose
(C) his
(D) whom

133. (A) examine
(B) pursue
(C) return
(D) abandon

134. (A) There it will be repaired at no charge.
(B) JMC cannot identify the component.
(C) It should be reported to the proper authorities.
(D) The new system replaced an unpopular one.

GO ON TO THE NEXT PAGE

Questions 135-138 refer to the following advertisement.

Let your stress melt away at Cedar Spa! All employees are certified in their various fields to ensure top-quality care. Our ------- are sold individually or in money-saving packages. Whether you're
135.
seeking skincare, a massage, or a beauty service, we're here to help. We have more positive comments ------- any other spa in town because we pay attention to every detail. Call us today at
136.
555-0132 to make a booking. Reservations are not mandatory. -------. We hope to see you at
137.
Cedar Spa soon. We promise you won't regret ------- our services.
138.

135. (A) measurements
(B) destinations
(C) treatments
(D) inspections

136. (A) as
(B) that
(C) where
(D) than

137. (A) We will inform you promptly if she is available.
(B) However, the waiting time could be long.
(C) Therefore, it is complimentary for every customer.
(D) You must notify us of the change in advance.

138. (A) tried
(B) try
(C) to be tried
(D) trying

280

Questions 139-142 refer to the following e-mail.

To: Naja Geisler
From: Azhar Sura
Date: October 13
Subject: Interest in Sergio Ortega

Dear Ms. Geisler,

I'm the owner of Page-by-Page Bookstore, a business that ------- promotes authors. As you are the literary agent for author Sergio Ortega, I'd like to extend an invitation for him to visit our store for a book signing. Many authors find this kind of event to be highly -------. We'll place a large order for Mr. Ortega's novel in advance. -------. Please let me know whether he's available and when. You should also keep our business in mind ------- you have other authors you represent who may be suitable for a visit.

Many thanks,

Azhar Sura

139. (A) activated
(B) actively
(C) active
(D) activity

140. (A) beneficial
(B) casual
(C) dependable
(D) qualified

141. (A) Books also make excellent gifts for special occasions.
(B) There are several popular titles to choose from.
(C) We do not want to risk running out.
(D) Many readers enjoyed getting to meet him.

142. (A) even though
(B) regardless of
(C) so that
(D) in case

Questions 143-146 refer to the following notice.

World-renowned artist Rolando Lombardi will give a talk at Victoria Gallery on August 15 at 7 P.M. He will discuss his ------- to become widely accepted in the art community. It was a long and difficult journey for him, and audience members will be inspired ------- his story. Tickets are available for $12 each and can be purchased at the door. Please bring ------- change if you plan to pay in cash. Additional donations will be collected at the entrance. -------. We hope to see a great crowd at this special event.

143. (A) struggle
     (B) reluctance
     (C) estimate
     (D) altitude

144. (A) to
     (B) by
     (C) of
     (D) for

145. (A) exacting
     (B) exactness
     (C) exact
     (D) exactly

146. (A) They will go toward community art projects.
     (B) We raised over five thousand dollars from the talk.
     (C) You will enjoy viewing these incredible paintings.
     (D) Both nights are expected to be entertaining.

PART 7

Directions: In this part you will read a selection of texts, such as magazine and newspaper articles, e-mails, and instant messages. Each text or set of texts is followed by several questions. Select the best answer for each question and mark the letter (A), (B), (C), or (D) on your answer sheet.

Questions 147-148 refer to the following notice.

Notice to Rio's customers:

Rio's restaurant is partnering with Wheely Meals, a company that provides delivery personnel for restaurants that do not have their own in-house delivery service. You can now get all of your Rio's favorites delivered right to your door anytime during Rio's hours of operation. Simply log on to www.wheely-meals.com and create an account. This can be done in less than five minutes! And for the month of June, for all Rio's customers whose orders are $35 or more, we'll throw in a free dish from our dessert menu.

147. Why was the notice written?
 (A) To acknowledge a partner's achievement
 (B) To introduce new menu items
 (C) To promote longer hours of operation
 (D) To announce a new service

148. How can customers get a free item in June?
 (A) By downloading an online coupon
 (B) By spending a certain amount
 (C) By placing multiple orders
 (D) By signing up for a membership

Questions 149-150 refer to the following text-message chain.

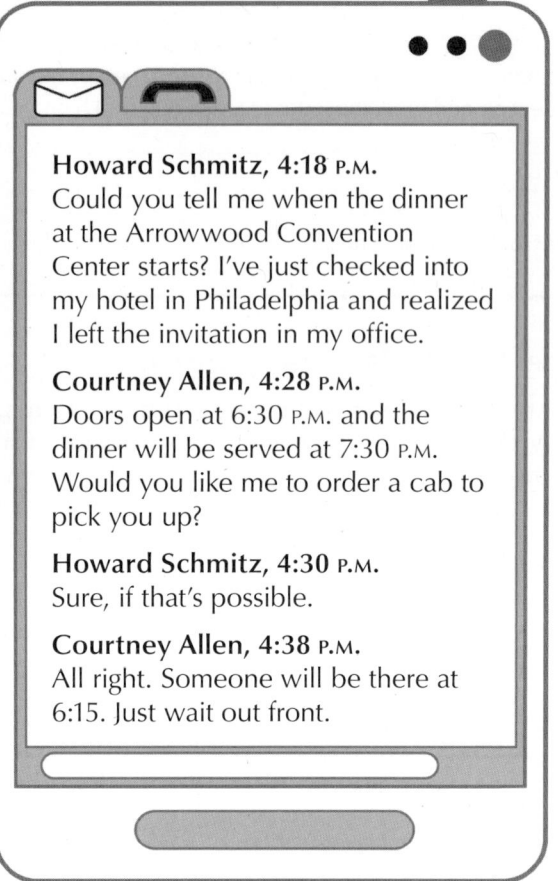

Howard Schmitz, 4:18 P.M.
Could you tell me when the dinner at the Arrowwood Convention Center starts? I've just checked into my hotel in Philadelphia and realized I left the invitation in my office.

Courtney Allen, 4:28 P.M.
Doors open at 6:30 P.M. and the dinner will be served at 7:30 P.M. Would you like me to order a cab to pick you up?

Howard Schmitz, 4:30 P.M.
Sure, if that's possible.

Courtney Allen, 4:38 P.M.
All right. Someone will be there at 6:15. Just wait out front.

149. Where is Mr. Schmitz now?

(A) At a convention center
(B) At an airport
(C) At a hotel
(D) At an office

150. At 4:30 P.M., what does Mr. Schmitz most likely mean when he says, "Sure, if that's possible"?

(A) He prefers to make his meal selection in advance.
(B) He wants his transportation arranged for him.
(C) He requests that Ms. Allen send an invitation.
(D) He would like to arrive at a site early.

Questions 151-152 refer to the following e-mail.

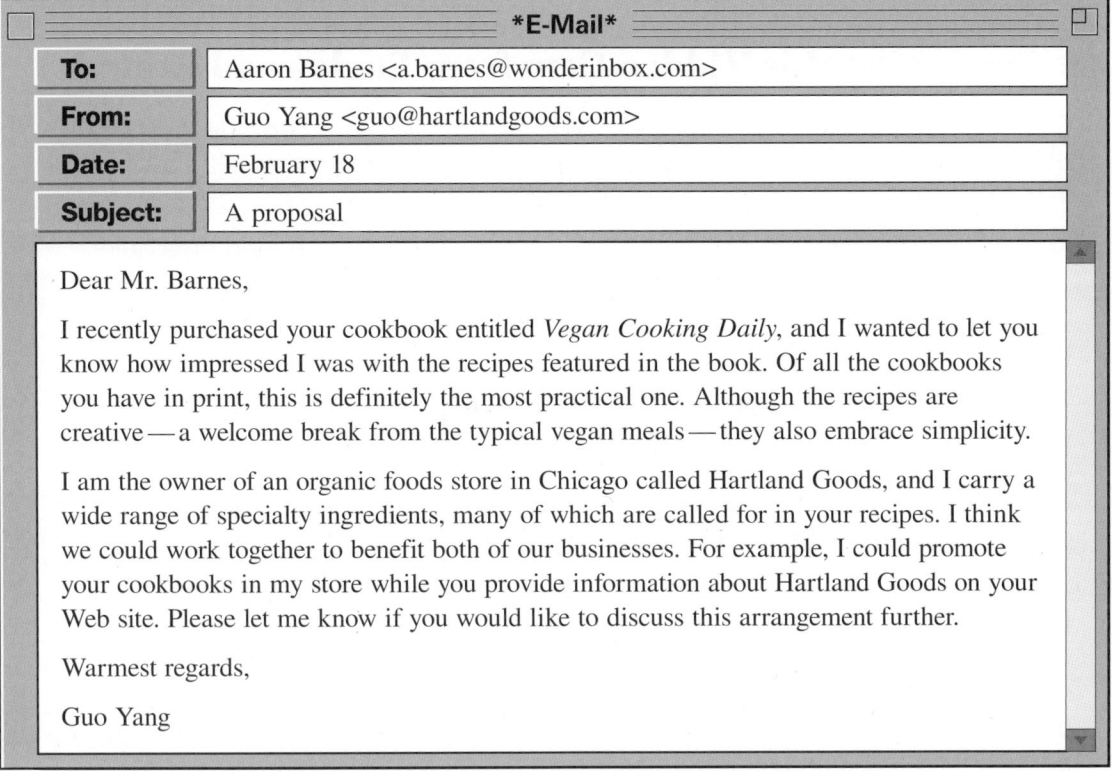

To: Aaron Barnes <a.barnes@wonderinbox.com>
From: Guo Yang <guo@hartlandgoods.com>
Date: February 18
Subject: A proposal

Dear Mr. Barnes,

I recently purchased your cookbook entitled *Vegan Cooking Daily*, and I wanted to let you know how impressed I was with the recipes featured in the book. Of all the cookbooks you have in print, this is definitely the most practical one. Although the recipes are creative—a welcome break from the typical vegan meals—they also embrace simplicity.

I am the owner of an organic foods store in Chicago called Hartland Goods, and I carry a wide range of specialty ingredients, many of which are called for in your recipes. I think we could work together to benefit both of our businesses. For example, I could promote your cookbooks in my store while you provide information about Hartland Goods on your Web site. Please let me know if you would like to discuss this arrangement further.

Warmest regards,

Guo Yang

151. What is implied about Mr. Barnes?
(A) He held a book-signing event.
(B) He is looking for new recipes.
(C) He has published several books.
(D) He gives public cooking demonstrations.

152. What does Ms. Yang propose doing?
(A) Upgrading a Web site
(B) Revising some recipes
(C) Providing free samples
(D) Forming a partnership

Questions 153-155 refer to the following advertisement.

Don't Miss this Hidden Gem from Englewood Realty!

Englewood Realty has been specializing exclusively in period homes for the past thirty years. We are pleased to present for sale the following property: 590 Patterson Road / Five-bedrooms, two-bathrooms

This stunning home built during the Victorian era is well-positioned on a quiet street in the sought-after neighborhood of West Garfield. It's near a bustling commercial area, where restaurants have really taken off in the past few years, so there are plenty of convenient dining options within walking distance.

The home has spacious rooms and plenty of natural light, as well as a sizeable yard to the rear with manicured gardens and mature trees. The first floor is comprised of an entrance hall, two living rooms, a dining room, a kitchen, and a study. Upstairs you will find five bedrooms—one of which is a master bedroom with its own master bathroom—and a second bathroom.

All fixtures and carpets throughout the home are less than twelve months old, as the current owners have completely remodeled the home. However, the work was completed with care, ensuring that the key original features of the home—such as the intricate woodwork along the banister and the cast iron fireplace in the front living room—have been retained, giving you the perfect balance between old-fashioned charm and modern amenities.

A complete inspection of the premises has been carried out by Jerry Vasquez, and there are no major repairs needed. We are happy to provide this information to potential buyers. If you are interested in viewing this home, please call 555-5168 to be put in touch with the real eatate agent dealing with the property. An open house event will be held on September 10 from 2 P.M. to 4 P.M.

153. What is indicated about Englewood Realty?
  (A) Its office is located on Patterson Road.
  (B) It deals solely with residential properties.
  (C) It will host open house events on September 10.
  (D) It has been in operation for forty years.

154. What is stated about the property?
  (A) Its selling price has been reduced.
  (B) It has five rooms on the first floor.
  (C) It is on the market for the first time.
  (D) It has been renovated in the past year.

155. Who most likely is Mr. Vasquez?
  (A) A building inspector
  (B) A real estate agent
  (C) A homeowner
  (D) A potential buyer

Questions 156-157 refer to the following e-mail.

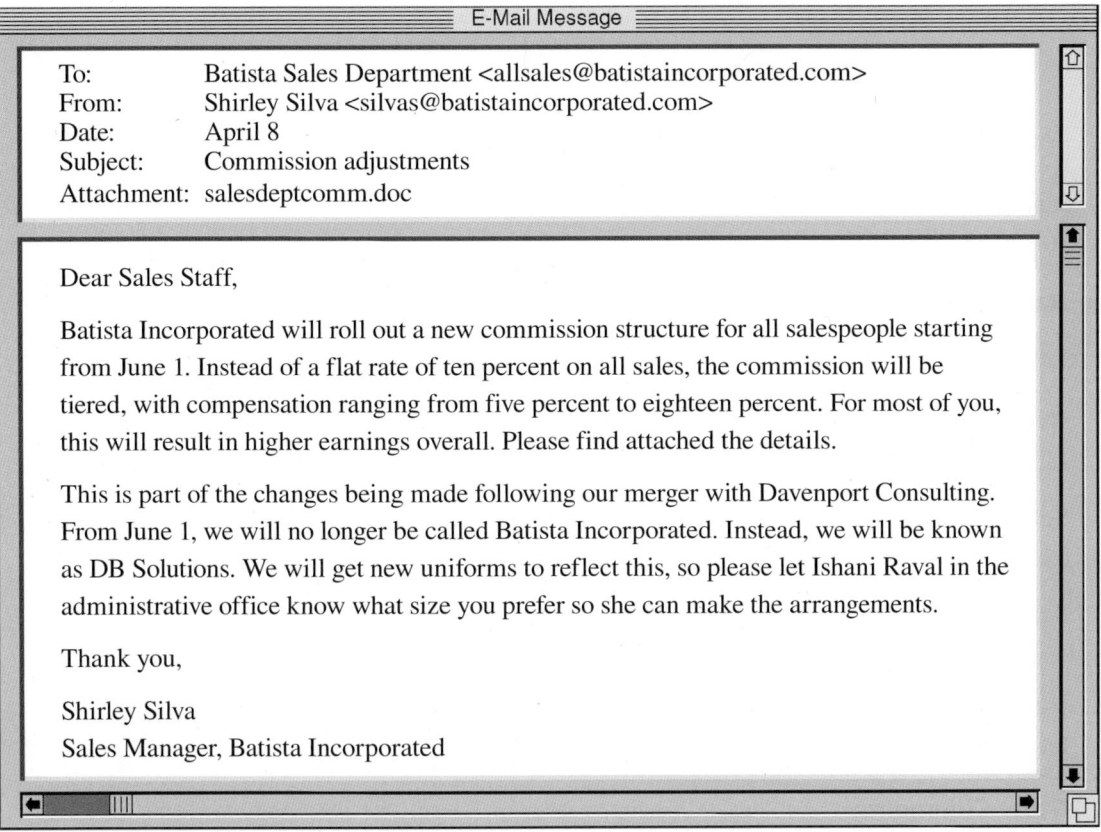

To: Batista Sales Department <allsales@batistaincorporated.com>
From: Shirley Silva <silvas@batistaincorporated.com>
Date: April 8
Subject: Commission adjustments
Attachment: salesdeptcomm.doc

Dear Sales Staff,

Batista Incorporated will roll out a new commission structure for all salespeople starting from June 1. Instead of a flat rate of ten percent on all sales, the commission will be tiered, with compensation ranging from five percent to eighteen percent. For most of you, this will result in higher earnings overall. Please find attached the details.

This is part of the changes being made following our merger with Davenport Consulting. From June 1, we will no longer be called Batista Incorporated. Instead, we will be known as DB Solutions. We will get new uniforms to reflect this, so please let Ishani Raval in the administrative office know what size you prefer so she can make the arrangements.

Thank you,

Shirley Silva
Sales Manager, Batista Incorporated

156. What is one purpose of the e-mail?
(A) To explain a change in payment
(B) To get opinions about a merger
(C) To recruit new salespeople
(D) To apologize for an error

157. What is Ms. Raval responsible for doing?
(A) Assigning new offices
(B) Preparing some clothing
(C) Planning a staff meal
(D) Arranging furniture delivery

Questions 158-160 refer to the following form.

Yonas Electronics Consumer Panel

We hope you enjoyed participating in our session for the YE Photo Printer, which is scheduled to hit the market next year. Please complete this form to provide your feedback. After you submit the form, you may go home, taking the printer you tested with you.

Name: Earl Hinkley   **Session:** July 14, 2 P.M.–5 P.M.

Rate each category from 1 (poor) to 5 (excellent) and share your comments.

Overall Appearance: 5 I liked the sleek design and the fact that it's available in both silver and black.

Setup: 5 It was easy to connect the printer to my smartphone without even having to refer to the manual.

Features: 4 Although it was compact enough to carry around in my pocket, because of its heavy weight, I don't think most people would do this as you anticipated.

Price: 3 For the quality of the photos, the price seems high. I would prefer to just print my photos on a traditional printer.

Other Comments: As for the feedback session itself, the discussion wasn't very productive because there were too many people in the group. So, even though we had sufficient time, some people felt too shy to share their opinions.

---

158. What is indicated about the consumer panel?

(A) Its session lasted for a total of two hours.
(B) Its purpose was to review a newly released product.
(C) It was held at the Yonas Electronics headquarters.
(D) Its participants were allowed to keep a device.

159. What is suggested about the product?

(A) It is sold with the YE smartphone.
(B) It comes in three colors.
(C) It is intended to be portable.
(D) It has a photo-scanning feature.

160. What did Mr. Hinkley like the least about the group session?

(A) The fee for participation
(B) The group size
(C) The duration of the session
(D) The session leader

Questions 161-163 refer to the following memo.

From: Riemi Saito, Office Manager
To: Randall Solutions Employees
Date: March 2
Re: Updates

Hello Everyone,

The meeting with Ogden Tech went even better than we had hoped. The general manager there, Sanjiv Nadar, has agreed to use our services for filling three open job positions. Let's use this opportunity to secure a major client. If we can impress Mr. Nadar with suitable candidates for these positions, we might be able to get a permanent contract with Ogden Tech. The company will open a second branch in Los Angeles, so they'll need about eighty new staff members by mid-May.

I will discuss this assignment further at the next staff meeting. I know we were supposed to meet on March 6, but I'd like to postpone it by two days, as I'll have more detailed information about Ogden Tech's needs by then. In addition,
Ms. Vasquez will leave for vacation next week. Therefore, please submit your monthly progress reports by March 9 instead of March 15 this month.

Thank you for your hard work!

Riemi Saito

161. Who most likely are the memo recipients?
(A) Job candidates
(B) Technology researchers
(C) Department managers
(D) Personnel recruiters

162. What is suggested about Ogden Tech?
(A) It will relocate its headquarters to Los Angeles.
(B) It is a long-time customer of Randall Solutions.
(C) It is facing financial difficulties.
(D) It has plans to expand its workforce.

163. When will Ms. Saito meet with the memo recipients?
(A) March 6
(B) March 8
(C) March 9
(D) March 15

Questions 164-167 refer to the following online chat discussion.

Nicolas Castro [2:04 P.M.]
Is your team working late? Do you still need me to approve overtime work for this evening so you can wrap up the market summary report for the new smartphone app?

Isabella Lanier [2:06 P.M.]
That's no longer needed.

Liu Qiao [2:07 P.M.]
We just handed in the final draft about an hour ago.

Nicolas Castro [2:08 P.M.]
Mr. Shaw will be pleased about that. He wasn't expecting it until tomorrow evening.

Isabella Lanier [2:09 P.M.]
Yeah, we thought he might want an additional day to go over the figures before he meets with Ms. Kao on Thursday.

Nicolas Castro [2:09 P.M.]
Do you think we'll get the investment funds from her?

Edgar Kotov [2:11 P.M.]
I do. Our research suggests that there aren't any similar apps on the market.

Liu Qiao [2:12 P.M.]
And because it is so easy to use, we think consumers will love it.

Isabella Lanier [2:13 P.M.]
Since the target market is young adults, it has a lot of potential for being popular on social media.

Nicolas Castro [2:14 P.M.]
That would save us a great deal of money on advertising.

Edgar Kotov [2:16 P.M.]
I was thinking the same thing.

Isabella Lanier [2:17 P.M.]
I guess we need to wait and see whether or not the project gets funded in the first place.

164. At 2:06 P.M., what does Ms. Lanier most likely mean when she writes, "That's no longer needed"?

(A) The product will not go on the market.
(B) A company policy has changed.
(C) The team members will not stay late.
(D) A summary does not need to be approved.

165. What is indicated about the market summary report?

(A) It was turned in early.
(B) It was created by Mr. Shaw.
(C) It was assigned at the last minute.
(D) It was for multiple products.

166. Who most likely is Ms. Kao?

(A) A smartphone salesperson
(B) A corporate investor
(C) A computer programmer
(D) A job candidate

167. What is suggested about the smartphone app?

(A) It will have a lot of competition.
(B) It is designed for social workers.
(C) It is currently popular on social media.
(D) Its advertising costs might be low.

Questions 168-171 refer to the following advertisement.

Ellison Motors

511 Austin Drive ▽ 793 18th Street ▽ 429 Stone Boulevard

Don't get saddled with high monthly loan payments on a car that is just decreasing in value. — [1] —. Lease a vehicle from Ellison Motors today and enjoy driving the latest models without the long-term risk. At Ellison Motors, we offer two-, three-, and five-year leases, so you can select the plan that best fits your budget and lifestyle. You can drive off the lot in a brand-new car with no money down, making manageable monthly payments that can be set up by direct debit. — [2] —. At the end of the lease term, return the vehicle and go shopping for a new one!

We have built a reputation for reliability over the years, and our service is top-notch. In fact, we received a perfect score on *Vehicle Insight* magazine, which has no affiliation with our company. Each vehicle is less than three years old, and we ensure the lowest possible prices by sourcing our fleet straight from the factory. That means we have set up the perfect system to pass the savings on to you. — [3] —.

At Ellison Motors, you can feel confident about your decision. That's because customers have a two-week grace period before the official contract goes into effect. We have the largest selection of vehicles of every type, from minivans to sports cars. — [4] —. Visit Ellison Motors today at one of our convenient locations in Pittsburgh.

168. What benefit of the service is mentioned?
(A) Customers may change vehicles mid-lease.
(B) Free driving lessons are included.
(C) No deposit is required by the customer.
(D) The lease duration can be extended.

169. What is suggested about Ellison Motors?
(A) It was favorably reviewed by an independent party.
(B) It has recently opened a third branch in Pittsburgh.
(C) It has the highest safety ratings in the industry.
(D) It is offering special discounts to new customers.

170. According to the advertisement, what does the company do to keep prices down?
(A) Automate its bookkeeping tasks
(B) Work directly with manufacturers
(C) Sell the vehicles after they are used
(D) Offer short-term leases only

171. In which of the positions marked [1], [2], [3], and [4] does the following sentence best belong?

"If you need help choosing one, our experienced employees can offer advice."

(A) [1]
(B) [2]
(C) [3]
(D) [4]

Questions 172-175 refer to the following article.

Norwalk Bank to Acquire Seifert Financial

February 19—In a press release issued yesterday, Seifert Financial announced that it will be purchased by Seattle-based Norwalk Bank. —[1]—. The transaction, one of the largest of its kind in the northwest region, will include the transfer of Seifert's $366 million in assets as well as its four branches operating in the Toronto area. The acquisition marks an important step in Norwalk's long-term goal of moving the business beyond U.S. borders and into Canada.

Norwalk's corporate lawyer, Robert Costner, reports that board members on both sides are highly motivated to ensure that a suitable arrangement is made as soon as possible. "The first round of negotiations will be held in March," Costner explained. "The final contract will be signed the following month. —[2]—." Norwalk currently has $1.2 billion in cash, investment funds, and other holdings, and the acquisition is expected to improve the company's position dramatically. "The strengths underlying Seifert's business model balance our current situation," observed Public Relations Director Seth Mabry. "Seifert's reputation for investment banking will provide the perfect complement to the services already offered at Norwalk. —[3]—."

Current customers of Seifert Financial will see no immediate change in branding after the agreement is finalized, though they will be able to use Norwalk's Web-based account system to make transfers, check account balances, and carry out other financial transactions. The goal is to have all accounts operating under the parent brand by the end of June. The management team at Norwalk will reassess the company's needs in July, and downsizing or a recruitment drive may be needed at that time. —[4]—.

172. Who is Mr. Costner?
 (A) A public relations employee
 (B) A board member
 (C) A legal professional
 (D) A company owner

173. When is an agreement expected to be finalized?
 (A) In March
 (B) In April
 (C) In June
 (D) In July

174. What is NOT indicated about Norwalk Bank?
 (A) It currently operates four branches.
 (B) It offers an online banking service.
 (C) It has plans to expand into Canada.
 (D) Its assets exceed one billion dollars.

175. In which of the positions marked [1], [2], [3], and [4] does the following sentence best belong?

 "Additionally, its employees' expertise in the residential mortgage market will be invaluable."

 (A) [1]
 (B) [2]
 (C) [3]
 (D) [4]

Questions 176-180 refer to the following invoice and e-mail.

Trenton Wholesale

Business Name: ECC
Phone Number: 859-555-0174
Shipping Address: 253 Stratford Park, Lexington, KY 40507
Billing Address: Same as above
Order Date: March 9

Point of Contact: Deborah Kemp
E-mail address: deborah@eccservices.net

Order #: 751275
Estimated Delivery Date: March 12

Ref. #	Brand / Item Description	Unit Size / Price	Qty	Total
T340	Spencer / Permanent Dye (black)	500 ml / $14.49	20	$289.80
R490	Spencer / Styling Gel	500 ml / $17.99	30	$539.70
W761	Spencer / Shampoo	500 ml / $18.49	35	$647.15
*D288	Spencer / Conditioner	500 ml / $18.49	30	$554.70
C492	Heatex / Hot Oil Treatment	500 ml / $23.99	15	$359.85

*Indicates out-of-stock item. It will not be sent with the rest of the products on the delivery date listed above. Instead, it will be dispatched as soon as it is available again (approximately 1 week).

Subtotal	$2,391.20
Tax	$143.47
Delivery	$35.00
Total	$2,569.67

E-mail

To: Trenton Wholesale <inquiries@trentonwholesale.com>
From: Deborah Kemp <deborah@eccservices.net>
Date: March 14
Subject: Order #751275

To Whom It May Concern:

I would like to inform you about two issues I had with my recent order, #751275. I placed my order over the phone, so I was surprised to discover that the Spencer Styling Gel, item R490, was nearly a dollar more than what is quoted in the catalog. I just got this catalog in the mail a few weeks ago, so I don't think it's outdated. I know that Trenton Wholesale was bought by another business recently, but I believe you have a responsibility to inform customers of these types of changes. I have been operating my business for over a decade and have never seen this kind of price increase without warning.

In addition, I would like to return the hot oil treatments I ordered. While the product seems to be effective, I really don't like the scent. I'll send the unopened bottles back at my own expense, in accordance with your return policy.

Sincerely,

Deborah Kemp
Owner, ECC

176. What kind of business most likely is ECC?
    (A) A housekeeping service
    (B) A hair salon
    (C) A fitness center
    (D) An art studio

177. What do the products ordered by Ms. Kemp have in common?
    (A) Their size
    (B) Their brand
    (C) Their unit price
    (D) Their delivery date

178. What is mentioned about product R490?
    (A) It has an outdated formula.
    (B) It did not arrive with the other items.
    (C) Its price was higher than expected.
    (D) It had an unpleasant scent.

179. Which product does Mr. Kemp want to return?
    (A) T340
    (B) W761
    (C) D288
    (D) C492

180. What is NOT indicated in the e-mail?
    (A) Trenton Wholesale is under new ownership.
    (B) Customers must pay shipping charges on returns.
    (C) Ms. Kemp's business is at least ten years old.
    (D) Trenton Wholesale accepts orders by mail.

GO ON TO THE NEXT PAGE

FINAL TEST

Questions 181-185 refer to the following e-mail and memo.

E-Mail message

To:	Joshua Wenzell <j_wenzell@odbsolutions.com>
From:	Ruth Hoffman <r_hoffman@odbsolutions.com>
Date:	August 23
Subject:	Lecture Schedule

Dear Mr. Wenzell,

I am currently working on the schedule for the company's Wednesday afternoon lecture series for September. We paused this weekly professional development series over the summer while the conference room was being remodeled. I was concerned that the work would run past the August 20 deadline, but I was pleased that didn't happen. I've evaluated the feedback from our employee questionnaire to find the topics that would be most interesting to our staff. So far, three out of the four speakers have confirmed. The fourth speaker, Maria Nugent, is only tentatively scheduled. If she is nominated for the Portland Award, she won't be able to visit our site, as this creates a scheduling conflict. In that case, I wouldn't replace her with anyone. I will send out a memo to the staff once everything is finalized.

Sincerely,

Ruth Hoffman

To: All ODB Solutions Staff
From: Ruth Hoffman
Date: August 30
RE: Please read

It is my pleasure to welcome as our guests a number of talented professionals who will take part in the ODB Solutions afternoon lecture series. These individuals are at the top of their fields, and they have the capacity to inspire and motivate others. All staff members are invited to attend these opportunities for professional development. Each talk will take place from 1 to 3 P.M., and the schedule for September will be as follows:

   Wednesday, September 9: Remigio Bianchi, "Time Management Tips"
   Wednesday, September 16: Henry Armstrong, "Hidden Customer Needs"
   Wednesday, September 20: Kunimi Ito, "Tech Solutions that Work"

There is no need to register in advance for these sessions, but please note that seating will be available on a first-come, first-served basis. In the case of overcrowding, some people may have to stand in the back. I hope you will all consider being in attendance.

181. What is Ms. Hoffman glad about?
(A) A lecture received positive reviews.
(B) A tight deadline was extended for the team.
(C) A renovation project was completed on time.
(D) A conference schedule was approved.

182. What does Ms. Hoffman say she has done?
(A) Sent payments to the speakers
(B) Printed some presentation materials
(C) Posted a schedule on a Web site
(D) Analyzed some survey results

183. What is the purpose of the memo?
(A) To update a production schedule
(B) To inform the staff about presentations
(C) To welcome new team members
(D) To invite employees to give a talk

184. In the memo, the word "capacity" in paragraph 1, line 3, is closest in meaning to
(A) function
(B) ability
(C) volume
(D) energy

185. What is implied about Ms. Nugent?
(A) She will give the first presentation in a series.
(B) Her talk will be moved to another date.
(C) She was nominated for an award.
(D) Her presentation was replaced by Remigio Bianchi's.

GO ON TO THE NEXT PAGE

Questions 186-190 refer to the following schedule and e-mails.

Spring Haven Health & Beauty Expo: February 3–4, LC Convention Center
A total of ten thousand visitors expected! Daily booths with cosmetics samples, make-up tutorials, recipe demonstrations, and exercise equipment to try.

Thursday, February 3
10 A.M. – Noon / Free Health Screenings sponsored by Spring Haven Hospital. Get your blood pressure, cholesterol level, and BMI [body mass index] checked by medical professionals.

1 P.M. – 4 P.M. / Tips on Improving Sleeping Habits by Grantson Furniture. Includes a drawing for a king-size mattress and bed frame.

Friday, February 4
9 A.M. – Noon / Shoulder and Neck Massages provided by Celadon Spa. Let your tension melt away with a complimentary ten-minute massage. You must sign up on the company's Web site at least 24 hours prior to the event, as space is limited.

2 P.M. – 4 P.M. / Secrets to Healthy Vision by Edwards Eye Clinic. Learn about lifestyle changes that can help you maintain your eyesight as you age.

Updated January 5

E-mail

To:	Jill Livingston <j.livingston@grantsonfurniture.com>
From:	Fernando Mora <moraf@springhavenhbe.com>
Date:	January 17
Subject:	Spring Haven Health & Beauty Expo

Dear Ms. Livingston,

I have great news about the schedule change that you asked for. I spoke to a representative at Edwards Eye Clinic, and he said that they would be willing to switch time slots with Grantson Furniture. They appreciate having some extra time for their activity, so it worked out perfectly. I will update our Web site this afternoon with the latest schedule. Additionally, regarding this year's attendance, the high number of confirmed attendees on our social media page tells us that there will be even more visitors than last year. I will send updated attendance figures to all exhibitors by the end of the week.

Sincerely,

Fernando Mora
Event Coordinator, Spring Haven Health & Beauty Expo

E-mail

To: Marcel Baum <m_baum@ruby-cosmetics.com>
From: Lucy Suffolk <l_suffolk@ruby-cosmetics.com>
Date: January 20
Subject: Upcoming expo

Dear Marcel,

Thanks again for agreeing to help me work at the company's booth at this year's Spring Haven Health & Beauty Expo. I just got an e-mail from the event coordinator, and he said that about 2,000 more people in total will be attending than originally expected. I'm going to prepare enough samples so we can give one to each person. This still might not be enough, but it's the best I can do considering the short time frame.

Lucy

---

186. What is mentioned about Celadon Spa's activity?

(A) It is the most popular event.
(B) Its participants must pay a fee.
(C) It will last for four hours.
(D) It requires advance registration.

187. What is indicated about Ms. Livingston?

(A) She will be unable to attend an event.
(B) She requested a schedule change.
(C) She should update some online details.
(D) She had a booth at last year's expo.

188. In the first e-mail, the word "tells" in paragraph 1, line 6, is closest in meaning to

(A) sets apart from
(B) speaks about
(C) gives information to
(D) looks for

189. When will a prize drawing most likely be held?

(A) On Thursday morning
(B) On Thursday afternoon
(C) On Friday morning
(D) On Friday afternoon

190. How many samples will Ms. Suffolk most likely prepare?

(A) 2,000
(B) 4,000
(C) 10,000
(D) 12,000

Questions 191-195 refer to the following advertisement, e-mail, and customer review.

Farias Coffee Makers: Get your perfect brew!

All Farias coffee makers use individual flavor pods to brew a wide range of coffees and teas on demand. Now you can drink the luxury coffee you want at home!

- **Farias Petite:** A compact version of our machine designed exclusively for small kitchens. / $99.99
- **Farias Select:** Features automatic cleaning cycle to reduce mineral buildup. / $129.99
- **Farias Bia:** The Farias Bia (brew in advance) allows you to preload the machine and start it from your smartphone. / $149.99
- **Farias Morning:** Brews two pods simultaneously in separate cups. Perfect for busy families. / $169.99

Available colors for all machines: Midnight Black (#101), Classic Silver (#117), Retro Red (#119), and Creamy Pearl (#134).

E-Mail message

To:	Deborah Simmons <simmonsd@crowndeptstore.com>
From:	Jack Herrera <j.herrera@fariasappliances.com>
Date:	August 8
Subject:	Farias Coffee Makers

Dear Ms. Simmons,

As the store manager, you must stay informed of any changes to our supply. Effective immediately, we have discontinued color #134 for all Farias appliances. According to our supply contract, we must provide ongoing support to our customers. Sales manager Michelle Vickrey has asked me to visit your store on August 15 to give a demonstration of the Farias Bia, which some customers are finding difficult to use despite reading the user manual. Actually, this task has been assigned to Raymond Perry, but I'm happy to come along as well to help you arrange the products in an eye-catching display. If there's anything else your store needs, just let me know.

Sincerely,

Jack Herrera
Southwest Product Support, Farias

www.crowndeptstore.com/customerfeedback

Username: joe77   Posted: August 31

Comments: I love the customer service I always get at Crown Department Store. I recently went there to buy a coffee maker. All of the sales representatives were busy, but the store manager noticed I was waiting, so she assisted me. Her advice helped me to decide which model to buy. I ended up purchasing a Farias Morning coffee maker, and I love it! I'll recommend this product and your store to others.

191. Which color is Farias no longer making for its coffee makers?
  (A) Midnight Black
  (B) Classic Silver
  (C) Retro Red
  (D) Creamy Pearl

192. In the e-mail, the word "asked" in paragraph 1, line 4, is closest in meaning to
  (A) invited
  (B) examined
  (C) questioned
  (D) demanded

193. What does Mr. Herrera offer to do?
  (A) Send some user manuals
  (B) Give a demonstration
  (C) Refund discontinued products
  (D) Set up a display

194. What is indicated about Ms. Simmons?
  (A) She recently renewed a contract.
  (B) She helped the reviewer make a decision.
  (C) She is the head of the sales team.
  (D) She requested advice from Mr. Herrera.

195. What is true about the product purchased by the reviewer?
  (A) It is able to be operated by a smartphone.
  (B) It can make more than one drink at a time.
  (C) It has a special feature for cleaning itself.
  (D) It is the smallest model sold by Farias.

Questions 196-200 refer to the following article, e-mail, and map.

May 14 — Edgeway, two-time winner of the National Food Award, is back again with another idea for consumers. The company has announced the launch of Misty Brew, a concentrated coffee mix that can be combined with water to make instant iced coffee. As iced drinks have become more popular at national coffee chains, Edgeway's CEO Sandra Jackson wanted the company's research team to create something that would follow the trend. In a short time, they worked out a way to bring the popular drink to people's homes in a fast and convenient form. With its reputation for unique and innovative products, it is no surprise that Edgeway continues to release high-quality foods and beverages that meet the needs of today's consumers.

Edgeway plans to take advantage of the hot summer season by not only advertising heavily in magazines and on social media, but also allowing shoppers to try the drink for free. As part of the launch, the company has hired hundreds of workers on a short-term basis to give out samples of Misty Brew in supermarkets across the country.

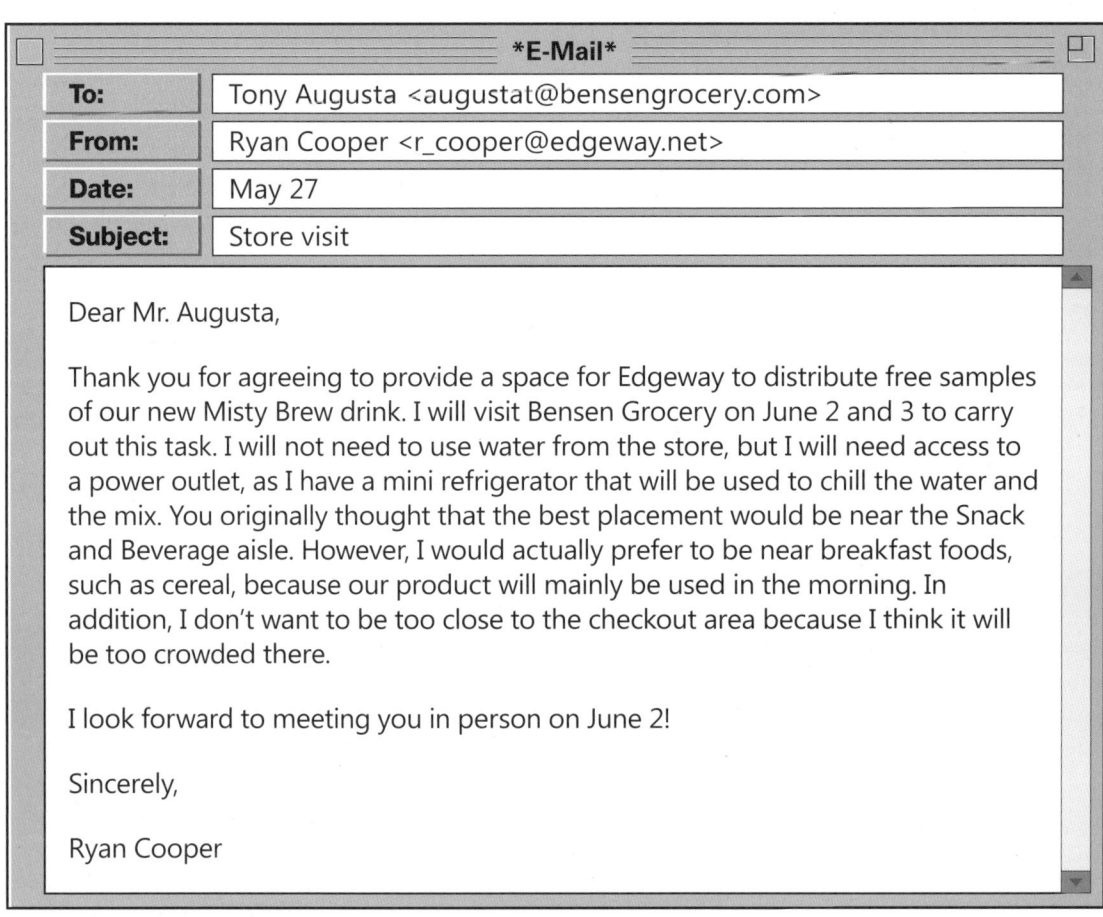

E-Mail

To: Tony Augusta <augustat@bensengrocery.com>
From: Ryan Cooper <r_cooper@edgeway.net>
Date: May 27
Subject: Store visit

Dear Mr. Augusta,

Thank you for agreeing to provide a space for Edgeway to distribute free samples of our new Misty Brew drink. I will visit Bensen Grocery on June 2 and 3 to carry out this task. I will not need to use water from the store, but I will need access to a power outlet, as I have a mini refrigerator that will be used to chill the water and the mix. You originally thought that the best placement would be near the Snack and Beverage aisle. However, I would actually prefer to be near breakfast foods, such as cereal, because our product will mainly be used in the morning. In addition, I don't want to be too close to the checkout area because I think it will be too crowded there.

I look forward to meeting you in person on June 2!

Sincerely,

Ryan Cooper

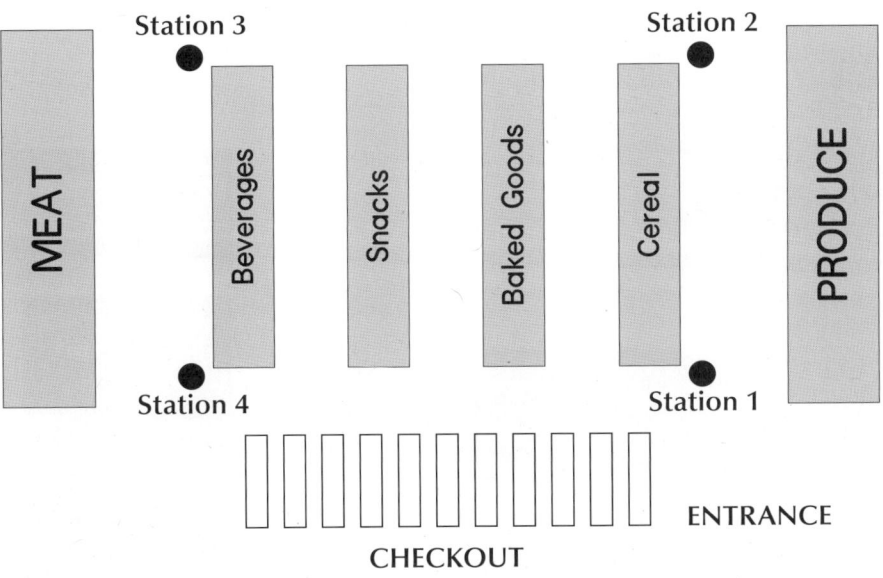

196. Why was the article written?

(A) To review the taste of a drink
(B) To announce the winner of an award
(C) To introduce a new product
(D) To explain a consumer report

197. In the article, the phrase "worked out" in paragraph 1, line 13, is closest in meaning to

(A) estimated
(B) devised
(C) outlined
(D) exercised

198. What is indicated about Edgeway?

(A) It is known for its creative ideas.
(B) It is the country's largest food company.
(C) It recently hired a new CEO.
(D) It sells beverages exclusively.

199. What is suggested about Mr. Cooper?

(A) He will visit the store three times.
(B) He is a temporary employee.
(C) He needs to be near a water tap.
(D) He used to work at Bensen Grocery.

200. Where would Mr. Cooper most likely want to be placed?

(A) Station 1
(B) Station 2
(C) Station 3
(D) Station 4

Stop! This is the end of the test. If you finish before time is called, you may go back to Parts 5, 6, and 7 and check your work.

ETS® & YBM 토익교재 로드맵

레벨	점수대	ETS TOEIC 시리즈	YBM TOEIC 시리즈
왕초보	450점 ~ 550점	토익 단기공략 550+	YBM ENGLISH Basics / YBM ENGLISH Basics Plus
입문 (초급)	550점 ~ 650점	토익기출 공식입문서 LC / 토익기출 공식입문서 RC / 토익 단기공략 650+	YBM 스타트 토익 LC / YBM 스타트 토익 RC / Jump Up TOEIC Basic LC·RC
기본 (중급)	750점 ~ 850점	토익기출 공식종합서 LC / 토익기출 공식종합서 RC / 토익 단기공략 750+	YBM 전략토익 LC / YBM 전략토익 RC / YBM 단기토익 700+ / Jump Up TOEIC Intermediate LC·RC
실전 (중·고급)	실전 모의고사	TOEIC 공식토익 LC / TOEIC Test 공식문제집 RC / 토익 정기시험 기출문제집 LC / 토익 정기시험 기출문제집 RC / 토익 정기시험 기출문제집 1 / 토익 정기시험 기출문제집 2 / 토익 정기시험 예상문제집 LC / 토익 정기시험 예상문제집 RC	YBM 실전토익 LC 1000 / YBM 실전토익 RC 1000 1 / YBM 실전토익 LC 1000 / YBM 실전토익 RC 1000 2
어휘 및 파트별	파트별 어휘	토익기출 VOCA / PART 7 실전전략	
스피킹	말하기	토익 스피킹 기출 단기공략 / 토익 스피킹 기출문제집 Speaking / 토익 스피킹 기출문제집	Interview English for Flight Attendants

YBM
전략토익
RC

정답 및 해설

PART 5-6

Unit 1 문장 구조

공식으로 해결하는 실전문제
본책 p. 21

1. (A)　2. (C)　3. (B)　4. (A)　5. (A)
6. (B)　7. (C)　8. (D)

1.
- 해설　주어 자리
  빈칸이 문장 맨 앞이자 동사 앞에 있으므로 주어 자리이다. 동명사가 될 수 있는 commuting은 복수동사 are 앞에 올 수 없으므로 명사 (A)가 정답이다.
- 번역　교통 체증이 예상되므로 출퇴근자들은 오늘 아침 평소보다 일찍 집을 나서도록 권고된다.
- 어휘　than usual 평소보다　heavy traffic 극심한 교통량　commuter 통근자　commute 통근하다

2.
- 해설　전치사의 목적어 자리
  빈칸은 전치사 for 뒤 목적어 자리이므로 동사(promote)와 형용사(promotional)는 답이 될 수 없다. '승진'을 뜻하는 명사 (C)가 정답이다.
- 번역　모든 직원들은 판매 목표를 지속적으로 달성할 경우 승진 자격이 주어진다.
- 어휘　eligible 자격이 되는　consistently 지속적으로　achieve 달성하다　sales target 판매 목표　promote 승진시키다, 홍보하다

3.
- 해설　주어 자리
  빈칸이 동사 continues 앞에 있고 문장의 주어인 Livewell Group과 동격을 이루는 주어 자리이므로 명사 (B)가 정답이다.
- 번역　다국적 건강 보험 제공업체인 리브웰 그룹은 건강 관리 이용에 대한 증가하는 수요를 지속적으로 충족시킨다.
- 어휘　insurance 보험　increasing 증가하는　access to ~에 대한 접근[이용]　healthcare 건강 관리　provide 제공하다　provider 제공자[제공업체]

4.
- 해설　주어 자리
  빈칸은 수식구인 for the first-quarter를 지우고 나면 동사 are 앞 주어 자리이므로 명사인 (A) earnings가 답이다. 빈칸 앞에 있는 소유격도 명사가 답임을 알려주는 단서가 된다.
- 번역　와이젠 식품 회사의 1/4분기 수익이 시장의 예상을 깰 것으로 예상된다.
- 어휘　quarter 분기　beat 이기다, 능가하다　expectation 예상　earnings 소득, 수입

5.
- 해설　there is/are 구문
  빈칸은 there is 뒤 주어 자리이므로 명사인 (A) access가 답이다. 명사 앞에는 명사를 수식해 주는 형용사(easy)가 자주 붙는 것도 알아두자.
- 번역　쇼핑 센터는 도시 중심부에 위치하고 있어서 대중 교통의 이용이 쉽다.
- 어휘　located in ~에 위치한　heart 중심부　public transportation 대중 교통　access 접근(하다)

6.
- 해설　목적어 자리
  빈칸은 타동사 identifies 뒤 목적어 자리이므로 명사인 (B) benefits가 답이다. 빈칸 앞에서 수식하는 「관사+형용사(the possible)」도 명사 자리임을 알려주는 단서가 된다.
- 번역　본 연구에서는 정규 항공사와 비교하여 수요 중심 비즈니스 항공이 가지는 가능한 혜택을 알아본다.
- 어휘　identify 알아보다　on-demand 수요 중심의　aviation 항공　as compared with ~와 비교하여　transportation 운송　beneficial 유익한　benefit 혜택; 유익하다

7.
- 해설　there is/are 구문
  that 이하 절에서 빈칸은 there are 뒤 주어 자리이므로 명사가 와야 한다. 동사 are와 수가 일치되어야 하므로 복수명사인 (D) limitations가 답이다.
- 번역　연구자들은 해양 생태계에 대한 불완전한 지식 탓에 자료에 한계가 있다는 점을 인정한다.
- 어휘　admit 인정하다　incomplete 불완전한　marine 해양의　ecosystem 생태계　limitation 한계　limitless 한이 없는

8.
- 해설　주어 자리
  빈칸은 맨 앞이면서, 수식구인 of Black Hills Institute를 지우고 나면 동사 will be 앞 주어 자리이므로 명사가 와야 한다. 명사인 (C)와 (D) 중, 문맥상 '그들의 근무와 헌신에 대해 인정받는다'고 했으므로 '직원들'을 뜻하는 (D)가 적절하다.
- 번역　블랙 힐스 협회의 직원들은 연례 직원 시상식 동안 수년 간의 근무와 헌신에 대해 인정받을 것이다.
- 어휘　recognize 인정하다　service 근무, 봉사　dedication 헌신, 전념　annual 매년의　reception 연회　employ 고용하다　employment 고용

공식으로 해결하는 실전문제
본책 p. 23

1. (D)　2. (C)　3. (D)　4. (A)　5. (B)
6. (C)　7. (A)　8. (B)

1.

해설 **동사 자리**
we가 주어, black and green olives가 목적어이고, 문장에 동사가 보이지 않는다. 빈칸이 동사 자리이므로 (D)가 정답이다.

번역 요청하시면 저희가 다양한 종류로 포장된 블랙 및 그린 올리브를 제공해 드립니다.

어휘 **upon request** 신청하면 **packaging** 포장 **provision** 공급

2.

해설 **자동사 자리**
빈칸 뒤에 전치사가 바로 오고 목적어가 없으므로 자동사가 들어가야 한다. come을 제외한 나머지 보기는 모두 타동사이다.

번역 플래테브에 의해서 제공되는 애완동물 사료는 다양한 맛으로 나오고 애완동물의 기호에 따라 맞춤 제작될 수 있다.

어휘 **pet** 애완동물 **come** (제품 등이) 나오다 **a variety of** 여러 가지의 **flavor** 풍미 **customize** 주문 제작하다 **suit** ~에 맞다 **preference** 선호

3.

해설 **동사 자리**
접속사 If 뒤로 연결된 절(you ~ software)에 동사가 보이지 않으므로 빈칸은 동사 자리이다. 따라서 동사인 (D)가 정답이다. 동명사[현재분사]인 experiencing, having experienced, to부정사인 to experience는 동사가 될 수 없다.

번역 소프트웨어를 설치하는 데 어려움을 겪는다면, Tech4U 지원 FAQ 페이지를 방문하세요.

어휘 **install** 설치하다 **support** 지원 **FAQ** 자주 묻는 질문 (= frequently asked questions)

4.

해설 **자동사 자리**
빈칸 뒤에 부사 hard가 오고 목적어가 없으므로 자동사가 답이다. work를 제외한 나머지 보기는 주로 타동사로 쓰이며, 의미상 가장 자연스러운 자동사 (A)가 정답이다.

번역 알렉스 비텔로는 5년 동안 카이드 회계 사에서 리스크 상담가로 열심히 일해왔다.

어휘 **risk** 위험 **consultant** 상담가 **attend** 참석하다 **hire** 고용하다

5.

해설 **자동사 자리**
빈칸 뒤에 전치사 according to가 오고 목적어가 없으므로 자동사가 답이다. proceed를 제외한 나머지 보기는 모두 타동사이므로 (B)가 정답이다.

번역 런던 마라톤은 태풍의 위협에도 불구하고 계획대로 진행될 것이다.

어휘 **according to** ~에 따라 **despite** ~에도 불구하고 **threat** 위협 **proceed** 진행하다[되다] **complete** 완료하다

6.

해설 **동사 자리**
접속사 that 뒤로 연결된 절, 즉 that절에 동사가 없으므로 빈칸은 동사 자리이다. 따라서 현재진행형 동사 (C) are functioning이 정답이다.

번역 코나 토이 공장의 보수관리 직원들은 생산 시스템이 제대로 기능하도록 분명히 한다.

어휘 **maintenance** 유지, 보수관리 **staff** 직원 **ensure** 반드시 ~하게 하다 **properly** 제대로 **functional** 실용적인, 기능 위주의 **function** 기능(하다)

7.

해설 **동사 자리**
문장에 동사가 보이지 않으므로 빈칸은 동사 자리이다. increased ~ competition이 주어이고 따라서 (A)가 정답이다.

번역 〈비즈니스 위클리〉에 따르면, 수용력 증대와 극심한 경쟁으로 항공사들이 운임을 올리지 못하고 있다.

어휘 **increased** 증가한 **capacity** 수용력 **intense** 극심한 **airline** 항공사 **raise** 올리다 **rate** 요금 **prevent A from -ing** A가 ~하지 못하도록 막다 **preventable** 막을 수 있는

8.

해설 **타동사 자리**
빈칸 뒤에 목적어 several ~ exhibitions가 있으므로 타동사가 답이다. holds를 제외한 나머지 보기는 모두 자동사이므로 정답은 (B)이다.

번역 호란 미술관은 신진 화가들과 협력하여 매년 여러 차례 기획 전시회를 연다.

어휘 **temporary** 일시적인 **in collaboration with** ~와 공동으로[협력해] **emerging** 떠오르는 **expire** 만료되다

공식으로 해결하는 실전문제 본책 p. 25

1. (B) 2. (D) 3. (B) 4. (A) 5. (D)
6. (A) 7. (C) 8. (C)

1.

해설 **보어 자리**
빈칸은 be동사 뒤 보어 자리이므로 형용사가 와야 하고 (B)가 정답이다. 빈칸 뒤에 목적어가 없으므로 necessitating은 답이 될 수 없다.

번역 장기적인 금융 성과를 내는 데에는 뛰어난 능력과 폭넓은 지식이 필수적이다.

어휘 **extensive** 폭넓은 **attain** 이루다 **long-term** 장기적인 **financial** 금융의 **necessitate** ~을 필요하게 하다 **necessary** 필수적인

2.
해설 목적격 보어 자리
빈칸은 5형식 동사 consider 뒤 목적어 the leadership training programs를 보충 설명하는 목적격 보어 자리이므로 형용사인 (D)가 정답이다. 참고로, quite은 부사로, 빈칸에 들어갈 형용사를 수식한다.

번역 쥬피터 사의 많은 직원들이 리더십 훈련 프로그램을 꽤 유용하다고 여긴다.

어휘 corporation 기업 quite 꽤

3.
해설 목적격 보어 자리
빈칸은 5형식 동사 find 뒤 목적어 the experience ~ Africa를 보충 설명하는 목적격 보어 자리이므로 형용사인 (B)가 답이다. 부사 truly는 rewarding을 수식하는 수식어다.

번역 남아프리카에서 자원봉사 프로젝트에 참여하는 경험이 정말 보람 있다는 것을 알게 될 것이다.

어휘 truly 정말로 reward 보상(하다) rewarding 보람 있는

4.
해설 보어 자리
빈칸은 2형식 동사 remain의 보어 자리이고, 주어 companies를 설명하는 형용사가 와야 하므로 (A)가 정답이다.

번역 마케팅 전문가인 론다 이거스는 회사들이 소셜 미디어에서 정치적으로 중립을 유지해야 한다고 말했다.

어휘 expert 전문가 state 말하다 politically 정치적으로 neutral 중립적인 neutralization 중립(화)

5.
해설 목적격 보어 자리
빈칸은 5형식 동사 deemed 뒤 목적어 some revisions를 보충 설명하는 목적격 보어 자리이므로 형용사인 (D)가 답이다.

번역 자료 수집 도구 및 절차를 사전 검사한 후, 연구 팀은 몇 가지 수정이 필요하다고 생각했다.

어휘 process 과정, 절차 deem 생각하다 revision 수정

6.
해설 보어 자리
빈칸은 2형식 동사 become의 보어 자리이고, 주어인 명사 changes를 설명하는 형용사가 와야 하므로 (A)가 답이다.

번역 장비의 사용 및 유지에 관한 회사 방침의 변경은 다음 주 월요일부터 효력이 있을 것이다.

어휘 policy 방침, 정책 maintenance 유지 equipment 장비 effective (규정 등이) 시행되는, 효력이 있는 effect 결과, 영향; (어떤 결과를) 가져오다

7.
해설 보어 자리
빈칸은 2형식 be동사의 보어 자리이고, 주어 consumption을 설명하는 형용사가 와야 하므로 명사 복수형인 lows는 답이 될 수 없다. lowly와 lowest도 형용사이지만 문맥상 적절하지 않다. 특히, 최상급인 lowest가 답이 되려면 앞에 the가 있어야 한다.

번역 지역 아동들의 식습관에 대한 연구로 신선한 식품의 섭취가 놀랄 만큼 낮다는 것이 밝혀졌다.

어휘 diet 식습관, 식사 consumption 소비 surprisingly 놀랄 만큼 low 낮은; 최저치 lowly 하찮은

8.
해설 5형식 동사 자리
목적어 the payment process 뒤에 목적격 보어로 형용사 easy가 있으므로 빈칸은 5형식 동사 자리임을 알 수 있다. 정답은 (C)이다.

번역 인포그래픽 서비스에 가입하시면, 귀사의 온라인 고객들을 위한 지불 절차를 쉽게 만드실 수 있습니다.

어휘 subscribe 가입(구독)하다 payment 지불 process 절차(과정)

YBM TEST

1. (D)	2. (C)	3. (D)	4. (C)	5. (D)
6. (B)	7. (B)	8. (C)	9. (D)	10. (A)
11. (A)	12. (C)	13. (A)	14. (C)	15. (B)
16. (A)	17. (D)	18. (A)	19. (B)	20. (D)

1.
해설 주어 자리
빈칸은 수식구인 for water skiing을 지우고 나면 동사 has led 앞 주어 자리이므로 명사인 (D) enthusiasm이 답이다. 빈칸 앞에 있는 소유격도 명사가 답임을 알려주는 단서가 된다.

번역 슐다 씨의 수상 스키에 대한 열정이 두 번 연속 위스콘신 수상 스키 선수권으로 이어졌다.

어휘 lead to ~로 이어지다 consecutive 연이은 championship 선수권 enthuse 열광하게 만들다 enthusiastic 열광적인 enthusiasm 열정

2.
해설 자동사 자리
빈칸 뒤에 부사가 바로 오고 목적어가 없으므로 자동사가 들어가야 한다. rise를 제외한 나머지 보기는 모두 타동사이다. 따라서 (C)가 정답이다.

번역 영향력 있는 스페인 애티튜즈 설문 조사 분석에 따르면 국민 건강 관리 서비스에 대한 만족이 상당히 상승했다.

어휘 satisfaction 만족 significantly 상당히 analysis 분석 influential 영향력 있는 attitude 태도 evaluate 평가하다

3.
해설 주어 자리
접속사 that으로 연결된 절(that ~ city)에서 동사 would 앞 주어 자리이므로 명사인 (D) efforts가 답이다. 빈칸 앞에 명사 수식어인 형용사 massive가 있는 것도 명사 자리임을 알려주는 단서가 된다.

번역 필라델피아 시장 험프리 펜은 신규 투자를 도시로 유치하기 위해 막대한 노력이 이루어질 거라고 말했다.

어휘 mayor 시장 state 말하다 massive 막대한 effortless 힘이 들지 않는 effort 노력

4.
해설 동사 자리
접속사 that으로 연결된 절(that ~ reception)에서 동사가 보이지 않으므로 빈칸에는 동사인 (C)가 들어가야 한다.

번역 보안 직원은 이 건물의 모든 방문자들이 반드시 접수처에 알리도록 해야 한다.

어휘 security 보안 personnel 직원들 make sure 반드시 (~하도록) 하다 reception 접수처 reporter 기자 report 알리다

5.
해설 명사 자리
소유격 뒤에는 명사가 와야 하므로 정답은 (D)이다.

번역 1925년 설립 이래로, 그린 유제품 사는 버터와 유제품의 제조를 선도해 온 업체이다.

어휘 leading 선두의 manufacturer 제조업체 dairy product 유제품 establish 설립하다 establishment 설립

6.
해설 보어 자리
빈칸은 be동사 뒤 보어 자리이고, 주어인 to carefully ~ attendees를 설명하는 형용사가 와야 하므로 (B)가 정답이다. it은 가주어이고 to carefully ~가 진주어이다.

번역 워크숍에 대비해 강사와 참가자들을 신중하게 맞추는 것이 중요하다.

어휘 preparation 준비 match 맞추다 instructor 강사 attendee 참가자

7.
해설 주어 자리
빈칸은 수식구인 of the graphic designer를 지우고 나면 동사 include 앞 주어 자리이므로 명사인 (B) responsibilities가 답이다. 빈칸 앞에 있는 관사 the도 명사가 답임을 알려주는 단서가 된다.

번역 그래픽 디자이너의 책무는 온라인 홍보를 위해 디자인을 개발하고 자료를 만드는 것을 포함한다.

어휘 material 자료 promotion 홍보 responsibility 책무 responsive 반응하는

8.
해설 진주어 자리
문장 맨 앞에 온 It은 가주어이므로 뒤에 진주어가 와야 한다. 진주어가 될 수 있는 to부정사와 that절 중, 빈칸 뒤에 절(we cannot provide ~)이 있으므로 (C) 접속사 that이 와야 한다.

번역 귀하의 선적물에 대해 대략적인 배송 시간을 알려드릴 수 없어 유감입니다.

어휘 unfortunate 유감스러운 approximate 대략적인 delivery 배송 shipment 선적물

9.
해설 목적격 보어 자리
빈칸은 5형식 동사 make 뒤의 목적어 its digital music player를 보충 설명하는 목적격 보어 자리이므로 형용사가 와야 하고 따라서 (D)가 답이다.

번역 사가 카르맨은 최신 기능을 추가함으로써 디지털 뮤직 플레이어를 더 매력적으로 만들었다.

어휘 up-to-date 최신의 feature 기능 attract 마음을 끌다 attractive 매력적인

10.
해설 자동사 자리
빈칸 뒤에 전치사가 바로 오고 목적어가 없으므로 자동사가 들어가야 한다. expire를 제외한 나머지 보기는 모두 타동사이다. 따라서 (A)가 정답이다.

번역 우리 데이터베이스 시스템은 당신의 오피스 올웨이즈 서비스 이용이 8월 31일에 만료된다는 것을 보여 준다.

어휘 indicate 보여 주다 subscription (서비스) 이용, 구독 expire 만료되다 install 설치하다 guarantee 보장하다

11.
해설 보어 자리
빈칸은 be동사 뒤 보어 자리이고, 주어인 Franco Guller watches를 설명하는 말이 와야 하므로 형용사인 (A)가 답이다. 부사 instantly는 형용사를 꾸며 주는 수식어다.

번역 프랑코 굴러 시계는 독특하고 아름다운 디자인으로 보는 즉시 눈에 띈다.

어휘 instantly 즉시 unique 독특한 recognizable 알아볼 수 있는 recognize 알아보다

12.
해설 목적어 자리
빈칸은 동사 publishes 뒤 목적어 자리이므로 명사인 (C)가 답이다. 바로 앞의 four(네 개의) 또한 다음에 명사가 나온다는 것을 알려주는 단서이다.

번역 〈가든데코〉 잡지는 매년 네 호의 잡지뿐 아니라 몇 년마다 한 번씩 특별판을 발행한다.

어휘 publish 출판하다 plus ~도 또한 edition (출판물의) 판 issue (잡지) 호; 발표하다, 발행하다

13.
해설 there is/are 구문
빈칸은 there are 뒤 주어 자리이므로 명사가 와야 하고, 동사 are와 수가 일치되어야 하므로 복수명사인 (A) signs가 답이다.

번역 세계 경제가 장기 침체 이후 마침내 성장 속도가 개선되는 걸 보게 되리라는 긍정적인 징후가 있다.

어휘 positive 긍정적인 pace 속도 recession 불황 sign 징후; 손으로 신호하다

14.
해설 목적격 보어 자리
빈칸은 to keep의 목적격 보어 자리로, fast와 함께 목적어 wireless internet connections를 보충 설명하므로 형용사인 (C)가 답이다.

번역 지하철에서 무선 인터넷 연결을 빠르고 안정적으로 유지하는 것은 쉽지 않다.

어휘 wireless 무선의 connection 연결 stability 안정 stabilize 안정시키다 stable 안정적인

15.
해설 보어 자리
빈칸은 2형식 동사 become 뒤 보어 자리이고, 주어인 Child safety car seats를 설명하는 형용사가 와야 하므로 (B)가 답이다. 부사 increasingly는 형용사를 꾸며 주는 수식어.

번역 어린이 안전 카시트는 점점 더 상용화되어 현재 6세 미만 어린이에게는 법적으로 요구되고 있다.

어휘 increasingly 점점 더 legally 법적으로 require 요구하다 common 흔한

16.
해설 진목적어 자리
5형식 동사 make 뒤에 가목적어 it과 목적격 보어 difficult가 있으므로 빈칸에는 진목적어 to부정사가 와야 한다. 따라서 (A)가 정답이다.

번역 데이터 저장의 발전으로 개인의 사생활을 침해하기가 어려워졌다.

어휘 advance 발전 storage 저장 privacy 사생활 violate 침해하다 violation 침해

17.
해설 보어 자리
빈칸은 be동사 뒤 보어 자리이고, 주어인 to develop ~ software를 설명하는 형용사가 와야 하므로 (D)가 답이다. it은 가주어이고 to develop ~ software가 진주어이다.

번역 회사가 오류 없는 소프트웨어를 개발하는 것은 비용이 너무 많이 들기 때문에 실현 가능하지 않다.

어휘 error-free 오류가 없는 costly 많은 비용이 드는 feasibility 실현 가능성 feasible 실현 가능한

18.
해설 타동사 자리
빈칸 뒤에 목적어 the Chinese market이 있으므로 타동사가 들어가야 한다. access를 제외한 나머지 보기는 모두 자동사이므로 (A)가 정답이다.

번역 펀플레이는 중국의 게임 대기업과 파트너 관계를 맺음으로써 중국 시장에 진출할 수 있다.

어휘 partner 파트너로 협력하다 giant 거대 기업, 거인 access 접근하다 proceed 진행하다 emerge 부상하다

19.
해설 동사 자리
문장에 동사가 보이지 않으므로 빈칸은 동사 자리이고 따라서 (B)가 정답이다.

번역 엇갈리는 반응이 있은 후, 시에서 가장 높은 건물의 설계자는 변경된 설계에 대해 설명했다.

어휘 mixed (의견이) 엇갈리는 reaction 반응 tower 높은 빌딩 revised 변경된 explanation 설명 explainable 설명할 수 있는

20.
해설 동사 자리
문장에 동사가 보이지 않으므로 빈칸은 동사 자리이다. 바로 뒤의 to부정사는 동사가 될 수 없다. (D)가 정답이다.

번역 그린 씨는 첫 레스토랑이 성공한 후 채식주의 식당을 추가로 열기로 결심했다.

어휘 vegetarian 채식주의자 decidedly 단호히

Part 6

문장 고르기 문제 1 - 대명사를 활용한다.

✚ 예제
본책 p. 28

Doris of Houston, TX
8월 19일에 쓴 의견

제 전화기를 업그레이드하고 싶어서 EZ 스마트폰을 샀어요. 예전 전화기와 비교해 이번 전화기에는 사용하기 흥미로운 앱이 더 많이 있고 카메라도 더 좋더라구요. 저는 기술에 강한 사람이 아닌데도 사용법을 배우기가 어렵지 않았어요. 전반적으로 EZ 스마트폰은 사용하기 즐거웠습니다. 친구들에게 그것을 틀림없이 추천할 거예요.

번역 (A) 서비스 이용이 내년에 만료돼요.
(B) 기꺼이 설문지를 작성할 거예요.
(C) 스마트폰을 그다지 많이 사용하지 않아요.
(D) 친구들에게 그것을 틀림없이 추천할 거예요.

어휘 comment 논평 upgrade 개선하다 compared with ~와 비교하여 application 앱

YBM TEST

본책 p. 29

1. (A)　2. (A)　3. (C)　4. (D)

알마 여행사와 다이버시티 여행 관리사의 합병

쿠퍼티노, 캘리포니아, 8월 4일 – 알마 여행사와 다이버시티 여행 관리사가 9월 1일자로 합병을 시행한다고 이번 주에 발표했다. 둘 다 여행 관리 업계에서 선도적인 업체들이다. 합산 총 연간 매출액이 7천만 달러가 넘는 이 새 회사는 국내에서 여섯 번째로 큰 규모의 여행 관리사가 될 것으로 예상된다. 현재 알마 여행사의 최고 경영자인 팻 호크가 두 회사의 합병을 이끌 것이며, 쿠퍼티노의 밀러 가에 있는 알마의 기존 건물에 본사를 두게 될 것이다.

"이번 합병으로 우리는 두 회사로부터 최고의 인재들과 경험을 한데 모을 수 있게 되었습니다. 높아진 구매력과 전문성, 더 넓어진 고객층으로 진짜 시장을 주도하는 뭔가를 만들 수 있는 멋진 기회를 갖게 될 것입니다."라고 호크 씨가 말했다.

어휘 management 관리 merge 합병하다 effective 시행되는, 효력이 있는 combined 결합된 gross 모두 합친 sales 매출액, 매출량 current 현재의 chief executive 최고 경영자 headquartered (~에) 본사가 있는 buying power 구매력 expertise 전문성, 전문 지식 customer base 고객층

1.
해설 문장 고르기
빈칸의 앞 문장에서 알마 여행사와 다이버시티 여행 관리사가 합병한다고 했으므로, 두 회사를 both로 받아 '두 회사는 여행 관리 업계에서 선도적인 업체들이다'라며 두 회사를 소개하는 (A)가 문맥상 자연스럽게 연결된다.

번역 (A) 둘 다 여행 관리 업계에서 선도적인 업체들이다.
(B) 다이버시티 여행 관리사는 30년이 넘은 회사이다.
(C) 회사는 재정적인 어려움을 겪었다.
(D) 다른 회사들이 내건 조건들은 거절되었다.

2.
해설 숫자 수식 부사
빈칸에는 숫자를 수식하기에 적절한 전치사가 와야 한다. 「over+숫자」는 '~가 넘는'이라는 뜻으로 '7천만 달러가 넘는 총판매액'을 뜻하므로 (A)가 정답이다. beneath(위치상 아래), even(심지어 ~조차), between(~ 사이에)은 의미상 적절하지 않다.

3.
해설 최상급
빈칸 앞에는 「the+서수」가 있고 뒤에는 비교 범위를 나타내는 in the country가 보이므로 최상급이 와야 한다. 의미상으로도 '전국에서 여섯 번째로 큰 여행사'가 적절하므로 (C)가 정답이다.

4.
해설 명사 어휘
opportunities(기회)는 뒤의 to부정사의 수식을 받아 '~할 기회'로 많이 쓰인다. '뭔가를 만들 멋진 기회를 가진다'로 의미상으로도 적절하므로 (D)가 정답이다.

어휘 substitute 대체물 exaggeration 과장 convenience 편리

Unit 2 명사

공식으로 해결하는 실전문제

본책 p. 33

1. (D)　2. (A)　3. (C)　4. (C)　5. (A)
6. (B)　7. (A)　8. (B)

1.
해설 주어 자리
빈칸은 관사 뒤이므로 명사가 와야 한다. 또한 수식구인 from the devastating financial crisis를 지우고 나면 동사(has been) 앞이므로 주어 자리, 즉 명사가 들어갈 자리이다. recover는 동사이므로 주어가 될 수 없고 명사인 (D)가 정답이다.

번역 형편없는 정부 정책으로 인해 혹독한 금융 위기로부터의 회복이 몹시 더뎠다.

어휘 devastating 엄청난 손상을 가하는 financial 금융의 crisis 위기 unusually 몹시 lengthy 매우 긴 policy 정책 recovery 회복

2.
해설 목적어 자리
빈칸은 동사 follow의 목적어 자리이므로 명사인 (A)가 정답이다.

번역 우리는 인턴 지망자들이 얼마나 지시사항을 잘 따르는지를 관찰하기 위해 테스트를 포함시키기로 결정했다.

어휘 prospective 장래의 instruction(s) 지시 instructive 유익한

3.
해설 목적어 자리
빈칸은 동사 provide의 목적어 자리이고, 앞에 수량 형용사(three)가 있으므로 명사가 와야 한다. 따라서 명사인 (C)가 정답이다.

번역 연구직에 지원하는 지원자들은 이전 고용주들로부터 받은 최소 세 장의 추천서를 제공해야 한다.

어휘 applicant 지원자 at least 최소한 previous 이전의 employer 고용주 refer 참고하다, 언급하다 reference 추천서

4.
해설 목적어 자리
빈칸은 전치사 for의 목적어 자리이므로 명사인 (C)가 정답이다.

번역 코넬은 훌륭한 기업가 정신을 인정받아 기업가 협회상을 수상했다.

어휘 entrepreneurial 기업가의 institution 협회 award 상 entrepreneurship 기업가 정신 excel 탁월하다 excellence 탁월함

5.
해설 목적어 자리
빈칸은 동사 has의 목적어 자리이고, 앞에 형용사 no가 있으므로 명사인 (A)가 정답이다. object도 명사로 물건이라는 뜻이 있지만 문맥상 적절하지 않다.

번역 그 기업은 평화로운 시위에는 반대하지 않는다고 주장한다.

어휘 corporation 기업 claim 주장하다 protest 항의, 시위 objection 반대 object 물건; 반대하다 objectify 객관화하다

6.
해설 소형명
빈칸은 동사 offered의 목적어 자리이고, 앞에 「소유격 + 형용사」가 있으므로 명사인 (B)가 정답이다.

번역 인사 부장이 엘리스 씨가 최우수 사원상을 수상한 것에 대해 진심 어린 축하를 전했다.

어휘 personnel 직원들, 인사과 director 이사 sincere 진심 어린 win (상 등을) 타다 outstanding 뛰어난 congratulation 축하 congratulatory 축하의

7.
해설 관(형)명
빈칸은 관사 뒤이고, 전치사 Following의 목적어 자리이므로 명사인 (A)가 정답이다.

번역 새로운 경영 절차를 확립하기 위해 1년간 지속됐던 프로젝트를 완료한 후, 모든 팀원들이 유급 휴가를 받게 될 것이다.

어휘 following ~후에 yearlong 1년간 지속되는 establish 수립하다 management 경영 process 절차 paid holiday 유급 휴가 completion 완료 complete 완성하다; 완벽한

8.
해설 관형명
빈칸은 「관사 + 형용사」 뒤이고, 동사 issued의 목적어 자리이므로 명사인 (B)가 정답이다.

번역 샘 어소시에잇츠는 최근 무역 박람회에서 있었던 현장 대리인의 행동에 대해 공식 사과 성명을 발표했다.

어휘 issue 발표하다 official 공식적인 behavior 행동 field 현장 representative 대리인, 대표 recent 최근의 trade 무역 fair 박람회 apologize 사과하다 apology 사과

✦ 공식으로 해결하는 실전문제
본책 p. 35

| 1. (A) | 2. (C) | 3. (C) | 4. (A) | 5. (D) |
| 6. (B) | 7. (D) | 8. (B) | | |

1.
해설 생김새(명사=동사)
빈칸은 동사 have의 목적어 자리이므로 명사인 (A)가 정답이다. access는 동사와 명사의 생김새가 같으므로 주의한다.

번역 ZED 회원으로서 당신은 방대한 지식과 경력 관련 정보를 접하게 될 것입니다.

어휘 resource 자원, 자료 access 접근; 접근하다

2.
해설 복합명사
빈칸은 전치사 in의 목적어 자리이고, 앞에 「한정사(this) + 형용사(open, international)」가 있으므로 명사가 와야 한다. 특히 design은 competition과 나란히 '디자인 대회'를 뜻하는 복합명사를 만들므로 명사인 (C)가 정답이다. design은 동사와 명사의 생김새가 같으므로 주의한다.

번역 본 국제 디자인 대회에서는 6개의 출품작이 "최우수 창작상"의 수상작으로 조명 받을 것이다.

어휘 entry 출품작 spotlight 집중 조명하다 winner 수상자[수상작] design competition 디자인 대회

3.
해설 생김새(명사=동사)
빈칸은 관사 뒤이므로 명사가 와야 한다. 또한 수식구인 of a camera flash를 지우면 동사 is의 주어 자리이므로 명사인 (C)가 정답이다. use는 동사와 명사의 생김새가 같고, '이용'이란 뜻일 때는 불가산명사이므로 복수형으로 쓸 수 없다.

번역 기념관에서는 항상 카메라 플래시의 사용이 엄격히 금지된다.

어휘 strictly 엄격히 prohibit 금지하다 at all times 항상 memorial 기념하기 위한

4.
해설 복합명사
빈칸은 동사 is의 주어 자리이므로 명사가 와야 한다. 앞에 있는 명사 staff job과 어울려 '직원 직무 능력'이라는 복합명사를 만드는 명사 (A)가 정답이다. performer도 명사이긴 하지만 의미상 적절하지 않다.

번역 직원 직무 능력은 생산성 유지 및 제고에 매우 중대한 요소 중 하나이다.

어휘 maintain 유지하다 productivity 생산성 performance 수행, 성과 performer 공연자, (일을) 수행하는 사람

5.
해설 생김새(명사=동사)
빈칸은 동사 will be 앞이므로 주어 자리이고, 앞에 「관사 + 형용사」가 있으므로 명사인 (D)가 정답이다. charge는 동사와 명사의 생김새가 같으므로 주의한다. (A)의 charges를 명사 복수형으로 볼 경우, 앞의 관사 an 때문에 적절하지 않다.

번역 만약 송장 날짜로부터 30일 이내에 결제가 이루어지지 않으면 추가 요금이 발생될 것이다.

어휘 payment 지불(금) invoice 송장 extra 추가의 incur (비용 등을) 발생시키다 charge 요금; 청구하다

6.
해설 복합명사
빈칸은 동사 are의 주어 자리이므로 명사가 와야 한다. 앞에 있는 명사 cost와 어울려 '비용 절감'이라는 복합명사를 만드는 명사 (B)가 정답이다.

번역 분석 보고서에 따르면, 사업이 계속 수익을 내기 위해서는 추가적인 비용 절감이 요구된다.

어휘 analysis 분석 further 추가의 profitable 수익이 나는 reduction 감소

7.
해설 생김새(명사=동사)
빈칸은 to부정사인 to provide의 목적어 자리이고, 앞에 명사 수식어인 형용사 continuous가 있으므로 명사인 (D)가 정답이다. support는 동사와 명사의 생김새가 같으므로 주의한다. 참고로 to부정사(to+동사원형)의 동사원형이 타동사일 경우, 타동사와 마찬가지로 뒤에 목적어를 취할 수 있다.

번역 안티바이러스 소프트웨어 회사들이 인터넷 사용자들에게 지속적인 지원을 제공할 것으로 기대된다.

어휘 antivirus 안티바이러스 firm 회사 continuous 지속적인 support 지원; 지원하다

8.
해설 복합명사
빈칸은 to increase의 목적어 자리이므로 명사가 와야 한다. 또한 앞에 있는 명사 employee와 더불어 '직원 생산성'이라는 복합명사를 만드는 명사가 필요하므로 (B)가 정답이다. product도 명사이긴 하나 의미상 적절하지 않다.

번역 이사회가 다음 주 목요일에 모여 직원 생산성을 향상시키기 위한 방안을 논의할 것이다.

어휘 board of directors 이사회 productivity 생산성 product 제품, 생산물

공식으로 해결하는 실전문제   본책 p. 37

1. (A) 2. (A) 3. (D) 4. (C) 5. (D)
6. (A) 7. (C) 8. (B)

1.
해설 동사와 수일치
빈칸은 단수동사인 has enjoyed 앞에 있는 주어 자리이므로 단수명사인 (A)가 정답이다.

번역 수년 동안, 관광은 꾸준한 성장을 누렸으며 세상에서 가장 빠르게 성장하는 경제 분야 중 하나가 되었다.

어휘 steady 꾸준한 sector 분야 tourism 관광, 관광 산업 tour 여행, 투어; 관광하다

2.
해설 불가산명사
빈칸은 소유격 your 뒤이므로 명사가 와야 한다. merchandise는 불가산명사이므로 복수형을 쓰지 않는다. 따라서 (A)가 정답이다.

번역 만약 상품에 대해 질문이 있으실 경우에는, 영수증에서 연락처를 확인하실 수 있습니다.

어휘 contact information 연락처 receipt 영수증 merchandise 상품; 판매하다

3.
해설 동사와 수일치
빈칸은 복수동사 give의 주어 자리이므로 복수명사인 (D)가 정답이다. architecture도 명사이지만 의미상 어색하다.

번역 우리 건축가들이 설계부터 비용까지 프로젝트의 모든 영역에 대해 안내를 제공합니다.

어휘 guidance 안내, 지도 aspect 측면 architecture 건축(물), 건축학 architect 건축가

4.
해설 동사와 수일치
수식구인 from our online store를 지우면 빈칸은 복수동사 are의 주어 자리이므로 복수명사인 (C)가 정답이다.

번역 일반적으로, 온라인 매장에서 주문된 상품은 구매일로부터 영업일 기준 3일 이내로 배송됩니다.

어휘 ship 운송하다 business day 영업일, 평일 purchase 구매 order 주문, 주문품; 주문하다

5.
해설 불가산명사
빈칸은 동사 has attracted의 목적어 자리이므로 명사가 와야 한다. interest는 '관심'을 뜻할 때는 불가산명사이므로 복수형을 쓰지 않는다. 따라서 (D)가 정답이다.

번역 밍센트럴 사는 수익이 상당히 오른 이후 여러 클라우드 기반 소프트웨어 공급업체들의 관심을 끌게 되었다.

어휘 cloud-based 클라우드 기반의 provider 공급업체 revenue 수익 rise 오르다 significantly 상당히

6.
해설 불가산명사
빈칸은 전치사 of의 목적어 자리이고, 앞에 형용사 hard의 수식을 받았으므로 명사가 와야 한다. work는 '일'을 뜻할 때는 불가산명사이므로 복수형을 쓸 수 없다. 따라서 (A)가 정답이다.

번역 안 박사와 그의 팀은 수개월간의 노고 끝에 새로운 스마트폰 앱을 성공적으로 출시했다.

어휘 manage to+동사원형 ~해내다 launch 시작[출시]하다 application 응용 프로그램, 앱 workable 실행 가능한

7.

해설 동사와 수일치
빈칸은 복수동사 are의 주어 자리이므로 복수명사인 (C)가 정답이다.

번역 가이드라인은 여러 학문 분야에서 일하고 있는 그룹들에 의해 방대하고 국제적인 자문 절차를 거쳐 개발된다.

어휘 multidisciplinary 여러 학문 분야에 걸친 vast 방대한 consultative 고문[상담]의 process 절차 guide 안내; 안내하다

8.

해설 가산명사 vs. 불가산명사
문맥상 전자제품에 대한 설명서라고 하는 것이 자연스러우므로 정답은 (B)이다. (A) information(정보)은 불가산명사이므로 앞에 a가 올 수 없고, (C) recipe(조리법)는 의미상 적절하지 않다. (D) instruction은 '설명'을 뜻할 때는 복수형으로 써야 한다.

번역 www.lcappliances.com에서 우리 가전제품에 대한 상세한 설명서를 다운로드하실 수 있습니다.

어휘 download 다운로드하다 detailed 상세한 appliance 가전제품 description 설명서 recipe 조리법 instruction(s) 지시, 설명

공식으로 해결하는 **실전문제**   본책 p. 39

| 1. (B) | 2. (D) | 3. (B) | 4. (A) | 5. (B) |
| 6. (A) | 7. (C) | 8. (B) | | |

1.

해설 가산명사 vs. 불가산명사
빈칸은 전치사 뒤 목적어 자리이고, 앞에 형용사 individual이 수식하므로 명사가 와야 한다. 형용사 앞에 한정사가 없으므로 가산 단수명사는 답이 될 수 없고, 복수명사인 (B)가 정답이다.

번역 훈련을 받은 사람들은 더 오랫동안 개별 업무에 집중할 수 있었다.

어휘 focus one's attention on ~에 주의를 집중하다 individual 개인의, 개별적인 task 업무

2.

해설 사람 명사 vs. 사물/추상명사
빈칸은 to부정사의 목적어 자리이므로 명사가 와야 한다. 앞에 한정사가 없으므로 가산 단수명사 investor(투자자)는 답이 될 수 없고, 불가산명사인 (D)가 정답이다. 참고로 to부정사(to+동사원형)의 동사원형이 타동사일 경우, 문장의 본동사(타동사)와 마찬가지로 뒤에 목적어를 취할 수 있다.

번역 정부가 이미 세금을 삭감했지만, 투자를 장려하기 위해서는 더 많은 것이 요구된다.

어휘 while ~이긴 하지만 encourage 장려하다 investment 투자

3.

해설 사람 명사 vs. 사물/추상명사
빈칸 앞에 소유격 your가 있으므로 명사가 와야 한다. 소유격 뒤에는 가산 단수명사(attendee, 참석자)와 불가산명사(attendance, 출석) 모두 답이 될 수 있다. 문맥상 '당신의 출석을 확인하기 위해'가 적절하므로 (B)가 정답이다.

번역 당신이 교육에 출석한 것을 확인하기 위해, 서류에 서명해야 한다.

어휘 confirm 확인하다 training session 교육 require 요구하다 sign 서명하다 form 서류, 서식 attendee 참석자 attendance 출석

4.

해설 사람 명사 vs. 사물/추상명사
빈칸은 「관사+형용사(skilled)」의 뒤이고, 앞에 있는 명사 excavator(굴착기)와 더불어 '굴착기 기사'라는 복합명사를 만들어 주는 명사가 필요하므로 (A)가 정답이다. operation(작업, 운영)은 문맥상 적절하지 않다.

번역 미리어드 머트리얼스는 현재 시 프로젝트 건으로 일할 숙련된 굴착기 기사를 구하고 있다.

어휘 currently 현재 skilled 숙련된 excavator 굴착기 civil 시민의 operator (기계 등을) 조작하는 사람

5.

해설 가산명사 vs. 불가산명사
빈칸은 동사 expect의 목적어 자리이므로 명사가 와야 한다. 앞에 한정사가 없으므로 가산 단수명사인 recruit(신입사원)는 답이 될 수 없다. 문맥상 '채용업자들이 이력서를 보고 ~할 것으로 기대하지 말아야 한다'가 적절하므로 (B)가 정답이다.

번역 구직자들은 채용업자들이 자신의 이력서를 보고 곧바로 그들의 구직활동을 지도해 줄 거라 기대하지 말아야 한다.

어휘 job seeker 구직자 résumé 이력서 immediately 즉시 recruit 모집하다; 신입사원 recruiter 채용자, 모집자

6.

해설 가산명사 vs. 불가산명사
빈칸은 전치사 of의 목적어 자리이므로 명사가 와야 한다. 빈칸 앞에 한정사가 없어서 가산 단수명사(purchaser, 구매자)는 답이 될 수 없으므로 (A)가 정답이다. 참고로, purchase는 '구입품'을 뜻할 때는 가산명사로 쓰인다.

번역 영수증을 분실한 경우, 구매의 증거로 은행의 입출금 내역서를 제공해도 된다.

어휘 in the event that ~할 경우에 receipt 영수증 bank statement 입출금 내역서 proof 증거 purchase 구매, 구매품; 구매하다 purchaser 구매자

7.

해설 가산명사 vs. 불가산명사
빈칸은 동사 can be의 주어 자리이므로 명사가 와야 한다. 앞에 한정사가 없으므로 가산 단수명사는 답이 될 수 없고, 복수명사인 (C)가 정답이다.

번역 비록 무료 배송은 제공되지 않지만, 200개 이상의 대량 주문에 대해서는 할인이 가능하다.

어휘 **shipping** 운송, 배송 **bulk** 대량, 대규모 **unit** (구성) 단위 **discount** 할인; 할인하다

8.

해설 **사람 명사 vs. 사물/추상명사**
수식구인 at the KeepLearn System을 지우고 나면 빈칸은 동사(are)의 주어 자리이므로 명사가 와야 한다. 앞에 한정사가 없을 때는 복수명사(employees, 직원)와 불가산명사(employment, 고용) 모두 답이 될 수 있는데, 문맥상 '직원들이 지속적인 교육 과정을 제공받는다'가 적절하므로 (B)가 정답이다.

번역 킵런 시스템의 직원들은 리더십 개발에 대한 지속적인 교육 과정을 제공받는다.

어휘 **provide** 제공하다 **continuing** 계속적인 **education** 교육 **course** 강좌 **development** 개발

YBM TEST

본책 p. 40

1. (C)	2. (B)	3. (C)	4. (D)	5. (C)
6. (B)	7. (A)	8. (B)	9. (C)	10. (D)
11. (A)	12. (D)	13. (B)	14. (D)	15. (B)
16. (B)	17. (C)	18. (C)	19. (A)	20. (D)

1.

해설 **가산명사 vs. 불가산명사**
빈칸은 동사 should visit의 주어 자리이다. 앞에 형용사 interested만 있고 한정사가 없으므로 가산 단수명사인 individual은 답이 될 수 없고 복수명사인 (C)가 정답이다.

번역 관심 있으신 분들은 멤버십 혜택에 대한 자세한 정보를 위해 우리 웹사이트를 방문하셔야 합니다.

어휘 **interested** 관심 있는 **detailed** 상세한 **benefit** 혜택 **individual** 개인; 개인의 **individuality** 개성

2.

해설 **사람 명사 vs. 사물/추상명사**
빈칸은 앞에 관사가 있고, 복수동사 are의 주어 자리이므로 복수명사가 와야 한다. 복수명사 negotiations(협상)와 negotiators(협상가) 중에서 문맥상 '협상이 진행 중이다'가 적절하므로 (B)가 정답이다.

번역 아직 합의가 이루어지지 않았으며 협상이 진행 중이다.

어휘 **reach an agreement** 합의에 이르다 **ongoing** 진행 중인 **negotiate** 협상하다 **negotiation** 협상

3.

해설 **복합명사**
'any research ------'은 begin의 목적어다. research activity가 복합명사로 '연구 활동'을 뜻하므로 (C)가 정답이다. (D) activation은 활성화라는 뜻으로 의미상 적절하지 않다.

번역 연구원들은 연구 활동을 개시하기 전에 부장으로부터 승인을 받아야 한다.

어휘 **obtain** 얻다 **approval** 승인 **department head** 부장, 부서장 **activate** 활성화시키다

4.

해설 **목적어 자리**
'be subject to(~의 대상이다)'에서 to는 전치사이다. 빈칸은 전치사 to의 목적어 자리이므로 명사인 (D)가 정답이다.

번역 우리의 제안은 가격 및 이용 가능성에 있어서 호텔의 확인을 받아야 한다.

어휘 **be subject to** ~의 대상이다 **in terms of** ~면에서 **availability** 이용 가능성 **confirmation** 확인 **comfirmative** 확증하는

5.

해설 **동사와 수일치**
빈칸은 「한정사(all)+형용사(anticipated)」 뒤이므로 명사가 와야 한다. 또한 수식구인 for your business trip을 지우면 복수동사 need의 주어 자리이므로 복수명사인 (C)가 정답이다.

번역 출장과 관련된 모든 예상되는 비용이 출장 승인 요청서에 포함되어야 한다.

어휘 **anticipated** 예상되는 **business trip** 출장 **request form** 신청서 **expense** 비용

6.

해설 **가산명사 vs. 불가산명사**
빈칸 앞 관사 a 뒤에는 가산 단수명사만 올 수 있으므로 (B) fee(수수료)가 정답이다. 나머지 보기는 모두 불가산명사이므로 a 뒤에 올 수 없다.

번역 우리 은행 방침이 일부 변경되어 수신 이체에 대해 4달러의 소정의 수수료가 부과될 것이다.

어휘 **policy** 방침 **charge** 부과하다 **incoming** 들어오는 **transfer** 이체 **fee** 수수료 **interest** 관심, 이익, 이자

7.

해설 **복합명사**
'All ------ letters'는 동사 must be의 주어이고, recommendation letter가 '추천서'를 뜻하는 복합명사이므로 (A)가 정답이다. 빈칸에는 명사 letters를 수식하는 형용사가 올 수도 있으나 recommendable(추천할 수 있는)은 의미상 적절하지 않다.

번역 모든 추천서는 온라인 신청서와 함께 전자상으로 제출되어야 한다.

11

어휘 submit 제출하다 electronically 전자상으로 along with ~와 함께 application 신청서 recommendation 추천

8.

해설 목적어 자리
빈칸은 to부정사 to make의 목적어 자리이므로 명사인 (B)가 정답이다. 참고로 to부정사(to+동사원형)의 동사원형이 타동사라면 뒤에 목적어를 취할 수 있다.

번역 전쟁기념관의 티켓은 구매가 한정되어 있으므로 방문객들은 한참 전에 예약하실 것을 권고드립니다.

어휘 availability 구입[이용] 가능성 memorial 기념의, 추도의 limited 한정된 in advance 미리 reserve 예약하다 reservation 예약

9.

해설 목적어 자리
빈칸은 동사 sent의 목적어 자리이므로 명사가 와야 한다. 명사 representative(직원)는 가산명사이므로 한정사가 없을 때는 복수 형태로 와야 한다. 따라서 복수명사 (C)가 정답이다.

번역 100여 곳의 회사가 재능 있는 학생들을 면접봐서 채용하기 위해 마드리드에서 개최된 채용 박람회에 직원들을 보냈다.

어휘 job fair 채용 박람회 talented 재능 있는 representative 대표, (회사를 대표하는) 직원 represent 대표하다

10.

해설 목적어 자리
빈칸은 전치사 for의 목적어 자리이므로, 가산명사의 복수형인 (D)가 정답이다. (C) delayer는 '지연하는 사람'을 뜻하는 가산명사로, 한정사 없이 단수 형태로는 쓸 수 없으므로 오답이다.

번역 배송과 관련해 우리는 불가항력적인 사건에 의해 발생된 지연에 관해서는 책임지지 않습니다.

어휘 with regard to ~에 관하여 shipment 배송 be liable for ~에 책임이 있다 beyond control 불가항력의 delay 지연; 미루다

11.

해설 목적어 자리
빈칸은 동사 will discuss의 목적어 자리이고, 형용사가 빈칸을 수식하므로 명사인 (A)가 정답이다. 참고로, 명사 앞에는 명사를 수식하는 형용사가 여러 개 올 수 있다.

번역 루머 금융 그룹의 사장 세라 큐리는 소기업의 경영주에게 적당한 포괄적인 금융 전략을 논의할 것이다.

어휘 comprehensive 포괄적인 financial 금융의 applicable to ~에 적당한, ~에 적용할 수 있는 strategy 전략 strategic 전략적인

12.

해설 사람 명사 vs. 사물/추상명사
빈칸은 동사 welcome의 목적어 자리이고, 앞에서 형용사 topical이 수식하므로 명사가 와야 한다. 앞에 한정사가 없으므로 가산 단수명사인 correspondent(통신원)는 답이 될 수 없고, 불가산명사인 (D)가 정답이다.

번역 〈월간 트렌즈〉의 편집자들은 주제와 상관없이 독자들이 보내는 시사성 있는 서신을 언제나 환영합니다.

어휘 editor 편집자 topical 시사와 관련된 correspond 서신을 주고 받다 correspondent 기자, 통신원 correspondence 서신

13.

해설 보어 자리+관사 수일치
빈칸은 2형식 동사(be동사) 뒤 보어 자리이고 주어 fundraiser (모금 행사)와 동격 관계이므로 명사가 와야 한다. 또한 앞에 a가 있으므로 단수명사인 (B)가 정답이다.

번역 지난 토요일에 있었던 모금 행사는 대성공이었고, 우리는 백만 달러 이상을 모금했다.

어휘 fundraiser 모금 행사 fantastic 환상적인, 굉장한 raise 모으다

14.

해설 복합명사+불가산명사
빈칸은 전치사 of의 목적어 자리이고, equipment(장비)는 sports와 함께 쓰여 '운동 장비(sports equipment)'를 뜻하는 복합명사가 된다. equipment는 불가산명사로 복수형은 쓸 수 없으므로 단수 형태인 (D)가 정답이다.

번역 프레코 사는 모든 선수들의 요구에 적합한 폭넓은 운동 장비를 제조하는 선두 기업이다.

어휘 manufacture 제조하다 comprehensive 종합적인 a range of 다양한 fit 맞다, 적합하다 athlete 운동선수

15.

해설 사람 명사 vs. 사물/추상명사
빈칸은 전치사 with의 목적어 자리이고, 명사 gardening(원예)과 더불어 복합명사를 만드는 명사가 필요하다. 앞에 한정사가 없으므로 가산 단수명사인 advisor(조언자)는 답이 될 수 없고 불가산명사인 (B)가 정답이다. gardening advice는 '원예 조언[정보]'을 뜻한다.

번역 우리는 회원들이 각자의 정원에서 기르기에 가장 좋은 식물을 알 수 있도록 개별 맞춤식 원예 조언을 제공한다.

어휘 provide A with B A에게 B를 제공하다 personalized 개인에게 맞춘 gardening 원예 advice 충고, 조언 advisory 조언의 advise 조언하다

16.
해설 사람 명사 vs. 사물/추상명사
빈칸은 관사 뒤이고, 동사 has led의 목적어 자리이므로 명사가 와야 한다. a 뒤에 올 수 있는 가산 단수명사 tourist(관광객)와 tour(견학) 중, 문맥상 '식품 가공 공장의 견학을 이끌었다'가 적절하므로 (B)가 정답이다.

번역 생산 관리자가 최근에 단골 고객들을 위한 식품 가공 공장의 견학을 이끌었다.

어휘 food processing 음식 가공 tour 여행, 견학

17.
해설 생김새(명사=동사)
빈칸은 한정사 All 뒤이고, 수식어 from the event를 지우면 동사 will be의 주어 자리이므로 명사가 와야 한다. All 뒤에는 복수명사나 불가산명사가 와야 하므로 복수명사인 (C)가 정답이다. proceeds(수익금)는 동사 proceed(진행하다)와 생김새가 같으므로 주의한다.

번역 행사 수익금은 전액 어린이 재단에 기부될 것이다.

어휘 procedure 절차 foundation 재단

18.
해설 동사와 수일치
빈칸은 복수동사 are의 주어 자리이고, 앞에 복수를 뜻하는 한정사 these가 있으므로 복수명사인 (C)가 정답이다.

번역 이 문서들은 대중들에게 공개되기 전에 선임 회계사들에 의해 검토될 것이다.

어휘 release 공개하다, 발표하다 examine 검토하다 senior 상위의 accountant 회계사 document 서류, 문서; 기록하다 documentation 문서화, 기록

19.
해설 관형명+관사와 수일치
빈칸은 전치사 at의 목적어 자리이고, 앞에 a가 있으므로 단수명사인 (A)가 정답이다.

번역 유펙스 물류에서는 뛰어난 물류 서비스를 합리적인 가격에 제공하는 것을 목표로 한다.

어휘 logistics service 물류 서비스 reasonable (가격이) 적당한 price 가격; 값을 매기다

20.
해설 목적어 자리
빈칸은 전치사 in의 목적어 자리이므로 명사가 와야 한다. in advance가 '미리, 사전에'를 뜻하는 관용 표현이고 문맥상 '사전에 신청서를 제출해야 한다'가 적절하므로 (D)가 정답이다. advancement(발전)는 의미상 적절하지 않다.

번역 〈시티 트리뷴〉에 행사를 홍보하길 원하는 지역 주민이나 단체들은 사전에 신청서를 제출할 것을 권고 드립니다.

어휘 resident 거주자, 주민 publicize 홍보하다 request form 신청서 advance 진전; 나아가다

Part 6

문장 고르기 문제 2 – 지시어를 활용한다.

예제
본책 p. 42

경영진이 올해 회계 연도 말까지 우리 사무실을 영구적으로 닫기로 결정했다는 사실을 발표하게 되어 유감입니다. 직원들 일부는 선택되어 본사로 발령이 날 예정입니다. 만약 당신이 이 명단에 들어간다면 곧 통지가 갈 것입니다. 고용이 종료되는 직원들은 관대한 보상 패키지를 받게 될 것이며, … 중략

번역 (A) 새로운 사업에 성공하시기를 바랍니다.
(B) 만약 당신이 이 명단에 들어간다면 곧 통지가 갈 것입니다.
(C) 저희는 이 사업을 더 이상 유지할 수 없었습니다.
(D) 본사 장소 선정이 미뤄졌습니다.

어휘 financial year 회계 연도 transfer 전근 보내다 compensation 보상

YBM TEST
본책 p. 43

| 1. (A) | 2. (C) | 3. (D) | 4. (B) |

1월 18일
칼라 홀러맨
몽고메리 가 440번지
샌프란시스코, 캘리포니아 94103

소득세 담당자께,

과세 연도 2016-2017년에 해당하는 소득세 초과 지급분에 대한 상환을 요청하고자 편지를 씁니다. 제 이전 고용주인 마우저 전자의 계산 착오로 저의 세금이 초과 지불되었습니다. 저의 계산에 근거하면, 저는 2,300달러를 초과로 지불했습니다. 의무적으로 납세해야 할 금액이 5,900달러인데도, 제가 총 8,200달러를 지불한 겁니다.

참고하실 수 있도록, 관련된 모든 서류를 동봉하는데, 마우저 전자에서의 전체 근무 이력과 납세 증빙 자료입니다. 이것이 귀하께서 저의 요청을 처리하는 데 충분한 정보라고 생각합니다. 추가 질문이 있으시면 chollerman@yahoo.net로 언제든 편하게 연락 주십시오.

어휘 income tax 소득세 officer 관리자, 담당자 request 요청하다 reimbursement 상환, 환급 overpayment 초과 지불(금) miscalculation 계산 착오 overpay 초과 지불하다 in excess 초과하여 whereas 반면에, ~임에도 be obliged to 부사적 의무적으로[어쩔 수 없이] ~하다 for one's reference 참고로 enclose 동봉하다 document 서류 work history 근무 내역, 이력 proof 증거 tax payment 납세, 납부 further 추가적인

1.

해설 분사구문
'------- my calculations'는 완전한 절에 덤으로 붙은 수식구로, 빈칸 뒤의 명사구(my calculations)를 절에 연결해야 하므로 전치사(Instead of ~ 대신에, Based on ~에 근거하여)가 답이 될 수 있다. 문맥상 '저의 계산에 근거하여'가 적절하므로 (A)가 정답이다. Likewise(마찬가지로)는 부사이므로 명사를 연결할 수 없고, As well as는 'A as well as B(B뿐만 아니라 A도)'로 쓰이므로 답이 될 수 없다.

2.

해설 형용사 어휘
'근무 내역 및 납세 증명을 제공해 줄 서류'를 꾸미는 형용사로는 relevant(관련 있는)가 가장 적절하다. 따라서 정답은 (C)이다.

어휘 numerous 많은 diverse 다양한 qualified 자격이 있는

3.

해설 형용사 자리
빈칸은 '관 ------- 명' 순서이고, 복합명사인 work history(근무 내역)를 수식하는 자리이므로 분사와 형용사가 올 수 있다. 문맥상 필요한 모든 것이 포함된 '완전한 근무 내역'을 뜻하므로 '완전한, 다 갖추어진'을 뜻하는 형용사 (D)가 정답이다.

4.

해설 문장 고르기
빈칸의 앞 문장에서 '나는 관련 서류를 모두 동봉했고, 이것이 완전한 자료가 되어 줄 것'이라고 했는데, 이것을 (B)에서 'this(이것)'라고 지칭해 충분한 정보가 되리라 생각한다고 했으므로 문맥상 (B)가 정답이다.

번역 (A) 소득세 신고서는 저의 회계사에 의해 제출되었습니다.
(B) 이것이 귀하께서 저의 요청을 처리하는 데 충분한 정보라고 생각합니다.
(C) 제가 세금 환급을 요청한 지 6개월이 지났습니다.
(D) 제가 잠시 동안 일에 복귀할 의사가 없음을 유념해 주세요.

Unit 3 대명사

공식으로 해결하는 실전문제 본책 p. 47

1. (B) 2. (C) 3. (D) 4. (D) 5. (B)
6. (A) 7. (A) 8. (B)

1.

해설 대명사 자리-주격
빈칸은 that절의 주어 자리이므로 주격인 (B)가 정답이다.

번역 켈리 스티븐슨은 시민회관 쪽 일을 마무리하는 것을 돕기 위해 더 많은 자원 봉사자들이 필요하다고 말했다.

어휘 volunteer 자원 봉사자 complete 완료하다 Community House 시민회관

2.

해설 대명사 자리-목적격
빈칸은 동사 will send의 목적어 자리이고, 단수명사 itinerary(일정표)를 대신하므로 정답은 (C)이다.

번역 더 자세한 일정표를 받기를 원하시면, 제가 전자상으로 그것을 보내드리겠습니다.

어휘 detailed 상세한 itinerary 일정표 electronically 전자상으로

3.

해설 대명사 자리-소유격
빈칸은 전치사 with의 뒤에 있긴 하지만, 빈칸 뒤에 명사가 있으므로 소유격이 와야 한다. 따라서 (D)가 정답이다.

번역 선임 UX 디자이너로서, 힐스 씨는 엔지니어링 및 제품 팀과 긴밀히 협력한다.

어휘 senior 상위의 UX 사용자 경험(= User Experience) closely 긴밀히 engineering 공학, 공학 기술

4.

해설 대명사 자리-목적격
빈칸은 전치사 of의 목적어 자리이므로 목적격인 (D)가 정답이다. 참고로, 재귀대명사는 주어 쪽 자리에는 오지 않는다.

번역 앞으로 몇 주 동안, 우리 중 몇 명은 시카고 출장 때문에 사무실을 비우게 될 것이다.

어휘 business trip 출장

5.

해설 대명사 자리-소유격
빈칸은 전치사 about의 뒤에 있긴 하지만, 빈칸 뒤에 「형용사+명사」가 보이므로 소유격이 와야 한다. 따라서 (B)가 정답이다.

번역 그렉 패터슨은 나디아 휘트먼과 함께 쓴 그의 신작 '유별난 아이'에 대해 이야기할 것이다.

어휘 eccentric 별난

6.

해설 대명사 자리-주격
빈칸은 if절의 주어 자리이므로 주격인 (A)가 정답이다.

번역 워크숍 참가자들은 웹 사이트에서 등록 여부를 확인할 수 있다.

어휘 participant 참가자 check 확인하다 register 등록하다

7.

해설 대명사 자리-소유격
빈칸은 전치사 in 뒤에 있긴 하지만, 빈칸 뒤로 명사가 있으므로 소유격이 와야 한다. 따라서 (A)가 정답이다. 형용사 own(자신의)은 소유격 뒤에 자주 붙어 소유격을 강조해 준다.

번역 세계건축협회 GCA의 모든 회원들은 자신들의 분야에서 성공한 전문가들이다.

어휘 organization 조직 accomplished 뛰어난 professional 전문가 field 분야

8.

해설 **대명사 자리-소유격**
빈칸에는 뒤에 명사가 있으므로 소유격이 와야 한다. 따라서 (B)가 정답이다. your application form이 동명사 submitting의 목적어로, 동명사는 동사와 마찬가지로 목적어를 취할 수 있다.

번역 지원서를 제출한 이후에는 추가적인 수정을 할 수 없습니다.

어휘 submit 제출하다 application form 신청서 further 추가의

공식으로 해결하는 실전문제
본책 p. 49

| 1. (B) | 2. (B) | 3. (D) | 4. (B) | 5. (C) |
| 6. (D) | 7. (B) | 8. (C) | | |

1.

해설 **재귀대명사-강조**
빈칸이 목적어 뒤에 있고, 빈칸이 없어도 완전한 절에서 주어 Ms. Duckworth를 강조하므로 재귀대명사인 (B)가 정답이다.

번역 덕워스 씨는 비록 디자이너는 아니지만 회사 로고를 직접 디자인했다.

어휘 even though 비록 ~일지라도

2.

해설 **재귀대명사**
빈칸은 전치사 among의 목적어 자리이고, 주어인 Nonprofit organizations를 대신해 주어와 목적어가 같으므로 재귀대명사인 (B)가 정답이다.

번역 비영리 기구는 그들 내부에서 자금을 분배하는 것이 금지된다.

어휘 nonprofit organization 비영리 기구[단체] prohibit A(목적어) from -ing A가 ~하는 것을 금지하다

3.

해설 **재귀대명사**
빈칸은 동사 consider의 목적어 자리이고, 주어인 she(Ms. Rowller)를 대신해 주어와 목적어가 같으므로 재귀대명사인 (D)가 정답이다.

번역 로울러 씨는 세 권의 베스트셀러 요리책의 작가이긴 하지만, 스스로를 전문 요리사로 생각하지 않는다.

어휘 author 작가 cookbook 요리책 cook 요리사

4.

해설 **재귀대명사**
빈칸은 to부정사(to introduce)의 목적어 자리이다. 명령문이기 때문에 주어인 you는 생략되었지만, 빈칸은 주어인 you를 대신해 주어와 목적어가 같으므로 재귀대명사인 (B)가 정답이다. 참고로, to부정사는 동사와 마찬가지로 목적어를 취할 수 있다.

번역 발표를 시작하기 전에, 간단명료하게 자신을 소개하는 것을 잊지 마세요.

어휘 brief 간단한 clear 명료한 manner 방식 presentation 발표

5.

해설 **재귀대명사-강조**
빈칸이 주어 뒤에 있고, 빈칸이 없어도 완전한 절에서 주어 Dr. Long을 강조하므로 재귀대명사인 (C)가 정답이다.

번역 롱 박사는 보안 위협으로부터 휴대전화를 보호해 주는 새로운 방화벽을 시연할 것이다.

어휘 demonstrate 시연하다 firewall 방화벽 security 보안 threat 위협

6.

해설 **재귀대명사-강조**
빈칸이 목적어 뒤에 있고, 빈칸이 없어도 완전한 문장에서 주어 You를 강조하므로 you의 재귀대명사인 (D)가 정답이다. the car engine은 동명사 replacing의 목적어로, 동명사는 동사와 마찬가지로 목적어를 취할 수 있다.

번역 자동차 엔진을 직접 교체하기보다는 우리의 기술자들에게 도움을 요청할 것을 권고드립니다.

어휘 ask for ~을 요청하다 assistance 도움 replace 교체하다

7.

해설 **재귀대명사-강조**
빈칸이 문장의 맨 뒤에 있고, 빈칸이 없어도 완전한 문장에서 주어 Director Anna Lopez를 강조하므로 재귀대명사인 (B)가 정답이다.

번역 애나 로페즈 이사는 항상 자신의 출장을 위한 교통 수단 및 숙소를 직접 예약한다.

어휘 director 이사 reservation 예약 transportation 교통편 accommodation 숙소 business trip 출장

8.

해설 **재귀대명사**
빈칸은 동사 has earned의 목적어 자리이고, 주어인 TechRecruit를 대신해 주어와 목적어가 같으므로 재귀대명사인 (C)가 정답이다. 참고로, earn은 4형식 동사(earn A B: A에게 B를 얻어 주다)로 목적어가 두 개 올 수 있다.

번역 테크리크루트는 회사가 번성하는 데 필요한 능력과 전문성을 가진 인재들을 제공한다는 평판을 얻어 왔다.

어휘 earn 얻다, 얻어 주다 reputation 평판 expertise 전문 지식 thrive 번성하다

공식으로 해결하는 **실전문제**   본책 p. 51

| 1. (D) | 2. (B) | 3. (D) | 4. (A) | 5. (B) |
| 6. (C) | 7. (B) | 8. (C) | | |

1.
해설 대명사-관용 표현
「by+재귀대명사」는 '혼자서'를 뜻한다. 문맥상 '혼자 참석할 것이다'이므로 재귀대명사인 (D)가 정답이다.

번역 다른 팀원들이 연수 세미나를 준비하느라 바쁘기 때문에 루이스 씨가 혼자 판매 컨퍼런스에 참석할 것이다.

어휘 attend 참석하다 training seminar 연수 세미나

2.
해설 대명사-those
빈칸은 전치사구 with nut allergies의 수식을 받아 '알레르기가 있는 사람들'을 의미하므로 (B)가 정답이다. We와 That은 주어 자리에 들어갈 수는 있지만, 뒤의 수식을 받아 '~한 사람들'로 쓰지 않는다.

번역 견과류 알레르기가 있으신 분들은 비행기가 출발하기 최소 48시간 전에 우리에게 알려주셔야 합니다.

어휘 nut 견과류 allergy 알레르기 notify 통지하다 prior to ~전에 flight 항공편 departure 출발

3.
해설 대명사-those/anyone
빈칸은 관계사절 who ~ competition의 수식을 받아 '작문 대회에 참가하고 싶은 사람'을 의미하므로 (D)가 정답이다. They는 주어 자리에 들어갈 수는 있지만, 일반적으로 뒤의 수식을 받아 '~한 사람'으로 쓰지 않는다. Whichever는 접속사이고, Other는 형용사이므로 주어 자리에 들어갈 수 없다.

번역 작문 대회에 참가하고 싶은 사람은 가능한 한 빨리 참가 신청서를 제출해야 한다.

어휘 participate in ~에 참가하다 submit 제출하다 entry from 참가 신청서

4.
해설 대명사-those
빈칸은 분사구 involved in supporting his Sports Foundation의 수식을 받아 '스포츠 재단을 후원하는 데 관련된 사람들'을 의미하므로 (A)가 정답이다. 원래 'those who were involved in ~(에 관여했던 사람들)'이었는데 'who were'가 생략된 것이다. them과 this는 전치사 to의 목적어 자리에 들어갈 수는 있지만, 뒤의 수식을 받아 '~한 사람들'로 쓰지 않는다.

번역 에드워드 듀란은 그의 스포츠 재단을 후원하는 데 관련된 사람들에게 깊은 감사를 표했다.

어휘 appreciation 감사 involved in ~에 관여한 foundation 재단

5.
해설 대명사-관용 표현
'on one's(소유격) own'은 '혼자서'를 뜻한다. 문맥상 '혼자서 사업을 시작했다'이므로 (B)가 정답이다.

번역 린다 호사키는 의류 소매업체인 룰루랜드를 떠난 후, 혼자서 사업을 시작했다.

어휘 apparel 의류 retailer 소매업체 on one's own 혼자서

6.
해설 대명사-those
빈칸은 분사구 unsatisfied with their jobs의 수식을 받아 '직업에 만족하지 못하는 사람들'을 의미하므로 (C)가 정답이다. these와 you는 전치사 for의 목적어 자리에 들어갈 수는 있지만 뒤의 수식을 받아 '~한 사람들'로 쓰지 않는다.

번역 바우어스는 구직자들과 자신의 직업에 만족하지 못하는 사람들을 위한 상담 서비스를 제공한다.

어휘 job seeker 구직자 unsatisfied 만족하지 못하는

7.
해설 대명사-관용 표현
「for+재귀대명사」는 '스스로'를 뜻한다. 문맥상 '스스로 볼 때까지'이므로 재귀대명사인 (B)가 정답이다.

번역 스스로 볼 때까지, 우리의 신형 냉방 시스템이 전기료를 그만큼 낮출 수 있다는 걸 믿기 힘들지도 모른다.

어휘 see for oneself 스스로 확인하다 lower 낮추다 bill 고지서, 고지액[청구서]

8.
해설 대명사 자리-소유격
빈칸은 전치사 by의 뒤에 있긴 하지만, 빈칸 뒤로 명사가 보이므로 소유격이 와야 한다. 따라서 (C)가 정답이다.

번역 후원 업체에 제출하기 전에 당신의 부장에게 모든 제안서를 검토 받도록 하세요.

어휘 proposal 제안서 review 검토하다 department head 부장 prior to ~전에 submission 제출 sponsor 후원 업체

공식으로 해결하는 **실전문제**   본책 p. 53

| 1. (C) | 2. (C) | 3. (C) | 4. (D) | 5. (D) |
| 6. (C) | 7. (D) | 8. (A) | | |

1.
해설 부정대명사
빈칸은 since절(since ~ company)을 제외한 나머지 절의 주어 자리이므로 형용사 All other는 답이 될 수 없다. Whoever는 '~한 사람은 (누구나)'라는 의미의 접속사이므로 뒤에 동사가 나와야 한다. 문맥상 '아무도 전화를 받을 수 없다'이므로 (C)가 정답이다. No one은 '아무도 ~않다'라는 뜻이다.

번역 내일은 우리 회사가 휴일이기 때문에 전화를 받을 사람이 없을 것이다.

어휘 available 이용 가능한

2.

해설 **부정대명사**
빈칸은 that절의 주어 자리이므로 they와 someone이 답이 될 수 있고, 문맥상 '런던 지사에서 온 누군가'를 뜻하므로 부정대명사 (C)가 정답이다.

번역 카메론 씨는 런던 지사에서 누군가가 공항으로 자신을 마중 나올 것이라고 연락을 받았다.

어휘 inform 알리다 pick up 태우러 가다

3.

해설 **부정대명사**
빈칸은 전치사 with의 목적어 자리이므로 보기 모두 답이 될 수 있지만, robots를 대신해 '로봇들 간에 서로 의사소통하다'를 뜻하므로 (C)가 정답이다.

번역 킹스 대학의 연구원들은 서로 의사소통하는 로봇을 만드는 작업을 하고 있다.

어휘 researcher 연구원 communicate with ~와 의사소통하다 each other 서로

4.

해설 **부정대명사**
some과 others는 짝꿍 표현으로, 빈칸 앞에 some이 있으므로 (D)가 정답이다. 빈칸은 전치사의 목적어 자리이므로 형용사인 other는 답이 될 수 없고, other one은 'the[any] other one(다른 것)'처럼 앞에 한정사(any/the)가 필요하다.

번역 카민스키 씨는 어떤 보험은 왜 다른 보험보다 훨씬 비싼지에 대해 조사하고 있다.

어휘 research 조사하다 insurance policy 보험 (증서)

5.

해설 **부정대명사**
빈칸은 while절(while ~ targets)을 제외한 나머지 절의 주어 자리이므로 us는 답이 될 수 없다. 빈칸은 sales representatives 중 일부를 대신하고, 문맥상 '소수만이 목표에 도달했다'를 뜻하므로 (D)가 정답이다.

번역 영업 사원들은 목표가 그다지 높지 않았는데도, 그 목표에 도달한 사람이 거의 없었다.

어휘 sales representative 영업 사원 relatively 비교적 modest 그다지 대단하지 않은 target 목표 manage to부정사 ~해내다

6.

해설 **부정대명사**
빈칸 앞에 'a+형용사'가 있고 문맥상 check를 대신한 '새로운 것[수표]'을 뜻하므로 (C)가 정답이다. that과 any는 앞에 관사가 올 수 없고, almost(거의)는 부사이므로 답이 될 수 없다.

번역 수표를 분실한 경우, 은행에 그 수표에 대한 지불 정지를 신청하고 새로운 수표를 발급 받아야 한다.

어휘 check 수표 lose 분실하다 stop payment 지불 정지 issue 발급하다

7.

해설 **부정대명사**
빈칸은 전치사 with의 목적어 자리이므로 형용사 every와 부사 nearly는 답이 될 수 없다. one과 another는 짝꿍 표현이고, '하나의 부품(one)'을 '또 다른 부품(another)'과 교환하는 것이므로 (D)가 정답이다.

번역 대규모의 조립 공정에서는 호환성 부품을 동종 군의 다른 것과 교체할 수 있다는 점이 도움이 된다.

어휘 assembly project 조립 공정 replace 교체하다 interchangeable 교체할 수 있는 part 부품 family (분류상의) 군, 과

8.

해설 **부정대명사**
빈칸은 전치사 to의 목적어 자리이므로 부사 mostly(대부분)는 답이 될 수 없다. whatever는 '~한 것은 무엇이든'이라는 뜻으로 '사물'을 의미하는 접속사이므로 적절하지 않다. 빈칸은 뒤에 있는 분사구 involved ~ product의 수식을 받아 '신제품 출시에 관여된 모든 사람'을 뜻하므로 (A)가 정답이다.

번역 해럴드는 신제품 출시에 관여된 모든 사람이 동의할 수 있는 마케팅 계획을 제안했다.

어휘 come up with 제안하다, 생각해내다 agreeable 동의할 만한 involved in ~에 관여한 launch 출시

YBM TEST

본책 p. 54

1. (C)	2. (B)	3. (B)	4. (A)	5. (A)
6. (D)	7. (A)	8. (A)	9. (A)	10. (C)
11. (A)	12. (C)	13. (D)	14. (B)	15. (C)
16. (D)	17. (B)	18. (A)	19. (B)	20. (B)

1.

해설 **대명사 자리-목적격**
빈칸은 전치사 of의 목적어 자리이고, critics(비평가들)를 대신하므로 (C)가 정답이다.

번역 푸드 트럭 운영자인 루크 카푸르는 많은 전문 비평가들이 몇 년에 걸쳐 미각을 개발하기 때문에 그들의 글을 존중한다.

어휘 value 소중히 생각하다 critic 비평가 writing 글 spend+시간+-ing ~하는 데 시간을 쓰다 taste 미각, 입맛

2.

해설 **대명사-관용 표현**
빈칸은 주어인 others(다른 사람들)를 대신하므로 (B)가 정답이다.

번역 그 연구는 어떤 사람들은 그룹으로 일할 때 최선의 결과를 내는 반면, 또 어떤 사람들은 혼자 일하는 것을 선호한다는 것을 보여준다.

어휘 **some, others** 어떤 사람들은, 또 어떤 사람들은 **prefer** 선호하다

3.
해설 **대명사-those**
빈칸은 분사구 interested ~ careers의 수식을 받아 '에너지 분야 경력에 관심 있는 사람들'을 의미하므로 (B)가 정답이다.

번역 밥슨 대학은 에너지 분야 경력에 관심 있는 사람들을 위해 국립 에너지 센터를 공개하는 행사를 열 것이다.

어휘 **hold** 개최하다 **open house** (집이나 기관 등을 개방하는) 공개 행사 **interested** 관심 있는 **career** 경력

4.
해설 **대명사 자리-목적격**
빈칸은 to부정사 to let의 목적어 자리이고 Mr. Bauers를 대신하므로 목적격 (A)가 정답이다.

번역 바우어스 씨에게 이메일을 보내서 세미나 일정에 대한 변경 사항을 알리세요.

어휘 **change** 변경, 변경 사항

5.
해설 **부정대명사**
빈칸은 전치사 to의 목적어 자리이므로 형용사 other는 답이 될 수 없다. one과 another는 짝꿍 표현이고, '하나(one)'의 계정에서 '다른 하나(another)'로 이동하는 것이므로 (A)가 정답이다.

번역 마음 커뮤니케이션스는 한 계정에서 다른 계정으로 한 번에 데이터를 옮기는 툴을 제공한다.

어휘 **tool** 도구, 툴 **migrate** 이동하다 **account** 계정 **(all) at once** 한 번에, 한꺼번에

6.
해설 **재귀대명사-강조**
수식구 across the country를 지우면 빈칸은 목적어 every office 뒤에 있고, 빈칸이 없어도 완전한 절에서 주어 Greg Foran을 강조하므로 재귀대명사인 (D)가 정답이다.

번역 CEO인 그렉 포란은 직원들과 알고 지내기 위해 전국에 있는 모든 지사를 정기적으로 방문한다.

어휘 **CEO** 최고경영자 **regularly** 정기적으로 **get to know** 알게 되다, 안면을 트다

7.
해설 **재귀대명사**
빈칸은 동사 has rebuilt의 목적어 자리이고, 주어인 Kow Inc.를 대신해 주어와 목적어가 같으므로 재귀대명사인 (A)가 정답이다.

번역 코우 사는 고객 서비스에 집중하여 혁신 회사로서 스스로를 성공적으로 다시 일으켜 세웠다.

어휘 **rebuild** 재건하다 **innovative** 혁신적인 **customer service** 고객 서비스

8.
해설 **대명사 자리-주격**
빈칸은 명사 all the furniture를 수식하는 관계대명사 that절에서 주어 자리이므로 주격인 (A)가 정답이다.

번역 에드와 가구의 이사진은 작년에 일본에서 판매했던 모든 가구를 회수하기로 결정했다.

어휘 **board** 이사회 **recall** 회수하다

9.
해설 **대명사-관용 표현**
「for+재귀대명사」는 '스스로'를 뜻한다. 문맥상 '아이들이 스스로 학습하도록 장려하다'이므로 재귀대명사인 (A)가 정답이다.

번역 보육원에서는 아이들이 스스로 학습하도록 장려함으로써 자립성을 기르도록 돕는다.

어휘 **child care** 보육 **provider** 공급업자 **independent** 독립적인 **encourage** 장려하다

10.
해설 **대명사-those/anyone**
빈칸은 동사 will vouch의 주어 자리이므로 형용사 Every는 답이 될 수 없다. 또한 관계사절 who ~ service의 수식을 받아 '우리의 음식공급 서비스를 경험한 사람'을 의미하므로 Those와 Anyone이 답이 될 수 있는데, who 뒤에 단수동사 has가 왔으므로 (C)가 정답이다.

번역 우리의 음식공급 서비스를 경험함 사람은 누구라도 우리의 우수한 서비스를 보증해 줄 것이다.

어휘 **catering** 음식 공급 **vouch for** (~이 확실함을) 보증하다 **quality** 질

11.
해설 **대명사 자리-소유격**
빈칸은 동사 announced 뒤에 있지만, 빈칸 뒤로 명사 plan이 있으므로 plan을 수식하는 소유격이 와야 한다. 따라서 (A)가 정답이다.

번역 정부가 학교에서 좀 더 많은 학생들에게 코딩을 배울 기회를 제공하기 위한 계획을 발표했다.

어휘 **code** (프로그램을) 코드화하다, 부호화하다

12.
해설 **부정대명사**
빈칸은 전치사 than의 목적어 자리이므로 형용사인 other는 답이 될 수 없다. some과 others는 짝꿍 표현으로, 앞에 some businesses가 있고 빈칸은 '다른 회사들'을 뜻하므로 (C)가 정답이다.

번역 그 연구는 어떤 회사들은 다른 회사들보다 경기 순환의 변화에 더 취약하다는 것을 보여준다.

어휘 **vulnerable to** ~에 취약한 **business cycle** 경기 순환

13.
해설 대명사 자리-주격
빈칸은 접속사 but 뒤로 연결된 절에서 주어 자리이므로 주격인 (D)가 정답이다.

번역 리사 크리지오는 3월 19일에 도쿄를 떠날 예정이었지만 이사회에 참석하기 위해 더 일찍 돌아올 것이다.

어휘 be scheduled to부정사 (일정상) ~할 예정이다, 일정을 잡다 board meeting 이사회 회의

14.
해설 대명사-관용 표현
'on one's(소유격) own'은 '혼자서'를 뜻한다. 문맥상 '혼자서 작업하다' 이므로 (B)가 정답이다.

번역 프로젝트 매니저가 우리에게 혼자 작업하기보다 팀으로서 함께 일할 것을 요구했다.

어휘 rather than ~보다는

15.
해설 재귀대명사-강조
수식구 of her business를 지우면 빈칸은 목적어 most aspects 뒤에 있고, 빈칸이 없어도 완전한 절에서 주어 Amelia Ortega를 강조하므로 재귀대명사인 (C)가 정답이다.

번역 개인 행사 기획자인 아멜리아 오르테가는 사업의 전 영역을 직접 처리하지만 일부에 있어서는 프리랜서들에게 도움을 받는다.

어휘 event planner 행사 기획자 handle 처리하다 aspect 영역 rely on ~에 의존하다 freelancer 프리랜서 issue 사안, 문제

16.
해설 대명사-those
빈칸은 분사구 applying for part-time positions의 수식을 받아 '시간제 근무 일자리에 지원하는 사람들'을 의미하므로 (D)가 정답이다. We는 주어 자리에 들어갈 수는 있지만 일반적으로 뒤의 수식을 받아 '~한 우리'로 쓰지 않는다.

번역 시간제 근무 일자리에 지원하는 사람들은 유급 휴가, 의료 보험 및 보너스와 같은 혜택을 받지 못할 것이다.

어휘 apply for ~에 지원하다 part-time 시간제의 position 일자리 paid vacation 유급 휴가 medical insurance 의료 보험

17.
해설 부정 대명사
빈칸은 전치사 to의 목적어 자리이므로 부사 mostly와 형용사 any other는 답이 될 수 없다. 문맥상 '스스로를 서로에게 소개한다'이므로 (B)가 정답이다.

번역 워크숍을 시작할 때 참가자들에게 스스로를 서로에게 소개할 기회가 주어질 것이다.

어휘 participant 참가자 one another 서로

18.
해설 재귀대명사
빈칸은 전치사 of의 목적어 자리이고, 주어인 The president를 대신해 주어와 목적어가 같으므로 재귀대명사인 (A)가 정답이다.

번역 나라 어패럴의 사장은 의류 소매업에서 그가 거둔 큰 성공에 대해 스스로를 매우 자랑스럽게 여긴다.

어휘 apparel 의류 retail 소매

19.
해설 대명사 자리-소유격
빈칸은 동사 implement 뒤에 있긴 하지만, 빈칸 뒤로 명사가 있으므로 소유격이 와야 한다. 따라서 (B)가 정답이다. 형용사 own(자신의)은 소유격 뒤에 붙어 소유격을 강조해 준다.

번역 우리는 6월 7일 월요일부터 우리의 모든 매장에서 새로운 식품 안전 검사를 실행할 것이다.

어휘 implement 실행하다 safety inspection 안전 검사, 안전 진단 outlet 매장

20.
해설 부정대명사
빈칸은 and로 연결되는 절의 주어 자리이므로 부사 nearly는 답이 될 수 없다. 또한 뒤에 복수동사 are가 있으므로 much와 it은 답이 될 수 없다. most는 복수명사 machines를 대신하므로 (B)가 정답이다. 참고로, most는 불가산명사를 대신할 때는 단수동사로 받는다.

번역 티버 피트니스 센터는 모든 종류의 운동 기구를 갖추고 있고, 대부분의 기구들이 최신식이다.

어휘 be equipped with ~을 갖추다 a (full) range of 다양한 state of the art 최신식의

Part 6

문장 고르기 문제 3 - 접속부사를 활용한다.

 예제
본책 p. 56

가족의 밤 모금행사

사람은 누구나 가정 내에서 안전할 권리가 있습니다. 로터스 여성 보호시설은 당신을 2월 15일에 깁스 휴양 센터에서 열릴 가족의 밤 모금행사에 초대하게 되어 기쁩니다. 지역 밴드인 영 패밀리 밴드가 공연할 예정입니다. 또한, 행사에는 나만의 타코 만들기 바도 있습니다. 입구에서 입장료 5달러를 내 주세요.

번역 (A) 마침내 저희가 교육 기회를 제공합니다.
(B) 지역 밴드인 영 패밀리 밴드가 공연할 예정입니다.
(C) 저희 웹 사이트 www.lotus.org를 확인하세요.
(D) 모두들 무료로 참가할 수 있다는 점을 유념하세요.

어휘 fundraiser 모금행사 shelter 피신처, 보호시설 recreation 오락 wellness 건강 additionally 추가로 admission 입장료

YBM TEST

본책 p. 57

1. (B) 2. (D) 3. (A) 4. (C)

건강과 안전 방침
작업 현장에서의 모바일 장치

이 방침은 작업 현장에서 모바일 장치의 사용과 관련된 부상을 줄이기 위한 절차를 수립하는 것을 목적으로 합니다. 작업 현장에서 모바일 장치를 사용하는 데에는 많은 위험이 따릅니다. 모바일 장치의 사용은 세심한 주의를 요구하는 작업 및 환경으로부터 직원들의 주의를 분산시킬 수 있습니다. 그러므로, 모바일 장치의 사용은 작업하는 동안 허용되지 않습니다.

작업 현장에서 모바일 장치의 사용을 제한함으로써 직원들의 집중력 수준을 상당히 높여줄 것입니다. 그 결과, 작업 능률이 개선될 것이고 모바일 장치를 사용함으로 인해 야기되는 부주의와 관련된 사고의 수가 감소할 것입니다.

이 정책은 프로젝트 경영 사업부에 의해 권한을 부여받은 사람을 제외한 모든 근로자 및 방문자에게 해당됩니다.

어휘 policy 정책, 방침 device 장치 worksite 작업장 establish 수립하다 procedure 절차 injury 부상 related to ~와 관련된 hazard 위험 associated with ~와 관련된 distract (주의를) 딴 데로 돌리다 surroundings 환경, 주변 restrict 제한하다 concentration 집중 quality 질 work performance 근무 실적 distraction 방해, 주의 산만함 apply to ~에 적용되다 authorized 인가 받은

1.
해설 문장 고르기

보기 (B)에의 접속부사 therefore(그러므로)는 인과 관계를 나타내므로, 앞 문장은 원인, 뒤 문장은 결과로 연결되어야 한다. 앞 문장에서 '작업 및 주변으로부터 직원들의 주의를 분산시킨다'며 모바일 장치 사용의 위험성을 얘기했다. 이어 빈칸에서 '그러므로 (이런 원인으로) 허용하지 않는다'는 결과로 연결되므로 (B)가 정답이다.

번역 (A) 관리자들은 지정된 안전 지역 중 한 곳에 있어야 합니다.
(B) 그러므로, 모바일 장치의 사용은 작업하는 동안 허용되지 않습니다.
(C) 전 직원은 근무 중에 승인 받은 안전모를 착용해야 합니다.
(D) 사고 및 부상은 관리자에게 즉시 보고되어야 합니다.

2.
해설 부사 어휘

'집중력 수준을 높여준다'에서 동사 '높여준다'를 수식하는 부사로는 significantly(상당히)가 가장 적절하다. 따라서 정답은 (D)이다.

어휘 intimately 친밀하게 permissibly 허용되어 exclusively 오로지

3.
해설 접속부사

앞뒤 문장의 연결 관계를 보여주는 접속부사를 고르는 문제이다. 앞 문장에서 '모바일 장치 사용의 제한이 직원의 집중력을 높여 줄 것이다'라고 했고, 뒤 문장에서 '작업 능률이 개선되고 사고도 줄 것이다'라고 했다. 즉 앞 문장 내용에 대한 결과를 이야기하는 것이므로 '그 결과'를 뜻하는 (A)가 정답이다.

어휘 in detail 상세하게 nevertheless 그럼에도 불구하고 even so 그렇다 하더라도

4.
해설 동명사

빈칸은 전치사 뒤이므로 명사나 동명사가 올 수 있고, 빈칸 뒤로 목적어 mobile devices가 있으므로 동명사인 (C)가 정답이다.

Unit 4 동사

공식으로 해결하는 실전문제
본책 p. 61

1. (B) 2. (D) 3. (A) 4. (B) 5. (A)
6. (D) 7. (C) 8. (C)

1.
해설 수일치

빈칸은 동사 자리이고 주어 Dr. Kelley가 3인칭 단수이므로 단수동사 (B)가 정답이다. 참고로 Business expert는 Dr. Kelley와 동격이다.

번역 비즈니스 전문가인 켈리 박사는 인도의 현재 마켓 트렌드를 논의하기 위해 투데이 쇼에 출현했다.

어휘 expert 전문가 current 현재의 trend 경향

2.
해설 수일치

빈칸은 that절(that ~ incorrect)의 동사 자리이고, 주어가 '부정대명사(some) of the 명사'이므로 명사인 information에 수를 일치시킨다. 불가산명사 information은 단수 취급하므로 단수동사인 (D)가 정답이다.

번역 박 씨는 그의 의료 차트에 있는 일부 정보가 부정확하다는 것을 알아챘다.

어휘 notice 알아채다 incorrect 부정확한

3.
해설 수일치

빈칸은 동사 자리이고, 주어가 '부정대명사(most) of the 명사'이므로 명사인 banks에 수를 일치시킨다. banks는 복수명사이므로 복수동사인 (A)가 정답이다.

번역 대부분의 은행은 적절한 담보를 제공할 수 없는 사람들에게 대출을 거절한다.

어휘 loan 대출 those ~한 사람들 suitable 적절한 guarantee 보장, 담보 refuse 거절하다

4.
해설 수일치

빈칸은 동사 자리이고 주어 workspace가 3인칭 단수이므로 단수동사 (B)가 정답이다.

번역 브리즈번의 유연한 작업 공간은 높은 수요 때문에 고객들로부터 높은 가격을 받는다.

어휘 flexible 유연한 workspace 작업 공간 demand 수요 command (당연히 받아야 할 것을) 받다

5.
해설 수일치
빈칸은 동사 자리이고 주어 Martin's work가 3인칭 단수이므로 단수동사 (A)가 정답이다.

번역 마틴의 작업은 회사 내에서 그의 관리자의 예상을 자주 넘어선다.

어휘 regularly 자주, 정기적으로 supervisor 관리자 surpass 능가하다

6.
해설 수일치
빈칸은 that절(that ~ errors)의 동사 자리이다. 주어가 '70% of the 명사'이고 70%는 부정대명사와 마찬가지로 전부나 일부를 가리키는 말이므로 명사인 credit reports에 수를 일치시킨다. credit reports는 복수명사이므로 복수동사인 (D)가 정답이다.

번역 금융 연구 법인에 의한 최근 연구는 신용 평가 보고서의 70% 이상이 오류가 있다는 것을 발견했다.

어휘 financial 금융의 research 연구 corporation 법인 credit report 신용 평가 보고서 contain 포함하다 container 용기

7.
해설 수일치
빈칸은 동사 자리이고 주어 interviewees가 복수이므로 복수동사 (C)가 정답이다.

번역 회사 방침에 따르면, 공정성을 보장하기 위해 모든 면접 대상자들은 정확하게 똑같은 질문을 받는다.

어휘 policy 방침 interviewee 면접 대상자 ensure 보장하다 fairness 공정성

8.
해설 수일치
빈칸은 동사 자리인데 주어가 복수명사 all guests이므로 복수동사 (C)가 정답이다.

번역 센트럴 호텔의 모든 투숙객은 체크인 시에 무료 환영 음료와 가벼운 다과를 받는다.

어휘 complimentary 무료의 refreshments 다과

공식으로 해결하는 실전문제 본책 p. 63

| 1. (D) | 2. (C) | 3. (B) | 4. (A) | 5. (C) |
| 6. (A) | 7. (C) | 8. (B) | | |

1.
해설 능동 vs. 수동
빈칸은 동사 자리이고 주어는 transfer이다. 뒤에 목적어가 없이 '전근이 연기되다'로 해석되므로 수동태인 (D)가 정답이다.

번역 판매 과장인 힐 씨의 뉴욕 지사 전근이 다음 달까지 연기되었다.

어휘 transfer 전근 sales manager 판매 과장 postpone 연기하다

2.
해설 능동 vs. 수동
빈칸은 be동사 뒤이므로 동사는 올 수 없고, 분사인 ing/p.p.가 올 수 있다. 빈칸 뒤에 목적어가 없고 '주문품이 발송된다'로 해석되므로 수동태인 (C)가 정답이다.

번역 귀하의 주문품이 내일 발송될 것이며 영업일 기준 3~5일 이내에 도착할 것입니다.

어휘 order 주문(품) business day 평일, 영업일

3.
해설 능동 vs. 수동
빈칸은 be동사 뒤이므로 동사는 올 수 없고, 분사인 ing/p.p.가 올 수 있다. 빈칸 뒤에 목적어 applications가 있고 '신청서를 받는다'로 해석되므로 능동태인 (B)가 정답이다.

번역 ORJA는 1월 3일부터 우주 비행사 후보자 프로그램의 신청서를 받을 것입니다.

어휘 application 신청서 astronaut 우주 비행사 candidate 후보자

4.
해설 5형식 동사 수동태+목적보어
빈칸은 동사 자리이고, 뒤에 목적어가 없으므로 수동태인 (A)가 정답이다. make는 5형식 동사이므로 수동태(be p.p.) 뒤로 목적보어인 형용사(available)가 남을 수 있다.

번역 이 웹 사이트의 자료들은 오직 개인적이고 비영리적인 용도로만 사용될 수 있게 되어 있다.

어휘 material 자료, 자재 available 이용 가능한 non-commercial 비영리적인

5.
해설 능동 vs. 수동
빈칸은 동사 자리이고 뒤에 목적어 the company's ~ conduct가 와서 '회사의 ~을 설명해 준다'로 해석되므로 능동태인 (C)가 정답이다.

번역 직원 안내서는 회사의 고용 정책과 전반적인 행동 수칙을 설명해 준다.

어휘 handbook 안내서 policy 정책 general 전반적인 rules of conduct 행동 수칙 outline 개요를 서술하다

6.

해설 **능동 vs. 수동**
빈칸은 조동사 may 뒤이므로 동사원형이 와야 하고, 뒤에 목적어가 없이 '제2판이 출판되지 않을 수 있다'로 해석되므로 수동태인 (A)가 정답이다.

번역 〈주택 백과사전〉의 제2판은 원래의 출판사에 의해 출판되지 않을 수도 있다.

어휘 **edition** (출판물의) 판 **encyclopedia** 백과사전 **housing** 주택 **original** 원래의 **publisher** 출판사 **publish** 출판하다

7.

해설 **능동 vs. 수동**
빈칸은 3인칭 단수주어 The national bank의 동사 자리이고, 뒤에 목적어 a strong 8% growth rate가 와서 '8%의 성장률을 예상한다'로 해석되므로 단수동사의 능동태인 (C)가 정답이다.

번역 국립 은행은 올해 국내 경제에 대해 8%의 높은 성장률을 예상했다.

어휘 **growth rate** 성장률 **domestic** 국내의 **project** 예상하다

8.

해설 **5형식동사**
모두 다 「has been+과거분사」 수동태로 되어 있다. 빈칸 뒤에 명사가 목적보어로 남아 있으므로 '수동태+목적보어'의 형태를 취할 수 있는 5형식 동사인 (B)가 정답이다. 다른 동사는 수동태 뒤로 명사가 연결되려면 전치사 as가 필요하다.

번역 노팅험에 있는 솔트 워터는 〈본 아페티〉 잡지에 의해 영국 최고의 식당으로 선정되었다.

어휘 **name A**(목적어) **B**(목적보어) A를 B라고 부르다 **recognize A as B** A를 B라고 인정하다

✚ 공식으로 해결하는 실전문제
본책 p. 65

| 1. (A) | 2. (A) | 3. (C) | 4. (D) | 5. (C) |
| 6. (D) | 7. (B) | 8. (B) | | |

1.

해설 **명령문**
등위접속사 and는 앞뒤의 동등한 성질의 구문을 연결하는 접속사이다. and 앞에 Please로 시작하는 명령문이 있으므로 and 뒤에도 명령문이 와야 한다. 따라서 동사원형인 (A)가 정답이다. 양쪽에 중복되는 단어는 생략할 수 있으므로 and 뒤에 please가 생략되었다.

번역 잠시 시간을 내서 의견 카드를 작성해 주시고 침대 테이블에 놓아 두세요.

어휘 **fill out** 작성하다 **comment** 논평, 지적 **leave** 남겨 두다

2.

해설 **조동사+동사원형**
빈칸은 조동사 would 뒤이므로 동사원형인 (A)가 정답이다.

번역 연구원들은 참가자들에게 그들의 개인 정보가 엄격하게 기밀로 유지될 것을 약속했다.

어휘 **researcher** 연구원 **assure** 확인하다 **participant** 참가자 **strictly** 엄격히 **confidential** 기밀의 **remain+형용사** ~인 상태로 있다

3.

해설 **현재 시제+수일치**
빈칸은 동사 자리이고, 앞에 일반적인 일임을 나타내는 부사 normally가 있으므로 현재 시제가 와야 한다. 또한 주어가 we이므로 복수동사인 (C)가 정답이다.

번역 파브 댄스웨어에서는 착용이나 세탁한 징후가 보이는 제품에 대해서는 보통 반품을 거절합니다.

어휘 **normally** 보통 **return** 반품 **item** 제품, 항목 **sign** 징후 **wear** 입다(wear-wore-worn) **wash** 세탁하다

4.

해설 **과거 시제**
빈칸은 동사 자리이고, 'in 2012(2012년에)'라는 특정한 과거 시점이 함께 쓰였으므로 (D)가 정답이다.

번역 비즈니스 네트워킹 그룹스는 2012년에 첫 오프라인 회원 모임을 가졌다.

어휘 **gathering** 모임 **hold** (회의, 행사 등을) 열다

5.

해설 **명령문**
문장에 동사가 없으므로 빈칸은 동사 자리이고, 앞에 주어가 없으므로 명령문이다. 따라서 동사원형인 (C)가 정답이다.

번역 기본 무선 연결을 설치하고 테스트하기 위해서는 아래의 지시를 주의 깊게 따르세요.

어휘 **instruction(s)** 지시 **set up** 설치하다 **wireless** 무선의 **connectivity** 연결

6.

해설 **과거 시제**
빈칸은 동사 can check의 목적어 역할을 하는 명사절(what ~ computer) 안에서 동사 자리이다. 절 안에 과거 시제를 알려주는 단서인 recently가 있으므로 (D)가 정답이다.

번역 우리의 오픈 세이브 파일즈 도구를 이용하시면, 최근에 컴퓨터에서 어떤 파일이 열렸는지를 확인할 수 있습니다.

어휘 **tool** 도구 **check** 확인하다

7.

해설 **조동사+동사원형**
빈칸은 조동사 can 뒤이므로 동사원형인 (B)가 정답이다. 조동사와 동사원형 사이에 부사가 낄 수 있다는 것도 알아두자.

번역 형편 없는 고객 서비스와 불만족한 직원들은 회사의 평판을 심하게 손상시킬 수 있다.

어휘 **poor** 형편 없는 **badly** 심하게 **reputation** 평판 **damage** 손상을 주다

8.

해설 과거 시제
빈칸은 동사 자리이고, 앞에 과거 시제를 알려주는 단서인 previously(이전에)가 있으므로 (B)가 정답이다.

번역 애틀랜타 은행의 새로 임명된 부사장인 찰스 존슨은 이전에 투자 상담 부서에서 이사로 근무했다.

어휘 appointed 임명된 vice president 부사장 previously 이전에 director 이사 serve 근무하다

공식으로 해결하는 실전문제   본책 p. 67

| 1. (B) | 2. (D) | 3. (D) | 4. (A) | 5. (A) |
| 6. (C) | 7. (A) | 8. (D) |

1.

해설 현재완료
빈칸은 동사 자리이고, 현재완료 시제의 단서인 over the last 7 years가 있으므로 현재완료 (B)가 정답이다.

번역 오직 세 개의 영화만으로, 케빈 앤더슨은 지난 7년 동안 세계적으로 칭송받는 감독으로 떠올랐다.

어휘 film 영화 acclaimed 찬사를 받고 있는 director 감독

2.

해설 미래 시제+태
빈칸은 동사 자리인데, 미래 시제의 단서인 next Tuesday가 있고 빈칸 뒤에 목적어가 없으므로 미래+수동태인 (D)가 정답이다.

번역 신제품 출시 행사가 다음 주 화요일 처칠 호텔의 연회장에서 열릴 것이다.

어휘 launch 출시 ball room 연회장

3.

해설 미래 시제
빈칸은 주어 the committee와 목적어 역할을 하는 명사절(who ~ project) 사이의 동사 자리이다. 미래 시제의 단서인 next meeting이 있으므로 미래 시제 (D)가 정답이다.

번역 다음 회의에서, 위원회는 누가 로저스 빌 지역 공원 디자인 프로젝트를 이끌지를 결정할 것이다.

어휘 committee 위원회

4.

해설 현재완료
수식구(of ~ our products)를 지우면 빈칸은 주어 The price의 동사 자리이다. 현재완료 시제의 단서인 「since+과거」가 있으므로 현재완료 (A)가 정답이다.

번역 우리 제품 대부분에 사용되는 주재료의 가격이 작년 이후 상당히 비싸졌다.

어휘 material 재료 significantly 상당히

5.

해설 현재완료
빈칸은 주절(Our ~ times)에서 동사 자리이고, 현재완료 시제의 단서인 「since+주어+과거동사」가 있으므로 현재완료 (A)가 정답이다.

번역 우리 가스 배관은 2년 전에 설치된 이래로 여러 번 검사를 받았다.

어휘 gas piping 가스 배관 install 설치하다 inspect 검사하다

6.

해설 현재완료
빈칸은 동사 자리이고, 현재완료 시제의 단서인 over the past 15 years가 있으므로 현재완료 (C)가 정답이다.

번역 스톡홀름-위크스는 지난 15년간 제조 분야에서 상당한 성장을 경험했다.

어휘 significant 상당한 manufacturing 제조업

7.

해설 미래 시제
빈칸은 동사 자리이고, 미래 시제 단서인 until further notice가 있으므로 미래 시제인 (A)가 정답이다.

번역 랜드 오브 버즈는 세균성감염증의 위험 때문에 추후 공지 때까지 일반인에게 문을 닫을 것이다.

어휘 until further notice 추후 공지가 있을 때까지 due to ~때문에 bacterial infection 세균성감염증

8.

해설 미래 시제
빈칸은 동사 자리인데, 미래 시제 단서인 As of January 2가 있고 빈칸 뒤에 목적어 extensive remodeling이 있으므로 능동 미래 시제 (D)가 정답이다.

번역 1월 2일부터, 호브 빌리지는 손님들에게 훨씬 더 멋진 스타일과 안락함을 제공하기 위해 대대적인 리모델링을 할 것이다.

어휘 as of ~부로 extensive 광범위한 comfort 편안함 undergo 겪다

공식으로 해결하는 실전문제   본책 p. 69

| 1. (A) | 2. (C) | 3. (D) | 4. (B) | 5. (C) |
| 6. (B) | 7. (C) | 8. (D) |

1.

해설 과거완료
빈칸은 주어 the store staff의 동사 자리이고, 과거완료의 단서인 「before+주어+과거동사」가 있다. '지역 관리자가 방문한 것'이 과거이고 상품을 정리한 것은 그 이전이므로 과거보다 이전 시제인 과거완료 (A)가 정답이다.

번역 지역 관리자가 상점을 방문하기 전에 상점 직원들은 선반에 진열된 상품을 깔끔하게 정리했다.

어휘 regional 지역의 merchandise 상품 neatly 깔끔하게 shelf 선반 arrange 정리하다

2.
해설 **과거완료**
빈칸은 주어 the human resources team의 동사 자리이고, 과거완료의 단서인 「by the time+주어+과거동사」가 왔다. '그들이 (과거에) 준비되었을 때' 이미 개발을 완료해 놓은 것이므로 과거보다 이전 시제인 과거완료 (C)가 정답이다.

번역 인사팀은 새로운 인턴을 모집할 준비가 되었을 때쯤 면접용 질문을 이미 개발했다.

어휘 human resources 인사과 by the time ~할 무렵에, ~할 때쯤 recruit 모집하다 intern 인턴, 인턴 사원

3.
해설 **시간/조건절 시제**
주절의 동사 will로 보아 미래에 대한 내용이지만, 빈칸은 조건 접속사 if절의 동사 자리이므로 미래 시제 대신 현재 시제가 와야 한다. 따라서 (D)가 정답이다.

번역 만약 제품에 결함이 있거나 파손된 경우 교체 혹은 환불해 드립니다.

어휘 replace 교체하다 refund 환불하다 defective 결함이 있는 damaged 파손된

4.
해설 **시간/조건절 시제**
주절의 동사 will로 보아 미래에 대한 내용이지만, 빈칸은 시간 접속사 as soon as절의 동사 자리이므로 미래 시제 대신 현재 시제가 와야 한다. 따라서 (B)가 정답이다.

번역 세부사항을 제출하자마자 등록 확인 메시지가 이메일로 발송될 것이다.

어휘 registration 등록 confirmation 확인 message 메시지 as soon as ~하자마자 details 세부사항

5.
해설 **시간/조건절 시제**
시간 접속사 while이 있는 절이 앞으로의 일정에 대한 내용이고 현재 시제 동사 is가 will be를 대신한 것이므로, 주절의 동사는 미래 시제가 되어야 한다. 따라서 미래 시제인 (C)가 정답이다.

번역 영업 부장은 연례 회의에 참석하기 위해 캘리포니아에 머무는 동안 그 지역의 사무실들을 방문할 예정이다.

어휘 sales director 영업 부장 annual 연례의 conference 회의

6.
해설 **과거완료**
빈칸은 주어 Ms. Graham의 동사 자리이고, 과거완료의 단서인 「before+과거(last year)」가 와서 '작년에 합류하기 전' 시점을 나타내므로 과거보다 이전 시제인 과거완료 (B)가 정답이다.

번역 그레이엄 씨는 작년에 우리 팀에 합류하기 전에 GT 그룹에서 수석 재무직을 맡았다.

어휘 senior 상위의 financial 금융의

7.
해설 **시간/조건절 시제+수일치**
주절의 동사 will로 보아 미래에 대한 내용이지만, 빈칸은 시간 접속사 when절의 동사 자리이므로 미래 시제 대신 현재 시제가 와야 한다. 주어가 you이므로 단수동사나 동사원형 be는 올 수 없다. 따라서 (C)가 정답이다.

번역 우리 웹 사이트에서 주문을 하자마자 전액 지불이 요청될 것입니다.

어휘 payment 지불 in full 전부 place an order 주문을 하다

8.
해설 **과거완료**
빈칸은 주어 Ms. Nolan의 동사 자리이다. 과거완료의 단서인 「before+주어+과거동사」가 와서 '소설이 출판된' 과거 시점보다 더 이전을 나타내므로 과거보다 이전 시제인 과거완료 (D)가 정답이다.

번역 놀런 씨는 자신의 소설을 출판하기 전에 원고를 전문적으로 교열 받았다.

어휘 publish 출판하다 have+A(목적어)+p.p. A를 ~하게 하다 manuscript 원고 professionally 전문적으로 copyedit (원고를) 교열하다

YBM TEST
본책 p. 70

1. (B)	2. (C)	3. (C)	4. (B)	5. (A)
6. (A)	7. (C)	8. (B)	9. (C)	10. (C)
11. (C)	12. (D)	13. (B)	14. (D)	15. (D)
16. (A)	17. (B)	18. (A)	19. (B)	20. (A)

1.
해설 **수일치**
빈칸은 동사 자리이므로 (A)와 (C)는 오답이며, 주어가 you이므로 복수동사 (B)가 정답이다. 또한, 시설 방문자에게 통상적으로 요구되는 규정을 설명하고 있으므로 현재 시제가 가장 적절하다.

번역 이 시설에 처음 방문하실 경우 요청에 따라 보안 직원에게 신분증을 제시하셔야 합니다.

어휘 facility 시설 present 제시하다 identification card 신분증 security staff 보안 직원 upon request 요청 시

2.
해설 **수일치**
빈칸은 동사 자리이고 주어 Dr. Wright가 3인칭 단수이므로 단수동사 (C)가 정답이다.

번역 비즈니스 경영 기사를 통해 라이트 박사는 조직에서 새로운 사업 시스템을 실행하는 데 대한 충고를 제공한다.

어휘 management 경영 article 기사 implement 실행하다, 시행하다 organization 조직

3.
해설 명령문
빈칸 앞에 please가 있으므로 명령문임을 알 수 있다. 따라서 동사원형인 (C)가 정답이다.

번역 기계는 거스름돈을 제공하지 않으므로 새 OK 여행 카드를 구매하실 때는 정확한 금액을 넣어 주세요.

어휘 change 거스름돈 exact 정확한 amount 금액 insert 삽입하다

4.
해설 시제+태
빈칸은 동사 자리이다. 앞에 next year가 있으므로 미래 시제가 와야 하고, 빈칸 뒤에 목적어 eligible employees가 있으므로 미래 시제+능동태인 (B)가 정답이다.

번역 내년부터 회사는 자격이 되는 직원들에게 4주간의 유급 가족 휴가를 제공할 것이다.

어휘 effective 시행되는, 효력을 발하는 eligible 자격이 되는 paid vacation 유급 휴가

5.
해설 조동사+동사원형
빈칸은 조동사 must의 뒤이므로 동사원형인 (A)가 정답이다.

번역 폐기물로 가득한 빨간색 생물학적 유해 물질 봉투는 지정된 용기에 두어야 한다.

어휘 biohazard bag 생물학적 유해 물질 봉투 waste 쓰레기, 폐기물 designated 지정된 receptacle 용기

6.
해설 현재 시제+태
빈칸은 동사 자리이고, 반복되는 일임을 나타내는 단서인 every year가 있으므로 현재 시제가 와야 한다. 또한 빈칸 뒤에 목적어 our operating license가 있으므로 능동태인 (A)가 정답이다.

번역 마이다스 오토 서비스에서는 정부 규정을 준수하기 위해 해마다 운영 허가를 갱신한다.

어휘 operating license 운영 허가 comply with ~을 준수하다 regulation 규제, 규정 renew 갱신하다, 새롭게 하다

7.
해설 과거완료
빈칸은 주어 Farmers Ltd.의 동사 자리이고, 과거완료의 단서인 「after+주어+___, 주어+과거동사」가 왔다. 제휴한 것이 과거(partnered)이고, 겪은 것은 그보다 이전이므로 빈칸은 과거보다 이전 시제인 과거완료 (C)가 정답이다.

번역 파머스 사는 생산 시설에 있어 운영상의 문제를 겪은 이후 콘트롤 어셈블리즈와 제휴했다.

어휘 operational 운영상의 issue 문제 facilities 시설 partner with ~와 협력하다

8.
해설 수일치
빈칸은 동사 자리이고, 주어가 '부정대명사(all) of the 명사'이므로 명사인 attendees에 수를 일치시킨다. attendees는 복수명사이므로 복수동사인 (B)가 정답이다.

번역 모든 참가자들은 참석하길 원하는 수업을 선택하도록 요구된다.

어휘 attendee 참가자 session (특정 활동) 시간

9.
해설 미래완료
빈칸은 주절(he ~ proposal)의 동사 자리이다. 미래완료의 단서인 「By the time+미래 내용」이 와서 '다음 주(미래)에 만날 때까지, 예산안을 ___하겠다'고 했다. 빈칸은 미래의 한 시점에 완료되는 시제를 나타내므로 미래완료인 (C)가 정답이다.

번역 윌슨 씨는 다음 주에 재무 이사를 만날 때까지 예산안을 완료할 것이다.

어휘 by the time ~할 때까지 financial 재무의 budget proposal 예산안

10.
해설 과거 시제
빈칸은 동사 자리이고, 앞에 과거 시제 단서인 Two weeks ago가 있으므로 (C)가 정답이다.

번역 2주 전에, WB 소프트웨어는 프리미어 프로Q 메시지 앱의 8.1.2 업데이트 버전을 출시했다.

어휘 application 앱 release 출시하다

11.
해설 현재완료
빈칸은 주어 many charity organizations의 동사 자리이고, 현재완료 시제의 단서인 in the past few years가 있으므로 현재완료 (C)가 정답이다.

번역 지난 몇 년간, 많은 자선 단체들이 재정상의 어려움에 직면해 어쩔 수 없이 문을 닫았다.

어휘 charity 자선 organization 단체 financial 재정적인 be forced to 부정사 ~하도록 강요받다

12.
해설 능동 vs. 수동
빈칸은 be동사 뒤이므로 동사는 올 수 없고, 분사인 ing/p.p.가 올 수 있다. 빈칸 뒤에 목적어가 없고 '최신 정보가 게시된다'로 해석되므로 수동태인 (D)가 정답이다.

번역 항공편 지연, 탑승구 변경과 같은 일정 관련 최신 정보는 공항 정보 화면에 즉시 게시될 것이다.

어휘 update 최신 정보 delay 지연 gate 탑승구 immediately 즉시 post 게시하다

13.
해설 시간/조건절 시제
주절의 동사 will로 보아 미래에 대한 내용이지만, 빈칸은 조건 접속사 if절의 동사 자리이므로 미래 시제 대신 현재 시제가 와야 한다. 따라서 (B)가 정답이다.

번역 우리 피트니스 센터에 회원으로 등록하시면 가든 광장에 주차 시 15% 할인을 받으실 수 있습니다.

어휘 membership 회원 register for ~에 등록하다

14.
해설 과거완료
빈칸은 주어 Ms. Hackett의 동사 자리이다. 과거완료의 단서인 「before+주어+과거동사」가 와서 '과거에 쇼를 진행한 것보다 더 이전'을 나타내므로 과거보다 이전 시제인 과거완료 (D)가 정답이다.

번역 해킷 씨는 볼티모어 TV 방송국에서 지역 토크쇼를 진행하기 전에 뉴스 프로그램에서 해고된 적이 있다.

어휘 host 진행하다 fire 해고하다

15.
해설 능동 vs. 수동
빈칸은 that절(that ~ society)의 동사 자리이고 빈칸 뒤에 목적어 reforms가 있으므로 능동태인 (D)가 정답이다.

번역 외교부 장관 강은 정부가 사회의 문화적 다양성을 함양하기 위한 개혁을 실시하고 있다고 말한다.

어휘 foreign minister 외교부 장관 reform 개혁 cultivate 양성하다 implement 실행하다, 시행하다

16.
해설 수일치
빈칸은 '부정대명사(each) of the 명사'의 동사 자리이다. 부정대명사 주어가 단수를 뜻하는 each이므로 단수동사인 (A)가 정답이다.

번역 각각의 제출된 제안서는 부동산 평가 위원회에 의해 검토되고 논의된다.

어휘 submit 제출하다 proposal 제안서 property 부동산 appraisal 평가 committee 위원회

17.
해설 현재완료
빈칸은 문장의 주절(Tom Collins ~ Dave Brown)의 동사 자리이고, 현재완료 시제의 단서인 「since+주어+과거동사」가 있으므로 현재완료 (B)가 정답이다.

번역 톰 콜린스는 굿라이프 보험사에 입사한 이래로 전설적인 영업 사원 데이브 브라운처럼 되기를 열망하고 있다.

어휘 legendary 전설의 sale agent 영업 사원 join 합류하다 insurance 보험 aspire to 부정사 ~하기를 갈망하다

18.
해설 시간/조건절 시제
조건 접속사 if가 있는 절이 의미상 미래를 나타내며 현재 시제의 동사 exceed가 will exceed를 대신한 것이므로, 주절의 동사는 미래 시제가 되어야 한다. 따라서 (A)가 정답이다.

번역 만약 수하물 허용량을 초과한다면 초과된 수하물에 대해 추가 요금을 지불해야 할 것이다.

어휘 exceed 초과하다 baggage allowance 수하물 허용량 additional 추가의 fee 요금, 수수료 excess 초과한 check (수하물을) 부치다

19.
해설 미래 시제
수식구(for ~ phones)를 지우면 빈칸은 동사 자리이고, 미래 시제 단서인 beginning next Monday가 있으므로 미래 시제인 (B)가 정답이다.

번역 다음 주 월요일부터, 텔레콤 큐브 휴대전화의 온라인 주문 기한이 원하는 픽업 날짜 전날 오후 5시까지로 연장될 것이다.

어휘 desired 바라는 extend 연장하다

20.
해설 수일치+태
빈칸은 동사 자리인데, 주어 The director가 3인칭 단수이고 빈칸 뒤에 목적어 every team member가 있으므로 단수동사+능동태인 (A)가 정답이다.

번역 이사는 모든 팀 구성원들이 다가오는 건설 프로젝트에 동등하게 기여할 것을 기대한다.

어휘 contribute to ~에 기여하다 equally 동등하게 upcoming 다가오는 construction 건설

Part 6

문장 고르기 문제 4 – 빈칸 주변의 동사와 명사를 활용한다.

 예제
본책 p. 72

> **블루윙 항공사 자주 묻는 질문**
>
> 만약 항공편이 취소되거나 지연된다면?
> 항공편이 취소된 경우, 환불을 요청할 수 있습니다. 국내선 항공권은 항공편이 90분 혹은 그 이상 지연될 경우 환불이 허용됩니다. 악천후, 파업, 보안상 폐쇄, 그 밖의 어떤 불가항력의 요인에 의해 항공편이 지연될 경우에는 오직 항공권 환불에 대한 의무만을 지며 숙소나 다른 보상은 제공되지 않습니다.

번역 (A) 항공편 정보가 이메일로 보내질 것입니다.
(B) 체크인 수속 후에 좌석이 배정될 것입니다.
(C) 예약을 확보하기 위해 신용 카드 정보를 요청 받을 것입니다.
(D) 항공편이 취소된 경우, 환불을 요청할 수 있습니다.

어휘 what if ~하면 어떻게 될까 domestic 국내의 inclement weather 악천후 labor strike 파업 security 보안 shutdown 폐쇄 beyond one's control 불가항력의 be obliged to 부정사 ~할 의무가 있다, ~하지 않을 수 없다 accommodation 숙소 compensation 보상

YBM TEST

본책 p. 73

1. (C) **2.** (A) **3.** (B) **4.** (D)

10월 21일
아이샤 첸 씨
해밀턴로드 59번지, 더넥, 뉴저지 주 07648

첸 씨께

보라 프리미엄 BBQ에서 최근에 구매해 주신 것에 대해 감사드립니다.

10월 20일에 BHL 익스프레스로 귀하의 주문품이 배송되었음을 알려드리게 되어 기쁩니다. 참고로 배송 조회 번호는 3873173242입니다.

우리의 모든 육류 제품은 최고의 최종 상품을 보장하기 위해 신선하게 포장되어 냉장 항공 화물로 배송됩니다. 우리의 명성은 신선한 상태로 배송되는 최고급 육류에 기초하고 있습니다. 만약 주문 상품에 문제가 있으시면 저희에게 알려주십시오. 환불해 드리거나 다음 주문에 해당 금액을 쓰실 수 있도록 해 드립니다.

귀하께 상품을 제공하게 되어 매우 기쁩니다. 향후에도 귀하를 도울 일이 생기면 망설이지 마시고 연락 주십시오.

유라 엘러슨
수석 고객 서비스 담당자

어휘 premium 고급의 BBQ 바비큐 via ~을 통해 express 속달 서비스 for your reference 참고로 tracking number 조회 번호 pack 포장하다 refrigerated 냉장한 airfreight 항공 화물 ensure 보장하다 credit (금액을) 기입하다, 입금하다 hesitate 망설이다 lead 선두(의) customer service representative 고객 서비스 담당자

1.

해설 명사 어휘
바로 다음 문장에서 '당신의 주문품이 배송되었다'고 했으므로 '최근 주문(order)에 대해 감사드린다'가 가장 적절하다. 따라서 (C)가 정답이다.

어휘 survey (설문) 조사 subscription 구독

2.

해설 동사 어휘
'주문 상품이 배송되었음을 ____하게 되어 기쁘다'는 내용이므로 inform(통지하다)이 문맥상 가장 잘 어울린다. 또한 「동사+A(사람)+that절」의 형태로 'A에게 ~라는 것을 ~하다'로 쓸 수 있는 동사는 보기 중 inform 뿐이다. 다른 동사는 동사와 that절 사이에 목적어(~에게)가 낄 수 없으며 respond는 자동사로 respond to(~에 응답하다)의 형태로 쓰인다. 따라서 (A)가 정답이다.

어휘 suggest 제안하다 explain 설명하다

3.

해설 문장 고르기
앞 문장에서 '최고의(best) 제품을 보장하기 위해 육류 제품(meat)이 신선하게(fresh) 포장되어 배송(shipped)된다고 했는데, (B)에서 이와 관련된 단어(premium-최고급 / meat-육류 / delivered-배송 / fresh-신선한)가 가장 많이 보인다. 내용상으로도 '신선하게 배송되는 최고급 육류로 명성을 쌓았다'는 것이므로 가장 자연스럽게 연결된다. 따라서 (B)가 정답이다.

번역 (A) 유감스럽게도, 귀하의 주문 상품이 일주일 정도 지연될 것입니다.
(B) 우리의 명성은 신선한 상태로 배송되는 최고급 육류에 기초하고 있습니다.
(C) 하지만, 그 제품은 재고가 소진되어 귀하의 주문을 처리할 수 없습니다.
(D) 우리는 개선을 위해 노력하고 있으므로 귀하의 의견이 소중하며 감사합니다.

4.

해설 가정법 도치
빈칸은 앞에 있는 명령문(Please ~ us) 뒤에 절(we ~ future)을 연결하는 자리이다. 빈칸 뒤 절의 동사가 동사원형 be인 것으로 보아 가정법 미래절(if+주어+should+동사원형~)에서 접속사 if가 생략되고 「should+주어+동사원형」이 되었음을 알 수 있다. 따라서 (D)가 정답이다. 다른 보기들은 동사원형 be가 올 수 없다.

Unit 5 To부정사 & 동명사

공식으로 해결하는 실전문제

본책 p. 77

1. (A) **2.** (B) **3.** (B) **4.** (C) **5.** (B)
6. (D) **7.** (D) **8.** (C)

1.

해설 to부정사-부사 역할
To ~ decision은 완전한 절 앞에 붙은 수식구이고, '옳은 결정을 내리기 위해'로 해석되므로 to부정사구가 되어야 한다. 빈칸 앞에 To가 있으므로 동사원형인 (A)가 정답이다.

번역 올바른 결정을 내리기 위해, 이사회는 더 상세한 정보가 필요했다.

어휘 board of directors 이사회 detailed 상세한

2.

해설 동사+목적어+to부정사
be required to do는 'require+목적어+to부정사'의 수동형이므로 빈칸에는 동사원형이 와야 한다. 따라서 정답은 (B)이다.

번역 조넉스 사의 모든 직원들은 이제 수기가 아니라, 전자상으로 출퇴근 기록부를 작성해야 한다.

어휘 timesheet 출퇴근기록부 electronically 전자상으로 manually 손으로 complete 작성하다, 기입하다

3.

해설 동사+목적어+to부정사
allow는 목적어 다음 목적격 보어 자리에 to부정사가 와야 하므로 (B)가 정답이다.

번역 스피디젯은 승객들이 예약 시 무료로 좌석을 선택하도록 허용한다.
어휘 for free 무료로 booking 예약

4.
해설 to부정사-부사 역할
완전한 절 뒤에 빈칸이 있고, 빈칸 뒤의 동사원형 provide를 연결해 '충분한 식음료를 제공하기 위해'로 해석되므로 (C)가 정답이다.
번역 레니 케이터링은 충분한 음식과 음료를 제공하기 위해 예상되는 손님 수를 미리 알아야 한다.
어휘 expected 예상되는 count 총수 in advance 미리 beverage 음료

5.
해설 to부정사-부사 역할
완전한 절 뒤에 빈칸이 있고, 빈칸 뒤에 남은 단어들과 함께 '수수료를 피하기 위해'로 해석되므로 (B)가 정답이다.
번역 연체 및 징수료를 피하려면 만기일까지 주차 위반 과태료를 내야 한다.
어휘 parking ticket 주차 위반 딱지 due date 만기일 late fee 연체료 collection fee 수금[징수] 수수료

6.
해설 동사+목적어+to부정사
'instruct+목적어+to부정사'의 수동형은 'be instructed to부정사'이므로 빈칸에는 to부정사가 와야 한다. 따라서 정답은 (D)이다.
번역 전 직원이 최근 수정된 안내서에 관해 강사가 이끄는 토론에 참석하도록 지시받는다.
어휘 instruct 지시하다 instructor-led 강사가 이끄는, 강의식의 revised 수정된 handbook 안내서 attendant 종업원

7.
해설 to부정사-부사 역할
in order to는 '~하기 위해서'를 뜻하는 to부정사구이므로 빈칸 뒤에는 동사원형이 와야 한다. 따라서 (D)가 정답이다.
번역 지불 서비스 제공업체들은 새로운 규정을 따르기 위해 보안 절차를 수정할 필요가 있다.
어휘 provider 공급업체 modify 수정하다 procedure 절차 regulation 규정 comply with ~을 준수하다

8.
해설 동사+목적어+to부정사
encourage는 목적어 다음 목적격 보어 자리에 to부정사가 와야 하므로 (C)가 정답이다.
번역 스미스 씨는 경품 추첨 행사가 고객들이 제품을 구매하도록 유도할 거라고 믿는다.
어휘 prize draw 상품[경품] 추첨, 제비뽑기 encourage 고무시키다 purchase 구매, 구매하다

공식으로 해결하는 실전문제
본책 p. 79

1. (A) **2.** (C) **3.** (A) **4.** (D) **5.** (D)
6. (B) **7.** (B) **8.** (A)

1.
해설 전치사 to+-ing
contribute 다음에 오는 to는 전치사 to이므로 뒤에 명사나 동명사가 와야 한다. 따라서 동명사인 (A)가 정답이다.
번역 린 씨의 지도력은 지역의 협력사들과 강한 유대를 구축하는 데 크게 기여했다.
어휘 leadership 지도력 contribute to ~에 기여하다 greatly 대단히 relationship 관계 local 현지의 partner 동업자

2.
해설 전치사 to+-ing
be dedicated 다음에 오는 to는 전치사 to이므로 뒤에 명사나 동명사가 와야 한다. 따라서 동명사인 (C)가 정답이다.
번역 아틀란티스 여행사는 여행자들에게 최고의 휴가 경험을 제공하는 데 전념합니다.
어휘 travel agency 여행사 be dedicated to ~하는 데 전념하다

3.
해설 형용사+to부정사
형용사 likely는 뒤에 to부정사가 붙어 '~할 것 같은'을 뜻하므로 (A)가 정답이다.
번역 갈수록 변동이 심한 강수량이 전국에 걸쳐 물 공급량에 영향을 줄 것 같다.
어휘 increasingly 점점 더 variable 변동이 심한 precipitation 강수량 be likely to부정사 ~할 것 같다 water 물 supply 공급

4.
해설 명사+to부정사
빈칸은 앞에 있는 명사를 뒤에서 수식하는 자리이고 특히, effort는 to부정사의 수식을 받아 '~하기 위한 노력'으로 쓰인다. 따라서 정답은 (D)이다.
번역 운영비를 아끼기 위한 노력으로, BNC 사는 종이를 쓰지 않는 회사가 되고자 한다.
어휘 in an effort to부정사 ~하기 위한 노력으로 operating expense 운영 비용 strive to부정사 ~하려고 애쓰다 paperless 종이를 쓰지 않는 save on ~을 절약하다

5.
해설 형용사+to부정사
be willing은 뒤에 to부정사가 붙어 '기꺼이 ~하다'를 뜻하므로 (D)가 정답이다.
번역 그 연구는 뛰어난 리더들은 기꺼이 위험을 감수하고 조직을 전진시킨다는 것을 보여준다.
어휘 exceptional (예외적으로) 우수한 take the risk 위험을 무릅쓰다 forward 앞으로

6.
해설 전치사 to + -ing
be committed 다음에 오는 to는 전치사 to이므로 뒤에 명사나 동명사가 와야 한다. 따라서 동명사인 (B)가 정답이다.

번역 D-갤러리의 큐레이터인 크리스 크롬은 장르 구분에 상관없이 예술을 조합하는 것에 몰두한다.

어휘 curator 큐레이터 be committed to ~에 전념하다 pull together 함께 모아 조화롭게 다루다 regardless of ~에 상관없이 genre 장르 classification 분류

7.
해설 명사 + to부정사
빈칸은 앞에 있는 명사를 뒤에서 수식하는 자리이다. 특히, opportunity는 to부정사의 수식을 받아 '~할 기회'로 쓰인다. 따라서 정답은 (B)이다.

번역 대회 수상자들은 BIO 비즈니스 포럼에서 발표할 기회를 얻게 될 것이다.

어휘 presentation 발표 forum 포럼, 토론회

8.
해설 전치사 to + -ing
look forward to에서 to는 전치사이므로 뒤에 명사나 동명사가 와야 한다. 명사 presentation은 뒤에 있는 명사 his ~ achievements로 연결될 수 없는 반면, 동명사 presenting은 이를 목적어로 취해 '실적을 발표하기'를 뜻하므로 (A)가 정답이다.

번역 선데이 파워의 재무 담당 최고 책임자는 주주총회에서 회사의 뛰어난 실적을 발표하기를 기대하고 있다.

어휘 chief financial officer 재무 담당 최고 책임자 look forward to ~을 기대하다 remarkable 놀랄 만한 achievement 성취, 업적 shareholder 주주

✚ 공식으로 해결하는 실전문제   본책 p. 81

1. (A) 2. (D) 3. (C) 4. (B) 5. (D)
6. (A) 7. (D) 8. (C)

1.
해설 동사 + 동명사
빈칸 앞에 있는 recommend는 동명사를 목적어로 갖는 동사이므로 정답은 (A)이다.

번역 공원이 매우 붐빌 수 있기 때문에 웹 사이트를 통해 미리 표를 구매할 것을 권고드립니다.

어휘 ticket 표 in advance 미리 crowded 붐비는

2.
해설 동사 + 동명사
빈칸 앞에 있는 suggests는 동명사를 목적어로 갖는 동사이므로 정답은 (D)이다.

번역 레밍턴 박사는 소셜 미디어에 소비하는 시간의 양을 제한할 것을 제안한다.

어휘 suggest -ing ~할 것을 제안하다 spend on ~에 시간을 쓰다

3.
해설 동사 + to부정사
빈칸 앞에 있는 has decided는 to부정사를 목적어로 갖는 동사이므로 정답은 (C)이다.

번역 경영진은 심사숙고 후 비용을 절감하기 위해 넥서스 여행사와의 계약을 종료하기로 결정했다.

어휘 consideration 숙고 management 경영진 cut cost 비용을 줄이다 terminate 종료하다

4.
해설 동사 + 동명사
빈칸 앞에 있는 mind는 동명사를 목적어로 갖는 동사이므로 정답은 (B)이다.

번역 제프 클락은 플라이 아시아 항공사의 최고 경영자이지만, 이코노미 좌석으로 여행하는 것을 꺼리지 않는다.

어휘 CEO 최고 경영자 mind -ing ~하기를 꺼리다 economy class 이코노미 좌석

5.
해설 동사 + to부정사
빈칸 앞에 있는 wish는 to부정사를 목적어로 갖는 동사이므로 정답은 (D)이다. 참고로 동사 wish는 those(~한 사람들)를 수식하는 관계사절(who ~ decision)에 속한 동사이다.

번역 젬프로는 구매 결정을 내리기 전에 제품을 사용해 보길 원하는 사람들을 위해 무료 체험을 제공한다.

어휘 free trial 무료 사용[체험] option 선택(권) those ~한 사람들

6.
해설 동사 + to부정사
빈칸 앞에 있는 strives는 to부정사를 목적어로 갖는 동사이므로 정답은 (A)이다.

번역 디지털웨이는 우리 지역의 모든 고객들에게 빠르고 믿을 수 있는 인터넷 연결 서비스를 공급하기 위해 항상 노력합니다.

어휘 strive to부정사 ~하려고 애쓰다 reliable 믿을 수 있는 connection 연결

7.
해설 동사 + to부정사
빈칸 앞에 있는 plans는 to부정사를 목적어로 갖는 동사이므로 정답은 (D)이다.

번역 AP 출판은 다음 주까지 이력서를 받고 나서 그 다음 주에 면접을 시행할 계획이다.

어휘 the week after 그 다음 주

8.
해설 동사 + 동명사
빈칸 앞에 있는 keeps는 동명사를 목적어로 갖는 동사이므로 정답은 (C)이다.

번역 바이마트 포도원은 남아메리카에서 가장 품질 좋은 와인의 선두 생산업체가 되는 것을 끊임없이 추구한다.

어휘 vineyard 포도밭 keep -ing ~을 계속하다 goal 목표 leading 선두의 producer 생산업체 pursue 추구하다

공식으로 해결하는 실전문제 　　　　　본책 p. 83

| 1. (D) | 2. (A) | 3. (D) | 4. (B) | 5. (C) |
| 6. (B) | 7. (B) | 8. (C) | | |

1.
해설 명사 vs. 동명사
빈칸은 전치사 뒤이므로 명사 혹은 동명사가 와야 하고, 빈칸 뒤에 목적어가 있으므로 동명사 (D)가 정답이다.

번역 파손된 상품을 포함한 배송물을 받은 직후, 최대 15일까지 반품하시면 전액 환불받으실 수 있습니다.

어휘 upon -ing ~하자마자 damaged 파손된 goods 상품 up to 최대 ~까지 return 반품하다 full refund 전액 환불 receipt 인수, 영수증

2.
해설 전치사+동명사
빈칸은 전치사 뒤이므로 동사는 올 수 없고 동명사인 (A)가 정답이다.

번역 인스톨-밴은 직원들이 회사 컴퓨터에 소프트웨어를 설치하는 것을 방지하기 위한 완벽한 해결책이다.

어휘 solution 해결책 prevent A(목적어) from -ing A가 ~하는 것을 막다[방지하다]

3.
해설 명사 vs. 동명사
빈칸은 전치사 뒤이므로 명사 혹은 동명사가 와야 하고, 빈칸 뒤에 목적어가 없으므로 명사 (D)가 정답이다.

번역 본 설명서는 방해받지 않고 데이터베이스 관리 시스템을 백업하는 방법을 알려준다.

어휘 manual 설명서 management 관리 interruption 중단, 방해

4.
해설 전치사+동명사
빈칸 앞에 전치사가 있고, 뒤로는 목적어 the retail price를 연결하므로 동명사인 (B)가 정답이다.

번역 이사회는 수요가 낮아질 것을 우려해 소매가를 인상하는 것에 대해 유보적인 입장을 표명했다.

어휘 board member 이사, 임원 reservation 유보, 주저함 retail price 소매 가격 lead to ~로 이어지다

5.
해설 명사 vs. 동명사
빈칸은 that절(that ~ operations)의 동사 would help의 주어 자리이므로 명사 혹은 동명사가 와야 하고, 빈칸 뒤에 목적어가 있으므로 동명사 (C)가 정답이다.

번역 울렛 밀턴의 사장은 회사를 두 개로 분리하는 것이 운영을 간소화하는 데 도움이 될 것이라고 말했다.

어휘 state 말하다 streamline 간소화하다 operation 운영

6.
해설 명사 vs. 동명사
빈칸은 전치사 뒤이므로 명사 혹은 동명사가 와야 하고, 빈칸 뒤에 목적어가 있으므로 동명사 (B)가 정답이다.

번역 우리의 온라인 과정은 기초적인 컴퓨터 능력을 향상시키는 데 관심 있는 사람들에게 이상적입니다.

어휘 course 강좌 ideal 이상적인 interested in ~에 관심 있는

7.
해설 명사 vs. 동명사
빈칸은 전치사 뒤이므로 명사 혹은 동명사가 와야 한다. 명사 application은 주로 가산명사로 '지원서'를 뜻하며, 지원 행위를 의미하지는 않으므로 문맥상 적절하지 않다. 반면, 동명사 applying은 '~에 지원하다(apply for)'를 뜻하는 자동사의 동명사라서 뒤에 목적어 없이 바로 전치사가 올 수 있으므로 (B)가 정답이다.

번역 일자리에 지원하기 전에, 이전 동료, 상사 혹은 고객과 같은 직업과 관련된 추천인 명단을 준비하는 것이 좋다.

어휘 professional 직업[업무]과 관련된 reference 추천인 former 예전의 colleague 동료 supervisor 관리자 client 고객 apply for ~에 지원하다 application 신청서

8.
해설 전시차+형용사+명사
빈칸에 들어갈 말이 명사 investments를 목적어로 취하는 동명사일 수도 있고, 명사 investments를 수식하는 형용사일 수도 있다. '상당한 투자 덕분에'가 문맥상 자연스러우므로 형용사인 (C)가 정답이다.

번역 제조 장비에 상당한 투자를 한 덕분에, 그 공장은 높은 수준의 생산성 신장을 달성했다.

어휘 thanks to ~ 덕분에 investment 투자 manufacturing 제조 productivity 생산성 considerable 상당한

YBM TEST 　　　　　본책 p. 84

1. (D)	2. (A)	3. (B)	4. (A)	5. (B)
6. (D)	7. (C)	8. (B)	9. (D)	10. (C)
11. (B)	12. (A)	13. (D)	14. (B)	15. (C)
16. (D)	17. (A)	18. (A)	19. (B)	20. (D)

1.

해설 **to부정사-부사 역할**
To ~ sales는 완전한 절 앞에 붙은 수식구이고, '온라인 판매를 늘리기 위해'로 해석되므로 to부정사구가 되어야 한다. 빈칸 앞에 To가 있으므로 동사원형인 (D)가 정답이다.

번역 온라인 판매를 늘리기 위해서는, 우리 고객들이 긍정적인 후기와 평가를 남기는 것이 중요하다.

어휘 **sales** 판매(량) **vital** 필수적인 **positive** 긍정적인 **review** 논평 **feedback** 피드백, 평가

2.

해설 **동사+목적어+to부정사**
'advise+목적어+to부정사'의 수동형은 'be advised to부정사'이므로 빈칸에는 to부정사가 와야 한다. 따라서 정답은 (A)이다.

번역 구직자들은 자격증을 따는 데 의지하기보다는 훌륭한 의사소통 및 문제 해결 능력을 계발하는 것이 좋다.

어휘 **job seeker** 구직자 **communication skill** 의사소통 능력 **problem solving skill** 문제 해결 능력 **instead of** ~ 대신에 **rely on** ~에 의존하다 **certificate** 자격증

3.

해설 **동사+to부정사**
빈칸 앞에 있는 decided는 to부정사를 목적어로 갖는 동사이므로 정답은 (B)이다.

번역 이사회는 가장 헌신적인 태도를 보여 준 구성원에게 매 회의마다 포상을 하기로 결정했다.

어휘 **board member** 이사, 임원 **reward** 보상 **commitment** 헌신

4.

해설 **동사+동명사**
빈칸 앞에 있는 enjoy는 동명사를 목적어로 갖는 동사이므로 정답은 (A)이다. 빈칸은 동사의 목적어 자리이므로 명사 reader도 올 수는 있지만 빈칸 뒤에 목적어(all ~ content)가 있으므로 답이 될 수 없고 해석상으로도 적절하지 않다.

번역 우리의 구독자들은 〈아이 모니〉 잡지의 모든 콘텐츠를 태블릿에서 디지털 판으로도 즐길 수 있다.

어휘 **subscriber** 구독자 **content** 내용물 **tablet** 태블릿 **access** 접근, 이용 **edition** (출판물의) 판

5.

해설 **동사+동명사**
빈칸 앞에 있는 discontinue는 동명사를 목적어로 갖는 동사이므로 정답은 (B)이다. 빈칸은 동사의 목적어 자리이므로 명사 offer도 올 수는 있지만 빈칸 뒤에 목적어(free ~ shipping)가 있으므로 답이 될 수 없다.

번역 경쟁 체인점인 베스트 숍 사와 달리, 올 마트 스토어즈는 다음 달부터 무제한 무료 배송을 제공하는 것을 중단할 것이다.

어휘 **unlike** ~와 달리 **discontinue** 중단하다 **unlimited** 무제한의

6.

해설 **주어 자리**
빈칸은 수식어 two hours before a flight을 지우면 동사 is의 주어 자리이다. 따라서 동사는 답이 될 수 없고 동명사인 (D)가 정답이다.

번역 국내선을 탈 경우, 반드시 비행 두 시간 전에 도착할 필요는 없다.

어휘 **flight** 항공편 **domestically** 국내에서

7.

해설 **전치사+명사**
빈칸은 전치사 뒤이므로 동사나 to부정사는 올 수 없고 동명사인 (C)가 정답이다. 빈칸 뒤에 목적어가 있으므로 명사는 답이 될 수 없다.

번역 근로자 고용에 드는 비용이 올라갈 것이라는 이유로 많은 소상공인들이 최저 임금을 인상하는 것에 대해 우려한다.

어휘 **concerned** 걱정하는 **minimum wage** 최저 임금 **hire** 고용하다 **raise** 올리다 **raiser** 올리는 사람[것]

8.

해설 **명사+to부정사**
빈칸은 앞에 있는 명사를 뒤에서 수식하는 자리이다. 특히, decision은 to부정사의 수식을 받아 '~하려는 결정'을 뜻한다. 따라서 정답은 (B)이다.

번역 소프트웨어 회사 넷클라우드는 온라인 광고 회사 너비를 인수하려는 결정을 발표했다.

어휘 **firm** 회사 **acquisition** 인수, 획득 **acquire** 인수하다

9.

해설 **to부정사-부사 역할**
완전한 절 뒤에 빈칸이 있고, 빈칸 뒤에 남은 단어들과 함께 '전액 환불을 받기 위해'로 해석되므로 (D)가 정답이다.

번역 고객이 전액 환불을 받기 위해서는 어떠한 청구 사항이라도 송장일로부터 15일 이내에 보고되어야 한다.

어휘 **claim** 청구 **report** 보고하다 **invoice** 송장, 청구서 **full refund** 전액 환불

10.

해설 **동사+목적어+to부정사**
urge는 목적어 다음 목적격 보어 자리에 to부정사가 와야 하므로 (C)가 정답이다.

번역 사이버 보안 전문가들은 사용자들이 좋은 안티바이러스 프로그램을 설치해 그들의 컴퓨터를 최신 사양으로 유지할 것을 권고한다.

어휘 **urge** 권고하다, 촉구하다 **anti-virus** 안티바이러스 **keep** 유지하다 **up-to-date** 최신의

11.
해설 명사 vs. 동명사
be subject to의 to는 전치사이므로 명사 혹은 동명사가 와야 하고, 빈칸 뒤로 목적어가 없으므로 동명사 changing은 답이 될 수 없다. 명사 changer(변경하는 사람)는 가산명사이므로 앞에 한정사가 없을 때는 복수 형태로 와야 하고, 문맥상으로도 적절하지 않다. 따라서 명사 (B)가 정답이다.

번역 모든 가격과 메뉴는 시장 상황이나 계절적 이용 가능성에 따라 변경될 수 있다.

어휘 be subject to ~의 대상이다 based on ~에 근거하여 seasonal 계절적인 availability 입수[이용] 가능성

12.
해설 동사+동명사
빈칸 앞에 있는 had finished는 동명사를 목적어로 갖는 동사이므로 정답은 (A)이다. 빈칸은 동사의 목적어 자리이므로 명사 writer도 올 수는 있지만 빈칸 뒤에 목적어(the first draft)가 있으므로 답이 될 수 없고 해석상으로도 적절하지 않다.

번역 제나 제임스는 그녀의 블로그에서 신작 소설 〈실버 에이지〉의 초고 집필을 끝냈다고 언급했다.

어휘 note 언급하다 draft 초고, 초안 upcoming 다가오는

13.
해설 동사+to부정사
빈칸 앞에 있는 is planning은 to부정사를 목적어로 갖는 동사이므로 정답은 (D)이다. 빈칸은 동사의 목적어 자리이므로 명사 opening(s)도 올 수는 있지만 이 경우 빈칸 뒤(its ~ branch)와 연결되지 못한다.

번역 싱가포르에 본사를 둔 홍보 회사인 링퐁 에이전시는 다음 달 서울에 첫 해외 지사를 개설할 계획이다.

어휘 public relations 홍보 firm 회사 based in ~에 기반을 둔 branch 지사 opening 시작, 개막

14.
해설 명사 vs. 동명사
빈칸은 전치사 After 뒤이므로 명사 혹은 동명사가 올 수 있다. 앞에 명사를 수식하는 형용사가 있으므로 명사 (B)가 정답이다. 참고로 동명사는 부사의 수식을 받으며 뒤에 목적어가 올 수 있다.

번역 방어 운전 교습을 성공적으로 마치고 나면 보험료 할인을 받을 수 있다.

어휘 defensive driving course 방어 운전 be eligible for ~에 자격이 있다 insurance 보험 completion 완료, 이수

15.
해설 동사+목적어+to부정사
be scheduled는 to부정사와 함께 '~할 예정이다'라는 뜻으로 쓰이므로 (C)가 정답이다.

번역 산체스 박사는 알츠하이머병에 관한 제12회 국제 컨퍼런스에서 개회사를 하기로 되어 있다.

어휘 be scheduled to부정사 ~할 예정이다 opening speech 개회사 Alzheimer's disease 알츠하이머병

16.
해설 명사 vs. 동명사
빈칸은 전치사 뒤이므로 명사 혹은 동명사가 와야 하고, 빈칸 뒤에 목적어가 있으므로 동명사 (D)가 정답이다.

번역 특정 기준을 충족시키는 사람들은 소득세를 면제받을 수 있다.

어휘 meet 충족시키다 specific 특정한, 구체적인 criteria 기준 be exempt from ~에서 면제되다 income tax 소득세

17.
해설 to부정사-부사 역할
완전한 절 앞 쪽에 빈칸이 있고, 빈칸 뒤의 동사원형 maintain을 연결해 '식품 안전 기준을 유지하기 위해'로 해석되므로 to부정사구가 되어야 한다. 따라서 정답은 (A)이다.

번역 식품 안전 기준을 유지하기 위해, 우리는 어떠한 남은 음식도 식당 외부로 반출되는 것을 허용하지 않습니다.

어휘 maintain 유지하다 safety standard 안전 기준 leftover (식사 후) 남은 음식

18.
해설 명사+to부정사
빈칸은 앞에 있는 명사를 뒤에서 수식하는 자리이다. 특히, proposal은 to부정사의 수식을 받아 '~하자는 제안'를 뜻한다. 따라서 정답은 (A)이다.

번역 강변 경기장을 건설하자는 제안은 주 정부의 승인을 필요로 한다.

어휘 waterfront 해안가 approval 승인 state government 주 정부

19.
해설 전치사 to + -ing
be committed to의 to는 전치사이므로 뒤에 명사나 동명사가 와야 한다. 빈칸 뒤에 목적어가 있으므로 동명사인 (B)가 정답이다.

번역 그린 브리즈는 재생 가능한 에너지원, 특히 풍력을 개발하는 것에 전념한다.

어휘 be committed to ~에 전념하다 renewable 재생 가능한 source 원천 developer 개발업자

20.
해설 명사 vs. 동명사
빈칸은 전치사 뒤이므로 명사 혹은 동명사가 와야 하고, 빈칸 뒤에 목적어가 있으므로 동명사 (D)가 정답이다.

번역 엘리자베스 데이턴은 연례 직원 시상식에서 한결같이 훌륭한 고객 서비스를 제공한 데 대해 상을 받을 것이다.

어휘 recognize 인정하다, 표창하다 annual 연례의 consistently 한결같이

Part 6

시제 문제 1 – 앞뒤 문장 동사의 시제를 확인한다.

✤ 예제
본책 p. 86

수신: 보아 베버리지 전 직원
발신: 노라 파메티

어제 회의에서, 보아 베버리지 사의 이사회가 회사 고위 경영진 구축을 위해 현재 의장 겸 최고 경영자인 휴 길버트에 대한 권고안을 만장일치로 승인했습니다. 새로운 조직 하에, 업무 총괄 책임자인 마이크 파킨슨이 다음 달부터 길버트 씨의 최고 경영자 직을 승계할 것입니다. 길버트 씨는 이사회 의장직을 계속 수행할 것입니다.

어휘 board of directors 이사회 unanimously 만장일치로 approve 승인하다 recommendation 권고 current 현재의 chairman 의장 chief executive officer 최고 경영자 (= CEO) senior 상위의 leadership 지도부, 지도자 structure 조직, 구조 chief operating officer 업무 총괄 책임자 succeed 승계하다 effective 시행하는 serve 근무하다

YBM TEST
본책 p. 87

| 1. (B) | 2. (A) | 3. (D) | 4. (A) |

패트릭 루이스
오처드 레인 215번지
샌프란시스코, 캘리포니아 92010

루이스 씨께,

밀린 임대료 납부에 대해 알려드리고자 편지를 보냅니다. 임대 계약서에 따르면, 당신은 매달 5일까지 임대료를 지불하기로 되어 있습니다. 하지만 우리 기록에 따르면 당신의 임대료 납부가 계속 늦어지고 있으며, 이는 계약 조건 위반에 해당합니다. 우리는 그러한 반복적인 지불 연체를 받아들일 수 없습니다. 지금부터 임대료가 제때에 납입되지 않을 경우, 우리는 당신이 우리 아파트에 더 이상 거주할 생각이 없는 것으로 간주할 것입니다.

만기일까지 임대료를 내실 것을 요청드립니다. 협조에 미리 감사드립니다.

낸시 바우어
부동산 관리인

어휘 inform A of B A에게 B를 알리다 delayed 지연된 rent 임대료, 집세 rental agreement 임대 계약(서) be supposed to부정사 ~하기로 되어 있다 on a regular basis 정기적으로 breach 위반 terms of the agreement 계약 조건 in time 제때에 assume 추정하다 due date 만기일, 기한 in advance 미리 property manager 부동산 관리인

1.
해설 수량형용사

빈칸은 가산 단수명사 calendar month를 수식하는 형용사 자리이므로 가산 복수명사와 쓰이는 all과 most는 답이 될 수 없다. 문맥상 '매(각각의) 달'을 의미하므로 (B)가 정답이다.

2.
해설 동사 시제

빈칸 주변을 살펴 보면 '지불이 연체되고 있음 → 매달 5일까지 지불해야 함 → 현재 기록에 따르면 → 임대료가 계속해서 늦게 ___ → 이는 계약 위반임'이라는 상황이다. 빈칸에는 과거부터 현재까지 임대료가 늦게 '지불되어 왔다'가 들어가야 적절하다. 따라서 현재완료 시제 (A)가 정답이다.

3.
해설 문장 고르기

빈칸의 앞 문장에서 '당신의 임대료 납부가 늦어지고 있다'고 했는데, 이를 (D)에서 지시어 such(그러한)로 받아 '그러한 반복적인 지불 연체'를 받아들일 수 없다고 한 것이 연결 관계가 적절하다. 또한 뒤이어서 지불이 다시 연체될 경우 일어날 일을 추가로 언급했으므로 (D)가 정답이다.

번역 (A) 지불은 현금으로만 받을 것입니다.
(B) 상승하는 주거비 때문에, 임대료를 올릴 필요가 있습니다.
(C) 당신은 새로운 세입자이기 때문에, 첫 번째 임대료를 면제해 드릴 겁니다.
(D) 우리는 그러한 반복적인 지불 연체를 받아들일 수 없습니다.

4.
해설 명사 어휘

앞 문장에서 '만기일까지 임대료를 낼 것을 요청한다'고 했으므로 빈칸에서는 이 요청에 대한 '협조'에 미리 감사한다는 내용이 와야 적절하다. 따라서 (A)가 정답이다.

어휘 renewal 갱신 solution 해결책

Unit 6 분사

✤ 공식으로 해결하는 실전문제
본책 p. 91

| 1. (A) | 2. (C) | 3. (A) | 4. (D) | 5. (B) |
| 6. (B) | 7. (D) | 8. (C) |

1.
해설 ing vs. p.p.

빈칸은 명사 costs를 앞에서 수식하는 분사 자리이고, costs(비용)는 '제안되는' 수동 관계이므로 (A)가 정답이다.

번역 옥스젬은 시스템 업그레이드를 위해 제안된 비용을 검토한 후, 진행 여부에 대한 최종 결정을 내릴 것이다.

어휘 review 검토하다 whether to부정사 ~할지 안 할지 proceed 진행하다

2.
해설 분사 자리

빈칸은 명사를 앞에서 수식하는 분사 자리이므로 동사나 명사는 답이 될 수 없고, 분사인 (C)가 정답이다. 참고로 rise는 동사(오르다)와 명사(상승)의 형태가 같다.

번역 상승하는 실업률은 보통 경기 둔화의 조짐으로 간주된다.

어휘 unemployment rate 실업률 regard A as B A를 B로 여기다 sign 조짐 weakening 약화되는

3.

해설 헷갈리는 분사
빈칸은 명사 number(수)를 수식하는 분사 자리이고, '한정된 수'로 해석되므로 (A)가 정답이다.

번역 지난 토요일에 한정된 수량의 마이크 운동화가 전국에 있는 가게에서 판매되었다.

어휘 sneakers 운동화 nationwide 전국적으로 limited 제한된

4.

해설 헷갈리는 분사
빈칸은 명사 visa application process(비자 신청 절차)를 수식하는 분사 자리이고, '복잡한 비자 신청 절차'로 해석되므로 (D)가 정답이다.

번역 와이저 제약회사는 외국인 직원을 위해 복잡한 비자 신청 절차와 관련하여 도움을 제공한다.

어휘 pharmaceutical 제약의 assistance 도움 complicate 복잡하게 만들다 complication 문제, 분규 complicated 복잡한

5.

해설 헷갈리는 분사
빈칸은 명사 landscape(풍경)를 수식하는 분사 자리이고, '주변의 풍경'으로 해석되므로 (B)가 정답이다.

번역 하이필즈 공원의 전망대는 근사한 전망의 주변 경관으로 유명하다.

어휘 observatory 전망대 view 전망 landscape 풍경 surround 둘러싸다 surrounding 주변의

6.

해설 ing vs. p.p.
빈칸은 명사 tickets를 앞에서 수식하는 분사 자리이고, tickets (입장권)는 '할인되는' 수동 관계이므로 (B)가 정답이다.

번역 TDF 회원들은 다양한 브로드웨이 공연의 입장권에 대해 특별 할인을 받는다.

어휘 access 접근(권), 이용 a variety of 다양한 performance 공연 discounter 할인점

7.

해설 ing vs. p.p.
빈칸은 명사 changes를 앞에서 수식하는 분사 자리이고, changes(변화)는 '예상되는' 수동 관계이므로 (D)가 정답이다.

번역 그 기사는 정부의 새로운 주택 정책에 관해 몇 가지 예상되는 변화를 다룬다.

어휘 address 다루다 housing policy 주택 정책

8.

해설 헷갈리는 분사
빈칸은 명사 town(마을)을 수식하는 분사 자리이고, '매력적인 마을'로 해석되므로 (C)가 정답이다.

번역 부뇰은 스페인의 축제인 라 토마티나가 매년 열리는 작지만 매력적인 마을이다.

어휘 be held 개최되다 inviting 매력적인, 솔깃한

공식으로 해결하는 실전문제 본책 p. 93

1. (D) 2. (D) 3. (C) 4. (B) 5. (A)
6. (B) 7. (C) 8. (A)

1.

해설 감정 분사
빈칸은 주어 Investors를 설명해 주는 분사 자리로, Investors (투자자)가 놀라움을 느꼈으므로 과거분사 (D)가 정답이다.

번역 투자자들은 커피 대기업 코피박스가 온라인 사업을 종료할 거라는 것을 알고 놀랐다.

어휘 investor 투자자 giant 거대 기업

2.

해설 명사 뒤 분사
빈칸은 명사 parking spaces(주차 공간)를 뒤에서 수식하는 분사 자리이고, 뒤에 목적어가 없이 '예약된'이라고 해석되므로 (D)가 정답이다.

번역 6월 둘째 주 동안, 공사로 인해 방문객들을 위해 마련된 주차 공간의 수가 제한될 것이다.

어휘 parking space 주차 공간, 주차장 limited 제한된 due to ~ 때문에 construction work 건설 공사 reserve 예약하다

3.

해설 명사 뒤 분사
빈칸은 명사 documents(서류)를 뒤에서 수식하는 분사 자리이고, 뒤에 목적어 its plans가 있으므로 (C)가 정답이다.

번역 시의회가 새로운 주민 회관을 건설하려는 계획을 설명하는 서류를 공개했다.

어휘 city council 시의회 release 공개하다 community center 주민 회관 outline 개요를 서술하다

4.

해설 감정 분사
빈칸은 주어 We를 설명하는 분사 자리로, 새 웹 사이트의 개설을 발표하게 되어 We(우리)가 흥분을 느끼므로 과거분사 (B)가 정답이다.

번역 실내 장식 추세에 대한 최신 정보를 다루게 될 새로운 스윗홈 웹 사이트의 개설을 발표하게 되어 매우 기쁩니다.

어휘 launch 개시 cover 다루다 latest 최신의 decorating 장식 trend 동향, 추세

5.
해설 명사 뒤 분사
빈칸은 명사 statement(성명서)를 뒤에서 수식하는 분사 자리이고, 뒤에 목적어가 없이 '발표된'이라고 해석되므로 (A)가 정답이다.

번역 스페이스 항공사의 CEO인 미라 누네즈는 월요일 아침에 발표된 그의 성명서에서 기내 직원들에 의해 부당한 대우를 받은 승객에게 사과했다.

어휘 statement 성명(서) CEO 최고 경영자 mistreat 홀대하다 crew 승무원 release (공개적으로) 발표하다

6.
해설 감정 분사/형용사
빈칸은 명사 features를 꾸미는 자리이다. features(특징)는 감동을 느끼지 않고 감동을 일으키는 원인이므로 과거분사 impressed(감동 받는)는 답이 될 수 없고 형용사인 (B) impressive(인상적인)가 정답이다.

번역 신작 XYZ 비디오 게임의 개발자들은 인상적인 새 특징들을 선보임으로써 새로운 플레이어들의 관심을 끌기를 기대하고 있다.

어휘 feature 특징 impressive 인상적인 impressed 감명 받은 impress 감동을 주다

7.
해설 명사 뒤 분사
빈칸은 명사 Fanali Louis를 뒤에서 수식하는 분사 자리이고, 뒤에 목적어가 없으므로 (C)가 정답이다.

번역 월드칙 디자인 상의 올해 수상자는 창의적인 사고와 실용적인 디자인으로 알려진 파날리 루이스이다.

어휘 winner 수상자 practical 실용적인 known for ~로 알려진[유명한]

8.
해설 명사 뒤 분사
빈칸은 주어 Anyone을 뒤에서 수식하는 분사 자리이다. 뒤에 목적어 an online application을 취해 '제출하는'으로 해석되므로 (A)가 정답이다.

번역 온라인 여권 신청서를 제출하는 사람은 누구라도 이름, 생년월일, 집 주소와 같은 개인 정보를 제공해야 한다.

어휘 application 신청서 passport 여권 such as ~와 같은

✚ 공식으로 해결하는 실전문제
본책 p. 95

| 1. (A) | 2. (D) | 3. (A) | 4. (A) | 5. (C) |
| 6. (D) | 7. (C) | 8. (A) | | |

1.
해설 부사절 접속사+분사
부사절 접속사 When 뒤에 주어가 없으므로 분사가 와야 하고, 빈칸 뒤로 목적어 potential customers가 있으므로 능동 분사인 (A)가 정답이다.

번역 잠재 고객을 만날 때는, 깔끔한 차림으로 정시에 도착하도록 하세요.

어휘 potential 잠재적인 dressed well 잘 차려 입은 turn up 나타나다 on time 정시에

2.
해설 분사구문
빈칸부터 customers까지는 완전한 절에 덤으로 붙은 수식구이므로 명사나 동사는 답이 될 수 없고, 분사구문으로 연결될 수 있다. hope는 to부정사를 목적어로 취하므로 능동 분사인 (D)가 정답이다.

번역 라니 그룹은 새 쇼핑센터를 개점할 예정이며, 젊은 고객층의 관심을 끌기를 바란다.

어휘 attract 끌어들이다 customer 고객

3.
해설 부사절 접속사+분사
부사절 접속사 While 뒤에 주어가 없으므로 분사가 와야 하고, 빈칸 뒤에 목적어 the seminar가 있으므로 능동 분사인 (A)가 정답이다.

번역 스위스 벨 호텔에서 열리는 세미나에 참석하는 동안, 무료 와이파이 서비스를 즐기실 수 있습니다.

어휘 while ~하는 동안

4.
해설 부사절 접속사+분사
부사절 접속사 as 뒤에 주어가 없이 빈칸으로 끝났고 '지시된'을 뜻하므로 수동 분사인 (A)가 정답이다.

번역 안전을 위해, 설명서를 꼼꼼히 읽고 지시된 대로 기계를 작동하세요.

어휘 manual 설명서 thoroughly 꼼꼼히 operate 작동하다 instruct 지시하다

5.
해설 분사구문
빈칸부터 history까지는 완전한 절에 덤으로 붙은 수식구이므로 동사는 답이 될 수 없고, 분사구문으로 연결될 수 있다. 빈칸 뒤에 목적어 him이 있으므로 능동 분사인 (C)가 정답이다. 참고로, 5형식 동사 make는 분사일 때도 같은 성질을 유지하므로 목적어(him) 뒤에 목적격 보어(the most-awarded musician)를 취했다.

번역 쇼 씨는 17개의 넷 음악상을 수상하여, 역사상 이 상을 가장 많이 수상한 음악인이 되었다.

어휘 awarded 상을 받은 musician 음악가

6.

해설 **부사절 접속사+분사**
부사절 접속사 When 뒤에 주어가 없으므로 분사가 와야 하고, 빈칸 뒤로 목적어가 없이 '질문을 받은'을 뜻하므로 수동 분사인 (D)가 정답이다.

번역 사임에 관한 소문에 대해 질문을 받았을 때 TG 에너지의 CEO인 렉스 밀러는 답변을 거절했다.

어휘 resignation 사임 rumor 소문 CEO 최고 경영자 decline 거절하다 comment 견해를 밝히다

7.

해설 **분사구문**
빈칸부터 reporter까지는 완전한 절에 덤으로 붙은 수식구이므로 명사나 동사는 답이 될 수 없고, 분사구문으로 연결될 수 있다. prefer는 to부정사를 목적어로 취하므로 능동 분사인 (C)가 정답이다.

번역 콕스 씨는 프리랜서 기자로 일하는 것을 선호하여, 〈모비오 저널〉의 일자리 제안을 거절했다.

어휘 reporter 기자

8.

해설 **분사구문**
빈칸부터 place까지는 완전한 절에 덤으로 붙은 수식구이므로 동사는 답이 될 수 없고, 분사구문으로 연결될 수 있다. 빈칸 뒤에 명사절 that절(that ~ in place)이 목적어 역할을 하므로 능동 분사인 (C)가 정답이다.

번역 모든 실험실 근로자는 장비를 꼼꼼히 점검하고, 안전장치들이 제자리에 있도록 해야 한다.

어휘 laboratory 실험실 inspect 점검하다 equipment 장비 safeguard 안전 장치

YBM TEST   본책 p. 96

1. (B)	2. (A)	3. (A)	4. (A)	5. (C)
6. (B)	7. (C)	8. (C)	9. (A)	10. (A)
11. (D)	12. (B)	13. (B)	14. (B)	15. (C)
16. (D)	17. (C)	18. (D)	19. (D)	20. (B)

1.

해설 **헷갈리는 분사**
빈칸은 명사 information(정보)을 수식하는 분사 자리이고, '상세한 정보'로 해석되므로 (B)가 정답이다.

번역 우리 웹 사이트에서 배송 선택 사항뿐 아니라 도구 및 서비스에 관한 상세한 정보를 확인할 수 있습니다.

어휘 as well as ~뿐 아니라 shipping 운송 option 선택(할 수 있는 것) detailed 상세한 detail 세부사항

2.

해설 **감정 분사**
빈칸은 주어 you를 설명하는 분사 자리로, you(당신)가 관심을 느끼므로 (A)가 정답이다. 참고로 'Should you be~'는 가정법 'If you should be~'에서 If가 생략되고 you와 should가 도치된 구문이다.

번역 만약 성수기 동안 추가 근무에 관심이 있으시면, 인사과의 도나에게 연락하세요.

어휘 shift 교대 근무 시간 busy season 성수기 personnel department 인사과[부] interested in ~에 관심이 있는 interest 관심; 관심을 끌다

3.

해설 **헷갈리는 분사**
빈칸은 명사 customers(고객)를 수식하는 분사 자리이고, '까다로운 고객들'로 해석되므로 (A)가 정답이다.

번역 오늘 세미나에서, 콴 박사는 까다로운 고객들을 효과적으로 다루는 기술에 대해 논할 것이다.

어휘 technique 기술 effectively 효과적으로 deal with ~을 다루다 demanding (다루기) 힘든, 요구가 많은 demand 요구하다

4.

해설 **분사구문**
빈칸부터 access까지는 완전한 절에 덤으로 붙은 수식구이므로 명사나 동사는 답이 될 수 없고, 분사구문으로 연결될 수 있다. 빈칸 뒤에 목적어가 없으므로 수동 분사인 (A)가 정답이다.

번역 오피스파인더는 냉방과 인터넷을 갖춘 사무실 공간을 임대하거나 매입합니다.

어휘 lease 임대하다 access 접근, 접속 equip 장비를 갖춰 주다 equipped with ~ 장비를 갖춘

5.

해설 **부사절 접속사+분사**
부사절 접속사 when 뒤에 주어가 없으므로 분사가 와야 하고, 빈칸 뒤에 목적어 the presentation이 있으므로 능동 분사인 (C)가 정답이다.

번역 발표를 준비할 때는 주제와 관련된 핵심 사안을 정하고 발표의 목적을 분명히 해야 한다.

어휘 determine 결정하다 identify 확인하다 related to ~와 관련된

6.

해설 **명사 뒤 분사**
빈칸은 명사 meat and meat products(육류 및 육류 제품)를 뒤에서 수식하는 분사 자리인데 뒤에 목적어가 없고 '소비되는'으로 해석되므로 수동 분사인 (B)가 정답이다.

번역 국내에서 소비되는 모든 육류 및 육류 제품의 거의 절반이 외국으로부터 수입된다.

어휘 **nearly** 거의 **domestically** 국내에서 **import** 수입하다 **consume** 소비하다

7.

해설 **감정 분사**
빈칸은 주어 We를 설명하는 분사 자리로, We(우리) 입장에서 '기쁨을 느끼는' 것이므로 (C)가 정답이다.

번역 귀하의 결혼식을 위해 귀하의 취향과 예산에 맞춰 메뉴를 만들게 되면 기쁘겠습니다.

어휘 **taste** 기호 **budget** 예산 **wedding ceremony** 결혼식 **delight** 기쁨; 기쁘게 하다 **delighted** 기뻐하는

8.

해설 **분사구문**
빈칸부터 world까지는 완전한 절에 덤으로 붙은 수식구이므로 명사나 동사는 답이 될 수 없고, 분사구문으로 연결될 수 있다. 빈칸 뒤에 목적어 factories가 있으므로 능동 분사인 (C)가 정답이다.

번역 스마트폰 대기업인 베니소프트는 생산 기지를 베트남으로 이전했고, 다른 나라에 있는 공장들을 닫았다.

어휘 **giant** 대기업 **relocate** 이전하다 **base** 기지

9.

해설 **헷갈리는 분사**
빈칸은 명사 applicants(지원자)를 수식하는 분사 자리이고, '자격을 갖춘 지원자들'로 해석되므로 (A)가 정답이다.

번역 훌륭한 자격을 갖춘 많은 지원자들이 단지 지원 관련 지침을 제대로 따르지 않아서 불합격 당한다.

어휘 **highly** 매우 **applicant** 지원자, 지원 **instruction(s)** 지시 **precisely** 정확히 **qualify** 자격을 부여하다 **qualified** 자격을 부여받은, 자격이 있는

10.

해설 **분사구문**
빈칸부터 firm까지는 완전한 절에 덤으로 붙은 수식구이므로 동사는 답이 될 수 없고, 분사나 to부정사로 연결될 수 있다. To win은 '계약을 따기 위해'로 목적을 의미하므로 의미상 적절하지 않다. '계약을 따내서'로 이유를 뜻하는 분사 (A)가 정답이다. '계약을 따낸' 시점은 문장의 시제(was rewarded)보다 앞선 시제이므로 완료형 분사 having p.p.를 쓴다.

번역 송 씨는 일본의 물류 회사에 트럭 500대를 공급하기로 계약을 체결해 상당한 보너스를 포상받았다.

어휘 **contract** 계약 **logistics** 물류 **firm** 회사 **reward** 보상하다 **substantial** 상당한

11.

해설 **감정 분사**
빈칸은 to keep의 목적어 our customers를 보충 설명하는 목적격 보어 자리이다. customers(고객)가 '만족을 느끼는' 것이므로 (D)가 정답이다.

번역 메이시 주얼리는 고객이 계속 만족할 수 있도록 끊임없이 새로운 디자인을 개발한다.

어휘 **jewelry** 보석류 **constantly** 끊임없이

12.

해설 **명사 뒤 분사**
빈칸은 명사 Steve Simon을 뒤에서 수식하는 분사 자리이고, 뒤에 목적어가 없이 '(~에 의해) 동반된'이라는 뜻이므로 수동 분사 (B)가 정답이다.

번역 WE 네트워크의 스티브 사이먼 사장은, 재무 담당 최고 책임자인 맷 펄롱과 함께, 합병을 논의하기 위해 팬 게임의 CEO인 마이클 톰슨과 만났다.

어휘 **chief financial officer** 재무 담당 최고 책임자 **merger** 합병 **accompany** 동행하다, 동반하다

13.

해설 **부사절 접속사+분사**
부사절 접속사 When 뒤에 주어가 없으므로 분사가 와야 하고, 빈칸 뒤로 목적어 a job application이 있으므로 능동 분사인 (B)가 정답이다.

번역 이메일로 입사지원서를 보낼 때는 이메일 메시지에 이력서와 자기소개서를 첨부하는 것을 잊지 마세요.

어휘 **job application** 입사 지원서 **via** ~을 통해 **attach** 첨부하다 **résumé** 이력서 **cover letter** 자기소개서

14.

해설 **헷갈리는 분사**
빈칸은 명사 population(인구)을 수식하는 분사 자리이고, '증가하는 인구'로 해석되므로 (B)가 정답이다.

번역 증가하는 고령 인구로 인해 치솟는 건강 관리 비용에 대한 우려가 있다.

어휘 **concern** 우려 **soaring** 급상승하는 **health care** 보건 **elderly** 연세 드신

15.

해설 **명사 뒤 분사**
빈칸은 명사 information(정보)을 뒤에서 수식하는 분사 자리이다. 뒤에 목적어가 없이 '요구되는'이라는 수동의 뜻이므로 (C)가 정답이다.

번역 급여 지급 부서는 당신이 소득세 신고서를 제출하기 위해 요구되는 모든 소득 정보를 준비하는 것을 도울 것이다.

어휘 **payroll department** 급여 지급 부서 **income** 소득 **file** 제출하다 **tax return** 소득세 신고서

16.
해설 감정 분사
빈칸은 목적어 it을 보충 설명하는 목적격 보어 자리이고, it은 'profits increased(수익이 증가한 점)'를 가리킨다. it이 '만족하게 만드는' 것이므로 만족을 유발하는 원인이므로 (D)가 정답이다.

번역 보험 회사의 직원들은 열심히 일한 결과 수익이 증가했을 때 이를 만족스럽게 생각했다.

어휘 insurance 보험 profit 수익 gratify 기쁘게 하다, 만족시키다

17.
해설 명사 뒤 분사
빈칸은 명사 tourists(관광객)을 뒤에서 수식하는 분사 자리이고, 뒤에 목적어 South Korea가 있으므로 (C)가 정답이다.

번역 한국을 방문하는 중국인 관광객의 수가 양국 간의 정치적 긴장 상태로 인해 급락했다.

어휘 plummet 급락하다 tension 긴장

18.
해설 분사구문
빈칸부터 costs까지는 완전한 절에 덤으로 붙은 수식구이므로 동사나 명사는 답이 될 수 없고, 분사구문으로 연결될 수 있다. 빈칸 뒤에 목적어 rising operating costs가 있으므로 능동 분사인 (D)가 정답이다.

번역 상승하는 운영비에 직면하여, BNDC는 남아메리카에 있는 모든 소매점을 닫기로 결정했다.

어휘 rising 상승하는 operating cost 운영비 retail 소매 face 직면하다

19.
해설 분사구문
빈칸부터 results까지는 완전한 절에 덤으로 붙은 수식구이므로 동사나 명사는 답이 될 수 없고, 분사구문으로 연결될 수 있다. 빈칸 뒤에 목적어가 없으므로 (D)가 정답이다.

번역 회사는 직원을 대상으로 한 설문 조사 결과를 토대로 근무시간 유연제를 도입할지를 결정할 것이다.

어휘 adopt 채택하다 flexible working 근무시간 유연제 based on ~에 근거하여 survey 설문 조사

20.
해설 부사절 접속사 + 분사
부사절 접속사 Once 뒤에 주어가 없으므로 분사가 와야 하고, 빈칸 뒤로 목적어가 없이 '승인된'을 뜻하므로 수동 분사인 (B)가 정답이다.

번역 일단 시의 건설 위원회에 의해 승인을 받고 나면, 91번 고속도로에 대한 확장 공사가 즉각 시작될 것이다.

어휘 once 일단 ~하면 expansion 확장 immediately 즉시

Part 6

시제 문제 2 – 문서 작성일도 단서가 된다.

예제
본책 p. 98

수신: 모니크 클로드⟨claude@bluesky.co.uk⟩
발신: 버나드 애쉬튼⟨ashton@gym.co.uk⟩
제목: 멤버십 갱신
날짜: 4월 5일

모니크 께,

이 편지는 당신의 체육관 멤버십이 3월 31일에 만료되었음을 알려 드리기 위한 고지입니다. 저희에게 당신의 멤버십은 귀중하므로, 멤버십을 갱신하시면 15% 할인을 제공함으로써 감사를 표할 기회로 삼고 싶습니다. 곧 다시 뵙기를 기대합니다.

버나드 애쉬튼

어휘 friendly 친절한 reminder 알림장, 상기시켜 주는 것 gym 체육관, 헬스 클럽 invaluable 귀중한 opportunity 기회 extend 베풀다 appreciation 감사 renewal 갱신 look forward to ~을 기대하다 expier 만료되다

YBM TEST
본책 p. 99

| 1. (C) | 2. (B) | 3. (A) | 4. (D) |

수신: smiller@fyimail.com
발신: bsmith@anachems.co.uk
날짜: 10월 15일
제목: 애너 케미컬 사에서의 첫날

밀러 씨께,

당신이 우리의 고용 제안을 받아들이기로 결정을 내려 우리 부서 모두가 기뻐했다는 점을 말씀드리고 싶습니다. 합의했던 대로, 당신은 11월 21일 월요일에 새 업무를 시작하게 될 것입니다. 오전 9시까지 이곳으로 오시면 됩니다.

우리는 직원에게 탄력 근무 시간제를 제공하고 있으며, 월요일에 오시면 당신의 표준 노동 시간에 대해 논의할 수 있습니다. 또한 당신은 신입 사원 멘토인 로버트 고어를 만나게 될 것입니다. 그는 당신이 회사와 새 부서를 잘 알아갈 수 있도록 도와줄 것입니다.

우리는 당신이 첫 일주일 동안 새로운 직무와 회사에 질 적응하는 것을 목표로 그에 알맞게 일정을 짜고 있습니다. <u>당신은 이번 주에 확정된 일정표를 받게 될 것입니다.</u>

질문이 있으시면, 저에게 편하게 이메일을 보내세요. 우리는 정말 당신과 함께 일하는 것을 기대하고 있습니다.

브랜든 스미스
관리 담당자

어휘 **corporation** 회사, 법인 **flexible working hours** 탄력 근무 시간제 **normal hours** (일·주·월 등의) 표준 노동시간 **get to know** 알게 되다 **aim to**부정사 ~하는 것을 목표로 하다 **orient** 적응시키다 **regarding** ~에 대해 **accordingly** 그에 맞게 **administrative** 관리[행정]의

1.

해설 **동사 어휘**
'우리의 제안을 ___하기로 결정해 기쁘다'고 했다. 뒤 문장에서 '11월 21일에 새 일을 시작할 것이고, 9시까지 출근하라'고 한 것으로 보아 제안을 accept(받아들이다)했음을 알 수 있다. 따라서 정답은 (C)이다.

2.

해설 **동사 시제**
이메일이 작성된 날짜는 10월 15일이고, 빈칸은 11월 21일 일어날 일에 대해 언급하고 있으므로 미래 시제인 (B)가 정답이다.

3.

해설 **접속부사**
빈칸은 앞뒤 문장의 연결 관계를 보여주는 접속부사를 고르는 문제이다. 앞 문장에서 '월요일에 근무 시간에 대해 논의할 것이다'라며 일정을 설명했고, 뒤 문장에서도 '멘토를 만날 것이다'라며 일정을 추가로 이야기하므로 '덧붙여'를 뜻하는 (A)가 정답이다.

어휘 **now that** ~이므로 **if so** 만약 그렇다면 **nevertheless** 그럼에도 불구하고

4.

해설 **문장 고르기**
앞 문장에서 '우리가 일정을 짜고 있다'고 했으므로 '확정된 일정표를 받게 될 것이다'로 연결되는 것이 가장 자연스럽다. 따라서 (D)가 정답이다.

번역 (A) 당신은 또한 고어 씨와 사무실을 공유할 것입니다.
(B) 우리는 실험실 보조원과 회의 일정을 정했습니다.
(C) 당신은 직원 배지를 받을 것입니다.
(D) 당신은 이번 주에 확정된 일정표를 받게 될 것입니다.

Unit 7 형용사 & 부사

공식으로 해결하는 실전문제
본책 p. 103

1. (A) 2. (A) 3. (C) 4. (D) 5. (B)
6. (D) 7. (B) 8. (C)

1.

해설 **명사 수식(관형명)**
빈칸은 명사 menu 앞에서 명사를 수식하는 자리이고, 〈관 ___ 명〉이므로 형용사 (A)가 정답이다.

번역 클래시코 피자리아는 꽤 합리적인 가격과 다양한 메뉴를 제공하기 때문에 항상 현지 식객들로 붐빈다.

어휘 **crowded** 붐비는 **local** 현지의 **diner** 식객 **fairly** 꽤 **reasonable** (가격이) 합리적인 **extensive** 폭넓은

2.

해설 **명사 수식(관부형명)**
빈칸은 명사 insight 앞에서 명사를 수식하는 형용사 자리이므로 형용사 (A)가 정답이다.

번역 PMC의 새 인턴근무 프로그램은 회사의 사업과 기업 문화에 대한 귀중한 통찰력을 제공한다.

어휘 **internship** 인턴근무 **insight** 통찰력

3.

해설 **명사 수식(관형형명)**
빈칸은 명사 skills 앞에서 명사를 수식하는 형용사 자리이므로 형용사 (C)가 정답이다. 「형용사+명사」 앞에는 명사를 수식하는 형용사가 또 올 수 있다.

번역 여러 다른 업무들의 균형을 잡아야 하는 경영주에게는 뛰어난 조직 능력이 중요하다.

어휘 **crucial** 중요한 **balance** 균형을 잡다, 균형 **duty** 직무, 의무 **organizational** 조직의, 조직하는

4.

해설 **~ly 형용사**
빈칸은 be동사 뒤에서 주어(doing so)를 설명하는 보어 자리이므로 형용사 (D)가 정답이다. 'is costed'는 '비용이 산출되다'로 의미상 적절하지 않다.

번역 경영진은 텔레비전 광고가 비용이 너무 많이 들기 때문에 포기하기로 결정했다.

어휘 **management** 경영진 **costly** (많은) 비용이 드는

5.

해설 **형용사 수식(관부형명)**
빈칸은 '관 ___ 형명' 순서로, 형용사 competitive(경쟁적인) 앞에서 형용사를 수식하는 부사 자리이므로 (B)가 정답이다.

번역 점점 더 경쟁적인 사업 환경에서 번창하기 위해서는 유연한 지도력이 필수적이다.

어휘 **flexible** 유연한 **leadership** 지도력 **essential** 필수적인 **thrive** 번창하다 **environment** 환경 **increasingly** 점점 더

6.

해설 **~ly 형용사**
빈칸은 명사 environment 앞에서 명사를 수식하는 형용사 자리이므로 형용사 (D)가 정답이다.

번역 직원들이 편안하고 친숙한 환경에서 일하도록 하는 것이 중요하다.

어휘 **ensure** 보장하다 **comfortable** 편안한 **environment** 환경 **friendly** 친숙한

7.
해설 주격 보어
빈칸은 be동사 뒤에서 주어인 명사 Consumers를 설명하는 형용사 자리이므로 형용사 (B)가 정답이다.

번역 소비자들은 사생활 침해에 대한 우려 때문에 온라인 회사에 개인 정보를 제공하기를 꺼린다.

어휘 privacy 사생활 concern 우려 be reluctant to부정사 ~하기를 꺼리다 reluctantly 마지못해서

8.
해설 ~ly 형용사
빈칸은 be동사 뒤에서 주어(global climate change)를 설명하는 보어 자리이므로 형용사 (C)가 정답이다. 'be likely to부정사(~할 것 같다)'를 암기하면 편하다.

번역 새로운 연구는 지구 기후 변화가 경제 성장에 부정적인 영향을 미칠 수 있다는 것을 보여준다.

어휘 adverse effect 악영향, 역효과

공식으로 해결하는 실전문제 (본책 p. 105)

| 1. (B) | 2. (A) | 3. (C) | 4. (D) | 5. (B) |
| 6. (A) | 7. (C) | 8. (D) | | |

1.
해설 형용사 vs. 분사
빈칸은 be동사 뒤에서 주어(Many ~ injuries)를 설명하는 보어 자리이므로 형용사 (B)가 정답이다. preventing(~을 예방하는)은 뒤에 목적어가 필요하고 prevention(예방)은 주어와 동격이 아니므로 답이 될 수 없다.

번역 많은 업무 현장의 사고 및 부상은 안전 지침과 규정이 주의하여 지켜진다면 예방 가능하다.

어휘 workplace 업무 현장 injury 부상 guideline 지침 regulation 규정 preventable 막을 수 있는

2.
해설 형용사 vs. 분사
빈칸은 명사 donation 앞에서 명사를 수식하는 형용사 자리이고, '상당한 기부'로 해석되므로 형용사 (A)가 정답이다. 참고로, sized는 '크기가 ~한', sizing은 명사로 '크기별로 모음'을 뜻한다.

번역 인버네스 주민 센터는 스코티아 은행으로부터 상당한 기부를 받았다.

어휘 community center 주민 센터 sizeable 상당 크기의 donation 기부

3.
해설 수량형용사
빈칸 뒤에 복수명사인 employees(직원)가 있으므로 (C)가 정답이다. each와 every는 가산 단수명사 앞, much는 불가산명사 앞에 온다.

번역 기술 연수 과정은 신입 사원들을 위한 것이지만, 관심 있는 직원들은 누구라도 참석을 환영합니다.

어휘 session 연수, 교육 intended for ~을 예상으로 하는, ~을 위해 만든

4.
해설 수량형용사
빈칸 뒤에 복수명사인 ~ opportunities(기회)가 있으므로 (D)가 정답이다. each와 every는 가산 단수명사 앞에 오고, a lot은 부사이므로 형용사 자리에 올 수 없다.

번역 벤 사는 자격증과 온라인 강의를 포함한 많은 경력 개발 기회를 제공한다.

어휘 career development 경력 개발 certificate 자격증 a lot 대단히

5.
해설 수량형용사
빈칸 뒤에 가산 단수명사인 entry(참가작)가 있으므로 (B)가 정답이다. all과 most는 복수명사 앞에 오고, whole은 단수명사 앞에 올 때는 반드시 whole 앞에 관사(a/the)가 있어야 한다.

번역 심사위원단이 각각의 대회 참가작을 검토하고 수상자를 선택할 것이다.

어휘 panel 패널, 집단 judge 심사위원 entry 출품작, 참가작 winner 수상자

6.
해설 형용사 vs. 분사
빈칸은 명사 information 앞에서 명사를 수식하는 형용사 자리이고, '추가적인 정보'로 해석되므로 형용사 (A)가 정답이다. 동사 further(발전시키다)에서 파생된 furthering이나 furthered는 적절하지 않다.

번역 대학원 입학에 관한 추가 정보를 원하시면, 신청서를 작성해 제출하세요.

어휘 postgraduate 대학원(생) admission 입학 complete 작성하다 submit 제출하다 request form 신청서 further 추가의, 더 이상의

7.
해설 형용사 vs. 분사
빈칸은 명사 feature 앞에서 명사를 수식하는 형용사 자리이고, '주목할 만한 특징'으로 해석되므로 형용사 (C)가 정답이다.

번역 스포텍의 첫 맨체스터 팀 셔츠의 가장 주목할 만한 특징은 빨간 모자이크 무늬다.

어휘 feature 특징 notable 주목할 만한

8.
해설 수량형용사
빈칸 뒤에 불가산명사인 attention(주의)이 있으므로 (D)가 정답이다. every는 가산 단수명사 앞, many와 few는 복수명사 앞에 온다.

번역 회계팀은 회사의 웹 사이트에 게시되는 정보의 정확성에 주의를 기울인다.

어휘 accounting 회계 pay attention to ~에 주의를 기울이다 accuracy 정확성 post 게시하다 corporate 기업의

공식으로 해결하는 **실전문제** 본책 p. 107

1. (B) 2. (B) 3. (D) 4. (C) 5. (B)
6. (A) 7. (B) 8. (D)

1.
해설 부사 자리
빈칸은 be동사와 p.p. 사이에서 located를 수식하므로 부사인 (B)가 정답이다.

번역 구스토 식당은 처철 광장에서 걸어갈 만한 거리에 편리하게 위치해 있다.

어휘 located 위치한 within walking distance 도보 거리 이내에

2.
해설 부사 자리
빈칸은 자동사 have responded로 끝난 완전한 절에 붙어 동사를 수식하므로 부사인 (B)가 정답이다.

번역 해피 밀 가맹점들은 신메뉴에 호의적으로 반응을 보여 임원진들이 크게 안도했다.

어휘 franchisee 가맹점 respond to ~에 반응하다 option 선택(할 수 있는 것) relief 안도 executive 경영 간부 favorably 호의적으로

3.
해설 부사 자리
빈칸은 조동사 will과 동사원형 사이에서 동사 send를 수식하므로 부사인 (D)가 정답이다.

번역 유폰 스케줄러는 전화기가 꺼져 있더라도 선택된 시간에 자동으로 메시지를 보낸다.

어휘 chosen 선택된 switch off 끄다 automated 자동화된 automatically 자동적으로

4.
해설 부사 자리
빈칸은 to부정사 to function을 수식하는 자리이다. to부정사에서 to 뒤의 동사는 동사일 때의 성질을 그대로 유지하는데, function은 자동사이므로 뒤에 목적어가 필요 없고 부사의 수식을 받는다. 따라서 부사인 (C)가 정답이다.

번역 생산 시설에 있는 모든 기계는 제대로 기능하기 위해 정기적인 유지 관리가 필요하다.

어휘 production facility 생산 시설, 생산 공장 maintenance 유지 관리 in order to ~하기 위해 function 기능하다 properly 제대로

5.
해설 부사 자리
빈칸은 완전한 절(whether절: whether ~ entered)에 덤으로 붙어 동사 has been entered를 수식하므로 부사인 (B)가 정답이다.

6.
해설 부사 자리
빈칸은 be동사와 형용사 사이에서 형용사 operational을 수식하므로 부사인 (A)가 정답이다.

번역 재리엇 호텔 밖 교차로의 새 신호등은 다음 주까지는 완전하게 가동되지 않을 것이다.

어휘 traffic light 신호등 intersection 교차로 outside 밖의 operational 가동의 fully 완전히

7.
해설 부사 자리
빈칸은 has p.p. 사이에서 p.p.인 increased를 수식하므로 부사인 (B)가 정답이다.

번역 새로운 조각 전시회의 개막 이후로 방문객의 수가 눈에 띄게 증가했다.

어휘 opening 개막 sculpture 조각 exhibition 전시회 noticeably 두드러지게

8.
해설 부사 자리
빈칸은 완전한 절(successful ~ contacted) 앞에 덤으로 붙어 있으므로 부사 자리이다. only는 부사이지만 명사(구)를 강조할 수 있다. '오직 합격한 지원자들만'이라는 뜻으로 명사구(successful candidates)를 강조하므로 (D)가 정답이다.

번역 지원자 수가 너무 많은 관계로, 오직 합격한 지원자들만 연락을 받게 될 것이다.

어휘 due to ~ 때문에 volume 용량, 수량 applicant 지원자 candidate 후보자

공식으로 해결하는 **실전문제** 본책 p. 109

1. (B) 2. (D) 3. (C) 4. (A) 5. (A)
6. (C) 7. (B) 8. (C)

1.
해설 ly가 붙어 뜻이 달라지는 부사
빈칸은 have been suspended(중단되었다)를 꾸미는 부사 자리이고, 문맥상 lately(최근에)가 어울린다. 따라서 (B)가 정답이다.

번역 신입 사원 오리엔테이션을 위한 준비로 리더십 교육은 최근에 중단되었다.

어휘 training session 연수, 교육 suspend (일시적으로) 중단하다 in preparation for ~을 준비하여 late 늦게, 늦은

41

2.
해설 ly가 붙어 뜻이 달라지는 부사
빈칸은 조동사 will과 동사 monitor 사이에서 monitor(관찰하다)를 수식하는 부사 자리이고, 문맥상 closely(자세히)가 어울리므로 (D)가 정답이다.

번역 코라텍의 직원은 적재 과정을 자세히 관찰하며 화물이 적절히 취급되도록 한다.

어휘 monitor 관찰하다 loading 적재 process 과정 ensure 보장하다 proper 적절한 handling 처리 cargo 화물 close 가까운, 가까이

3.
해설 접속부사
빈칸은 주어 the sales와 동사 turned 사이에서 문장을 수식하는 부사 자리이다. 문맥상 콤마(,) 앞뒤가 서로 상반되는 내용으로 연결되므로 '그럼에도 불구하고'를 의미하는 (C)가 정답이다.

번역 전기 자전거에 대한 초기의 열광적인 반응에도 불구하고 판매는 저조한 것으로 드러났다.

어휘 despite ~에도 불구하고 initial 초기의 enthusiasm 열광 turn out ~임이 드러나다 poor 형편 없는 moreover 게다가 neither (둘 중) 어느 것도 아닌 except ~을 제외하고

4.
해설 접속부사 vs. 접속사
빈칸은 절(the Bangkok ~ short-staffed)과 절(it ~ employees) 사이에서 두 절을 연결하는 접속사 자리이므로 (A)가 정답이다. Despite(~에도 불구하고)는 전치사, Furthermore(더욱이)는 부사, In addition(게다가)은 부사이므로 절을 연결할 수 없다.

번역 방콕 지사는 현재 직원이 부족한데도 불구하고, 직원들의 헌신 덕분에 순조롭게 운영되고 있다.

어휘 currently 현재 short-staffed 직원이 부족한 run 운영되다 dedication 헌신

5.
해설 ly가 붙어 뜻이 달라지는 부사
빈칸은 완전한 절 뒤에 덤으로 붙어 뒤의 전치사구(because of ~ SUV)를 수식하는 부사 자리이고, 문맥상 largely(주로)가 어울리므로 (A)가 정답이다.

번역 미아 모터스의 판매가 급증한 것은 주로 신모델 Max-3 SUV 차량의 성공적인 출시 덕분이다.

어휘 sale 판매(량) surge 급증하다 launch 출시

6.
해설 접속부사 vs. 접속사
절(Carla ~ time)과 절(is ~ policy)을 등위접속사 and가 연결하고 있으며, and 뒤의 절에서 앞 절과 동일한 주어(Carla)가 생략된 구조이다. 빈칸이 없어도 완전한 문장이므로 전치사나 접속사는 들어갈 수 없고, 부사가 와야 한다. 부사 instead는 의미상 적절하지 않고, 인과관계를 나타내는 부사 (C)가 정답이다.

번역 칼라는 파트 타임으로 근무하므로 가게 방침에 따라 유급 휴가를 받을 수 있는 자격이 되지 않는다.

어휘 ineligible 자격이 되지 않는 paid vacation 유급 휴가 according to ~에 따라 instead 대신에

7.
해설 접속부사 vs. 접속사
빈칸은 절(Mr. Juntana ~ spring)과 절(he ~ representative) 사이에서 두 절을 연결하는 접속사 자리이므로 (B)가 정답이다. After all(결국)과 Furthermore(더욱이)는 부사, Prior to(~에 앞서)는 전치사이므로 절을 연결할 수 없다.

번역 준타나 씨는 지난봄, 우리 회사의 밴쿠버 지사에 합류했을 때 판매 사원으로 근무했다.

어휘 sales representative 판매 사원

8.
해설 ly가 붙어 뜻이 달라지는 부사
빈칸은 관계사절(that ~ users) 내의 be동사와 p.p. 사이에서 recommended(추천되는)를 수식하는 부사 자리이고, 문맥상 highly(매우)가 어울리므로 (C)가 정답이다.

번역 넥선은 모든 사용자들에게 적극 권장되는 소프트웨어 업데이트를 공개했다.

어휘 release 공개하다, 출시하다 high 높은, 높게 height 높이

YBM TEST
본책 p. 110

1. (A)	2. (B)	3. (C)	4. (C)	5. (B)
6. (A)	7. (D)	8. (C)	9. (C)	10. (B)
11. (D)	12. (B)	13. (A)	14. (A)	15. (D)
16. (C)	17. (B)	18. (A)	19. (C)	20. (D)

1.
해설 부사 자리
빈칸은 be동사와 -ing 사이에서 searching을 수식하므로 부사인 (A)가 정답이다.

번역 프리먼 리소시즈에서는 우리의 전문가 인력에 합류할 새로운 전문가들을 끊임없이 찾고 있습니다.

어휘 search for ~을 찾다 specialist 전문가 expert 전문가 pool 이용 가능 인력 continually 끊임없이

2.
해설 명사 수식(관부형명)
빈칸은 복합명사 weather conditions 앞에서 명사를 수식하는 자리이므로 형용사 (B)가 정답이다.

번역 건설 프로젝트를 계획할 때는 공사 일정과 생산성에 영향을 미칠 수 있는 계절적인 기상 조건을 고려해야 한다.

어휘 construction 건설 planning 계획 수립 take into account ~을 고려하다 productivity 생산성 seasonal 계절적인

3.
해설 수량형용사
빈칸 뒤에 가산 단수명사인 member(회원)가 있고 동사도 단수동사(is)로 받았으므로 (C)가 정답이다. all, most, other는 복수명사나 불가산명사 앞에 온다.

번역 모든 피트니스 센터 회원은 등록 후 한 달 동안 무료 개인 강습을 받을 수 있습니다.

어휘 fitness 피트니스 클럽 센터 be eligible for ~에 자격이 되다 registration 등록

4.
해설 형용사 vs. 분사
빈칸은 명사 plan 앞에서 명사를 수식하며, 〈관 ___ 명〉이므로 형용사 자리이다. practicing(활동하고 있는)과 practical (현실적인) 중 문맥상 적절한 (C)가 정답이다.

번역 베트남의 건축 및 건설업계는 국내 수요에 대응하기 위해 현실적인 계획을 개발했다.

어휘 construction 건설 industry 산업 respond to ~에 대응하다 domestic 국내의

5.
해설 접속부사 vs. 접속사
빈칸은 절(the film ~ critics)과 절(it ~ audience) 사이에서 두 절을 연결하는 접속사 자리이므로 (B)가 정답이다. Nonetheless(그럼에도 불구하고), However(하지만), Consequently(따라서)는 부사이므로 절을 연결할 수 없다.

번역 영화 〈파 어웨이〉는 평론가들에 의해 높은 평가를 받았지만, 많은 관객을 끌어들이는 데는 실패했다.

어휘 film 영화 highly 매우 critic 평론가 audience 관객

6.
해설 ~ly 형용사
빈칸은 명사 fashion 앞에서 명사를 수식하며, 〈관 ___ 명〉이므로 형용사 자리이다. 따라서 형용사인 (A)가 정답이다. 'in an orderly fashion[manner](질서 정연하게)'라는 표현을 기억해 두자.

번역 논리 정연하게 의견을 발표하는 능력 덕분에 해킷 씨가 공개 토론회에서 회사 대표로 선택되었다.

어휘 represent 대표하다 panel 패널, 전문 토론자들 present 발표하다 fashion 방식 orderly 질서 정연한

7.
해설 목적격 보어
빈칸은 5형식 동사 make의 목적어 electric cars를 보충 설명해 주는 목적격 보어 자리이므로 형용사인 (D)가 정답이다.

번역 뭄버그 에너지의 조사는 하락하는 배터리 비용이 전기 자동차를 10년 이내에 좀 더 구매 가능하게 만들어 줄 거라는 점을 보여준다.

어휘 indicate 보여주다 falling 하락하는 cost 비용 electric 전기의 decade 10년 affordable (가격이) 감당할 만한

8.
해설 ly가 붙어 뜻이 달라지는 부사
빈칸은 has p.p. 사이에서 changed(바뀌다)를 수식하는 부사 자리이고, 문맥상 hardly(거의 아니다)가 어울리므로 (C)가 정답이다.

번역 아니미 사의 로고는 60여 년 전에 디자인된 이후로 거의 바뀌지 않았다.

어휘 logo 로고 since ~한 이래로 more than ~이상 harden 굳어지다

9.
해설 형용사 수식(관부형명)
빈칸은 〈관 ___ 형명〉 순서로, 형용사 acceptable(받아들일 수 있는) 앞에서 형용사를 수식하는 부사 자리이므로 부사인 (C)가 정답이다.

번역 아르곤 사는 12번 고속도로에 대해 합리적으로 받아들일 수 있는 입찰가를 제시한 유일한 회사였다.

어휘 present 제시하다 bid 입찰가, 가격 제시 reasonably 합리적으로

10.
해설 명사 수식(관부형명)
빈칸은 명사 documents 앞에서 명사를 수식하는 자리이고, 〈관 ___ 명〉이므로 형용사 (B)가 정답이다.

번역 학비 보조금을 신청하려면 모든 관련 서류와 함께 신청서를 학자금 대출과로 우편으로 보내야 한다.

어휘 apply for ~에 지원하다 grant 보조금 mail (우편으로) 보내다 application form 신청서 along with ~와 함께 document 서류 financial aid 학자금 지원 relevant 관련 있는

11.
해설 부사 자리
빈칸은 수동태 be p.p.로 끝난 완전한 절 뒤에 덤으로 붙어 전치사구(to your desired bank account)를 수식하므로 부사인 (D)가 정답이다.

번역 세금 환급액은 한 달 후 곧장 당신이 원하는 은행 계좌로 이체될 것입니다.

어휘 tax refund 세금 환급액 transfer 이체하다 desired 바라는 account 계좌 directly 곧장

12.
해설 수량형용사
빈칸 뒤에 가산 단수명사인 discrepancy(불일치)가 있으므로 (B) any(어떤 ~라도)가 정답이다. many와 several은 복수명사 앞에 오고, others는 대명사이므로 오답이다. 참고로, discrepancy는 불가산명사로 쓰이는 경우도 있으나 '수량의 불일치'처럼 그 대상이 명확하고 구체적일 때는 주로 가산명사로 쓴다.

번역 배송물을 모두 확인한 후, 어떠한 수량 불일치도 있을 경우 공급업체에게 즉시 보고해야 한다.

어휘 delivery 배달, 배달된 물건 fully 완전히 quantity 수량 report 보고하다 immediately 즉시 supplier 공급업체 discrepancy 불일치, 불일치하는 점

13.
해설 부사 자리
빈칸은 수식구(to *Huffington Daily Post*)를 지우면 주어 subscribers와 동사 receive 사이에서 동사를 수식하는 자리이므로 부사인 (A)가 정답이다.

번역 모든 〈허핑턴 데일리 포스트〉지의 구독자들은 COL 미디어 그룹으로부터 정기적으로 최신 정보를 받습니다.

어휘 subscriber 구독자 update 최신 정보[소식] regularly 정기적으로

14.
해설 ly가 붙어 뜻이 달라지는 부사
빈칸은 to부정사 to work를 수식하는 부사 자리이고, 문맥상 closely(밀접하게)가 어울리므로 (A)가 정답이다. 참고로, to부정사에서 to 뒤의 동사는 동사일 때의 성질을 그대로 유지하는데, work는 자동사이므로 뒤에 목적어가 필요 없고 부사의 수식을 받는다.

번역 박 씨는 그의 팀원들에게 함께 긴밀히 협력해 컨퍼런스를 준비하라고 지시했다.

어휘 organize 준비[조직]하다 conference 회의, 학회 closely 밀접하게, 친밀하게 close 가까운, (거리가) 가까이

15.
해설 부사 자리
빈칸은 완전한 절 뒤에 덤으로 붙어 동사 be sent를 수식하므로 부사인 (D)가 정답이다.

번역 주문품이 배송되는 대로, 배송 조회 번호가 귀하의 이메일 주소로 즉시 발송될 것입니다.

어휘 once ~하자마자 order 주문(품) ship 운송하다 tracking number 추적 번호 immediately 즉시

16.
해설 부사 자리
빈칸은 완전한 절 뒤에 덤으로 붙어 동사 read를 수식하므로 부사인 (C)가 정답이다.

번역 책장을 조립하고 설치하기 전에 설명서를 꼼꼼히 읽으세요.

어휘 instruction(s) 설명 attempt 시도하다 assemble 조립하다 install 설치하다 bookshelf 책장 carefully 주의 깊게

17.
해설 ~ly 형용사
빈칸은 명사 manner 앞에서 명사를 수식하며, 〈관 ___ 명〉이므로 형용사 자리이다. 따라서 형용사인 (B)가 정답이다. 'in a timely manner(시기적절하게)'를 암기하면 편하다.

번역 고객 문의에 제때에 대응하지 못하면 어떠한 종류의 사업이라도 부정적인 영향을 받을 것이다.

어휘 failure to부정사 ~하지 못함 respond to ~에 대응하다 inquiry 문의 manner 방식 negative 부정적인 impact 영향 timely 시기적절한

18.
해설 ly가 붙어 뜻이 달라지는 부사
빈칸은 완전한 절(that절: that ~ resume)에 덤으로 붙어 자동사 resume을 수식하는 부사 자리이고, 문맥상 shortly(곧)가 어울리므로 (A)가 정답이다.

번역 국립 철도청의 최고 홍보 책임자인 제레미 발테즈는 보수 공사가 이미 시작했고 서비스가 곧 재개될 거라고 말했다.

어휘 chief 최고의 public relations 홍보 repair work 보수 공사 resume 재개되다 shortly 얼마 안 있어, 곧

19.
해설 접속부사 vs. 접속사
절(Ms. Kaminsky ~ Moscow)과 절(could ~ meeting)을 등위접속사 and가 연결하고 있고, and 뒤의 절에서 앞 절과 동일한 주어(Ms. Kaminsky)가 생략된 구조이다. 빈칸이 없어도 완전한 문장이므로 전치사나 접속사는 들어갈 수 없고, 부사가 와야 한다. 따라서 부사인 (C)가 정답이다.

번역 카민스키 씨는 모스크바로 가는 비행기를 놓쳤고 그로 인해 업무 회의에 제때 참석할 수 없었다.

어휘 miss 놓치다 flight 항공편 make it 해내다, (시간에) 맞추다 on time 기간을 어기지 않고

20.
해설 목적격 보어
빈칸은 to keep의 목적어 patients' medical records를 설명하는 목적격 보어 자리이므로 형용사인 (D)가 정답이다. to부정사에서 to 뒤에 오는 동사는 동사일 때의 성질을 그대로 유지한다는 점을 알아두자.

번역 스탠퍼드 의료 센터는 모든 직원들이 환자들의 의료 기록을 기밀로 유지할 것을 엄격히 요구한다.

어휘 medical 의료의 strictly 엄격히 keep (~한 상태로) 유지하다 confide 비밀을 털어놓다 confidential 기밀의

Part 6

접속부사 문제는 앞뒤 문장의 관계를 따진다.

 예제

본책 p. 112

여름 강좌 휴강

주방 구역의 보수공사로 인해 우리의 인기 있는 쿡 투게더 프로그램의 여름 강좌를 개설하지 못하게 되었음을 발표하게 되어 유감입니다. 하지만, 가을에는 여러분을 다시 뵙기를 기대합니다. 가을 강좌 등록은 7월 초에 시작될 것입니다. 그때 저희와 다시 확인하시거나 우리 이메일 명단에 등록하셔서 가을 등록에 관한 최신정보와 알림을 받아 보세요.

어휘 **break** 중단, 휴식 (기간) **regret to**부정사 ~하게 되어 유감이다 **run** 운영하다 **session** (특정 활동의) 시간, 회기 **renovation** 보수 공사 **look forward to** ~하기를 기대하다 **registration** 등록 **commence** 시작하다 **then** 그때 **sign up for** ~에 등록하다 **update** 최신 정보 **notification** 통지, 알림 **concerning** ~에 관해 **unfortunately** 불행히도 **specifically** 구체적으로

YBM TEST
본책 p. 113

1. (B)　2. (A)　3. (D)　4. (C)

주문 취소 정책

E-Traders.com에서 주문하신 것을 취소하시려면 이메일 주소 cancel@etraders.com이나 전화번호 1-800-1259-4577을 통해 고객 지원 부서로 연락하셔야 합니다. 물품이 아직 배송되지 않은 한 주문 취소를 수용하도록 모든 노력을 기울일 것입니다. 주문을 취소하기 위해 고객 지원 부서로 연락하실 때는, 귀하의 이름 및 연락처뿐 아니라 주문 번호를 알려주실 수 있도록 준비해 주세요. 물품이 이미 배송되었다면 주문은 취소될 수 없음을 유의해 주십시오. 이 경우에는 환불을 위해 반품을 요청하실 수 있습니다. 반품에 따른 배송 비용은 청구될 것입니다.

어휘 **cancellation** 취소 **policy** 정책 **place an order** 주문을 하다 **customer support** 고객 지원 **division** 부서 **via** ~을 통해 **as long as** ~하는 한 **ship** 배송하다 **note** 유의하다 **item** 물품 **refund** 환불

1.

해설 **to부정사**

빈칸은 명사 effort를 뒤에서 수식하는 자리이고, effort는 주로 to부정사의 수식을 받아 '~하기 위한 노력'을 뜻한다. to accommodate는 빈칸 뒤의 명사 the cancellation을 목적어로 연결해 '취소를 수용하기 위한 노력'을 뜻하며 effort를 적절히 수식하므로 (B)가 정답이다. to accommodate를 '수용하기 위해'라는 '목적'의 뜻으로 볼 수도 있다. 이때는 to부정사가 동사(make)를 수식한다고 본다.

2.

해설 **상관접속사**

빈칸은 완전한 절(please ~ number)에 명사구(your name and contact information)를 연결하는 자리이므로 부사는 들어갈 수 없다. 상관접속사 as well as는 빈칸 뒤의 명사구를 연결해 '당신의 이름과 연락처뿐 아니라 주문 번호도'를 뜻하므로 (A)가 정답이다. 참고로, additionally(추가로), as well(또한), also(또한)는 부사이다.

3.

해설 **접속부사**

빈칸은 앞뒤 문장의 연결 관계를 보여주는 접속부사를 고르는 문제이다. 앞 문장에서 '제품이 배송된 경우 취소될 수 없다'는 규정을 이야기하고, 뒤 문장에서 '환불을 위해 반품을 요청할 수 있다'며 앞 문장에서 언급한 상황이 일어날 경우 고객이 할 수 있는 일을 설명하므로 '이 경우'를 뜻하는 (D)가 정답이다.

어휘 **in contrast** 그에 반해서 **furthermore** 게다가 **finally** 마침내

4.

해설 **문장 고르기**

빈칸 앞 문장에서 '환불을 위해 제품을 반품할 수 있다'고 했으므로 반품 및 환불과 관련된 내용이 이어져야 자연스럽다. '반품 배송료가 청구될 것이다'라며 반품 조건을 안내하는 (C)가 정답이다.
(A) 우리의 재고품은 하루 사이에도 크게 변동될 수 있습니다.
(B) 설명서에서 주문을 취소하는 방법을 알려드릴 것입니다.
(C) 반품에 따른 배송 비용은 청구될 것입니다.
(D) 배송 비용만이 유일한 문제는 아닙니다.

Unit 8 전치사

공식으로 해결하는 실전문제
본책 p. 117

1. (B)　2. (A)　3. (C)　4. (D)　5. (D)
6. (C)　7. (A)　8. (B)

1.

해설 **전치사 자리**

빈칸은 완전한 절에 명사구(further notice)를 연결하는 자리이므로 전치사인 (B)가 정답이다.

번역 아무르 강의 제퍼슨 다리는 추후 통지 때까지 보수 공사를 위해 폐쇄될 것이다.

어휘 **repair** 보수 **until further notice** 추후 통지 때까지

2.

해설 **전치사 자리 + 기간 vs. 시점**

주어를 수식하고 있는 관계사절(who ~ hours)를 지우면 빈칸은 완전한 절에 명사구(the peak season)를 연결하는 자리이므로 전치사가 와야 하고, 빈칸 뒤 명사 season은 기간을 나타내므로 기간 전치사인 (A)가 정답이다.

번역 성수기 동안 추가 근무를 하는 모든 직원들은 유급 휴가를 받게 될 것이다.

어휘 **extra** 추가의 **peak season** 성수기 **paid holiday** 유급 휴가

3.

해설 **기간 vs. 시점**

빈칸 뒤에 기간을 나타내는 명사가 있고, 문맥상 '지난 두 달 동안'을 의미하므로 기간 전치사 (C)가 정답이다.

번역 판촉 활동 덕분에 지난 두 달간 우리의 스마트폰 판매가 급증했다.

어휘 **dramatically** 극적으로 **promotion** 홍보, 판촉 (활동)

4.

해설 **전치사 자리**

빈칸은 완전한 절(Overnight ~ allowed)에 명사구(prior authorization)를 연결하는 자리이므로 전치사인 (D)가 정답이다.

번역 야간 주차는 주차 관리실로부터 받은 사전 승인 없이는 허용되지 않습니다.

어휘 overnight 야간의 prior 사전의 authorization 허가

5.
해설 기간 vs. 시점
빈칸 뒤 명사 event(행사)는 기간을 나타내고, 문맥상 '모금 행사 내내'가 자연스러우므로 (D)가 정답이다.

번역 주스와 기타 무알코올 음료가 모금 행사 내내 무료로 이용 가능합니다.

어휘 non-alcoholic 무알코올의 beverage 음료 available 이용 가능한 for free 무료로 fundraising 모금

6.
해설 전치사 자리
빈칸은 완전한 절에 동명사구(interviewing ~ candidates)를 연결하는 자리이므로 전치사가 와야 하고, 의미상 '면접한 후'가 적절하므로 (C)가 정답이다.

번역 상위 4명의 후보자를 면접한 후, 사장은 리차드슨 씨를 지점장으로 고용하기로 결정했다.

어휘 candidate 후보자 president 사장 hire 고용하다 branch 지사, 지점

7.
해설 기간 vs. 시점
빈칸은 절(While ~ trip)에 명사구(two weeks)를 연결하므로 전치사 자리이다. 또한 two weeks(2주)는 기간을 나타내고, 문맥상 '2주 동안'이 자연스러우므로 기간 전치사 (B)가 정답이다.

번역 응우옌 씨가 2주간 출장 가 있는 동안, 김 씨가 그녀의 업무를 대신할 것이다.

어휘 away 자리에 없는 business trip 출장 take over (업무 등을) 인계 받다 responsibility 맡은 일

8.
해설 전치사 자리
빈칸은 완전한 절(Economists ~ change)에 명사구(the jobless figures)를 연결하는 자리이므로 전치사인 (B)가 정답이다.

번역 경제 전문가들은 다음 주에 정부가 발표할 실업자 수치에 큰 변동이 없을 것으로 예상한다.

어휘 economist 경제 전문가 significant 상당한 the jobless 실업자들 figure 수치 release 공개하다

공식으로 해결하는 **실전문제**
본책 p. 119

| 1. (B) | 2. (C) | 3. (C) | 4. (C) | 5. (A) |
| 6. (C) | 7. (D) | 8. (B) | | |

1.
해설 전치사+동명사
Upon은 빈칸 뒤의 동명사구 'submitting~'과 어울려 '제출하자마자'를 의미하므로 (B)가 정답이다. 참고로 during은 뒤에 동명사가 오지 않는다.

번역 주문을 제출하자마자, 당신은 우리로부터 주문 번호를 포함한 주문 확인 이메일을 받게 될 것입니다.

어휘 submit 제출하다 confirmation 확인 upon -ing ~하자마자

2.
해설 동사+목적어+전치사
빈칸 앞에 동사 submit는 전치사 to와 짝을 이뤄 'submit A to B(A를 B에게 제출하다)'를 의미하며 be submitted to는 수동태로 변환된 형태이다. 따라서 정답은 (C)이다.

번역 음식 판매상 면허 신청서는 시 보건 부서에 직접 제출되어야 한다.

어휘 application 신청서 food vendor 음식 판매상 license 면허 submit 제출하다 directly 바로

3.
해설 전치사+명사
between은 빈칸 뒤 명사구 '9 A.M. and 3 P.M.'과 어울려 '9시와 3시 사이에'를 의미한다. 따라서 (C)가 정답이다.

번역 배터리 파크에서 매 시간 출발하는 페리 노선은 겨울에는 아침 9시부터 오후 3시 사이에 이용 가능합니다.

어휘 hourly 매 시간마다의 ferry 연락선, 페리 available 이용 가능한

4.
해설 전치사+명사
빈칸은 완전한 절에 명사구(the country)를 연결하므로 전치사 자리이다. 또한 across는 빈칸 뒤 명사구 'the country'와 어울려 '전국에 걸쳐'를 의미하므로 (C)가 정답이다.

번역 올 여름, 우슬라 바이든은 그녀의 새 책을 홍보하기 위해 전국에 걸쳐 16개 도시를 방문할 것이다.

어휘 promote 홍보하다

5.
해설 동사+목적어+전치사
빈칸 앞의 동사 forward는 전치사 to와 짝을 이뤄 'forward A to B(A를 B에게 전달하다)'를 의미하며 be forwarded to는 수동태로 변환된 형태이다. 따라서 정답은 (A)이다.

번역 새로운 무선 연결 유틸리티가 진단 테스트를 위해 기술 지원 부서에 전달되었다.

어휘 wireless 무선의 connection 연결 utility 유틸리티(컴퓨터의 소프트웨어) forward 전달하다 technical 기술의 support 지원 diagnostic 진단의

6.
해설 전치사+명사
as는 빈칸 뒤의 직함을 나타내는 명사구 'a general manager'와 어울려 '총괄 관리자로서'를 의미한다. 따라서 (C)가 정답이다.

번역 티민즈 씨는 암스테르담에 새로 개설하는 지사에서 총괄 관리자로 일할 것이다.

어휘 general 전반적인 manager 관리자 branch 지점

7.

해설 동사+목적어+전치사
빈칸 앞의 동사 provide는 전치사 with와 짝을 이뤄 'provide A witih B(A에게 B를 제공하다)'를 뜻하며, '회원에게 고품질 상품을 제공한다'로 의미상으로도 적절하므로 (D)가 정답이다.

번역 민스크 식료품 체인점에서는 우리 회원들에게 고품질 상품을 경쟁력 있는 가격에 제공합니다.

어휘 grocery 식료품 chain 체인점 quality 질, 고급의 goods 상품 competitive 경쟁력 있는

8.

해설 동사+목적어+전치사
빈칸 앞 동사 choose는 전치사 from과 짝을 이뤄 'choose A from B(B에서 A를 고르다)'가 되므로 (B)가 정답이다.

번역 2월 1일부로, 귀하는 저희의 온라인 제품 카탈로그에서 어떤 물품이라도 선택할 수 있게 될 것입니다.

어휘 effective+날짜 ~부터

공식으로 해결하는 실전문제   본책 p. 121

1. (A) 2. (A) 3. (C) 4. (C) 5. (B)
6. (C) 7. (C) 8. (A)

1.

해설 구전치사
빈칸은 완전한 절에 명사구(a new WMA study)를 연결하는 자리이므로 전치사가 와야 한다. 문맥상 '연구에 따르면'이 적절하므로 (A)가 정답이다.

번역 새로운 WMA 연구에 따르면, 전 세계적으로 휴대폰 이용자의 수가 곧 50억을 넘을 것이라고 한다.

어휘 study 연구 mobile cellular 무선 휴대폰 subscriber 이용자 surpass 초과하다 billion 10억 shortly 곧 provided that 만약 ~라면

2.

해설 분사형 전치사
빈칸은 완전한 절에 명사구(the number ~ state)를 연결하는 전치사 자리이고, 문맥상 '수에 관한 정보'가 적절하므로 (A)가 정답이다.

번역 아이오와 직업 안내서는 아이오와 주에서 일하고 있는 사람들의 수에 관한 정보를 포함하고 있다.

어휘 occupational 직업의 handbook 안내서 state 주

3.

해설 구전치사
빈칸은 완전한 절에 명사구(all ~ reservations)를 연결하는 전치사 자리이고, 문맥상 '항공 및 호텔 예약과 더불어'가 적절하므로 (C)가 정답이다.

번역 트레블위더스는 항공 및 호텔 예약과 더불어 비자 신청도 처리할 수 있다.

어휘 handle 처리하다 flight 항공권 reservation 예약

4.

해설 분사형 전치사
빈칸은 완전한 절에 명사구(the tight deadline)를 연결하는 자리이고, 문맥상 '빡빡한 마감일을 고려하여'가 적절하므로 전치사 (C)가 정답이다.

번역 빡빡한 마감일을 고려해 제때에 프로젝트를 마무리하는 것을 돕도록 더 많은 직원이 그 팀에 배정될 것이다.

어휘 tight 빡빡한 deadline 마감일 assign 배정하다 complete 완료하다 on time 정시에 given ~을 고려할 때

5.

해설 구전치사
빈칸은 앞에 있는 완전한 절(you ~ experience)에 뒤에 남은 'to every aspect'를 연결하는 자리이다. pertaining은 to와 함께 전치사(pertaining to: ~에 관련된)를 만들어 명사구(every aspect)를 자연스럽게 연결한다. 따라서 (B)가 정답이다.

번역 탑 엔터프라이즈에서 당신은 성공적인 사업 운영의 모든 측면에 관해 매우 실용적인 기술과 경험을 습득할 것이다.

어휘 acquire 습득하다 highly 매우 practical 실용적인 aspect 측면 run 경영하다

6.

해설 분사형 전치사
빈칸은 완전한 절에 명사구(a guided tour)를 연결하는 전치사 자리이고, 문맥상 '가이드가 딸린 투어 후에'가 적절하므로 (C)가 정답이다.

번역 우리 포도주 양조장을 가이드와 함께 둘러보신 후에 우리의 가장 인기 있는 와인을 맛볼 기회를 갖게 될 것입니다.

어휘 guided 안내인이 딸린 tour 여행, 견학 winery 포도주 양조장 following ~ 후에, ~에 뒤이어

7.

해설 구전치사
빈칸은 완전한 절에 명사구(the condition)를 연결하는 전치사 자리이고, 문맥상 '상태에 근거하여'가 적절하므로 (C)가 정답이다.

번역 서니힐즈 스토어즈에서는 현지 농산물의 가격이 상품의 상태에 따라 결정됩니다.

어휘 local 현지의 produce 농산물 determine 결정하다 goods 상품 adjacent to ~에 인접한 in spite of ~에도 불구하고 based on ~에 근거하여 such as ~와 같은

8.

해설 분사형 전치사
빈칸은 완전한 절에 명사 fees를 연결하는 전치사 자리이고, 문맥상 '수수료를 포함하여'가 적절하므로 (A)가 정답이다.

번역 블루리본 항공사의 웹 사이트는 항공편 일정과, 추가 및 중량 초과 수하물에 대한 요금을 포함한 수하물 요금을 열거한다.

어휘 airways 항공사 list 열거한다 flight 항공편 baggage 수하물 fee 수수료, 요금 additional 추가의 overweight 중량 초과의

공식으로 해결하는 실전문제
본책 p. 123

| 1. (A) | 2. (C) | 3. (C) | 4. (D) | 5. (A) |
| 6. (B) | 7. (C) | 8. (B) | | |

1.
해설 방향 vs. 위치
빈칸은 완전한 절에 명사구(the country)를 연결하는 전치사 자리이고, '___ the country'는 명사 outlets의 고정된 위치를 수식하므로 위치 전치사인 (A)가 정답이다.

번역 온라인 거대기업 글로브존은 전국에 걸쳐 100곳 이상의 소매점을 운영한다.

어휘 giant 거인, 대기업 operate 운영하다 more than ~ 이상의 retail outlet 소매점

2.
해설 방향 vs. 위치
'___ Shrewsbury Street'는 명사 restaurant의 고정된 위치를 수식하므로 위치 전치사인 (C)가 정답이다.

번역 애나 퐁홍은 다음 달에 임대 계약이 만료될 때 슈루즈버리 가에 있는 그녀의 식당을 닫기로 결정했다.

어휘 lease 임대차 계약 expire 만료되다

3.
해설 전치사 for
빈칸은 완전한 절에 명사구(first-time home buyers)를 연결하므로 전치사 자리이고, 문맥상 빈칸 뒤 명사 '생애 최초 주택 구입자들'은 앞 명사 loan rates and terms(대출 금리 및 조건)의 대상을 나타내므로 (C)가 정답이다.

번역 누리 은행은 신용 평가가 좋은 생애 최초 주택 구입자들을 위해 매력적인 대출 금리와 조건을 제공한다.

어휘 loan rate 대출 금리 terms 조건 buyer 구매자 credit 신용

4.
해설 전치사 for
문맥상 빈칸 뒤 명사 '큰 행사'는 앞에 있는 명사 The Honor Hall이 완벽하게 쓰일 수 있는 용도를 나타내므로 (D)가 정답이다.

번역 코렉스 컨벤션 센터의 아너홀은 수백 명이 참석하는 대규모 행사에 완벽하다.

어휘 guest 손님

5.
해설 방향 vs. 위치
문맥상 '한강(the Han River)이 흐르는 방향을 따라 조깅한다'는 내용이므로 방향 전치사인 (A)가 정답이다.

번역 달하트 씨는 매일 아침 신선한 공기를 즐기기 위해 서울의 한강을 따라 조깅을 한다.

어휘 go jogging 조깅하러 가다

6.
해설 전치사 for
빈칸은 완전한 절에 명사구(its ~ dishes)를 연결하는 전치사 자리이고, 문맥상 빈칸 뒤 명사 '혁신적이고 맛있는 요리'는 최고로 선정된 데 대한 이유를 나타내므로 (B)가 정답이다.

번역 제이 키친은 매우 혁신적이고 맛있는 요리로 시드니에서 최고의 식당으로 선정되었다.

어휘 vote 선출하다, 투표하다 innovative 혁신적인 dish 요리

7.
해설 전치사 for
문맥상 빈칸 뒤 명사 '도움'은 앞 명사 Requests(요청서)의 목적을 나타내므로 (C)가 정답이다.

번역 해외 출장 예약을 도와달라는 요청서는 출발 날짜 5주 전에 제출되어야 한다.

어휘 request 요청(서) business travel 출장 submit 제출하다 prior to ~ 전에 departure 출발

8.
해설 방향 vs. 위치
문맥상 '주차 구역에 차를 주차한다'는 움직임이 없는 고정된 상태를 의미하므로 위치 전치사인 (B)가 정답이다.

번역 JH 센터의 모든 방문객들은 지정된 방문자 주차 구역에 차량을 주차해야 한다.

어휘 vehicle 차량 designated 지정된 area 지역

YBM TEST
본책 p. 124

1. (A)	2. (C)	3. (A)	4. (B)	5. (B)
6. (C)	7. (D)	8. (B)	9. (B)	10. (D)
11. (D)	12. (B)	13. (A)	14. (B)	15. (A)
16. (D)	17. (D)	18. (A)	19. (A)	20. (C)

1.
해설 전치사 자리
빈칸은 완전한 절에 명사구(the implementation)를 연결하는 자리이므로 전치사가 와야 한다. benefit은 from과 어울려 '~로부터 혜택을 얻다'를 뜻하므로 (A)가 정답이다.

번역 피어슨 씨가 우리의 새로운 인사(HR) 소프트웨어의 실행으로 당신의 직원들이 어떻게 혜택을 얻게 될지를 설명해 줄 것입니다.

어휘 **benefit from** ~로부터 혜택을 얻다 **implementation** 실행 **HR** 인사과(= Human Resources)

2.
해설 **기간 vs. 시점**
빈칸 뒤에 시점을 나타내는 명사가 있고, 문맥상 '~전에 작성하세요'를 의미하므로 (C)가 정답이다.

번역 시에라 음악 축제에서 자원봉사할 기회에 관심 있으시면 6월 9일 전에 우리의 Contact Us 페이지를 작성해 주세요.

어휘 **volunteer** 자원봉사하다 **festival** 축제 **fill out** 기입하다

3.
해설 **전치사 for**
문맥상 빈칸 뒤 명사 '초보자들'은 앞 명사구 'simple recipes(간단한 조리법)'의 대상을 나타내므로 (A)가 정답이다.

번역 수잔 램지의 새 요리책에는 초보자들을 위한 간단한 조리법이 다양하게 있다.

어휘 **a diverse range of** 다양한 범위의 **recipe** 조리법 **beginner** 초보자

4.
해설 **분사형 전치사**
빈칸은 완전한 절에 명사구(part-time employees)를 연결하는 자리이므로 전치사가 필요하다. 따라서 전치사인 (B)가 정답이다.

번역 주 20시간 미만으로 일하는 파트 타임 근로자들을 제외한 베라시티의 모든 직원들은 퇴직금 제도에 대한 자격이 된다.

어휘 **be eligible for** ~에 자격이 되다 **retirement plan** 퇴직금 제도 **per** ~당 **exclusively** 독점적으로, 오로지 **exclusion** 제외

5.
해설 **동사+목적어+전치사**
빈칸 앞의 동사 distribute는 전치사 to와 짝을 이뤄 'distribute A to B(A를 B에게 배포하다)'를 의미하며 be distributed to의 수동태로 전환된 형태이다. 따라서 (B)가 정답이다.

번역 교육이 시작되기 전에 모든 참가자들에게 설문지가 배포될 것이다.

어휘 **questionnaire** 질문 **form** 양식 **distribute** 배포하다 **participant** 참가자 **training session** 교육, 연수

6.
해설 **구전치사**
빈칸은 완전한 절에 명사구(a malfunction)를 연결하는 전치사 자리이므로 구전치사인 (C)가 정답이다.

번역 페샤와르의 거주자들은 지난밤 전력 공급 불량으로 인한 예상치 못한 정전으로 고초를 겪었다.

어휘 **resident** 거주자 **suffer** 고통받다 **unexpected** 예상하지 못한 **power outage** 정전 **malfunction** 고장, 불량 **power supply** 전력 공급

7.
해설 **전치사+명사**
at은 빈칸 뒤 시간을 나타내는 명사구 '8 P.M.'과 어울려 '저녁 8시에'를 의미한다. 따라서 (D)가 정답이다.

번역 밥 스테이턴 사장의 연설 직후 저녁 8시에 대회 수상자가 발표될 것이다.

어휘 **winner** 수상자 **competition** 대회 **announce** 발표하다 **speech** 연설 **president** 사장

8.
해설 **전치사 자리**
빈칸은 완전한 절에 명사구(the company)를 연결하는 자리이므로 전치사인 (B)가 정답이다.

번역 회사 전체에 걸쳐 낡은 사무장비를 에너지 효율적인 새 기종으로 교체할 계획이다.

어휘 **replace** 교체하다 **equipment** 장비 **energy-efficient** 에너지 효율적인 **model** 기종 **additionally** 추가로 **altogether** 전적으로, 모두 함께 **in advance** 미리

9.
해설 **기간 vs. 시점**
빈칸은 완전한 절에 명사구(just a few years)를 연결하므로 전치사가 와야 한다. 또한 빈칸 뒤 명사 years는 기간을 나타내며 문맥상 '몇 년 만에'를 의미하므로 기간 전치사인 (B)가 정답이다.

번역 단 몇 년 만에 스마트폰 게임은 어디에서나 정말 흔히 볼 수 있게 되었다.

어휘 **common** 흔한 **sight** 광경 **everywhere** 어디에나 **in** ~ 안에, ~가 지나서

10.
해설 **방향 vs. 위치**
'___ the ~ tunnel'은 빈칸 앞 passing을 수식해 '터널을 통과해 지나는'이라는 뜻이 된다. 기차가 움직이는 방향을 나타내므로 방향 전치사 (D)가 정답이다.

번역 세계에서 가장 긴 철도 터널을 통과하는 기차가 매일 아침 취리히에서 출발한다.

어휘 **depart** 출발하다 **through** ~을 관통하는

11.
해설 **기간 vs. 시점**
빈칸은 완전한 절에 명사구(the second quarter)를 연결하는 자리이므로 전치사가 와야 한다. 또한 빈칸 뒤에 기간을 나타내는 명사가 있고, 문맥상 '2/4분기 동안'을 의미하므로 기간 전치사인 (D)가 정답이다.

번역 미국에서 가장 큰 주택 수리 소매점 업체인 퀸피셔는 2/4분기 동안 판매가 하락했다고 보고했다.

어휘 **home improvement** 주택 수리[개조] **retailer** 소매업체 **quarter** 분기

12.
해설 방향 vs. 위치
빈칸은 that절 안에서 뒤에 있는 명사구(the southern area)를 연결해 주어인 million businesses를 수식하는 전치사 자리이다. '__ the southern area'가 회사(businesses)의 고정된 위치를 수식하므로 위치 전치사인 (B)가 정답이다.

번역 스퀴웨더의 분석은 남부 지역의 50만여 회사가 허리케인 마비의 영향을 받을 것임을 보여준다.

어휘 analytics 분석(론) impact 영향을 미치다

13.
해설 동사+목적어+전치사
빈칸 앞의 동사 congratulate는 전치사 on과 짝을 이뤄 'congratulate A on B(B에 대해 A를 축하하다)'를 뜻하며, 의미상으로도 뛰어난 성과에 대해 Ms. Larson을 축하하는 것이므로 '~에 관해'를 뜻하는 전치사 (A)가 정답이다.

번역 지난 화요일에 열렸던 연말 회의에서, 사장은 직접 라슨 씨의 뛰어난 성과를 치하했다.

어휘 year-end 연말의 hold 열다 personally 직접, 개인적으로 remarkable 뛰어난 achievement 업적, 성과 overall 전반적으로

14.
해설 구전치사
빈칸은 완전한 절에 동명사구(limiting ~ grants)를 연결하는 전치사 자리로 문맥상 '장학금을 제한하는 대신'이 적절하므로 (B)가 정답이다.

번역 재단 이사회는 장학금을 제한하는 대신 개인 기부자들로부터 금융 지원을 받기로 결정했다.

어휘 limit 제한하다 scholarship grant 장학금 foundation 재단 board 이사회 seek 구하다 financial 금융의 donor 기부자

15.
해설 구전치사
빈칸은 완전한 절에 명사구(Bill's substantial contribution)를 연결하는 전치사 자리이고, 문맥상 'Bill의 상당한 기여를 고려해 볼 때'가 적절하므로 (A)가 정답이다.

번역 빌이 판매 신장에 상당히 기여한 점을 고려해 볼 때, 그가 지역 관리자로 빠르게 승진한 것은 놀랍지가 않다.

어휘 substantial 상당한 contribution 기여 rapid 빠른 promotion 승진 considering ~을 고려하면

16.
해설 전치사+명사
among은 빈칸 뒤 복수명사로 된 구 'the leading advertising agencies'와 어울려 '선두 광고 기획사들 사이에'를 의미한다. 따라서 (D)가 정답이다.

번역 샤프 크랙 스튜디오는 독일에서 선두 광고 기획사들 사이에 들어간다.

어휘 leading 선두의 agency 대행사

17.
해설 구전치사
빈칸은 Since절(Since ~ schedule) 내에서 완전한 절(the renovation ~ completed)에 명사 schedule을 연결하는 전치사 자리이고, 문맥상 '일정보다 앞서'가 어울리므로 (D)가 정답이다. 'ahead of schedule(일정보다 앞서)'는 관용표현으로 암기해 둔다.

번역 보수공사가 일정보다 앞서 완료되었기 때문에, 다음 주에 가게를 다시 열 수 있다.

어휘 since 때문에 renovation 보수공사 complete 완료하다 ahead of ~에 앞서 reopen 다시 열다

18.
해설 전치사 for
문맥상 빈칸 뒤 명사 '노고와 헌신'은 앞 명사 'appreciation(감사)'의 이유를 나타내므로 (A)가 정답이다.

번역 사장은 프로젝트 팀원들의 노고와 헌신에 깊은 감사를 표했다.

어휘 appreciation 감사 hard work 노고 dedication 헌신

19.
해설 전치사+동명사
before는 빈칸 뒤 동명사구 'clicking~'과 어울려 '클릭하기 전에'를 의미한다. 따라서 (A)가 정답이다.

번역 이메일이 민감하거나 기밀 정보를 포함할 경우, 발신 버튼을 누르기 전에 주소를 반드시 확인하세요.

어휘 contain 포함하다 sensitive 민감한 confidential 기밀의 make sure to부정사 반드시 ~하다

20.
해설 동사+목적어+전치사
빈칸 앞의 동사 discourage는 전치사 from과 짝을 이뤄 'discourage A from B(A가 B하는 것을 말리다)'를 뜻한다. '직원들이 초과 근무나 집에 일감을 가져가는 것을 말리다'라는 의미이므로 (C)가 정답이다.

번역 버클리 리서치의 연구는 직원들이 초과 근무를 하거나 집으로 일감을 가져가는 것을 자제시킬 때 회사가 이득을 본다는 것을 보여준다.

어휘 indicate 보여주다 benefit 이득을 얻다 work extra hours 시간 외 근무를 하다 discourage A(목적어) from -ing A가 ~하지 못하게 하다

Part 6

대명사 문제는 빈칸의 앞 문장에서 명사를 찾는다.

예제
본책 p. 126

출장 비용 환급 요청서에 관한 지침

본인의 출장일에 부합하는 출장 비용 환급 요청서를 회사 인트라넷 사이트에서 다운로드해야 합니다. 서류는 엑셀 파일이므로 직접 계산을 할 필요는 없습니다. 또한 "읽기 전용" 파일이므로, 서류를 작성하기 전에 본인의 컴퓨터에 저장해야 합니다. 만약 컴퓨터에 서류를 저장하는 데 문제가 있으시면 내선번호 4175번으로 기술 지원 팀에 연락하세요.

어휘 instruction(s) 지시 regarding ~에 관해 travel expense 출장 비용 reimbursement 환급 form 서류 양식 download 다운로드하다 correspond with ~와 부합하다, ~에 해당하다 intranet 내부 전산망 thus 그러므로 calculation 계산 save 저장하다 fill out 작성하다 technical 기술의 support 지원 extension 내선 번호

YBM TEST
본책 p. 127

| 1. (B) | 2. (A) | 3. (D) | 4. (C) |

캘리포니아, 샌 라파엘에서 최고의 개인 창고 시설이 필요하시다면, Easy Self Storage만 보시면 됩니다. 우리의 최신식 시설은 보안과 편리함을 결합해 당신에게 편안한 보관 장소를 제공합니다. 우리는 또한 귀하의 쉽고 빠른 입주를 위해 현장에서 포장 자재도 판매합니다.

Easy Self Storage는 고객들이 우리의 창고 서비스에 만족할 수 있도록 하는 데 전념합니다. 모든 창고 시설은 전문 직원들이 관리하는 냉난방 및 통풍 시스템을 갖추고 있습니다. 우리는 창고 대여에서부터 짐을 옮기는 것까지 모든 것을 도와드립니다. 창고 시설을 고르는 데 도움이 필요하세요? 언제든지 편하게 연락하시면 합리적인 선택을 하실 수 있도록 갖고 계신 물건을 평가해 드리겠습니다.

어휘 self-storage facility 개인 창고 시설 further 더 멀리 state-of-the-art 최신식의 combine 결합하다 security 보안 convenience 편리함 provide 제공하다 comfortable 편안한 space 공간 storage 보관 keep 유지하다 customer 고객 satisfied 만족한 unit (상품) 단위 be equipped with ~을 갖추고 있다 air-conditioning 냉난방 ventilation 통풍 manage 관리하다 expert 전문가 rental 대여 assistance 도움 select 선택하다 be delighted to부정사 ~하게 되어 기쁘다 assess 평가하다 belongings 소유물, 소지품 informed choice (정보와 지식에 근거한) 합리적인 선택

1.

해설 대명사
빈칸은 대명사를 고르는 문제이다. 지문이 광고문이고 앞에 따로 언급된 명사가 없으므로 광고를 낸 측은 'I/we', 광고의 대상은 'you'로 지칭하면 된다. 문맥상 '우리 시설이 ___에게 편안한 보관 장소를 제공한다'고 했으므로 빈칸은 광고의 대상인 (B)가 정답이다.

2.

해설 문장 고르기
(A)에 연결 관계를 보여주는 부사인 also가 있으므로 빈칸 앞 문장과 적절하게 연결되었는지 확인해 본다. 'also(또한)'는 추가를 나타내므로 앞 문장과 비슷한 내용이 나와야 한다. 앞 문장에서 보안과 편리함 같은 창고 시설의 장점을 이야기하고 있고 (A)에서 포장재를 판매해 입주가 쉽고 빠르다는 장점을 추가로 이야기하므로 자연스럽게 연결된다. 따라서 (A)가 정답이다.

번역 (A) 우리는 또한 귀하의 쉽고 빠른 입주를 위해 현장에서 포장 자재도 판매합니다.
(B) 귀하의 물품이 필요하실 때는 언제든지 온라인 목록을 사용해 물품을 회수하세요.
(C) 보관 장소에서 해충 및 설치류를 예방하기 위해 해충 방제 서비스 업체를 고용하셔야 합니다.
(D) 업무 특성상 귀하의 개인 정보를 요청할 수도 있습니다.

3.

해설 능동 vs. 수동
빈칸은 be동사 뒤 보어 자리이므로 동사는 올 수 없고, 명사나 분사가 가능하다. 명사 commitments(전념)는 주어 we와 동격이 아니므로 답이 될 수 없고, 빈칸 뒤에 목적어가 없어서 수동태가 되어야 하므로 과거분사인 (D)가 정답이다. 'be committed to -ing(~에 전념하다)'라는 관용표현으로 암기하면 더 편하다.

4.

해설 형용사 어휘
빈칸은 choice(선택)를 꾸미는 형용사를 고르는 문제이고, '창고 시설을 선택할 때 도움이 되도록 소지품을 평가해 준다'는 말은 선택 시 도움이 되는 정보를 제공해 준다는 뜻이므로 '(정보 등을) 잘 알고 있는'을 뜻하는 (C) informed가 정답이다.

어휘 exclusive 독점적인, 전용의 evident 분명한 additional 추가의

Unit 9 접속사

공식으로 해결하는 실전문제
본책 p. 131

| 1. (A) | 2. (B) | 3. (C) | 4. (C) | 5. (D) |
| 6. (A) | 7. (D) | 8. (B) | | |

1.

해설 부사절 접속사
빈칸 앞뒤로 절이 두 개가 있으므로 접속사가 와야 한다. 따라서 부사절 접속사 (A)가 정답이다.

번역 에펠 씨는 고객 서비스 상담원으로 일했기 때문에 까다로운 고객들을 다루는 방법을 안다.

어휘 deal with ~을 다루다 demanding 까다로운 representative 직원, 대리인

2.
해설 부사절 접속사
빈칸 뒤에 절이 두 개가 있으므로 절과 절을 연결하는 접속사가 하나 필요하다. 따라서 부사절 접속사인 (B)가 정답이다. 참고로, 등위접속사는 문장 맨 앞에 오지 않으므로 So는 답이 될 수 없다.

번역 애니잡 클럽에 등록하면 전국에서 가장 큰 일자리 데이터베이스를 이용할 수 있다.

어휘 register for ~에 등록하다 access 접근, 이용(권) database 데이터베이스

3.
해설 부사절 접속사
빈칸은 완전한 절(the traffic ~ area)에 완전한 절(the city ~ charge)을 추가로 연결하는 자리이므로 부사절 접속사인 (C)가 정답이다. 참고로, 등위접속사는 문장 맨 앞에 오지 않으므로 But은 답이 될 수 없다.

번역 시가 교통 혼잡 부담금을 도입한 이후로, 중심부의 교통량이 감소했다.

어휘 congestion 혼잡 charge 요금 volume 양

4.
해설 부사절 접속사
문장 안에 절이 총 세 개가 있으므로 접속사가 두 개 필요하다. 따라서 부사절 접속사인 (C)가 정답이다. 참고로, 첫 번째 접속사는 가주어-진주어의 명사절 접속사 that이고, 두 번째인 빈칸은 뒤의 절(you finalize ~)을 바로 앞에 있는 절(you have ~)에 연결하는 자리이다.

번역 구매를 확정하기 전에 부동산을 점검받도록 하는 것이 중요하다.

어휘 property 부동산 inspect 점검하다 finalize 마무리 짓다

5.
해설 부사절 접속사
빈칸 뒤로 절이 2개가 있으므로 절과 절을 연결하는 접속사가 하나 필요하다. 따라서 부사절 접속사인 (D)가 정답이다.

번역 마라톤으로 도로가 폐쇄되는 동안 많은 도시내 버스들이 대안 도로로 운행될 것이다.

어휘 marathon 마라톤 alternative 대안의 route 길

6.
해설 부사절 접속사
빈칸 뒤로 절이 두 개가 있으므로 절과 절을 연결하는 접속사가 하나 필요하다. 따라서 부사절 접속사인 (A)가 정답이다. 참고로, Yet은 부사(아직) 외에 등위접속사도 되지만, 등위접속사는 문장 맨 앞에 오지 않으므로 Yet은 답이 될 수 없다.

번역 입장권이 남을 경우, 우리는 행사 당일에 입구에서 입장권을 팔 수도 있다.

어휘 at the door 입구에서 nor ~ 또한 아니다

7.
해설 부사절 접속사
빈칸 뒤로 절이 두 개가 있으므로 절과 절을 연결하는 접속사가 하나 필요하다. 따라서 부사절 접속사인 (D)가 정답이다.

번역 우리 헤어 케어 제품의 초기 판매가 좋았음에도 불구하고 지난 6개월간 판매가 점차 하락했다.

어휘 initial 초기의 gradually 점차 decline 줄어들다

8.
해설 부사절 접속사
문장 안에 절이 총 세 개가 있으므로 접속사가 두 개 필요하다. 첫 번째 절(Please note)과 두 번째 절(players ~ servers)은 접속사 that이 연결하고 있고, 세 번째 절(maintenance~)을 연결하는 접속사가 하나 더 필요하다. 따라서 부사절 접속사인 (B)가 정답이다.

번역 보수 작업이 완료될 때까지 플레이어들은 WinnerZ 서버에 연결할 수 없음을 유의해 주세요.

어휘 connect 연결하다, 접속하다 server 서버 maintenance 유지, 보수 complete 완료된

◆ 공식으로 해결하는 **실전문제**   본책 p. 133

1. (B)   2. (B)   3. (A)   4. (D)   5. (A)
6. (C)   7. (C)   8. (D)

1.
해설 부사절 접속사
빈칸 뒤로 절이 두 개 있으므로 절과 절을 연결하는 접속사가 하나 필요하다. 따라서 부사절 접속사인 (B)가 정답이다.

번역 팀이 네 명의 직원만으로 구성되어 있다는 점을 감안하면 계약을 달성한 데 있어 그들의 성과는 놀랍다.

어휘 consist of ~로 구성되다 achievement 성취 secure 확보하다 contract 계약 considering ~을 고려하면

2.
해설 부사절 접속사
보기가 모두 부사절 접속사이므로 자리 파악할 필요 없이 바로 해석을 통해 답을 고른다. 문맥상 '표를 구매할 때, 쉽게 가입할 수 있다'가 적절하므로 (B)가 정답이다.

번역 매표소나 온라인으로 입장권을 구매할 때 유레일 멤버십에 쉽게 가입할 수 있다.

어휘 sign up for ~에 가입하다 ticketing booth 매표소

3.
해설 부사절 접속사
보기가 모두 부사절 접속사이므로 자리 파악할 필요 없이 바로 해석을 통해 답을 고른다. 문맥상 '만약 시장 진출을 고려한다면'이 적절하므로 (A)가 정답이다.

번역 해외 시장으로 진출을 고려한다면 우리는 해외 출장 예산을 늘려야 한다.

어휘 budget 예산 look to ~을 고려해 보다 expand 확장하다 overseas 해외의 assuming 만약 ~하면, ~라고 가정한다면

4.
해설 부사절 접속사
빈칸 뒤로 절이 두 개 있으므로 절과 절을 연결하는 접속사가 하나 필요하다. 따라서 부사 Therefore(그러므로)는 답이 될 수 없고, 등위접속사 So는 문장 앞에 오지 않으므로 답이 될 수 없다. 부사절 접속사 (B)와 (D) 중 문맥상 '시간이 한정되어 있기 때문에'가 적절하므로 (D)가 정답이다.

번역 발표에 배정된 시간이 한정되어 있기 때문에 발표 시간이 15분을 넘기지 않도록 해야 한다.

어휘 allocate 할당하다 limited 한정된

5.
해설 부사절 접속사
빈칸 뒤로 절이 두 개 있으므로 절과 절을 연결하는 접속사가 하나 필요하다. 접속사 (A)와 (C) 중에서 문맥상 'Jeremy가 사임하자마자'가 적절하므로 (A)가 정답이다.

번역 제레미 코빈이 5월에 IBC 의장직에서 사임하자마자 샤우브 씨가 그의 자리를 대신할 것이다.

어휘 resign 사임하다 post 직책 chairman 의장 take one's place ~ 자리를 대체하다

6.
해설 부사절 접속사
빈칸은 앞에 있는 절(Ms. Potter ~ director)에 뒤의 절(she ~ expert)을 연결하는 접속사 자리이므로 부사 additionally(추가적으로)는 답이 될 수 없다. 남은 보기 중 문맥상 '디자인 전문가였다는 점을 고려해 볼 때'가 적절하므로 (C)가 정답이다. 참고로 맨 앞 주어 It은 가주어이고, 진주어 that절(that Ms. Potter ~)의 that은 생략된 상태다.

번역 포터 씨는 디자인 전문가였다는 점을 고려해 볼 때 마케팅 이사로 임명되었다는 것이 놀라웠다.

어휘 appoint 임명하다 expert 전문가

7.
해설 부사절 접속사
빈칸 뒤로 절이 두 개 있으므로 절과 절을 연결하는 접속사가 하나 필요하다. 따라서 부사절 접속사인 (C)가 정답이다.

번역 프로젝트가 일정대로 진행되면 우리는 올해 상당한 보너스를 기대할 수 있다.

어휘 according to ~에 따라 substantial 상당한 provided that 만약 ~라면

8.
해설 부사절 접속사
빈칸 뒤로 절이 두 개이므로 절과 절을 연결하는 접속사가 하나 필요하다. 따라서 전치사구 As a result(결과적으로)는 답이 될 수 없고 남은 부사절 접속사 보기 중 문맥상 '허리케인이 미칠 영향을 고려한 후, 결정을 내렸다'가 적절하므로 (D)가 정답이다.

번역 조직 위원회가 허리케인 젬마의 잠재적 영향을 고려한 후, 리더십 세미나를 취소하기로 결정했다.

어휘 organizing 조직 committee 위원회 take into consideration ~을 고려하다 potential 잠재적인 impact 영향

공식으로 해결하는 **실전문제**   본책 p. 135

1. (A) **2.** (B) **3.** (D) **4.** (A) **5.** (C)
6. (B) **7.** (D) **8.** (C)

1.
해설 명사절 접속사
동사가 두 개(asked, was)이고 빈칸이 동사의 목적어 자리, 즉 명사 자리에 있는 것으로 보아 명사 자리에 절이 들어갔다는 단서이므로 빈칸은 명사절 접속사 자리이다. 빈칸 뒤에 완전한 절이 왔으므로 which는 답이 될 수 없고 (A)가 정답이다.

번역 고용 결정을 내리기 전에 인사 부장은 존스 씨가 여전히 그 일자리에 관심이 있는지 물었다.

어휘 personnel 인사과, 직원 position 일자리 hiring 고용

2.
해설 명사절 접속사
동사가 두 개(has decided, will release)이고 빈칸이 동사의 목적어 자리, 즉 명사 자리에 있는 것으로 보아 명사 자리에 절이 들어갔다는 단서이므로 빈칸은 명사절 접속사 자리이다. 빈칸 뒤로 완전한 절이 왔으므로 what은 답이 될 수 없고 (B)가 정답이다.

번역 게이머들이 준 피드백의 결과로서, 경영진은 올해 새 게임을 출시하지 않을 것을 결정했다.

어휘 feedback 피드백 management 경영진 release 출시하다

3.
해설 명사절 접속사
동사가 두 개(will give, has been decided)이고 빈칸이 주어 자리, 즉 명사 자리에 있는 것으로 보아 명사 자리에 절이 들어갔다는 단서이므로 빈칸은 명사절 접속사 자리이다. 따라서 명사절 접속사 (D)가 정답이다.

번역 누가 암스테르담 도시 포럼에서 기조 연설을 할지는 아직 결정되지 않았다.

어휘 keynote speech 기조 연설 urban 도시의 forum 포럼

4.
해설 명사절 접속사
동사가 두 개(can tell, are)이고 빈칸이 동사의 목적어 자리, 즉 명사 자리에 있는 것으로 보아 명사 자리에 절이 들어갔다는 단서이므로 빈칸은 명사절 접속사 자리이다. 따라서 명사절 접속사 (A)가 정답이다.

번역 면허를 소지한 우리 대리인들이 정확히 어떤 보험이 당신의 개인적인 의료 요구에 가장 적합한지 알려줄 수 있습니다.

어휘 licensed 면허를 가진 insurance 보험 suitable 적합한

5.
해설 명사절 접속사
동사(will decide)의 목적어 자리, 즉 명사 자리에 빈칸이 있고 뒤에 to부정사가 있으므로 빈칸은 명사 자리에 들어가 to부정사구를 연결할 수 있는 명사절 접속사 자리이다. 따라서 (C)가 정답이다. 「명사절 접속사+주어+동사」에서 주어를 생략해 「명사절 접속사+to부정사」로 축약할 수 있다.

번역 정부는 내수 경기 진작을 위해 최저 임금을 인상할지를 결정할 것이다.

어휘 government 정부 raise 올리다 minimum wage 최저 임금 boost 북돋우다 domestic 국내의 whether to부정사 ~인지 아닌지

6.
해설 명사절 접속사
동사가 두 개(describes, are)이고 빈칸이 동사의 목적어 자리, 즉 명사 자리에 있는 것으로 보아 명사 자리에 절이 들어갔다는 단서이므로 빈칸은 명사절 접속사 자리이다. 빈칸 뒤에, be동사(are) 뒤로 보어가 빠진 불완전한 절이 왔으므로 how나 if는 답이 될 수 없고 (B)가 정답이다.

번역 이 웹 페이지는 시의 실업 수당을 받기 위한 자격에 대한 기본 요건이 무엇인지를 설명한다.

어휘 describe 서술하다 requirement 요건 eligibility 자격 unemployment allowance 실업 수당

7.
해설 명사절 접속사
동사가 두 개(will proceed, is)이고 빈칸이 전치사의 목적어 자리, 즉 명사 자리에 있는 것으로 보아 명사 자리에 절이 들어갔다는 단서이므로 빈칸은 명사절 접속사 자리이다. 빈칸 뒤로 완전한 절이 왔으므로 what은 답이 될 수 없고 (D)가 정답이다.

번역 주립 공원의 보수 작업은 예산 합의가 이루어지는지에 상관없이 진행될 것이다.

어휘 maintenance 유지, 보수 proceed 진행되다 regardless of ~에 상관없이 budget 예산

8.
해설 명사절 접속사
동사가 두 개(explained, can benefit)이고 빈칸이 동사의 목적어 자리, 즉 명사 자리에 있는 것으로 보아 명사 자리에 절이 들어갔다는 단서이므로 빈칸은 명사절 접속사 자리이다. 따라서 명사절 접속사 (C)가 정답이다.

번역 일자리 기회 세미나 동안, 모랄레스 박사는 대회 참가가 경력에 어떤 식으로 도움이 되는지를 설명했다.

어휘 opportunity 기회 participate in ~에 참가하다

✦ 공식으로 해결하는 **실전문제** 본책 p. 137

| 1. (B) | 2. (A) | 3. (C) | 4. (B) | 5. (D) |
| 6. (C) | 7. (D) | 8. (A) |

1.
해설 부사절 접속사
빈칸 앞뒤로 절이 2개가 있으므로 접속사가 와야 한다. 따라서 부사절 접속사 (B)가 정답이다.

번역 관리자가 필요하다고 여길 때는 언제든지 물류창고 직원은 재고 조사를 할 수 있어야 한다.

어휘 warehouse 물류창고 take inventory 재고 조사를 하다 deem 여기다

2.
해설 관계대명사
빈칸 앞에 사람 대명사 someone이 있고 빈칸 뒤에 주어가 빠진 절이 와서 someone을 수식하므로 사람 주격 관계대명사가 와야 한다. 따라서 (A)가 정답이다.

번역 우리 WidU24 상점은 저녁과 주말에 일할 수 있는 사람을 구하고 있다.

어휘 look for ~을 구하다

3.
해설 관계대명사
빈칸 앞에 사물 명사 plan이 있고 빈칸 뒤에 주어가 빠진 절이 와서 plan을 수식하므로 사물 주격 관계대명사가 와야 한다. 따라서 (C)가 정답이다.

번역 우리는 프로젝트 팀의 출장 비용을 포함한 예산안을 만들어야 한다.

어휘 budget 예산 include 포함하다 expense 비용

4.
해설 명사절 접속사
동사가 두 개(will offer, downloads)이고 빈칸이 전치사의 목적어 자리, 즉 명사 자리에 있는 것으로 보아 명사 자리에 절이 들어갔다는 단서이므로 빈칸은 명사절 접속사 자리이다. 따라서 명사절 접속사 (B)가 정답이다.

번역 미라트 호텔은 예약 앱을 처음으로 다운로드하는 사람은 누구든 크리스마스 특별 패키지를 무료로 제공할 것이다.

어휘 reservation 예약 app 앱

5.
해설 관계대명사
빈칸 앞에 사물 명사 things가 있고 빈칸 뒤에 주어가 빠진 절이 와서 things를 수식하므로 사물 주격 관계대명사가 와야 한다. 따라서 (D)가 정답이다.

번역 내구성과 신뢰성은 우리 노트북 컴퓨터를 경쟁사 제품과 구별 짓는 두 가지이다.

어휘 durability 내구성 reliability 신뢰성 distinguish 구별하다 competitor 경쟁자

6.
해설 부사절 접속사
빈칸 뒤로 절이 두 개가 있으므로 접속사가 와야 한다. 등위접속사 But은 문장 맨 앞에 오지 않으므로 답이 될 수 없고 부사절 접속사 (C)가 정답이다. 특히 접속사 자리에 빈칸이 있고 빈칸 바로 뒤에 형용사나 부사가 올 경우 however가 답이 되어 '아무리 (형/부)할지라도'를 뜻한다.

번역 아무리 주의 깊게 비용이 계산될지라도, 실제 프로젝트 비용은 견적액과 차이가 날 수 있다.

어휘 calculate 계산하다 actual 실제의 differ 다르다 estimate 견적, 견적액

7.
해설 관계대명사
빈칸 앞에 사물 명사 festival이 있고 빈칸 뒤에 주어가 빠진 절이 와서 festival을 수식하므로 사물 주격 관계대명사가 와야 한다. 따라서 (D)가 정답이다.

번역 관광청은 국내와 해외 관광객 모두의 관심을 끄는 연례 등 축제를 개최해 왔다.

어휘 bureau 부서, 국 lantern 손전등 domestic 국내의

8.
해설 부사절 접속사
빈칸 앞뒤로 절이 두 개가 있으므로 접속사가 와야 한다. 따라서 부사절 접속사 (A)가 정답이다.

번역 산호세와 주변 지역에서 임차할 주택을 구해야 할 때는 언제든 우리가 도움을 제공할 수 있습니다.

어휘 assistance 도움 rent 임차하다, 임대하다 surrounding 주위의 in consequence 결과적으로 compared to ~와 비교해

✦ 공식으로 해결하는 실전문제   본책 p. 139

| 1. (B) | 2. (A) | 3. (D) | 4. (D) | 5. (A) |
| 6. (D) | 7. (C) | 8. (C) |

1.
해설 관계대명사
명사 bag 뒤에 빈칸이 있고, 빈칸 뒤에 명사(total dimensions)로 시작하면서 주어(나 목적어)가 빠지지 않은 절(total ~ 158cm)이 와서 bag을 수식하므로 소유격 관계대명사인 (B)가 정답이다.

번역 총 치수가 158cm를 초과하는 가방은 모두 특대형으로 취급될 것이다.

어휘 dimension 크기, 치수 exceed 초과하다 treat 취급하다 oversized 특대의, 크기가 초과하는

2.
해설 관계대명사
「사람 명사(150,000명), 부정대명사(many)+of」 뒤로 빈칸이 있고, 빈칸 뒤로 사람 명사(150,000명) 중 일부에 대해 서술하는 절이 왔으므로 관계대명사 (A)가 정답이다.

번역 영국 시민권 신청자 수는 15만 명 이상이며 그 중 다수가 중국인이다.

어휘 applicant 지원자 citizenship 시민권

3.
해설 관계대명사
명사 student 뒤에 빈칸이 있고, 빈칸 뒤에 명사(request)로 시작하면서 주어(나 목적어)가 빠지지 않은 절(request ~ refused)이 와서 student를 수식하므로 소유격 관계대명사인 (D)가 정답이다.

번역 기간 연장에 대한 요청이 거절된 학생은 강의 마감일까지 작업물을 제출해야 한다.

어휘 extension (기간) 연장 refuse 거절하다

4.
해설 관계대명사
「,(콤마) 부정대명사(none)+of」 뒤로 빈칸이 있고, 빈칸 뒤로 선행사인 사람 명사(employees) 중 일부에 대해 수식하는 절이 왔으므로 관계대명사 (D)가 정답이다. 선행사와 관계대명사절은 나란히 오는 것이 일반적이지만 반드시 그런 것은 아니므로 이 경우, 해석을 통해 관계대명사절이 수식하는 명사를 찾아야 한다.

번역 여러 직원들이 베트남 지사의 일자리에 관심을 보였는데, 그 중 누구도 결혼하지 않았다.

어휘 express 표현하다 interest 관심 branch 지사

5.
해설 관계대명사
명사 instructor 뒤에 빈칸이 있고, 빈칸 뒤에 명사(native language)로 시작하면서 주어(나 목적어)가 빠지지 않은 절이 와서 instructor를 수식하므로 소유격 관계대명사인 (A)가 정답이다. 참고로 관계부사 when은 앞에 시간 명사, where는 앞에 장소 명사가 와야 한다.

번역 ELL 학원에서는 모국어가 영어인 경력 있는 강사를 구하고 있다.

어휘 seek 구하다 experienced 경력 있는 native language 모국어

6.
해설 관계대명사
빈칸 앞에 명사 companies가 있고 빈칸 뒤에 이 명사를 수식하는 내용의 절이 왔으므로 관계대명사절임을 알 수 있다. 'most of which'가 빈칸에 들어가면 사물 명사 companies 중 일부를 수식하는 관계대명사절로 연결이 자연스러우므로 (D)가 정답이다.

번역 인도의 신생기업 환경은 많은 회사들을 끌어들이고 있는데, 그들 대부분은 기술 분야 회사들이다.

어휘 startup 신생 벤처 기업, 스타트업 ecosystem 생태계 sector 분야 inasmuch as ~이므로, ~인 것을 보면

7.
해설 관계대명사
빈칸 앞뒤로 절이 두 개 있으므로 반드시 접속사가 하나 필요하다. 따라서 관계대명사 (C)가 정답이다. 참고로, 관계사절은 「전치사+목적격 관계대명사+완전절」의 형태로 앞 명사를 수식하기도 하며, 여기서는 「with which+완전절」이 선행사 produce를 수식한다.

번역 우리 식당은 현지 농부들로부터 신선한 유기농 농산물을 공급받으며, 그 농산물로 식사가 준비된다.

어휘 local 현지의 supply 공급하다 organic produce 유기농 농산물

8.
해설 관계대명사
명사 NEZ 뒤에 빈칸이 있고, 빈칸 뒤에 명사(anti-virus software)로 시작하면서 주어(나 목적어)가 빠지지 않은 절이 와서 NEZ를 수식하므로 소유격 관계대명사인 (C)가 정답이다.

번역 이넬 전자그룹은 NEZ라는 현지 소프트웨어 공급업체와 협력하는데, 그 회사의 안티바이러스 소프트웨어는 아시아에서 널리 사용되고 있다.

어휘 vendor 공급업체

YBM TEST
본책 p. 140

1. (C)	2. (D)	3. (A)	4. (D)	5. (B)
6. (D)	7. (B)	8. (D)	9. (B)	10. (A)
11. (C)	12. (D)	13. (A)	14. (B)	15. (B)
16. (C)	17. (D)	18. (D)	19. (A)	20. (C)

1.
해설 부사절 접속사
빈칸은 완전한 절(Please ~ ready)에 완전한 절(you ~ assistance)을 추가로 연결하는 자리이므로 부사절 접속사인 (C)가 정답이다.

번역 기술 지원을 요청할 때는 일련번호를 준비해 주세요.

어휘 serial number 일련번호 assistance 도움 otherwise 그렇지 않으면

2.
해설 관계대명사
빈칸 앞에 사물 명사 businesses가 있고 빈칸 뒤에 주어가 빠진 절이 와서 businesses를 수식하므로 사물 주격 관계대명사가 와야 한다. 따라서 (D)가 정답이다.

번역 한국 무역 기구는 해외 시장에서 기회를 찾고 있는 회사들에게 실용적인 충고를 제공한다.

어휘 practical 실용적인 seek 구하다 overseas 해외의

3.
해설 명사절 접속사
동사가 두 개(should be, will be)이면 절도 두 개 있다는 뜻이므로 반드시 접속사가 필요하다. 또한 빈칸이 절(public ~ facility)을 통째로 이끌고 동사(will be)의 주어 자리, 즉 명사 자리에 있는 것으로 보아 명사 자리에 절이 들어갔다는 단서이므로 빈칸은 명사절 접속사 자리이다. 따라서 (A)가 정답이다.

번역 스포츠 시설을 건설하는 데 공공 자금이 사용되어야 할지 아닐지는 오늘 밤 의회 회의에서 논의될 것이다.

어휘 public 공공의 fund 자금 facility 시설 council 의회

4.
해설 부사절 접속사
빈칸 뒤로 절이 두 개가 있으므로 절과 절을 연결하는 접속사가 하나 필요하다. 따라서 부사절 접속사인 (D)가 정답이다. 등위접속사는 문장 맨 앞에 오지 않으므로 For와 So는 답이 될 수 없다.

번역 스마트폰 판매가 회복되었기 때문에 모니아 디스플레이는 전력으로 차세대 OLED 디스플레이 생산을 가동할 것이다.

어휘 pick up 회복되다 operate 운영하다 generation 세대 at full capacity 전력으로

5.
해설 부사절 접속사
보기가 모두 부사절 접속사이므로 자리 파악할 필요 없이 바로 해석을 통해 답을 고른다. 문맥상 앞뒤 절이 반대되는 내용으로 연결되므로 '~인 반면'을 뜻하는 (B)가 정답이다. 참고로, once는 부사절 접속사(일단 ~하면) 외에 부사(한 번, 한때)도 된다.

번역 YZ 그룹 소유의 다른 건물들 대부분이 여행객들을 대상으로 하는 반면 새 호텔은 주로 업무상 출장객들을 대상으로 한다.

어휘 cater to ~ 구미에 맞추다, ~에게 필요한 것을 제공하다 property 부동산 own 소유하다 target 목표로 삼다

6.
해설 명사절 접속사
동사가 두 개(volunteers, will enjoy)이고 빈칸이 주어 자리, 즉 명사 자리에 있는 것으로 보아 명사 자리에 절이 들어갔다는 단서이므로 빈칸은 명사절 접속사 자리이다. 따라서 '~한 사람은 누구나'를 뜻하는 명사절 접속사 (D)가 정답이다.

번역 영화제에서 자원봉사하는 사람은 누구든 무료 입장권과 점심 식사를 받을 것이다.

어휘 volunteer 자원봉사 하다

7.
해설 관계대명사
명사 Artists 뒤에 빈칸이 있고, 빈칸 뒤에 명사(entries)로 시작하면서 주어(나 목적어)가 빠지지 않은 절(entries ~ competition)이 와서 Artists를 수식하므로 소유격 관계대명사인 (B)가 정답이다.

번역 출품작이 대회에 선택된 작가들은 8월 말까지 이메일로 통보를 받을 것이다.

어휘 entry 출품작 select 선택하다 competition 대회 via ~을 통해

8.
해설 관계대명사
「사물 명사(companies), 부정대명사(all)+of」 뒤로 빈칸이 있고, 빈칸 뒤로 companies의 전부(all)를 서술하는 절이 왔으므로 관계대명사 (D)가 정답이다.

번역 블레어 씨는 다수의 신생 기업에 상당한 금액을 투자했는데 그들 모두 유망한 것으로 간주된다.

어휘 considerable 상당한 amount 액수 multiple 다수의 startup 신생 벤처 기업, 스타트업 promising 유망한

9.
해설 부사절 접속사
빈칸 뒤로 절이 두 개가 있으므로 절과 절을 연결하는 접속사가 하나 필요하다. 접속사 보기인 (A), (B), (D) 중에서 문맥상 앞뒤 절이 서로 반대되는 내용이므로 '비록 ~하지만'을 뜻하는 (B)가 정답이다.

번역 공공 자전거를 이용할 수 있도록 함으로써 자전거 타기를 시에서 장려하고 있지만 대부분의 사람들은 시내에서 이동하는 데 계속 차를 이용했다.

어휘 encourage 장려하다 available 이용 가능한

10.
해설 부사절 접속사
빈칸 앞뒤로 절이 두 개가 있으므로 접속사가 와야 한다. 따라서 부사절 접속사 (A)가 정답이다.

번역 회사는 라지브 씨의 장기 주택이 마련될 때까지 그에게 임시 거처를 제공할 것이다.

어휘 temporary 임시의 accommodation 숙소 long-term 장기적인 housing 주택 arrange 마련하다, 준비하다

11.
해설 관계대명사
빈칸 앞에 사람 명사 student가 있고 빈칸 뒤에 주어가 빠진 절이 와서 student를 수식하므로 사람 주격 관계대명사가 와야 한다. 따라서 (C)가 정답이다.

번역 캠퍼스에서 행사를 계획하는 학생은 누구나 2주 전에 행정실로 요청서를 제출해야 한다.

어휘 administration 행정, 행정처 in advance 미리

12.
해설 명사절 접속사
동사가 두 개(indicates, are)이고 빈칸이 동사의 목적어 자리, 즉 명사 자리에 있는 것으로 보아 명사 자리에 절이 들어갔다는 단서이므로 빈칸은 명사절 접속사 자리이다. 빈칸 뒤로 완전한 절이 왔으므로 what은 답이 될 수 없고 (D)가 정답이다.

번역 이 설문조사는 소비자의 거의 3분의 1이 사회적 책임을 지는 회사의 제품에 대해 더 지출할 의향이 있다는 것을 보여준다.

어휘 indicate 보여주다 nearly 거의 a third 3분의 1 socially 사회적으로

13.
해설 관계대명사
문장에 동사가 두 개(based, was conducted)인 것으로 보아 절도 두 개이므로 반드시 접속사가 필요하다. 따라서 관계대명사 (A)가 정답이다. 참고로, 관계사절은 「전치사+목적격 관계대명사+완전절」의 형태로 앞 명사를 수식하기도 하는데, 여기서 'on which+완전절(the company ~ policy)'은 선행사 market survey를 수식하고 있다.

번역 회사가 가격 방침의 근거로 둔 시장 조사는 타사 조사에 의해 실행되었다.

어휘 survey 조사 base A on B A의 근거를 B에 두다 conduct 실행하다 third-party 제3자의 research firm 리서치 회사

14.
해설 부사절 접속사
빈칸 앞뒤로 절이 두 개가 있으므로 접속사가 와야 한다. 따라서 부사절 접속사 (B)가 정답이다. 특히 접속사 자리에 빈칸이 있고 빈칸 바로 뒤에 형용사나 부사가 올 경우 however가 답이 되어 '아무리 (형/부)할지라도'를 뜻한다.

번역 외국 통화에 투자하는 것은 아무리 철저하게 계획된다 할지라도 상당한 손실을 볼 가능성이 높다.

어휘 investment 투자 foreign currency 외화 involve 수반하다 substantial 상당한 loss 손실 thoroughly 철저히 regardless 개의치 않고

15.
해설 부사절 접속사
빈칸 앞뒤로 절이 두 개가 있으므로 접속사가 와야 한다. 부사절 접속사 as와 등위접속사 but 중 문맥상 빈칸 뒤의 절이 앞 절의 이유를 나타내므로 '~ 때문에'를 뜻하는 (B)가 정답이다.

번역 컨퍼런스에 관심 있는 사람들은 표가 빨리 매진될 것으로 예상되기 때문에 사전에 구입하도록 권고된다.

어휘 in advance 사전에 sell out 매진되다

16.
해설 관계대명사
빈칸 앞에 사람 명사 Sophia Fowler가 있고 빈칸 뒤에 주어가 빠진 절이 와서 Sophia Fowler를 수식하므로 사람 주격 관계대명사가 와야 한다. 따라서 (C)가 정답이다.

번역 새로운 급여 시스템을 개발하는 데 크게 기여한 소피아 파울러는 수석 회계사로 승진되었다.

어휘 contribute 기여하다 significantly 상당히 payroll 총급여 대상자, 총 급여액 accountant 회계사

17.
해설 부사절 접속사
문장 안에 절이 두 개가 있으므로 접속사가 필요하다. 두 번째 절(solutions ~ Thursday)과 첫 번째 절(We ~ time)을 연결하는 접속사가 하나 더 필요하다. 따라서 부사절 접속사인 (D)가 정답이다.

번역 목요일에 있을 이사회 전에 저조한 판매에 대한 해결책을 찾아야 한다는 점을 감안하면 우리는 시간이 부족하다.

어휘 **short of** ~가 부족한 **solution** 해결책 **board meeting** 이사회 (회의) **considering** ~을 고려하면

18.

해설 **관계대명사**
명사 Individuals 뒤에 빈칸이 있고, 빈칸 뒤에 명사(incomes)로 시작하면서 주어(나 목적어)가 빠지지 않은 절(incomes ~ $200,000)이 와서 Individuals를 수식하므로 소유격 관계대명사인 (D)가 정답이다.

번역 소득이 20만 달러 이상인 사람들은 개정된 세법에서 35%의 새로운 과세 등급에 들어가게 될 것이다.

어휘 **individual** 개인 **income** 소득 **tax bracket** 과세 등급 **revised** 개정된 **tax system** 세법, 세제

19.

해설 **부사절 접속사**
빈칸 앞뒤로 절이 두 개가 있으므로 접속사가 와야 한다. 따라서 부사절 접속사인 (A)가 정답이다.

번역 사전에 저희에게 알려주신다면 담당 의사가 검진하는 동안 음성을 녹취하실 수 있습니다.

어휘 **sound recording** 녹음 **check-up** 검진 **physician** 의사 **notify** 알리다 **in advance** 사전에 **provided that** 만약 ~라면

20.

해설 **명사절 접속사**
동사가 두 개(need, are)이고 빈칸이 to부정사(to define)의 목적어 자리, 즉 명사 자리에 있는 것으로 보아 명사 자리에 절이 들어갔다는 단서이므로 빈칸은 명사절 접속사 자리이다. 빈칸 뒤에, be동사(are) 뒤로 보어가 빠진 불완전한 절이 왔으므로 whether나 that은 답이 될 수 없고 (C)가 정답이다.

번역 제품을 개발할 때는 목표하는 소비자가 누구인지를 분명히 해야 한다.

어휘 **define** 분명히 밝히다 **consumer** 소비자

Part 6

어휘 문제는 빈칸의 앞뒤 문장에 정답과 유의어가 있다.

예제
본책 p. 142

우리의 지면판 체험 구독에 등록하시고 월간 잡지 두 부를 무료로 받아 보세요. 당월 호를 즉시 우편으로 보내 드리고, 이후 한 권을 또 보내 드립니다. 두 달 후, 우리가 송장을 보내 드리면 그때 유료 구독을 취소하시거나 시작하실 수 있습니다.

어휘 **register for** ~에 등록하다 **trial** 체험 **print** 지면 **subscription** 구독 **copy** (신문 등의) 한 부 **monthly** 월간의 **mail** 우편물을 발송하다 **current** 현재의 **right away** 즉시 **invoice** 송장, 청구서 **either A or B** A이거나 B인 **cancel** 취소하다 **paid** 유급의, 유료의

YBM TEST
본책 p. 143

1. (B) 2. (C) 3. (D) 4. (A)

4월 9일

랄르 펄리
샌타 모니카 대로 9602번지
비벌리힐스, 캘리포니아 90210

펄리 씨께,

3월 31일에 저는 당신에게 홈워드가123번지 아파트 3B의 깨진 창문을 일주일 이내에 손보지 않는다면, 직접 수리를 받도록 해 비용에 대한 상환을 청구할 것이라고 통보했습니다. 제 요청이 무시되었으므로 저는 유리 보수 서비스 업체인 글래스 닥터를 불러 4월 8일에 문제가 해결되도록 했습니다.

수리 작업에 포함된 자재 및 인건비 $180에 대한 송장을 동봉합니다. 제 다음 달 집세에서 그 금액을 공제할 것입니다.

존 커켈라

어휘 **fail to** 부정사 ~하지 못하다 **broken** 깨진 **arrange for** ~을 준비하다 **seek** 추구하다 **reimbursement** 상환, 변제 **fix** 고치다 **copy** 사본 **invoice** 송장, 청구서 **material** 자재 **labor** 노동 **involved** 관여된 **amount** 금액

1.

해설 **동사 시제**
편지가 작성된 날짜는 4월 9일이고, 빈칸은 3월 31일 일어난 일에 대해 언급하고 있으므로 과거 시제인 (B)가 정답이다.

2.

해설 **명사 어휘**
빈칸이 있는 절에서 '깨진 창문을 수리(take care of)하지 않으면 내가 직접 ___를 받아 비용을 청구하겠다'고 했고, 뒤 문장에서도 '내가 수리 서비스 업체(repair service)를 불러 수리를 받았다(fixed)'는 내용으로 연결되므로 문맥상 '수리'를 뜻하는 (C)가 정답이다.

어휘 **purchase** 구매 **reservation** 예약

3.

해설 **분사 도치**
빈칸은 수식구(for the cost ~ of $180)를 지우면, 원래 'a copy of the invoice is enclosed'에서 분사 enclosed가 절 앞으로 나오면서 주어(a copy of the invoice)와 동사(is)가 도치된 구문이다. 따라서 (D)가 정답이다. enclosed는 도치 구문으로 자주 쓰이므로 암기하면 편하다. 참고로 명사 enclosure(동봉된 것)는 가산명사이므로 앞에 한정사가 없이는 단수 형태로 빈칸 자리에 들어갈 수 없다.

4.

해설 문장 고르기:
빈칸 앞 문장에서 '자재 및 인건비 180달러에 대한 송장을 첨부한다'고 했고, (A)의 that amount는 180달러를 의미하므로 정답은 (A)이다.

번역 (A) 제 다음 달 집세에서 그 금액을 공제할 것입니다.
(B) 수리 작업이 이루어지도록 시간을 정해 주세요.
(C) 그것을 빨리 수리해 주시는 것이 중요합니다.
(D) 지불된 금액에 대한 영수증을 제게 주셔야 합니다.

Unit 10 특수구문

공식으로 해결하는 실전문제   본책 p. 147

| 1. (B) | 2. (B) | 3. (C) | 4. (D) | 5. (A) |
| 6. (D) | 7. (A) | 8. (C) | | |

1.

해설 상관접속사
빈칸 앞에 있는 both는 and와 짝을 이루므로 (B)가 정답이다.

번역 신입 사원을 채용할 때 우리는 내부와 외부 후보자들 둘 다 고려한다.

어휘 recruit 채용하다 internal 내부의 external 외부의 candidate 후보자

2.

해설 등위접속사
등위접속사는 빈칸 앞뒤로 대등한 성분을 연결하는데, 등위접속사 and 뒤로 명사 passion이 있으므로 빈칸에도 명사가 와야 한다. 따라서 (B)가 정답이다.

번역 성공적인 사회자가 되기 위해서 당신은 확신과 열정을 가지고 이야기하는 법을 배워야 한다.

어휘 presenter 사회자 passion 열정 confidence 확신 confidential 기밀의

3.

해설 상관접속사
빈칸 뒤에 있는 or는 either와 짝을 이루므로 (C)가 정답이다.

번역 달리 언급된 바 없으면, IT 교육은 목요일이나 금요일 중에 열릴 것이다.

어휘 otherwise 달리 state 언급하다 training session 교육

4.

해설 등위접속사
빈칸은 앞의 전치사구(at the boarding gate)와 뒤의 전치사구(at the check in counter)를 대등하게 연결하는 등위접속사 자리이고 문맥상 '~와'가 어울리므로 (D)가 정답이다.

번역 항공사들은 탑승구와 탑승 수속 창구에서 승객들에게 사진이 있는 신분증을 보여줄 것을 요구할 수 있다.

어휘 present 제시하다 ID 신분증(= identification) boarding 탑승

5.

해설 상관접속사
빈칸 앞에 있는 neither는 nor와 짝을 이루므로 (A)가 정답이다.

번역 워크숍 출석률이 70% 미만일 경우, 당신은 수료증이나 회사로부터의 비용 환급 둘 다 받을 수 없을 것이다.

어휘 certificate 증명서 reimbursement 환급, 상환 expense 비용

6.

해설 상관접속사
빈칸 뒤의 but also는 not only와 짝을 이루므로 (D)가 정답이다.

번역 드래곤 라이더는 유럽에서 가장 큰 규모의 모바일 게임일 뿐 아니라 가장 인기 있는 게임이기도 하다.

어휘 mobile game 모바일 게임

7.

해설 등위접속사
등위접속사는 빈칸 앞뒤로 대등한 성분을 연결하는데, 등위접속사 and 앞에 동사원형 look이 있으므로 빈칸에도 동사원형이 와야 한다. 따라서 (A)가 정답이다. 참고로 'look and ____'은 to help의 목적보어 자리이고, help는 목적보어 자리에 동사원형이나 to부정사가 올 수 있다.

번역 우리의 목표는 고객들이 우리의 다양한 건강 및 미용 제품을 이용해 외모와 건강을 증진시키도록 돕는 것이다.

어휘 aim 목표 extensive 폭넓은 range 범위

8.

해설 등위접속사
빈칸은 주어 we가 생략되고 남은 '동사+목적어~' 구문을 앞뒤로 동등하게 연결하므로 등위접속사 자리이고 문맥상 '그리고'가 어울리므로 (C)가 정답이다.

번역 이노테크는 제품을 신중하게 선택하고 우리 고객들에게 최선의 가격을 제시한다.

어휘 product 제품 offer ~에게 …을 제공하다

공식으로 해결하는 실전문제   본책 p. 149

| 1. (C) | 2. (B) | 3. (A) | 4. (D) | 5. (B) |
| 6. (D) | 7. (A) | 8. (B) | | |

1.

해설 원급 비교
빈칸 앞뒤로 as ~ as가 보이므로 원급이고, 빈칸 앞의 as와 수식구(for the vacant position)를 지우면 빈칸은 be동사의 보어 자리이므로 형용사인 (C)가 정답이다.

번역 팀의 다른 어떤 구성원들만큼이나 라이나도 그 공석에 자격이 있다.

어휘 vacant 비어 있는 position 일자리 qualified 자격이 있는

2.

해설 원급 비교

빈칸 앞에 있는 the same은 as와 짝을 이루어 '~와 같은'을 뜻하므로 (B)가 정답이다.

번역 오늘 벨은 예전 사양과 같은 가격으로 새로운 10.5 인치 B-Pad를 선보였다.

어휘 introduce 새로운 상품을 내놓다 all-new 전적으로 새로운 previous 이전의

3.

해설 원급 비교

as ~ as 사이에 빈칸이 있으므로 원급이 와야 하고 문맥상 '16달러만큼 낮은 가격'을 뜻하므로 '낮은'을 뜻하는 (A)가 정답이다.

번역 이지 카 렌털스로 하루 16달러의 환상적인 싼 가격에 세상을 탐험하세요.

어휘 explore 탐험하다 rate 가격 per ~당 lowly 하찮은

4.

해설 원급 비교

as ~ as 사이에 빈칸이 있으므로 원급이고, as ~ as 사이에는 형용사나 부사만 올 수 있으므로 challenges(동사, 명사)는 답이 될 수 없고 형용사인 (D)가 정답이다.

번역 재능 있는 직원들을 보유하는 것은 처음에 그들을 채용하는 것만큼이나 어렵다.

어휘 retain 보유하다 talented 재능 있는 recruit 채용하다

5.

해설 원급 비교

as ~ as 사이에 빈칸이 있으므로 원급이고 빈칸 앞의 as와 부사 수식구(about twice)를 지우면 빈칸은 be동사의 보어 자리이므로 형용사인 (B)가 정답이다.

번역 모요다는 연료 소모 면에서 연료 전지 자동차가 휘발유로 작동하는 자동차의 약 두 배만큼 효율적이라고 주장한다.

어휘 claim 주장하다 fuel-cell 연료 전지의 gas-powered 휘발유로 작동하는 in terms of ~의 면에서

6.

해설 원급 비교

빈칸 뒤에 '복수명사+as'가 있으므로 원급 비교구문을 만들기 위해서는 'as+many'가 필요하다. 따라서 (D)가 정답이다.

번역 송 박사는 임상 의학 및 수술에 관한 세미나가 끝난 후 가능한 한 많은 질문에 답변하려고 노력했다.

어휘 clinical medicine 임상 의학 surgery 수술

7.

해설 원급 비교

as ~ as 사이에 빈칸이 있으므로 원급이고 빈칸 앞의 as를 지우면 빈칸은 완전한 to부정사구에 덤으로 붙은 수식어 자리이므로 부사인 (A)가 정답이다.

번역 화학 물질을 가능한 한 안전하게 보관하기 위해, 실험실에서 잡동사니는 최소한으로 유지되어야 한다.

어휘 store 보관하다 chemical 화학 물질 clutter 잡동사니 laboratory 실험실

8.

해설 원급 비교

빈칸 앞뒤로 as ~ as가 보이므로 형용사나 부사가 들어갈 수 있고, 빈칸 앞의 as를 지우면 빈칸은 to make의 목적격 보어 자리이므로 형용사인 (B)가 정답이다.

번역 회사는 고객 서비스 부서가 가능한 고객의 요구에 즉각 대응하도록 만드는 것을 목표로 삼았다.

어휘 aim 목표하다 needs 요구, 필요사항 responsive 즉각 대응하는

공식으로 해결하는 실전문제 본책 p. 151

1. (C) 2. (A) 3. (D) 4. (D) 5. (B)
6. (C) 7. (A) 8. (B)

1.

해설 비교급 비교

빈칸 뒤에 비교급을 알려주는 단서인 than이 보이고, 빈칸은 be동사의 보어 자리이므로 형용사 비교급인 (C)가 정답이다.

번역 우리의 새로운 엔터프라이즈 솔루션즈는 사실상 다른 어떤 자원 관리 시스템보다 더 융통성이 있다.

어휘 virtually 사실상 resource 자원 flexible 융통성 있는, 유연한

2.

해설 비교급 비교

빈칸 뒤에 비교급이 있으므로 '훨씬'이란 뜻으로 비교급을 강조하는 부사인 (A)가 정답이다.

번역 회비가 인상되었기 때문에 넷필름즈에서 영화를 보는 것은 훨씬 더 비싸졌다.

어휘 fee 수수료 increase 인상되다

3.

해설 최상급 비교

빈칸 앞에는 the, 뒤에는 비교 범위를 나타내는 in the world가 있고, '세계에서 가장 많이 학습된'을 뜻하므로 최상급인 (D)가 정답이다. 참고로 by far는 최상급을 강조하는 부사로 쓰인다.

번역 에듀 리서치의 조사에 따르면 영어는 세계적으로 단연코 가장 많이 학습하는 외국어이다.

어휘 by far 단연코 commonly 흔히

4.

해설 최상급 비교

빈칸 앞에는 the, 뒤에는 최상급의 단서가 되는 수식어인 available이 있고, '가장 폭넓은'을 뜻하므로 최상급인 (D)가 정답이다.

번역 베스트 가전제품에서는 여러분께 최고의 가격과 가장 다양한 제품을 제공합니다.

어휘 **selection** 선택, 선택 가능한 것들 **available** 이용[구입] 가능한

5.
해설 비교급 비교
빈칸은 비교급 강조 부사인 even(훨씬)의 수식을 받았으므로 비교급인 (B)가 정답이다.

번역 오피스월드는 구매자들에게 제품을 훨씬 더 매력적으로 만들기 위해 가격을 낮출 계획이다.

어휘 **lower** 낮추다 **even** 훨씬

6.
해설 비교급 비교
빈칸 뒤에 비교급을 알려주는 단서인 than이 보이므로 비교급인 (C)가 정답이다.

번역 전기 자동차는 가솔린 엔진 차량보다 더 조용히 주행하므로 보행자들이 차량이 오는 것을 듣기 어렵다.

어휘 **electric** 전기의 **petrol** 휘발유, 가솔린 **pedestrian** 보행자

7.
해설 최상급 비교
빈칸 앞에 최상급의 단서가 되는 'the + 서수(the third)'가 있고, '세 번째로 가장 인기 있는'을 뜻하므로 최상급인 (A)가 정답이다.

번역 체어마스터는 〈데코데일리〉에 의해 세 번째로 가장 인기 있는 가구 브랜드로 선정되어 자랑스럽다.

어휘 **rank** (순위를) 매기다 **brand** 브랜드, 상표

8.
해설 형용사 자리
빈칸은 '관사 + 부사 _____ 명사'의 순서로 명사를 수식하는 자리이므로 형용사인 (B)가 정답이다. 참고로 most는 최상급을 나타낼 때는 '가장, 최고로'를 뜻하는 부사이다.

번역 최후의 전사 VII은 야후 온라인 게임이 지금까지 개발한 가장 성공적인 게임이다.

어휘 **ever** (최상급 강조) 역대, 지금까지

◆ 공식으로 해결하는 실전문제   본책 p. 153

| 1. (D) | 2. (D) | 3. (A) | 4. (B) | 5. (A) |
| 6. (C) | 7. (C) | 8. (B) | | |

1.
해설 가정법
빈칸은 If절의 동사 자리이고, 상대절의 동사(would have qualified)가 가정법 과거완료 시제인 것으로 보아 had p.p.가 와야 한다. 따라서 (D)가 정답이다.

번역 블랙 삭스가 한 게임만 더 이겼더라면, 챔피언스 리그 준결승전에 진출할 자격을 얻었을 것이다.

어휘 **qualify for** ~에 자격을 얻다 **semifinal** 준결승

2.
해설 가정법 도치
빈칸 뒤가 '주어 + 동사원형 ~, 주어 will ~'이고, 문맥상 '교육을 받으면 ~'으로 가정하는 내용이므로 'If you should take'에서 If가 생략되어 'Should you take'가 된 것임을 알 수 있다. 따라서 (D)가 정답이다. 접속사 Unless는 문맥상 적절하지 않아 답이 될 수 없다.

번역 방어 운전 교육을 받으시면 자동차 보험료의 5퍼센트를 할인받을 수 있는 자격이 주어집니다.

어휘 **defensive driving** 방어 운전 **qualify for** ~에 자격을 얻다 **insurance rate** 보험료

3.
해설 가정법
빈칸 앞의 If절 동사(had purchased)가 가정법 과거완료 시제이므로 빈칸에 들어갈 동사도 시제 일치가 되어야 하고, 빈칸 뒤에 목적어가 있으므로 가정법 과거완료 능동태인 (A)가 정답이다.

번역 만약 출발하기 3주 전에 표를 구매했더라면 10퍼센트의 할인을 받았을 것이다.

어휘 **purchase** 구매하다 **prior to** ~에 앞서 **departure** 출발

4.
해설 가정법 도치
콤마(,) 뒤 절의 동사가 가정법 과거완료 시제인 것으로 보아 빈칸이 있는 절은 'If + 주어 + had p.p.'가 되어야 하는데 동사 자리에 had가 빠진 것으로 보아 if가 생략되고 'Had + 주어 + p.p.'로 도치되었음을 알 수 있다. 따라서 (B)가 정답이다.

번역 이사회가 신차 모델의 디자인을 승인했다면 생산이 이미 시작되었을 것이다.

어휘 **board** 이사회 **approve** 승인하다

5.
해설 가정법 도치
빈칸 뒤가 '주어 + 동사원형 ~, 명령문'이고, 문맥상 '도움이 필요하면 ~'으로 가정하는 내용이므로 'If you should require'에서 If가 생략되어 'Should you require'가 된 것임을 알 수 있다. 따라서 (A)가 정답이다. 접속사 Because는 문맥상 적절하지 않다.

번역 추가로 도움이 필요하시면 언제든지 주저 마시고 연락 주세요.

어휘 **further** 추가의 **assistance** 도움 **hesitate** 망설이다

6.
해설 가정법
빈칸 앞 If절의 동사(had been followed)가 가정법 과거완료 시제이고 빈칸에 들어갈 동사도 시제 일치가 되어야 하므로 가정법 과거완료 시제인 (C)가 정답이다. 빈칸 뒤에 목적어가 없으므로 (A)는 정답이 될 수 없다.

번역 안전 예방책이 엄격하게 준수되었다면, 참혹한 사고를 피할 수 있었을 것이다.

어휘 safety precaution 안전 예방책 strictly 엄격히 devastating 참혹한 accident 사고 avoid 피하다

7.
해설 가정법 도치
의문문이 아닌 평서문이 Should로 시작한 것으로 보아 가정법 도치 문장임을 알 수 있다. 'Should+주어' 다음에는 동사원형이 와야 하므로 (C)가 정답이다.

번역 오류 메시지가 다시 나타나면, 추가적으로 조사할 수 있도록 우리 고객센터로 전화 주세요.

어휘 investigate 조사하다 further 더

8.
해설 가정법
빈칸 앞 If절의 동사(should encounter)가 가정법 미래 시제이므로 상대절의 동사로는 'will/may/can+동사원형'이나 명령문이 와야 한다. 빈칸 앞에 명령문을 뜻하는 please가 있으므로 동사원형인 (B)가 정답이다.

번역 검색하는 동안 어려움이 있으시면 연락용 서식을 제출하셔서 저희에게 알려주세요.

어휘 encounter 접하다, 마주치다 browse 둘러보다, 검색하다 notify 알리다, 통고하다

YBM TEST
본책 p. 154

1. (C)	2. (B)	3. (C)	4. (C)	5. (A)
6. (B)	7. (A)	8. (A)	9. (D)	10. (D)
11. (B)	12. (A)	13. (A)	14. (B)	15. (D)
16. (D)	17. (D)	18. (A)	19. (C)	20. (C)

1.
해설 상관접속사
빈칸은 앞의 명사 newsletter와 뒤의 명사 opportunities를 연결하는 자리이므로 부사는 답이 될 수 없다. 따라서 '기회(opportunities)뿐 아니라 소식지도'라는 뜻으로 두 명사를 자연스럽게 연결하는 상관접속사 (C)가 정답이다.

번역 BI 네트워크의 회원은 현지 회사들과 조우할 기회를 가질 뿐 아니라 월간 비즈니스 소식지도 받는다.

어휘 newsletter 회보, 소식지 likewise 마찬가지로 moreover 게다가 as a result 결과적으로

2.
해설 비교급 비교
빈칸 뒤에 비교급이 있으므로 '훨씬'이란 뜻으로 비교급을 강조하는 부사인 (B)가 정답이다.

번역 인사 부장은 다니엘 루이스의 경력이 빌 로텍의 경력보다 훨씬 더 인상적이라고 생각했다.

어휘 personnel director 인사 부장 career 경력 impressive 인상적인

3.
해설 최상급 비교
빈칸 앞에는 the, 뒤에는 비교 범위를 나타내는 among international students가 있고, '해외 학생들 사이에서 가장 널리 사용되는'을 뜻하므로 최상급인 (C)가 정답이다.

번역 넷 타임스에 따르면 '세계 대학 순위'는 해외 학생들 사이에서 가장 널리 통용되는 순위표이다.

어휘 ranking 순위(표)

4.
해설 원급 비교
as ~ as 사이에 빈칸이 있으므로 형용사나 부사가 들어갈 수 있고, 빈칸 앞의 as를 지우면 빈칸은 be동사의 보어 자리이므로 형용사인 (C)가 정답이다.

번역 직원 평가는 가능한 포괄적이어서, 성과를 평가하는 데 필요한 모든 영역을 포함해야 한다.

어휘 evaluation 평가 cover 다루다, 포괄하다 essential 필수적인 rate 평가하다 performance (업무) 성과 comprehensive 폭넓은, 포괄적인

5.
해설 상관접속사
빈칸은 앞의 to부정사구(to reduce ~ business)에 뒤의 to부정사구(to stop ~ completely)를 연결하는 자리이고, 빈칸 뒤의 not은 but과 짝을 이루므로 (A)가 정답이다. 참고로, 'B, but not A'는 'not A but B(A가 아니라 B)'와 같다.

번역 하야스는 원자력 산업에서 완전히 철수하는 것이 아니라 사업의 규모를 줄이기로 결정했다.

어휘 reduce 줄이다 nuclear energy 원자력 industry 산업

6.
해설 가정법 도치
의문문이 아닌 평서문이 Should로 시작한 것으로 보아 가정법 도치 문장임을 알 수 있다. 'Should+주어' 다음에는 동사원형이 와야 하므로 (B)가 정답이다.

번역 누구라도 서식을 다운로드할 때 문제를 경험할 경우 우리는 이메일로 서식을 보내야 할 것이다.

어휘 form 서식 via ~을 통해

7.
해설 원급 비교
빈칸 뒤에 '복수명사+as'가 있으므로 원급 비교 구문을 만들기 위해서는 'as+many'가 필요하다. 따라서 (A)가 정답이다.

번역 그린테이블은 유기농 제품 이용 고객을 늘리기 위해 가능한 많은 자원을 새로운 블로그를 만드는 데 할애하고 있다.

어휘 allocate 할당하다 resource 자원 drive 몰아가다 traffic 고객 수(규모) as many+복수명사+as possible 가능한 많은 ~

8.
해설 등위접속사
등위접속사는 빈칸 앞뒤로 대등한 성분을 연결한다. 등위접속사 and 앞이 명령문으로 수식구(before September 30)를 지우면 동사원형 register가 있으므로 and 뒤 빈칸에도 동사원형이 와야 한다. 따라서 (A)가 정답이다.

번역 경력 개발 컨퍼런스에 9월 30일 전에 등록하시고 얼리버드 할인을 받으세요.

어휘 register 등록하다 early bird 얼리버드(일찍 오는 사람) career 경력 receipt 영수(증)

9.
해설 원급 비교
as ~ as 사이에 빈칸이 있으므로 형용사나 부사가 들어갈 수 있고, 빈칸 앞의 as와 부사 수식구(nearly twice)를 지우면 빈칸은 be동사(are)의 보어 자리이므로 형용사인 (D)가 정답이다.

번역 M2 비즈니스의 연구는 요즘 사무직 근로자들이 1970년대의 사무원들보다 거의 두 배만큼 생산적이라는 점을 보여준다.

어휘 nearly 거의 twice 두 배 counterpart 상대, 대응 관계에 있는 사람[것] productive 생산적인

10.
해설 가정법 도치
의문문이 아닌 평서문이 Had로 시작한 것으로 보아 가정법 과거완료의 도치 문장임을 알 수 있다. 'Had+주어' 다음에는 과거분사가 와야 하므로 (D)가 정답이다(If Mr. Long had known → Had Mr. Long known).

번역 롱 씨는 16번 고속도로가 보수 작업 중이라는 것을 알았다면 차를 가지고 출근하지 않았을 것이다.

어휘 road work 도로 공사 underway 진행 중인

11.
해설 only 도치
문두가 'Only+ 부사구'로 시작하고 있으므로 '주어+동사'가 '동사+주어' 순으로 도치된다. 문장에 동사가 없고 빈칸 뒤에 to부정사가 있으므로 (B)가 정답이다(you are able to see → are you able to see).

번역 우리의 철도 예약 앱의 사용을 통해서만 막판 할인 기회를 확인하실 수 있습니다.

어휘 app 앱 last minute 막판 be able to부정사 ~할 수 있다

12.
해설 가정법
빈칸 앞 If절의 동사(had not upgraded)가 가정법 과거완료 시제이고 빈칸에 들어갈 동사도 시제가 일치되어야 하므로 가정법 과거완료 시제인 (A)가 정답이다.

번역 사무실이 컴퓨터의 방화벽 설정을 업그레이드하지 않았다면 악성 코드의 공격으로 인한 손상의 규모가 막대했을 것이다.

어휘 firewall 방화벽 setting 설정 scale 규모 damage 손상 malware 악성 코드, 악성 소프트웨어 enormous 막대한

13.
해설 원급 비교
as ~ as 사이에 빈칸이 있으므로 원급이고, 빈칸 앞의 as를 지우면 빈칸은 완전한 절에 덤으로 붙은 수식어 자리이므로 부사인 (A)가 정답이다.

번역 우리는 당신의 반려동물이 가능한 편하게 여행할 수 있도록 전문화된 반려동물 운송 서비스를 제공합니다.

어휘 specialized 전문화된 pet 애완동물, 반려동물 transportation 운송

14.
해설 상관접속사
빈칸 앞의 either는 or와 짝을 이루므로 (B)가 정답이다.

번역 우리 항공사는 예약 후 24시간 이내에 추가 수수료 없이 예약을 완전히 취소하거나 변경할 수 있도록 할 것이다.

어휘 entirely 완전히 at no extra cost 추가 비용 없이

15.
해설 가정법 도치
콤마(,) 뒤 절의 동사가 가정법 과거완료 시제인 것으로 보아 빈칸이 있는 절은 'If+주어+had p.p.'가 되어야 하는데 동사 자리에 had가 빠진 것으로 보아 If가 생략되고 'Had+주어+p.p.'로 도치 되었음을 알 수 있다. 따라서 (D)가 정답이다.

번역 로우헤드 씨가 두 달 전에 무역 박람회에 참석했더라면 네슬라의 창립자인 로미오 머스크를 만날 기회가 있었을 것이다.

어휘 trade fair 무역 박람회 founder 창립자

16.
해설 비교급 비교
빈칸 뒤에 비교급을 알려주는 단서인 than이 보이므로 비교급인 (D)가 정답이다.

번역 일반적으로 대기업들은 소기업들보다 더 관대한 직원 복리 후생을 제공할 여유가 있다.

어휘 in general 일반적으로 can afford to부정사 ~할 여유가 있다 benefits package 복리 후생 제도

17.
해설 등위접속사
빈칸은 'All new staff members are required to'가 생략되고 남은 '동사원형+목적어' 구문을 앞뒤로 동등하게 연결하므로 등위접속사 자리이고 문맥상 '그리고'가 어울리므로 (D)가 정답이다.

번역 모든 신입 사원들은 출근 첫날 리셉션을 방문해 연락처를 제공해야 한다.

어휘 reception 접수처, 리셉션 details 세부사항

18.
해설 최상급 비교
빈칸 앞에는 the, 뒤에는 비교 범위를 나타내는 in the world가 있고, '세계에서 가장 활발한'을 뜻하므로 최상급인 (A)가 정답이다.

번역 한국 온라인 게임 산업은 세계에서 가장 활발한 곳 중 하나로 급부상했다.

어휘 industry 산업 rapidly 빠르게 emerge 부상하다 dynamic 활발한, 역동적인 dynamism 활력

19.
해설 가정법 도치
빈칸 뒤가 '주어+동사원형 ~, 명령문'이고, 문맥상 '취소를 원하면 ~'으로 가정하는 내용이므로 'If you should wish'에서 If가 생략되어 'Should you wish'가 된 것임을 알 수 있다. 따라서 (C)가 정답이다.

번역 HDN 케이블의 이용을 취소하기를 원하신다면 취소 양식을 작성하셔서 저희에게 돌려주세요.

어휘 subscription (서비스) 이용 complete 작성하다 cancellation 취소

20.
해설 가정법
빈칸은 If절의 동사 자리이고, 상대절의 동사(could have been prevented)가 가정법 과거완료 시제인 것으로 보아 had p.p.가 와야 한다. 따라서 (C)가 정답이다.

번역 공항이 소프트웨어를 정기 점검했더라면 수하물 시스템 고장은 예방될 수 있었을 것이다.

어휘 regular 정기적인 maintenance 유지 보수 baggage 수하물 failure 고장 prevent 예방하다

Part 6

문법 문제는 한 문장 안에서 해결한다.

 예제

본책 p. 156

테일러 씨께,

저희 회사 워크숍에서 강연하시기로 동의해 주셔서 감사합니다. 워크숍에 대해 몇 가지 기본적인 정보를 드리기 위해 이 편지를 씁니다. 잠정 결정된 안건도 동봉해 드렸습니다. 6월 12일 오후 3시에 의사소통 전략에 관한 강연을 하시게 될 예정입니다.
강연이 매우 기대됩니다.

제인 W. 맥킨
메트로폴리탄 사 인사 부장

어휘 enclosed 동봉된 tentative 잠정적인 agenda 안건 be scheduled to부정사 ~할 예정이다 communication 의사소통 strategy 전략 look forward to ~을 기대하다 HR 인사과(= Human Resources) director 이사

YBM TEST
본책 p. 157

1. (A)　**2.** (C)　**3.** (A)　**4.** (D)

글: 사무엘 루이스 (12월 26일) - 〈보스턴 타임즈〉는 디자인 담당자인 에이미 브라운을 부편집장으로 승진시킨다는 내용을 수요일에 발표했다. 보스턴 출신으로 매사추세츠 대학을 졸업한 브라운 씨는 BBS 방송 그룹에서 디자이너로서 일하기 시작했고 〈파인 아츠〉 잡지사에서 아트 디렉터로 근무했다. 그녀는 6년 전에 홈 부문 아트 디렉터로 〈보스턴 타임즈〉에 합류했다. 2년 후, 그녀는 디자인 책임자로 임명되었다. 그녀는 신문 지면과 웹 사이트의 외관을 책임지고 있는 65명의 아트 디렉터, 그래픽 아티스트, 웹 디자이너 등으로 구성된 팀을 감독하는 일을 계속할 것이다. 승진은 1월 1일자로 시행된다.

어휘 deputy editor 부편집장 native 토박이 career 경력 serve 근무하다 section 부문 oversee 감독하다 responsible for ~을 책임지는[담당하는] appearance 외관 promotion 승진

1.
해설 관계사
수식구(of Boston City)를 지우면 빈칸은 주어 Ms. Brown의 동격으로 온 명사 A native를 뒤에서 수식하는 자리이다. 빈칸 뒤에 명사가 남아 있으므로 이를 목적어로 연결하면서 A native를 수식할 수 있는 '주격관계사+동사' 형태가 적합하다. '명사(선행사)+주격관계사+동사'에서 동사는 선행사에 수를 일치시켜야 하는데, A native는 3인칭 단수이므로 복수동사 attend는 답이 될 수 없다. 또한 뒤에서 Amy Brown의 경력을 순차적으로 소개하고 있는 것으로 보아 '대학을 다녔고 일을 시작했고 경력을 쌓아왔다'의 순서로 과거 시제가 적절하다. 따라서 (A)가 정답이다.

2.
해설 명사 자리
빈칸은 전치사 as의 목적어 자리이므로 명사 자리이고, 앞에 관사 a가 있으므로 단수명사가 와야 한다. 또한 문맥상 '디자이너로서 경력을 시작했다'가 적절하므로 (C)가 정답이다.

3.
해설 문장 고르기
빈칸 앞 문장은 '그녀가 6년 전 입사해 아트 디렉터가 되었다'고 하고, 뒤 문장은 앞으로 그녀가 할 일을 이야기하고 있다. 따라서 빈칸에는 그 사이에 있었던 일인 '2년 후, 그녀는 디자인 디렉터가 되었다'가 들어가면 시간의 흐름에 따라 일어난 일을 자연스럽게 연결해 주므로 (A)가 정답이다.

번역 (A) 2년 후, 그녀는 디자인 책임자로 임명되었다.
(B) 편집위원단은 그녀가 신문사에 합류하는 것을 환영한다.
(C) 그녀는 일을 쉴 필요가 있다고 느꼈다.
(D) 그녀는 지난 달에 편집장 자리에서 물러났다.

4.
해설 형용사 어휘
주어인 promotion(승진)을 수식하는 형용사 어휘를 고르는 문제이다. 빈칸이 있는 문장과 바로 앞 문장만으로 단서를 파악하기 어려우므로 문맥 전체를 살펴야 한다. 지문의 전반부에서 12월 26일에 Amy Brown의 승진을 발표하면서 Amy의 약력을

소개했고 향후의 계획까지 이야기하고 있으므로 '승진은 1월 1일부터 시행된다'가 적절하다. 따라서 (D)가 정답이다.

어휘 available 이용 가능한 promising 촉망되는, 유망한 undecided 결정되지 않은 effective (특정 일자부터) 시행되는

Unit 11 어휘 1

공식으로 해결하는 실전문제
본책 p. 159

1. (B) 2. (C) 3. (D) 4. (A) 5. (A)
6. (C) 7. (C) 8. (D)

1.
해설 **제안/요구 동사+that절**
빈칸은 that절의 동사 자리이고, that 앞에 제안/요구 동사인 request가 있으므로 'should+동사원형'에서 should가 생략된 동사원형이 와야 한다. 따라서 (B)가 정답이다.

번역 블루젯 항공사는 승객들이 비행기 탑승 시 음료를 가져올 것을 요청한다.

어휘 passenger 승객 on board 탑승한

2.
해설 **자동사+전치사**
빈칸 뒤로 목적어가 보이지 않고 전치사 as가 있으므로 전치사 as와 어울려 '~로 근무하다'를 뜻하는 자동사 (C)가 정답이다.

번역 켈리 맥케이 씨는 2009년에 우리 팀에 합류한 이후 투자 자문위원으로 근무했다.

어휘 investment 투자 advisor 자문위원

3.
해설 **제안/요구 동사+that절**
빈칸은 that절의 동사 자리이고, that 앞에 제안/요구 동사인 suggested가 있으므로 'should+동사원형'에서 should가 생략된 동사원형이 와야 한다. 또한 빈칸 뒤에 목적어가 없으므로 수동태임을 알 수 있다. 따라서 (D)가 정답이다.

번역 행정 국장인 와타나베 씨는 현행 통보 절차가 간소화되어야 한다고 제안했다.

어휘 chief 최고위의 administrator 행정 관리자 notification 통보 procedure 절차

4.
해설 **필수 형용사+that절**
빈칸 뒤로 보이는 that절의 동사가 주어와 수일치가 되지 않고 동사원형이므로 '필수 형용사+that+주어+should+동사원형'에서 should가 생략된 구문임을 알 수 있다. 따라서 필수 형용사인 (A)가 정답이다.

번역 마케팅 팀의 모든 직원들이 연례 국제 마케팅 동향 컨퍼런스에 참석하는 것이 중요하다.

어휘 present 참석한 annual 연례의

5.
해설 **자동사+전치사**
빈칸 뒤로 목적어가 보이지 않고 전치사 for가 있으므로 전치사 for와 어울려 '~에 지원(신청)하다'를 뜻하는 자동사 (A)가 정답이다.

번역 무료 수업에 특별 예약을 신청하시려면 등록 카드를 작성하세요.

어휘 reservation 예약 session (특정 활동을 위한) 시간 complete 작성하다 registration 등록

6.
해설 **자동사+전치사**
빈칸 뒤로 목적어가 보이지 않고 전치사 with가 있으므로 전치사 with와 어울려 '~와 연락하다'를 뜻하는 자동사 (C)가 정답이다.

번역 뉴욕에 연락 사무소를 개설함으로써 회사는 미국 내의 지사들과 연락을 더 잘 할 수 있다.

어휘 liaison office 연락 사무소 branch 지사 separate 분리하다 inform 알리다 communicate 연락하다 focus 집중하다

7.
해설 **제안/요구 동사+that절**
빈칸은 that절의 동사 자리이고, that 앞에 제안/요구 동사인 ask가 있으므로 'should+동사원형'에서 should가 생략된 동사원형이 와야 한다. 따라서 (C)가 정답이다.

번역 지원서를 제출하기 전에 모든 정보를 꼼꼼히 검토할 것을 요청드립니다.

어휘 application 지원(서) submission 제출

8.
해설 **자동사+전치사**
빈칸 뒤 전치사 in과 어울려 '~에 참석하다'를 뜻하는 자동사 (D)가 정답이다. attend가 '참석하다'라는 의미로 쓰일 때는 타동사이므로 in 앞에 오지 않는다.

번역 회계 부서의 전 직원은 새로운 회계 소프트웨어를 위한 교육에 참석해야 한다.

어휘 accounting 회계 training session 교육 (과정)

공식으로 해결하는 실전문제
본책 p. 161

1. (D) 2. (B) 3. (B) 4. (A) 5. (D)
6. (A) 7. (C) 8. (C)

1.
해설 **목적어가 '~에게'인 동사**
빈칸 뒤로 '사람목적어+that절'이 와서 '승리한 참가자들에게 that~을 알리다'로 해석되므로 (D)가 정답이다. 다른 보기의 동사들은 that절과 동사 사이에 목적어가 올 수 없다.

번역 픽타그램 사진 경연 대회의 조직자들은 수상자들에게 상을 받게 될 것임을 통보할 것이다.

어휘 organizer 조직자 winning 승리한 contestant 참가자

2.
해설 동사+명사
extend(연장하다)는 'operating hours(영업 시간), deadline(마감일)' 등과 짝을 이뤄 '~기간을 연장하다'로 자주 출제된다. 빈칸 뒤에 operating hours가 목적어로 왔고 '야간 운행 시간을 연장한다'로 문맥상 적절하므로 (B)가 정답이다.

번역 시티 메트로는 주요 국경일에 야간 운행 시간을 90분 늘릴 것이다.

어휘 operating 운영 major 주요한 magnify 확대하다 obtain 얻다

3.
해설 동사+명사
빈칸 뒤의 목적어가 its plan이므로 목적어가 '~에게'로 해석되는 inform과 remind는 적절하지 않다. 문맥상 '회사의 계획을 발표했다'가 적절하므로 (B)가 정답이다.

번역 오늘 스포츠 소매업체인 아레카스는 8월부터 80개의 점포를 닫을 계획임을 발표했다.

어휘 retailer 소매업체

4.
해설 동사+명사
빈칸 앞의 동사 expressed(표현하다)는 주로 감정을 나타내는 말이 목적어로 와서 '~감정을 표현하다'로 출제된다. 보기 중 감정을 뜻하는 'appreciation(감사)'와 짝을 이뤄 '감사를 표했다'로 해석이 자연스러우므로 (A)가 정답이다.

번역 윌리엄 에버렛 시장은 공공 보건 프로젝트에 참가하는 자원봉사자들의 솔선수범에 감사를 표했다.

어휘 volunteer 자원봉사자 willingness 기꺼이 함 abundance 풍부

5.
해설 동사+명사
attract(마음을 끌다)는 목적어 customers(고객)와 짝을 이뤄 '고객을 유치하다'로 자주 출제된다. '고객을 유치하기 위한 노력으로'로 문맥상으로도 적절하므로 (D)가 정답이다.

번역 빅 테크놀로지스는 새로운 고객들을 유치하기 위한 노력으로 새 컴퓨터의 가격을 약 380달러로 책정했다.

어휘 price 가격을 매기다 inform 알리다 refer to 참고하다 promote 홍보하다, 승진시키다

6.
해설 목적어가 '~에게'인 동사
빈칸 뒤로 '사람목적어+on+명사'가 와서 목적어가 '을/를'이 아닌 '~에게'로 해석되어 '투자자들에게 ~에 대해 충고하다'를 나타내므로 (A)가 정답이다. advise는 'advise A on B(A에게 B에 대해 충고한다)'로 자주 쓰이므로 암기해 둔다.

번역 내일 세미나에서 매튜 리 박사는 첨단산업 관련주에 대해 투자자들에게 자문해 주는 방법을 주제로 다룰 것이다.

어휘 address 다루다 investor 투자자 hi-tech 첨단산업 stock 주식

7.
해설 동사+명사
present(수여하다)는 목적어 award(상)와 짝을 이뤄 '상을 수여하다'로 자주 출제된다. 'present the ~ Award'가 수동태로 전환되어 'the ~ Award'가 주어 자리에 있고, 문맥상 '상이 수여될 것이다'로 적절하므로 (C)가 적절하다.

번역 올해의 앱 개발자 상은 전세계의 2000명의 참가자 중에서 선택된 수상자들에게 수여될 것이다.

어휘 dedicate 전념하다 demonstrate 보여주다 present 수여하다 relate 관련시키다

8.
해설 목적어가 '~에게'인 동사
빈칸 뒤로 '사람목적어+that절'이 와서 '승객들에게 that~을 보장한다'로 해석되므로 (C)가 정답이다. 다른 보기의 동사들은 that절과 동사 사이에 목적어가 오지 않는다.

번역 크루즈 아메리카는 여행이 꼼꼼하게 준비되고 종합 보험에 가입되어 있다는 점을 승객들에게 보장한다.

어휘 passenger 승객 meticulously 꼼꼼하게 insured 보험에 가입된

공식으로 해결하는 실전문제
본책 p. 163

1. (D)　2. (A)　3. (C)　4. (B)　5. (B)
6. (C)　7. (A)　8. (D)

1.
해설 동사 A 전치사 B
빈칸 뒤 전치사 to는 attribute와 짝을 이뤄 'attribute A to B(A를 B 덕으로 돌리다)'로 쓰인다. '성공적 출시를 팀 덕으로 돌리다'로 문맥상으로도 적절하므로 (D)가 정답이다.

번역 크로포드 씨는 신제품 라인의 성공적인 출시를 열심히 일해 준 자신의 팀 덕으로 돌렸다.

어휘 launch 출시 hardworking 열심히 일하는 finalize 마무리하다

2.
해설 전치사 덩어리
빈칸 뒤 walking distance(도보 거리)는 전치사 within(이내에)과 짝을 이뤄 '도보 거리 이내에'를 뜻한다. 따라서 (A)가 정답이다.

번역 로열 리마 리조트는 피어슨 공항으로부터 도보 거리 이내에 편리하게 위치해 있다.

어휘 conveniently 편리하게 distance 거리

3.

해설 **동사 A 전치사 B**
빈칸 뒤 전치사 to는 match와 짝을 이뤄 'match A to B(A를 B에 맞추다)'로 쓰인다. '이력서와 자기소개서를 요건에 맞춘다'로 문맥상으로도 적절하므로 (C)가 정답이다.

번역 잡서포터의 상담가들은 구직자들이 이력서와 자기소개서를 각 일자리의 요건에 맞출 수 있도록 돕는다.

어휘 **consultant** 상담가 **job seeker** 구직자 **requirement** 요건

4.

해설 **동사 A 전치사 B**
빈칸 뒤 전치사 with는 present와 짝을 이뤄 'present A with B(A에게 B를 수여하다)'로 쓰인다. 'present A with B'가 수동태로 전환되어 'be presented with' 형태로 쓰였으며, 'Michael Rosella가 감사패를 수여받다'로 문맥상으로도 적절하므로 (B)가 정답이다.

번역 마이클 로셀라는 20년 근속을 인정받아 DPC의 사장인 찰스 데이터로부터 감사패를 수여받았다.

어휘 **appreciation plaque** 감사패 **in recognition of** ~을 인정하여 **service** 근무 **commit** 전념하다 **relate** 관련시키다

5.

해설 **전치사 덩어리**
빈칸 앞의 전치사 on은 명사 basis와 짝을 이루고, 'on a regular basis'는 '정기적으로'를 뜻하며 문맥상으로도 적절하므로 (B)가 정답이다.

번역 음식을 준비하고 제공하는 모든 회사들은 정기적으로 공공 식품 안전 기관의 검사를 받아야 한다.

어휘 **serve** 제공하다 **inspect** 검사하다 **organization** 기관 **assortment** 모음, 종합 **base** 맨 아래 부분 **overhaul** 점검, 정비

6.

해설 **전치사 덩어리**
'in the ____ future'의 형용사 자리에는 near나 foreseeable이 들어가 '가까운 미래'를 뜻한다. 따라서 (C)가 정답이다.

번역 엑스프린츠의 최고 책임자는 가까운 미래에 일본의 스마트폰 회사와의 거래가 발표될 것으로 기대한다고 말했다.

어휘 **chief executive** 최고 책임자 **involve** 관련시키다 **surrounding** 주위의 **nearby** 인근의

7.

해설 **동사 A 전치사 B**
빈칸 뒤 전치사 to는 direct와 짝을 이뤄 'direct A to B(A를 B에게 보내다)'로 쓰인다. 'direct A to B'가 수동태로 전환되어 'be directed to' 형태로 '불만이 직속 상사에게 보내져야 한다'로 문맥상으로도 적절하므로 (A)가 정답이다.

번역 직원 및 직원 서비스에 대한 불만은 해당 직원의 직속 상사에게 전달되어야 한다.

어휘 **complaint** 불만 **regarding** ~에 관한 **immediate** 직속의 **supervisor** 관리자

8.

해설 **전치사 덩어리**
'for your convenience'는 '편의를 위해'를 뜻하는 빈출 표현이다. 문맥상으로도 '편의를 위해, ~한 기능을 추가했다'로 적절하므로 (D)가 정답이다.

번역 당신의 편의를 위해, 우리는 당신의 휴대폰이 여러 개의 프로그램을 동시에 가동할 수 있도록 하는 기능을 추가했습니다.

어휘 **feature** 특징 **multiple** 다수의 **concurrently** 동시에 **occurrence** 발생 **elevation** 승진 **combination** 결합

공식으로 해결하는 **실전문제**   본책 p. 165

1. (D) **2.** (B) **3.** (D) **4.** (B) **5.** (A)
6. (D) **7.** (A) **8.** (C)

1.

해설 **형용사+to부정사**
be동사와 to부정사 사이에 빈칸이 있으므로 'be likely to(~할 것 같다)'가 유력하다. '코스가 취소될 것 같다'로 문맥도 적절하므로 (D)가 정답이다.

번역 일본어 A 레벨 코스는 낮은 등록률로 인해 취소될 가능성이 있다.

어휘 **cancel** 취소하다 **registration** 등록 **typical** 전형적인

2.

해설 **동사+목적어+to부정사**
be동사와 to부정사 사이에 빈칸이 있으므로 'be expected to(~할 것으로 예상되다)'가 적절하며 '주문품이 도착할 것으로 예상된다'로 해석도 자연스럽다. 따라서 (B)가 정답이다.

번역 우리가 지난 주에 페이퍼 밀 스토어에서 주문한 물품이 내일 오후까지 도착할 것으로 예상된다.

어휘 **place an order** 주문하다 **relate** 관련시키다

3.

해설 **동사+목적어+to부정사**
be동사와 to부정사 사이에 빈칸이 있으므로 'be scheduled to(~할 예정이다)'가 적절하며 'Mr. Cordell은 강연을 할 예정이다'로 해석도 자연스럽다. 따라서 (D)가 정답이다.

번역 휴스턴 비즈니스 협회의 창립자인 코델 씨는 불확실한 시기에 주식 시장에서 금융 손실을 최소화하는 방법에 대해 강연할 예정이다.

어휘 **founder** 창립자 **deliver a talk** 강연하다 **minimize** 최소화하다 **loss** 손실 **uncertain** 불확실한 **stock** 주식

67

4.

해설 명사+to부정사
수식구(for small business owners)를 지우면 빈칸은 to부정사 수식을 받는 자리이고 문맥상 '서로 연결될 기회'가 적절하므로 '기회'를 뜻하는 (B)가 정답이다.

번역 소셜 네트워크 서비스 회사인 스몰 얼쓰는 소규모 자영업자들이 온라인상으로 서로 연결될 수 있도록 좋은 기회를 제공한다.

어휘 owner 소유주 recruiter 채용업체 industry 산업 entrance 입구

5.

해설 명사+to부정사
전치사 in과 to부정사 사이에 빈칸이 있으므로 'in an effort to(~하기 위한 노력으로)'가 유력하다. '직원 생산성을 높이기 위한 노력으로'로 문맥도 적절하므로 (A)가 정답이다.

번역 직원 생산성을 높이기 위한 노력으로 회사는 보상 프로그램을 고려하고 있다.

어휘 productivity 생산성 incentive 보상(우대)책 operation 영업 achievement 업적

6.

해설 형용사+to부정사
be동사와 to부정사 사이에 빈칸이 있으므로 'be reluctant to(~하길 망설이다)'가 유력하다. 'Ms. Kasai는 새 프로젝트를 맡길 망설인다'로 문맥도 적절하므로 (D)가 정답이다.

번역 카사이 씨는 다음 달에 휴가를 계획하고 있기 때문에 새 프로젝트를 맡기를 꺼린다.

어휘 take on (일을) 맡다 responsive 즉각 대응하는 aware 알고 있는 knowledgeable 많이 아는

7.

해설 동사+목적어+to부정사
빈칸은 '목적어+to부정사' 앞이므로 목적보어로 to부정사가 오는 enabled가 적절하며 '직원들이 균형을 이룰 수 있도록 해 준다'로 해석도 자연스럽다. 따라서 (A)가 정답이다.

번역 탄력근무시간제는 직원들이 더 나은 일과 삶의 균형을 이룰 수 있도록 해 준다.

어휘 flexible working hours 탄력근무시간제 achieve 달성하다 balance 균형 emerge 부상하다

8.

해설 동사+목적어+to부정사
빈칸은 '목적어+to부정사' 앞이므로 목적보어로 to부정사가 오는 encourages가 적절하며 '구매자들이 더 많이 쓰도록 장려한다'로 해석도 자연스럽다. 따라서 (C)가 정답이다.

번역 온라인 소매 대기업인 나라존은 무료 배송을 제공함으로써 구매자들의 더 많은 소비를 장려한다.

어휘 retailer 소매업체 shipping 배송 feature 특별히 포함하다 acquire 습득하다

YBM TEST
본책 p. 166

1. (D)	2. (B)	3. (C)	4. (C)	5. (A)
6. (D)	7. (D)	8. (C)	9. (B)	10. (B)
11. (B)	12. (A)	13. (B)	14. (C)	15. (A)
16. (A)	17. (D)	18. (B)	19. (C)	20. (C)
21. (B)	22. (D)	23. (A)	24. (A)	25. (B)
26. (A)	27. (D)	28. (B)		

1.

해설 필수 형용사+that절
빈칸 뒤로 보이는 that절의 동사가 주어와 수일치가 되지 않고 동사원형이므로 '필수 형용사+that+주어+should+동사원형'에서 should가 생략된 구문임을 알 수 있다. 따라서 필수 형용사인 (D)가 정답이다.

번역 정기적인 안전 및 성능 검사가 모든 생산 장비에 필수적으로 행해지도록 해야 한다.

어휘 regular 정기적인 inspection 검사 automated 자동화된 disrupted 중단된

2.

해설 동사+명사
빈칸 뒤의 목적어가 the benefits이므로, 주로 사람목적어가 와서 '~에게'로 해석되는 convinces는 적절하지 않다. 문맥상 '혜택을 설명한다'가 적절하므로 (B)가 정답이다.

번역 우리의 새로운 15분 온라인 회의는 식품 및 제약 제조업체에 엑스레이 검사의 혜택을 설명한다.

어휘 webinar 온라인 회의 inspection 검사 pharmaceutical 제약 insert 삽입하다 convince 납득시키다

3.

해설 자동사+전치사
빈칸 뒤로 목적어가 보이지 않고 전치사 with가 있으므로 전치사 with와 어울려 '~를 준수하다'를 뜻하는 자동사 (C)가 정답이다.

번역 모든 부서 관리자들은 직원들이 회사 방침을 준수하도록 하는 것을 책임진다.

어휘 ensure 반드시 ~하게 하다 policy 방침 observe 준수하다 dedicate 전념하다 respond 응답하다

4.

해설 명사+to부정사
빈칸은 to부정사의 수식을 받는 자리이고 문맥상 '긍정적인 감정을 떠올리게 하는 능력'이 적절하므로 '능력'을 뜻하는 (C)가 정답이다.

번역 세계적으로 유명한 건축가인 대니얼 크레이그 씨는 건물에서 긍정적인 감정을 불러일으키는 능력으로 찬사를 받는다.

어휘 renowned 유명한 architect 건축가 ~로 칭찬 받다 evoke 떠올려 주다 emotion 감정

68

5.
해설 동사+명사
submit(제출하다)는 주로 서류와 짝을 이뤄 '~서류를 제출하다'로 자주 출제된다. 빈칸 뒤에 your request(당신의 요청서)가 목적어로 왔고 '요청서를 제출하세요'로 문맥상 적절하므로 (A)가 정답이다.

번역 CEPT 제품을 이용하는 데 도움이 필요하시면 우리의 온라인 지원 센터로 요청서를 제출하세요.

어휘 assistance 도움 request 요청(서) detach 떼다 apply 지원하다 vacate 비우다

6.
해설 동사+명사
make는 decision(결정)과 짝을 이뤄 '결정을 내리다'로 자주 출제되며, '취소할지에 대해 결정을 내리지 않았다'로 문맥상 적절하므로 (D)가 정답이다.

번역 정부는 원자력 발전소의 건설을 취소할지에 대해 아직 결정을 내리지 않았다.

어휘 have yet to 아직 ~하지 않았다 whether ~인지 아닌지 nuclear power plant 원자력 발전소 precaution 예방책 preference 선호 strategy 전략

7.
해설 동사 A 전치사 B
빈칸 뒤 전치사 into는 expand와 짝을 이뤄 'expand A into B(A를 B로 확장시키다)'로 쓰인다. '여객선 운항을 새 목적지로 확장한다'로 문맥상으로도 적절하므로 (D)가 정답이다.

번역 보스턴 해운 회사는 여객선 운항을 인근 해안 도시를 포함한 새로운 목적지로 확장할 계획이다.

어휘 ferry 여객선 destination 목적지 nearby 인근의 coastal 해안의

8.
해설 동사+목적어+to부정사
빈칸은 '목적어+to부정사' 앞이므로 목적보어로 to부정사가 오는 reminded가 적절하며 '참가자들이 평가서를 작성할 것을 상기시켰다'로 해석도 자연스럽다. 따라서 (C)가 정답이다.

번역 사회자는 워크숍이 끝날 때 참가자들이 평가서를 작성할 것을 상기시켰다.

어휘 presenter 사회자 participant 참가자 complete 작성하다 evaluation form 평가서 declare 선언하다 specify 명시하다

9.
해설 전치사 덩어리
빈칸 뒤 further notice(추후 통지)는 until과 짝을 이뤄 'until further notice(추후 통지 때까지)'로 쓰인다. 문맥상으로도 '추후 통지 때까지 회의가 연기되었다'로 적절하므로 (B)가 정답이다.

번역 뜻밖에 일정이 겹치는 바람에 마을 의회 회의가 추가 통지 때까지 연기되었음을 유의하세요.

어휘 council 의회 postpone 연기하다 unforeseen 뜻밖의 scheduling conflict 일정 겹침

10.
해설 동사+명사
address(다루다, 고심하다)는 주로 문제나 걱정거리 등과 짝을 이뤄 '문제/걱정거리를 다루다(고심하다)'로 자주 출제된다. 빈칸 뒤에 concerns(우려)가 목적어로 왔고 '우려 사항을 고심하다'로 문맥상 적절하므로 (B)가 정답이다. 참고로, 다른 보기의 동사들은 모두 자동사이므로 뒤에 목적어가 올 수 없다.

번역 비록 당신이 회사의 안전 책임자라 하더라도 안전 관련 우려 사항은 당신의 직속 상사와 먼저 상담해야 한다.

어휘 concern 우려 immediate 직속의

11.
해설 동사 A 전치사 B
빈칸 뒤 전치사 into는 divide와 짝을 이뤄 'divide A into B(A를 B로 나누다)'로 쓰인다. '연구 목표를 세 범주로 나눈다'로 문맥상으로도 적절하므로 (B)가 정답이다.

번역 STC 실험실의 선임 연구원은 연구 목표를 세 개의 다른 범주로 나눈다.

어휘 senior 상위의 laboratory 실험실 objective 목표 category 범주

12.
해설 동사+목적어+to부정사
be동사와 to부정사 사이에 빈칸이 있으므로 'be urged to(~하도록 권고된다)'가 적절하며 '건설 근로자들은 추가적인 예방 조치와 휴식을 취하도록 권고된다'로 해석도 자연스럽다. 따라서 (A)가 정답이다.

번역 건설 근로자들은 지역의 기온이 급등함에 따라 추가적인 예방 조치와 휴식을 취하도록 권고된다.

어휘 precaution 예방 조치 temperature 기온 soar 급등하다

13.
해설 자동사+전치사
빈칸 뒤로 목적어가 보이지 않고 전치사 on이 있으므로 전치사 on과 어울려 '~에 집중하다'를 뜻하는 자동사 (B)가 정답이다.

번역 바얏 은행은 추가로 지사를 개설할 계획이 없으며 온라인 뱅킹 서비스를 성장시키는 데 집중할 것이다.

어휘 branch 지사 operate 운영하다 benefit 유익하다 propose 제안하다

14.
해설 목적어가 '~에게'인 동사
빈칸 뒤로 '사람목적어+that절'이 와서 '참가자들에게 that~을 알리다'로 해석되므로 (C)가 정답이다. 다른 보기의 동사들은 that절과 동사 사이에 목적어가 오지 않는다.

번역 참가자들에게 지난 워크숍의 모든 프로젝트가 우리의 웹 사이트에 업로드되었음을 알리게 되어 기쁩니다.

어휘 participant 참가자 upload 업로드하다

69

15.

해설 동사 A 전치사 B
빈칸 뒤 전치사 for는 reimburse와 짝을 이뤄 'reimburse A for B(A에게 B에 대해 환급해 주다)'로 쓰인다. 'reimburse A for B'가 수동태로 전환되어 'be reimbursed for' 형태로 '출장 비용에 대해 환급 받기 위해서'로 문맥상으로도 적절하므로 (A)가 정답이다.

번역 출장 비용을 환급 받기 위해서 직원들은 모든 원본 영수증과 함께 출장 비용 보고서를 제출해야 한다.

어휘 expense 비용 along with ~와 함께 original 원래의 receipt 영수증 entitle 자격을 주다 obtain 얻다

16.

해설 전치사 덩어리
빈칸 앞의 전치사 upon은 receipt(수령)과 짝을 이뤄 '수령하자마자'로 자주 쓰인다. '경보를 받자마자'로 해석도 적절하므로 (A)가 정답이다.

번역 경보를 받자마자 우리의 훈련된 보안 시스템 운영자들이 귀사의 보안 정책에 따라 행동을 취할 것이다.

어휘 alert 경보 security 보안 operator 운영자 in accordance with ~에 따라서 corporate 기업의 entry 입장 appeal 항소, 매력

17.

해설 동사+목적어+to부정사
빈칸은 '목적어+to부정사' 앞이므로 목적보어로 to부정사가 오는 allow가 적절하며 '멤버들이 등록하도록 허용할 것이다'로 해석도 자연스럽다. 따라서 (D)가 정답이다.

번역 와인 자격증 세미나는 공간이 한정되어 있으므로, 일반인에 자리를 제공하기 전에 우리 멤버들이 등록할 수 있도록 허용할 것입니다.

어휘 space 공간 limited 한정된 certification 증명, 증명서 부여 register 등록하다 spot 자리 cooperate 협력하다 reflect 반영하다, 반사하다 include 포함하다

18.

해설 제안/요구 동사+that절
빈칸 뒤로 보이는 that절의 동사가 주어와 수일치가 되지 않고 동사원형이므로 '제안/요구 동사+that+주어+should+동사원형'에서 should가 생략된 구문임을 알 수 있다. 따라서 제안/요구 동사인 (B)가 정답이다.

번역 영업부 과장은 그가 컨퍼런스로 떠나기 전에 숙소 및 교통편이 준비될 것을 요청했다.

어휘 accommodation 숙소 transportation 교통편 arrange 준비(주선)하다 indicate 나타내다 reserve 예약하다

19.

해설 전치사 덩어리
빈칸 앞의 전치사 in은 advance와 짝을 이뤄 'in advance (사전에)'로 자주 쓰인다. '사전에 예약을 한다'로 해석도 적절하므로 (C)가 정답이다.

번역 우리 식물원은 방문객들이 많기 때문에 사전에 예약할 것을 강력히 권고 드립니다.

어휘 volume 양, 수량 botanical garden 식물원 reservation 예약 series 연속, 시리즈 agency 대행사

20.

해설 형용사+to부정사
be동사와 to부정사 사이에 빈칸이 있으므로 'be bound to(반드시 ~하다)'가 유력하다. '가격이 반드시 떨어진다'로 문맥도 적절하므로 (C)가 정답이다.

번역 지역의 인구가 감소하고 있다는 점을 고려해 볼 때 시간이 가면서 부동산 가격이 반드시 하락할 것이다.

어휘 given ~을 고려해 볼 때 population 인구 region 지역 decline 감소하다 property 부동산

21-24

> 〈더 뮤지엄 익스플로러〉는 버밍엄의 많은 박물관에서 진행 중인 행사를 소개하는 라디오 토크쇼이다. 매주마다 박물관 한 곳이 특집으로 구성될 것이며, 각 박물관은 대략 두 달마다 한 번 정도 다루어질 것이다. 매주, 그 주의 특집 박물관에서 나온 초대 손님이 토크쇼에 나와 전시회나 특정 행사의 테마와 같은 주제를 이야기할 것이다. 초대 손님은 박물관 직원이나 전시회 출품자가 될 것이다.
>
> 본 프로그램은 매주 90분 간 방송될 것이다. 그것은 같은 주 동안 한 번 재방송될 수도 있다. 우리의 DJ 베키 앤더슨 씨는 청취자들이 전화를 걸어 질문을 하고 그들이 관심 있을 만한 전시회나 행사를 알아낼 수 있도록 장려할 것이다. 〈더 뮤지엄 익스플로러〉는 청취자들이 버밍엄의 문화 생활에 좀 더 직접적으로 연결될 수 있도록 하는 것을 목표로 한다.

어휘 museum 박물관 explorer 탐험가 showcase 소개하다 ongoing 진행 중인 occur 일어나다 per ~당 allow 허용하다 cover 다루다 feature 특별히 포함하다, 특징으로 삼다 discuss 논의하다 theme 테마 exhibition 전시회 specific 특정한 exhibitor 전시회 출품자 broadcast 방송하다 weekly 매주의 encourage 장려하다 exhibit 전시회 interested 관심 있는 intend to ~할 의도이다 provide 제공하다 direct 직접적인 connection 연결 cultural 문화의

21.

해설 동사 능동 vs.수동
빈칸 앞에 조동사가 있으므로 동사원형이 와야 한다. 또한 빈칸 뒤에 목적어가 없고 '박물관 한 곳이 특집으로 구성될 것이다'로 해석되므로 수동태인 (B)가 정답이다.

22.

해설 부사 자리
빈칸은 뒤에 있는 부사 once 앞에 덤으로 붙어 once를 수식하므로 (D)가 정답이다. 특히 approximately는 숫자 앞에서 숫자 수식 부사로 자주 출제된다.

23.

해설 명사 어휘
'전시회나 특정 행사의 테마와 같은 ___을 토론한다'고 했으므로 문맥상 topic(주제)이 가장 적절하다. 따라서 (A)가 정답이다.

어휘 benefit 혜택 composition 구성 article 기사

24.

해설 문장 고르기
빈칸 앞 문장에서 '본 프로그램은 매주 90분 간 방송될 것이다'라고 했고, (A)에서 프로그램을 it으로 받아 재방송될 수 있다고 했으므로 자연스럽게 연결된다. 따라서 (A)가 정답이다.

번역 (A) 그것은 같은 주 동안 한 번 재방송될 수도 있다.
(B) 그 쇼는 박물관 후원자들에 의해 부분적으로 제작될 것이다.
(C) 〈더 뮤지엄 익스플로러〉는 2개의 주요 청취자 그룹을 목표로 삼는다.
(D) 청취자들은 너무 바빠서 실제로 박물관에 갈 수 없을지도 모른다.

25-28

수신: 듀란트 에너지 사의 모든 관리자들
발신: 케빈 듀란트
날짜: 4월 6일
제목: 특별 회의

우리 회사의 운영에 상당한 영향을 미칠 수도 있는 경제 및 금융 여건에 많은 진전이 있었습니다. 이러한 변화하는 상황에 대처하기 위해 우리는 즉각적인 조치를 취해야 합니다. 그러므로, 우리는 특별 회의를 소집하기로 결정했습니다.

4월 11일 오전 11시에 회의실 C에서 회의가 개최될 것입니다. 우리 토론에 기여할 수 있는 어떠한 정보라도 있으면 주저하지 말고 회의로 가져오세요. 회의 안건에 관한 첨부파일을 동봉하니 확인하시기 바랍니다. 관리자급 직원은 전원 회의에 참석해야 합니다. 만약 일정이 겹치거나 다른 어떠한 이유로 회의에 참석할 수 없다면 내게 사전에 알려주세요.

어휘 development 개발, 새로이 전개된 국면 economic 경제의 financial 금융의 situation 상황 significant 중요한 impact 영향 operation 운영 immediate 즉각적인 measure 조치 deal with 다루다 changing 변화하는 circumstance 상황 conference room 회의실 contribute 기여하다 significantly 상당히 discussion 토론 mandatory 의무적인 managerial 관리의 present 출석한 be unable to ~할 수 없는 scheduling conflict 일정이 겹침 inform 알리다 beforehand 사전에

25.

해설 관계사
빈칸은 뒤에 있는 절을 연결해 앞에 있는 명사 situation을 수식하는 자리이므로 관계사가 와야 한다. 또한 빈칸 뒤의 절에 주어가 빠져 있으므로 주격 관계사인 (B)가 정답이다.

26.

해설 접속부사
보기 (A)의 접속부사 'therefore(그러므로)'는 인과 관계를 나타내므로, 앞 문장은 원인, 뒷 문장은 결과로 연결되어야 한다. 앞 문장에서 '변화하는 상황에 대처하기 위해 즉각적인 조치를 취해야 한다'고 했고, '그러므로 특별 회의를 소집하기로 결정했다'는 앞 내용에 대한 결과로 자연스럽게 연결되므로 (A)가 정답이다.

번역 (A) 그러므로, 우리는 특별 회의를 소집하기로 결정했습니다.
(B) 회사는 곧 현재 상황으로부터 회복될 것입니다.
(C) 이는 우리가 상황이 곧 호전될 것이라고 자신하기 때문입니다.
(D) 우리는 이것이 단지 임시 조치일 뿐이라는 것을 보장드립니다.

27.

해설 접속부사
빈칸은 앞뒤 문장의 연결관계를 보여주는 접속부사를 고르는 문제이다. 앞 문장에서 '회의에 의무적으로 참석해야 한다'라고 했는데, 뒷 문장에서 '참석 못할 경우 사전에 연락 달라'며 앞 내용과 반대되는 상황을 이야기하므로 '하지만'을 뜻하며 역접관계를 나타내는 (D)가 정답이다.

28.

해설 명사 어휘
'일정 ___이든 다른 이유든 회의에 참석 못할 경우'라고 했으므로 빈칸에 들어갈 말은 회의 불참 이유가 되면서 '일정'과 복합명사를 이뤄 '일정이 겹침'을 뜻하는 (B)가 정답이다.

어휘 suggestion 제안 request 요청 claim 주장

Unit 12 어휘 2

공식으로 해결하는 실전문제   본책 p. 171

| 1. (A) | 2. (D) | 3. (B) | 4. (D) | 5. (A) |
| 6. (B) | 7. (B) | 8. (C) | | |

1.

해설 닮은꼴 형용사
빈칸은 명사 benefits를 수식하는 자리이므로 사람의 감정 상태를 나타내는 satisfied(만족한)와 태도를 나타내는 considerate(사려 깊은)은 적절하지 않다. 문맥상 '비슷한 복지를 제공해서 두 회사 사이에서 결정을 못 하고 있다'가 적절하므로 (A)가 적절하다.

번역 DLC Contractors, Inc.와 Yuma Associates, Inc. 두 회사 모두 비슷한 복지를 제공하므로 Ms. Long은 여전히 두 곳의 일자리 제안 사이에서 결정을 내리지 못했다.

어휘 benefits 복지 혜택 comparable 비슷한 reflected 반영된

2.

해설 형용사+전치사
빈칸 주변이 'are ___ to'이므로 'be subject to(~의 영향을 받는, ~에 해당하다)'인지 확인한다. '모든 제품은 철저한 검사를 받는다'로 적절하므로 (D)가 정답이다.

번역 미켈 텍스타일의 캄보디아 공장에서 생산된 모든 제품은 배송되기 전에 철저한 검사를 받는다.

어휘 goods 제품 thorough 철저한 inspection 검사 fragile 손상되기 쉬운 subjective 주관적인 cautious 조심스러운

3.
해설 형용사+전치사
빈칸 주변이 'are _____ for'이므로 'be eligible for(~에 자격이 되다)'인지 확인한다. '~한 고객들은 무료 배송에 자격이 된다'로 적절하므로 (B)가 정답이다.

번역 온라인으로 최소 50달러를 주문하신 고객들은 무료 배송에 자격이 됩니다.

어휘 value 가치 standard 기준 shipping 배송 convenient 편리한 verified 확인된 valuable 소중한

4.
해설 형용사+전치사
빈칸 뒤 전치사 to는 responsive와 짝을 이루어 '~에 즉각 대응하는'을 뜻한다. '회사가 변화하는 산업에 즉각 대응하게 만들기 위한 노력'으로 문맥상 적절하므로 (D)가 정답이다.

번역 운영을 간소화하려는 AT 엔터프라이즈의 계획은 회사가 변화하는 산업에 좀 더 즉각적으로 대응하도록 만들려는 노력의 일부이다.

어휘 streamline 간소화하다 operation 운영 observant 관찰력 있는 forceful 단호한 responsive 즉각 대응하는

5.
해설 닮은꼴 형용사
빈칸은 명사 Internet connections(인터넷 연결)를 수식하는 자리이고, 인터넷 연결을 수식하는 말로는 'reliable(믿을 만한)'이 가장 적절하므로 (A)가 정답이다. 'reliant(의지하는)'와 혼동하지 않도록 주의한다.

번역 위토피아는 고객들에게 믿을 만한 인터넷 서비스를 제공하므로 서비스가 끊길까봐 걱정할 필요가 없습니다.

어휘 connection 연결 interruption 중단 considerable 상당한 courteous 공손한

6.
해설 형용사 어휘
빈칸은 주어 the smartphone market을 수식하는 자리이고, '새 회사들이 다른 브랜드들로부터 고객을 유치하려고 노력한다'는 내용으로 보아 '스마트폰 시장'을 수식하는 말로는 '경쟁이 있는'이 가장 적절하므로 (B)가 정답이다.

번역 공고한 브랜드들로부터 고객을 유치하기 위해 노력하는 새 회사들로 인해 스마트폰 시장은 점점 경쟁이 치열해지고 있다.

어휘 increasingly 점점 lure 유혹하다 established 자리 잡은 domestic 국내의 steady 꾸준한 frequent 빈번한

7.
해설 형용사+전치사
빈칸 주변이 'has been _____ with'이므로 'be pleased with(~에 기뻐하다)'인지 확인한다. '경영진이 결과에 기뻐한다'로 적절하므로 (B)가 정답이다.

번역 회사의 경영진은 새로운 OLED TV 세트를 위한 적극적인 광고의 결과에 기뻐한다.

어휘 vigorous 활발한 impressive 인상적인 reflected 반영된 enjoyable 즐거운

8.
해설 닮은꼴 형용사
빈칸은 one-week membership(일주일 멤버십)을 수식하는 자리이고, 일주일 멤버십을 수식하는 말로는 'complimentary(무료의)'가 가장 적절하므로 (C)가 정답이다. 'complimentary'는 'free'로 자주 패러프레이징 되며 complementary(상호보완적인)와 혼동하지 않도록 주의한다.

번역 무료 일주일 멤버십에 자격이 되시려면 우리 피트니스 센터를 처음으로 이용하시는 분이어야 합니다.

어휘 be eligible for ~에 자격이 되다 variable 변동이 심한 subsequent 그 다음의 promising 유망한

✦ 공식으로 해결하는 실전문제   본책 p. 173

| 1. (C) | 2. (B) | 3. (B) | 4. (A) | 5. (B) |
| 6. (A) | 7. (D) | 8. (D) | | |

1.
해설 형용사+명사
빈칸 뒤 time은 형용사 limited와 짝을 이뤄 '한정된 시간'을 뜻하는 빈출 표현이다. 문맥상 '한정된 시간 동안만 할인받을 수 있다'로 적절하므로 (C)가 정답이다.

번역 모비아의 스마트워치는 현재 한정된 시간 동안만 온라인스토어에서 할인된 가격으로 구입 가능하다.

어휘 available 이용(구입) 가능한 limited 한정된 prominent 중요한

2.
해설 in+명사+전치사
빈칸 주변이 'in _____ of'이므로 'in recognition of(~을 인정하여)'인지 확인한다. '당신이 애용해 준 점을 인정하여'로 문맥상 적절하므로 (B)가 정답이다. replacement도 in replacement of(~을 대신하여)로 쓰이지만 문맥상 어울리지 않는다.

번역 애용해 주신 대한 답례로 당신에게 75파운드 상당의 상품권을 드리게 되어 기쁩니다.

어휘 loyal 충성스러운 patronage 애용 gift certificate 상품권 worth ~의 가치가 있는 replacement 교체

3.
해설 형용사+명사
leading(선도적인)은 '회사, 제조업체, 브랜드' 등과 자주 짝을 이루어 '선도 업체'를 뜻하는 빈출 형용사이다. 빈칸 뒤의 manufacturers(제조업체들)와 어울려 '선도 업체들 중 하나가 되었다'로 문맥상 적절하므로 (B)가 정답이다.

번역 메이콘 테크놀로지의 혁신을 향한 전념이 회사가 선진 컴퓨터 칩의 선도 제조업체들 중 하나가 될 수 있게 해 주었다.

어휘 commitment 전념 innovation 혁신 advanced 선진의 selective 선택적인 rigorous 철저한 delicate 연약한

4.

해설 in+명사+전치사

빈칸 주변이 'in _____ with'이므로 'in cooperation with(~와 협력하여)'인지 확인한다. 'Lindberg School of Education과 협력하여 디자인된'으로 문맥상 적절하므로 (A)가 정답이다.

번역 Birmingham City Schools는 Lindberg School of Education과 협력하여 디자인된 교육 프로그램을 채택할 계획이다.

어휘 adopt 채택하다 placement 취업 알선 institution 기관 reputation 평판

5.

해설 형용사+명사

outstanding(뛰어난)은 주로 '업적, 경력, 성과, 작업(작품)' 등과 자주 짝을 이루는 형용사이다. 빈칸 뒤의 poetry(시)는 일종의 작품, 성과이므로 outstanding과 잘 어울리며 '뛰어난 시'로 의미도 적절하다. 따라서 (B)가 정답이다.

번역 케이티 페리스는 뛰어난 시를 쓸 수 있는 잠재력을 입증해 한 재단 장학금의 가장 어린 수상자가 되었다.

어휘 recipient 수령인 foundation 재단 grant 보조금 demonstrate 입증하다, 보여주다 potential 잠재력 relative 상대적인 numerous 많은 transitional 과도기의

6.

해설 in+명사+전치사

빈칸 주변이 'in the _____ of'이므로 'in the vicinity of(~의 근처에)'인지 확인한다. '~ 해변 근처에 위치한'으로 문맥상 적절하므로 (A)가 정답이다. majority도 in the majority of(~의 대부분에)로 쓸 수 있지만 문맥상 어울리지 않는다.

번역 멜러하이드의 아름다운 금빛 해변에 가까이 위치한 에버그린 호텔은 안락함을 제공합니다.

어휘 comfort 안락 majority 다수 direction 방향 immediacy 신속성

7.

해설 in+명사+전치사

빈칸 주변이 'in _____ with'이므로 'in compliance with(~을 준수하여)'인지 확인한다. '용수 사용 규정을 준수하여'로 문맥상 적절하므로 (D)가 정답이다.

번역 농장주들이 용수 이용 규정을 준수하도록 하기 위해 지침이 수립되었다.

어휘 guideline 지침 establish 수립하다 ensure 보장하다 owner 소유주 regulation 규정 activation 활성화 achievement 성취 permission 허가

8.

해설 형용사+명사

빈칸은 areas(지역)를 수식하는 자리이고, 장소 명사를 꾸미는 형용사로는 surrounding(주변의)이 가장 적절하므로 정답은 (D)이다. surrounding은 area와 자주 짝을 이루므로 'the surrounding area'를 통째로 암기하도록 한다.

번역 에브리존 와이어리스는 허리케인 어마가 강타한 채팀과 주변 지역의 고객들에게 최대 2GB의 무료 데이터를 제공하고 있습니다.

어휘 hurricane 허리케인 compatible 호환이 되는 supplementary 보충의 consequential ~에 따른

공식으로 해결하는 **실전문제** 본책 p. 175

| 1. (B) | 2. (A) | 3. (C) | 4. (A) | 5. (D) |
| 6. (C) | 7. (B) | 8. (C) | | |

1.

해설 부사 짝꿍 표현

immediately는 after 앞에 자주 붙어 'after~'구문을 수식하며 '~한 후 즉시'를 뜻한다. '검사가 끝난 직후'로 문맥상 자연스러우므로 (B)가 정답이다.

번역 롸이트 씨는 검사가 완료된 직후 부동산 소유주를 만나기로 했다.

어휘 arrange 마련하다, 주선하다 property 부동산 owner 소유주 inspection 검사

2.

해설 부사 짝꿍 표현

정도를 나타내는 부사 slightly(약간)는 증가/감소 의미의 동사를 주로 수식한다. 빈칸은 '감소'를 뜻하는 동사 fell을 수식하는 자리이고 '약간 떨어졌다'로 문맥상 적절하므로 (A)가 정답이다.

번역 면화의 평균 가격이 부진한 수요의 영향을 받아 약간 떨어졌다.

어휘 average 평균의 raw 가공되지 않은 cotton 면직물 affect 영향을 미치다 sluggish 부진한 demand 수요 simultaneously 동시에 availably 얻을 수 있게

3.

해설 현재+빈도부사

빈칸 앞의 동사가 현재 시제이므로 부사 typically가 잘 어울린다. '점검이 보통 밤에 행해진다'로 문맥상 적절하므로 (C)가 정답이다.

번역 정례적인 항공기 점검은 5시간 이상 소요되며 보통 밤에 행해진다.

어휘 routine 정례적인 aircraft 항공기 maintenance 유지 보수 formerly 이전에 loosely 느슨하게 typically 보통 previously 이전에

4.

해설 현재+빈도부사

빈칸 앞의 동사가 현재 시제로 평소 반복적으로 일어나는 일에 대해 언급하고 있으므로 빈도부사가 잘 어울린다. '정기적으로 평가할 수 있게 해 준다'로 문맥상 적절하므로 (A)가 정답이다.

번역 핀텍의 분기별 성과 평가는 매니저들로 하여금 직원들의 업무 수행을 정기적으로 평가할 수 있게 해 준다.

어휘 quarterly 분기별 performance 성과 review 평가 assess 평가하다 inconclusively 결정적이 아니고

5.

해설 현재+빈도부사

빈칸 앞의 동사가 현재 시제이므로 부사 generally가 잘 어울린다. '일반적으로 사용되는 가스'로 문맥상 적절하므로 (D)가 정답이다.

번역 린덴 파워는 화학 처리 공정에 일반적으로 사용되는 공업용 가스의 선두 공급업체이다.

어휘 leading 선두의 supplier 공급업체 industrial 공업용의 chemical processing 화학 처리 obediently 고분고분하게 persistently 고집스레 considerately 사려 깊게 generally 일반적으로

6.

해설 부사 짝꿍 표현

빈칸 앞의 'unless+p.p.(~되지 않으면)'와 잘 어울리는 부사는 '달리'를 뜻하는 otherwise이다. '달리 언급되지 않으면~'으로 문맥상 적절하므로 (C)가 정답이다.

번역 달리 언급되지 않으면, 일정표에 나와 있는 모든 시간은 현지 시간을 나타낸다.

어휘 state 언급하다 itinerary 일정표 represent 나타내다 local 현지의 occasionally 가끔 otherwise 달리

7.

해설 현재+빈도부사

빈칸 뒤의 동사가 현재 시제이므로 빈도부사 occasionally가 잘 어울린다. '가끔 프로젝트를 외부에 위탁한다'로 문맥상 적절하므로 (B)가 정답이다.

번역 와우 어카운팅은 운영비를 절감하기 위해 복잡한 IT 프로젝트를 가끔 외부에 위탁한다.

어휘 outsource 외부에 위탁하다 complex 복잡한 reduce 줄이다 operating expense 운영비 occasionally 가끔 somewhat 약간

8.

해설 부사 짝꿍 표현

at least(최소한)는 숫자와 잘 어울리는 부사이다. 빈칸 뒤에 숫자 50이 있고, 문맥상 '최소한 50명을 수용할 수 있는'이 적절하므로 (C)가 정답이다.

번역 휴 허먼은 핀리 씨의 퇴임식을 위해 최소 50명의 손님을 수용할 수 있는 장소를 물색 중이다.

어휘 venue 장소 accommodate 수용하다 retirement 은퇴 even so 그렇기는 하지만

YBM TEST

본책 p. 176

1. (C)	2. (A)	3. (D)	4. (C)	5. (A)
6. (C)	7. (C)	8. (B)	9. (C)	10. (D)
11. (B)	12. (D)	13. (A)	14. (A)	15. (B)
16. (B)	17. (A)	18. (D)	19. (D)	20. (D)
21. (C)	22. (A)	23. (B)	24. (D)	25. (D)
26. (C)	27. (D)	28. (B)		

1.

해설 in+명사+전치사

빈칸 주변이 'in ____ of'이므로 'in anticipation of(~을 예상하여)'인지 확인한다. '배송이 급증할 것을 예상하여'로 문맥상 적절하므로 (C)가 정답이다. receipt도 in receipt of(~을 받은)로 쓰이지만 문맥상 어울리지 않는다.

번역 배송 물량이 급증할 것을 예상해 Fastwheels는 휴가철 동안 배송을 도울 임시 근로자 약 300명을 고용할 것이다.

어휘 surge 급증 temporary 임시의 estimate 견적 strategy 전략 receipt 영수증, 수령

2.

해설 부사 짝꿍 표현

nearly(거의)는 숫자와 잘 어울리는 부사이다. 빈칸 뒤에 숫자 25가 있고, 문맥상 '거의 25분이 걸린다'로 적절하므로 (A)가 정답이다.

번역 여객선 터미널에서 리조트까지는 고속도로에 교통량이 적을 때는 거의 25분이 걸린다.

어휘 ferry 여객선 nearby 인근의

3.

해설 현재+빈도부사

빈칸 뒤의 동사가 현재 시제이므로 빈도부사가 잘 어울린다. '주기적으로 이메일 뉴스레터를 보낸다'로 문맥상 적절하므로 (D)가 정답이다.

번역 뮤 퍼니싱은 고객들에게 신제품과 최신 가구 트렌드를 주로 보여주는 이메일 뉴스레터를 주기적으로 발송한다.

어휘 highlight 강조하다 latest 최신의 briefly 잠시, 간단히 periodically 주기적으로

4.

해설 형용사+전치사

빈칸 주변이 'are ____ from'이므로 'be exempt from(~를 면제받다)'인지 확인한다. 문맥상 '등록을 면제받는다'가 적절하므로 (C)가 정답이다. separate도 'be separate from(~와 분리되다)'으로 from과 잘 어울리지만 문맥상 어울리지 않는다.

번역 시의회는 최대 5000달러 이하의 연간 소득이 있는 현지 장인들은 새로운 세법 하에 사업자 등록에서 면제된다고 밝혔다.

어휘 artisan 장인 income 소득 registration 등록 tax 세금 skillful 숙련된 respective 각자의 separate 분리된

5.

해설 형용사+명사
빈칸은 store policy(가게 방침)을 수식하는 자리이고, 가게 방침을 수식하는 형용사로는 'revised(개정된)'이 가장 적절하므로 (A)가 정답이다. revised는 특히 'policy, schedule, plan, edition' 등과 자주 짝을 이룬다.

번역 개정된 가게 방침의 사본이 전 올라이트 직원들에게 일주일 내로 배포되어야 한다.

어휘 copy 사본 policy 방침 distribute 배포하다 pure 순수한 obliged 고마운 slight 약간의

6.

해설 부사 짝꿍 표현
빈칸은 위치를 뜻하는 located를 수식하는 자리이므로 centrally(중앙에)가 잘 어울린다. 따라서 (C)가 정답이다. centrally 이외에도 located를 수식하는 부사로 'conveniently (편리하게), ideally(이상적으로)'도 암기해 두자.

번역 빅토리아 역은 런던의 중심부에 위치해 있어서 도시 내 대부분의 장소로 편리하게 이동할 수 있다.

어휘 located 위치한 access 접근 location 장소 formerly 이전에 intentionally 의도적으로

7.

해설 닮은꼴 형용사
빈칸은 명사 advantages(이점)를 수식하는 형용사 자리이고, '이점'을 수식하는 말로는 'various(다양한)'가 가장 적절하므로 (C)가 정답이다. 'variable(변하기 쉬운)'과 혼동하지 않도록 주의한다.

번역 Z-Mobile은 정규 고객에게 추가 서비스에 대한 15% 할인과 같은 다양한 혜택을 제공한다.

어휘 regular 정기적인 advantage 이점 additional 추가의 variety 다양성 vary 서로 다르다

8.

해설 부사 짝꿍 표현
빈칸은 to부정사 수식구(to prevent~)를 지우면, 완전한 절에 덤으로 붙어 동사 change를 수식하는 부사 자리이므로 접속사인 as soon as는 답이 될 수 없다. 문맥상 '의심이 들면, 즉시 비밀번호를 변경해야 한다'가 적절하므로 (B)가 정답이다.

번역 만약 로그인 정보가 도난되었다고 의심이 든다면, 당신의 계정에 무단접근을 예방하기 위해 즉시 비밀번호를 변경해야 합니다.

어휘 suspect 의심하다 stolen 도난 당한 prevent 예방하다 unauthorized 승인되지 않은 access 접근 prominently 현저히

9.

해설 부사 짝꿍 표현
정도를 나타내는 부사 significantly(상당히)는 증가/감소 의미의 동사를 주로 수식한다. 빈칸은 '증가'를 뜻하는 increase를 수식하는 자리이고 '상당히 증가할 것으로~'로 문맥상 적절하므로 (C)가 정답이다.

번역 매우 성공적인 광고 덕분에 제노텍은 해당 분기 동안 수익이 상당히 증가할 것으로 예상한다.

어휘 advertising 광고 revenue 수익 current 현재의 quarter 분기 evenly 고르게 exclusively 오로지 eagerly 간절히

10.

해설 미래+shortly
빈칸 앞의 동사가 미래 시제이므로 '곧'이라는 뜻으로 미래를 나타내는 shortly가 잘 어울린다. '곧 당신에게 돌아올 것이다'로 문맥상 적절하므로 (D)가 정답이다.

번역 질문에 답변이 늦어 죄송합니다만 우리의 고객 서비스 책임자가 곧 답변을 드릴 것입니다.

어휘 delay 지연 head 책임자 cooperatively 협조적으로 permissibly 허용되어 abruptly 갑자기 shortly 곧

11.

해설 형용사+전치사
빈칸 뒤 전치사 of는 capable과 짝을 이루어 '~할 수 있는'을 뜻한다. '간단한 대화를 할 수 있는 로봇'으로 문맥상 적절하므로 (B)가 정답이다.

번역 판타지아 백화점은 간단한 대화를 할 수 있는 로봇을 본점에서 선보일 것이라고 월요일에 발표했다.

어휘 introduce 소개하다 conversation 대화 defective 결함이 있는 practical 실용적인 perceptive 통찰력이 있는

12.

해설 닮은꼴 형용사
빈칸은 명사 conditions(환경, 상황)를 수식하는 자리이고, '정부의 집념이 외국인 투자를 위한 ___ 환경을 조성했다'는 내용으로 보아 '환경'을 수식하는 말로는 '유리한, 좋은'이 가장 적절하므로 (D)가 정답이다.

번역 기업 친화적인 세제 개편에 대한 정부의 집념이 제조 산업에 있어 외국인 투자에 유리한 환경을 조성했다.

어휘 government 정부 commitment 전념 reform 개혁 investment 투자 variable 변하기 쉬운 considerable 상당한 proposed 제안된 favorable 유리한, 좋은

13.

해설 형용사+명사
sizable(상당한 크기의)은 주로 '수요(demand), 시장(market)' 등과 짝을 이루어 '상당한 규모의 수요/시장'의 구문으로 출제된다. 빈칸 뒤의 demand와 어울려 '상당한 수요가 있는 것 같다'로 문맥상 적절하므로 (A)가 정답이다.

번역 새 케이폰에 대한 상당한 수요가 있어 보이는 반면 1000달러가 넘는 높은 가격은 방해 요인이 될 수 있다.

어휘 **demand** 수요 **hindrance** 방해 요인 **spacious** 넓은

14.
해설 부사 짝꿍 표현
정도를 나타내는 부사 markedly(두드러지게)는 증가/감소 의미의 동사를 주로 수식한다. 빈칸은 '증가'를 뜻하는 동사 have increased를 수식하는 자리이고 '두드러지게 증가했다'로 문맥상 적절하므로 (A)가 정답이다.

번역 화이트 박사의 연구는 북태평양에서 대형 폭풍의 빈도와 강도가 두드러지게 증가해 왔다는 것을 보여준다.

어휘 **reveal** 드러내다 **frequency** 빈도 **intensity** 강도 **extreme** 극심한 **dividedly** 분리되어 **intimately** 친밀히 **consequently** 그 결과

15.
해설 in+명사+전치사
빈칸 주변이 'in ____ with'이므로 'in accordance with(~에 따라서)'인지 확인한다. '규정에 따라서'로 문맥상 적절하므로 (B)가 정답이다.

번역 새로운 비자 규정에 따라 오직 국외로 나가는 티켓이 있는 사람들만 여행객 비자를 발급받게 될 것이다.

어휘 **regulation** 규정 **onward ticket** 해외로 나가는 티켓 **grant** 수여하다

16.
해설 형용사+전치사
빈칸 주변이 'is ____ on'이므로 'be dependent on(~에 의존하는, ~에 달려 있는)'인지 확인한다. '공원 조성이 자금 조성에 달려 있다'로 적절하므로 (B)가 정답이다.

번역 그린힐 로에 새 공원을 조성하는 것은 민간 부문의 협력사들로부터의 자금 조성에 달려 있다.

어휘 **financing** 자금 조성 **private** 사적인 **sector** 부문 **dependable** 믿을 만한 **distinguished** 유명한

17.
해설 부사 짝꿍 표현
빈칸 앞뒤의 unless와 p.p.는 주로 otherwise(달리)의 수식을 받아 '달리 ~되지 않으면(unless otherwise p.p.)'을 뜻한다. 문맥상 '달리 통보되지 않으면'으로 적절하므로 (A)가 정답이다.

번역 달리 통지 받지 않는 한, 전 직원들은 아침 10시에 교육에 참석해야 한다.

어휘 **notify** 통지하다 **training session** 교육 **indeed** 정말 **accordingly** 그에 맞춰 **briefly** 짧게, 간단히

18.
해설 형용사+명사
reasonable(합리적인)은 특히 토익에서 '가격(price/rate)'을 자주 수식하는 형용사이고, '합리적인 가격에 여행할 수 있다'로 문맥상 적절하므로 (D)가 정답이다.

번역 폴라리스의 올유캔플라이 클럽 멤버십이 있으면 보너스 마일을 받을 수 있을 뿐 아니라 합리적인 가격으로 여행하실 수 있습니다.

어휘 **mile** 마일 **renowned** 유명한 **loose** 헐거운 **relevant** 관련 있는 **reasonable** 합리적인

19.
해설 형용사+명사
빈칸 앞의 형용사 detailed(상세한)는 특히 '정보, 설명'과 짝을 자주 이루며, '코스에 대한 상세한 정보를 원하면'으로 문맥도 적절하므로 (D)가 정답이다.

번역 우리의 졸업생 교육 과정에 대한 상세한 설명을 원하시면 https://dsf.uni.ac.de에서 온라인 카탈로그를 이용하실 수 있습니다.

어휘 **detailed** 상세한 **graduate** 졸업생 **journal** 저널, 잡지 **admission** 입학 **description** 설명

20.
해설 in+명사+전치사
빈칸 주변이 'in ____ with'이므로 'in conjunction with(~와 함께)'인지 확인한다. '다른 판매 판촉행사와 함께'로 문맥상 적절하므로 (D)가 정답이다.

번역 10% 할인 쿠폰은 개별적으로만 사용 가능하고 다른 판촉 행사와 함께 중복 할인은 안 된다는 점에 유의하십시오.

어휘 **individually** 개별적으로 **promotion** 판촉 **application** 신청, 지원 **courtesy** 공손함 **in conjunction with** ~와 함께

21-24

> 백사장과 도보 거리에 있으며 근사한 바다가 보이는 이 넓고 현대적인 스타일의 주택에서 당신은 환상적인 삶을 누리게 될 것입니다. 이 주택은 널찍한 3개의 침실과 2개의 고급스러운 욕실, 매끈하고 현대적인 주방, 그리고 자연스럽게 이어지는 식사 공간과 뒤쪽의 조용한 파티오로 구성되어 있습니다. 부부용 침실에는 욕실과 드레스룸이 딸려 있습니다. 이는 부부가 사적인 공간을 누릴 수 있게 해 줍니다. 게다가 이 방의 통유리를 통해 보이는 반짝거리는 바다는 당신을 도시 생활의 스트레스로부터 벗어나게 해 줄 것입니다.
>
> 이 집은 투숙객들이 해변과 다양한 카페, 식당들을 가까이 즐길 수 있도록 이상적인 곳에 위치해 있습니다. 당신이 가족 휴가를 계획하고 있든지 개인적인 주말 휴가를 계획하고 있든지 간에 이 집은 완벽한 선택이 될 것입니다.

어휘 **wonderful** 멋진 **stylishly** 멋지게 **contemporary** 현대의 **residence** 주택 **stunning** 근사한 **ocean** 해양 **located** 위치한 **within walking distance** 도보 거리에 있는 **floor plan** 평면도 **include** 포함하다 **spacious** 넓은 **luxurious** 고급스러운 **sleek** 매끈한 **modern** 현대의 **flow** 흐르다 **dining room** 식당 **private** 사적인 **rear** 뒤의 **patio** 파티오 **master bedroom** 안방 **wardrobe** 옷장 **en suite** 욕실이 딸린 **moreover** 게다가 **sparkling** 반짝거리는 **ceiling** 천장 **escape** 탈출하다

21.
해설 전치사 어휘
'백사장과 도보 거리 ___ 위치해 있다'에서 '도보 거리'를 가장 자연스럽게 연결하는 전치사는 '이내에(within)'이므로 (C)가 정답이다. within walking distance(도보 거리 이내에)는 자주 나오는 표현이므로 암기해 두면 편하다.

22.
해설 문장 고르기
빈칸의 앞 문장에서 '부부용 침실에는 욕실과 드레스룸이 딸려 있다'고 했고 (A)에서 This는 앞 문장 내용 전체를 받아 '이러한 점이 부부가 사적인 공간을 누릴 수 있게 해 준다'며 앞 문장의 내용에 대한 장점을 부연설명하며 자연스럽게 연결되므로 (A)가 정답이다.

번역 (A) 이는 부부가 사적인 공간을 누릴 수 있게 해 줍니다.
(B) 위층에는 호화롭게 꾸며진 침실이 있습니다.
(C) 이 곳은 대가족을 위한 꿈의 집입니다.
(D) 당신은 집을 구경하기 위해 약속을 잡을 수 있습니다.

23.
해설 대명사
'도시 생활의 스트레스에서 벗어나게 해 준다'는 광고문을 읽는 사람, 즉 당신(you)을 대상으로 한 말이므로 (B)가 정답이다.

24.
해설 명사 어휘
'이 집은 위치가 좋아서 투숙객들이 해변과 다양한 카페, 식당과 가까운 ___을 즐길 수 있게 해 준다'라며 집의 위치에 대해서 설명하고 있으므로 '근접(가까움)'을 뜻하는 (D)가 정답이다.

어휘 intimacy 친밀함 locality (~가 있는) 곳 majority 다수

25-28

6월 27일

제시카 페레즈
우드랜드 드라이브 7440번지
인디애나폴리스, 인디애나 주, 46278

제시카 님께,

8월 1일을 잠정 시작일로 당신에게 디어본 카운티의 산림 프로그램 코디네이터 직으로의 전근을 제안하게 되어 기쁩니다. 당신의 복지 혜택은 이번 전근으로 인해 변경되지 않을 것입니다. 건강 보험 보장이나 연금 분담금은 중단 없이 제공될 것입니다.

당신이 새 직위에 적응하는 것을 돕기 위해 제가 평가를 통한 성과 면담을 실행할 것입니다. 평가는 첫 해 동안 여러 번 주기적으로 이루어질 것입니다. 새 직위나 직무 수행에 대해 질문이 있으시면 언제든 제게 연락하세요.

새 자리에 선택되신 것을 축하드리며 당신과 함께 인디애나 주민들을 위해 일하게 되어 몹시 기대됩니다.

루이스 해밀턴
인사과 부장

어휘 be pleased to ~하게 되어 기쁘다 transfer 전근 position 직위 forest 숲 coordinator 코디네이터, 조정자 anticipated 예상된 interruption 중단 health insurance 건강 보험 coverage 보장 pension 연금 contribution 분담금, 기여 assist 돕다 transition 이행, 과도 performance 성과 discussion 면담, 토론 evaluation 평가 conduct 행하다 look forward to ~하길 기대하다 serve (서비스를) 제공하다 regards 안부 Personnel 인사과

25.
해설 동사 어휘
빈칸 뒤로 목적어 두 개가 와서 '당신에게 전근을 ___하게 되어 기쁘다'라고 했으므로 4형식 동사인 offer(~에게 …를 제안하다)가 적절하다. 또한 '산림 프로그램 코디네이터 직의 예상되는 시작 일자가 8월 1일'이라고 했고, 뒤 문장에서 '복지 혜택도 변동이 없이 제공될 것'이라며 전근으로 인해 뒤따르는 사항에 대해서도 설명하고 있으므로 이미 전근이 결정되어 '제안'하는 상황임을 알 수 있다. 따라서 (D)가 정답이다.

26.
해설 문장 고르기
앞 문장에서 '전근을 제안한다'고 한 내용을 (C)에서 this transfer로 받아 '이번 전근으로 인해 복지 혜택이 변경되지 않는다'고 했고, 뒷 문장에서 '건강 보험 보장이나 연금 분담금이 중단되지 않을 것이다'라며 복지 혜택에 대해서 자세히 설명하고 있으므로 연결이 자연스럽다. 따라서 (C)가 정답이다.

번역 (A) 전 직원이 전근 기회에 지원할 자격이 있습니다.
(B) 당신은 최소 3장의 추천서를 제출해야 할 것입니다.
(C) 당신의 복지 혜택은 이번 전근으로 인해 변경되지 않을 것입니다.
(D) 공고된 일자리와 관련된 당신의 질문은 비밀로 남을 것입니다.

27.
해설 동사 시제
앞 뒤 문장 모두 미래 시제(will)로 전근과 관련되어 앞으로 일어날 상황에 대해 설명하고 있는 문장이므로 빈칸이 있는 문장도 미래 시제로 연결되어야 자연스럽다. 따라서 정답은 (D)가 정답이다.

28.
해설 부사 자리
빈칸은 수동태로 끝나는 완전한 절에 덤으로 붙어 동사 'will be conducted'를 수식하므로 부사 (B)가 정답이다.

PART 7

CHAPTER 1 문제 유형

Unit 1 주제/목적 문제

 예제
본책 p. 182

Q. 무엇이 광고되고 있는가?
(A) 보관 서비스
(B) 주거용 건물

더 작은 집으로 이사를 하실 건가요? 없애고 싶지 않은 소유물을 지나치게 갖고 계신가요? 그렇다면 콘리 엔터프라이즈가 해결책입니다. 저희는 여러분의 가구, 서류, 전자 제품 등을 보관할 수 있는, 온도 조절이 되는 다양한 크기의 창고를 제공합니다.

YBM TEST
본책 p. 183

1. (B) 2. (C) 3. (A)

[1-3] 이메일

수신: 티아 헤스터 〈t_hester@houmafinancial.com〉
발신: 병민 최 〈b_choi@houmafinancial.com〉
날짜: 5월 18일
내용: 주목해 주세요

헤스터 씨께,

사분기 회의에서 할당 받으셨던 업무에 관해 씁니다. 고객 리드 처리에 관한 새 정책을 시행하는 데 있어서 **1훌륭하게 일해 주신 데 대해 진심으로 감사드립니다**. 우리는 작년에 실적 기반 리드(PBL) 시스템을 시도했습니다. 한 달 지나자 성공의 기미가 보였죠. **2하지만 세 달간 사용한 후, 우리는 이 프로그램을 포기했습니다**. 너무 경쟁적이고, 일부 직원들은 공정한 대우를 받지 못하는 것 같다며 심지어 그만두기도 했기 때문입니다.

1당신이 개발한 시스템은 훨씬 훌륭합니다. 직원들은 잠재 고객들이 공평하게 배당된다고 느낍니다. 이는 전반적인 업무 만족도는 물론 팀워크를 향상시키는 데 도움이 되고 있습니다. 당신을 팀장으로 승진시킨 게 올바른 결정이었다는 게 분명합니다.

3지사 책임자 트레보 파스코 씨와 저와 함께 모여 당신의 다른 아이디어를 얘기하는 거 괜찮으시겠죠. 그에게 전화해서 스케줄을 알아보고 다시 연락드리겠습니다. 그동안, 계속해서 잘 일해 주시기 바랍니다!

어휘 **assign** (임무를) 맡기다, 배정하다 **quarterly** 분기별의 **implement** (정책을) 시행하다 **handle** 처리하다 **lead** 리드(고객이나 영업 기회가 될 수 있는 잠재적인 사람 또는 물건) **performance-based** 실적 기반의 **promising** 유망한, 성공 가능성이 보이는 **abandon** 버리다, 포기하다 **competitive** 경쟁적인 **quit** 그만두다 **equally** 동등하게 **superior** 우월한 **potential** 잠재적인 **distribute** 배분하다 **job satisfaction** 직무 만족 **promote** 승진[승격]시키다 **get together** 모이다 **in the meantime** 그동안에

1.
번역 이메일의 주요 목적은 무엇인가?
(A) 직원 환영
(B) 감사 표시
(C) 정책 도입
(D) 업무 할당

해설 주제/목적
첫 번째 단락의 '훌륭하게 일해 주신 데 대해 진심으로 감사드립니다(I would like to offer my sincere thanks for the wonderful job you did)', 두 번째 단락의 '당신이 개발한 시스템은 훨씬 훌륭합니다(The system you developed is far superior)'에 감사의 마음이 드러나므로 (B)가 정답이다.

2.
번역 PBL 시스템은 얼마나 오랫동안 사용되었는가?
(A) 1개월
(B) 2개월
(C) 3개월
(D) 4개월

해설 세부사항
첫 번째 단락에서 '하지만 세 달간 사용한 후, 우리는 이 프로그램을 포기했습니다(However, after three months of use, we abandoned the program)'라고 했으므로 (C)가 정답이다.

3.
번역 최 씨가 파스코 씨에게 연락을 하는 이유는 무엇일 것 같은가?
(A) 직접 만나는 약속을 잡으려고
(B) 사업을 위한 재정 지원을 의논하려고
(C) 승진 대상으로 헤스터 씨를 추천하려고
(D) 초과 근무 일정을 승인받으려고

해설 추론
마지막 단락에서 '지사 책임자 트레보 파스코 씨와 저와 함께 모여 당신의 다른 아이디어를 얘기하는 거 괜찮으시겠죠(I know that you would like to get together with Branch Director Trevor Pasco and me to discuss some of your other ideas)'라는 말로 직접 만나자고 제안하고 있으므로 (A)가 정답이다.

Paraphrasing
지문의 get together with Branch Director Trevor Pasco and me → 정답의 an in-person meeting

Unit 2 세부사항 문제

예제
본책 p. 184

Q1. 베벨 씨는 누구인가?
(A) 지사장
(B) 행사 기획자

Q2. 7월 25일에 어떤 일이 일어날까?
(A) 등록 기간이 끝날 것이다.
(B) 직원들이 회사 야유회에 갈 것이다.

키니 컨설팅의 연례 회사 야유회가 7월 31일 금요일에 샐리나스 포도원에서 열립니다. 마리 베벨 씨가 필요한 모든 준비를 마쳤습니다. 우리는 사무실에서 셔틀 버스를 타고 가서 포도원에서 점심을 먹은 후, 이어 도보 여행을 하게 됩니다. 늦어도 7월 24일까지 신청해야 한다는 점에 주목해 주십시오. 모두 다 즐거운 시간 갖기를 바랍니다!

YBM TEST

본책 p. 185

1. (D) 2. (D) 3. (B) 4. (A)

[1-4] 편지

리넷 뮬러
세인트 앤드류스 레인
캠던, 뉴저지 주 08102
12월 29일

뮬러 씨께,

발렌티노 프리 클리닉을 대표해, 저희 이상을 위해 기부해 주신 데 대해 깊은 감사를 표하고자 합니다. 귀하와 같은 주민들의 관대한 지원 덕분에, 수백 저소득 가구와 개인들이 필요한 의료 조치를 받을 수 있습니다. **1지난 한 해 동안 저희는 정부 보조금과 개인 기부금을 통해 거의 380,000달러를 모금했습니다.** 저희 기본적인 운영 예산은 295,000달러이며, 이 돈은 치료 프로그램(180,000달러), 의료 장비 구입(65,000달러), 보험(30,000달러), 건물 유지(15,000달러), 그리고 관리비 및 잡비(5,000달러)에 쓰입니다.

2병원의 20년 역사상 처음으로 예산에 잉여금이 발생했기 때문에, 1지난 5년간 위시 리스트에 있던 사업에 자금을 충당할 수 있게 되었습니다. 저희 자원봉사자 의사와 간호사들이 병원 영업 시간 중에 더 많은 환자를 볼 수 있게 더 많은 진료실을 둘 수 있도록, **1기존 건물을 증축할 계획입니다. 3이 새 구역은 유명한 건축 설계 회사인 랜슬롯 주식회사의 코디 패리시 씨가 설계할 예정입니다.** 그는 수많은 공공 사업에서 일했고 제한된 공간을 최대한 활용하는 데 아주 특별한 재능이 있습니다. 건설 사업은 봄에 시작되고, 건설 공사로 인해 병원 폐쇄가 필요한 날에는 드레이턴 병원에서 일부 공간을 우리에게 빌려주기로 합의했습니다.

여러분의 도움이 없었다면, 이 놀라운 사업은 절대 가능하지 않았을 겁니다. **4저희는 해마다 메르카도 홀 연회장에서 특별 만찬을 들면서 직원 및 독지가 여러분의 공헌을 기념합니다. 올해는 1월 28일 토요일 오후 6시 30분으로 예정돼 있습니다. 참석해 주시길 바랍니다.**

타이 렌

어휘 on behalf of ~을 대신[대표]해서 appreciation 감사 donation 기부 cause 목표, 이상, 대의명분; (사회 정치적인 운동을 하는) 단체 medical 의료의 attention 보살핌, 치료 raise (돈을) 모으다 grant (정부에서 주는) 지원금 operating budget 운영 예산 treatment 치료 upkeep 유지 administration 관리 miscellaneous expenses 잡비 surplus 잉여금, 흑자 fund 자금을 대다 extension 확장, 증축한 방 consultation room 진찰실 physician 의사 opening hours 영업 시간 exceptional 특출한 make the best use of ~을 최대한 활용하다 necessitate 필요하게 만들다 closure 폐쇄 contribution 기여, 공헌 donor 기부자

1.

번역 렌 씨가 뮬러 씨에게 편지를 쓴 이유는?
(A) 자선 단체에 재정적 기부를 해 달라고 요청하려고
(B) 충고를 해 준 데 대해 뮬러 씨에게 감사하려고
(C) 진료 약속 예약 방법을 알려주려고
(D) 기금이 어떻게 사용됐는지 최신 소식을 전하기 위해

해설 주제/목적
첫 번째 단락에서 '지난 한 해 동안 저희는 거의 380,000달러를 모금했습니다(Over the past year, we raised nearly $380,000)'라고 말하면서 돈의 지출 내역을 밝혔고, 두 번째 단락에서는 잉여금을 5년간 미뤄 왔던 '기존 건물을 증축하는 데(adding an extension to our building)' 사용할 것이라고 말하고 있으므로 (D)가 정답이다.

2.

번역 렌 씨의 기관은 운영을 시작한 지 얼마나 되었는가?
(A) 5년
(B) 10년
(C) 15년
(D) 20년

해설 세부사항
두 번째 단락에서 '병원의 20년 역사상 처음으로 예산에 잉여금이 발생했기 때문에(As we have a surplus in our budget for the first time in the clinic's two-decade history)'라는 말에 병원이 20년 된 것을 알 수 있으므로 (D)가 정답이다.

3.

번역 패리시 씨는 어디에서 일하는가?
(A) 컨벤션 센터
(B) 건축 회사
(C) 약국
(D) 병원

해설 세부사항
두 번째 단락에서 '이 새 구역은 유명한 건축 설계 회사인 랜슬롯 주식회사의 코디 패리시 씨가 설계할 예정입니다(The new section of the building will be designed by Cody Farrish from Lancelot Incorporated, a popular architecture design firm)라고 했으므로 (B)가 정답이다.

Paraphrasing
지문의 architecture design firm
→ 정답의 an architectural firm

4.

번역 뮬러 씨는 무엇을 해 달라고 요청받는가?
(A) 연례 연회 참석
(B) 회의 일정 잡기
(C) 사회 단체에 돈을 내겠다고 약속하기
(D) 초대하기

해설 **세부사항**
마지막 단락에서 '저희는 해마다 메르카도 홀 연회장에서 특별 만찬을 들면서 직원 및 독자 여러분의 공헌을 기념합니다(Each year, we celebrate the contributions of our staff and donors with a special dinner in the ballroom of Mercado Hall)'라면서 '참석해 주시길 바랍니다(We hope you can be there)'라고 요청했으므로 (A)가 정답이다.

Paraphrasing
지문의 Each year → 정답의 annual

Unit 3 의도 파악 문제

 예제   본책 p. 186

Q. 오후 1시 27분에 포르틸로 씨가 "다시는 거기에 주문하지 않을 거예요."라고 쓸 때 그 의도는 무엇인가?
(A) 그녀는 물품을 늦게 받았다.
(B) 그녀는 품질에 실망했다.

에드가 르보, 1:23 P.M.
휴스턴 문구에서 운송품 받았어요?

키라 포르틸로, 1:24 P.M.
네, 오늘 아침에 받고 사인했어요. 주문한 거 모두 정확해요.

에드가 르보, 1:26 P.M.
좋아요. 휴스톤 문구 이용하는 게 이번이 처음이잖아요. 품질은 어때요?

키라 포르틸로, 1:27 P.M.
다시는 거기에 주문하지 않을 거예요.

에드가 르보, 1:28 P.M.
어쩐지 가격이 너무 낮더라고요.

YBM TEST   본책 p. 187

1. (A)   2. (C)

[1-2] 문자 메시지

브루노 세카다	11:35 A.M.
조이스 실바 씨 건으로 이메일 보낸 거 받았어요? 그녀는 최근 폭풍으로 인한 집 손상 때문에 배상을 청구했어요. **1**하지만 집주인 관련 우리 정책에서는 자연 재해는 보상하지 않죠?	

서연 김	11:38 A.M.
폭풍 피해는 보상되고, 홍수 피해는 안 됩니다. 그러니까 괜찮은 거죠.	

브루노 세카다	11:39 A.M.
좋습니다. 그럼 실바 씨의 요청을 진행시키면 되겠네요.	

서연 김	11:40 A.M.
작업이 벌써 진행됐나요?	

브루노 세카다	11:41 A.M.
네, 손상된 게 지붕이라서요. 실바 씨가 건설회사를 바로 다음 날 방문하게 했고, 이미 그 쪽에 지불도 다 했어요. 문제가 되나요?	

서연 김	11:42 A.M.
사실, **2**그게 우리한테는 더 나아요. 그녀가 제출한 청구서를 검토해서 비용이 적절한지 꼭 확인하고, **1**배상액 수표를 발행하기만 하면 되거든요.	

브루노 세카다	11:43 A.M.
좋습니다. 그렇게 처리하겠습니다.	

어휘 **put in a claim for damage** 손해 배상을 청구하다 **homeowner** 주택 소유자, 집주인 **policy** 정책; 보험증권 **cover** (손실에 대해 보험에서) 보상[보장]하다 **natural disaster** 자연 재해 **move forward** 진전시키다 **carry out** 수행하다 **invoice** 청구서 **make sure** 반드시 ~하도록 하다 **reasonable** (가격이) 적절한 **issue a check** 수표를 발행하다 **reimbursement** 배상, 상환 **take care of** ~을 처리하다

1.

번역 화자들은 어디서 일할 것 같은가?
(A) 보험회사
(B) 실내 장식 회사
(C) 기상대
(D) 건설회사

해설 **추론**
오전 11시 35분에 세카다 씨가 '집주인 관련 우리 정책에서는 자연 재해는 보상하지 않죠?(But our homeowners policy doesn't cover natural disasters, does it?)'라고 물었고, 11시 42분에 김 씨가 '배상액 수표를 발행하기만 하면(issue a reimbursement check)'이라고 말했다. 정책, 보상 등의 말로 미루어 (A)가 정답이다.

2.

번역 오전 11시 42분에 김 씨가 "그게 우리한테는 더 나아요"라고 쓴 의미는?
(A) 어떤 비용이 예상했던 것보다 적게 들었다.
(B) 세카다 씨가 실바 씨에게 옵션을 선택하도록 장려해야 한다.
(C) 어떤 절차가 완수하기에 쉬울 것으로 예상된다.
(D) 회사를 보호하기 위해 규제가 생겼다.

해설 **의도 파악**
이미 다른 쪽에서 지불을 다 마쳤다는 말에 '그게 우리한테는 더 낫다'며 '그녀가 제출한 청구서를 검토해서 비용이 적절한지 꼭 확인하고, '배상액 수표를 발행하기만 하면 되거든요(Then we just have to review the invoice she submits, make sure that it's reasonable, and issue a reimbursement check)'라고 했다. 절차가 오히려 수월해졌다는 뜻이므로 (C)가 정답이다.

Unit 4 NOT / TRUE 문제

예제
본책 p. 188

클리프사이드 스파

영업 시간: 월-금요일, 오전 8시-오후 9시
서비스*: 마사지, 얼굴 관리, 손톱 손질, 제모

마사지
스웨덴식 마사지: 1시간, 1시간 30분
타이 마사지: 30분, 1시간
뜨거운 돌 마사지: 1시간

*전 직원이 주에서 허가를 받았으며 추가 자격증 과정도 이수했습니다.

Q1. 마사지에 관해 명시된 것은?
 (A) 미리 예약해야 한다.
 (B) 지속 시간이 각기 다르다.

Q2. 클리프사이드 스파에 관해 사실인 것은?
 (A) 직원들이 충분한 자격을 갖추고 있다.
 (B) 매일 문을 연다.

YBM TEST
본책 p. 189

1. (A) 2. (C) 3. (A)

[1-3] 웹 페이지

www.felosaairlines.com

| 홈 | 항공편 예약 | 수하물 정책 | 상용 고객 클럽 | 연락처 |

펠로사 항공 수하물 정책

2-A연방항공협회의 원칙에 따라 수하물 정책을 일반이 이용할 수 있게 공개합니다. **1-C**종이 항공권 이용 승객의 경우는, 이 조건들이 항공권 뒷면에도 인쇄되어 있습니다. 탑승 수속을 신속하게 하기 위해 초과 수하물에 대해서는 예약할 때 비용을 지불해 주시기를 간곡히 권합니다. **1-A**신용카드가 탑승 창구에서 받는 유일한 지불 형태라는 점 기억해 주십시오.

일반 가방: 최대 치수(길이+폭+높이) 62인치, 최대 무게 50파운드

	첫 번째 가방	두 번째 가방	세 번째 가방
3-C이코노미석 승객	25달러	50달러	불가
3-A퍼스트 클래스석 승객	무료	25달러	50달러

2-D, 3-B펠로사 항공은 여행 성수기 때 가방의 수를 제한할 권리가 있다는 점을 주지해 주십시오. 가방 개수 제한을 실행할 경우 승객들은 적어도 출발 48시간 전에 이메일로 통지 받게 됩니다.

중량 초과/크기 초과 가방

	중량 초과: 51-90파운드	중량 초과: 91파운드 이상	크기 초과: 63-100인치 (길이+폭+높이)	크기 초과: 101-120인치 (길이+폭+높이)
모든 승객	75달러	수용 불가*	75달러	85달러

2-C*예외: 하드 케이스에 넣은 첼로, 기타, 금관악기 등

중량 초과와 크기 초과 수하물의 경우 짐이 지연되지 않도록 하기 위해 **1-D**적어도 출발 2시간 전에 수하물을 부쳐 주십시오. 의문사항이 있으면 **3-D**언제든지 고객 서비스부에 1-800-555-0147번으로 연락하시든지, 여기를 클릭해 온라인 질문을 제출해 주십시오.

어휘 frequent flyer (항공사의) 상용 고객 in compliance with ~의 명령[원칙]에 따라 aviation 항공 publicly 공개적으로 terms (계약의) 조건 make payments for ~을 지불하다 excess 초과한 expedite 신속하게 처리하다 check-in 탑승 수속 dimension 치수 width 폭 weigh 무게가 ~이다 up to 최대 ~인 reserve the right to 부정사 ~할 권한을 지니다 notify 알리다, 통지하다 prior to ~에 앞서 restriction 규제 in place 가동하는, 가동 준비가 된 overweight 중량이 초과하는 oversized 지나치게 큰 check in 수하물을 부치다 ensure 보장하다 inquiry 질문, 문의

1.

번역 펠로사 항공의 탑승 카운터에 대해 명시된 것은?
 (A) 한 가지 지불 형태만 처리할 수 있다.
 (B) 상용 고객을 위한 우선적인 줄이 있다.
 (C) 모든 승객에게 종이 티켓을 발행한다.
 (D) 출발 2시간 전에 문을 연다.

해설 Not/true
첫 번째 단락에서 '신용카드가 탑승 창구에서 받는 유일한 지불 형태라는 점 기억해 주십시오(Please note that credit cards are the only form of payment accepted at the check-in counter)'라고 밝혔으므로 (A)가 정답이다. (B) 상용 고객에 대한 언급은 없고, (C)의 경우는 '종이 항공권 이용 승객의 경우는(For passengers using paper tickets)'이라고 일부를 언급했을 뿐 모든 승객이라는 단서는 없고, (D)에서 말하는 '출발 2시간 전'의 경우도 '늦어도 이때까지는 짐을 맡기라'고 했지 이때 문을 여는 것은 아니므로 모두 정답이 아니다.

Paraphrasing
지문의 the only form of payment accepted
→ 정답의 only process one payment type

2.

번역 무게 제한에 관해서 사실인 것은?
 (A) 연방항공협회에서 규제한다.
 (B) 승객의 항공권에 따라 다르다.
 (C) 악기에는 적용되지 않는다.
 (D) 여행 성수기에는 줄어든다.

해설 Not/true
두 번째 표 밑에 '예외:하드 케이스에 넣은 첼로, 기타, 금관악기(Exception: cellos, guitars, brass horns, etc. in hard-shell cases)'라고 되어 있으므로 (C)가 정답이다. (A)의 경우 연방항공협회 규정 준수는 '수하물 정책을 공개(making our baggage policy publicly available)'하는 것과 관련이 있지 초과 수하물에 관한 것은 아니므로 사실이 아니다. (B)의 경우, 첫 번째 표에서 보면 이코노미석인지 퍼스트 클래스석인지에 따라 가방 개수에는 차이가 있지만, 두 번째 표에서 보면 크기 및 중량에 대한 제한 규정은 모든 승객이 똑같으므로 역시 사실이 아니다. 중간 단락에서 여행 성수기 때 '가방의 수(the number of bags)'를 제한한다고 했으므로 무게 제한을 낮춘다는 (D)도 사실이 아니다.

Paraphrasing
지문의 cellos, guitars, brass horns
→ 정답의 musical instruments

81

3.

번역 펠로사 항공에 대해 명시되지 않은 것은?
(A) 퍼스트 클래스석 승객들은 위탁 수하물에 대해 돈을 지불하지 않아도 된다.
(B) 연중 어느 때인지에 따라 가방의 수를 제한할 수 있다.
(C) 이코노미석 승객에게 두 개의 가방만 위탁하도록 허락한다.
(D) 고객 서비스 부서를 24시간 이용할 수 있다.

해설 Not/true
첫 번째 표에서 퍼스트 클래스석 승객도 두 번째 가방부터는 추가 요금을 낸다고 되어 있으므로 (A)가 정답이다. 중간 단락 '펠로사 항공은 여행 성수기 때 가방의 수를 제한할 권리가 있다(Felosa Airlines reserves the right to limit the number of bags during the peak travel season)'라고 한 부분에 (B)가 명시되어 있다. 첫 번째 표에서 이코노미석의 경우는 '세 번째 가방(Third Bag)'이 '불가(Not available)'라고 했으므로 (C)도 명시되어 있다. 마지막 단락 '언제든지 고객 서비스부에 연락하라(contact our customer service department anytime by calling)'라는 부분에 (D)가 명시되어 있다.

Paraphrasing
지문의 limit the number of bags during the peak travel season → 보기의 restrict the number of bags depending on the time of year
지문의 contact our customer service department anytime → 보기의 customer service department is available twenty-four hours a day

Unit 5 동의어 문제

예제
본책 p. 190

Q. 첫 번째 단락, 일곱 번째 줄의 "back up"과 의미상 가장 가까운 것은?
(A) 복사하다
(B) 뒷받침하다

노턴 씨께,

저는 블루베리 베이커리를 운영합니다. 사업체가 커져서 최근에 대출 신청을 했는데 오늘 아침 제 신청이 받아들여지지 않았다는 통보를 받았습니다. 이 통보를 거의 이해할 수가 없습니다. 제 사업은 높은 수익을 냈고 지난 2년간의 과세 서류를 제공해서 그 주장을 입증도 했습니다.

YBM TEST
본책 p. 191

1. (B) **2.** (C) **3.** (A) **4.** (D)

[1-4] 기사

자르비스 디자인이 한 단계 도약하다

1월 18일 – [1]날렵하면서 세련된 운동복과 신발로 유명한 자르비스 디자인이 테이트 주식회사와 협력하여 테크놀로지가 결합된 운동화를 제품에 추가하려고 한다. 얼핏 보면 두 회사는 어울리지 않는 짝으로 보인다. 자르비스 디자인은 쿠르트 자르비스 씨에 의해 설립되었다. [2]그는 샌프란시스코의 윌슨 디자인 스쿨에서 학위를 받고 졸업했고, 그곳 디자인 회사에서 유급 인턴직을 맡아 한 후, 자금을 모아 시카고에서 자신의 회사를 열었다. 한편, 테이트 주식회사는 킴벌 테이트 씨에 의해 뉴욕에서 설립되었다. 이 회사는 자동차 생산 공장으로 시작했지만 약 10년 전에 GPS 장비 생산으로 방향을 돌렸다.

[1]GPS가 결합된 운동화를 개발하기 위해 두 회사는 각자가 제시할 수 있는 최상의 것을 이용하고 있다. [3-A, 3-C]이 신발의 데모 제품(당시 제품명이 없었음)이 지난달 시애틀에서 열린 '세계 건강과 미용 박람회'에 처음 모습을 드러냈다. 회사 대표 직원들이 이 신발이 어떻게 걸은 거리, 평균 속도, 소모된 칼로리 같은 요소들을 추적할 수 있는지를 시연했다. 이 신발은 심지어 달리는 사람의 유형에 따라 발생 가능한 문제점까지 알아챌 수 있다. [3-A]JDT-360(이 제품에 붙여진 이름)의 개발에는 수백만 달러가 소요되었지만 [4]이 사업은 일단 3월에 제품이 시장에 풀리면 곧바로 수익이 나는 쪽으로 돌아설 것으로 예상된다. JDT-360 사전 주문이 이미 자르비스 디자인 웹 사이트에서 접수되고 있다. 신발은 온라인과 모든 주요 백화점에서 판매될 예정이다.

어휘 sleek (모양이) 매끄럽고 날렵한 athletic clothing 운동복 footwear 신발 team up with ~와 협력하다 enabled ~를 사용해 가동하는 running shoe 운동화 at first glance 언뜻 보기에는 unlikely 예상 밖의, 있음직하지 않은 take on (임무를) 떠맡다 fashion house 의류 회사 raise funds 자금[기금]을 모으다 automotive 자동차 manufacturing plant 생산 공장 transition 바뀌다, 변천하다 unnamed 이름이 없는, 이름이 확인되지 않은 representative 대표 demonstrate (실례를 들어가며) 보여주다 track 추적하다 cover (특정 거리만큼) 걷다, 이동하다 identify 확인하다, 찾아내다 issue 문제점 profitable 수익성이 있는 hit the shelves 가게에 나오다, 구입할 수 있게 되다

1.

번역 기사는 주로 무엇에 관한 것인가?
(A) 지도부 교체
(B) 사업 협력
(C) 시장 동향
(D) 패션쇼

해설 주제/목적
첫 번째 단락에서 '자르비스 디자인이 테이트 주식회사와 협력하여 테크놀로지가 결합된 운동화를 제품에 추가하려고 한다(Jarvis Designs, ~, is teaming up with Tate Incorporated to add a technology-enabled running shoe to its line)'라는 말로 시작해 두 회사 연혁을 간략히 소개했고, 두 번째 단락에서는 '두 회사는 각자가 제시할 수 있는 최상의 것을 이용해 GPS가 결합된 운동화를 개발했다(The two firms are using the best that each has to offer to develop a GPS-enabled athletic shoe)'라는 말로 시작해 합작 제품을 소개하고 있다. 결국, 두 회사가 협력해 신제품 운동화를 개발했다는 내용이므로 (B)가 정답이다.

2.

번역 자르비스 씨는 어디에서 처음 패션 분야 일을 했는가?
(A) 시카고
(B) 뉴욕
(C) 샌프란시스코
(D) 시애틀

해설 **세부사항**

첫 번째 단락에서 '그는 샌프란시스코의 윌슨 디자인 스쿨에서 학위를 받고 졸업했고, 그곳 디자인 회사에서 유급 인턴직을 맡아 한 후(who graduated with a degree from the Wilson School of Design in San Francisco, taking on a paid internship at a fashion house there)'라고 자르비스 씨의 초기 경력을 설명했다. 샌프란시스코에서 학교도 졸업하고 패션 회사에서도 일했으므로 (C)가 정답이다.

3.

번역 JDT-360에 대해 명시된 것은?
(A) 이름이 몇 차례 바뀌었다.
(B) 킴벌 테이트 씨가 디자인했다.
(C) 국제 박람회에서 처음 소개되었다.
(D) 회사에서 가장 잘 팔리는 제품이다.

해설 **Not / true**

두 번째 단락에서 '이 신발의 데모 제품(당시 제품명이 없었음)이 지난 달 시애틀에서 열린 '세계 건강과 미용 박람회'에 처음 모습을 드러냈다(A demo version of the shoe, unnamed at the time, was debuted at ~ Expo)'라고 했고, 몇 줄 아래 JDT-360라는 신발 이름이 처음 등장하는 곳에는 '이 제품에 붙여진 이름(the name given to the product)'이라는 부연 설명이 나온다. 즉, 이 신제품 신발은 엑스포에서 이름이 없는 채로 처음 선보였고, 이후 정식 이름을 얻은 것이므로 (A)는 명시된 바가 없고, (C)가 정답이다. (B)는 언급된 바가 없고, (D)의 경우는 아직 판매가 시작되지 않아 알 수 없다.

Paraphrasing

지문의 was debuted at the International Health and Beauty Expo → 정답의 was first shown at an international expo

4.

번역 두 번째 단락 열세 번째 줄의 "turn"과 의미상 가장 가까운 것은?
(A) 확실하게 하다
(B) 곡선으로 움직이다
(C) 해결하다
(D) 어떤 상태로 되다

해설 **동의어**

해당 문장은 '이 사업은 일단 3월에 제품이 시장에 풀리면 곧바로 수익이 나는 쪽으로 돌아설 것으로 예상된다(the project is expected to turn profitable quickly once it hits the shelves in March)'라고 해석된다. 여기서 turn은 '~해지다, ~한 상태로 되다'라는 뜻이므로 (D)가 정답이다.

Unit 6 추론 문제

예제
본책 p. 192

Q1. 폴라드 씨에 대해 암시된 것은?
(A) 저녁 식사 메뉴를 염두에 두었다.
(B) 바워 씨에게 제안을 달라고 요청했다.

수신: 카산드라 폴라드
발신: 크리스 바워

중국 투자자들 방문을 준비하느라 바쁜 거 잘 알고 있어요. 월요일에 얘기를 나누고 나서, 저녁 식사 후에 그들을 데려갈 장소를 생각하고 있는 중이에요. 아직도 추천이 필요하다고 당신이 말해서요. 세계 춤 전시회에 가는 건 어때요?

Q2. 이 정보는 어디에서 가장 보게 될 것 같은가?
(A) 사용 설명서
(B) 여행자 가이드

저희 제품을 구매해 주셔서 감사합니다. 다음 정보를 꼼꼼히 읽으시면 저희 제품의 특징을 최대한 활용하실 수 있을 겁니다.

YBM TEST
본책 p. 193

1. (B) 2. (A) 3. (B) 4. (C)

[1-4] 기사

2월 18일 – 1엘크뷰 시 관리들이 애크런 호수의 수은 오염 수치 감소를 목표로 하는 야심찬 사업을 발표했다. 해리슨 대학 연구원들이 지난 30년 동안 매년 호수의 유독성을 감시해 왔는데, 최근 보고서에서는 호수의 물과 주변 토양의 수은 수치가 높게 나타났다. 4-D호수의 북쪽 해안에 접해 있는 땅이 산업 용도 지구로 지정되어 있기 때문에, 이곳의 물은 근처 공장에서 배출되는 오염물질에 취약하다. 최근 법정 소송에서는, 3형광 전구를 생산하는 멜렌데즈 메뉴팩처링이 오염의 주요 원인이라고 밝혔다. 납세자들은 이 회사가 이 땅의 전체 복구 비용을 내야 할 것이라는 것을 알고 안도했으며, 작업은 올해 후반기에 진행될 것으로 보인다.

엘크뷰 시의원들은, 약 1억 달러가 소요될 것으로 추정되는 '애크런 호수 복원 계획(ALRP)'을 감독하기 위한 분과 위원회를 지명했다. 2"우리는 이 사업이 조심스럽게 시행되도록 하기 위해 전문가들과 면밀하게 협조하고 있습니다." 위원회 회장인 조슈아 헤스터 씨가 말했다. 4-B"호수 안과 주변에는 셀 수 없이 많은 식물과 동물 종이 살고 있습니다. 그래서 우리는 필요 이상으로 이들의 서식지를 교란시키는 건 피하고 싶습니다."

이 사업은 3단계로 이루어지며, 4-A호수 현지의 편의시설들은 절차상 부분적으로 출입이 금지될 것이다. 첫 번째 단계는 호수 안과 주변에서 가져온 흙과 물 샘플들을 시험하는 2개월 기간이다. 두 번째 단계는 4개월에 걸쳐 호수 바닥을 준설하게 되는데 오염된 침전물을 제거하고 위험 폐기물에 관한 규제 조항에 따라 이를 처리하기 위해서다. 세 번째 단계는 자연의 균형을 회복하기 위해 물속의 수생 식물들을 옮겨 심는 것으로 이루어진다. 마지막 단계는 3년까지 걸릴 수 있다.

 aimed at ~을 목표로 한 mercury contamination 수은 오염 monitor 감시하다 toxicity 독성, 유독성 elevated 높은, 높아진 border 경계에 접해 있다 be zoned for ~지구로 정해지다 susceptible to ~에 민감한[취약한] pollutant 오염 물질 court case 법정 소송 (사례) fluorescent light bulb 형광 전구 taxpayer 납세자 relieved 안도한 restoration 복구, 복원 get underway 진행되다 oversee 감독하다 remediation 개선, 복원 project (비용 등을) 추정하다 implement 시행하다 disturb 교란시키다 habitat 서식지 consist of ~로 이루어지다 on-site 현장의 amenities

편의시설 off limits 출입 금지의 dredge 준설하다, (하천 등의) 바닥을 파내다 sediment 침전물 dispose of ~을 처리하다 hazardous 위험한 waste 폐기물 replant 옮겨 심다 submersed 물속에 잠긴 aquatic plant 수중 식물, 수초

1.

번역 기사의 목적은 무엇인가?
(A) 자연 교육 프로그램을 설명하기 위해
(B) 정화 노력을 강조하기 위해
(C) 투자 사업을 홍보하기 위해
(D) 지역의 모금행사를 소개하기 위해

해설 주제/목적
첫 번째 단락에서 '엘그뷰 시 관리들이 애크런 호수의 수은 오염 수치 감소를 목표로 하는 야심찬 사업을 발표했다(Elkview city officials have announced an ambitious project aimed at reducing mercury contamination levels at Akron Lake)'라는 말로 시작해 호수의 오염 실태를 얘기했고, 두 번째 단락에서는 오염 제거 사업을 구체적으로 설명했다. 따라서 (B)가 정답이다.

Paraphrasing
지문의 an ambitious project aimed at reducing mercury contamination levels
→ 정답의 a cleanup effort

2.

번역 헤스터 씨는 누구일 것 같은가?
(A) 시위원회 위원
(B) 대학교수
(C) 회사 대변인
(D) 연구 과학자

해설 추론
두 번째 단락에서 "우리는 이 사업이 조심스럽게 시행되도록 하기 위해 전문가들과 면밀하게 협조하고 있습니다." 위원회 회장인 조슈아 헤스터 씨가 말했다("We are working closely with specialists ~" said Joshua Hester, the head of the committee)'라고 한 데서 헤스터 씨가 위원회 일원인 것을 알 수 있다. 바로 앞 문장에 이 위원회는 '엘크뷰 시위원회'라고 언급돼 있으므로 (A)가 정답이다.

3.

번역 ALRP에 대해 암시된 것은?
(A) 토양 침식을 막아 줄 것이다.
(B) 민간에 의해 자금이 조달될 것이다.
(C) 제조 회사에 의해 개발되었다.
(D) 통틀어 3년이 걸릴 것으로 보인다.

해설 추론
첫 번째 단락에서 멜렌데즈 메뉴팩처링이 오염의 주요 원인으로 밝혀졌다고 말하면서 '납세자들은 이 회사가 이 땅의 전체 복구 비용을 내야 할 것이라는 것을 알고 안도했으며(Taxpayers were relieved to discover that the company will be required to pay for the entire restoration of the site)'라고 덧붙였다. 기업에서 복구 비용을 댄다는 것이므로 (B)가 정답이다. 호수의 오염 제거가 주목적이므로 (A)는 틀리고, 제조회사는 오염원으로 언급된 것이 전부이므로 (C)도 틀리고, 3단계 사업에만 3년이 걸리므로 (D)도 틀리다.

Paraphrasing
지문의 the company will be required to pay for the entire restoration → 정답의 It will be privately funded

4.

번역 애크런 호수에 대해 암시되지 않은 것은?
(A) 일시적인 시설 폐쇄가 있을 것이다.
(B) 다양한 야생생물이 살고 있다.
(C) 식수 공급원을 오염시켰다.
(D) 산업 지구 근처에 위치한다.

해설 추론
세 번째 단락 '호수 현지의 편의시설들은 절차상 부분적으로 출입이 금지될 것이다(the lake's on-site amenities will be off limits)라고 한 부분에 (A)가 나와 있고, 두 번째 단락 '호수 안과 주변에는 셀 수 없이 많은 식물과 동물 종이 살고 있습니다(There are countless plant and animal species)'라고 한 부분에 (B)가, 첫 번째 단락 '호수의 북쪽 해안에 접해 있는 땅이 산업 용도 지구로 지정되어 있기 때문에(As the land bordering the northern shore of the lake is zoned for industrial use)'라고 한 부분에 (D)가 암시되어 있다. 식수와 관련된 언급은 없으므로 (C)가 정답이다.

Paraphrasing
지문의 the lake's on-site amenities will be off limits
→ 보기의 have temporary facility closures
지문의 countless plant and animal species
→ 보기의 the home of a variety of wildlife
지문의 the land bordering the northern shore of the lake is zoned for industrial use → 보기의 located near an industrial district

Unit 7 문장 삽입 문제

예제

본책 p. 194

리베라 카펫

계획의 규모와 상관없이, 리베라 카펫에서는 새로운 바닥 전면 카펫으로 여러분 가정에 멋과 매력을 더하도록 도와 드릴 수 있습니다. 저희는 업계에서 가장 경험이 많은 설치 직원을 보유하고 있다는 확고한 평판을 얻고 있습니다. 따라서 작업된 것이 여러 해 갈 거라고 확신하셔도 됩니다. 언제든지 전화하셔서 무료 가정 방문 상담을 예약하세요. 방문해서, 저희 직원 중 하나가 방 크기를 재고 견적서를 드릴 것입니다. 그런 다음, 편한 시간에 저희 매장에 오셔서 제품 샘플을 보세요. 일단 결정을 하시면, 계약서에 서명하고 3일 이내에 작업을 시작할 수 있습니다. 여러분을 위해 일할 수 있기를 고대합니다!

Q1. [1], [2], [3], [4]로 표시된 곳 중에서 다음 문장이 가장 적합한 곳은?
"그런 다음, 편한 시간에 저희 매장에 오셔서 제품 샘플을 보세요."
(A) [1]
(B) [2]
(C) [3]
(D) [4]

Q2. [1], [2], [3], [4]로 표시된 곳 중에서 다음 문장이 가장 적합한 곳은?
"언제든지 전화하셔서 무료 가정 방문 상담을 예약하세요."
(A) [1]
(B) [2]
(C) [3]
(D) [4]

YBM TEST
본책 p. 195

1. (C)　**2.** (D)　**3.** (C)

[1-3] 이메일

수신: 〈tenantlist@creeksideapts.com〉
발신: 〈osborneh@creedsideapts.com〉
날짜: 8월 13일
내용: 중요한 안내

크릭사이드 아파트 세입자 여러분께,

건물에 대한 지속적인 개선 작업의 일환으로, 시 전력회사 직원에게 우리 건물 변압기 보수를 시행할 수 있도록 하기 위해 약속을 잡았습니다. 작업은 8월 20일 수요일 오후 2시에서 약 4시까지 이루어질 것입니다. **1**안전상의 이유로, 이 시간에는 전 건물에 대한 전기가 차단되어야 합니다. 이것이 끼칠 불편에 대해 미리 사과드립니다.

데이터를 잃지 않기 위해, 당일 오후 2시 전에 컴퓨터 전원을 꺼 주실 것을 당부드립니다. **3**문을 꼭 닫아 놓기만 하면 냉장고와 냉동고 안에 있는 물건에 미칠 영향에 대해서는 걱정하실 필요가 없습니다. 최대 4시간까지는 온도가 유지되며, 작업 시간은 최대 2시간 지속될 것으로 예상됩니다. 이런 경우라면 음식이 상하는 일은 없을 겁니다.

다음 세입자 회의 때 향후 건물 개선 계획이 밝혀질 겁니다. 회의는 8월 28일 목요일 오후 7시 레크리에이션 룸으로 일정이 잡혔습니다. **2**다음 회의 때 의논돼야 할 주제들 목록이 첨부된 것을 보시고 추가돼야 할 것이 있다면 제게 연락 주십시오.

헤더 오스본
건물 관리자, 크릭사이드 아파트

어휘 tenant 세입자 ongoing 지속적인, 진행 중인 upgrade (장비·건물 등에 대한) 개선 representative 직원, 대표 municipal 시의 utility company (전기·가스 등을 공급하는) 공익 기업 maintenance 유지, 보수 transformer 변압기 shut off (엔진·전기 등을) 멈추다, 차단하다 in advance 미리 inconvenience 불편함 power down 전원을 차단하다 freezer 냉동고 maintain 유지하다

1.
번역 이메일의 목적은 무엇인가?
(A) 세입자들에게 안전 규정을 상기시키려고
(B) 새 단장 작업에 관해 알리려고
(C) 세입자들에게 예정된 정전에 관해 알려 주려고
(D) 새로운 아파트 정책을 설명하려고

해설 주제/목적
첫 번째 단락에서 변압기 공사가 있을 것이라는 안내에 이어 '이 시간에는 전 건물에 대한 전기가 차단되어야 합니다(the electricity to the entire building must be shut off

during this period)'라고 했고, 두 번째 단락에서 구체적인 행동 요령을 설명했으므로 (C)가 정답이다.

2.
번역 오스본 씨는 자신의 이메일에 무엇을 포함시켰는가?
(A) 검사 일정표
(B) 안전 수칙 목록
(C) 동의서
(D) 회의 안건

해설 세부사항
세 번째 단락 '다음 회의 때 의논돼야 할 주제들 목록이 첨부된 것을 보시고 추가돼야 할 것이 있다면 제게 연락 주십시오(Please see the attached list of topics that are to be discussed at the next meeting and let me know if anything needs to be added)'라고 말한 데서 회의 안건을 첨부했음을 알 수 있으므로 (D)가 정답이다.

Paraphrasing
지문의 list of topics that are to be discussed at the next meeting → 정답의 a meeting agenda

3.
번역 [1], [2], [3], [4]로 표시된 곳 중에서 다음 문장이 가장 적합한 곳은?
"이런 경우라면 음식이 상하는 일은 없을 겁니다."
(A) [1]
(B) [2]
(C) [3]
(D) [4]

해설 문장 삽입
삽입 문장에서 말하는 '이런 경우'가 무엇을 가리키는지 찾으면 된다. 두 번째 단락에서 '문을 꼭 닫아 놓기만 하면(as long as you keep the doors shut) 냉장고 안의 음식에 영향을 미치지 않는다고 했고, 냉장고 온도가 4시간 유지되고 작업은 2시간 걸린다고 했다. 이 모든 경우에 이어 삽입 문장이 들어가는 게 자연스러우므로 (C)가 정답이다.

Unit 8 연계 문제

 예제1
본책 p. 196

	스미스 브라더스 배관 설비 사원 작업 보고서	
작업 번호	주소	작업 내역
303	파인 스트릿 428번지	리틀턴 세탁기 설치
306	크릭 로드 23번지	ADR 식기 세척기 설치

수신: 스미스 브라더스 배관 설비
발신: 샌드라 브런스윅

어제 파인 스트릿 428번지, 제 집에서 배관 공사를 받았습니다. 기사님이 제시간에 도착해서 적시에 작업을 마쳤습니다.

Q1. 브런스윅 씨는 어떤 상표 가전제품을 소유하고 있는가?
(A) 리틀턴
(B) ADR

예제2
본책 p. 197

수신: 제나 심즈
발신: 데이빗 실바, 모다르 여행사

안녕하세요 심즈 씨,

동봉된 송장을 확인하세요. 귀하께서 5월 9일에 왕복으로 다녀오신 세븐 시스터즈 절벽 여행 때 발생한 추가 경비가 반영되도록 수정하였습니다.

모다르 여행사 송장

날짜: 5월 28일
청구서 수령인: 제나 심즈

내역	수량	가격
남부 영국 패키지 여행	1	1,270파운드
추가 여행	1	113파운드
	총액	1,383파운드

Q2. 모다르 여행사는 왜 심즈 씨에게 113파운드를 청구했는가?
(A) 심즈 씨가 여행 기간을 연장했다.
(B) 심즈 씨가 세븐 시스터즈의 명소를 여행했다.

YBM TEST
본책 p. 198

1. (B) **2.** (D) **3.** (C) **4.** (A) **5.** (A)

[1-5] 일정표 + 의견서 + 이메일

포트 디아즈: 페리 일일 시간표

클리어워터 페리즈에서는 승객 여러분의 편의를 위해 운행 시간을 지키려고 노력하고 있습니다. 하지만, 혹독한 기상조건에서는 연착이나 취소가 있을 수 있다는 점을 기억해 주십시오.

목적지	출발 시간	운임*: 성인 / 어린이
그랜스터	오전 8:05	25유로 / 13유로
워시번	오전 11:30	18유로 / 8유로
3소머빌	**오후 1:25**	12유로 / 6유로
첼름스퍼드	오후 5:50	20유로 / 10유로

***1** 페리를 자주 이용하는 승객은, 소지자에게 20% 할인가로 여행할 수 있게 해 주는 EZ 패스를 신청하세요.

https://www.clearwaterferries.com/feedback

클리어워터 페리즈 고객 의견서

고객 이름: 나탈리 밀른   이메일 주소: nataliem@kzservices.com

의견 형태: [X] 문의   [X] 불만   [ ] 제안   [ ] 기타

의견:
1최근 제 클리어워터 페리즈 EZ 패스에 문제가 있었습니다. 6월 20일 포트 디아즈에서 페리에 승선하는데, 부두 입구에 있는 카드 스캐너가 제 패스를 읽지 않으려고 했어요. 작동시키려고 몇 차례 시도해 본 후에, 그리고 한 직원의 도움까지 받은 후에, 승선권을 구매해야 한다는 얘기를 들었습니다. **5**다행히, 목적지까지 가는 승선권을 살 만큼의 현금이 있었어요. **2**차액에 대해 환불을 받을 수 있다고 생각합니다. 그래서 이것을 어떻게 하면 되는지 알고 싶습니다. 제 EZ 패스 번호는 38492입니다.

수신: 나탈리 밀른 〈nataliem@kzservices.com〉
발신: 클리어워터 페리즈 안내 〈info@clearwaterferries.com〉
날짜: 6월 23일
주제: 클리어워터 페리즈 고객 의견

밀른 씨께,

클리어워터 페리즈를 대표해, 귀하가 최근 포트 디아즈에서 실망스러운 경험을 하신 데 대해 사과드리고 싶습니다. 유감스럽게도, **4**그곳의 카드 판독기가 매우 오래돼서 항상 요구되는 대로 기능을 하지는 않습니다. 기계들을 대체하는 작업을 지금 진행 중입니다. 저희 기록에 따르면 **3**기계가 귀하의 여행일 오후 1시 직후에 부두에서 귀하의 카드를 인식했습니다. 하지만 무슨 이유에서인지 입장을 허락하지는 않았습니다. 저희 환불 정책은, **5**현금 구매에 대해서는 EZ 패스 신청 시 기록된 주소로 수표로 환불금을 보내고, 신용카드 구매에 대해서는 신용카드 계좌로 상환 지불을 하는 것입니다. 영업일 기준 10일 이내에 차액에 대해 환불 받을 것을 예상하시면 됩니다. 이를 통해 문제가 만족스럽게 해결되기를 희망합니다.

세바스찬 러셀

어휘 endeavor 노력하다 service (교통수단) 운행편 delay 지연, 연착 cancellation 취소 severe 혹독한 destination 목적지, 행선지 fare 운임 frequently 수시로 holder 소지자 customer feedback 고객 의견 issue 문제; 발급하다 dock 부두 assistance 도움 assume 추정하다 get a refund 환불을 받다 (price) difference 차액 on behalf of ~을 대표해서 apologize for ~을 사과하다 disappointing 실망스러운 function 기능하다 in the process of -ing ~하는 중인 acknowledge 인정하다 presence 존재 shortly after ~ 직후 refund policy 환불 정책 by check 수표로 registration 등록, 신청 reimbursement 변제, 상환 resolve 해결하다 to one's satisfaction ~의 마음에 들게

1.
번역 밀른 씨에 대해 암시된 것은?
(A) 평일에 여행했다.
(B) 페리를 자주 이용한다.
(C) 교통카드를 분실했다.
(D) 포트 디아즈에서 일한다.

해설 연계
고객 의견서의 의견 란에서 '최근 제 클리어워터 페리즈 EZ 패스에 문제가 있었습니다(I recently had an issue with my Clearwater Ferries EZ-Pass)'라고 말한 것으로 보아 밀른 씨는 이미 EZ 패스를 구입했다. 그런데 시간표에서 '페리를 자주 이용하는 승객은, ~ EZ 패스를 신청하세요(Passengers who frequently travel on the ferry may apply for an EZ-Pass)'라고 말했다. 밀른 씨가 페리를 자주 이용한다는 것을 유추할 수 있으므로 (B)가 정답이다.

2.
번역 의견서 첫 번째 단락 다섯 번째 줄의 "assume"과 의미상 가장 가까운 것은?
(A) 수락하다
(B) 깨닫다
(C) 확인하다
(D) 생각하다

해설 동의어
해당 문장은 '차액에 대해 환불을 받을 수 있다고 생각합니다'라고 해석된다. 여기서 assume은 '생각하다'라는 뜻으로 쓰였으므로 '생각하다, 추측하다'를 뜻하는 (D)가 정답이다.

3.
번역 밀른 씨의 여행 목적지는 어디일 것 같은가?
(A) 그랜스턴
(B) 워시번
(C) 소머빌
(D) 헬름스퍼드

해설 연계
이메일에서 '기계가 귀하의 여행일 오후 1시 직후에 부두에서 귀하의 카드를 인식했습니다(the machine did acknowledge the presence of your card at the dock shortly after 1 P.M. on your date of travel)'라고 말한 데서 밀른 씨가 오후 1시쯤에 기계를 통과했음을 알 수 있다. 위의 시간표에서 보면 바로 직후인 오후 1:25에 출발하는 페리가 소머빌 행이라고 나와 있다. 따라서 (C)가 정답이다.

4.
번역 러셀 씨는 포트 디아즈에 관해 무엇을 언급하는가?
(A) 장비가 오래되었다.
(B) 직원들이 교육을 더 받아야 한다.
(C) 현재 건설 중이다.
(D) 낮에는 붐빈다.

해설 세부사항
이메일에서 포트 디아즈에 관해 얘기하며 '그곳의 카드 판독기가 매우 오래돼서 항상 요구되는 대로 기능을 하지는 않습니다(the card-reading machines there are very old and do not always function as required)'라고 했다. 따라서 (A)가 정답이다.

Paraphrasing
지문의 the card-reading machines there are very old
→ 정답의 Its equipment is outdated

5.
번역 밀른 씨의 환불에 대해 사실인 것은?
(A) 수표로 발급될 것이다.
(B) 전체 승선권 가격에 대해서일 것이다.
(C) 이미 밀른 씨에게 보내졌다.
(D) 신용카드 내역서에 나올 것이다.

해설 연계
밀른 씨가 의견서에서 '현금으로 표를 샀고, 차액을 환불 받을 수 있을 것(I had enough cash ~ for the difference)'이라고 말했고, 이메일에서 안내된 환불 정책 부분에서는 '현금 구매에 대해서는 EZ 패스 신청 시 기록된 주소로 수표로 환불금을 보낸다(Our refund policy is to send refunds by check to the address listed on the EZ-Pass registration for cash purchases)'라고 되어 있다. 밀른 씨는 승선권을 현금으로 구매하는 바람에 20퍼센트 할인을 받지 못했으므로 그 차액을 수표로 환불을 받게 될 것이고 정답은 (A)가 된다.

CHAPTER 2 지문 유형

Unit 1 편지 / 이메일

예제
본책 p. 200

수신: 아유미 네기시 〈negishiayumi@marquettepost.com〉
발신: 마리아나 카발칸티 〈m.cavalcanti@benitassolar.com〉

네기시 씨께,

지난주 약속 때 만나뵈서 기뻤습니다. 태양 전지판 설치 적합성 여부에 관해 당신의 주택을 평가하기 위해서였죠. 지붕의 크기와 위치 때문에, 제 생각에는 15개 전지판 식이 적절할 것 같습니다.
말씀해 주신 에너지 사용에 비추어 봤을 때, 월별로 대략 56%의 에너지 요금 절감을 기대하실 수 있습니다. 향후에는 이 시스템으로 매달 훨씬 더 많은 비용을 절약할 수 있을 것입니다.
이 건을 계속 진행하실 생각인지 알려주십시오.

마리아나 카발칸티
컨설턴트, 베니타스 솔라

어휘 assess 평가하다 property 재산, 건물 suitability 적합성 appropriate 적절한 go forward with ~을 계속 추진하다

Q1. 카발칸티 씨가 네기시 씨에게 편지를 쓴 이유는 무엇인가?
(A) 청구액 지불을 요청하려고
(B) 방문에 따른 후속 조치로

Q2. 네기시 씨에 대해 암시된 것은?
(A) 에너지 절약에 관심이 있다.
(B) 에너지 사용료가 과다하게 청구되었다.

YBM TEST
본책 p. 201

1. (C)	2. (A)	3. (B)	4. (C)	5. (D)
6. (C)	7. (A)	8. (B)	9. (C)	10. (B)
11. (A)	12. (C)	13. (C)	14. (C)	15. (D)
16. (A)	17. (C)	18. (C)	19. (C)	20. (B)
21. (A)	22. (D)	23. (B)	24. (D)	25. (A)
26. (C)	27. (A)			

[1-2] 이메일

수신: 직원 명부 〈staff@pemberton1.com〉
발신: 셰리 플린 〈sflynn@pemberton1.com〉
날짜: 11월 23일
내용: 다음 차례 강습

여러분 안녕하세요,

펨버튼이 12월 10일에, 문을 열게 된다는 걸 알리게 되어 기쁩니다. **1스키와 폴을 챙겨 오지 않을 사람들은, 반드시 필요한 장비를 개장일 이전에 현장 상점에서 예약하세요.** 지금까지 온라인 예약에 비추어 보면, 우리는 전에 이 스포츠를 해보지 않은 사람을 많이 포함해 여러 개의 큰 그룹을 맞이하게 될 것 같습니다. 그러므로, **1초보자 단계가 다른 해처럼 스키장의 40%가 아니고 약 75%를 차지할 것으로 예상하셔야 합니다.** 시즌 첫 몇 주간은 특히 정신 없이 바쁠 것입니다. 그래서 **1,2여러분 중 누군가 초과 근무를 할 사람이 필요합니다. 그렇게 하는 데 관심이 있다면 케슬린 클락 씨에게 kclark@pemberton1.com으로 이메일 주십시오.**

고맙습니다!

셰리 플린

어휘 open for business 영업하는 pole (스키) 폴 be sure to 부정사 반드시 ~하다 on-site 현장의 based on ~에 근거해 make up (전체 중 한 부분을) 이루다, 차지하다 hectic 정신없이 바쁜 pick up extra shift 초과 근무를 하다

1.
번역 이메일 수령인은 누구이겠는가?
(A) 요리 강사들
(B) 음악 교사들
(C) 스키 강사들
(D) 웨이트 트레이너들

해설 추론
스키 초보자들이 많을 것이고 굉장히 바빠질 거라고 말하면서, '여러분 중 누군가 초과근무를 할 사람이 필요합니다. 그렇게 하는 데 관심 있으면 이메일 주십시오(we need some of you to pick up extra shifts. If you are interested in doing so, please send an e-mail)'라고 요청했다. 이메일 수령인이 스키 학습자를 위해 일하는 사람임을 알 수 있으므로 (C)가 정답이다.

2.
번역 직원들은 클라크 씨에게 왜 이메일을 보내야 하는가?
(A) 추가 근무를 하겠다고 자원하려고
(B) 장비를 예약하려고
(C) 납세 서류를 작성하려고
(D) 개선을 위한 제안을 공유하려고

해설 세부사항
'여러분 중 누군가 초과근무를 할 사람이 필요합니다. 그렇게 하는 데 관심이 있다면 케슬린 클락 씨에게 kclark@pemberton1.com으로 이메일 주십시오(we need some of you to pick up extra shifts. If you are interested in doing so, please send an e-mail to Kathleen Clark at kclark@pemberton1.com)'라고 했으므로 (A)가 정답이다.

Paraphrasing
지문의 pick up extra shifts
→ 정답의 work additional hours

[3-5] 이메일

수신: 조디 오브레곤 〈j.obregon@eastonsales.com〉
발신: 황 라오〈h.lao@eastonsales.com〉
날짜: 2월 3일
내용: 휴대폰 업데이트

오브레곤 씨께,

회사의 휴대전화 건으로 제게 맡기신 업무에 대해 응답하기 위해 메일을 씁니다. **3요청하신 대로, 어떤 것이 우리 필요에 가장 적합할지 결정하기 위해 여러 공급자의 수많은 휴대전화 패키지 계약 조건을 검토했습니다. 4포뮬러 통신사 사용을 권하신 것으로 알고 있는데요.** 그들이 무제한 통화 시간에 매력적인 월별 요금을 제공하기는 하지만, 그 패키지에는 이용자당 데이터가 500 메가바이트만 포함되어 있습니다. **4이 한도가 넘으면 데이터 비용이 매우 비싸집니다.** 직원들이 할당량을 쉽게 초과해 요금이 예산에서 많이 벗어날 수도 있습니다.

포뮬러 패키지보다 그다지 많이 비싸지 않으면서 데이터는 훨씬 더 후한, 팁스 모바일도 생각해 봤습니다. 하지만, 고객평을 검토해 보니까 그럴 가치가 있는 것 같지 않습니다. **5팁스 모바일은 통화가 중간에 끊어지는 경우나 서비스가 안 되는 지역이 많은 것으로 알려져 있습니다.** 무엇보다, 우리 영업에 부정적인 영향을 끼치지 않기 위해 신뢰할 만한 것이 필요합니다. 그래서, 이것 또한 저희에게 좋은 대안은 아닙니다.

현재의 계약이 만료될 때까지는 꼭 결정을 하지 않아도 되기 때문에, 이 일을 고민할 시간은 좀 더 있습니다. 다음 주 초에 다시 최신 사항을 알려 드리겠습니다.

황 라오

어휘 follow-up on ~에 대해 후속[추가] 조치를 하다 assign (책임을) 맡기다 terms and conditions (계약의) 조건 provider 공급자 suit one's needs 요구에 적합하다 monthly rate 월별 요금 exceed 초과하다 allotted amount 할당량 bill 청구서, 청구금액 budget 예산 generous 후한 look into 들여다보다, 조사하다 dropped call 전화통화 중 연결이 끊어지는 현상 expire (기한이) 만료되다 work on ~에 애를 쓰다, ~에 대해 작업을 하다

3.
번역 라오 씨는 무엇을 해 달라고 요청 받았는가?
(A) 직원들에게 전화 나눠주기
(B) 전화 패키지 조사하기
(C) 휴대전화 특성 시험하기
(D) 전화 수리 이행하기

해설 세부사항
두 번째 문장에서 '요청하신 대로, ~ 여러 공급자의 수많은 휴대전화 패키지 계약 조건을 검토했습니다(As requested, I have reviewed the terms and conditions of a number of cell phone packages from various providers)'라고 했고, 포뮬러 통신사(Formula Communications)와 팁스 모바일(Tibbs Mobile) 패키지를 비교하는 것이 주요 내용이므로 (B)가 정답이다.

Paraphrasing

지문의 reviewed the terms and conditions of a number of cell phone packages
→ 정답의 research phone packages

4.

번역 라오 씨는 오브레곤 씨의 제안을 왜 거절하는가?
(A) 더 이상 나오지 않는다는 것을 알기 때문에
(B) 충분한 관련 정보를 얻을 수가 없어서
(C) 과비용을 유발할 수 있다고 생각해서
(D) 시행하는 데 너무 많은 시간이 걸릴까 걱정돼서

해설 세부사항
세 번째 문장에서 '포뮬러 통신사 사용을 권하신 것으로 알고 있는데요(I know you recommended using Formula Communications)'라면서, 그 제안의 문제점을 지적하고 있다. '데이터 비용이 매우 비싸진다(the cost of data becomes very expensive),' '요금이 예산에서 많이 벗어날 수도 있다(pushing the bill way over budget)' 등으로 미루어 (C)가 정답이다.

Paraphrasing

지문의 data becomes very expensive, pushing the bill way over budget → 정답의 lead to overspending

5.

번역 [1], [2], [3], [4]로 표시된 곳 중에서 다음 문장이 가장 적합한 곳은?
"무엇보다, 우리 영업에 부정적인 영향을 끼치지 않기 위해 신뢰할 만한 것이 필요합니다."
(A) [1]
(B) [2]
(C) [3]
(D) [4]

해설 문장 삽입
삽입 문장에서 '우리 영업에 부정적으로 영향을 미칠(negatively affect our business)'것을 피하자고 했는데, 이는 [4] 바로 앞에 나오는 '통화가 중간에 끊어지는 경우나 서비스가 안 되는 지역이 많은(having a lot of dropped calls and out-of-service areas)' 것을 가리킨다. 따라서 [4], 즉 (D)가 정답이다.

[6-9] 편지

크리스토퍼 머피
윌킨슨 거리 861번지
프랭클린, 매사추세츠 주 02038

3월 2일

머피 씨께,

저희 기록에 귀하는 최근 저희 매장에서 로미타 사의 전기구동 안락의자를 구입하신 것으로 나와 있습니다. 저희는 제조사로부터 **6L-980 모델이 시장에서 정리되고 있다는 통보를 받았습니다. 즉시 이행된다는 통보로, 잠재적인 화재 위험 때문입니다.** 전력 공급 장치의 피복 부분이 반복 사용으로 쉽게 뜯어질 수 있어, 사용자가 노출된 전선에 접촉할 경우 잠재적인 감전의 위험이 있습니다. **7이는 가죽과, 겉천을 씌우는 모델 둘 다에 해당 됩니다.** 아직까지 부상이 보고된 적은 없으나, 회사 측에서는 소비자를 위해 신중을 기하기로 했습니다. 이 제품은 전국적으로 저희 5개 전 매장 내 보이드 퍼니처에서, 그리고 기타 가구 소매점들에서 판매됐습니다.

6고객들은 전액 환불을 받고 의자들을 반품할 수 있습니다. 3월 5일과 6일에는 매장 내에서 직접 반송 행사를 벌일 예정입니다. 이 기간에는, 자신의 제품을 들고 와서 현장에서 환불 조치를 받을 수 있습니다. 아니면, 3월 10일부터, 로미타 사가 가정 방문 수거 서비스를 제공합니다. 의자를 주요 지역의 생산 공장으로 직접 우송할 수도 있습니다. **8이를 위한 주소는 동봉한 서류에 제공되었습니다. 9어떤 옵션을 선택하시든지, 환불 요구 의사는 늦어도 4월 25일까지 제출되어야 합니다.** 고객께서는 문제가 해결된 새로운 안락의자가 5월 15일부터 판매될 예정임을 기억해 주십시오.

배상 청구서를 다운로드 하시려면 www.boydfurniture.com/documents를 방문하십시오. 프린터를 이용할 수 없으면 로미타 사의 핫라인 1-800-555-0184번으로 연락해 청구서를 요청하세요.

보이드 가구 고객 서비스 팀

동봉

어휘 power-operated 전기로 구동하는 recliner (등받이와 발판을 조절할 수 있는) 안락의자 manufacturer 제조업체 remove 치우다, 없애다 effective (조치 등이) ~부터 시행되는 potential 잠재적인 fire hazard 화재 위험 casing 포장, 싸개 power supply 전력 공급 장치 pose a risk 위험을 제기하다, 위험 요소가 되다 electrical shock 감전 come into contact with ~와 접촉하다 exposed 노출된 upholstered (소파 등에) 겉천을 씌우는[댄] thus far 이제까지는 err on the side of caution 지나치다 싶을 정도로 조심하다 for one's sake ~을 위해서 retailer 소매상 full refund 전액 환불 in-store 매장 내의 drop-off (상점 등에) 직접 가져다 주는 on-site 현장에서 residential 주택의, 주거의 enclosed 동봉된 claim (권리로서) 요구하다 no later than (시한) ~가 넘지 않게 issue (해결해야 할) 문제 resolve 해결하다 claim form 배상 청구서

6.

번역 편지의 목적은 무엇인가?
(A) 고객의 피드백을 요청하려고
(B) 기기의 특징을 소개하려고
(C) 제품의 리콜을 알리려고
(D) 품질 보증 정보를 설명하려고

해설 주제/목적
첫 번째 단락의 'L-980 모델이 시장에서 정리되고 있다는 통지를 받았습니다. 즉시 이행된다는 통보로, 잠재적인 화재 위험 때문입니다(model L-980 is being removed from the market—effective immediately—due to a potential fire hazard)'라고 한 부분에서 제품에 문제가 있음을 알 수 있다. 두 번째 단락에서는 '고객들은 전액 환불을 받고 의자들을 반품할 수 있습니다(Customers can return the chairs for a full refund)'라는 말로 시작해 반품 방식을 설명하고 있으므로 (C)가 정답이다.

7.

번역 L-980 모델에 대해 암시된 것은?
(A) 한 종류 이상의 커버로 생산되었다.
(B) 디자인이 결과적으로 손상되었다.
(C) 오직 보이드 퍼니처에서만 구할 수 있다.
(D) 5개 국가에서 판매된다.

해설 추론
첫 번째 단락에서, L-980 모델이 잠재적인 감전 위험(posing a potential risk of electrical shock)이 있다고 하면서, '이는 가죽과, 겉천을 씌우는 모델 둘 다에 해당됩니다(This applies to both the leather and the upholstered versions)'라고 했다. 둘 다 커버(covering)에 해당되므로 (A)가 정답이다.

Paraphrasing
지문의 the leather and the upholstered versions
→ 정답의 more than one covering

8.

번역 편지와 함께 무엇이 포함되었는가?
(A) 반송 라벨
(B) 우편 주소
(C) 상점 목록
(D) 배상 청구서

해설 세부사항
두 번째 단락에서 의자를 생산 공장으로 직접 우송할 수도 있다면서, '이를 위한 주소는 동봉한 서류에 제공되었습니다(the address for which is provided on the enclosed document)'라고 밝혔으므로 (B)가 정답이다. (D)의 배상 청구서는 별도로 다운로드해야 한다.

9.

번역 머피 씨는 언제까지 조치를 취해야 하는가?
(A) 3월 5일
(B) 3월 10일
(C) 4월 25일
(D) 5월 15일

해설 세부사항
두 번째 단락 뒷부분에서 '어떤 옵션을 선택하시든지, 환불 요구 의사는 늦어도 4월 25일까지 제출되어야 합니다(No matter which option you choose, your intention to claim a refund must be submitted no later than April 25)'라고 했으므로 (C)가 정답이다.

[10-13] 이메일

수신: 디클랜 버지스
발신: 푸옹 응우옌
날짜: 7월 15일
내용: 베트남 그룹 투어

버지스 씨께,

두옹 여행사를 대표해, 귀하가 5일간의 베트남 여행을 위해 예약하신 그룹 투어 패키지에 관한 편지를 씁니다. 귀하의 보증금과 여권 정보를 받았고, **12**시드니에서 7월 20일에 출발해 7월 24일에 돌아가는, 시드니-호치민 시간 왕복 비행권을 예약했습니다. 하지만, **10**귀하의 여행 계획에 약간의 변동이 있을 것 같습니다. 여행 중 둘째 날 7월 21일에, 투어 참가자들에게 선택 투어를 할 수 있게 할 계획입니다. 저희는 오페라 투어(동 코이 거리의 오페라 하우스 투어), 박물관 투어(전쟁 박물관 투어), 사원 투어(티엔 허우 사원 투어)의 가이드 투어를 제공하는 현지 독립 여행사와 함께 일합니다. **11**이들 당일 투어는 각각 최소 15인의 참가자가 필요합니다. 그런 이유로 오페라 투어가 취소되었습니다. 이것은 귀하가 선택한 액티비티이므로, **10, 13**저희는 귀하를 다른 투어 중 하나로 재예약을 해야 합니다. 제가 입장권을 예약할 수 있도록 어떤 것을 원하시는지 이메일 답장 주십시오. 귀하의 자리를 확보하기 위해 가능한 빨리 해야만 합니다.

제가 보낸 여행 계획서상의 액티비티 일정 중 나머지의 경우는, 모두 예정대로 진행될 것입니다. 과거 참가자들의 제안에 근거해, **12**벤탄 시장 여행이 투어 마지막 날 오전, 공항으로 향하기 전에 있을 것입니다. 이 액티비티 일정으로 여러분이 가족이나 친구들을 위한 선물을 살 걱정 없이 투어의 다른 부분을 즐길 수 있게 되기를 희망합니다.

푸옹 응우옌

어휘 on behalf of ~을 대표[대신]해서 deposit 보증금 round-trip 왕복의 participant 참가자 tour operator 여행사 guided 가이드가 인솔하는 daily tour 당일 투어 cancel 취소하다 re-book 다시 예약하다 as for ~에 대해 말하자면 remainder 나머지 pick up 사다, 집어 들다 souvenir 기념품

10.

번역 이메일의 목적은 무엇인가?
(A) 서비스 이용료를 요청하려고
(B) 여행 일정을 변경하려고
(C) 여권 번호를 확인하려고
(D) 투어 패키지를 홍보하려고

해설 주제/목적
첫 번째 단락에서 여행 일정에 변동사항이 생겼다고 말하면서, '다른 투어 중 하나로 재예약을 해야 합니다. 제가 입장권을 예약할 수 있도록 어떤 것을 원하시는지 이메일 답장 주십시오(we need to re-book you ~ Please e-mail me back to let me know which one prefer so that I can reserve your ticket)'라고 요청했다. 일정 변경을 위한 것이므로 (B)가 정답이다.

Paraphrasing
지문의 re-book you for one of the other tours
→ 정답의 revise a travel itinerary

11.

번역 오페라 투어에 대해 암시된 것은?
(A) 진행하기에는 신청자가 너무 적었다.
(B) 응우옌 씨의 회사에서 운영한다.
(C) 나쁜 날씨 때문에 취소되었다.
(D) 버지스 씨에게 추가 요금을 요구한다.

해설 **추론**

첫 번째 단락 중간 부분에서 '이들 당일 투어는 각각 최소 15인의 참가자가 필요합니다. 그런 이유로 오페라 투어는 취소가 되었습니다(These daily tours must have a minimum of fifteen participants each. Therefore, the Opera Tour has been canceled)'라고 했다. 인원 부족으로 취소된 것이므로 (A)가 정답이다.

12.

번역 버지스 씨는 어떤 날에 시장을 방문할 것인가?
(A) 7월 20일
(B) 7월 21일
(C) 7월 24일
(D) 7월 25일

해설 **세부사항**

두 번째 단락에서 '벤탄 시장 여행이 투어 마지막 날 오전, 공항으로 향하기 전에 있을 것입니다(the trip to Ben Thanh Market will take place on the final day of the tour, in the morning before you head to the airport)'라고 한 것으로 보아 시장은 마지막 날에 방문한다. 다시 첫 번째 단락에서 확인해 보면 '시드니에서 7월 20일에 출발해 7월 24일에 돌아가는(departing Sydney on July 20 and returning on July 24)'이라는 말이 나온다. 투어의 마지막 날, 즉 시장 방문하는 날이 7월 24일이므로 (C)가 정답이다.

13.

번역 [1], [2], [3], [4]로 표시된 곳 중에서 다음 문장이 가장 적합한 곳은?
"귀하의 자리를 확보하기 위해 가능한 한 빨리 해야만 합니다."
(A) [1]
(B) [2]
(C) [3]
(D) [4]

해설 **문장 삽입**

삽입 문장은 '자리 확보(guarantee you a spot)'가 필요하고, 그것도 '가능한 빨리' 해야 한다며 재촉하는 의도이다. '재예약이 필요하니 원하는 걸 이메일로 알려 달라'고 요청한 다음에 들어가는 것이 자연스럽다. 따라서 (C)가 정답이다.

[14-17] 편지

즈왈라 나야르
아보 광고
머스그레이브 거리 528번지
오클라호마 시티, 오클라호마 주 73102

나야르 씨께,

저는 엔더비 사의 선임 광고 매니저로, **14**우리 팀의 주요 멤버인 마라 파도베시 씨를 대신해 편지를 씁니다. 귀사의 빈 자리에 지원한 파도베시 씨를 추천하고자 합니다. 저는 파도베시 씨와 지난 5년간 함께 일했으며, 그녀의 업무 수행에 지속적으로 감동을 받았습니다. **15-A**그녀는 불과 2년 만에 인턴에서 팀 리더로 성장한 유일한 직원입니다. 덧붙여, **15-C**그녀는 정식 경영 교육을 받은 적이 없음에도 불구하고 팀을 순조롭게 맡아 이끌 줄 압니다.

수년간 그녀가 보여준 업무 수준은 어느 누구에게도 뒤지지 않습니다. **16**그녀가 지역 레스토랑 개업식 때 디자인한 전단을 동봉합니다. 그녀의 독창성을 확인하실 수 있을 겁니다. 의뢰인이 최종 결과에 굉장히 만족했고 더 많은 일을 가지고 수시로 저희 회사를 찾아 옵니다. 그러니까 직접적으로 파도베시 씨의 노력을 통해 저희는 고정 고객을 확보한 셈이고, 이것은 수많은 사례 중 하나일 뿐입니다. **17**파도베스키 씨와 그녀의 팀은 메츠 애슬레틱스를 위한 광고 개발도 맡아 했습니다. 언제든 그걸 꼭 보셔야 합니다. 보시면, 광고가 보는 이들의 시선을 사로잡는다는 데 동의하시리라 생각합니다.

직원 모두가 파도베시 씨를 밝은 미래를 가지고 **15-B**주도적으로 일해 나가는 사람이라고 믿고 있습니다. 그녀가 더 이상 엔더비 사 직원이 아니게 된다면 우리는 슬플 것입니다. 하지만 그녀의 진로가 그녀를 새로운 방향으로 이끌 것이라고 생각합니다.

혹시 이 일에 관해 더 의논하기 원하신다면, 시간 편하실 때 555-0174, 내선번호 20으로 자유롭게 연락 주십시오.

철수 정

어휘 **endorsement** (공개적인) 인정, 보증, 추천 **job opening** (구인이 필요한) 빈 자리 **impressed** 좋은 인상을 받은, 감동 받은 **performance** (업무 등의) 수행 **work one's way up** (서서히) 성장하다 **formal** 정식의 **managerial** 경영 **take charge of** (책임을) 맡다 **exhibit** 보이다 **second to none** 아무에게도 뒤지지 않는, 아주 훌륭한 **flyer** 광고지, 전단 **grand opening** 개업, 개장 **immensely** 굉장히 **secure** 얻어내다, 확보하다 **commercial** (상업) 광고 **capture** (관심 등을) 사로잡다 **self-starter** 자발적[주도적]으로 일하는 사람 **career path** 진로 **availability** 이용 가능성, 시간이 됨

14.

번역 무엇에 관한 편지인가?
(A) 채용 홍보
(B) 일자리 지원
(C) 동료 추천
(D) 일자리 제안 거절

해설 **주제/목적**

첫 번째 문장에서 '우리 팀의 주요 멤버인 마라 파도베시 씨를 대신해 편지를 씁니다. 귀사의 빈 자리에 지원한 파도베시 씨를 추천하고자 합니다(I am writing on behalf of Mara Padovesi, a key member of our team. I would like to provide an endorsement for Ms. Padovesi, who has applied for the job opening at your company)'라고 했고, 이어 파도베시 씨의 업무 능력과, 그와 헤어지는 아쉬움 등을 얘기하고 있으므로, 동료를 위해 취업을 추천하는 글임을 알 수 있다. 따라서 (C)가 정답이다.

Paraphrasing

지문의 provide an endorsement for Ms. Padovesi
→ 정답의 recommending a colleague

15.

번역 파도베시 씨에 대해 언급되지 않은 것은?
(A) 다른 사람들보다 빨리 승진했다.
(B) 의욕적인 사람으로 여겨진다.
(C) 타고난 지도력을 지니고 있다.
(D) 더 이상 엔더비 사의 직원이 아니다.

해설 **Not / true**

첫 번째 단락의 '그녀는 불과 2년 만에 인턴에서 팀 리더로 성장한 유일한 직원입니다(She is the only staff member to have worked her way up from intern to team leader in just two years)'에 (A)가, 세 번째 단락의 '주도적으로 일해 나가는 사람(a self-starter)'에 (B)가, 첫 번째 단락, '그녀는 정식 경영 교육을 받은 적이 없음에도 불구하고 팀을 순조롭게 맡아 이끌 줄 압니다(although she has never received formal managerial training, she has been able to take charge of a team with ease)'에 (C)가 언급되어 있다. 세 번째 단락에서 '그녀가 더 이상 엔더비 사 직원이 아니게 된다면 우리는 슬플 것입니다(We would be disappointed if she were no longer part of the Enderby Incorporated staff)'라고 한 것은, '만약 다른 회사로 떠난다면'이라는 가정이므로 엔더비 사의 직원이 아니라는 (D)는 언급된 바 없다.

Paraphrasing

지문의 a self-starter → 보기의 a motivated individual

16.

번역 정 씨는 편지와 함께 무엇을 보냈는가?

(A) 홍보용 인쇄물
(B) 가용 인력 일정표
(C) 고용 계약서
(D) 신청서 양식

해설 **세부사항**

두 번째 단락, '그녀가 지역 레스토랑 개업식 때 디자인한 전단을 동봉합니다(Enclosed is a flyer that she designed for a local restaurant's grand opening)'라고 한 부분에서 홍보용 전단을 동봉했음을 알 수 있으므로 (A)가 정답이다.

Paraphrasing

지문의 a flyer → 정답의 leaflet

17.

번역 [1], [2], [3], [4]로 표시된 곳 중에서 다음 문장이 가장 적합한 곳은?
"언제이든 그걸 꼭 보셔야 합니다."
(A) [1]
(B) [2]
(C) [3]
(D) [4]

해설 **문장 삽입**

삽입 문장 '그걸 꼭 보셔야 합니다(sure to catch it)'에서 말하는 '그것'은 [3]번 바로 앞, '파도베스키 씨와 그녀의 팀은 메츠 애슬레틱스를 위한 광고 개발도 맡아 했습니다(Ms. Padovesi and her team were also responsible for developing a commercial for Metz Athletics)'에서 가리키는 '광고'이다. [3]번 문장 뒤에 나오는 '보시면(When you do)'에서 다시 한 번 확인할 수 있으므로 (C)가 정답이다.

[18-22] 전단+편지

민주주의 중요성 연합

여러분의 목소리를 전달할 수 있게 도와줍니다

민주주의 중요성 연합(DMA)은 모든 단계에 걸쳐 공정한 선거를 보장하는 일에 헌신하면서, 보다 엄격한 신분 규제 현안들을 다루고, 부재 투표자들을 위한 기간을 줄이고, 후보자 선택에 더 많은 기술을 도입해 나가고 있습니다. **18**밀러 카운티에 선거 등록이 되어 있는 분이라면, DMA 회원들이 법률 전문가들과 함께 여러분의 의견을 듣고, 최상의 논점들을 선거 관료들에게 제시하고자 합니다. 비록 지역 단위로라도, **19**저희는 사람들이 수동적으로 민주주의에 참여하는 데 익숙해지는 것을 원치 않습니다.

20토론회는 10월 3일 금요일 오후 7시 코트라이트 홀에서 열립니다. 누구나 참석할 수 있으며, DMA 회원이 아니어도 되고, 좌석은 선착순으로 이용 가능합니다. 아니면, 여러분의 의견을 r.klein@dmamiller.com으로 로버트 클라인 씨에게 보내주셔도 됩니다. **21**가장 훌륭한 의견들을 DMA의 위원회에서 선정하며, 이 의견들은 행사 때 이번 행사를 총괄할, 시장 다릴 어빈 씨가 큰 소리로 읽게 됩니다. 우리는 다양한 관점의 의견들이 포함될 수 있도록 노력을 기울일 것입니다. **20**행사 전 과정은 녹화되어 2시간 분량의 비디오로 전체 영상이 그 다음 주에 DMA 웹사이트에 게시될 예정입니다.

셰리 레논
콜드웰 거리 970번지
무어랜드, 오클라호마 주 73852

레논 씨께,

저희 위원회는 투표 절차에 관해 귀하가 제출한 의견이, 이 주제와 관련해 열린 대화를 용이하게 한다는 우리의 사명을 위해, 건설적이면서 뛰어난 통찰을 담고 있다고 느꼈습니다. 귀하가 10월 3일 행사에 참여하실 수 없어서 유감입니다. 하지만 **21**귀하가 제출한 것이 선정되어 토론에 포함되게 되었습니다. **22**이 행사가 비디오로 온라인에 게재될 것이므로, 귀하의 발언을 사용할 수 있다는 공식적인 허가를 저희에게 주셨으면 합니다. 동봉한 서류를 작성하셔서 제공된 봉투를 이용해 반송해 주십시오. 이는 9월 20일이 넘지 않게 진행되어야 합니다. 혹시 질문이나 우려사항이 있으면 주저 없이 555-0199번으로 제게 연락해 주십시오.

로버트 클라인
DMA 부회장

동봉

어휘 **be dedicated to** ~에 헌신하다 **ensure** 보장하다 **tackle** 맞서다, (솔직하게) 다루다 **ID** 신분 확인(= identification) **regulation** 규정, 규제 **timeframe** 기간 **absentee voter** 부재 투표자 **incorporate** 포함시키다, 합하다 **put forth** 제시하다, 제안하다 **official** 관료, 고위 공무원 **get used to** ~에 익숙해지다 **passively** 수동적으로 **seating** 자리 **on a first come, first served basis** 선착순으로 **alternatively** 그렇지 않으면 **oversee** 감독하다, 관장하다 **endeavor** 노력하다 **perspective** 관점 **proceedings** 진행되는 일[행사]; (회의 등의) 공식 기록 **in their entirety** 전부 **procedure** 절차 **insightful** 통찰력이 있는 **constructive** 건설적인 **facilitate** 쉽게[원활하게] 해주다 **submission** 제출, 제출물 **remark** 언급, 발언 **fill out** 작성하다

18.
번역 전단은 어떤 수령인을 대상으로 하는가?
(A) 법률 전문가
(B) 정치인 후보자
(C) 등록된 선거인
(D) 선거 종사자

해설 세부사항
전단 첫 번째 단락에서 '밀러 카운티에 선거 등록이 되어 있는 분이라면, DMA 회원들이 법률 전문가들과 함께 여러분의 의견을 듣고(If you are registered to vote in Miller County, DMA members want to hear from you, along with their legal experts)' 싶다고 말한 것으로 보아 대상이 선거 등록자임을 알 수 있으므로 (C)가 정답이다.

19.
번역 전단에서 첫 번째 단락 여섯 번째 줄의 "used"와 의미상 가장 가까운 것은?
(A) 운용되는
(B) 재활용되는
(C) 익숙해진
(D) 격감된

해설 동의어
해당 문장은 '우리는 사람들이 수동적으로 민주주의에 참여하는 데 익숙해지는 것을 원치 않습니다(we don't want people getting used to passively participating in democracy)'라는 의미로 해석된다. 여기서 used는 '익숙한'이라는 뜻이므로 (C)가 정답이다. get used to는 '~에 익숙해지다'라는 의미로 쓰인다.

20.
번역 10월 3일 행사에 대해 명시된 것은?
(A) DMA 회원만 참여할 수 있다.
(B) 오후 9시에 끝날 것으로 보인다.
(C) 실시간으로 온라인에서 스트리밍 될 예정이다.
(D) 입장권이 빨리 매진될 것 같다.

해설 Not / true
전단 첫 번째 단락 '토론회는 10월 3일 금요일 오후 7시 코트라이트 홀에서 열립니다(The debate will take place at Courtright Hall on Friday, October 3, at 7 P.M.)'에서 시작 시간이 오후 7시임을 알 수 있다. 또한 두 번째 단락 '행사 전 과정은 녹화되어 2시간 분량의 비디오로 전체 영상이 그 다음 주에 DMA 웹 사이트에 게시될 예정입니다(The proceedings will be recorded and posted in their entirety as a two-hour video)'에서 행사 소요시간이 2시간임을 알 수 있다. 따라서 행사는 9시에 끝나게 되므로 (B)가 정답이다.

21.
번역 레논 씨에 관해 사실은 것은?
(A) 그녀의 의견이 시 관료에 의해 낭독될 것이다.
(B) 그녀가 제출한 것은 일부 수정이 필요하다.
(C) 그녀의 DMA 회원자격이 승인되었다.
(D) 그녀의 제안이 단체의 회보에 실릴 것이다.

해설 연계
레논 씨에게 보내는 이메일에서 '귀하가 제출한 것이 선정되어 토론에 포함되게 되었습니다(your submission has been selected to be included in the discussion)'라고 했고, 앞의 전단에서 '가장 훌륭한 의견들을 DMA의 위원회에서 선정하며, 이 의견들은 행사 때 이번 행사를 총괄할, 시장 다릴 어빈 씨가 큰 소리로 읽게 됩니다(The best ones will be selected by a committee ~ will be read aloud at the event by the city's mayor, Daryl Irvine)'라고 밝혔다. 따라서 레논 씨의 글을 시장이 읽게 될 것이므로 (A)가 정답이다.

Paraphrasing
지문의 by the city's mayor → 정답의 by a city official

22.
번역 클라인 씨는 편지에 무엇을 포함시켰는가?
(A) 투표 카드
(B) 팸플릿
(C) 입장권
(D) 동의서

해설 세부사항
이메일에서 발언을 사용할 수 있는 공식 허가를 달라며 '동봉한 서류를 작성하셔서 제공된 봉투를 이용해 반송해 주십시오(Please fill out the enclosed document and return it using the envelope provided)'라고 요청했다. 동봉한 서류는 사용 허가와 관련된 것임을 알 수 있으므로 (D)가 정답이다.

Paraphrasing
지문의 official permission to use your remarks → 정답의 consent
지문의 enclosed document → 정답의 form

[23-27] 일정표 + 이메일 + 이메일

톨레도 광장 행사
8월 17일 시작 주

8월 17일, 일요일 9 A.M. – 5 P.M.: 광장 운동의 날
배구, 미니 골프, 암벽타기 등으로 몸을 움직이면서 활기를 유지하세요. 23모든 액티비티는 무료입니다. 하지만 높은 수요 때문에 긴 줄을 예상하셔야 합니다.

8월 19일, 화요일, 1 P.M. – 4 P.M.: 남성 합창단 축제
지역 곳곳에서 모인 남성 합창단들이 광장에서 아카펠라 공연을 펼칩니다. 야외 좌석을 선착순으로 이용할 수 있습니다.

268월 22일, 금요일, 7 P.M. – 9 P.M.: 마을 애완견 대회
시 웹 사이트를 통해 시합에 참가하세요(참가비 5달러). '가장 웃기는 개,' '최고 꾀쟁이,' '최고 멋쟁이' 등 다양한 범주로 상이 수여됩니다.

8월 23일, 토요일, 2 P.M. – 3:30 P.M.: 서머타임 퍼레이드
24행진 음악 부대(드럼 악대, 학교 밴드 등), 그리고 지역 비영리 단체에서 만든 가장 행렬 장식차들과 함께 여름을 축하하세요. 27퍼레이드는 시청에서 시작해 톨레도 광장에서 끝이 나며, 광장에 음식 판매대가 설치될 것입니다

수신: 마야 와이즈만 〈wmaya@snappypost.net〉
발신: 아니시 나야르 〈nayaranish@valley-mail.com〉
날짜: 8월 11일
내용: 다가오는 행사

안녕하세요 마야,

24다가오는 서머타임 퍼레이드에 쓸 가장행렬 차량을 준비하는 게 기다려져요. 필요한 장식과 물품들을 구매해 줘서 고마워요. 행렬 차량 꾸미는 걸 돕겠다고 서명한 우리 모든 동료들은 이번 토요일(8월 16일) 오후 2시에 듀발 빌딩에서 만날 예정이에요. 필요하다면 다음 주 일 끝나고 다시 만나서 마무리 손질을 할 수도 있고요. **26마테우스 리비에로 씨가 16일에만 도와줄 수 있고 퍼레이드에는 못 온답니다. 애완견 대회에 심사위원으로 나가게 돼서 한 주 내내 바쁠 거 같아요. 25회사에서는 우리 노고를 다음 주 회보에 기사로 실어줄 거예요.** 그러니까 잊지 말고 행렬 차량 꾸미는 과정 사진을 많이 찍어야 돼요.

토요일에 봅시다!

아니시

수신: 아니시 나야르 〈nayaranish@valley-mail.com〉
발신: 마야 와이즈만 〈wmaya@snappypost.net〉
날짜: 8월 12일
내용: 답신: 다가오는 행사

아니시에게,

좋은 소식입니다! **27퍼레이드 때 우리를 도와줄 사람을 하나 뽑았어요. 홍보부의 르네 한 씨예요.** 장식하는 것은 도와줄 수 없지만 퍼레이드 때 행렬차 옆에서 같이 걸으면서 사탕을 나눠줄 수 있어요. **27퍼레이드 당일에 출발 지점에서 우리와 만나면 될 거예요.**

마야

어휘 get moving 움직이다 choir 합창단 a cappella 아카펠라(무반주 노래) on a first come, first served basis 선착순으로 enter a competition 시합에 나가다 entry fee 참가비 grooming 몸단장 marching 행진하는, 행군하는 nonprofit 비영리의 float (시가 행진 때 등장하는) 장식 차량 stall 판매대, 노점 set up 설치하다 upcoming 다가오는 supplies 공급 물품 coworker 동료 put on the finishing touches 마무리 손질을 하다 judge 심사원 carry an article 기사를 싣다 recruit 모집하다 publicity 홍보, 홍보부 pass out 나눠주다

23.
번역 광장 운동의 날에 대해 명시된 것은?
(A) 승자들에게 상이 수여될 것이다.
(B) 참가자들은 오랫동안 기다려야 할 수도 있다.
(C) 팀 사전 등록을 해야 한다.
(D) 명목상의 참가비를 내야 할 것이다.

해설 Not / true
'모든 액티비티는 무료입니다. 하지만 높은 수요 때문에 긴 줄을 예상하셔야 합니다(All activities are free, but expect long lines due to the high demand)'라고 했으므로 (B)가 정답이다. (A)의 수상과 (D)의 참가비에 관한 언급은 모두 마을 애완견 대회(Community Dog Show)에서 나온다.

Paraphrasing
지문의 expect long lines → 정답의 wait a long time

24.
번역 나야르 씨에 관해 암시된 것은?
(A) 남성 합창단의 단원이다.
(B) 행사에 참석할 수 없을 것이다.
(C) 장식들을 살 계획이다.
(D) 비영리 단체에서 일한다.

해설 연계
일정표의 서머타임 퍼레이드에서 '행진 음악 부대, 그리고 지역 비영리 단체에서 만든 가장 행렬 장식차들과 함께 여름을 축하하세요(Celebrate summer with marching musical groups ~ as well as floats made by local nonprofit groups)'라고 말한 것으로 보아, 비영리 단체에서 장식차를 만드는 걸 알 수 있다. 또한, 나야르 씨가 발신한 첫 번째 이메일과, 수신한 두 번째 이메일을 보면 나야르 씨가 동료 마야 씨와 함께 퍼레이드 때 쓸 장식차를 만드는 일에 관해 얘기하고 있으므로 (D)가 정답이다.

25.
번역 첫 번째 이메일 첫 번째 단락 일곱 번째 줄에서 "carry"와 의미상 가장 가까운 것은?
(A) 출판하다
(B) 유지하다
(C) 가지고 오다
(D) 수락하다

해설 동의어
해당 문장은 '회사에서는 우리 노고를 다음 주 회보에 기사로 실어줄 거예요(The company is going to carry an article about our efforts in the next newsletter)'라고 해석되는데, 여기서 carry는 '보도하다'라는 뜻이 자연스러우므로 (A)가 정답이다.

26.
번역 리비에로 씨는 언제 행사에 참석할 것인가?
(A) 8월 17일
(B) 8월 19일
(C) 8월 22일
(D) 8월 23일

해설 연계
첫 번째 메일에서 마테우스 리비에로 씨가 퍼레이드에 못 온다면서 '애완견 대회에 심사위원으로 나가게 돼서 한 주 내내 바쁠 거 같아요(He is going to be a judge in the dog show and will be busy all week)'라고 했다. 일정표에서 보면 마을 애완견 대회는 8월 22일로 나와 있으므로 (C)가 정답이다.

27.
번역 한 씨는 8월 23일에 어디서 나야르 씨와 와이즈만 씨를 만날 것인가?
(A) 시청
(B) 듀발 빌딩
(C) 톨레도 광장
(D) 한 씨의 사무실

해설 연계

와이즈만 씨가 나야르 씨에게 보내는 두 번째 이메일에서 '퍼레이드 때 우리를 도와줄 사람을 하나 뽑았어요. 홍보부의 르네 한 씨예요(I recruited one more person to help us at the parade, Renee Hahn from the publicity department),' 그리고 '퍼레이드 당일에 출발 지점에서 우리와 만나게 될 거예요 (She will just meet us at the starting point on the day of the parade)'라고 말했다. 퍼레이드에서 세 사람이 모이는 것을 알 수 있다. 일정표의 서머타임 퍼레이드 항목을 보면 '퍼레이드는 시청에서 시작해(The parade will start at City Hall)'라고 장소가 나와 있으므로 (A)가 정답이다.

Unit 2 공지/회람/광고

예제

본책 p. 212

고객 공지 사항:
오늘은 매장 내에서, 특히 중앙 출입문 근처에서, 걸음걸이에 조심해 주십시오. 폭우로 인해 많은 물자국이 생겨버렸기 때문입니다.
고객 여러분은 입구에 놔둔 우산 넣는 무료 비닐 봉지가 보일 것입니다. 현재 물기가 있는 곳을 닦아내는 작업을 하고 있습니다. 저희에게 알려주고 싶은 곳을 발견하시면 직원에게 말씀해 주세요. 고맙습니다.

어휘 **complimentary** 무료의 **mop up** (물기를) 닦아내다, 훔치다 **damp** 축축한, 눅눅한

Q. 고객들이 직원에게 얘기를 해야 하는 이유는?
(A) 물품을 찾는 데 도움을 얻으려고
(B) 물기가 있는 장소를 알려주려고

YBM TEST

본책 p. 213

1. (C)	2. (A)	3. (A)	4. (D)	5. (A)
6. (B)	7. (A)	8. (B)	9. (B)	10. (B)
11. (C)	12. (A)	13. (C)	14. (D)	15. (C)
16. (D)	17. (B)	18. (C)	19. (C)	20. (B)
21. (D)	22. (C)	23. (C)	24. (D)	25. (B)
26. (B)				

[1-2] 공지

건설 공사 공지

5월 17일부터, 해밀 애비뉴 12번 거리와 34번 거리 사이 구간에서 도로 건설이 있을 예정입니다. 작업자들이 차도의 일부 구간을 재포장함은 물론, 움푹 패인 곳과 연석도 손을 볼 것입니다. **1-A**시끄러운 기계 소리로 야기될 혼란에 대해 미리 사과드립니다. **1-D**건설 공사 중에는 차량 운행이 엣셀 로드 쪽으로 돌아가게 됩니다. 공사 중에는 해밀 애비뉴에 주차가 금지됩니다. **2**이 지역의 주민들께서는 555-0156번으로 전화해 주변 지역 다른 도로에 주차할 수 있는 일시적인 주차권을 요청하십시오. **1-B**공사는 대략 14일 이내에 마무리 될 것입니다. 참고 협조해 주셔서 감사합니다.

교통국

어휘 **carry out** 수행하다 **pothole** 도로의 움푹 패인 곳 **curb** 연석(보도 가장자리를 따라 차도와 경계를 이루는 돌) **resurface** (도로를) 재포장하다 **roadway** 차도 **in advance** 미리 **disruption** 혼란 **reroute** 다른 길로 변경하다 **resident** 주민 **short-term** 단기적인 **parking pass** 주차권 **approximately** 대략 **patience** 인내 **cooperation** 협조

1.
번역 공사에 대해 언급되지 않은 것은?
(A) 소음 폐해를 일으킬 수도 있다.
(B) 약 2주가 걸릴 것이다.
(C) 도로 확장에 도움이 될 것이다.
(D) 도로 우회를 요구한다.

해설 Not / true
'시끄러운 기계 소리로 야기될 혼란에 대해 미리 사과드립니다(We apologize in advance for disruptions caused by the loud machinery)'에서 소음 얘기가, '공사는 대략 14일 이내에 마무리 될 것입니다(The work will be completed within approximately fourteen days)'에서 기간 얘기가, '건설 공사 중에는 차량 운행이 엣셀 로드 쪽으로 돌아가게 됩니다(During construction, traffic will be rerouted to Edsel Road)'에서 우회 도로 얘기가 나왔다. 도로 확장에 대한 언급은 없으므로 (C)가 정답이다.

Paraphrasing

지문의 disruptions caused by the loud machinery
→ 보기의 noise disturbances
지문의 approximately fourteen days
→ 보기의 about two weeks
지문의 traffic will be rerouted
→ 보기의 requires road detours

2.
번역 주민들은 왜 제공된 번호로 전화를 걸어야 하는가?
(A) 임시 주차권을 요청하려고
(B) 건설 공사 문제점을 신고하려고
(C) 공사에 대한 의견을 공유하려고
(D) 향후 건설 계획에 관해 문의하려고

해설 세부사항
'이 지역의 주민들께서는 555-0156번으로 전화해 주변 지역 다른 도로에 주차할 수 있는 일시적인 주차권을 요청하십시오(Residents in the area should call 555-0156 to ask for a short-term pass to park on other streets in the neighborhood)'라고 말했으므로 (A)가 정답이다.

Paraphrasing

지문의 ask for a short-term pass to park
→ 정답의 request a temporary parking pass

95

[3-5] 메모

수신: 콘웨이 엔터프라이즈 전 직원
발신: 데보라 아담스
날짜: 9월 25일

관리부를 대표해서 가장 최근의 간부 회의 결과를 발표하겠습니다. 간부들은 직원들에게 동기를 부여하기 위한 아이디어를 자유롭게 집단 토론했습니다. 영업부장은 융통성 있는 휴가 시간제를 제안했고, **3인사부장은 덜 엄격한 금요일 복장 코드를**, 경리부장은 매주 팀 점심을 제안했습니다.

시간을 두고 이 모든 변화를 도입하겠지만, **3케리 스튜어트 씨의 제안부터 시작하려고 합니다. 따라서, 410월 1일부터 시작해, 직원들은 금요일에 마음대로 편안한 옷을 입고 출근할 수 있습니다. 11월 말까지는 시험 단계로 새 정책을 실행할 것입니다.** 그때 가서, 우리는 직원들에게 의견을 들어보려고 합니다. 평상복을 고를 때는, 반바지의 경우 리넨이나 기타 질 좋은 옷감으로 만들어진 경우 입어도 되고, 상태가 좋은 청바지도 허용되고, 치마와 드레스도 평소와 마찬가지로 허용된다는 점 유의해 주세요. **5운동화와 발가락 부분이 트인 신발은 신지 마시기 바랍니다.**

협조해 주셔서 감사합니다. 모든 질문은 직속 상관에게 바로 해 주십시오.

어휘 on behalf of ~를 대표해서 administrative 관리의, 행정의 management 경영, 경영진 brainstorm 브레인스토밍하다, 자유롭게 집단 토론하다 flexible 유연한, 융통성 있는 HR 인사부 (= human resources), 인적 자원 strict 엄격한 be welcome to 부사적 자유롭게 ~하다 implement (정책 등을) 실행하다 on a trial basis 시험 삼아 feedback 반응, 의견 shorts 반바지 linen 리넨, 아마 섬유 fine 질 좋은, 섬세한, 촘촘한 material 옷감 jeans 청바지(= blue jeans) sneakers (밑창이 고무로 된) 운동화 open-toed shoes 발가락 부분이 트인 신발 direct ~을 보내다 immediate supervisor 직속 상관

3.
번역 스튜어트 씨는 어떤 부서에서 일하는가?
(A) 인사부
(B) 영업부
(C) 관리부
(D) 회계부

해설 세부사항
두 번째 단락에서 '케리 스튜어트 씨의 제안부터 시작하려고 합니다. 따라서, 10월 1일부터 시작해, 직원들은 금요일에 마음대로 편안한 옷을 입고 출근할 수 있습니다(we will start with Kerry Stewart's idea. Therefore, beginning from October 1, employees are welcome to wear casual clothing to the office on Fridays)'라고 했고, 첫 번째 단락에서 '인사부장은 덜 엄격한 금요일 복장 코드를 제안했다(HR director proposed a less strict dress code on Fridays)'라고 했다. 스튜어트가 금요일 복장 아이디어를 냈고, 그 아이디어를 낸 사람이 인사부장이므로 (A)가 정답이다.

4.
번역 시험 기간은 얼마나 걸릴까?
(A) 약 2주
(B) 약 4주
(C) 약 6주
(D) 약 8주

해설 세부사항
두 번째 단락에서 '10월 1일부터 시작해, 직원들은 금요일에 마음대로 편안한 옷을 입고 출근할 수 있습니다. 11월 말까지는 시험 단계로 새 정책을 실행할 것입니다(beginning from October 1, employees are welcome to wear casual clothing to the office on Fridays. We will implement the new policy on a trial basis until the end of November)'라고 했으므로 2개월간 시험 기간이다. (D)가 정답이다.

5.
번역 시험 기간 중 금요일에 허용되지 않는 의복은?
(A) 샌들
(B) 반바지
(C) 치마
(D) 청바지

해설 세부사항
두 번째 단락 마지막의 '운동화와 발가락 부분이 트인 신발은 신지 마십시오(Please do not wear sneakers or open-toed shoes)'라고 한 부분에서 샌들이 금지됨을 알 수 있으므로 (A)가 정답이다.

Paraphrasing
지문의 open-toed shoes → 정답의 sandals

[6-9] 메모

수신: 모든 직원들
발신: 아담 레너드, 사무장
날짜: 6월 3일
내용: 휴가 신청

이제 여름이 되었으므로 많은 7월 휴가 신청이 예상됩니다. **6휴가 신청은 희망하는 휴가 날짜 전 달에 서면으로 작성되어야 합니다. 7일반적으로는, 25일까지 휴가 신청서를 제출해야 합니다. 하지만, 23일에 제가 출장으로 나가 있을 것이므로 이번 달에 한해서만 한 주 일찍 신청서를 받아야겠습니다.**

9모든 신청서를 다 수용하도록 최선을 다하겠습니다. 하지만, 이것이 모든 경우에 가능하지는 않다는 점을 이해해 주십시오. 이 점 매우 죄송합니다. 여러분 모두가 즐겁고 여유 있는 휴가를 보내기를 바랍니다만, 우리가 7월 중에 일손이 달리는 것은 원치 않는다는 점을 명심하셔야 합니다. **8저의 제1의 목표는 이 시기에 고객 서비스가 저해되지 않도록 하는 겁니다.** 여러분의 휴가 신청이 단축되거나 거부된다면, 바로 이런 이유 때문입니다. 궁금한 점 있으면 제게 직접, 혹은 직속 상관에게 물어보십시오.

아담 레너드

어휘 now that ~이니까 underway 진행 중인 time off 휴식, 휴가 in writing 서면으로 prior to ~에 앞서 hand in 제출하다 go out of town (출장 등으로) 도시를 떠나다 accommodate (의견 등을) 수용하다 keep in mind 명심하다 short-staffed 직원이 부족한, 일손이 달리는 suffer 악화되다 shorten 단축하다

6.

번역 메모의 주요 목적은 무엇인가?
(A) 실수를 사과하려고
(B) 절차를 설명하려고
(C) 상점 폐쇄 날짜를 확정하려고
(D) 휴가 일정을 발표하려고

해설 주제/목적
첫 단락에서 '휴가 신청은 희망하는 휴가 날짜 전 달에 서면으로 작성되어야 합니다(Requests for time off should be made in writing in the month prior to your desired vacation days)'라며 신청 방식과 시간을 언급했고, 이후 휴가 신청 시 고려할 점을 설명하고 있으므로 (B)가 정답이다.

7.

번역 이번 달 신청서 제출 마감일은 언제인가?
(A) 6월 18일
(B) 6월 23일
(C) 6월 25일
(D) 6월 30일

해설 세부사항
첫 번째 단락에서 '일반적으로는, 25일까지 휴가 신청서를 제출해야 합니다. 하지만, 23일에 제가 출장으로 나가 있을 것이므로 이번 달에 한해서만 한 주 일찍 신청서를 받아야겠습니다(Usually, you have until the 25th of the month to hand in the Vacation Request Form. However, since I'll be going out of town on the 23rd, I need them one week early this month only)'라고 했다. 일반 마감일인 25일보다 한 주 앞당겨진 것이므로 (A)가 정답이다.

8.

번역 메모에 따르면, 레너드 씨의 최우선 순위는 무엇인가?
(A) 휴가 기간 연장
(B) 서비스 수준 유지
(C) 직원들의 팀워크 향상
(D) 신규 사업 유치

해설 세부사항
두 번째 단락에서 '저의 제1의 목표는 이 시기에 고객 서비스가 저해되지 않도록 하는 겁니다(My number one goal is to make sure our customer service does not suffer during this time)'라는 말로 서비스의 중요성을 강조했으므로 (B)가 정답이다.

Paraphrasing
지문의 my number one goal → 질문의 top priority
지문의 our customer service does not suffer
→ 정답의 Maintaining a desired service level

9.

번역 [1], [2], [3], [4]로 표시된 곳 중에서 다음 문장이 가장 적합한 곳은?
"하지만, 이것이 모든 경우에 가능하지는 않다는 점을 이해해 주십시오."
(A) [1]
(B) [2]
(C) [3]
(D) [4]

해설 문장 삽입
[2]번 앞에서 '모든 신청서를 다 수용하도록 최선을 다하겠습니다(I will do my best to accommodate all requests)'라고 한 후 갑자기 [2]번 다음부터는 '이 점 매우 죄송합니다(I'm very sorry about this)'라고 사과한다. 이 사과에 이어, 휴가를 제한할 수밖에 없는 이유가 설명되고 있다. 따라서 [2]에는 죄송한 이유가 나오는 게 자연스러우므로 (B)가 정답이다.

[10-12] 광고

맥시즈

기념일, 생일, 특별한 날, 어떤 날을 기념하든 맥시즈가 해결해 줍니다. **10저희 꽃과 화분 식물들이 어떤 방이든 안을 밝게 해 줍니다.** 그리고 이 꽃들은 사랑하는 이들에게 당신이 그들을 생각하고 있다는 것을 보여주는 최상의 방법입니다. 저희는 모든 제품에 무료 배달 서비스를 제공하며, 이 서비스에는 여러분 일정에 맞춰 저녁이나 주말도 포함됩니다. 그리고 지난 주에, 저희는 더 많은 고객님들에게 더 나은 서비스를 제공하기 위해 새로운 정책을 도입했습니다. **11블루 스프링스 이내로만 발송하는 것이 아니라, 저희는 이제 벨스빌 전 구역을 포함한, 시외 20 마일의 지역까지 배달할 수 있게 되었습니다.** 그게 전부가 아닙니다. **126월 이내 어느 때나 주문을 해 주세요. 그러면 추가 비용 없이 무료 축하 카드를 받으실 수 있습니다.** 오늘 555-0169번으로 저희에게 전화 주시거나, 로미타 드라이브 4981번지에 잠시 들르셔서 저희 친절한 직원들과 얘기를 나눠 보세요.

어휘 **potted plant** 화분에 심은 식물 **initiative** 계획, 시작 **limits** 경계, 범위 **greeting card** 인사 카드, 축하 카드 **at no extra cost** 추가 비용 없이 **stop in** 잠시 들르다

10.

번역 어떤 종류의 업체를 광고하고 있는가?
(A) 조경 회사
(B) 꽃가게
(C) 실내 디자인 회사
(D) 파티 기획 서비스

해설 세부사항
첫 번째 단락 '저희 꽃과 화분들이 어떤 방이든 안을 밝게 해 줄 것입니다(Our flowers and potted plants brighten up the interior of any room)'라고 한 데서 꽃을 취급하는 곳임을 알 수 있으므로 (B)가 정답이다.

11.

번역 맥시즈에 관해 언급된 것은?
(A) 영업 시간을 연장했다.
(B) 벨스빌에 최근 지사를 열었다.
(C) 배달 지역을 확장했다.
(D) 새 직원들을 찾고 있다.

해설 Not/true
두 번째 단락에서 '블루 스프링스 이내로만 발송하는 것이 아니라, 시외 20 마일의 지역까지 배달할 수 있게 되었습니다(Instead of sending out items only within Blue Springs, we now can deliver them to locations up to 20 miles outside the city limits)'라고 말했다. 이것은 블루 스프링스에서 그 너머까지로 지역을 확장한다는 말이므로 (C)가 정답이다. 고객의 일정에 맞춰 저녁이나 주말에도 배달을 한다고 했지만 이것이 영업 시간 연장은 아니므로 (A)는 언급된 바 없다.

Paraphrasing

지문의 send them up to 20 miles outside the city limits
→ 정답의 expanded its delivery area

12.

번역 광고에 따르면, 7월 1일에 무슨 일이 있을까?
(A) 특가 판매가 끝난다.
(B) 제품의 가격이 오를 것이다.
(C) 기념일을 축하할 것이다.
(D) 온라인 주문 방식이 시작될 것이다.

해설 세부사항
두 번째 단락에서 '6월 이내 어느 때나 주문을 해 주세요. 그러면 추가 비용 없이 무료 축하 카드를 받으실 수 있습니다(Place an order anytime within June, and you'll get free greeting card at no extra cost)'라고 했다. 한시적으로 무료 카드를 제공하는 특가 판매가 6월 말까지 하고 끝날 것이므로 (A)가 정답이다.

Paraphrasing

지문의 get free greeting card at no extra cost
→ 정답의 A special offer

[13-16] 광고

크레센트 센터에서 직원을 구합니다!

13크레센트 센터에서는 투손 지역에서 파트타임으로 일할 물리 치료사를 찾고 있습니다. 여러분은 환자 치료 및, 치료에 있어서의 다학문적 접근 방식에 전념하는 역동적인 팀에 소속될 것입니다. 크레센트 센터에서는 스스로 일정을 정하고 적절하다고 느끼는 대로 약속을 잡을 수 있는 자율성을 갖게 됩니다. 14저희는 노인들을 대상으로 한 최대의 물리 치료 공급자라는 점을 자랑스럽게 생각하며, 실제 이들 노인층이 저희 고객 기반의 대다수를 이루고 있습니다. 이 직업은 개인 가정집 방문을 필요로 하며, 그렇기 때문에 16-C일관되게 약속 시간에 제대로 도착할 수 있도록 차를 소유하고 있어야 합니다. 맡은 바 임무는 환자에 따라 다르겠지만, 모든 경우에 진단 평가, 진전 상황 기록, 치료 계획 개발이 포함될 것입니다.

혜택으로는 경쟁력 있는 시급과 특정 실적 목표에 이르렀을 때 주어지는 연간 보너스, 15크레센트 센터에서 여러분 투자 금액의 최대 6%를 대는 회사 퇴직금 적립 설계, 충분한 휴가 시간 등이 포함됩니다. 크레센트 센터 직원들은 또한 에퍼슨 대학과 코헨 협회를 통해서 전문 자격 인증 프로그램에 할인을 받을 자격이 주어집니다.

적임 지원자는 16-A물리치료과 석사학위와 아리조나 주 물리치료 위원회에서 발급하는 유효한 자격증을 소지해야 하며, 이것을 인터뷰에 앞서 입증을 받아야 합니다. 입원 환자 환경이든, 외래 환자 진료 환경이든 16-D 최소 2년간의 경험이 있는 지원자들을 우대합니다. 16-B환자와 쉽고 자신감 있게 대화하고, 더불어 명확한 서신으로 후속 처리를 해 나가는 능력은 필수입니다.

이 직책에 지원하시려면, visit www.crescentcenter.net/careers를 방문해 온라인 신청서를 작성하고, 취업참조번호 T-3049를 적어야 합니다. 3월 31일까지 지원서를 받고, 인터뷰는 그 다음 주에 일정을 잡게 됩니다.

어휘 physical therapist 물리 치료사 dedicated to ~에 전념하는 multidisciplinary 여러 학문 분야에 걸친 autonomy 자율성 see fit 맞다고 보다 senior citizen 노인 make up 차지하다 private residence 개인 가정 diagnostic assessment 진단 평가 document 상세하게 기록하다 progress 진전 benefits 특전, 혜택 competitive wage 경쟁력 있는 임금(비슷한 직종이나 업무를 기준으로 평균 또는 평균 이상) performance 실적, 성과 corporate 법인의, 기업의 retirement plan 퇴직금 적립 설계 match (자금을) 대다 ample 충분한 eligible (가질) 자격이 있는 certification 자격, 자격 인증 valid 유효한 validate (사실임을) 인정하다, 승인하다 preference 우대, 우선권 inpatient 입원 환자 outpatient 외래 환자 setting 환경 confidently 자신 있게 follow-up 후속 조치를 취하다 correspondence 서신

13.

번역 어떤 종류의 직책을 광고하는가?
(A) 체육 강사
(B) 병원 관리자
(C) 의료 전문가
(D) 관계 치료사

해설 주제/목적
첫 문장에서 '크레센트 센터에서는 투손 지역에서 파트타임으로 일할 물리 치료사를 찾고 있습니다(Crescent Center is currently seeking a part-time physical therapist to work in the Tucson area)'라며 광고 대상을 밝혔고, 이어 환자(patient), 치료(treatment) 등의 말로 구체적인 업무를 설명하고 있으므로 (C)가 정답이다.

Paraphrasing

지문의 physical therapist
→ 정답의 medical professional

14.

번역 크레센트 센터에 대해 명시된 것은?
(A) 최근에 투손에 사무소를 열었다.
(B) 직원들이 상을 받았다.
(C) 현재 몇 직책을 구인 중이다.
(D) 서비스를 주로 노인들이 이용한다.

해설 Not/true
첫 번째 단락에서 '저희는 노인들을 대상으로 한 최대의 물리 치료 공급자라는 점을 자랑스럽게 생각하며, 실제 이들 노인층이 저희 고객 기반의 대다수를 이루고 있습니다(We are proud to be the largest provider of physical therapy treatments to senior citizens, who make up the vast majority of our client base)'라고 했으므로 (D)가 정답이다.

Paraphrasing

지문의 senior citizens → 정답의 the elderly

15.

번역 이 직책의 혜택으로 언급된 것은?
(A) 넉넉한 유급 휴가
(B) 자격증 프로그램 비용 상환
(C) 퇴직 적립금 고용주 분담
(D) 분기별 실적 보너스

해설 Not/true
두 분째 단락에서 여러 혜택 중 하나로 '크레센트 센터에서 여러분 투자 금액의 최대 6%를 대는 회사 퇴직금 적립 설계(corporate retirement plan with Crescent Center matching up to 6% of what you invest)'를 언급했으므로 (C)가 정답이다. '충분한 휴가 시간(ample vacation time)'만 언급했으므로 (A)는 틀리고, '전문 자격 인증 프로그램의 할인(discounts on specialty certification programs)'만을 언급했으므로 (B)도 틀리고, '연간 보너스(annual bonuses)'라고 했으므로 (D)도 사실과 다르다.

16.

번역 이 직책의 필수 조건이 아닌 것은?
(A) 석사 학위
(B) 뛰어난 의사소통 능력
(C) 믿을 만한 교통수단
(D) 최소 2년의 경력

해설 세부사항
세 번째 단락에서 '최소 2년간의 경험이 있는 지원자들을 우대합니다(Preference will be given to candidates with at least two years of experience)'라고 말했는데, 이는 우대 사항이지 필수 조건은 아니므로 (D)가 정답이다.

Paraphrasing
지문의 a Master of Physical Therapy degree
→ 보기의 a postgraduate degree
지문의 the ability to easily and confidently converse
→ 보기의 excellent communication skills
지문의 car → 보기의 transportation

[17-21] 메모+보고서

수신: 샌드파이퍼 짐 전 직원
발신: 엘렌 웨일랜드, 매니저
내용: 구내 매점

2월 6일

샌드파이퍼 짐이 건물 확장 공사를 마쳤기 때문에, 우리 공간을 최대한 활용하는 방법을 찾아보고자 합니다. 그래서, 로비 구역 일부를 에너지바, 주스, 단백질 분말을 판매하는 구내 매점으로 전환할 계획입니다. **17**17번 가의 VTX 짐에도 비슷한 매점이 있습니다. 그래서 우리도 고객들이 비슷한 편의시설을 이용할 수 있도록 하고자 합니다.

18우리 체육관에서 어떤 것을 취급해야 할지 결정하기 위해 지금 시중에 나와 있는 여러 브랜드의 에너지바를 검토하고 있습니다. 그 결과를 요약해 첨부한 게 보일 텐데요. 우리가 네 개의 옵션을 제안하는 게 좋을 것 같습니다. **19**상품 공급 과정이 너무 복잡해지는 걸 막기 위해서, 네 개가 넘는 건 좋지 않다고 생각합니다. 일반적으로, **21**우리 멤버들은 고단백 스낵에 관심이 많습니다. 근육량을 유지하도록 하는 데 기여하기 때문이죠. **20**우선, 피크 이용 시간대에만 매점을 열 생각입니다. 더 오래 열어두는 걸 정당화할 만큼 매출이 높아지면 차후에 영업시간을 연장할 것입니다.

샌드파이퍼 짐 제품 검토

보고 날짜: 2월 10일   편집자: 엘렌 웨일랜드
분류: 에너지바

상표	단백질*	당분*
에이스 바	12 g	10 g
아이언 존	18 g	5 g
LL-펌프	10 g	26 g
누-골드	16 g	20 g
21샘프톤	21 g	8 g

*1회분 60그램 기준으로 계산함. 바의 크기는 45-85그램.

우리는 단백질바 또는 주스 음료 중 어느 것이 **20**피크타임인 오전 5시 30분 - 7시 30분에 운동하는 사람들에게 더 인기 있는지 확인하기 위해 매출을 면밀히 감시할 것입니다.

어휘 expansion 확장 make the best use of ~을 최대한 활용하다 convert 변환하다, 개조하다 concession stand 구내 매점 equivalent 동등한 amenities 편의시설 carry (품목으로) 가지고 있다[취급하다] in an effort to 부정사 ~하기 위한 노력[조치]로 keep A from -ing A가 ~하는 것을 막다 exceed 초과하다 contribution 기여 muscle mass 근육량 to begin with 우선 justify 정당화시키다 hours of operation 운영 시간 serving 1인분, 1회 분량 range A from B 범위가 A에서 B에 걸치다 monitor 추적 관찰하다

17.

번역 업소에서 변화를 시도하려는 이유는 무엇인가?
(A) 건축 사업을 위한 기금을 조성하려고
(B) 경쟁사와 똑같은 서비스를 제공하려고
(C) 간접비를 줄이려고
(D) 회원들의 요구에 응하려고

해설 세부사항
첫 번째 단락에서 '17번 가의 VTX 짐에도 비슷한 매점이 있습니다. 그래서 우리도 고객들이 비슷한 편의시설을 이용할 수 있도록 하고자 합니다(VTX Gym on 17th Street has a similar stand, so we want to make sure that our members have access to equivalent amenities)'라는 말로 매점 설치 이유를 밝혔으므로 (B)가 정답이다.

18.

번역 메모에서, 두 번째 단락 두 번째 줄의 "carry"와 의미상 가장 가까운 것은?
(A) 승인하다
(B) 들어 올리다
(C) 공급하다
(D) 운송하다

해설 동의어
해당 문장은 '우리 체육관에서 어떤 것을 취급해야 할지 결정하기 위해 지금 시중에 나와 있는 여러 브랜드의 에너지바를 검토하고 있습니다(I am reviewing the various brands of energy bars on the market to determine which ones we should carry at our gym)'라는 의미로 해석된다. 여기서 carry는 '품목으로 취급하다'라는 뜻이고 '공급하다'와 의미상 동일하므로 (C)가 정답이다.

19.

번역 웨일랜드 씨는 제공되는 에너지바들의 종류에 대해 무엇을 암시하는가?
(A) 시간이 지나면서 꾸준히 늘어날 것이다.
(B) 입수 가능한 물건의 수에 근거했다.
(C) 주문을 단순화하기 위해 몇 개가 넘지 않아야 한다.
(D) 회원들의 선호도에 따라 결정될 것이다.

해설 추론
두 번째 단락에서 '상품 공급 과정이 너무 복잡해지는 걸 막기 위해서 네 개가 넘는 건 좋지 않다고 생각합니다(In an effort to keep the process of supplying the goods from getting too complicated, I don't think it's a good idea to exceed four)'라고 했다. 적은 수량으로 공급을 쉽게 하겠다는 뜻이므로 (C)가 정답이다.

Paraphrasing
지문의 keep the process of supplying the goods from getting too complicated → 정답의 simplify ordering

20.

번역 구내 매점에 대해 암시된 것은?
(A) 로커룸 근처에 위치하게 될 것이다.
(B) 처음에는 이른 아침에 문을 열 것이다.
(C) 풀타임 멤버들에게는 할인을 해 줄 것이다.
(D) 에너지바 회사 직원들로 종업원이 충원될 것이다.

해설 연계
메모 두 번째 단락에서 '우선은, 피크 이용 시간대에만 매점을 열 생각입니다(To begin with, we will only open the concession stand during the peak usage time)'라고 했다. 보고서에서 피크타임을 오전 5시 30분 - 7시 30분으로 보았으므로 이른 아침에 문을 연다고 한 (B)가 정답이다.

Paraphrasing
지문의 to begin with → 정답의 initially
지문의 during our peak time of 5:30 A.M. to 7:30 A.M. → 정답의 in the early morning

21.

번역 샌드파이퍼 짐 멤버들 사이에서는 어떤 상표가 가장 인기가 있겠는가?
(A) 에이스 바
(B) 아이언 존
(C) 누-골드
(D) 잼프톤

해설 연계
메모의 두 번째 단락에서 '우리 멤버들은 고단백 스낵에 관심이 많습니다(our members are interested in high-protein snacks)'라고 말했다. 제품 보고서의 표에서 보면 단백질 함량이 가장 높은 상표는 잼프톤이므로 (D)가 정답이다.

[22-26] 공지+이메일+기사

배역진에게 알리는 일정 변경 공지

11월 14일

22로저 키니 씨가 오늘 아침 자기 일을 끝내려면 예상보다 시간이 더 필요하다고 알려 와서, 우리는 아직 무대 구역을 쓸 수 없습니다. 저는 감독과 의논을 했고, 우리는 최종 총연습을 11월 16일 오후 7시로 옮기기로 결정했습니다. 기자들도 참석할 겁니다. **23**총연습 전에 의상 디자이너를 방문해 옷이 잘 맞는지 최종 점검을 하고 필요하다면 수정을 받으세요.

11월 15일에는 변동 사항을 미처 알지 못한 기자들과 짧은 인터뷰가 있을 겁니다. 욜란다 바이어스 씨와 기타 주연자 몇몇이 출연자를 대표해 나가겠다고 나서 주었습니다.

-제나 프래지어, 극장 매니저

수신: 노라 라이샌더 〈n.lysander@brighamtribune.com〉
발신: 제나 프래지어 〈jenna@bradfordtheater.com〉
날짜: 11월 14일
내용: 공연 변경

라이샌더 씨께,

마지막 순간에 변경을 하게 돼서 정말 죄송하지만, 〈홀리데이 하모니스〉 총연습을 내일로 미뤘습니다. **22**전기 기사가 무대 조명을 수리하는 중이고, 공사가 아직 마무리되지 않았습니다. **25**저희는 당신이 11월 16일 오후 7시에 공연에 참석해 주시기를 바랍니다. **24**제가 손님 명단에 이름을 올려놨기 때문에 들어오실 때 입장권은 제시하지 않아도 됩니다. **25**총연습 날짜였던 11월 15일 오후 7시에는 간단한 인터뷰를 열 예정입니다. 출연진과 얘기를 나눌 수 있는 유일한 기회가 될 텐데요. 11월 16일 쇼 대신, 혹은 쇼와 더불어, 원하시는 대로 인터뷰에 참석하실 수 있습니다.

제나 프래지어, 극장 매니저

〈홀리데이 하모니스〉가 당신의 마음을 노래하게 합니다
글: 노라 라이샌더

〈홀리데이 하모니스〉는 1960년대를 배경으로 한 뮤지컬 코미디로, 미국 중서부 작은 도시 출신의 젊은 대학 졸업생 도나 플린이 유럽으로 여행을 떠나 모험을 발견하는 내용이다. 너무 아름다운 의상 디자인과 매력적인 음악 때문에 〈홀리데이 하모니스〉는 틀림없이 폭넓은 관중을 만족시킬 것이다. **25, 26**하지만 진정으로 이 뮤지컬을 남다르게 만드는 것은 쇼에 등장하는 재능 있는 가수와 댄서들이다. "전 이처럼 독특한 작품에 등장하게 돼서 기뻐요." **25**주연 여배우 로지타 프로보 씨는 이번 주 초 인터뷰에서 이렇게 말했다. "관객들도 우리처럼 재미있어 하셨으면 좋겠습니다." 〈홀리데이 하모니스〉는 오늘 저녁 브래드포드 극장에서 6주간의 공연을 시작한다.

어휘 cast (연극 등의) 출연자들 dress rehearsal (의상을 갖추고 하는) 총연습 costume 의상 adjustment 수정 accommodate (변화·상황 등을) 수용하다, 대응하다 volunteer to 부정사 ~하겠다고 자진해서 나서다 represent 대표하다 postpone 연기하다 electrician 전기 기사 lights 조명 present 제시하다 welcome to 부정사 자유롭게 ~하다 college graduate 대학 졸업자 stunning 놀라운, 아름다운 enchanting 매력적인 be sure to 부정사 반드시 ~하다 set A apart A를 남다르게[돋보이게] 만들다 quirky 독특한, 기이한 production (연극·오페라 등의) 제작, 작품 run (장기적인) 공연, 상연

22.
번역 키니 씨는 누구일 것 같은가?
(A) 극장 매니저
(B) 주연 배우
(C) 전기 기사
(D) 기자

해설 연계
극장 매니저가 쓴 공지의 첫 번째 단락에서 '로저 키니 씨가 오늘 아침 자기 일을 끝내려면 예상보다 시간이 더 필요하다고 알려 와서, 우리는 아직 무대 구역을 쓸 수 없습니다(Roger Kinney informed me this morning that more time is needed to complete his work than expected, so we are still unable to use the stage area)'라고 했고, 같은 사람이 쓴 메일에서 '전기 기사가 무대 조명을 수리하는 중이고, 공사가 아직 마무리되지 않았습니다(An electrician is fixing our stage lights, and the project is not yet completed)'라고 했다. 키니 씨가 전기기사이고 무대 조명을 수리 중이라는 것을 알 수 있으므로 (C)가 정답이다.

23.
번역 모든 배역진은 무엇을 해 달라고 요청받는가?
(A) 리허설 시간 확인
(B) 인터뷰 자발적 참여
(C) 의상 맞추기
(D) 무대 구역 청소

해설 세부사항
공지의 첫 번째 단락에서 '총연습 전에 의상 디자이너를 방문해 옷이 잘 맞는지 최종 점검을 하고 필요하다면 수정을 받으세요(Please visit the costume designer before the rehearsal for a final check that your costume fits correctly and to receive adjustments if necessary)'라고 했으므로 (C)가 정답이다.

24.
번역 프래지어 씨는 라이샌더 씨를 위해 무엇을 했는가?
(A) 인터뷰 질문을 마련했다.
(B) 출입증을 부쳐 주었다.
(C) 극장까지 가는 길안내를 보내 주었다.
(D) 목록에 이름을 올려 주었다.

해설 세부사항
프래지어 씨가 라이샌더 씨에게 보내는 이메일에서 '제가 손님 명단에 이름을 올려놓았기 때문에 들어오실 때 입장권은 제시하지 않아도 됩니다(You will not have to present an entrance pass to get in, as I have put your name on our guest list)'라고 했으므로 (D)가 정답이다.

Paraphrasing
지문의 put your name on our guest list
→ 정답의 added her name to a list

25.
번역 라이샌더 씨에 대해 암시된 것은?
(A) 드라마보다 뮤지컬을 더 좋아한다.
(B) 최소한 두 차례 브래드포드 극장을 방문했다.
(C) 매주 공연 평을 한다.
(D) 〈홀리데이 하모니스〉 감독과 인터뷰를 했다.

해설 연계
11월 15일에 예정되었던 총연습이 16일로 미루어지고, 15일은 대신 인터뷰만 하게 된 상황이다. 극장 매니저가 라이샌더 씨에게 쓴 이메일에서 '저희는 당신이 11월 16일 오후 7시에 공연에 참석해 주시기를 바랍니다(We hope you can join us at 7 P.M. on November 16 for the performance)'라며 공연에 초대했다. 그리고 나서 '11월 15일 오후 7시에는 간단한 인터뷰를 열 예정입니다. ~ 11월 16일 쇼 대신, 혹은 쇼와 더불어 원하시는 대로 인터뷰에 참석하실 수 있습니다(~ You are welcome to attend the interview instead of, or in addition to, the November 16 show)'라고 말했다. 즉 총연습과 인터뷰 둘 다 초대한 셈이다. 그런데 마지막으로 라이샌더 씨가 쓴 기사를 보면 공연 감상에 따른 평이 나오고, 주연 여배우 인터뷰 내용도 나온다. 따라서 공연과 인터뷰를 둘 다 봤을 것으로 추측할 수 있으므로 (B)가 정답이다.

26.
번역 라이샌더 씨는 공연에서 무엇이 가장 마음에 들었는가?
(A) 음악
(B) 출연진
(C) 무대 디자인
(D) 의상

해설 세부사항
기사에서 '하지만 진정으로 이 뮤지컬을 남다르게 만드는 것은 쇼에 등장하는 재능 있는 가수와 댄서들이다(But what really sets it apart is the gifted singers and dancers in the show)'라고 했으므로 (B)가 정답이다.

Paraphrasing
지문의 the gifted singers and dancers in the show
→ the cast

Unit 3 문자 메시지 / 온라인 채팅

예제
본책 p. 222

제인 버킨 [10:42 A.M.]
모두 안녕하세요. 도움이 필요합니다. 회의실 영사기가 작동을 안 해요.

피터 파커 [10:44 A.M.]
또 시작이네요.

마르코 베라티 [10:44 A.M.]
점심 시간 전에 모든 준비가 갖춰져 있어야 하는데.

제인 버킨 [10:48 A.M.]
피터, 와서 좀 봐 주겠어요?

피터 파커 [10:49 A.M.]
가는 중입니다.

마르코 베라티 [10:51 A.M.]
제인 빼고, 모두 준비됐나요?

피오나 로페즈 [10:53 A.M.]
네. 모두 좋습니다.

어휘 in order 제대로 된, 만반의 준비가 갖춰진 on one's way 가는 중인

Q. 오전 10시 49분에 파커 씨가 "가는 중입니다"라고 쓴 의미는?
(A) 버킨 씨를 도우러 가는 중이다.
(B) 점심 식사를 위해 베라티 씨를 만날 예정이다.

YBM TEST
본책 p. 223

1. (B)	2. (B)	3. (D)	4. (B)	5. (B)
6. (D)	7. (C)	8. (C)	9. (D)	10. (B)
11. (B)	12. (D)	13. (A)	14. (C)	15. (B)
16. (A)	17. (A)	18. (C)		

[1-2] 문자 메시지

다니엘 콘리 [1:01 P.M.]
지금 시내로 들어가는 중인데요. **1내 기차가 40분 연착할 거 같아요.** 아무래도 웨이드와 씨의 회의에 제시간에 도착하려면 회의장으로 바로 가야 할 거 같습니다.

매티 벨트런 [1:03 P.M.]
네. 난 아직도 사무실에 있어요. 뭐 가져다 줄 거 있어요?

다니엘 콘리 [1:06 P.M.]
네. 내 책상에 5페이지짜리 자료가 있는데요. **2그거 복사 좀 해 줄 사람이 필요해요.**

매티 벨트런 [1:08 P.M.]
2내가 시간이 있어요.

다니엘 콘리 [1:10 P.M.]
고맙습니다! 블레이크 역에 도착하면 다시 문자 보낼게요.

어휘 head back to ~로 돌아가다 conference center 회의장 handout 유인물, 배포 자료 make copy of ~의 사본을 만들다

1.
번역 콘리 씨는 어디서 메시지를 보냈을 것 같은가?
(A) 블레이크 역
(B) 기차 안
(C) 회의장
(D) 사무실

해설 추론
오후 1시 1분에 콘리 씨가 돌아가는 중이라며 '하지만 내 기차가 40분 연착할 거 같아요(but my train is going to arrive about forty minutes late)'라고 했다. 콘리 씨가 현재 기차 안에서 메시지를 보냈다고 짐작할 수 있으므로 (B)가 정답이다. 참고로, 기차를 타기 위해 역에 와 있다고 생각할 수도 있지만 블레이크 역은 콘리 씨가 내리려는 행선지이므로 (A)는 맞지 않다.

2.
번역 오후 1시 8분에 벨트런 씨가 "내가 시간이 있어요"라고 쓴 의미는?
(A) 콘리 씨를 태우러 나오겠다.
(B) 서류를 복사해 주겠다.
(C) 자료를 작성해 주겠다.
(D) 웨이드 씨와 연락하겠다.

해설 의도 파악
오후 1시 6분에 '내 책상에 5페이지짜리 자료가 있는데. 그거 복사 좀 해 줄 사람이 필요해요(There is a five-page handout on my desk. But I'll need someone to make copies of it)'라고 말하자, 그에 대한 대답으로 시간이 있다고 했다. 즉, 자료 복사를 도와줄 수 있다는 뜻이므로 (B)가 정답이다.

[3-4] 문자 메시지

야말 솔랭키 12:38 P.M.
다이애나, 3층은 어떻게 되고 있어요?

다이애나 브리스톨 12:40 P.M.
3계획대로 오후 2시까지 여기 모든 객실 청소 마칠 수 있게 잘되고 있어요. 왜요?

야말 솔랭키 12:41 P.M.
오후 1시에 블레이클리 여행사에서 오는 단체 관광객이 있는데, 그 시간에 입실을 하고 싶어할 거예요.

다이애나 브리스톨 12:42 P.M.
4좀 더 일찍 문자 메시지를 주지 그랬어요. 그럼 일 우선 순위를 다르게 했을 텐데.

야말 솔랭키 12:43 P.M.
4그래도 소용 없었을 거예요.

다이애나 브리스톨 12:44 P.M.
뭐 좋은 생각 있어요?

야말 솔랭키 12:45 P.M.
그럼요. 하던 일 잘 하시구요, 손님들이 오면 내가 상황을 설명할게요.

어휘 on track 제대로 진행되고 있는 check in 입실 수속을 하다, 체크인하다 prioritize 우선 순위를 정하다 find out 해답을 얻다, 문제를 해결하다

3.
번역 브리스톨 씨는 어디에서 근무할 것 같은가?
(A) 운송 회사
(B) 레스토랑
(C) 여행사
(D) 호텔

해설 추론
오후 12시 40분에 브리스톨 씨가 '계획대로 오후 2시까지 여기 모든 객실 청소 마칠 수 있게 잘되고 있어요(We're on track to have all guest rooms up here cleaned by 2 P.M. as planned)'라고 말한 데서 객실 청소를 담당하고 있음을 알 수 있다. 이어 상대방도 '단체 관광객 맞이(We've got a tour group)', '입실 수속(check in)' 등을 언급했다. 호텔에서 근무한다고 추론할 수 있으므로 (D)가 정답이다.

4.
번역 오후 12시 43분에 솔랭키 씨가 "그래도 소용 없었을 거예요"라고 쓴 의미는?
(A) 브리스톨 씨의 업무 우선순위에 동의하지 않는다.
(B) 마지막 순간에 어떤 정보를 얻었다.
(C) 일을 어떻게 해야 하는지 모른다.
(D) 필요한 연락처를 잃어버렸다.

해설 **의도 파악**

오후 12시 42분에 '좀 더 일찍 문자 메시지를 주지 그랬어요(I wish you would have texted sooner)'라고 아쉬워하는 말에 '그래도 소용 없었을 거예요'라고 대답했다. 그러면서 마지막에 자기가 알아서 처리하겠다는 의도로 말을 마무리했다. 갑자기 상황이 바뀌었거나, 무슨 말을 들었다고 추측할 수 있으므로 (B)가 정답이다.

[5-6] 문자 메시지

크리스 분, 2:25 P.M.
내 차가 고장 나서 그러는데요, 3시 현대 회화 전시회 투어에 20분쯤 늦을 거 같아요. 내 대신 해줄 수 있을까요?

유나 리, 2:27 P.M.
미안하지만, 나도 그 시간에 투어가 있어요.

크리스 분, 2:28 P.M.
5사람이 너무 많아져서 두 투어 참가자를 합할 수는 없을 것 같은데요.

유나 리, 2:29 P.M.
네, 5그게 문제예요. 6비디오 프로젝터를 설치해서 당신 도착할 때까지 그 그룹이 예술 역사에 관한 단편 영화를 보게 하는 건 어떨까요?

크리스 분, 2:30 P.M.
그러면 되겠네요. 6필한테 준비시켜 달라고 할게요. 고마워요!

어휘 **cover** (없는 사람의 일을) 대신하다 **combine** 결합시키다 **participant** 참가자 **issue** (해결해야 할) 문제 **set up** 설치하다 **work** 효과가 있다, 작용을 하다

5.

번역 오후 2시 29분에 리 씨가 "그게 문제예요"라고 쓴 의미는?
(A) 참가자들이 늦을까 봐 걱정된다.
(B) 그룹이 너무 커질 거라고 생각한다.
(C) 미술 전시회는 익숙하지 않다.
(D) 자신에게 필요한 비디오를 찾을 수가 없다.

해설 **의도 파악**

크리스 분 씨가 오후 2시 28분 메시지에서 '사람이 너무 많아져서 두 투어 참가자를 합할 수는 없을 것 같은데요(I guess we can't combine the participants from the two tours because there will be too many people)'라고 말하자 '네 그게 문제예요(Yes, that's the issue)'라고 호응했으므로 (B)가 정답이다.

Paraphrasing

지문의 there will be too many people
→ 정답의 a group will be too big

6.

번역 필은 무엇을 해 달라고 요청 받을까?
(A) 참가자의 질문에 응답하기
(B) 정보가 담긴 비디오 편집하기
(C) 박물관 투어 제공하기
(D) 장비 설치하기

해설 **세부사항**

유나 리 씨가 오후 2시 29분 메시지에서 '비디오 프로젝터를 설치해서 당신 도착할 때까지 그 그룹이 예술 역사에 관한 단편 영화를 보게 하는 건 어떨까요?(How about setting up the video projector and having your group watch the short film on art history until you arrive?)'라고 제안하자 크리스 분이 '필한테 준비시켜 달라고 할게요(I'll ask Phil to get it ready)'라고 대답했다. 필에게 프로젝터를 준비시키겠다는 의미이므로 (D)가 정답이다.

Paraphrasing

지문의 the video projector → some equipment

[7-10] 온라인 채팅

하니타 팬딧 [1:08 P.M.]
지난 사분기 우리 항공사 실적에 관한 통계 수치를 검토하는 중인데요. 7분실 수하물 수치가 유난히 낮아 보여요. 검토하신 건가요?

마릴린 킨스만 [1:09 P.M.]
네. 그 숫자는 정확해요. 짐을 맡긴 승객과 함께 행선지에 도착하지 못한 가방 숫자가 급격히 준 걸 확인했어요.

카케루 산와 [1:10 P.M.]
그거 좋은 소식이네요. 8이런 긍정적인 변화를, 손에 잡고 쓰는 새 스캐너 덕분으로 돌릴 수 있을 거예요. 수하물 팀에서 쓰는 거요. 직원들이 어떤 가방이든 실시간으로 검사할 수 있어서, 잘못 놓인 가방들을 되돌려 보내기가 쉬워졌죠.

레오 로스 [1:11 P.M.]
솔직히, 초기 비용이 너무 높아서 난 처음에 회의적이었는데, 지금은 완전히 찬성입니다.

카케루 산와 [1:13 P.M.]
그렇죠, 9그걸 사기로 한 건 옳은 결정이었어요.

마릴린 킨스만 [1:14 P.M.]
9고마워요. 계획대로 잘 되고 있다니 다행이에요.

하니타 팬딧 [1:15 P.M.]
그렇게 낮은 가방 분실률이면, 우리 기록을 업계 최고로 만들어 주네요.

레오 로스 [1:18 P.M.]
10다음 광고 캠페인에 그 점을 이용해야겠네요. 여행자들은 우리가 얼마나 신뢰할 만한지 알고 싶을 거예요. 종종 그게 최종 티켓 가격보다 더 중요하기도 하니까요.

하니타 팬딧 [1:19 P.M.]
그거 타당한 지적이네요. 10누녜스 씨와 얘기해서 그 팀이 이 새 소식을 어떻게 담아낼 수 있을지 봐야겠어요.

어휘 **in the process of** ~하는 중인 **statistics** 통계, 통계 자료 **performance** 실적, 성과 **figure** 수치 **lost luggage** 분실 수하물 **decline** 감소 **destination** 행선지, 목적지 **check in** 수하물[짐]을 부치다 **attribute A to B** A를 B의 덕분[탓]으로 돌리다 **handheld** 손에 들고 쓰는 **redirect** 되돌려 보내다 **misplace** 잘못 두어 못 찾다 **skeptical** 회의적인 **upfront cost** (계약 · 사업의) 초기 비용 **on board** 편승하는, 지지하는 **relieved** 안도하는 **reliable** 신뢰할 만한 **valid** 타당한, 근거 있는 **incorporate** 포함하다

7.
번역 오후 1시 8분에 팬딧 씨가 "검토하신 건가요?"라고 쓴 의미는?
(A) 소포가 도착하기를 기다리고 있다.
(B) 다른 사람들이 실적 보고서를 읽기를 권한다.
(C) 일부 자료에 실수가 있다고 생각한다.
(D) 자신이 완수한 업무에 대한 반응을 원한다.

해설 의도 파악
'분실 수하물 수치가 유난히 낮아 보여요(The figure for lost luggage seems unusually low)'라고 하면서 검토 여부를 확인하고 있다. 비정상적으로 낮아 무언가 의심이 된다는 의미이므로 (C)가 정답이다.

Paraphrasing
지문의 figure → 정답의 some data

8.
번역 회사가 서비스를 향상시키는 데 도움이 된 것은 무엇인가?
(A) 운영자에게 더 많은 권한을 준 것
(B) 숙련된 직원들을 고용한 것
(C) 새로운 장비를 사용한 것
(D) 교육 프로그램을 개선한 것

해설 세부 사항
오후 1시 10분 카케루 산와 씨가 '이런 긍정적인 변화를, 손에 잡고 쓰는 새 스캐너 덕분으로 돌릴 수 있을 거예요(We can attribute this positive change to the new handheld scanners used by the baggage team)'라는 말로 스캐너에 공을 돌렸고, 스캐너 덕분에 짐 분실률이 줄고, 곧 서비스 향상으로 이어졌다는 내용이 이어지므로 (C)가 정답이다.

Paraphrasing
지문의 the new handheld scanners
→ 정답의 new equipment

9.
번역 킨스만 씨에 대해 암시된 것은?
(A) 수정된 계획을 발표할 것이다.
(B) 문제를 빨리 해결했다.
(C) 비용을 걱정했다.
(D) 구매 결정을 했다.

해설 추론
오후 1시 13분에 산와 씨가 '그걸 사기로 한 건 옳은 결정이었어요(it was the right decision to buy them)'라고 칭찬했는데 이어서 킨스만 씨가 고맙다고 말했으므로 그가 내린 결정임을 알 수 있고 정답은 (D)가 된다.

10.
번역 누네즈 씨는 어떤 부서에서 일할 것 같은가?
(A) 인사부
(B) 마케팅부
(C) 경리부
(D) 영업부

해설 추론
오후 1시 18분에 레오 로스 씨가 '다음 광고 캠페인에 그 점을 이용해야겠네요(We should use that point in our next ad campaign)'라고 하자, 팬딧 씨가 '누네즈 씨와 얘기해서 그 팀에서 이 새 소식을 어떻게 담아낼 수 있을지 봐야겠어요(I'll talk to Ms. Nunez to see how she and her team can incorporate this new information)'라고 호응했다. 광고 캠페인 건으로 누네즈 씨와 의논하겠다는 것이므로 (B)가 정답이다.

[11-14] 온라인 채팅

산딥 라벨 [9:12 A.M.]
모두 안녕하세요. 곧 있을 이번 금요일 투자자들과의 회의에 관해 최근 소식을 알려드리려고요.

테레사 뮬러 [9:13 A.M.]
어떻게 되고 있죠?

산딥 라벨 [9:15 A.M.]
재무 보고서를 인쇄해서 전문성 있게 멋진 파일 꾸러미에 넣고 싶었어요. **11그렇게 할 수는 있는데, 인쇄 예산 잡은 거의 대략 세 배가 들어요.** 파일 하나당 30달러 정도래요.

한나 아처 [9:16 A.M.]
그렇게 비쌀 줄 몰랐는데요.

산딥 라벨 [9:17 A.M.]
나도요. **11그래서 내가 거기 견적서 받고 정말 실망했어요.**

키릴 라자레브 [9:18 A.M.]
내 친구가 윌리엄스버그에 인쇄소를 갖고 있는데. 거기서 인쇄를 하게 해서 택배로 받을 수도 있을 거 같아요.

한나 아처 [9:19 A.M.]
그거 괜찮겠네요. **12전화 해서 구체적으로 우리 프로젝트가 비용이 얼마나 들지 알아봐 줄래요?**

키릴 라자레브 [9:20 A.M.]
12그러죠.

산딥 라벨 [9:21 A.M.]
테레사, 수정된 수치가 반영된 최종안이 9월 18일 이전에 필요해요. **13그리고 꼼꼼하게 교정을 보지 않은 채 제출하면 안 된다는 거 명심하세요.**

테레사 뮬러 [9:22 A.M.]
9그렇게는 안 해요. 걱정할 필요 없습니다.

산딥 라벨 [9:23 A.M.]
고마워요! 회의 날 오전에 모두 만나서 모든 게 제대로 되는지 챙기도록 합시다.

키릴 라자레브 [9:24 A.M.]
14모두 참석하지는 못하니까 난 회의를 기록할게요.

한나 아처 [9:25 A.M.]
고마워요, 키릴. **14틈 나는 대로 그걸 볼게요.**

어휘 update (갱신된) 최신 소식 upcoming 다가오는 professionally 전문적으로 packet (파일) 꾸러미 budget 예산을 세우다 estimate (비용) 추정, 견적(서) letdown 실망, 실망스러운 일 print shop 인쇄소 by courier 택배로 promising 유망한, 성공 가능성이 있는 specific 구체적인, 특정한 final draft 최종안 updated (최종으로) 수정된 figures 수치 make a submission 제출하다(= submit) proofread 교정을 보다 meticulously 꼼꼼하게 dare 감히 ~하다 make sure 반드시 ~하게 하다 in order 제대로 된

11.

번역 라벨 씨가 실망한 이유는 무엇인가?
(A) 인쇄된 파일들이 배달이 안 되었다.
(B) 서비스 비용이 예상보다 비싸다.
(C) 일부 투자자들이 제안을 거절했다.
(D) 프로젝트가 마감일을 맞추지 못할 수도 있다.

해설 세부사항
라벨 씨가 오전 9시 15분에 파일 꾸러미 얘기를 하면서 '그렇게 할 수는 있는데, 인쇄 예산 잡은 거의 대략 세 배가 들어요(We can do this, but it's nearly triple what we budgeted for printing)'라고 했고, 이어 9시 17분에 '그래서 내가 거기 견적서 받고 정말 실망했어요(That's why getting their estimate was a real letdown)'라고 했다. 알고 보니 너무 비싸서 실망스럽다는 의미이므로 (B)가 정답이다.

12.

번역 라자레브 씨는 무엇을 해 달라고 요청 받았나?
(A) 동료들을 프로젝트에 배정하기
(B) 믿을 만한 택배 찾기
(C) 회의에서 발표 주도하기
(D) 가격 세부 정보 확보하기

해설 세부사항
라자레브 씨가 오전 9시 18분에 친구가 운영하는 인쇄소 얘기를 하자, 9시 19분에 아처 씨가 '전화 해서 구체적으로 우리 프로젝트가 얼마나 들지 알아봐 줄래요(Would you call to find out how much it would be for our specific project?)'라고 요청했고, 라자레브 씨가 이를 수락했다. 가격 정보를 받아오라는 것이므로 (D)가 정답이다.

Paraphrasing
지문의 find out how much it would be
→ 정답의 get some pricing details

13.

번역 오전 9시 22분에 몰러 씨가 "그렇게는 안 해요"라고 쓴 의미는?
(A) 서류를 면밀히 검토할 계획이다.
(B) 일정을 변경하지 않겠다고 약속한다.
(C) 기밀 정보를 누설하지 않을 것이다.
(D) 최종안을 이미 보냈다.

해설 의도 파악
'그리고 꼼꼼하게 교정을 보지 않은 채 제출하면 안 된다는 거 명심하세요(And remember that you should not make a submission without proofreading it meticulously)'라고 라벨 씨가 주의를 주자 '그렇게 안 한다'고 대답했다. 결국 꼼꼼하게 읽어 보겠다는 의미이므로 (A)가 정답이다.

Paraphrasing
지문의 proofreading it meticulously
→ 정답의 check a document carefully

14.

번역 금요일에 누가 회의에 불참할 것인가?
(A) 라벨 씨
(B) 몰러 씨
(C) 아처 씨
(D) 라자레브 씨

해설 세부사항
오전 9시 24분에 라자레브 씨가 '모두 참석하지는 못하니까 난 회의를 기록할게요(I'll be recording the meeting since not everyone can be there)'라고 말하자 아처 씨가 고맙다며 '틈 나는 대로 그걸 볼게요(I'll watch it as soon as I get the chance)'라고 대응했다. 아처 씨가 회의에 참석하지 못한다는 의미이므로 (C)가 정답이다.

[15-18] 온라인 채팅

카말 타네자 [10:24 A.M.]	
아시겠지만, 15쇼나 메뉴팩처링과의 계약 협상차 곧 싱가포르로 출장 가시는 건으로 에메랄드 호텔을 예약했습니다. 지금 항공편을 알아보고 있는데, 특별히 선호하시는 거 있어요?	
알베르토 바즈 [10:25 A.M.]	
첫 번째 회의가 6월 8일이라서, 그 전 날에 도착해야 하는데, 몇 시에 도착할지는 난 전혀 상관없어요.	
네자 하메드 [10:26 A.M.]	
하지만, 에메랄드 호텔에서 제공되는 공항 셔틀이 없다는 걸 우리가 명심해야 돼요. 그래서, 16너무 늦게 도착하는 건 원치 않아요, 시내 버스가 운행을 마친 다음에 말죠. 그 지역의 경우는 오후 11시 정도라고 알고 있어요.	
카말 타네자 [10:27 A.M.]	
그건 문제 없어요. 오후 6시쯤에 닿게 되는 항공편이 있습니다. 그렇게 되면, 17숨 돌릴 시간이 있고 근처 레스토랑에서 저녁식사도 할 수 있어요.	
알베르토 바즈 [10:29 A.M.]	
17그게 우리가 돈 내야 되면 안 되는데.	
카말 타네자 [10:30 A.M.]	
걱정 마세요. 그렇지 않아요. 17모든 경비는 우리 회사에서 지불됩니다.	
네자 하메드 [10:31 A.M.]	
그거 다행이에요. 우리가 쓴 거는 영수증을 챙겨야 하겠네요, 그렇죠?	
카말 타네자 [10:32 A.M.]	
법인 신용카드로 지불되는 건 빼고요. 하지만 어떤 이유에서 현금으로 지불한다면 차후 변제를 위해 영수증을 가지고 있어야 합니다.	
알베르토 바즈 [10:34 A.M.]	
좋습니다. 그렇게 하죠.	
카말 타네자 [10:35 A.M.]	
예약을 위해서 당신의 여권 세부정보를 파일에 가지고 있습니다. 18아주어 항공 사은 프로그램 회원이시면, 비행 마일 점수를 얻을 수 있게 단골고객 번호를 이메일로 보내 주십시오.	

어휘 upcoming 다가오는 negotiation 협상 preference 선호, 선호하는 것 run (대중교통 노선이) 운행하다 be on (음식·티켓 등을) ~가 지불해야 하는 expense 돈, 비용 cover (비용을) 부담하다 firm 회사 receipt 영수증 charge 청구, 청구액 corporate 기업의, 법인의 in cash 현금으로 retain 간직하다 reimbursement 상환, 변제 frequent flyer (특정 항공사의) 단골 고객

15.

번역 바즈 씨와 하메드 씨가 싱가포르로 여행을 가는 이유는?
(A) 취업 인터뷰를 하기 위해
(B) 사업상의 계약을 협상하기 위해
(C) 생산 현장을 돌아보기 위해
(D) 파트너에게 연수를 제공하기 위해

해설 세부사항
오전 10시 24분에 타네자 씨가 '쇼나 메뉴팩처링과의 계약 협상차 곧 싱가폴로 출장 가시는 건으로 에메랄드 호텔을 예약했습니다(I've booked Emerald Hotel for your upcoming trip to Singapore for the contract negotiations with Shona Manufacturing)'라고 출장 얘기를 꺼내면서 채팅이 시작된다. 이어 바즈 씨, 하메드 씨가 여행에 관해 얘기를 나누고 있으므로 (B)가 정답이다.

Paraphrasing
지문의 the contract negotiations
→ 정답의 a business arrangement

16.

번역 하메드 씨는 무엇을 우려하는가?
(A) 대중교통이 운행하지 않을 때 도착하는 것
(B) 연결 비행편이 출발한 후 늦게 도착하는 것
(C) 너무 이른 아침에 공항에서 출발하는 것
(D) 호텔 셔틀 좌석을 미리 예약하는 것

해설 세부사항
오전 10시 26분에 하메드 씨가 '너무 늦게 도착하는 건 원치 않아요, 시내 버스가 운행을 마친 다음에 말이죠(I don't want to arrive too late, after the city buses stop running)'라고 말한 것으로 보아 시내 버스가 끊길까 봐 걱정하고 있으므로 (A)가 정답이다.

Paraphrasing
지문의 the city buses → 정답의 public transportation

17.

번역 오전 10시 29분에 바즈 씨가 "그거 우리가 돈 내야 되면 안 되는데"라고 쓴 의미는?
(A) 회사에서 식사비를 지불해야 한다고 생각한다.
(B) 쇼나 메뉴팩처링이 항공권을 예약해 주기를 원한다.
(C) 업무를 완수할 시간이 있을 거라고 생각하지 않는다.
(D) 어떤 레스토랑을 방문할지 결정하기가 어렵다.

해설 의도 파악
바로 앞에서 타네자 씨가 '숨 돌릴 시간이 있고 근처 레스토랑에서 저녁식사도 할 수 있어요(you'll have time to relax and have some dinner at a nearby restaurant)'라고 식사 얘기를

꺼내자 이렇게 말했고, 이어 타네자가 걱정 말라며 '모든 경비는 우리 회사에서 지불됩니다(All expenses will be covered by our firm)'라고 안심을 시키고 있다. (A)가 정답이다.

18.

번역 타네자 씨는 어떤 정보를 요청하는가?
(A) 주문 번호
(B) 여권 번호
(C) 회원 번호
(D) 신용카드 번호

해설 세부사항
카말 타네자 씨가 10시 35분에 '아주어 항공 사은 프로그램 회원이시면, 비행 마일 점수를 얻을 수 있게 단골 고객 번호를 이메일로 보내 주십시오(If you're a member of the Azure Airlines Rewards Program, e-mail me your frequent flyer number so you can earn miles for your flight)'라며 고객 번호를 요청했으므로 (C)가 정답이다.

Paraphrasing
지문의 your frequent flyer number
→ 정답의 A membership number

Unit 4 웹 페이지 / 안내문

예제
본책 p. 232

판매합니다: 트레일러가 달린 중고 보트

판매자: 테렌스 와이엇   연락처: t.wyatt@ilangmail.com
원하는 가격: 8,500달러   게시일: 3일 전

5년 정도 된 18피트 켈베이 중고 쾌속정을 판매하려고 합니다. 가솔린 동력의 8기통 엔진이 달려 있고, 최근에 정비사에게 점검도 받았습니다.
반대로, 트레일러의 바퀴들은 상당히 닳아서 가능한 한 빨리 새것으로 교체해야 합니다.

어휘 asking price 호가, 원하는 가격 seaworthy 항해에 적합한 vessel 배 relocate 이주하다 undergo 받다, 겪다 inspection 조사, 점검 conversely 반대로 worn 닳은, 낡은 at the first opportunity 기회가 닿는 대로, 가능한 한 빨리

Q. 새 소유주에게 무엇을 하라고 권하는가?
(A) 가능한 한 빨리 타이어를 교체할 것
(B) 엔진 검사를 받을 것

YBM TEST
본책 p. 233

1. (B)	2. (A)	3. (C)	4. (D)	5. (A)
6. (C)	7. (C)	8. (D)	9. (D)	10. (B)
11. (D)	12. (D)	13. (C)	14. (C)	15. (D)
16. (B)	17. (B)	18. (D)	19. (A)	20. (D)
21. (D)	22. (B)	23. (B)	24. (D)	25. (A)
26. (C)	27. (D)			

[1-2] 웹 페이지

```
https//www.maloyappliances/customerfeedback

주방용품    >>    식기 세척기    >>    토피카-80

글: 산드라 휴버트                    10월 4일
```

양심상 토피카-80을 추천하지는 못하겠습니다. 이 상품을 구입하기 전에 여러 상표와 모델을 놓고 아주 많은 조사를 했고, **1결국 토피카-80으로 결정했습니다. '라이트 사이클' 때문이었는데, 이것이 일반적인 식기 세척기 사이클보다 훨씬 적은 전기를 소모한다고 홍보되었거든요.** 사실 기계 성능은 회사의 주장에 미치지 못했습니다. '라이트 사이클'의 짧은 운행 시간으로 전력 소모가 굉장히 줄어든 건 사실이지만, 그릇들이 완전히 씻겨서 나오지 않았습니다. 결과적으로, 그릇을 다시 씻어야 했고, 이것이 그나마 절약된 돈을 무효로 만들어 버렸습니다.

이 문제 외에도, 가동 중에 기계 아래 물이 고이는데, 자격 있는 배관공이 설치했기 때문에 이게 설치 잘못은 아니라고 생각합니다. **2다행히, 이 식기 세척기는 아직 품질보증이 되고, 그래서 제 필요에 더 잘 맞는 것을 가질 수도 있습니다.**

어휘 **kitchen appliance(s)** 주방용품 **dishwasher** 식기 세척기 **in good conscience** 양심상, 양심에 걸려서 **carry out** 수행하다 **a great deal of** 많은 양의 **prior to** ~에 앞서서 **settle on** ~을 결정하다 **due to** ~ 때문인 **promote** 홍보하다 **live up to** (기대 등에) 부응하다 **claim** 주장 **running time** (시작부터 끝까지) 운전 시간 **thoroughly** 철저히 **rewash** 다시 닦다 **negate** 무효로 하다 **saving** 절약 **issue** (해결해야 할) 문제 **pool** (물이) 고이다, 웅덩이를 만들다 **in operation** (기계가) 가동 중인, 운영 중인 **installation** 설치 **setup** 설치 **perform** (일을) 수행하다 **licensed** 자격 있는, 면허가 있는 **plumber** 배관공 **warranty** 품질보증 **based on** ~에 근거해 **process** 과정, 절차

1.

번역 휴버트 씨는 왜 토피카-800을 구입하기로 결정했는가?
(A) 제조사에서 품질 보증을 한다.
(B) 에너지 효율성이 높게 설정되어 있다.
(C) 저장 공간이 넓다.
(D) 싼 가격에 나온다.

해설 세부사항
첫 번째 단락에서 '결국 토피카-800으로 결정했습니다. '라이트 사이클' 때문이었는데, 이것이 일반적인 식기 세척기 사이클보다 훨씬 적은 전기를 소모한다고 홍보되었거든요(eventually settling on the Topeka-80 due to its Light Cycle, which was promoted as consuming far less electricity than average dishwasher cycles)'라고 말한 것으로 미루어 전기 소모 때문에 구입한 것이므로 (B)가 정답이다.

Paraphrasing
지문의 consuming far less electricity
→ 정답의 an energy-efficient setting

2.

번역 휴버트 씨에 관해 암시된 것은?
(A) 제품을 돌려줄 생각이다.
(B) 일부 수리를 할 것이다.
(C) 기계를 잘못 설치했다.
(D) 고객 서비스부에 연락을 했다.

해설 추론
두 번째 단락에서 품질보증을 언급하며 '다행히 ~ 제 필요에 더 잘 맞는 것을 가질 수 있습니다(Fortunately ~ I can get something that better suits my needs),'라고 했으므로 기계를 계속 쓸 생각은 없는 것으로 짐작할 수 있다

Paraphrasing
지문의 get something that better suits my needs
→ 정답의 return a device

[3-5] 안내문

벌링턴 지역 서비스

3벌링턴 시에서는 주민들이 정규 쓰레기 수거에서 다루기에는 너무 큰 오래된 냉장고, 전자레인지, 오븐, 세탁기, 기타 가전제품과 가구 등을 처리할 수 있도록 '대형 품목 수거' 서비스를 제공합니다.

수거를 신청하기 위해서는:
- www.burlington.gov/services31을 방문해 양식을 작성하세요. 한 번에 수거할 물건이 최소한 세 개 있어야 합니다. 요금은 웹 사이트 상에서 신용카드로 미리 지불하고, 원하는 수거일을 정하실 수 있습니다.

수거일 이전에:
- 버리려는 물건들을, 평소에 일반 쓰레기 및 정원 쓰레기가 수거되는 연석 근처에 놓아두세요. 반드시 이 물건들이 인도 진입을 막지 않도록 해 주십시오.
- **4전선코드는 각 가전제품 옆면에 테이프로 단단히 고정시켜 주십시오.**
- 확인 페이지를 프린트해서 물건들 중 하나에 테이프로 붙여 주세요.

5시 근로자가 여러분의 요청된 수거품을 예정 날짜에 치워 가지 않을 경우, 위생 담당 매니저 키스 디본 씨에게 555-6725, 내선 22번으로 전화주세요. 우리가 수거하는 품목의 전체 목록을 보시려면 산드라 폭스 씨에게 sfox@burlington.gov로 이메일 주십시오.

어휘 **bulky** 부피가 큰 **collection** (폐물·쓰레기 등의) 수거 **resident** 주민 **get rid of** ~을 없애다 **microwave** 전자레인지 **appliance(s)** 가전제품 **garbage** 쓰레기 **at a time** 한 번에 **in advance** 미리 **prior to** ~에 앞서 **curb** 연석(보도 가장자리를 따라 길게 차도와의 경계를 이루는 돌) **trash** 쓰레기 **yard waste** (잘라낸 풀 등의) 정원 쓰레기 **block** (진입을) 막다 **sidewalk** 보도 **secure** (단단히) 고정시키다 **power cord** 전선 코드 **confirmation page** 확인 페이지(신청, 구매 등의 절차가 완료되었음을 알리는 페이지) **remove** 치우다 **sanitation** 위생

3.

번역 안내문은 주로 무엇에 관한 내용인가?
(A) 소지품 검사 받기
(B) 정원 쓰레기 재활용
(C) 큰 물건들 처리하기
(D) 주방용품 설치하기

해설 주제/목적
첫 문장에서 '벌링턴 시에서는 주민들이 정규 쓰레기 수거에서 다루기에는 너무 큰 오래된 냉장고, 전자레인지, 오븐, 세탁기, 기타 가전제품과 가구 등을 처리할 수 있도록 대형 품목 수거 서비스를 제공합니다(The city of Burlington offers a Bulky Collection service so that residents may get rid of old refrigerators, ~ that are too big for the regular garbage service)'라며 안내문을 보내는 목적을 밝혔다. 이어 구체적인 처리 방식을 설명하고 있으므로 (C)가 정답이다.

Paraphrasing
지문의 get rid of old refrigerators, microwaves, ovens, washing machines, and other appliances and pieces of furniture ➜ 정답의 disposing of large items

4.

번역 주민들은 방문일 이전에 무엇을 해야 하는가?
(A) 인도에서 쓰레기를 쓸어낸다.
(B) 물건들을 철저하게 닦는다.
(C) 확인 번호를 요청한다.
(D) 전선 코드를 테이프로 붙여 놓는다.

해설 세부사항
세 번째 단락의 사전에 해야 할 일 부분에서 '전선코드는 각 가전제품 옆면에 테이프로 단단히 고정시켜 주십시오(Secure the power cord to the side of each appliance with tape)'라고 했으므로 (D)가 정답이다.

Paraphrasing
지문의 power cord ➜ 정답의 electrical cords
지문의 secure with tape ➜ 정답의 tape down

5.

번역 주민들이 디본 씨에게 연락해야 하는 이유는?
(A) 서비스가 이행되지 않았다는 것을 알리기 위해
(B) 방문일을 변경하기 위해
(C) 보다 상세한 목록을 요청하기 위해
(D) 지불을 준비하기 위해

해설 세부사항
마지막 단락 '시 근로자가 여러분의 요청된 수거품을 예정 날짜에 치워가지 않을 경우, 위생 담당 매니저 키스 디본 씨에게 전화 주세요(If city workers did not remove your requested collection on the scheduled day, please call Sanitation Manager Keith Devon)'라고 한 부분에서 서비스 불이행 때문임을 알 수 있으므로 (A)가 정답이다.

Paraphrasing
지문의 city workers did not remove your requested collection ➜ 정답의 a service was not performed
지문의 call ➜ 정답의 report

[6-9] 웹 페이지

www.concordlandscaping.com [검색]

| 홈 | 비포 & 애프터 갤러리 | 고객 의견 | **6회사 소개** | 방문 약속 잡기 |

6,8-B콩코드 조경은 1992년 레너드 콩코드 씨와 그의 아들 아서 콩코드 씨에 의해 설립되었으며, 이 둘이 지금까지 운영을 감독하고 있습니다. 초기에는 업체라고 해야 트럭 한 대와 두 명의 직원이 고작이었습니다. 그때 이후로 저희는 **6**계속 성장해 프레스턴 시티와 애너하임에 지사를 둔 존경 받는 기업이 되었습니다. **8-C**저희는 조경업계에서 5년 이상 일한 사람들로 20명의 상근 직원 팀을 두고 있고, 계절적으로 임시 직원도 고용합니다.

저희는 1회 공사로, 또는 유지 보수를 위한 지속적인 방식으로 여러분의 가정이나 회사를 방문할 수 있습니다. **6**저희는 잔디 보존, 비료 주기, 조경 설계, 나무 및 관목 다듬기, 땅 파기 등의 서비스를 제공합니다. **7**올해 3월에는 가로톱과 스텀프 그라인더를 구입해 나무 제거 서비스도 시작할 수 있게 되었습니다.

저희는 고객뿐만 아니라 지역사회를 위해서도 봉사하는 것이 목표입니다. 프레스턴 시티와 애너하임의 공원들에서 청소 사업을 벌여 나가고 있고, **6, 8-A**불우한 이들을 위해 봉사하는 자선단체에 재정 지원도 하고 있습니다. 저희는 또한, 민간 기업들 사이에서 공평한 고용 관행을 추구하는, '비즈니스 평등 조합'의 일원임을 자랑스럽게 여깁니다.

마당의 모습을 가꾸는 데 관심이 있든, 나무와 마구 자란 관목들을 제거하는 데 관심이 있든, 저희는 도움을 드릴 수 있습니다. 온라인으로, 또는 555-0177번으로 전화하셔서 약속을 잡으세요. **9**과거와 현재 콩코드 조경 고객들의 의견을 돌아보고 싶으시면 여기를 클릭하세요.

어휘 landscaping 조경 establish 설립하다 oversee 감독하다 operation 운영 crew 함께 일하는 팀[조] seasonal 계절적인 one-time 한 번에 끝나는 on an ongoing basis 지속적으로 maintenance 유지, 보수 fertilize 비료를 주다 bush 관목 trimming 다듬기, 가지치기 excavation 땅파기, 터파기 cross-cut saw 가로톱 stump grinder 스텀프 그라인더 (그루터기 등을 갈거나 잘게 자르는 데 쓰는 도구) removal 제거 aim to부정사 ~하는 것을 목표로 하다 make a contribution 기여하다 financial 재정적인 charity 자선 단체 ensure 보장하다 practice 관행 shrub 관목 overgrown 무성하게[제멋대로] 자란 browse 둘러보다

6.

번역 웹 페이지 안내문의 목적은 무엇인가?
(A) 회사의 업적들을 강조
(B) 새로운 서비스 소개
(C) 기업 개요 소개
(D) 조경 정보 공유

해설 주제/목적
이 페이지는 ABOUT US 즉, 회사를 소개하는 페이지이다. 첫 번째 단락에서 설립 연도(Concord Landscaping was established in 1992 by Leonard Concord and his son, Arthur Concord)와 성장세(have grown) 등 역사를 소개하고 있고, 두 번째 단락에서는 제공하는 서비스의 종류(We provide services for ~)를, 세 번째 단락에서는 비영리적인 활동을 얘기하고 있으므로 (C)가 정답이다.

7.

번역 콩코드 조경이 올해 장비를 구입한 이유는?
(A) 높은 고객 수요에 대응하기 위해
(B) 안전 규정을 준수하기 위해
(C) 새로운 서비스를 제공하기 위해
(D) 두 번째 지점을 열기 위해

해설 세부사항
두 번째 단락에서 '올해 3월에는 가로톱과 스텀프 그라인더를 구입해 나무 제거 서비스도 시작할 수 있게 되었습니다(In March of this year, we purchased a cross-cut saw and a stump grinder so that we could start offering tree removal as well)'라고 말했으므로 서비스 확장이 목표임을 알 수 있다. 따라서 (C)가 정답이다.

Paraphrasing
지문의 start offering tree removal as well
→ 정답의 provide a new service

8.

번역 콩코드 조경에 대해 언급되지 않은 것은?
(A) 비영리 단체에 기부해 왔다.
(B) 가족이 운영하는 기업이다.
(C) 경험을 갖춘 상근직 직원들을 고용한다.
(D) 고객에게 식물을 판매한다.

해설 Not/true
세 번째 단락의 '자선단체에 재정 지원도 하고 있습니다(we have made financial contributions to charities)'에 (A)가, 첫 번째 단락의 '콩코드 조경은 1992년 레너드 콩코드 씨와 그의 아들 아서 콩코드 씨에 의해 설립되었으며, 이 둘이 지금까지 운영을 감독하고 있습니다(~ established in 1992 by Leonard Concord and his son, Arthur Concord, and the two still oversee operations today)'에 (B)가, 첫 번째 단락 '저희는 조경업계에서 5년 이상 일한 사람들로 20명의 상근 직원 팀을 두고 있고(~ a team of twenty full-time employees, ~ for five years or more)에 (C)가 나와 있다. 판매에 관한 언급은 전혀 없으므로 (D)가 정답이다.

Paraphrasing
지문의 made financial contributions to charities
→ 보기의 made donations to nonprofits
지문의 have a team of twenty full-time employees
→ 보기의 employs experienced full-time workers

9.

번역 웹 페이지 방문자는 링크를 클릭함으로써 무엇을 할 수 있는가?
(A) 과거 사업들의 사진을 본다.
(B) 월간 회보 구독 신청을 한다.
(C) 약속 일정을 잡는다.
(D) 고객의 의견을 읽는다.

해설 세부사항
마지막 단락에서 '과거와 현재 콩코드 조경 고객들의 의견을 돌아보고 싶으시면 여기를 클릭하세요(If you'd like to browse comments from past and current Concord Landscaping customers, click here)'라고 했으므로 (D)가 정답이다.

Paraphrasing
지문의 browse comments from customers
→ 정답의 read opinions from customers

[10-13] 안내문

⟨블루 플래닛⟩ 가이드라인   최종 수정일: 6월 1일

자연보호구역, 자연 현상, 토착 식물상과 동물상 **10**스냅 사진을 찍어 본 적이 있으세요? 그렇다면 ⟨블루 플래닛⟩ 매거진에서 여러분이 필요합니다! 저희는 지속적으로 디지털 사진을 제출받습니다. **11**프랜서들의 기고 사진이 저희 미디어 콘텐츠의 30퍼센트를 차지하며, 저희는 매우 다양한 사람들의 작업을 종합할 수 있는 가능성을 반깁니다. 사진 파일은 submissions@blueplanetmag.com으로 보내시면 됩니다.

제출 작품을 효율적으로 처리할 수 있도록 다음의 가이드라인을 준수해 주십시오:
- 파일은 JPEG 포맷이어야만 합니다. 다른 포맷으로 저장된 사진들을 가지고 있다면 무료로 이용할 수 있는 온라인 파일 변환기가 많이 있습니다.
- 최소 1800 x 1200의 픽셀이 요구됩니다.
- 사진은 본인의 작품이어야 하며 다른 사람의 저작권을 침해해서는 안 됩니다. **12**각 사진에는 서명된 법적 양도서가 수반되어야 하는데, 귀하의 사진을 사용하고 복제할 수 있는 가시적인 허락을 ⟨블루 플래닛⟩에 주는 서류입니다.
- 워터마크가 있는 사진은 받지 않습니다. 사진 바로 아래 설명에 여러분이 사진 찍은 사람임을 제대로 표시해 넣을 것입니다.
- 사진은 원본 상태여야 하므로, 편집 소프트웨어를 이용해 변경하면 안 됩니다.

13여러분의 작품이 출판될 수 있도록 선정되면, — 인쇄 버전이든, 온라인 버전이든, 또는 둘 다이든 — 저희가 이메일을 통해 연락을 드립니다. 모든 제출 작품에 대해 경쟁력 있는 시장가격에 따라 금전적인 보상이 제공됩니다. 저희는 많은 양의 작품을 받기 때문에 모든 문의에 응답할 수는 없습니다. 양해해 주셔서 감사합니다.

어휘 take a snapshot 스냅 사진을 찍다 nature reserve 자연보호구역 phenomena 현상 native 토착의 flora 식물상 fauna 동물상 submission 제출, 제출물 on an ongoing basis 지속적으로 contribution (원고·작품 등의) 기고 make up (부분을) 차지하다 prospect (일어날 일에 대한) 전망, 가능성 incorporate 포함[통합]시키다 a wide range of 광범위한 adhere to ~을 준수하다 process 처리하다 converter 컨버터, 변환 장치 infringe on ~을 침해하다 copyright 저작권법 accompanied by ~를 수반하는, ~가 뒤따르는 release (권리 등의) 양도 explicit 명백하게 표현된, 겉으로 드러내는 reproduce 복사[복제·재생]하다 watermark (빛에 비쳐야 보이는) 투명 무늬, 워터마크(저작권 정보 등을 식별할 수 있도록 디지털 이미지나 오디오 및 비디오 파일에 삽입한 비트 패턴) credit (기여도가 있다고) 인정하다 caption 캡션(사진 밑에 붙이는 짧은 설명) alter 변경하다 editing 편집 compensation 보상 competitive 경쟁력 있는 inquiry 문의

10.

번역 안내문은 누구를 대상으로 한 것이겠는가?
(A) 인터넷 블로거들
(B) 사진작가들
(C) 잡지 구독자들
(D) 환경 과학자들

109

해설 추론
첫 단락 '스냅 사진을 찍어 본 적이 있으세요? 그렇다면 〈블루 플래닛〉 매거진에서 여러분이 필요합니다! 저희는 지속적으로 디지털 사진을 제출받습니다(Do you have experience taking snapshots of ~? Then *Blue Planet* magazine needs you! We accept submissions of digital images on an ongoing basis)'라고 말한 데서 사진 작품을 구하는 중임을 알 수 있고, 이하에서 사진 작품 제출 방식을 구체적으로 설명하고 있으므로 (B)가 정답이다.

11.

번역 첫 번째 단락 세 번째 줄의 "make up"과 의미상 가장 가까운 것은?
(A) 상쇄하다
(B) 발명하다
(C) 준비하다
(D) 해당하다

해설 동의어
해당 문장은 '프리랜서들의 기고 사진이 저희 미디어 콘텐츠의 30퍼센트를 차지하며(Contributions from freelancers make up approximately thirty percent of our media content)'라고 해석된다. 여기서 make up은 '~을 차지하다'라는 뜻이므로 '~에 해당하다[상당하다]'를 뜻하는 (D)가 정답이다.

12.

번역 모든 제출 작품에는 무엇이 요구되는가?
(A) 견본 계약서
(B) 수수료
(C) 캡션 글
(D) 양도 계약서

해설 세부사항
두 번째 단락에서 '각 사진에는 서명된 법적 양도서가 수반되어야 하는데, 귀하의 사진을 사용하고 복제할 수 있는 가시적인 허락을 〈블루 플래닛〉에 주는 서류입니다(Each image must be accompanied by a signed legal release, a document that gives *Blue Planet* explicit permission to use and reproduce your image)'라고 밝혔으므로 (D)가 정답이다.

Paraphrasing
지문의 a signed legal release → 정답의 a release form

13.

번역 블루 플래닛에 관해 명시된 것은?
(A) 한 달에 한 번 출간된다.
(B) 모든 문의에 응답을 한다.
(C) 두 가지 형태로 이용할 수 있다.
(D) 국립공원 방문에 관한 조언을 해 준다.

해설 Not/true
세 번째 단락에서 '여러분의 작품이 출판될 수 있도록 선정되면, — 인쇄 버전이든, 온라인 버전이든, 또는 둘 다이든 — 저희가 이메일을 통해 연락을 드립니다(If your work is selected for publication—either in the print version, online, or both—we will contact you via e-mail)'라고 말한 것으로 미루어 종이와 온라인 두 종류로 잡지가 출판됨을 알 수 있다. (C)가 정답이다.

Paraphrasing
지문의 either in the print version, online, or both → 정답의 in two formats

[14-17] 웹 페이지

www.riverdaleinst.com

| 홈 | 교육과정 | 교수 소개 | 등록 | 연락처 |

리버데일 비즈니스 인스티튜트

리버데일 비즈니스 인스티튜트는 전문가 교육의 선두 주자로, 미래를 준비시키는 수준 높은 강의와 폭넓은 교육과정을 통해 여러분이 직업 목표를 성취할 수 있도록 도와줍니다. **14**우리는 비즈니스 개발 교육 협회(ABDE)의 완전한 승인을 받았으며, 이 협회에 의한 인가 기한 연장을 해마다 별 문제없이 승인받고 있습니다. 우리는 고등 교육 기관으로서 — 주와 국가에서 요구하는 — 모든 기준을 충족하고 있으며 교수들은 각자의 분야에서 널리 인정받고 있습니다.

새 교육 과정은 매 학기마다 시작되며, 경제학, 재정, 기업의 책임, 마케팅 같은 주제를 다룹니다. 인기 있는 수업들은 빨리 마감되므로 빠른 신청을 권합니다. **15**로스앤젤레스 캠퍼스에서 수업을 듣는 게 적절하지 않다면, 똑같은 교육 자료가 원격학습 프로그램을 통해서도 이용 가능합니다. 필요한 것은 오직 믿을 만한 인터넷 접속뿐입니다.

리버데일 비즈니스 인스티튜트를 선택하시면, 진정으로 미래의 문을 열어 주는 교육을 받고 있다고 확신할 수 있습니다. **17**우리 졸업생들은 같은 업계에서 가장 높다고 할 수 있는 성공률을 기록하고 있습니다. 사실, 우리 학생들의 95퍼센트가 졸업 6개월 이내에 일을 찾습니다. 이는 82퍼센트라는 전국 평균과 비교해도 손색이 없는 수치입니다.

리버데일 비즈니스 인스티튜트에 관해 더 알고 싶으시면 info@riverdaleinst.com에 이메일을 보내 **16**안내 꾸러미 파일을 요청하시면 원하는 주소로 우송될 것입니다. 그 안에는 우리 교수단의 약력, 다가오는 학기의 수업 시간표, 수업료 관련 상세 정보가 포함되어 있습니다.

커리어 이동을 걸 준비가 되셨나요? 지금 온라인으로 신청하세요! 위의 '등록' 탭을 클릭하셔서 온라인 신청서를 작성하세요. 양식을 완성하는 데 약 20분이 걸리고, 신청을 접수했다는 이메일 확인을 받게 될 겁니다.

어휘 **meet** (요구·기준·목표 등을) 충족시키다 **instruction** 강의 **comprehensive** 포괄적인 **curriculum** 교육과정 **accredited** 인가 받은, 공인된 **renewal** (인가·계약 등의) 기한 연장 **interruption** 중단, 방해 **criteria** 기준 **federal** 연방 정부의 **faculty** 교수단 **respective** 각각의 **semester** (2학기제의) 학기 **corporate** 기업의 **registration** 등록, 신청 **distance learning** 원격 학습 **rest assured** 확신하다, 믿고 안심하다 **favorably** 호의적으로, 유리하게 **preferred** 선호되는, 원하는 **fee** (서비스에 대한) 이용료 **jump-start** (다른 차 배터리에 연결시켜) 시동을 걸다; (작동하지 않는 시스템을) 움직이게 하다 **confirmation** 확인, 확인서

14.

번역 리버데일 비즈니스 인스티튜트에 대해 암시된 것은?
(A) 직원 규모를 늘릴 계획이다.
(B) 전국 곳곳에 캠퍼스가 있다.
(C) 공식 인가 절차를 통과했다.
(D) 예전에 ABDE 소유였다.

해설 추론
첫 번째 단락 '우리는 비즈니스 개발 교육 협회(ABDE)의 완전한 승인을 받았으며, 이 협회에 의한 인가 기한 연장을 해마다 별 문제없이 승인받고 있습니다(We are fully accredited by ~ (ABDE), and our renewal by this body has been approved year after year without interruption)'라는 부분에서 계속 승인을 받고 있음을 알 수 있으므로 (C)가 정답이다.

Paraphrasing
지문의 fully accredited
→ 정답의 passed an official recognition process

15.

번역 교육과정에 대해 언급된 것은?
(A) 작은 팀들을 중점적으로 취급한다.
(B) 1년에 3회 제공된다.
(C) 모두 다 기업 소유주들이 강의한다.
(D) 두 가지 형태로 수강할 수 있다.

해설 Not / true
두 번째 단락에서 '로스앤젤레스 캠퍼스에서 수업을 듣는 게 적절하지 않다면, 똑같은 교육 자료가 원격학습 프로그램을 통해서도 이용 가능하며(If attending classes ~ the same material is available through our distance learning program)'라고 말했다. 캠퍼스와 원격 프로그램, 두 가지 방식으로 교육이 이루어짐을 알 수 있으므로 (D)가 정답이다.

16.

번역 웹 페이지에 따르면, 안내 꾸러미에 포함된 것은?
(A) 설문 카드
(B) 수업 시간표
(C) 캠퍼스 지도
(D) 신청서 양식

해설 세부사항
네 번째 단락에서 안내 꾸러미를 요청하라면서 '그 안에는 우리 교수단의 약력, 다가오는 학기 수업 시간표, 수업료 관련 상세 정보가 포함되어 있습니다(It includes biographies of our faculty, a timetable for the upcoming semester's classes, and details about our fees)'라고 안내 꾸러미 안의 내용을 설명했으므로 (B)가 정답이다.

Paraphrasing
지문의 a timetable for the upcoming semester's classes → 정답의 a class schedule

17.

번역 [1], [2], [3], [4]로 표시된 곳 중에서 다음 문장이 가장 적합한 곳은?
"사실, 우리 학생의 95퍼센트가 졸업 6개월 이내에 일을 찾습니다."
(A) [1]
(B) [2]
(C) [3]
(D) [4]

해설 문장 삽입
세 번째 단락에서, 이곳 졸업생들의 성공률이 업계 최고(one of the highest success rates)라고 한 다음, [2]에서 그 구체적인 수치 95퍼센트(ninety-five percent)를 언급하고, 그 다음에 82퍼센트라는 전국 평균과 비교(compares favorably to the national average of just eighty-two percent)하는 문장 흐름이 자연스럽다. 따라서 (B)가 정답이다.

[18-22] 공지 + 온라인 양식

사우스사이드 스위트 세입자에게 알리는 공지

7월 1일부터, 사우스사이드 스위트는 외부에 위탁해 보수 작업을 하게 됩니다. 서비스를 이용하시려면 www.ortizmaintenance.com/request에서 필요한 서류를 작성해 주십시오. **21**요청하실 때는, 가전제품(해당되는 경우)의 상표 및 일련번호는 물론 수리가 되어야 하는 방을 반드시 적어 주세요. 정상 근무 시간 중에서 여러분이 참석 가능한 시간, 그리고 얼마나 빨리 수리가 완료되어야 하는지도 알려 주셔야 합니다. **22**수리할 때 참석할 수 없는 경우, 기술자가 여러분 댁 들어가도록 허락한다는 것을 보여 주기 위해 박스에 표시를 해야 합니다. 이 경우에는, 임대 사무소의 커비 패트리치오 씨가 기술자를 따라갈 겁니다. 오티스 메인터넌스의 직원들은 그들이 정한 약속시간을 지키기 위해 최선을 다할 것입니다. **18**하지만, 만약 더 다급한 일이 발생할 경우 여러분과의 약속을 연기해야 할 수도 있습니다. 질문은 오티즈 메인터넌스 매니저인 존 듀몬트 씨에게 555-4531번으로 하시면 됩니다. 수리가 필요한 손상에 대해 여러분이 책임이 있을 경우에는, 우리 회계사인 클라라 크루즈 씨가 관련 비용을 청구할 것임을 명심해 주십시오. 협조해 주셔서 감사합니다.

www.ortizmaintenance.com/request

| 홈 | 업체 소개 | 신청 | 연락처 |

오티즈 메인터넌스 신청서

건물 이름과 호수: 사우스사이드 스위트, 322호
이름: **20, 21**로렐 토지어   전화번호: (466) 555-0179
19신청일: 7월 26일   **22**가능한 시간(평일 오전 9시-오후 6시): 없음
22 ✓ 오티즈 메인터넌스 기술자가 나의 부재시 내 집에 들어오는 것을 허락함

21-B수리가 필요한 구역/기기: 침실에 있는 가르골라 상표 에어컨

문제 설명: 기계를 켜면 타는 냄새가 분명하게 납니다. 지금은 전혀 그 방에서 에어컨을 사용하지 않고 있는데, 더운 날씨 때문에 이것이 매우 불편합니다. **19**제가 계약을 갱신하던 지난 달에 집주인이 기존 식기 세척기와 에어컨을 떼어내고 새것을 설치했기 때문에 이 기계에 문제가 있다는 게 놀랍습니다. **20**저는 내일 7일간 해외 휴가 여행을 떠나 2일에 돌아옵니다. 그래서, **21-A**가능하다면 8월 2일 오전까지는 이 문제가 해결되면 좋겠습니다.

어휘 **outsource** (작업을) 외부에 위탁하다 **maintenance** 유지, 보수 **serial number** (제품) 일련번호 **appliance** 가전제품 **applicable** 타당한, 적용되는 **available** 시간이 되는 **business hours** 영업 시간, 근무 시간 **present** 참석한 **rental** 임대, 임차 **accompany** 동행하다 **pressing** 긴급한 **arise** 발생하다 **postpone** 연기하다 **direct** ~에게 보내다[향하다] **damage** 손상 **bill** 청구서를 보내다 **relevant** 관련 있는 **description** 설명, 묘사 **noticeable** 뚜렷한 **landlord** 집주인 **install** 설치하다 **renew** 갱신하다, (계약을) 연장하다 **resolve** 해결하다

18.

번역 공지에 따르면, 작업 약속이 연기될 수 있는 이유는 무엇일까?
(A) 작업이 국경일과 겹치면
(B) 부품을 주문할 필요가 있으면
(C) 신청서를 잘못 작성하면
(D) 더 급한 일이 나타나면

해설 세부사항
공지에서 '하지만, 만약 더 다급한 일이 발생할 경우 여러분과의 약속을 연기해야 할 수도 있습니다(However, if a more pressing matter arises, they may have to postpone your appointment)'라고 했으므로 (D)가 정답이다.

Paraphrasing
지문의 if a more pressing matter arises
→ 정답의 If more urgent work comes along

19.

번역 에어컨에 관해 언급된 것은?
(A) 6월에 교체되었다.
(B) 식기 세척기와 같은 상표이다.
(C) 토지어 씨의 집에 있는 유일한 것이다.
(D) 오랫동안 문제점을 보이고 있었다.

해설 Not / true
신청일(Date of Request)이 7월인데 지난달에 식기세척기와 에어컨을 새로 설치했다(the landlord took out both the old dishwasher and air conditioner and installed new ones last month)고 했으므로 (A)가 정답이다.

20.

번역 토지어 씨에 대해 사실인 것은?
(A) 8월 2일에 업체와 연락할 예정이다.
(B) 수시로 해외에서 근무한다.
(C) 아파트 임차 계약을 갱신하기를 원한다.
(D) 한 주간 휴가를 보낼 것이다.

해설 Not / true
신청서에서 '저는 내일 7일간 해외 휴가 여행을 떠나 2일에 돌아옵니다(Tomorrow I am leaving for an overseas vacation for seven days, returning on the 2nd)'라고 밝혔으므로 (D)가 정답이다.

Paraphrasing
지문의 leaving for an overseas vacation for seven days → 정답의 take a one-week vacation

21.

번역 공지에서 요청한 정보 중 토지어 씨가 제공하지 않은 것은?
(A) 얼마나 빨리 일이 끝날 필요가 있는지
(B) 어떤 방에 보수 공사가 필요한지
(C) 얼마나 오래 전에 문제가 발생했는지
(D) 기계의 일련번호는 무엇인지

해설 연계
공지에서 '가전제품의 상표 및 일련번호, 수리가 되어야 하는 방, 얼마나 빨리 수리가 완료되어야 하는지 등을 적으라(When making a request ~ how soon you need the repair completed)'고 했다. 토지어 씨의 신청서 마지막에 '8월 2일 오전까지는 이 문제가 해결되면 좋겠다(I would like this matter resolved by the morning of August 2)라는 말에서 (A)를 밝혔고, 신청서 앞 부분의 '수리가 필요한 구역 / 기기: 침실에 있는 가르골라 상표 에어컨(Area / Device in Need of Repair: Gargola brand air conditioning unit in the bedroom)'에서 (B)도 밝혔다. 하지만 여기서 기기의 상표까지는 나오지만 일련번호는 나오지 않으므로 (D)가 정답이다. (C)는 공지에서 요청한 정보가 아니므로 정답이 될 수 없다.

22.

번역 패트리치오 씨에 관해 암시된 것은?
(A) 보수과의 과장이다.
(B) 기술자와 함께 토지어 씨의 집을 방문할 것이다.
(C) 토지어 씨에게 수리비 청구서를 보낼 것이다.
(D) 8월에 수리를 하게 될 것이다.

해설 연계
공지에서, 수리하는 날 주인이 참석하지 못하는 경우에는 '임대 사무소의 커비 패트리치오 씨가 기술자를 따라갈 겁니다(Kirby Patricio from the rental office will accompany the technician)'라고 말했다. 그런데 신청서 상단을 보면 Availability에 None으로 기재되어 있고, 다음 행에 있는 '부재 시에 정비 기술자가 집에 들어오는 것을 허락함(I consent to an Ortiz Maintenance technician entering my home while I am absent)'을 표시하는 칸에 체크가 되어 있으므로 정답은 (B)이다.

[23-27] 웹 페이지 + 이메일 + 이메일

www.gusmanmotivation.com/tour

앤서니 구스만 전국 투어

동기를 부여하는 연사 **26앤서니 구스만 씨는 헨리 사(社)에서 근무를 시작했지만** 자신의 진정한 열정은 사람들과 직접적으로 함께하는 것이라는 걸 발견했습니다. 10년 전 로스앤젤레스에 구스만 연구소를 설립한 이후 앤서니 씨는 그곳에서 매진되는 강좌를 맡아 강의하고 있습니다. **23그의 재능에 대한 수요가 계속 높아지자, 그는 순회하며 일일 워크숍을 통해 자신의 메시지를 전달하기로 결정했습니다.**

일일 워크숍은 구스만 씨의 '핵심 다섯 가지'를 바탕으로 전개됩니다. 이는 성공을 이루기 위한 그의 다섯 가지 요점으로, 같은 이름의 그의 베스트셀러 책에 개요가 설명되어 있습니다. **24참가자들은 이 워크숍을 최대한 활용하기 위해 이 요점들을 사전에 숙지하는 게 좋습니다.**

6월 투어 날짜

25시애틀: 6월 8일(셀턴 컨벤션 센터)
6월 11일(타바레스 플라자)
댈러스: 6월 13일(펄 호텔)
애틀랜타: 6월 18일(화이트테일 홀)
6월 20일(더 챔버스)
보스턴: 6월 25일(소토 컨퍼런스 센터)

티켓 관련 정보는 각 행사장에 연락하세요.
7월과 8월에 더 많은 날짜가 추가될 것이며, **27투어는 8월 31일까지 계속됩니다.**

수신: 앤서니 구스만 〈anthony@gusmanmotivation.com〉
발신: 세라 네이젤 〈s.nagel@snyderincorporated.com〉
날짜: 7월 5일
내용: 개인적인 출연

구스만 씨께,

제 이름은 세라 네이젤이고, 운송업에 종사하는 고객들과 주로 일하는 26광고 회사 UBP의 선임 광고 기획 담당자입니다. 25지난달에 저는 당신의 일일 워크숍에 참석하는 대단한 특권을 누렸습니다. 당신의 투어 중 두 번째 것이었죠. 저는 이 행사가 유익하고 고무적이었다고 생각했습니다. 그래서 저의 직원들 교육 행사를 위해 저희 사무실로 당신을 초대하고 싶습니다. 이 같은 개인적인 출연도 하시는지 알려 주십시오.

세라 네이젤

수신: 세라 네이젤 〈s.Nagel@snyderincorporated.com〉
발신: 앤서니 구스만 〈anthony@gusmanmotivation.com〉
날짜: 7월 6일
내용: 답신: 개인적인 출연

네이젤 씨께,

워크숍에서 좋은 경험을 하셨다니 기쁩니다. 그리고 그곳에서 배운 것이 귀하의 경력을 더욱 발전시키고 직장에서 자신감을 주는 데 도움이 되기를 희망합니다. UBP에서의 개인적인 출연을 제안한 귀하의 아이디어는 매우 흥미롭습니다. 지금까지 그런 활동은 제 사업 계획의 일부로 삼아 본 적이 없습니다. 하지만 그렇다고 가능한 일이 아니라는 의미는 아닙니다. 26특히 제가 헨리 사(社)에 있었던 덕분에 귀하의 분야에 특별한 이해를 가지고 있기 때문이죠. 27현재는 투어 때문에 바쁘지만, 완료하는 대로 며칠 이내로, 우리가 이 문제를 좀 더 들여다볼 수 있게 다시 이메일 보내겠습니다.

앤서니 구스만

어휘 motivational 동기 부여의, 동기를 부여하는 passion 열정, 열정적으로 하는 것 sold out 매진된 on the road 순회하는 fundamental 기본, 핵심 outline 개요를 설명하다 be familiar with ~을 잘 알다, ~와 친숙하다 make the most of ~을 최대한 이용하다 venue 공연장, 행사장 account executive 광고 기획 담당자(광고 대행사에서 광고주와의 연락 및 기획업무를 담당하는 책임자) transportation industry 운수산업, 운송업 privilege 특혜, 특권 informative 정보를 주는, 유익한 inspirational 영감을 불러 일으키는, 고무적인 appearance 출연 further 발전시키다; 더욱 더 confidence 자신감 intriguing 매우 흥미로운 thus far 지금까지 insight 이해, 통찰(력) completion 완료

23.
번역 구스만 씨에 대해 암시된 것은?
(A) 일부 강의를 온라인으로 제공한다.
(B) 처음으로 투어를 하고 있다.
(C) 투어 기간 중에 네 개 도시만을 방문할 것이다.
(D) 로스앤젤레스에 두 번째 지사를 열 계획이다.

해설 추론
웹 페이지 첫 번째 단락에서, '그의 재능에 대한 수요가 계속 높아지자, 그는 순회하며 일일 워크숍을 통해 자신의 메시지를 전달하기로 결정했습니다(Because the demand for his talents has grown, he has decided to take his message on the road with a one-day workshop)'라고 했다. 순회 공연을 새롭게 결정한 것이므로 (B)가 정답이다.

Paraphrasing
지문의 take his message on the road
→ 정답의 going on tour

24.
번역 일일 워크숍에 대해 암시된 것은?
(A) 참가자에게 무료로 베스트셀러 책을 준다.
(B) 티켓을 구스만 연구소에서 구입할 수 있다.
(C) 회사 중역들만을 위해 설계되었다.
(D) 참가자들은 사전에 약간의 개념을 학습하는 게 좋다.

해설 추론
웹 페이지 두 번째 단락에서 구스만 씨의 핵심 이론을 설명하면서 '참가자들은 이 워크숍을 최대한 활용하기 위해 이 요점들을 사전에 숙지하는 게 좋습니다(Audience members should be familiar with these points already in order to make the most of the workshop)'라고 말했다. 사전 학습이 필요하다는 말이므로 (D)가 정답이다.

Paraphrasing
지문의 Audience members should be familiar with these points
→ 정답의 Its attendees should learn some concepts

25.
번역 네이젤 씨는 어디에서 구스만 씨의 워크숍에 참가했는가?
(A) 시애틀
(B) 댈러스
(C) 애틀랜타
(D) 보스턴

해설 연계
첫 번째 이메일에서 네이젤 씨는 구스만 씨의 워크숍에 갔었다며 '당신의 투어 중 두 번째 것이었죠(the second one of your tour)'라고 말한다. 웹 페이지의 일정을 보면 시애틀에서 워크숍을 처음 시작하고 6월 8일과 6월 11일 두 차례에 걸쳐서 한다. 따라서 두 번째 워크숍 장소는 시애틀이므로 (A)가 정답이다.

26.
번역 네이젤 씨와 구스만 씨는 어떤 공통점을 가지고 있는가?
(A) 같은 도시에서 살고 근무한다.
(B) 헨리 사에서 근무한 적이 있다.
(C) 둘 다 마케팅 분야에 경험이 있다.
(D) 둘 다 워크숍에서 사업 성공에 관해 가르친다.

해설 연계
첫 번째 메일에서 네이젤 씨는 '광고 회사 UBP의 선임 광고 기획 담당자입니다(I am a senior account executive at UBP, an advertising firm)라고 자신을 소개했다. 두 번째 메일에서 구스만 씨는, 워크숍 요청을 고려해 보겠다며 '특히 제가 헨리 사(社)에 있었던 덕분에 귀하의 분야에 특별한 이해를 가지고 있기 때문이죠'라고 말했다. 구스만 씨가 일했던 헨리 사가 네이젤 씨와 같은 분야를 다루는 곳이라고 추측할 수 있다. 광고 회사라고 했으므로 (C)가 정답이다.

Paraphrasing

지문의 an advertising firm → 정답의 the marketing field

27.

번역 구스만 씨는 무엇을 할 것 같은가?
(A) 워크숍 티켓에 대량 할인가를 제공한다.
(B) 네이젤 씨를 동료에게 보낸다.
(C) UBP를 위해 온라인 강의를 준비한다
(D) 9월에 네이젤 씨에게 연락한다.

해설 연계

두 번째 이메일에서 구스만 씨가 '완료하는 대로 며칠 이내로, 우리가 이 문제를 좀 더 들여다볼 수 있게 다시 이메일 보내겠습니다(I will e-mail you again within a few days of its completion so that we may look into the matter further)'라고 했다. 워크숍 일정이 끝나면 며칠 이내에 연락을 하겠다는 말인데, 공지의 일정 부분에서 보면 '투어는 8월 31일까지 계속됩니다(with the tour running until August 31)'라고 나와 있다. 9월 초에 연락할 것이므로 (D)가 정답이다.

Paraphrasing

지문의 e-mail you → 정답의 contact Ms. Nagel

Unit 5 기사 / 발표문

예제

본책 p. 244

타버리 트리뷴
글: 홀리 렌즈, 3월 12일

낮은 수익률 예측에 이어, 타버리 메뉴팩처링은 노동 생산성 향상을 겨냥한 일련의 조치를 발표했다. 첫 번째는 다음 달부터 시작하는 탄력 근무제 도입이 될 것이다.

이 계획은 또한 여름이 끝날 무렵부터 모든 부서에 보너스 제도를 도입하는 것도 포함된다.

업계 관측자들은 이 조치가 원하는 결과를 만들어낼지에 관해 의견이 엇갈린다. "타버리가 시장 쪽에서 이윤 폭이 좁기 때문에 이 프로그램을 장기간 원활하게 유지하기 위한 비용을 상쇄하려면 노동 생산성의 상당한 증가가 필요할 것입니다." 시장 전문가 프랭크 게리 씨는 이렇게 말했다.

어휘 step 조치 aimed at ~을 겨냥한 output 생산량, 생산고 flexible working hours 탄력적인 근무시간제 scheme 계획 profit margin 이윤 폭 offset 상쇄하다 prolonged (시간이) 오래 걸리는

Q1. 주로 무엇에 관한 기사인가?
(A) 탄력적인 지불 방식 도입
(B) 직원 생산성 향상

Q2. 기사에 따르면, 게리 씨는 어떤 문제점을 언급하는가?
(A) 수행 목표가 실현 가능하다고 생각되지 않는다.
(B) 변화를 장기적으로 유지하기에는 너무 비용이 많이 들 수 있다.

YBM TEST

본책 p. 245

1. (D)	2. (C)	3. (B)	4. (C)	5. (D)
6. (B)	7. (B)	8. (B)	9. (D)	10. (A)
11. (B)	12. (C)	13. (A)	14. (B)	15. (A)
16. (A)	17. (C)	18. (D)	19. (C)	20. (A)
21. (A)	22. (B)	23. (D)	24. (B)	25. (C)
26. (A)	27. (C)	28. (D)	29. (B)	

[1-3] 기사

오래된 건물의 새로운 변화

애플턴, 10월 15일 – 역사적인 저택인 맥도걸 영지의 감독 레오나 헬름 씨가 저택 출입문을 휠체어가 접근할 수 있도록 하는 계획을 발표했다. 이 넓은 건물은 일반인 출입구가 6개 있다. 이들 중 4개의 입구는 현재 계단을 통해서만 접근할 수 있다. 공사가 끝나는 대로 모든 출입문에는 경사로가 생길 것이다. 시 규정에는 현재 건물당 한 개의 휠체어용 경사로를 의무로 하고 있다. 하지만, **1**헬름 씨는 이 변화가 더 많은 사람들, 특히 예전에 혼자 힘으로는 여러 동의 건물을 돌아보는 데 어려움을 겪었던 사람들을 이 저택으로 오게 할 수 있기를 희망한다. 공사 기간 중에는 안전상의 이유로 저택 전체가 폐쇄된다. **3**헬름 씨는 수입 감소를 최소화하기 위해 가장 방문객이 적은 달에 공사를 할 계획이다.

예상되는 사업 비용은 25,000달러이다. 헬름 씨가 시에서 보조금을 받고자 했다가 실패하자, 애플턴 관광 클럽 회원들이 자발적으로 나서 이 사업을 후원하는 모금 행사를 열었다. 유감스럽게도, 참가자는 많지 않았다. 헬름 씨와 그의 팀은 개인에게 기부금을 받기 위해 지역사회로 손을 뻗었다. 이 방식은 성공을 거두었다. **2**지역의 여성 사업가인 신시아 윌킨스 씨가 이들의 목표에 동조해 매우 후하게 기부를 해 주었기 때문인데, 필요한 자금의 거의 80%에 해당하는 액수이다. 이 공사는 내년에 진행될 예정이며, **3**연초에 바로 시작해서 1월 31일이면 마무리된다.

어휘 manor 영지, 영주의 주택 wheelchair accessible 휠체어가 접근할 수 있는 upon ~즉시(= on) completion 완성 ramp 경사로, 램프 attract 끌어들이다 have difficulty -ing ~하는 데 애를 먹다 wing (건축의) 부속 건물, 동 minimize 최소화하다 revenue 수입 grant (정부나 단체에서 주는) 보조금 fundraiser 모금 행사 turnout 참가자 수 reach out to ~에게 손을 뻗다, ~에게 접근하다 donation 기부 cause 이상, 목표, (사회적인 운동을 하는) 단체 account for (부분을) 차지하다 get underway 진행을 시작하다

번역 기사에 따르면 수리를 하는 이유는 무엇인가?
(A) 건물을 원래 설계 상태로 되돌리기 위해
(B) 대기 시간을 줄이기 위해
(C) 안전 규정을 준수하기 위해
(D) 더 많은 방문객을 끌어들이기 위해

해설 세부사항

첫 번째 단락에서 '헬름 씨는 이 변화가 더 많은 사람들, 특히 예전에 혼자 힘으로는 여러 동의 건물을 돌아보는 데 어려움을 겪었던 사람들을 이 저택으로 오게 할 수 있기를 희망한다(Helm hopes the change will attract more people to the site, especially those who previously had difficulty exploring the various wings on their own)'라고 했으므로 (D)가 정답이다.

114

Paraphrasing

지문의 attract more people to the site
→ 정답의 attract more visitors

2.

번역 맥도걸 영지는 사업을 위한 자금의 대부분을 어디서 얻었나?
(A) 시 보조금
(B) 자체 일반 예산
(C) 개인 기부자
(D) 클럽의 모금 행사

해설 세부사항
두 번째 단락 '지역의 여성 사업가인 신시아 윌킨스 씨가 이들의 목표에 동조해 매우 후하게 기부를 해 주었기 때문인데, 필요한 자금의 거의 80%에 해당하는 액수이다(as local businesswoman Cynthia Wilkins made a very generous donation to the cause that accounted for nearly eighty percent of the funds needed)'에서 한 개인이 80%를 낸 것을 알 수 있으므로 (C)가 정답이다.

3.

번역 맥도걸 영지에 대해 암시된 것은?
(A) 건설 기술이 있는 자원 봉사자를 찾고 있다.
(B) 1월에 가장 적은 수의 방문객을 받는다.
(C) 애플턴 관광 클럽의 회합 장소이다.
(D) 1년 운영 예산이 25,000달러이다.

해설 추론
첫 번째 단락에서 '헬름 씨는 수입 감소를 최소화하기 위해 가장 방문객이 적은 달에 공사를 할 계획이다(Helm plans to do this during the slowest month to minimize revenue loss)'라고 했고, 두 번째 단락에서 '연초에 바로 시작해서 1월 31일이면 마무리된다(beginning shortly after the first of the year and reaching completion by January 3)'라고 했다. 방문객이 가장 적은 1월에 공사한다는 말이므로 (B)가 정답이다. (D)의 25,000달러는 예산이 아니라 사업 비용이다.

[4-7] 기사

그레이더빌 관리들이 갈매기를 상대로 행동에 들어가다

5월 18일 — 그레이더빌 시 관리들이 록웰 해변 지역을 중점 대상으로 해, 시에 서식하는 갈매기 개체 수를 줄이기 위한 계획을 발표했다. 갈매기들은 해변을 찾는 사람들에게 오랫동안 골칫거리였으며, 잠재적으로 질병을 옮길 수도 있다. **4지난 여름 그레이더빌 방문자들이 기록적인 숫자로 이 문제에 불만을 나타냈으며 시에 조치를 촉구했다.**

이 계획에는 갈매기들을 해변에서 쫓아내 다른 곳에서 둥지를 틀도록 유인하기 위해 훈련받은 개들을 이용하는 방법이 포함될 것이다. **7다른 해변 지역들에서 이 방법을 이용해 최고 97%까지 갈매기 수를 감소시킨 바 있다.** 그것은 활동이 가장 활발한 시간대에 이용하면 가장 효과가 있다. 시 근로자들은 또한 해변 근처의 창턱이나 옥상에 뾰족한 것들을 놔둬 갈매기들이 내려앉지 못하게 할 예정이다.

5웨이턴 대학의 과학자들은 이 지역의 갈매기 개체 수를 연구해 왔으며 몇 년간 이 수치를 추적하고 있다. "우리 계산에 따르면," 웨슬리 루이스 씨는 말했다. "단 3년 전과 비교해 갈매기 수가 60% 증가했어요." 이는 일부러이든 음식물 쓰레기를 밖에 내놓아서든, 갈매기들에게 먹이를 주는 사람들한테 부분적으로 원인이 있는데요, 이것이 더 많은 새들을 끌어들이기 때문입니다. 그것이 바로 갈매기들이 예전 어느 때보다 많은 시간을 도시에서 보내는 이유입니다."

6마당에 음식 찌꺼기를 놔두는 사람이나 뚜껑 없이 쓰레기통에 음식을 버리는 사람들은 첫 번째 위반의 경우 50달러, 반복 위반일 때는 최고 300달러의 벌금을 부과 받게 될 것이다. 관리들은 이 조치가 사람들이 도시 갈매기들에게 먹이원을 제공하지 못하게 막기를 바란다.

어휘 take action against ~에 대해 조치를 취하다 seagull 갈매기 initiative 계획 nuisance 성가신 것, 골칫거리 beachgoer 수시로 해변에 가는 사람 potentially 잠재적으로 prompt (행동을 하도록) 재촉하다 chase off ~에서 쫓아내다 nest 둥지를 틀다 spike (못이나 징처럼) 뾰족한 것, 못 windowsill 창턱 rooftop 옥상 perch (무엇의 끝에) 걸터앉다 track 추적하다 figures 수치 compared to ~와 비교해서 partially 부분적으로 feed 먹이를 주다 on purpose 일부러 food waste 음식물 쓰레기 food scrap 음식 찌꺼기 trash can 쓰레기통 lid 뚜껑 fine 벌금을 물리다 offense 범행, 범죄 subsequent 뒤 이은 deter 단념시키다, 방해하다

4.

번역 도시가 이 계획을 시행하게 만든 원인은 무엇인가?
(A) 새로운 정부 규제
(B) 보건 검사 불합격
(C) 관광객들의 불만
(D) 예산 흑자

해설 세부사항
첫 번째 단락 '지난 여름 그레이더빌 방문자들이 기록적인 숫자로 이 문제에 불만을 나타냈으며 시에 조치를 촉구했다(Visitors to Graderville complained about the problem in record numbers last summer, prompting action from the city)'라고 말한 데서 관광객들의 불만이 계기가 됐음을 알 수 있으므로 (C)가 정답이다.

Paraphrasing

지문의 Visitors to Graderville complained about the problem → Complaints from tourists

5.

번역 루이스 씨에 대해 암시된 것은?
(A) 동물의 권리에 관심이 있다.
(B) 그레이더빌의 시 관리이다.
(C) 연구를 공표했다.
(D) 대학에서 일한다.

해설 추론
세 번째 단락에서, 웨이턴 대학에서 갈매기 연구를 하고 있다고 말하면서 '우리 계산에 따르면(According to our calculations)'이라는 말로 시작해 연구 관련자가 그 연구 내용을 설명했다. 이 설명에 '웨슬리 루이스 씨는 말했다(said Wesley Lewis)'라고 언급자를 덧붙였으므로 루이스 씨가 웨이턴 대학 관계자임을 알 수 있다. 따라서 정답은 (D)이다. (C)의 경우, 연구 결과를 공표했는지 여부는 나와 있지 않다.

115

6.

번역 기사에 따르면, 그레이더빌에서 사람들이 왜 벌금형을 받을 것인가?
(A) 공해물질을 물속에 버려서
(B) 식품을 부적절하게 처리해서
(C) 갈매기 둥지를 망가뜨려서
(D) 개장 시간 이후에 해변에 머물러서

해설 세부사항
네 번째 단락에서 '마당에 음식 찌꺼기를 놔두는 사람이나 뚜껑 없이 쓰레기통에 음식을 버리는 사람들(People who leave food scraps on the ground or those who throw away food in trash cans without a lid)' 즉, 음식 처리를 제대로 못하는 사람에게 벌금을 부과하겠다고 했으므로 (B)가 정답이다.

Paraphrasing
지문의 leave food scraps on the ground or throw away food in trash cans without a lid
→ 정답의 disposing of food improperly

7.

번역 [1], [2], [3], [4]로 표시된 곳 중에서 다음 문장이 가장 적합한 곳은?
"그것은 활동이 가장 활발한 시간대에 이용하면 가장 효과가 있다."
(A) [1]
(B) [2]
(C) [3]
(D) [4]

해설 문장 삽입
두 번째 단락의 [2] 바로 앞에 갈매기를 쫓는 데 개를 이용하는 방법이 효과를 보고 있다는 말이 나온다. 심지어 97%까지 감소시켰다고 했는데, 이 말에 바로 이어 삽입 문장이 들어가는 게 가장 자연스러우므로 (B)가 정답이다.

[8-11] 기사

> 8월 9일 — 칠와 섬의 국내 문제 관리국 대변인은 '칠와 인 포커스(CIF) 착수'를 발표했다. 이 섬의 연간 방문객을 앞으로 3년에 걸쳐 최소 25% 늘리는 것을 임무로 하는 프로그램이다. 공적 자금 백만 달러 이상이 CIF에 할당되었는데, 이것이 섬의 자연의 아름다움과 세계 수준의 숙박시설을 보여주는 광고를 전 세계에 내보낼 수 있게 함으로써 여행 부문에서 자극제 역할을 해 줄 것이다. 11권위 있는 전 세계 여행 박람회 참가를 위해서도 자금이 제공될 예정인데, 이 박람회들은 매우 유익할 것으로 기대된다. 런던에서의 것이 특히 이득이 될 것으로 예상된다. 비교적 알려지지 않은 섬인 칠와가 브랜드 인지도에서 큰 진전을 이뤄 '꼭 봐야 하는' 행선지가 될 수 있는 기회를 갖게 된 것이다.
> "우리가 이 산업을 지원하는 게 꼭 필요합니다." 이 프로그램을 선두 지휘하는 제랄드 샘프스 씨는 말했다. "910년 전에 해외 여행자에 대한 서비스 산업은 우리 지역 국내 총생산의 단 5%를 차지했습니다. 하지만 그건 우리가 공산품 부문의 고용에서 크게 이익을 얻고 있을 때였습니다. 시간이 흐르면서 생산 시설들이 서서히 폐쇄되었기 때문에, 우리는 자원을 긍정적인 미래 전망이 있는 산업으로 전환해야 하고, 안정적인 경제를 창출하기 위해 선제적인 접근을 해야 합니다."
> 섬을 둘러싸고 있는 흰 모래 해변 같은 인기 있는 해변 명소들을 홍보하는 것 외에, 10이 프로그램은 주로 시골인 섬의 안쪽 지역 장소들도 알리게 될 것이다. 이 지역은 휴일 모험 여행 패키지 상품을 위한 미개발 시장으로 여겨진다. 가처분 소득이 있는 보다 젊은 여행자들이 사람들의 발길이 닿지 않는 곳을 방문하는 데 관심을 가질 것이기 때문이다. 칠와 주민들은 www.chilwaif.org를 방문해 이 프로그램에 대한 반응을 남겨 줄 것을 요청받고 있다.

어휘 launch 개시, 출발 public fund 공금, 공적 자금 allocate 할당하다 stimulus 자극 run an advertisement 광고를 내다 showcase (유리하게) 보여주다 accommodations 숙박 시설 capital 자금 prestigious 명성 있는, 일류의 beneficial 유익한, 이로운 stride 큰 걸음, 진전 brand recognition 브랜드 인지도 imperative 꼭 해야 하는, 아주 중요한 spearhead 선두 지휘하다 account for (특정 비율을) 차지하다 gross domestic product 국내 총생산(GDP) benefit 이익을 보다 industrial goods 공산품 production facilities 생산 시설[설비] shift 이동하다 outlook (앞날에 대한) 전망 proactive 상황을 앞서서 끌고 가는 publicize 널리 알리다 predominantly 대개, 주로 interior 내륙, (안쪽의) 중앙부 untapped 손대지 않은, 미개발의 disposable income (세금, 연금 등을 제외한) 가처분 소득 off the beaten path 사람들의 발길이 닿지 않은

8.

번역 기사는 무엇에 관한 것인가?
(A) 섬의 폭풍 피해 복구 계획
(B) 관광 산업 부양을 위한 노력
(C) 오염물질 감소를 위한 프로그램
(D) 관광객 활동의 새로운 추세

해설 주제/목적
'섬의 연간 방문객을 앞으로 3년에 걸쳐 최소 25% 늘리는 것을 임무로 하는 프로그램(a program whose mission is to increase the number of annual visitors to the island by a minimum of twenty-five percent over the next three years)'에 관한 언급으로 기사를 시작했고, 세 번째 단락에서도 해변 명소(seaside attractions)와 휴일 모험 여행 패키지 상품(adventure holiday packages) 등의 말로 여행 홍보 프로그램에 대해 설명하고 있으므로 (B)가 정답이다.

9.

번역 기사에 따르면 칠와의 변한 점은 무엇인가?
(A) 주민들이 여행을 더 많이 하기 시작했다.
(B) 인구가 상당한 증가를 보였다.
(C) 지역 법률이 외국인들의 방문을 더 쉽게 해준다.
(D) 한때 생산직이 더 많았다.

해설 세부사항
두 번째 단락에서, 10년 전 이 지역의 국내 총생산 얘기를 하면서 '하지만 그건 우리가 공산품 부문의 고용에서 크게 이익을 얻고 있을 때였습니다(but that was when we benefited heavily from employment in the industrial goods sector)'라고 했다. 10년 전에는 공산품 부문의 고용에 많이 의존했다는 의미이고 따라서 생산직이 많았을 것이므로 (D)가 정답이다

10.

번역 섬의 중앙 지역에 대해 암시된 것은?
(A) 거의 시골 지역으로 이루어져 있다.
(B) 인기 있는 행선지가 되었다.
(C) 섬의 공항이 있는 곳이다.
(D) 훌륭한 해안가 전망을 가지고 있다.

해설 **추론**

세 번째 단락에서, 명소만 홍보하는 게 아니라 '주로 시골인 섬의 안쪽 지역 장소들도 알릴(publicize destinations in the island's predominantly rural interior)' 것이라는 말을 했다. 안쪽 지역(interior)을 '주로 시골인(predominantly rural)'이라고 묘사했으므로 (A)가 정답이다.

Paraphrasing

지문의 predominantly rural
→ 정답의 mainly comprised of countryside

11.

번역 [1], [2], [3], [4]로 표시된 곳 중에서 다음 문장이 가장 적합한 곳은?
"런던에서의 것이 특히 이득이 될 것으로 예상된다."

(A) [1]
(B) [2]
(C) [3]
(D) [4]

해설 **문장 삽입**

두 번째 단락 [2] 바로 앞에서, '권위 있는 전 세계 여행 박람회 참가(participation in prestigious travel exhibitions around the world)가 매우 유익할(highly beneficial) 것'이라고 말했는데, 바로 뒤에 구체적으로 런던 박람회가 특히 그렇다는 삽입 문장이 들어가는 게 자연스러우므로, (B)가 정답이다.

[12-15] 발표문

12가장 최근의 주 선거에서 통과한 찬반 투표 법안 때문에, 1퍼센트의 판매세가 특정 구매에 부과될 것으로 보인다. 주 전역에 걸쳐 고속도로와 교각들을 개선하는 개발 계획에 자금을 대기 위해서이다. 이 프로그램 지지자들은 이 법안이 기업주들에게 유인력 있는 상황을 만들어, 신생 기업과 큰 체인들을 끌어들일 것으로 기대한다. "현재 상황에서는, 기업들이 우리 주 안에 사업 부지를 확보하는 걸 꺼려합니다. 15나쁜 도로 상태가 수송을 신뢰할 수 없게 만들기 때문이죠. 형편없는 도로 안전 기록 또한 장래의 투자자들을 망설이게 하고 있다. 15이 프로그램을 통해 이런 장애물을 제거함으로써, 우리는 사업 개발에 더욱 적합해지고 자원도 최대한 활용할 수 있게 됩니다." 법안의 초안을 설계한 주 상원의원 모리스 레비는 이렇게 말했다. "비영리적인 목적으로 도로망을 이용하는 운전자들 또한 훌륭한 운전 도로, 더 넓은 차선, 강화된 다리 등의 이점을 누릴 수 있게 될 겁니다."

세금 인상으로 만들어진 기금은 지역 단위로 배분될 것이다. 각 지역은 이 자금을 활용할 가장 좋은 방식을 결정하기 위해 기반시설 확충 위원회를 임명할 예정이다. 13주에서도 원안 계획 및 인력 추천의 형태로 지원을 하겠지만, 각 위원회가 자신의 지역을 책임지며 다른 곳에 보고를 하지 않아도 될 것이다.

투표자들이 세금 인상을 승인한다는 게 다소 이상하기는 하지만, 이 법안은 86퍼센트라는 압도적인 다수의 찬성, 14퍼센트 반대로 통과되었다. 14"이 안을 승인함으로써 투표자들은 이 변화가 그들의 최상의 이익이 된다는 것을 이해하고 있음을 보여준 겁니다." 레비 씨는 설명했다. "14건설 부문의 취업 기회가 단기적으로 늘어날 테고요, 이 변화가 다른 산업에도 장기적인 성장을 자극할 것이고, 주 전체에 더 많은 일자리를 제공하게 될 겁니다."

어휘 **ballot measure** 찬반 투표가 필요한 제안 법안 **sales tax** 판매세 **fund** 자금을 대다 **initiative** 계획 **supporter** 지지자 **bring in** 관여시키다 **start-up** 스타트업, 신생 벤처 기업 **reluctant to** 부사부 ~하기를 꺼리는 **roadway** 도로 **transportation** 운송 **obstacle** 장애물 **suited for** ~에 적합한 **make the most of** ~을 최대한 이용하다 **resources** 자원 **draft** 초안을 작성하다 **motorist** 운전자 **non-commercial** 비영리적인 **superior** 우수한, 우월한 **reinforced** 보강된, 강화된 **generate** 발생시키다 **disperse** 분배하다, 분산시키다 **infrastructure** 기반시설 **ascertain** 결정하다, 확인하다 **template** 원안, 견본 **personnel** 직원들, 인력 **overwhelming** 압도적인 **majority** 다수 **in favor** 찬성하는 **opposed** 반대하는 **demonstrate** 보여주다 **in the short-term** 단기적으로 **spur** 박차를 가하다, 자극하다 **long-term** 장기적인

12.

번역 발표문의 목적은 무엇인가?
(A) 선거 결과에 이의를 제기하려고
(B) 안전 규정상의 바뀐 점을 명확히 하려고
(C) 개선안을 간략하게 설명하려고
(D) 계획을 위한 지지를 얻으려고

해설 **주제/목적**

첫 번째 문장에서 '법안 통과로 판매세 도입이 시작될 것(sales tax will be added)'이고, 그 목적은 개발 계획 재정 지원(to fund a development initiative)'이라고 개발 계획을 소개한 후 개발의 이점을 설명했다. 두 번째 단락에서는 '자금이 지역 단위로 배분된다(The funds ~ dispersed at the regional level)'며 개발 계획 자금 운용 방식을 언급했고, 세 번째 단락에서는 '더 많은 일자리(greater employment)' 등의 말로 개발의 장기 전망을 얘기했으므로 (C)가 정답이다.

Paraphrasing

지문의 a development initiative
→ 정답의 an improvement plan

13.

번역 지역 단위 위원회에 대해 사실일 것 같은 것은?
(A) 독자적으로 결정을 내린다.
(B) 모임이 일반인에게 공개된다.
(C) 레비 씨에 의해 임명될 것이다.
(D) 위원들은 주에서 급여를 받을 것이다.

해설 **추론**

두 번째 단락에서 '각 위원회가 자신의 지역을 책임지며 다른 곳에 보고를 하지 않아도 될 것이다(each committee will be responsible for its own region and will not be required to report to another body)'라는 말로 위원회의 독립성을 강조했고, 주에서는 '원안 계획 및 인력 추천의 형태로(in the form of planning templates and personnel recommendations) 지원만 한다'고 했으므로 결정은 위원회에 달려 있음을 추론할 수 있다. 따라서 (A)가 정답이다.

117

14.

번역 레비 씨에 따르면, 투표자들은 왜 법안을 지지했는가?
(A) 환경 상태를 개선해 줄 것이므로
(B) 지역에 더 많은 일자리를 창출해 줄 것이므로
(C) 전반적인 과세 부담을 줄여 줄 것이므로
(D) 노동 생산성을 극대화시켜 줄 것이므로

해설 세부사항

세 번째 단락에서 '자신들의 이익에 부합한다는 걸 알기 때문에 (understand that the change is in their best interest)' 찬성한다고 하면서, 그 이익을 '취업 기회(Job opportunities),' 주 전체의 '더 많은 일자리(greater employment)' 등으로 표현했다. 결국 투표자들은 일자리 창출에 관심이 있다는 말이므로 (B)가 정답이다.

Paraphrasing

지문의 provide greater employment throughout the state → 정답의 create more local jobs

15.

번역 [1], [2], [3], [4]로 표시된 곳 중에서 다음 문장이 가장 적합한 곳은?
"형편없는 도로 안전 기록 또한 장래의 투자자들을 망설이게 하고 있다."
(A) [1]
(B) [2]
(C) [3]
(D) [4]

해설 문장 삽입

[1] 바로 앞에서, 기업들이 이 주에서 사업하기를 꺼려하는 첫 번째 이유로, '나쁜 도로 상태가 수송을 신뢰할 수 없게 만들기 때문이죠(because the poor condition of our roadways makes transportation unreliable)'라며 도로 상태를 지적했다. 두 번째 이유로 삽입 문장의 '안전상의 이유'가 들어가면 삽입 문장 다음에 '이런 장애물(these obstacles)을 제거함으로써'라는 말과도 자연스럽게 이어지므로 (A)가 정답이다.

[16-19] 기사

조이아가 식품산업 틈새 시장에서 최고의 자리에 오르다

9월 30일 - 조이아가 건강 스낵 식품 회사들 중 선도회사로서 프리즐랜드 스낵을 앞질렀다. CEO인 카밀 클라인 씨는 지난주 '식품 유통업자 컨퍼런스'에서 자신이 갑작스럽게 성공 대열에 합류하게 된 것과 관련해 연설했는데, 그녀는 이 성공이 혁신과, 협동, 공감에 의해 동력을 얻었다고 말한다. **16이 회사가 연간 수입의 5퍼센트를 비영리 단체에 기부하기 때문에 조이아는 분명히 "건강과 지역사회"라는 슬로건에 부합하고 있다.**

클라인 씨는 식품업계에서 15년간 일해 오고 있다. **17그녀는 뉴욕의 매우 높이 평가 받는 대학인 콘코르디아에서 기업 경영학을 공부했고**, 반에서 최우수 학생으로 졸업했다. 그녀는 에이커스 퀴진에서 일자리를 잡았는데, 조리 포장되어 전자레인지로 준비해 먹는 식사의 생산자로는 전국에서 가장 규모가 큰 곳 중 하나였다. 7년 후에, 그녀는 회사를 떠나 조이아를 세웠다.

"저는 에이커스 퀴진에서의 경험에 매우 감사합니다." 클라인 씨는 최근 인터뷰에서 말했다. 업계 내부의 일 돌아가는 상황을 볼 수 있는 통찰력을 주었는데, 그것은 제 새로운 사업에 매우 중요했습니다." **17저는 콘코르디아에 다니던 시절에 조이아에 대한 아이디어를 얻었어요, 하지만 그 아이디어를 추진해 나갈 수 있는 자신감을 갖게 된 건 에이커스 퀴진에서 일하면서였어요."**

클라인 씨는 인지된 시장의 틈새를 근간으로 해서 사업안을 만들었다. "사람들이 점점 더 건강을 의식하게 되니까, **19건강 스낵 식품들의 인기가 굉장히 커졌습니다. 하지만 진정으로 당분이 없는 상품은 구할 수 없었습니다. 대부분이 꿀을 함유하고 있었죠.** 하지만 영양 과학자들의 연구로, 꿀이 고과당 콘 시럽 및 기타 감미료와 매우 비슷하게 우리 몸 속에서 분해된다는 게 드러났습니다. 이 관찰에 근거해, 클라인 씨는 그래놀라 바인 그라노고를 만들어 냈고, **18조이아의 기술자들이 아이들, 성인, 운동선수, 당뇨병 환자, 노인 등의 영양 요건에 특별히 맞춰 수없이 다양한 그래놀라 상품을 개발하고 있다.** 소비자들은 조이아가 앞으로 몇 년간 슈퍼마켓의 주요 식품이 될 것을 기대해도 좋을 것 같다.

어휘 niche 틈새, 틈새 시장 overtake 앞지르다 meteoric 유성의, 혜성처럼 빠른 fuel 연료를 공급하다, 북돋우다 compassion 동정심, 연민 annual revenue 연간 소득 live up to (기대 등에) 부응하다 pre-packaged 조리 포장된 microwavable 전자레인지로 조리할 수 있는 grateful for ~에 감사하는 insight into ~에 대한 통찰력 inner 안쪽의 working 작동 (방식) invaluable 귀중한 move forward 나아가다, 전진하다 perceive 인지하다 gap 틈, 틈새 health-conscious 건강을 의식하는 nutrition 영양 break down 분해되다 fructose 과당 sweetener 감미료 in response to ~에 대한 응답으로 granola 그래놀라(곡물, 견과류, 말린 과일 등을 혼합한 시리얼) tailor (특정 목적에) 맞추다 diabetic 당뇨병의, 당뇨병 환자 the elderly 노인들 staple 주식, (일상에서) 아주 중요한 것

16.

번역 클라인 씨에 대해 명시된 것은?
(A) 자기 회사 수익의 일부를 기부한다.
(B) 15년간 CEO로 일해 왔다.
(C) 경쟁자의 회사를 사들였다.
(D) 영양학 학위를 가지고 있다.

해설 Not/true

첫 번째 단락에서 클라인 씨가 CEO로 있는 회사를 얘기하면서 '이 회사가 연간 수입의 5퍼센트를 비영리 단체에 기부하기 때문에(With the company contributing five percent of its annual revenue to nonprofit organizations)'라고 말했으므로 (A)가 정답이다. (B)의 15년이라는 숫자는 식품업계에서 일한 기간이고, 기업 경영학을 전공했다고 했으므로 (D)도 틀린 진술이다.

Paraphrasing

지문의 the company contributing five percent of its annual revenue
→ 정답의 donates a portion of her company's profits

17.

번역 클라인 씨는 사업 아이디어를 처음에 어디에서 얻었는가?
(A) 컨퍼런스 참석 중에
(B) 에이커스 퀴진에 근무하면서
(C) 대학 재학 중에
(D) 사업 파트너를 찾는 과정에서

해설 세부사항

세 번째 단락에서 '저는 콘코디아에 다니던 시절에 조이아에 대한 아이디어를 얻었어요(I got the idea for Joyia during my days at Concordia)'라고 말했는데, 두 번째 단락에서 확인해 보면 '그녀는 뉴욕의 매우 높이 평가 받는 대학인 콘코디아에서 기업 경영학을 공부했고(She studied business management at Concordia)'라고 언급했다. 콘코디아 대학 재학 중에 아이디어를 얻은 것이므로 (C)가 정답이다.

Paraphrasing

지문의 during my days at Concordia
→ 정답의 While attending university

18.

번역 그라노고에 대해 암시된 것은?
(A) 재료를 국내에서 공급받는다.
(B) 주로 건강 식품 상점에서 판매된다.
(C) 포장재가 유기농 재료로 만들어진다.
(D) 다양한 요구에 맞출 수 있게 여러 제조방식을 가지고 있다.

해설 추론

네 번째 단락 '조이아의 기술자들이 아이들, 성인, 운동선수, 당뇨병 환자, 노인 등의 영양 요건에 특별히 맞춰 수없이 다양한 그래놀라 상품을 개발하고 있다(Joyia's technicians have developed numerous varieties tailored specifically to the nutritional requirements of children, adults, athletes, diabetics, and the elderly)'라고 한 데서 대상별로 제조방식이 다름을 추론할 수 있으므로 (D)가 정답이다.

Paraphrasing

지문의 numerous varieties tailored specifically to the nutritional requirements
→ 정답의 different formulas for various needs

19.

번역 [1], [2], [3], [4]로 표시된 곳 중에서 다음 문장이 가장 적합한 곳은?
"하지만 진정으로 당분이 없는 상품은 구할 수 없었습니다."
(A) [1]
(B) [2]
(C) [3]
(D) [4]

해설 문장 삽입

네 번째 단락의 [3] 바로 앞에서 '건강 스낵 식품들의 인기가 굉장히 커졌습니다(the popularity of healthy snack foods grew significantly)'라고 했고, 바로 다음에 삽입 문장이 오고, 그 다음에 '대부분이 꿀을 함유하고 있었죠(Most contained honey)'라는 부연 설명이 이어지는 게 자연스럽다. 따라서 (C)가 정답이다.

[20-24] 기사+발표문

설문조사 결과가 베로 사에 좋은 징조가 되다

1월 7일 - 전국 호텔 협회(NHA)에서 시행한 연례 설문 조사에서 **20레날도 지토 씨가 설립한 베로 사(社)가 자신의 분야에서 5년 연속으로 누구**나 부러워하는 최고의 위치에 오른 것으로 드러났다. 설문조사는 수천 명의 호텔 손님들을 대상으로 했는데, 이들은 고객 서비스, 객실 수준, 전반적인 가치, 편의시설 같은 요소에 근거해 호텔 체험에 등급을 매겨 달라는 요청을 받았다. NHA의 리스트에서 인정을 받은 대다수 호텔은, 많아진 노출과 개선된 대중적 인지도 덕분에 다음 해에 눈에 띄는 성장을 체험했다. **21베로 사는 무역 및 산업 전문가에게 봉사하는 것을 목표로 하는 호텔 중에서 가장 성과가 좋았다.** 이 회사는 충성도가 높은 고객 기반을 가지고 있는데, 설문 조사의 한 의견에서 드러난다. "나는 베로 사의 건물에서 묵을 수 없다면 여행 계획을 재고한다," 설문 응답자로 여행을 자주 다니는 아델라인 드웟 씨는 이렇게 말했다.

"우리는 이 결과에 정말 만족합니다." **24베로 사의 CFO 미누 팬디 씨는 말했다.** "우리의 일차적인 초점은 고객들의 안락함과 편리함에 맞춰져 있습니다. 그리고 NHA의 순위는 우리의 노고가 성과를 내고 있다는 걸 확인해 줍니다."

언론 행사에서 이야기하는 자리에서, 베로 사의 회장 킬론 틸만 씨 또한 이 결과에 만족을 표했다. "**22보스턴에 있는 본사에서 시작해, 가장 최근 문을 연 댈러스 지점을 포함해 전국적으로 확장을 해 나가면서, 우리는 고객을 위해 세계적인 수준의 보살핌을 제공한다는 것에서 한치의 흔들림도 없었습니다.**" 틸만 씨는 말했다.

직원 공지

제로드 코넬리 씨를 위한 은퇴 기념 연회

베로 사에서 20년 이상 봉직한 후, CEO 제로드 코넬리 씨가 다음 달 자신의 임무를 벗고 은퇴를 합니다. **22그의 공헌을 기념하기 위한 연회가 10월 7일 금요일 회사 본사에서 열립니다.** 뷔페 저녁식사가 제공되며, 코넬리 씨가 참석자들에게 연설을 할 예정입니다. 모든 직원들의 참석을 환영합니다. 하지만 식사와 좌석을 적절히 준비하기 위해 참가 공지가 필요합니다. **23내선번호 22번으로 지아 바이 씨에게 전화해 자신의 좌석이 마련될 수 있게 해 주세요.**

지난 세월에 걸친 코넬리 씨의 노고에 감사하며, 그가 가족과 보다 많은 시간을 보내기 위해 은퇴를 하는 데 있어 모든 것이 잘되기를 빕니다. **24회사의 CFO가 코넬리 씨를 대신할 예정이며,** 이 둘은 이번 변화를 가능한 순조롭게 하기 위해 함께 협력하고 있습니다.

어휘 **bode** 징조가 되다 **coveted** 탐내는, 부러워하는 **consecutive** 연이은 **rate** 등급을 매기다 **amenities** 편의시설 **notable** 현저한 **publicity** (대중에게) 알려짐 **perception** 인지 **aimed at** ~를 목표로 하는 **respondent** 응답자 **outcome** 결과 **CFO** 최고 재무 관리자(= Chief Financial Officer) **confirm** 확인시키다 **pay off** 성과가 있다 **expand** 확장하다 **waver** 흔들리다, 약해지다 **banquet** 연회 **celebrate** 기념하다 **contribution** 공헌 **address** 연설하다 **attendee** 참석자 **make arrangements for** (행사 등을) 준비하다 **proper** 적절한 **set aside** (나중에 쓰기 위해) 따로 떼어 두다 **transition** 이행, 전이

20.

번역 기사의 목적은 무엇인가?
(A) 한 기업체의 업적을 보고하려고
(B) 호텔 규정의 변경을 공지하려고
(C) 한 호텔의 연구 노력을 설명하려고
(D) 업계 협회 회원을 모집하려고

해설 **주제/목적**

첫 문장 'Renaldo Zito 씨가 설립한 베로 사가 자신의 분야에서 5년 연속으로 누구나 부러워하는 최고의 위치에 오른 것으로 드러났다(Vero Incorporated, founded by Renaldo Zito, has attained the coveted top spot in its category for the fifth consecutive year)'라는 말로 시작해, 이 호텔이 어떤 노력으로 고객들의 높은 평가를 받고 있는지를 설명하는 기사이므로 (A)가 정답이다.

Paraphrasing

지문의 attained the coveted top spot
→ 정답의 a business's achievement

21.

번역 베로 사에 대해 명시된 것은?
(A) 비즈니스 여행자들에게 서비스를 한다.
(B) 직원들이 정기적으로 교육을 받는다.
(C) 그 업계에서 요금이 가장 낮다.
(D) 단골 고객 보상 프로그램을 운영한다.

해설 **Not/true**

첫 번째 단락의 '베로 사는 무역 및 산업 전문가에게 봉사하는 것을 목표로 하는 호텔 중에서 가장 성과가 좋았다(Vero Incorporated performed best among hotels aimed at serving trade and industry professionals)'라는 말에서 무역 및 산업 전문가들이 주요 고객임을 알 수 있으므로 (A)가 정답이다.

Paraphrasing

지문의 serving trade and industry professionals
→ 정답의 caters to business travelers

22.

번역 10월 7일 행사에 대해 명시된 것은?
(A) 상 배부가 있을 것이다.
(B) 보스턴에서 열릴 것이다.
(C) 상근직 직원들만을 대상으로 할 것이다.
(D) 라이브 음악이 연주될 것이다.

해설 **연계**

공지문에서 '그의 공헌을 기념하기 위한 연회가 10월 7일 금요일 회사 본사에서 열립니다(A banquet to celebrate his contributions will be held at the company headquarters on Friday, October 7)'라고 했고, 기사 두 번째 단락에서 '보스턴에 있는 본사에서 시작해(from our headquarters in Boston)'라는 언급이 있었다. 행사는 본사에서 열리고, 본사는 보스턴에 있음을 알 수 있으므로 (B)가 정답이다. 공지문 첫 번째 단락에서 '모든 직원들(All staff members)'을 환영한다고 했으므로 (C)는 틀린 진술이다.

23.

번역 직원들이 바이 씨에게 전화를 해야 하는 이유는?
(A) 발표에 자원하기 위해
(B) 우편물 수신자 명단에 들어가기 위해
(C) 저녁 식사를 고르기 위해
(D) 자리를 확보하기 위해

해설 **세부사항**

공지문 첫 번째 단락에서 '내선번호 22번으로 지아 바이 씨에게 전화해 자신의 좌석이 마련될 수 있게 해 주세요(Call Jia Bai at extension 22 to have a seat set aside for you)'라고 했으므로 (D)가 정답이다.

Paraphrasing

지문의 to have a seat set aside for you
→ 정답의 To reserve a spot

24.

번역 누가 코넬리 씨의 역할을 대신 맡을 것인가?
(A) 드윗 씨
(B) 팬디 씨
(C) 틸만 씨
(D) 지토 씨

해설 **연계**

공지문의 두 번째 단락에서 '회사의 CFO가 코넬리 씨를 대신할 예정이며(The company's CFO will replace Mr. Connelly)'라고 말했는데, 기사에서 확인해 보면 '베로 사의 CFO 미누 팬디 씨는 말했다(said Minu Pandey, Vero Incorporated's CFO)'라며 그의 말을 인용한 부분이 나온다. CFO 미누 팬디 씨가 새 역할을 맡게 될 것이므로 (B)가 정답이다.

[25-29] 기사+웹 사이트+후기

프랭클린 시티 레스토랑: 최고 순위
글: 체첼리아 카실라스

이번 주말에는 평범한 것에서 기억할 만한 것으로 여러분의 식사를 한 단계 높여 보는 게 어떨까요? 아래 장소 중 하나에 가셔서 잊지 못할 식사 체험을 해 보세요!

코미다: 코미다는 정통 스페인 음식과 전통 음악 라이브 공연을 제공합니다. 중앙 식사 공간에서는 25**멋있는 도시 전망이 바라보입니다.**

베니스 그릴: 양이 푸짐한 1인분, 신선한 해산물, 라이브 음악을 원한다면 베니스 그릴을 방문하세요. 26**레스토랑이 바로 해안가에 자리 잡고 있어서** 25**식사를 하면서 아름다운 스타피시 만을 바라볼 수 있습니다.**

더 가든: 옥상 테라스에서 맛있는 중국 음식을 차려 내며, 이 테라스가 손님들에게 25**독특한 시각으로 프랭클린 시티를 바라볼 수 있는 훌륭한 기회를 줄 것입니다.** 이 지역의 아마추어 음악가들이 레스토랑에서 수시로 연주를 합니다.

원더 카페: 프랭클린 시티 아쿠아리움에 위치하는 원더 카페는 카페 벽 3면이 수족관 벽면으로 되어 있어 식사 손님들이 25**탱크 안에 있는 상어들과 기타 야생생물들의 멋진 모습을 볼 수 있습니다.** 29**정오 이전까지 식사를 마친 손님들께는 수족관 할인 입장권을 드립니다.**

www.franklincity.gov/tourism/events

프랭클린 시티 행사: 7월 10일 시작 주

7월 10일, 일요일: 프랭클린 시티 농산물 시장, 워릭 공원
[오전 8시-오후 4시]
신선한 지역산 과일과 채소를 슈퍼마켓보다 싼 가격으로 구입하세요.

7월 12일, 화요일: **26노래 대회, 베니스 그릴**
[오후 7시-오후 9시]
베니스 그릴 티셔츠를 얻을 수 있는 기회를 위해 재주를 뽐내 보세요.

7월 15일, 금요일: 고전 영화 시리즈, 몬태규 극장
[오후 7시 30분-오후 9시 30분]
감독 제임스 포크너 씨의 드라마 〈트위스티드 라이즈〉 상영

7월 16일, 토요일: 야외 예술과 문화 페스티벌, 세네카 공원
[오전 10시-오후 5시]
그림 그리는 모습을 구경하고, 그림을 구입하고, 전통 춤 공연을 즐기세요.

---

www.travelreportcard.net

의견 남기기 ≫ 사우스웨스트 지역 ≫ 프랭클린 시티

글: 로이스 잉글우드   날짜: 7월 20일   추천: 네

7월 9일에서 7월 16일까지 프랭클린 시티에서 휴가를 보냈습니다. 몇 가지 휴가 대안을 고려했지만 **27제 집에서 가깝기 때문에 결국 프랭클린 시티로 결정을 했습니다.** 편리하게 두 시간 운전 거리라서, 이것이 여행 비용도 줄여 주었습니다. 그것 이외에도, 저는 **27, 28지역 경제를 지원하기 위해 근처로 여행을 하는 게 언제나 좋다는 생각을 가지고 있습니다.** 여행 중에, 농산물 시장과 기타 관광지들 방문했던 게 좋았습니다. **29저는 특히 수족관의 원더 카페에 감명을 받았습니다. 음식이 훌륭했을 뿐만 아니라 할인 입장권도 받았습니다.**

어휘 top pick 최우수 순위 mundane 지나치게 평범한 authentic 정통의 live performance 라이브 공연 spectacular 장관인 portion 1인분 shoreline 해안가 rooftop patio 옥상 테라스 perspective 시각, 전망 aquarium 아쿠아리움 tank 탱크, 수조 diner 식당에서 식사하는 사람 screening 상영 demonstration (직접 시연해 보이는) 시범 설명 ultimately 결국 proximity to ~에 가까움 residence 거주, 거주지 cut down on (비용 등을) 줄이다 admission pass 입장권

25.

번역 모든 레스토랑에 포함되는 특징은 무엇인가?
(A) 광범위한 메뉴
(B) 라이브 음악
(C) 훌륭한 전망
(D) 푸짐한 1인분

해설 세부사항
기사의 네 개 레스토랑을 소개하는 부분에서, '멋진 도시 전망(a spectacular view of the city),' '아름다운 스타피시 만(beautiful Starfish Bay),' '독특한 시각으로 프랭클린 시티를 바라볼 수 있는 훌륭한 기회(a great opportunity to see Franklin City from a unique perspective),' '탱크 안에 있는 상어들과 기타 야생생물들의 멋진 모습(a perfect view of the sharks and other wildlife in the tank)'이라고 멋진 전망이 빠지지 않고 들어가므로 (C)가 정답이다. (B) 라이브 음악도 답이 될 것 같지만 원더 카페에서 공연이 있는지에 대한 언급이 없으므로 오답이다.

26.

번역 노래 대회에 대해 사실인 것은?
(A) 연안 근처에서 열렸다.
(B) 승자들에게 상품권을 제공했다.
(C) 매주 열린다.
(D) 식사 손님들이 판정을 했다.

해설 연계
웹 사이트에 보면 7월 12일, 화요일 행사에 '노래 대회, 베니스 그릴(Singing Contest, Benny's Grill)'이라고 되어 있고, 기사에서 확인해 보면 레스토랑 베니스 그릴을 소개하는 부분에서 '레스토랑이 바로 해안가에 자리 잡고 있어서(Because the restaurant is located right on the shoreline)'라고 설명되어 있다. 노래 대회가 해안가에 있는 베니스 그릴에서 열린 것이므로 (A)가 정답이다.

Paraphrasing
지문의 on the shoreline → 정답의 near a coastline

27.

번역 후기에 따르면, 잉글우드 씨가 프랭클린 시티를 방문하기 원했던 이유는?
(A) 그곳 호텔의 쿠폰을 가지고 있어서
(B) 친구의 추천을 받아서
(C) 멀리까지 갈 필요가 없었기 때문에
(D) 사는 곳에서 값싼 항공편이 있어서

해설 세부사항
'제 집에서 가깝기 때문에(due to its proximity to my place of residence)'라는 지리적인 이유와 '지역 경제를 지원하기 위해 근처로 여행을 하는 게 언제나 좋다(it is always better to travel nearby to support the local economy)'라는 생각에서 프랭클린 시티를 선택했다고 했다. 가까운 휴가지를 선호한다는 것을 알 수 있으므로 (C)가 정답이다.

28.

번역 후기에서, 첫 번째 단락 네 번째 줄의 "hold"와 의미상 가장 가까운 것은?
(A) 점유하다
(B) 쥐다
(C) 소유하다
(D) 지니다

해설 동의어
해당 문장은 '지역 경제를 지원하기 위해 근처로 여행을 하는 게 언제나 좋다는 생각을 가지고 있습니다'라고 해석된다. 여기서 hold는 '(생각을) 지니다, 유지하다'로 보는 게 자연스러우므로 (D)가 정답이다.

29.

번역 잉글우드 씨에 대해 암시된 것은?
(A) 휴가 기간을 늘리기로 결정했다.
(B) 오전에 원더 카페에서 식사를 했다.
(C) 농산물 시장에서 구매를 했다.
(D) 수족관을 두 차례 방문했다.

해설 연계

후기에서 수족관의 원더 카페가 특히 좋았다며 '할인 입장권도 받았습니다(I also received a discounted admission pass)'라고 말했고, 기사에서 원더 카페 부분을 보면 '정오 이전까지 식사를 마친 손님들께는 수족관 할인 입장권을 드립니다(A discount admission ticket to the aquarium is given to diners who complete their meal before noon)'라고 되어 있다. 즉, 원더 카페에서 오전에 식사를 하고 수족관 할인 입장권을 받아 수족관을 구경했다고 추측할 수 있으므로 (B)가 정답이다.

Paraphrasing

지문의 complete their meal before noon
→ 정답의 ate at Wonder Café in the morning

Unit 6 기타 양식

 예제 본책 p. 256

에잇 스트릿 서점에서는, 5년간 영업을 해 온 것을 축하하며 소중한 고객 여러분께 특가 상품을 제공하고자 합니다. 4월 3일부터 9일까지 계산할 때 이 쿠폰을 제시하면 다음의 염가 혜택을 받으실 수 있습니다:

양장본 책을 2권 구입하면, 세 번째 책은 무료

이 쿠폰은, 거의 할인 판매를 하지 않는 신간 및 교과서를 포함해 어떤 책에도 이용할 수 있습니다. 이용해 주셔서 감사합니다!

* 가장 비싼 책 두 권은 정가입니다. 어떤 할인가도 적용되지 않습니다.

어휘 **special deal** 특가 상품, 특별 판매 **valued** 소중한 **checkout** 계산대 **release** 발간, 발간물 **valid** 유효한

Q. 쿠폰에 명시된 것은?
(A) 쿠폰은 3일간 유효하다.
(B) 가장 저렴한 품목이 무료일 것이다.

YBM TEST 본책 p. 257

1. (B)	2. (D)	3. (D)	4. (B)	5. (B)
6. (C)	7. (D)	8. (B)	9. (A)	10. (D)
11. (C)	12. (D)	13. (D)	14. (C)	15. (D)
16. (D)	17. (B)	18. (C)	19. (D)	20. (A)
21. (C)	22. (D)	23. (D)	24. (C)	

[1-2] 목차

사회 심리학 저널

322호

목차

편집장 모니카 코니어스 씨의 편지 · · · · · · · 2
테크놀로지가 인간 관계에 미치는 영향 · · · · · 3
긍정적인 자아상에 있어서 대중매체의 영향 · · · 16
1로즈버드 상 수상자, 다크샤 로디 씨와의 대담 · · 28

불안감 감소를 위한 전략: 대학 사례 연구 · · · 41
2직업 환경에서 협력적인 단체 행동 · · · · · · 56

원고 제출은 editor@journalofsp.com으로 해 주세요. 출판이 고려되는 저자에게만 연락이 갈 것입니다.

어휘 **effect of A on B** A가 B에 미치는 영향 **mass media** 대중매체 **self-image** 자아상 **recipient** 수령인, 수상자 **strategy** 전략 **anxiety** 불안감 **case study** 사례 연구 **cooperative** 협력적인 **group behavior** 단체 행동 **professional** 직업의, 전문직의 **setting** 환경 **submission** (서류 등의) 제출 **publication** 출판

1.

번역 로디 씨는 누구인가?
(A) 경제 기자
(B) 수상자
(C) 구직자
(D) 대학 교수

해설 세부사항

목차 네 번째 줄에서 '로즈버드 상 수상자, 다크샤 로디 씨와의 대담(Interview with Daksha Lodi, Recipient of the Rosebud Prize)'이라고 했으므로 (B)가 정답이다.

Paraphrasing

지문의 Recipient of the Rosebud Prize
→ 정답의 An award winner

2.

번역 독자들은 함께 일하는 것에 관해 어디서 찾아볼 수 있는가?
(A) 3페이지
(B) 16페이지
(C) 41페이지
(D) 56페이지

해설

질문의 함께 일하기(working together)는 목차 마지막 줄의 '직업 환경에서 협력적인 단체 행동(Cooperative Group Behavior in a Professional Setting)'과 의미가 통한다. 페이지가 56으로 표시되어 있으므로 (D)가 정답이다.

[3-4] 안내 소책자

밸리 요리학교

4월 수업[최종 확정] : 매주 화요일 오후 6시 30분- 8시 30분

3밸리 요리학교에서는 보다 많은 신청자를 수용하기 위해 4월에 중급을 두 부분으로 나눴습니다. 등록은 3월 16일까지 받습니다.

초급 /	엘리자베스 윈스테드 강사
	칼 사용법, 위생, 수프
4중급 /	타카히로 후지무라 강사
	소스, 시즈닝 선택, 불에 굽기
중상급 /	존 보이드 강사
	생선 졸이기, 디저트, 수제 파스타

	고급 /	바네사 사니 강사
		페이스트리, 해산물, 메뉴 짜기

어휘 culinary 요리의 session (회의, 교육 등의) 기간 updated 최신 정보의 split 나누다, 쪼개다 intermediate level 중급 accommodate 수용하다 registration 등록, 등록자 enrollment 등록, 등록생, 입회 sanitation 위생 seasoning 양념, 시즈닝(맛과 향을 증가시키기 위해 소금, 후추, 특히 허브를 넣어 만듦) grilling (불에) 굽기 poaching (생선) 졸이기, (계란) 수란 만들기

3.

번역 밸리 요리학교가 시간표를 조정한 이유는 무엇인가?
(A) 중급 학생들이 반을 통과하지 못해서
(B) 일부 교실이 수리 중이어서
(C) 강사 하나가 학생들을 가르칠 수 없어서
(D) 등록생 수가 늘어나서

해설 세부사항
두 번째 줄의 '밸리 요리학교에서는 보다 많은 신청자를 수용하기 위해 4월에 중급을 두 부분으로 나눴습니다(Valley Culinary School has split the intermediate level into two sections for April to accommodate the higher registration)'라고 말한 데서 수강생이 늘어났음을 알 수 있고, 실제로 과목 안내표에 중급이 상하 둘로 나눠져 있으므로 (D)가 정답이다.

4.

번역 누가 학생들에게 허브 선택에 대해 가르칠 것인가?
(A) 윈스테드 씨
(B) 후지무라 씨
(C) 보이드 씨
(D) 사니 씨

해설 세부사항
중하급반 강습 내용 중에 포함되는 시즈닝(seasoning)에서는 허브를 많이 이용한다. 중하급반 강사가 타카히로 후지무라 씨(Taught by Takahiro Fujimura)라고 되어 있으므로 (B)가 정답이다.

[5-7] 설문지

빛나는 미소 치과
고객 설문지

시간을 내서 빛나는 미소 치과 이용에 관한 질문에 응답해 주셔서 감사합니다. 여러분의 반응은 저희 서비스 개선을 향상시키는 데 도움이 됩니다.

환자 이름: 미란다 아브너   방문 일자: 2월 5일
재방문 환자: ☑ 네   ☐ 아니오
5치과 의사: ☑ 크리스토퍼 메디나 박사
              ☐ 에벌린 초 박사
              ☐ 제니스 브루스터 박사

위에 기록된 정보가 정확합니까? ☑ 네   ☐ 아니오
그렇지 않다면, 정정된 사항을 여기에 적어 주세요.: _____

아래 항목에 대해 1(나쁨)에서 10(훌륭함)까지 등급을 매겨 주세요.

쉬운 예약: 5   영업 시간의 편리함: 6
주차 공간 이용: 9   **6-C**전반적인 청결도: 10
대기 시간: 9   접수 담당자: 8
치과 의사: 10   약속 절차: 9

의견: 전반적으로, 약속된 진료 중에 시간을 아주 잘 보냈습니다. 한 가지 불만이라면, 검사 받기 위해 의사에게 보내졌을 때 방을 찾느라 애를 먹었습니다. **7**환자들이 검사실을 더 쉽게 찾을 수 있도록 문 위에 큰 간판을 붙여 놓으면 더 좋을 것 같습니다.

어휘 correction 정정, 정정한 것 rate 평가하다, 등급을 매기다 scale 등급 hours of operation 운영[영업] 시간 availability 이용[입수] 가능 cleanliness 청결 receptionist 접수 담당자 appointment (업무·진료상의) 약속 procedure 절차 complaint 불만

5.

번역 밝은 미소 치과에 대해 명시된 것은?
(A) 아브너 씨에게 경품 당첨 자격을 줄 것이다.
(B) 직원으로 둘 이상의 치과 전문의를 두고 있다.
(C) 재방문하는 환자에게는 할인을 해 준다.
(D) 수리를 했다.

해설 Not / true
설문지의 치과의사(Dentist) 난에 이름이 셋 올라와 있으므로 의사가 둘 이상이라고 말한 (B)가 정답이다.

Paraphrasing
지문의 Dentist → 정답의 dental professional

6.

번역 아브너 씨에 대해 암시된 것은?
(A) 약속된 진료를 위해 오래 기다려야 했다.
(B) 밝은 미소 치과에 처음 온 환자이다.
(C) 시설의 청결함에 만족했다.
(D) 주차장을 찾느라 고생을 많이 했다.

해설 추론
등급 평가에서 '전반적인 청결도(Overall cleanliness)'에 최고 점수 10점을 준 것으로 보아 (C)가 정답이다. '대기 시간(Waiting time)'에 9점을 준 것으로 보아 (A)는 틀리고, 설문지의 '재방문 환자(Returning Patient)' 항목에서 'Yes'에 표시했으므로 (B)도 틀리다. 등급 매기기의 '주차 공간 이용(Parking Availability)' 항목에서 9점을 주었으므로 (D)도 틀린 진술이다.

7.

번역 아브너 씨는 어떻게 변화할 것을 제안하는가?
(A) 로비 공간에서 만나기
(B) 건물로 가는 길 안내하기
(C) 검사실 확장하기
(D) 방에 분명하게 표시하기

해설 세부사항
의견란에서 검사실 찾는 데 애를 먹었다며 '환자들이 검사실을 더 쉽게 찾을 수 있도록 문 위에 큰 간판을 붙여 놓으면 더 좋을 것 같습니다(It would be better if you put large signs above the doors so patients can find the exam rooms more easily)'라고 제안했다. 분명한 표시를 하라는 뜻이므로 (D)가 정답이다.

Paraphrasing
지문의 put large signs above the doors
→ 정답의 Marking rooms clearly

[8-10] 양식

조안스 케이터링
주문서

8 고객/회사 이름: 조슈아 리코/미라쥐 굿즈   **전화 번호:** 555-0193
9 행사 날짜/시간: 10월 6일/오전 11시 30분   **장소:** 레드우드 센터
손님 수: 80명   **필요한 서비스원:** 0명

해당되는 곳에, 각 음식의 필요한 숫자를 표시하세요.

점심 세트 메뉴
에피타이저: 속을 채운 버섯
샐러드: 시저 샐러드
메인 요리: [72] 치킨 페투치니 알프레도 파스타
　　　　　 [8] 시금치와 리코타 라비올리*
디저트: [40] 브라우니　　　[40] 망고 타르트

음료** (2개 선택): ☑ 커피 ☐ 차 ☑ 아이스 레모네이드 ☐ 소다

10-B *채식주의자에게 적합
**레몬을 첨가한 물도 제공됨

배달 형태: ☐ 조안스 케이터링이 배달(추가 요금 적용)
　　　　　8 ☑ 고객이 직접 가져감
　　　　　　위의 이름과 다를 경우 알려 주세요: _____
　　　　　☐ 연회장 직원이 가져감
　　　　　☐ 기타(상세히): _____

9 행사 5일 전에 반액 지불이 되어야 합니다. 나머지는 행사 3일 이후 지불합니다.

10-D 고객 주: 이 주문은 직원 오찬을 위한 것입니다. 저희 동료 중 하나가 땅콩 알레르기가 있기 때문에, 제공되는 음식 안에 땅콩이 들어가지 않도록 확인해 주십시오. 음식 설명 부분에서 땅콩을 못 보기는 했지만, 다시 확인하고 싶습니다.

어휘　catering (연회 등을 위한) 음식 공급업　venue (콘서트, 스포츠, 행사 등이 열리는) 장소　server 서빙하는 사람　applicable 해당되는　appetizer 전채, 에피타이저　stuffed (음식) 속을 채워 넣은　entrée 메인 요리, 주요 요리　fettuccini 길고 납작한 파스타　alfredo 알프레도(버터와 치즈가 많이 들어간 소스)　ricotta 리코타(이탈리아산 치즈의 일종)　ravioli 라비올리(고기, 야채, 치즈 등으로 속을 채워 만두처럼 만든 파스타)　beverage 음료　iced 얼음을 넣은　soda 탄산음료　surcharge 추가 요금　remainder 나머지　due 지불해야 하는　luncheon 오찬

confirm 확인하다　description 설명　double-check 재확인하다

8.
번역 미라쥐 굿즈는 어떻게 식사를 받을 것인가?
(A) 음식 공급업자가 배달해 줄 것이다.
(B) 리코 씨가 직접 가져갈 것이다.
(C) 레드우드 센터가 운송해 줄 것이다.
(D) 리코 씨의 동료가 가져갈 것이다.

해설 세부사항
배달 형태에서 '고객이 직접 가져감(Customer Pick-up)'에 표시했고, 위의 이름과 다르면 알려 달라고 했는데 아무 표시가 없다. 맨 위 이름으로 올라가 보면 '고객/회사 이름: 조슈아 리코/미라쥐 굿즈(Customer/Company Name: Joshua Rico/Mirage Goods)'라고 되어 있다. 즉, 미라쥐 굿즈사(社)의 조슈아 리코 씨가 음식을 찾아갈 것이므로 (B)가 정답이다.

Paraphrasing
지문의 Customer Pick-up
→ 정답의 be picked up by Mr. Rico

9.
번역 리코 씨는 언제 첫 번째 지불을 해야 하는가?
(A) 10월 1일
(B) 10월 5일
(C) 10월 6일
(D) 10월 9일

해설 세부사항
아래 부분에서 '행사 5일 전에 반액 지불이 되어야 합니다(A half-payment must be made five days before the event)'라고 명시했고, 다시 위를 확인하면 '행사 날짜/시간(Date/Time of Event)' 항목에 10월 6일이라고 적혀 있다. 10월 6일 기준으로 5일 전에 우선 반액을 내야 하므로 (A)가 정답이다.

10.
번역 리코 씨에 대해 사실인 것은?
(A) 주문에 대해 다량 주문 할인을 받을 자격이 있다.
(B) 모든 음식이 채식주의자에게 적합하기를 바란다.
(C) 행사에서 물과 따뜻한 음료만 주문할 계획이다.
(D) 특정 재료가 빠질 것을 분명히 하고 싶어 한다.

해설 Not/true
마지막의 고객 주(Customer Notes)에서 땅콩을 빼 달라며, 위에 적힌 사항에서 확인했지만 재차 요청한다고 하고 있으므로 (D)가 정답이다. (B)의 경우 별표(*)가 되어 있는 항목만 '채식주의자에게 적합한(Suitable for vegetarians)' 것이므로 틀린 진술이다.

Paraphrasing
지문의 confirm that there are no peanuts in the dishes served → 정답의 make sure that a certain ingredient is excluded

[11-14] 일정표

어빙빌 축제
주말 일정표

11어빙빌 읍은 1878년 8월 20일에 헌장에 의해 공식적으로 설립되었습니다. 그리고 이제 또 다시 이 특별한 날을 기념할 순간이 왔습니다! 아래 활동으로 함께 재미있게 즐겨 보세요.

8월 19일, 토요일
오전 10시 장식 행렬 차량, 밴드, 댄서들이 타운 곳곳을 이리저리 돌아다닙니다. 시청에서 출발해 세딜로 경기장을 거쳐 **12**할리혹 공원에서 끝이 날 것입니다. 예상 경로 지도를 시 웹 사이트에서 다운로드 받을 수 있습니다. **12**시장 애슐리 마르티노 씨가 퍼레이드가 끝나는 곳에서 정오 무렵에 연설을 할 예정입니다. 마을의 단체들은 퍼레이드에 참가하려면 555-0133번으로 리디아 부어히스 씨에게 전화 주십시오.

오전 11시 할리혹 공원과 근처 마켓 공원에서 음식 판매대를 운영합니다.
–오후 7시 지역의 인기 음식은 물론 이국적인 전 세계 음식을 맛보세요.

오후 2시 네 개 연령대로 나뉘는 재미있는 **14-B**3대 3 배구 토너먼트에서 여러분의 배구 실력을 자랑해 보세요. 등록하려면 어빙빌 지역 주민회관을 방문하세요.

오후 6시 **13**마켓 공원에서 열리는 어빙빌 최초의 밴드 경연. 밴드를 출전시키려면 시청에서 서류를 작성해 주세요.

8월 20일, 일요일
오전 10시 어빙빌 화가 로시타 베네벤티 씨의 단계별 지도로 **14-A**자신만의 아크릴화 그리는 법을 배워 보세요. 재료비는 15달러입니다. 사전 등록을 하지 않아도 됩니다.

오후 2시 **14-D**어빙빌 전역의 제빵사들이 최고의 파이와 케이크를 가지고 나오고, 우승자는 핀첨 가전에서 만든 최첨단 오븐을 받게 됩니다! 판정이 끝나면 무료 디저트가 제공될 것입니다. 도널드 길모어 씨에게 dgilmore@irvingville.gov로 이메일을 보내 경연에 참가하세요.

오후 4시 다가오는 시의회 선거의 후보자들을 만나 보세요. 어빙빌의 기자 바이올렛 쇼 씨가 마켓 공원 무대에서 이들과 인터뷰를 할 것입니다.

어휘 charter 헌장, 인가서 commemorate 기념하다 occasion (특정한) 경우, 때 float (퍼레이드 때 쓰기 위한) 장식 차량 weave one's way 이리저리 누비며 나아가다 approximately 대략 sample 맛보다, 시식하다 exotic 이국적인, 독특한 cuisine 요리법, 요리 sign up 등록하다 fill out a form 서식을 작성하다 enter 출전[참가]시키다 acrylic painting 아크릴화 instructions 지시, 설명 material 재료 baker 제빵사 state-of-the-art 최신의, 최첨단 upcoming 다가오는 city council 시의회

11.
번역 어빙빌 축제에 대해 암시된 것은?
(A) 읍의 사업을 위해 모금을 할 것이다.
(B) 처음으로 열리고 있다.
(C) 읍의 설립을 축하한다.
(D) 관광산업을 홍보하려는 의도로 열린다.

해설 추론
첫 문장에서 '어빙빌 읍은 1878년 8월 20일에 헌장에 의해 공식적으로 설립되었습니다. 그리고 이제 또 다시 이 특별한 날을 기념할 순간이 왔습니다!(The town of Irvingville was officially established by charter on August 20, 1878, and it's time once again to commemorate this special occasion!)'라고 말한 후 이어 행사 일정을 자세히 소개하고 있다. 설립을 기념해 축제를 여는 것을 알 수 있으므로 (C)가 정답이다. '이제 또 다시(once again)'라는 말로 미루어 처음 여는 행사는 아니므로 (B)는 답이 될 수 없고, 마을 주민들만을 대상으로 하므로 (D)도 틀린 진술이다.

12.
번역 마르티노 씨는 어디에서 연설을 할 예정인가?
(A) 마켓 공원
(B) 시청
(C) 세딜로 경기장
(D) 할리혹 공원

해설 세부사항
8월 19일, 토요일, 오전 10시 일정에서, '시장 애슐리 마르티노 씨가 퍼레이드가 끝나는 곳에서 연설할 예정(Mayor Ashley Martino will give a speech at the end of the parade route)'이라고 했고, 바로 앞에서 행렬은 할리혹 공원에서 끝난다고 했다. 할리혹 공원에서 연설을 하게 될 것이므로 (D)가 정답이다.

13.
번역 음악인들은 어떻게 행사 참가 신청을 할 수 있을까?
(A) 연락 번호로 전화해서
(B) 이메일을 보내서
(C) 어빙빌 주민 센터를 방문해서
(D) 직접 서류를 작성해서

해설 세부사항
8월 19일, 오후 6시 일정을 보면 '밴드를 출전시키려면 시청에서 서류를 작성해 주세요(Fill out a form at City Hall to enter your band)'라고 했다. 시청에 가서 서류를 써야 하므로 (D)가 정답이다.

Paraphrasing
지문의 Fill out a form at City Hall
→ 정답의 completing a form in person

14.
번역 어빙빌 축제에서 열리는 활동으로 명시되지 않은 것은?
(A) 그림 수업
(B) 스포츠 경연
(C) 정치 토론
(D) 제빵 경연 대회

해설 Not / true
두 번째 날, 오후 4시 행사에서 시의원 후보자와 기자의 인터뷰가 있을 것이라고 말했지만, 정치 토론에 관한 언급은 없으므로 (C)가 정답이다. 두 번째 날 오전 10시의 '아크릴화(acrylic painting)' 수업에 (A)가, 첫 번째 날 오후 2시의 '3대 3 배구 토너먼트' 경연에 (B)가, 두 번째 날 오후 2시의 '제빵사(bakers), 우승자(winner), 경연(competition)' 등의 말에 (D)가 명시되었다.

[15-19] 송장+이메일

미첼 코퍼레이션
주문 확인서

고객: 멜리사 라인하트	배송 주소: 휠러 드라이브 622번지, 애크런, 오하이오 주 44304
발송일: 10월 16일	배달 유형: 일반 (영업일 기준 2-3일)
16할인 클럽 회원: 네	주문 번호: 26505
지불: 5981번으로 끝나는 신용카드로 전액 지불	

품목/상표	**15**제품 설명	개당 가격	수량	총액
485 / 호라이즌	다목적 표면 스크럽제 [11온스]	일반가: 1.99달러 회원가: 9.99달러	2개	19.98달러
091 / **17**와팍	극세사 천 수건 [24묶음]	일반가: 15.99달러 회원가: 14.99달러	1개	14.99달러
337 / 필즈	목재 가구 광택제 [13.8온스]	일반가: 12.99달러 회원가: 9.99달러	1개	9.99달러
262 / 슈미트	욕실 항균 스프레이 [30온스]	일반가: 16.99달러 회원가: 15.99달러	3개	47.97달러
모든 품목은 함께 배송될 예정입니다. 혹시 주문과 관련해 문제가 있을 경우 inquiries@mitchellco1.com로 저희에게 연락 주십시오.			배송료	3.95달러
			세금	5.57달러
			총액	102.45달러

수신: inquiries@mitchellco1.com
발신: rinehartm@ciscomail.com
날짜: 10월 25일
내용: 주문 번호 26505

관계자 여러분께:

미첼 코퍼레이션에 최근 주문했다가(주문 번호 26505) 빠진 제품에 대해 항의했던 것과 관련해 다시 씁니다. **18**제가 수령하면서 배달물을 확인했을 때, 개리 타보 씨가 빠진 물건을 알게 되었고, 보고를 하겠다고 말했습니다. 하지만 그 이후 그에 관해 아무 말도 듣지 못했습니다. **19-C**귀사의 고객 서비스부 쪽으로 이 문제를 알렸더니, 그곳 직원이 이메일을 보내라고 제안했습니다. **17**빠진 물건은 극세사 천 수건 묶음이고, 가능한 한 빨리 이것이 보내졌으면 좋겠습니다. **19-B**지난 달에 귀사에서 많은 신제품을 출시했고, 이로 인해 주문 처리가 더 복잡해진다는 거 알고 있습니다. 하지만 **19-A**제가 과거에 귀사에서 보았던 높은 수준의 고객 서비스를 여전히 기대하고 있습니다.

이 문제에 대한 빠른 응답을 감사드립니다.

멜리사 라인하트

어휘 **shipping** 배송, 배송료 **dispatch** 발송 **paid in full** 전액 지불된 **all-purpose** 다목적, 다용도의 **surface scrub** 표면 스크럽제(때 묻은 표면을 문질러서 닦기 위한 세제) **microfiber cloth** 극세사 천 **polish** 광택제 **antibacterial** 항균성의 **issue** (처리해야 할) 문제 **follow up on** 후속 조치를 취하다 **make a complaint** 항의를 제기하다 **missing** 분실된, 빠진 **receipt** 수령, 인도 **representative** (회사를 대표하는) 직원 **fulfill an order** 주문을 처리하다, 주문품을 조달하다 **complicated** 복잡한 **prompt** 즉각적인

15.
번역 미첼 코퍼레이션은 어떤 종류의 상품을 판매하는가?
(A) 가전제품
(B) 캐주얼 의류
(C) 목재 가구
(D) 청소용품

해설 세부사항
송장의 '제품 설명(Product Description)'에서 보면 표면 스크럽제(surface scrub), 극세사 천 수건(Microfiber cloth towels), 목재 가구 광택제(Wooden furniture polish), 욕실 항균 스프레이(Bathroom antibacterial spray) 등 모두 청소에 쓰이는 용품들이 나온다. 따라서 (D)가 정답이다.

16.
번역 라인하트 씨가 주문한 상품 전체에 관해 사실인 것은?
(A) 세금이 면제되었다.
(B) 수수료 없이 배달되었다.
(C) 10월 16일에 도착했다.
(D) 할인 받을 자격이 있다.

해설 Not/true
송장 세 번째 줄의 '할인 클럽 회원' 여부에 Yes라고 했고, 표에서 개당 가격과 전체 금액을 확인해 보면 일반(reg)과 회원(member) 중에서 회원가를 적용해 싸게 해 준 것을 알 수 있다. 따라서 (D)가 정답이다. 세금(Tax)이 $5.57로 나와 있으므로 (A)는 틀리고, 배송료(Shipping)가 $3.95로 나와 있어 (B)도 사실이 아니다. (C)의 경우, 두 번째 줄에 '발송일(Dispatch Date)'이 10월 16일이라고 나와 있고, 송장 윗부분에서 배달은 영업일 기준 2-3일이 걸린다고 했으므로, 역시 사실이 아니다.

17.
번역 라인하트 씨의 주문 중에서 어떤 상표가 빠졌는가?
(A) 호라이즌
(B) 와팍
(C) 필즈
(D) 슈미트

해설 연계
이메일에서 '빠진 물건은 극세사 천 수건 묶음이고(The missing item is the pack of microfiber cloth towels)'라고 말했는데, 앞의 표에서 확인해 보면 극세사 천 수건 묶음의 상표명은 와팍(Wapak)이라고 되어 있다. (B)가 정답이다.

18.
번역 타보 씨는 누구일 것 같은가?
(A) 제품 생산자
(B) 고객 서비스부 직원
(C) 배달원
(D) 업체 소유주

해설 추론
이메일에서 '제가 수령하면서 배달물을 확인했을 때, 개리 타보 씨가 빠진 물건을 알게 되었고, 보고를 하겠다고 말했습니다(When I checked the delivery at the time of receipt, Gary Tabor noted the missing item and said he would make a report)'라고 했다. 물건을 받는 자리에 있었고, 회사에 보고할 위치에 있으므로 배달원으로 추론할 수 있다. 따라서 (C)가 정답이다.

19.

번역 이메일에서 언급되지 않은 것은?
(A) 라인하트 씨는 전에 미첼 코퍼레이션에서 물건을 산 적이 있다.
(B) 미첼 코퍼레이션은 최근에 제품 종류를 확대했다.
(C) 라인하트 씨는 자신이 한 주문의 문제점을 이미 알렸다.
(D) 미첼 코퍼레이션은 제품에 대해 환불을 해 줘야 한다.

해설 Not / true
이메일에서 빠진 물건을 알려주며 '가능한 한 빨리 이것이 보내졌으면 좋겠습니다(I would like them to be sent as soon as possible)'라고 했을 뿐, 환불에 관한 언급은 없었으므로 (D)가 정답이다. '과거에 귀사에서 보았던 높은 수준의 고객 서비스(the high level of customer service that I've seen from you in the past)'에 (A)가, '지난 달에 귀사에서 많은 신제품을 출시했고(you introduced a lot of new products last month)'에 (B)가, '귀사의 고객 서비스부 쪽으로 이 문제를 알렸는데(I reported the issue to your customer service line)'에 (C)가 언급되었다.

[20-24] 기사 + 이메일 + 평면도

지역사회에서 원예 박람회를 준비하다

원예 용품과 장비들을 선보이는 지역 원예 박람회가 4월 15일 토요일에 제페다 컨벤션 홀에서 열릴 예정이다. **20작년의 첫 박람회는 세실 센터에서 열렸지만, 올해는 행사의 인기 때문에 더 넓은 공간이 필요해졌다.** 행사 기획자들은, 비록 올해는 그 중 아주 일부에 그칠 것으로 예상되지만, 향후 5년 이내에 입장객 수를 2만 명으로 끌어올리기를 희망한다.

박람회는 나무와 꽃(1층), 비료와 잡초 처리(2층), **23도구와 장비(3층),** 액세서리와 야외 가구(4층) 등, 네 개 층에 걸쳐 범주별로 부스를 열 것이다. **21박람회에서 부스를 임차하는 판매 회사들은 수천 명의 원예 애호가들이 자사 제품과 만나게 되는 기회를 얻게 될 것이다.** 이들은 또한 로고와 업체 설명을 엑스포 웹 사이트에 게시하게 되는데, 웹 사이트는 1년 내내 운영될 예정이다. 이 같은 기본적인 혜택 이외에도, 추가 회비를 내는 '프리미엄 상인'들은 엑스포 TV 광고와 홍보용 전단에 이름이 언급될 것이다. 출입구 가까이에는 이들의 로고가 담긴 현수막을 붙여, 방문객들을 부스로 안내하게 된다. 2월 25일 이전에 신청하는 업체들은 자신의 부스 배치를 선택할 수 있다. 그 이후에는 행사 기획자에 의해 부스가 할당된다.

판매사와 방문객에 관한 정보는 www.gardeningex.com에서 확인할 수 있다.

수신: 제리 아이버슨 〈j_iverson@alvarezincorporated.net〉
발신: 타이 징 〈t_xing@alvarezincorporated.net〉
날짜: 2월 23일
내용: 지역 원예 박람회

안녕하세요 제리,

다가오는 지역 원예 박람회에 알바레즈 사(社)를 지금 등록했어요. 4월 15일에 열리는 거죠. **22프리미엄 옵션으로 했는데 혜택들이 충분히 추가 비용을 낼 만한 거 같아서요.** 우리 로고와 회사 정보를 이번 주 중으로 행사 주최측에 보내려고 해요. 박람회 인기 때문에, 이건 우리 회사에게는 아주 좋은 기회가 될 거예요. **23우리 대표 제품인 잔디 깎는 기계의 판매를 신장시키는 건 물론이고 가스로 작동하는 신제품 생울타리 다듬는 기계를 홍보하기에도 말이죠.**

우리 부스의 위치를 골라야 해요. 이용 가능한 자리 지도를 첨부합니다. **24아주 비슷한 상품들을 갖고 있기 때문에 HBR 바로 옆에 배치되는 건 원치 않아요. 그것만 빼고는 에스컬레이터 쪽으로 가능한 한 가까운 게 좋을 거 같아요.** 어떻게 생각하는지 알려주세요.

타이

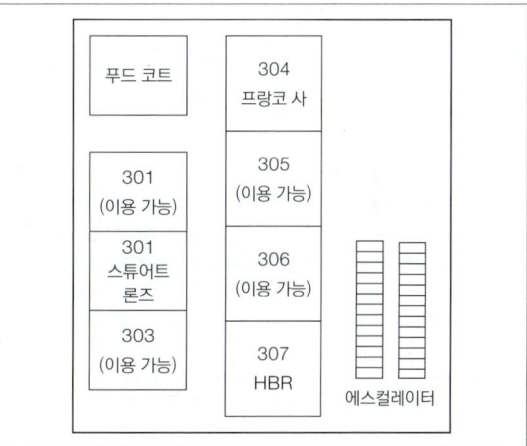

어휘 showcase 진열장, (최선의 상태로) 보여주는 것 gardening supplies 원예 용품 attendance 참석자, 참석자 수 fraction (아주 적은) 일부 feature (영화, 전시 등에) 등장시키다 fertilizer 비료 weed treatment 잡초 처리 vendor 행상, 판매 회사 enthusiast 열광적인 팬 encounter 맞닥뜨리다 in operation 가동[운영] 중인 premium (품질이) 높은, 고급스러운 mention 언급하다 commercial 광고 promotional flyer 광고 전단 banner 현수막 direct ~로 안내하다 placement 배치 go for ~으로 선택하다 well worth ~의 가치가 충분한 organizer 주최자 gas-powered 가스로 작동하는 hedge trimmer 생울타리 다듬는 기계 boost 북돋우다 lawn mower 잔디 깎는 기계 slot 구멍, 틈, 자리 position 배치하다, 자리를 잡다

20.

번역 지역 원예 박람회에 대해 명시된 것은?
(A) 두 번째로 열린다.
(B) 방문객에게 입장료를 부과한다.
(C) 마지막 순간에 위치가 바뀌었다.
(D) 원예 기술에 대해 시범 설명을 해 줄 것이다.

해설 Not/true
기사 첫 번째 단락에서 '작년의 첫 박람회는 세실 센터에서 열렸지만, 올해는 행사의 인기 때문에 더 넓은 공간이 필요해졌다(Last year's debut expo was held at the Cecil Center, but this year required a larger space due to the popularity of the event)'라고 말했다. 작년에 첫 번째, 올해 두 번째 행사이므로 (A)가 정답이다. 위치가 바뀌기는 했지만 마지막 순간에 변경되었다는 말은 없으므로 (C)는 틀리다. 출연하는 판매 회사에 참가 비용이 있지만 방문객에게 입장료가 있다는 말은 없고, 도구와 장비를 판매할 뿐 기술 시연에 관한 말은 없으므로 (B)와 (D)도 명시되지 않은 진술이다.

21.

번역 기사에 따르면, 올해는 모든 판매사들이 어떤 혜택을 받을 수 있는가?
(A) 로고가 실린 현수막
(B) 2만 방문객에게 접근할 수 있음
(C) 웹 사이트를 통한 지속적인 노출
(D) TV 광고 출연

해설 세부사항
기사 두 번째 단락에서 '부스를 임차하는 판매 회사들(Vendors who rent booths),' 즉 참가하는 모든 판매사는 '로고와 업체 설명을 엑스포 웹 사이트에 게시하게(have their logo and business description posted on the expo's Web site)' 된다고 했다. 또한 웹 사이트는 '1년 내내 운영될(remain in operation year-round)' 것이므로 (C)가 정답이다.

Paraphrasing
지문의 posted on the expo's Web site, which will remain in operation year-round
→ 정답의 Ongoing publicity on a Web site

22.

번역 이메일에서, 첫 번째 단락 두 번째 줄의 "went for"와 의미상 가장 가까운 것은?
(A) 도착했다
(B) 여행했다
(C) 잡았다
(D) 선택했다

해설 동의어
해당 문장은 '프리미엄 옵션으로 했는데 혜택들이 충분히 추가 비용을 낼 만한 거 같아서요'라고 해석된다. 여기서 went for는 여러 옵션 중 프리미엄으로 '선택했다'라고 보는 게 자연스러우므로 (D)가 정답이다.

23.

번역 알바레즈 사에 대해 암시된 것은?
(A) 조기 등록 마감일을 놓쳤다.
(B) 비용을 줄이려고 노력 중이다.
(C) 전에 박람회에 참석한 적이 있다.
(D) 3층에 부스를 갖게 될 것이다.

해설 연계
이메일 첫 번째 단락에서, '우리 대표 제품인 잔디 깎는 기계의 판매를 신장시키는 건 물론이고 가스로 작동하는 신제품 생울타리 다듬는 기계를 홍보하기에도 좋은 기회가 될 거예요(this will be ~ to promote our new gas-powered hedge trimmer as well as boost sales for our classic lawn mower)'라고 했다. 원예 장비를 주로 취급하는 회사임을 알 수 있는데, 기사 첫 번째 단락에서 보면 '도구와 장비(Tools & Equipment)'를 3층에 전시한다고 나와 있다. 따라서 (D)가 정답이다.

24.

번역 징 씨는 어떤 부스를 예약하고 싶어 할 것 같은가?
(A) 301호
(B) 303호
(C) 305호
(D) 306호

해설 연계
이메일에서 좋은 부스의 조건으로 'HBR 바로 옆에 배치되는 건 싫고(We don't want to be positioned right next to HBR),' '에스컬레이터 쪽에 가능한 한 가까운 게 좋다(we'd better be as close to the escalators as possible)'라고 했다. 도면에서 보면 에스컬레이터 옆 이용 가능한(available) 두 개의 부스 중에서 305호 부스를 선택할 것이다. (C)가 정답이다.

FINAL TEST

본책 p.276

101. (C)	102. (D)	103. (C)	104. (A)	105. (D)
106. (D)	107. (B)	108. (B)	109. (B)	110. (C)
111. (A)	112. (B)	113. (A)	114. (A)	115. (B)
116. (C)	117. (D)	118. (B)	119. (D)	120. (A)
121. (C)	122. (B)	123. (A)	124. (D)	125. (B)
126. (B)	127. (B)	128. (B)	129. (C)	130. (C)
131. (B)	132. (B)	133. (C)	134. (A)	135. (C)
136. (D)	137. (B)	138. (D)	139. (B)	140. (A)
141. (C)	142. (D)	143. (A)	144. (A)	145. (C)
146. (A)	147. (D)	148. (B)	149. (C)	150. (B)
151. (C)	152. (B)	153. (C)	154. (D)	155. (A)
156. (A)	157. (B)	158. (C)	159. (C)	160. (B)
161. (D)	162. (B)	163. (B)	164. (C)	165. (A)
166. (B)	167. (D)	168. (C)	169. (A)	170. (B)
171. (D)	172. (C)	173. (B)	174. (A)	175. (C)
176. (B)	177. (A)	178. (C)	179. (D)	180. (C)
181. (C)	182. (D)	183. (D)	184. (B)	185. (C)
186. (D)	187. (B)	188. (D)	189. (D)	190. (D)
191. (D)	192. (A)	193. (C)	194. (B)	195. (B)
196. (C)	197. (B)	198. (A)	199. (B)	200. (B)

PART 5

101.
해설 명사 어휘
배달되고, 주소가 붙어 있는 것이므로 정답은 (C) package(소포)이다. (D) speech의 경우는 'deliver a speech(연설을 하다)'의 형태로 쓰이지만 여기서는 전체적인 문맥에 맞지 않는다.

번역 소포는 잘못된 주소가 붙여져 있었기 때문에 제시간에 배달되지 않았다.

어휘 deliver 배달하다 on time 제시간에 label 라벨을 붙이다

102.
해설 인칭대명사의 격-주격
밑줄부터 planned까지는 앞의 the event를 수식하는 관계대명사절이다. 목적격 관계대명사 that이 생략되고, 바로 이어 빈칸에 주어가 들어가야 하므로 주격 인칭대명사인 (D) they가 정답이다.

번역 행사 기획자들은 자신들이 기획한 행사의 참가자 수에 만족했다.

어휘 event planner 행사 기획자 be pleased with ~에 만족하다 attendance 참석자, 참석자 수

103.
해설 인칭대명사의 격-소유격
'for routine employee evaluation(일상적인 직원 평가를 위해서)'가 이미 의미상 완성된 구이므로 빈칸에 주어나 목적어 등이 올 수 없다. 뒤의 명사(evaluation)를 수식하는 소유격이 필요하다. 정답은 (C) her(그녀의)이다.

번역 플로렌스 씨는 월요일에 자신의 일상적인 직원 평가를 위해 본사에 들러야 한다.

어휘 report to ~에게 보고하다, ~에 출두하다 head office 본사 routine 늘 하는, 일상적인 employee evaluation 직원 평가(서)

104.
해설 동사 어휘
베이커리가 큰 상업 공간을 만들거나(creates), 주문하는(orders) 것은 의미상 어색하다. 구입하는(purchases) 것도 곧 이전한다고 했으므로 어색하다. 정답은 (A) occupies(공간을 차지하다[점유하다])이다.

번역 홈타임 베이커리는 시내의 큰 상업 공간을 차지하고 있지만, 곧 이전할 것이다.

어휘 commercial space 상업 공간[구역] relocate 이전하다

105.
해설 형용사의 비교급
빈칸에는 동사 is를 설명하는 보어로 형용사가 필요하다. narrowing은 '좁아지는'이라는 뜻의 현재분사, 즉 형용사로 볼 수 있지만 than 이하의 내용과 어울렸을 때 의미상 어색하다. 바로 뒤의 than으로 미루어 비교급이 와야 하므로 정답은 (D) narrower(더 좁은)이다.

번역 살라자르 가는 근처 대다수 다른 거리보다 더 좁기 때문에 주차가 허용되지 않는다.

어휘 parking 주차 neighborhood 근처

106.
해설 명사 어휘
판매 대가로 지불되는 것이므로 occasion(경우, 때), extension(확장), impression(인상)은 의미상 적절하지 않다. 정답은 (D) commission((위탁 판매 대가로 받는) 수수료, 커미션)이다.

번역 콜센터 직원들이 하는 각 판매에 대해 적은 수수료가 월 단위로 지불된다.

어휘 make a sale 판매를 하다 on a monthly basis 월 단위로

107.
해설 전치사 어휘
'the end of the month(월말)'와 어울려 쓸 수 있는 전치사는 'at the end of the month(월말에),' 'toward the end of the month(월말 무렵에)'이다. during은 'during the summer months(여름철 동안)'에서처럼 '~동안, ~내내'라는 뜻으로 쓰이고, between은 '~사이에'라는 뜻으로 쓰인다. among(~중에)은 시간과 함께 쓰이지 않는다. 따라서 정답은 (B) toward(~무렵에, ~즈음에)이다.

번역 도슨 씨는 합병에 관한 더 많은 정보를 월말 무렵에 얻을 수 있을 것이라고 말했다.

어휘 merger 합병 available 입수[이용]할 수 있는

108.

해설 부사 자리-과거분사 수식

controlled(통제되는)는 과거분사로 형용사와 같은 역할을 하기 때문에, 형용사 tight(단호한), 명사 tightness(단호함), 동사 tighten(엄격하게 하다)의 수식을 받을 수가 없다. 부사의 수식을 받아야 하기 때문에 정답은 (B) tightly(단호하게, 철저하게)이다.

번역 그 나라의 국경들은 질병에 걸린 식물과 동물들을 들여오지 못하도록 철저히 통제된다.

어휘 border 국경 control 통제하다 diseased 병에 걸린 bring in 들여오다

109.

해설 부사 어휘

동사(be used)를 수식하는 부사 자리이기 때문에 형용사 another(다른, 또 하나의)는 정답에서 제외된다. 앞에 only로 미루어 정답은 (B) once(한 번)이다. only once는 '단 한 번만'이라는 뜻이다. again(다시)과 either(또한)는 의미상 어색하다.

번역 밴쿠버행 연착 항공편 승객에게 발행된 할인 쿠폰은 한 번만 사용될 수 있다.

어휘 issue 발행하다 delayed 연착한 flight 비행편, 항공편

110.

해설 전치사 어휘

빈칸에는 an error와 함께 쓰여 의미가 통하는 전치사가 와야 하기 때문에 형용사 due(예정된)는 정답에서 제외된다. '오류 때문에' 완료되지 못 한 것이므로 정답은 (C) because of(~때문에)이며, due to와 같은 뜻이다. rather than(~라기보다는)과 since(~이래로)는 의미상 어울리지 않는다.

번역 창고의 재고 파악 업무는 컴퓨터 시스템의 오류 때문에 완료될 수 없었다.

어휘 inventory 재고, 재고 목록, 재고 파악 warehouse 창고 complete 완료하다 error 실수, 오류

111.

해설 형용사 어휘

소유물이 많지 않기 때문에 널찍한(spacious), 분실한(missing), 휴대용의(portable) 아파트를 찾는다는 건 의미상 어색하다. 정답은 (A) furnished(가구가 비치되어 있는)이다.

번역 브레넌 씨는 자신의 소유물을 많이 갖고 있지 않기 때문에 가구가 비치된 아파트를 찾고 있다.

어휘 belongings 소유물

112.

해설 동사의 시제

the Shea Corporation이 주어, 빈칸은 동사 자리이므로 introducing과 being introduced는 정답에서 제외된다. next quarter(다음 분기)라는 미래시제와 함께 쓰였으므로 정답은 (B) will introduce이다.

번역 고객 만족도를 높이기 위한 노력으로 셰 코퍼레이션은 다음 분기에 새로운 교육 정책을 도입할 것이다.

어휘 in an effort to 부정사 ~하기 위한 노력으로 customer satisfaction 고객 만족 measure 조치, 정책 quarter (넷으로 나눈) 분기

113.

해설 형용사 어휘

택시 대신 셔틀 버스를 이용하는 것을 광범위한(extensive), 기대하는(expectant), 도달할 수 없는(unreachable) 대안이라고 말할 수는 없다. 정답은 (A) affordable((가격이) 적절한)이다.

번역 라이머 역에서 공항 셔틀을 타는 건 개인 택시 서비스를 이용하는 것의 적절한 대안이다.

어휘 alternative to ~에 대한 대안 private 개인 전용의

114.

해설 형용사 어휘

공평한(fair) 대회를 위해 필요한 심판이므로 정답은 (A) impartial(공정한)이다. probationary(견습 중인), impulsive(충동적인), mutual(상호간의)은 모두 의미상 어색하다.

번역 모든 참가자들에게 공평한 미술대회를 만들기 위해서는 공정한 심사위원을 고용하는 것이 중요하다.

어휘 fair 공평한 participant 참가자 hire 고용하다 judge 심사위원

115.

해설 전치사의 목적어-동명사

전치사 on(~에 관한) 다음에는 명사형이 와야 하므로 동사인 (A) operates와 (D) operate(가동시키다)는 빈칸에 올 수 없다. 바로 뒤의 the construction equipment가 '건설 장비를'이라는 뜻의 목적어 역할을 하므로 빈칸에는 명사이면서 동시에 동사 역할을 하는 것, 즉 동명사가 와야 한다. 따라서 (B) operating이 정답이다. 참고로 (C) operation의 경우는 operation of의 형태로 쓰이면 어법상 맞는다.

번역 신입사원들에게 배부된 설명서는 건설 장비를 안전하게 가동시키는 것에 대한 조언을 담고 있다.

어휘 manual (사용) 설명서 contain 담고 있다 tip 조언, 정보 construction equipment 건설장비[기계]

116.

해설 명사 자리-목적어

빈칸에는 employee와 함께 동사 improve의 목적어로 쓰일 명사가 필요하므로 형용사인 motivational(동기부여의)과 motivated(동기부여 받은, 의욕적인), 부사인 motivationally는 정답에서 제외된다. 정답은 (C) motivation(자극, 동기부여)이다.

번역 매장의 총지배인은 직원 동기부여를 향상시키기 위한 방법을 배우려고 강의를 들었다.

어휘 general manager 총지배인 attend a lecture 강의를 듣다

117.
해설 부사절 접속사 자리
앞뒤에 완전한 문장이 있으므로 빈칸에는 이 둘을 연결하는 접속사가 와야 한다. 전치사 despite(~에도 불구하고)는 정답에서 제외되고, while(~하는 동안)과 once(일단 ~하면)는 의미상 어색하다. 정답은 (D) unless(~하지 않으면)이다.

번역 직원들은 감독자에게 먼저 승인을 받지 않으면 늦게까지 일한 것에 대해 초과근무 수당을 받지 못할 것이다.

어휘 overtime payment 초과근무 수당 stay late 늦게까지 있다 approval 승인

118.
해설 부사 자리-동사 수식
빈칸에는 동사(are)를 수식하는 부사가 와야 하므로 전치사인 beside(~옆에)와 among(~사이에)은 답이 될 수 없다. further는 '(거리상)으로 더 멀리, (정도가) 더 심하게'라는 뜻이므로 의미상 어색하다. 정답은 (A) nearby(가까운 곳에)이다.

번역 그 호텔에는 자체 레스토랑이 없지만 가까운 곳에 훌륭한 식사 장소가 몇몇 있다.

어휘 fine 훌륭한, 세련된 dining establishment 식사 장소, 식사 시설

119.
해설 부사 자리-과거분사 수식
noticed(주목 받는)는 과거분사로 형용사와 마찬가지로 부사의 수식을 받는다. 따라서 형용사 scarce(드문)와 명사 scarcity(부족)는 정답에서 제외된다. 정답은 (D) scarcely(거의 ~하지 않다)이다.

번역 국가 차원에서는 거의 인식되지 못했지만, 그 공장의 폐쇄는 스프링 시티 지역 경제의 급격한 하락을 야기했다.

어휘 notice 알다, 주목하다 national 국가의 closure 폐쇄 decline 감소, 하락

120.
해설 접속사-명사절
빈칸 이하가 동사 determine의 목적절(명사절)이다. just as(꼭 ~인 것처럼), as if(마치 ~인 것처럼), whereas(~인 반면에)는 부사절을 이끄는 접속사이며 의미상으로도 어색하다. 'whether A or B(A인지 B인지)' 구문이므로 정답은 (A) whether이다.

번역 문제가 제조상의 결함으로 야기되었는지 고객의 부주의로 야기되었는지 밝히는 게 어려웠다.

어휘 determine 결정하다, 밝히다 manufacture 제조하다 defect 결함 carelessness 부주의

121.
해설 지시형용사와 한정사-수
donor가 주어이고 동사는 is listed이다. 빈칸에는 donor를 수식하는 말이 와야 하는데 anyone(누구나)은 대명사로 뒤의 명사를 수식할 수 없고, those와 some은 뒤에 복수형이 나와야 하므로 정답에서 제외된다. 정답은 (C) each(각각의)이다.

번역 모금 캠페인에 기여한 각 기부자는 이 자선 단체의 웹 사이트에 등재되어 있다.

어휘 donor 기여자, 기부자 contribute to ~에 기부[기여]하다 fundraising 모금, 기금 조성 charity 자선 단체

122.
해설 명사 자리-주어/수의 일치
make가 문장의 동사이고 빈칸에는 주어가 와야 하므로 committed는 답이 될 수 없다. 동명사 주어(committing)와 단수 주어(commitment)는 동사가 단수(makes)일 때 쓸 수 있으므로 역시 정답에서 제외된다. 정답은 (B) commitments이다. commitment to는 '~에 대한 헌신'을 뜻한다.

번역 환불 보장과 품질보증 같은 고객에 대한 헌신이 리마트를 그토록 인기 있게 만들어 준다.

어휘 money-back guarantee 환불 보장 quality assurance 품질 보증

123.
해설 전치사 어휘
빈칸에는 its competitors를 받는 전치사가 와야 하기 때문에 접속사 although(비록 ~일지라도)는 정답이 될 수 없다. throughout(~의 곳곳에)과 since(~이래로)는 의미상 어색하다. 정답은 (A) unlike(~와 달리)이다.

번역 VLC 베버리지스는 경쟁사들과 달리 자사 카페인 음료에 대한 수요가 계속 증가하고 있다.

어휘 caffeinated 카페인이 함유된 competitor 경쟁자, 경쟁사

124.
해설 동사구 어휘
지사를 방문하는 것은 진척 상황을 '확인하기' 위한 것이어야 하므로 정답은 (D) check up on(~을 확인하다)이다. get rid of(~을 없애다), come up with(~을 생각해 내다), run out of(~을 다 써버리다)는 의미상 어색하다.

번역 아렐라노 소프트웨어의 CEO는 지사에서의 진척 상황을 확인하기 위해 분기별로 지역 사무소들을 방문한다.

어휘 regional 지역의 quarterly 분기별로 progress 진전, 진척 상황 branch 지사

125.
해설 동사의 형태-조동사 + 동사원형
조동사(should) 다음에는 동사의 원형이 와야 하므로 compiling과 compiled는 정답에서 제외된다. be compiled는 수동태(정리되다, 편집되다)이므로 의미상 어색하다. 정답은 (B) have compiled인데, should have + 과거분사는 '~했어야 했다'라는 뜻이다.

번역 부서 책임자들은 수상자 지명을 위해 추천할 직원들의 명단을 정리해 두었어야 했다.

어휘 department head 부서장, 부서 책임자 recommend 추천하다 nomination 지명, 추천

126.
해설 명사 어휘
빈칸에는 a number of(수많은)의 수식을 받는 명사가 와야 하므로 부사 chemically(화학적으로)는 정답에서 제외된다. 약품의 개선을 위해 상의하는 대상이 빈칸에 나와야 하므로 chemistry(화학)와 chemicals(화학 약품)도 의미상 어색하다. 정답은 (B) chemists(화학자)이다.

번역 웨스트버리 제약은 진통제 개발을 어떻게 해야 할지에 대해 의견을 구하고자 수많은 화학자와 상의를 했다.

어휘 **pharmaceutical** 제약; 제약의 **consult** 상담하다, 상의하다 **pain medication** 진통제

127.
해설 부사 어휘
동사 voted를 수식해 의미가 통하는 부사를 찾는 문제이다. '만장일치로 선출하다'가 가장 자연스러우므로 정답은 (C) unanimously(만장일치로)이다. traditionally(전통적으로), approximately(대략), innocently(결백하게)는 의미상 어색하다.

번역 이사회 위원들은 자리가 채워지는 동안 폴 채프먼 씨를 임시 CEO로 임명하는 데 만장일치로 찬성했다.

어휘 **board** 이사회 **appoint** 임명하다 **interim** 임시의, 과도의 **fill** (일자리에 사람을) 채우다

128.
해설 과거분사-명사 수식
밑줄 앞에 관사 the가 있고 밑줄 뒤에 명사 pieces가 있다. the pieces만으로도 의미가 통하므로 그 사이에 동사(customizes와 customize)는 들어갈 수 없다. 빈칸에는 pieces를 수식하는 말이 필요한데, customize(주문 제작하다)의 현재분사형인 customizing(주문 제작하는)은 의미상 적절하지 않고, 과거분사인 customized(주문 제작된)이 의미상 적절하다. 정답은 (A) customized(주문 제작된)이다.

번역 트레저 퍼니처의 고객들은 주문 제작된 제품은 되팔 수 없기 때문에 반품이 허용되지 않는다.

어휘 **return** 반품하다 **resell** 되팔다

129.
해설 부사 어휘
'those (who are) linked to hiring'은 '고용과 관련된 사람들'이라는 뜻이고, 빈칸에는 linked를 수식해 의미가 통하는 부사가 필요하다. 정답은 (C) indirectly(간접적으로)이다. insincerely(진실성 없이), inefficiently(비효율적으로), insecurely(불안정하게) 등은 모두 의미상 어색하다.

번역 관리 팀은 인사과 직원, 그리고 고용과 간접적으로 관련된 사람들 다 분기별 워크숍에 참석할 것을 권장했다.

어휘 **management** 경영, 관리 **encourage A(목적어) to**부정사 A에게 ~하라고 권장하다 **personnel department** 인사과 **linked to** ~와 관련된 **hire** 고용하다 **attend** 참석하다 **quarterly** 4분기의, 분기별로

130.
해설 동사 어휘
빈칸 뒤의 his ankle로 미루어 정답은 (C) sprained(삐었다)이다. 'sprain one's ankle(발목을 삐다)'이라는 표현을 알아두자. enforce(강요하다, 집행하다), obstruct(방해하다), comply(준수하다)는 의미상 적절하지 않다.

번역 지역사회 소프트볼 토너먼트에서 제이슨 호손 씨는 공을 잡으려고 점프했다가 발목을 삐었다.

어휘 **ankle** 발목

Part 6

131-134

자동차 거대 기업이 리콜을 발표하다

자동차 제조사인 JMC는 자사 차량 중 하나를 잠재적인 안전 위험 때문에 리콜한다고 발표했다. 이 리콜은 작년에 출시되어 캐나다와 미국에서 판매된 우르버나이트 모델을 **131**포함한다. 회사 대변인은 이 차량의 충격 감지 센서가 제대로 작동하지 않아, 이로 인해 충돌 시 에어백이 부풀어오르지 못하게 될 수 있다고 보고했다. 그레고리오 멘도사 씨 – **132**그의 팀이 에어백 시스템을 개발함 –가 이 결함으로 야기된 부상에 대해 사과를 했다. 영향을 받은 차량을 소유한 사람은 누구나 그 차를 구입 장소에 **133**가져다 주어야 한다. **134**그곳에서 무료로 수리를 받게 될 것이다.

어휘 **manufacturer** 제조사 **due to** ~때문에 **potential** 잠재적인 **cover** 다루다, 포함하다 **release** 출시하다 **distribute** 유통시키다 **spokesperson** 대변인 **crash sensor** 충격 감지 센서 **malfunction** 제대로 작동하지 않다 **failure to** 부정사 ~을 제대로 하지 못함 **inflate** (공기나 가스로) 부풀다 **collision** 충돌 **apologize for** ~에 대해 사과하다 **injury** 부상 **defect** 결함 **affected** 영향을 받은, 걸린 **return** 돌려보내다 **at no charge** 비용 청구 없이

131.
해설 동사 자리
This recall이 주어, the Urbanite model이 목적어이고 빈칸에는 동사가 들어가야 한다. covering과 to cover는 동사가 아니므로 정답에서 제외되고, 리콜이 특정 모델을 '포함하는' 것이지 '포함되는' 것은 아니므로 수동태인 is covered도 답이 될 수 없다. 정답은 (B) covers(포함하다)이다.

132.
해설 관계대명사-소유격
Gregorio Mendoza가 주어, apologized가 동사이고, 빈칸에서 system까지는 주어를 보충 설명하는 삽입절이다. 삽입절이 주어, 동사, 목적어를 갖춘 완전한 문장이므로 빈칸에 주격이나 목적격 관계대명사(that, whom)는 필요하지 않다. '멘도사의' 팀이라는 소유격의 의미이므로 소유격 관계대명사 (B) whose가 정답이다. (C) his(그의)의 경우, 같은 소유격으로 의미상으로는 통하지만, 별개 문장이 아닌 한 문장으로 연결해서 쓸 때는 관계대명사를 써야 한다.

132

133.

해설 동사 어휘
뒤에 '구입 지점으로'라는 말이 나오므로 (C) return(돌려보내다)이 정답이다. examine(조사하다), pursue(추구하다), abandon(버리다)은 의미상 적절하지 않다.

134.

번역 (A) 그곳에서 무료로 수리를 받게 될 것이다.
(B) JMC는 부품을 찾을 수 없다.
(C) 그것은 해당 당국에 보고되어야 한다.
(D) 새로운 시스템이 인기 없는 시스템을 대체했다.

해설 문맥에 맞는 문장 고르기-주제 및 바로 앞 문장과의 관계 파악
문제 차량이 유통되어 리콜을 해 준다는 것이 글의 취지이다. 바로 앞에서 해당 차량을 판매처로 가지고 가라고 했으므로, 이어 수리를 해 준다는 말이 나와야 한다. 따라서 (A)가 정답이다.

135-138

체다 스파에서 스트레스를 사라지게 하세요! 모든 직원이 다양한 각 분야에서 자격을 갖추고 있어 최고 수준의 서비스를 보장합니다. 저희 **135처치들은** 개별적으로 또는 비용이 절약되는 패키지로 판매됩니다. 피부 관리, 마사지, 뷰티 서비스, 어떤 것을 원하시든지 저희가 도와드립니다. 저희는 시내의 어떤 다른 **136스파보다** 더욱 긍정적인 평을 듣고 있습니다. 모든 세세한 것에 신경을 쓰기 때문이죠. 오늘 555-0132번으로 전화 주셔서 예약하세요. 예약이 필수는 아닙니다. **137하지만 대기 시간이 길 수도 있습니다.** 체다 스파에서 곧 뵙기를 바랍니다. 저희 서비스를 **138이용한 것을** 절대 후회하지 않으실 것을 약속드립니다.

어휘 melt away 서서히 사라지다 certified 자격증[면허]를 가지고 있는 ensure 보장하다 individually 개별적으로 positive 긍정적인 make a booking 예약하다 mandatory 의무적인 regret 후회하다

135.

해설 명사 어휘
스파에서 개별적으로 또는 패키지로 제공되는 것이므로 정답은 (C) treatments(처치, 치료)이다. measurements(측정, 치수), destinations(목적지), inspections(점검)는 의미상 통하지 않는다.

136.

해설 비교급
빈칸 앞에 more positive(보다 긍정적인)라는 비교급 형용사가 나온다. 뒤의 여타 스파와 비교하고 있으므로 정답은 (D) than(~보다)이다.

137.

번역 (A) 그녀가 시간이 되면 즉시 알려 드리겠습니다.
(B) 하지만, 대기 시간이 길 수도 있습니다.
(C) 그러므로, 그것은 모든 고객에게 무료입니다.
(D) 변동 사항은 미리 저희에게 알려 주셔야 합니다.

해설 문맥에 맞는 문장 고르기-바로 앞 문장과의 관계 파악
바로 앞에서 예약이 필수는 아니라고 했고, 바로 뒤에서는 곧 뵙고 싶다고 했으므로 (B)가 정답이다. 즉, 예약이 필수는 아니지만 오래 기다리지 않으려면 예약을 하는 게 더 좋다는 의도이다.

138.

해설 준동사-동명사
동사 regret 다음에 또 다른 동사가 올 수 없으므로 try는 정답에서 제외된다. regret은 동명사와 함께 쓰여 '~한 것을 후회하다'라는 뜻이 되므로 정답은 (D) trying(시도하기)이다.

139-142

수신: 네이자 가이슬러
발신: 아자르 수라
날짜: 10월 13일
주제: 세르지오 오르테가 씨에 대한 관심

가이슬러 씨께,

저는 저자들을 **139적극적으로** 홍보하는 사업체, 페이지 바이 페이지 서점의 주인입니다. 당신이 저자 세르지오 오르테가 씨의 대리인이기 때문에, 책 사인회를 위해 저희 서점을 방문해 달라는 초대장을 그를 대신해 보내드리고자 합니다. 여러 저자분들이 이 같은 행사를 매우 **140유익하다** 고 여깁니다. 오르테가 씨의 소설을 미리 다량 주문해 놓을 생각입니다. **141다 떨어지는 모험을 감수하고 싶지 않아서요.** 그가 시간이 되는지, 그리고 언제인지 알려 주시기 바랍니다. 또한 당신이 대리하는 다른 저자들 중에서 방문에 적합할지도 모르는 저자들이 **142있을 경우** 저희 업체를 기억해 주십시오.

아자르 수라

어휘 promote 홍보하다 author 저자 literary agent 작가 대리인(작가를 위해 출판, 계약, 판매, 홍보 등의 일을 대리해 줌) extend an invitation 초대장을 보내다 place an order 주문하다 in advance 미리 available 시간이 되는 keep in mind 마음에 담고 있다, 명심하다 in case ~한 경우에 (대비해) represent 대표하다, 대리하다

139.

해설 부사 자리
'that ~ authors'가 a business를 수식하는 형용사절이다. 절 안에서 주격 관계대명사 that이 주어, promotes가 동사이므로 그 사이 빈칸에는 동사를 수식하는 부사가 와야 한다. 따라서 형용사인 activated(활성화된)와 active(활발한), 명사인 activity(활동)는 어법상 맞지 않으며, 정답은 (B) actively(활발하게, 적극적으로)이다.

140.

해설 형용사 어휘
밑줄에는 this kind of event를 설명하는 말이 온다. this kind of event가 막연하게 모든 종류의 사인회를 가리키므로 (B) casual(격식이 없는, 우연한), dependable(신뢰할 수 있는), qualified(자격이 있는)는 의미상 어색하다. 사인회 행사를 '매우 유익하다'고 보는 것이 가장 자연스러우므로 정답은 (A) beneficial(유익한)이다.

141.

번역 (A) 책들은 또한 특별한 날을 위한 훌륭한 선물이 됩니다.
(B) 고를 만한 인기 있는 책들이 일부 있습니다.
(C) 다 떨어지는 모험을 감수하고 싶지 않아서요.
(D) 많은 독자들이 그를 만나는 걸 즐겼습니다.

해설 **문맥에 맞는 문장 고르기-바로 앞 문장과의 관계 파악**
바로 앞에서 미리 다량으로 책을 주문해 두겠다고 했으므로, 이어 다량 주문하는 이유를 밝히는 (C)가 정답이다. 소설 한 권에 해당하는 (A)나 (B) 모두 의미상 적절하지 않다.

142.

해설 **부사절 접속사**
빈칸에는 앞 뒤 두 개의 완전한 문장을 연결하는 접속사가 필요하기 때문에 전치사인 regardless of(~와 상관없이)는 정답에서 제외된다. '방문에 적합한 다른 저자가 있을 경우'라는 의미이므로 정답은 (D) in case(~할 경우, 만약 ~라면)이다. even though(비록 ~일지라도)와 so that(~하기 위해서)은 의미상 어색하다.

143-146

세계적으로 유명한 화가 롤란도 롬바르디가 8월 15일 오후 7시에 빅토리아 갤러리에서 강연을 할 예정입니다. 그는 미술계에서 널리 인정받기 위한 자신의 **143분투**에 관해 얘기할 것입니다. 그에게는 길고도 어려운 여행이었으며, 청중들도 그의 **144이야기에서** 영감을 얻게 될 것입니다. 입장권은 한 장에 12달러에 이용할 수 있으며 입구에서 구입하면 됩니다. 현금으로 지불하실 계획이면 **145정확한** 잔돈을 가지고 오십시오. 입구에서 추가적인 기부금이 모금될 예정입니다. **146이들은 지역사회의 미술 사업에 쓰이게 됩니다.** 이 특별한 행사에서 많은 분들을 만날 수 있기를 바랍니다.

어휘 world-renowned 세계적으로 유명한 give a talk 강연을 하다 inspire 고무시키다, 영감을 주다 available 손에 넣을 수 있는 change 잔돈 in cash 현금으로 additional 추가의 donation 기부, 기부금 collect (기금, 세금 등을) 모금하다

143.

해설 **명사 어휘**
화가로서 널리 인정받기까지 그가 겪었던 것을 얘기한다는 뜻이므로 정답은 (A) struggle(분투, 고생)이다. reluctance(꺼림), estimate(추산), altitude(고도)는 의미상 어색하다.

144.

해설 **전치사 어휘**
바로 앞에 수동태 동사 be inspired가 있다. '그의 이야기에 의해 감동받다'라는 뜻이 되어야 하므로 정답은 (B) by(~에 의해서)이다.

145.

해설 **형용사 자리**
bring이 동사이고 change(잔돈)가 목적어로, 가운데 빈칸에는 change를 수식하는 형용사가 들어가야 한다. bring change가 '잔돈을 가지고 오다'라는 뜻인데, 그 사이에 형용사 exact가 들어가면 '정확한 잔돈을 가지고 오다'가 된다. 따라서 정답은 (C) exact이다. 명사인 exactness(정확함), 부사인 exactly(정확하게)는 어법상 어색하고, exacting은 '힘든'이라는 뜻의 또 다른 형용사로 의미상 어울리지 않는다.

146.

번역 (A) 이들은 지역사회의 미술 사업에 쓰이게 됩니다.
(B) 저희는 강연에서 5000달러 이상을 모금했습니다.
(C) 여러분은 이 놀라운 그림들 감상을 즐기게 될 것입니다.
(D) 두 날 저녁 다 재미있을 것으로 기대됩니다.

해설 **문맥에 맞는 문장 고르기-바로 앞 문장과의 관계 파악**
바로 앞 문장에서 모금을 할 예정이라고 했으므로, 그 다음에는 모금의 쓰임새를 밝히는 게 자연스럽다. 따라서 (A)가 정답이다.

Part 7

147-148 공지문

리오 고객에게 알림

리오 레스토랑은 자체적인 사내 배달 서비스를 갖추지 못한 레스토랑에 배달 인력을 공급하는 회사, 윌리 밀즈와 손을 잡게 되었습니다. **147이제 영업 시간 중에 여러분이 리오에서 좋아하는 음식을 모두 바로 집 앞까지 배달 받으실 수 있습니다.** www.wheely-meals.com에서 로그인하고 계정만 만드시면 됩니다. 이 작업은 5분 이내에 끝낼 수 있습니다! 그리고 **1486월달에는 주문이 35달러 이상인 모든 리오의 고객께, 저희 디저트 메뉴 중에서 무료 음식을 덤으로 드립니다.**

어휘 personnel 직원, 인력 in-house 사내의, 매장 내의 get+A(목적어)+과거분사 A가 ~되게 하다 hours of operation 운영[영업] 시간 account 계좌, 계정 throw in 덤으로 주다

147.

번역 공지문을 쓴 이유는 무엇인가?
(A) 동업자의 업적을 인정하려고
(B) 새로운 메뉴 품목을 소개하려고
(C) 영업 시간 연장을 홍보하려고
(D) 새로운 서비스를 알리려고

해설 **주제/목적**
'새 파트너와 손을 잡아서 이제 영업 시간 중에 여러분이 리오에서 좋아하는 음식을 모두 바로 집 앞까지 배달 받으실 수 있습니다(You can now get all of your Rio's favorites delivered right to your door anytime during Rio's hours of operation)'라고 했다. 배달 서비스를 새로 시작한다는 의미이므로 (D)가 정답이다.

148.

번역 고객들은 6월에 어떻게 무료 품목을 얻을 수 있을까?
(A) 온라인 쿠폰을 다운로드해서
(B) 일정 액수만큼 사용해서
(C) 여러 가지 주문을 해서
(D) 회원 가입을 해서

해설 **세부사항**
'6월달에는 주문이 35달러 이상인 모든 리오의 고객께, 저희 디저트 메뉴 중에서 무료 음식을 덤으로 드립니다(And for the month of June, for all Rio's customers whose orders are $35 or more, we'll throw in a free dish from our dessert menu)'라고 했다. 35달러가 넘게 구입하면 되는 것이므로 (B)가 정답이다.

Paraphrasing
지문의 whose orders are $35 or more
→ By spending a certain amount

149-150 문자 메시지

> 하워드 슈미츠, 4:18 P.M.
> 애로우드 컨벤션 센터 저녁 식사가 언제 시작하는지 알려 주실 수 있을까요? **149**필라델피아의 호텔에 지금 막 들어왔는데, 초대장을 사무실에 두고 온 걸 알았어요.
>
> 코트니 앨런, 4:28 P.M.
> 문은 오후 6시 30분에 열고, 식사는 오후 7시 30분에 제공됩니다. **150**택시가 당신을 태우러 가게 부탁해 놓을까요?
>
> 하워드 슈미츠, 4:30 P.M.
> 좋죠. 가능하다면요.
>
> 코트니 앨런, 4:38 P.M.
> 좋습니다. 6시 15분에 누군가 그리 갈 테니까. 바로 밖에서 기다리시면 됩니다.

어휘 **check into** (호텔에) 들다, 체크인하다 **cab** 택시 **pick up** (차에) 태우다, 태우러 가다

149.
번역 슈미츠 씨는 지금 어디에 있는가?
(A) 컨벤션 센터
(B) 공항
(C) 호텔
(D) 사무실

해설 **세부사항**
오후 4시 18분에 슈미츠 씨가 '필라델피아의 호텔에 지금 막 들어왔는데(I've just checked into my hotel in Philadelphia)'라고 말한 것으로 보아 지금 호텔에 있으므로 (C)가 정답이다.

150.
번역 오후 4시 30분에 슈미츠 씨가 "좋죠. 가능하다면요"라고 쓴 의미는?
(A) 미리 식사 선택을 하기를 원한다.
(B) 자신을 위해 교통편이 마련되기를 원한다.
(C) 앨런 씨에게 초대장을 보내 달라고 요청한다.
(D) 일찍 장소에 도착하고 싶다.

해설 **의도 파악**
바로 앞에서 '택시가 당신을 태우러 가게 부탁해 놓을까요?(Would you like me to order a cab to pick you up?)'라고 묻는 질문에 그렇게 해 달라는 것이므로 (B)가 정답이다.

Paraphrasing
지문의 order a cab to pick you up
→ 정답의 his transportation arranged for him

151-152 이메일

> 수신: 아론 바네스 〈a.barnes@wonderinbox.com〉
> 발신: 구오 양 〈guo@hartlandgoods.com〉
> 날짜: 2월 18일
> 주제: 제안
>
> 바네스 씨께,
>
> 〈매일의 채식 요리〉라는 제목의 당신의 요리책을 최근에 구입했는데, 제가 그 책에 나와 있는 조리법에 얼마나 감동을 받았는지 알려드리고 싶었습니다. **151**당신이 출판한 모든 요리책 중에서 이 책이 단연코 가장 실용적인 책입니다. 조리법들이 독창적이면서도(전형적인 채식주의 식사와는 환영할 만한 차이점), 단순함을 포함하고 있습니다.
>
> 저는 시카고에 하틀랜드 굿즈라는 유기농 식품점을 가지고 있습니다. 다양한 특산 재료를 취급하는데, 그 중 많은 부분이 당신의 조리법에 필요한 것이었어요. **152**저는 두 사업 모두에 이익이 될 수 있도록 저희가 협력할 수 있지 않을까 생각합니다. 예를 들어, 제가 당신의 책을 제 상점에서 홍보하고 당신은 하틀랜드 굿즈에 대한 정보를 당신의 웹 사이트에 제공할 수 있습니다. 이 같은 방식에 관해 좀 더 의논하실 의향이 있는지 알려주십시오.
>
> 구오 양

어휘 **entitled** ~라는 제목의 **vegan** (계란, 유제품 등도 먹지 않는) 엄격한 채식주의자 **recipe** 조리법 **feature** (영화, 전시, 책 등에) 등장시키다 **in print** (절판되지 않고) 출간되는, 출판되어 나온 **definitely** 틀림없이 **practical** 실용적인 **break** 변화, 단절 **embrace** 끌어안다, 수용하다 **simplicity** 단순함 **organic food** 유기농 식품 **carry** (상점에서 물품을) 취급하다 **wide range of** 다양한 범위[종류]의 **specialty** 특산품, 특선품 **ingredient** (음식의) 재료 **call for** 필요로 하다 **arrangement** (처리) 방식, 계획

151.
번역 바네스 씨에 관해 암시된 것은?
(A) 책 사인회 행사를 열었다.
(B) 새로운 요리법을 찾고 있다.
(C) 여러 책을 출판했다.
(D) 공개 요리 시범을 보인다.

해설 **추론**
첫 번째 단락에서 '출판된 당신의 모든 요리책 중에서 이 책이 단연코 가장 실용적인 책입니다(Of all the cookbooks you have in print, this is definitely the most practical one)'라고 말한 것으로 미루어 이미 여러 권의 요리책을 출판했음을 알 수 있으므로 (C)가 정답이다.

152.
번역 양 씨는 무엇을 할 것을 제안하는가?
(A) 웹 사이트 업그레이드
(B) 몇몇 요리법 변경
(C) 무료 샘플 제공
(D) 동업 관계 형성

해설 세부사항

두 번째 단락에서 '저는 두 사업 모두에 이익이 될 수 있도록 저희가 협력할 수 있지 않을까 생각합니다(I think we could work together to benefit both of our businesses)'라는 말로 동업을 제안하면서, 이어 동업 방식을 예를 들어 설명했다. 따라서 (D)가 정답이다.

Paraphrasing

지문의 work together to benefit both of our businesses → 지문의 Forming a partnership

153-155 광고

잉글우드 부동산이 보유한 숨겨진 보석을 놓치지 마세요!

153잉글우드 부동산은 지난 30년간 특정 시대 주택만을 전문으로 취급해 왔습니다. 저희는 다음 건물을 매물로 내놓게 되어 기쁩니다: 페터슨 로 590번지, 방 5개, 욕실 2개

빅토리아 시대에 지어진 매우 아름다운 이 주택은 인기 있는 웨스트 카필드 지역의 한적한 거리라는 좋은 위치를 차지하고 있습니다. 지난 몇 년간 레스토랑들이 성공을 거두고 있는, 부산한 상업 지구 가까이 집이 있기 때문에, 수많은 편리한 식사 선택권이 걸어갈 만한 거리에 있는 셈이죠.

이 주택은 널찍한 방들과 풍부한 자연광을 가지고 있습니다, 뒤쪽 넓은 마당에 잘 가꾸어진 정원과 크게 자란 나무들이 있는 건 물론이고요. 1층은 현관 홀, 2개의 거실, 식당, 주방, 서재로 이루어져 있습니다. 2층에는 5개의 침실(그 중 하나가 주 욕실이 딸린 주 침실)과 두 번째 욕실이 있습니다.

154현재 주인들이 집을 전면 수리했기 때문에 집 곳곳의 붙박이 세간과 카펫들은 12개월이 채 안 됐습니다. 하지만, 수리 작업이 조심스럽게 진행되어, 집안의 중요한 원래 특징들, 예를 들어 난간의 정교한 목재 세공과 앞쪽 거실의 주철 난로 등이 그대로 보존되고 있으며, 이것이 여러분에게 예스러운 매력과 현대적인 편의 사이의 완벽한 균형을 느끼게 해 줍니다.

155제리 바스케스 씨에 의해 주택 경내에 대한 완벽한 검사가 이루어졌으며, 크게 수선이 필요한 사항은 없습니다. 저희는 이 같은 정보를 장래의 구매자에게 알리게 되어 기쁩니다. 집을 둘러보시는 데 관심이 있으면 555-5168번으로 전화해 이 건물을 취급하는 부동산 중개인과 연락을 취하십시오. 오픈 하우스 행사는 9월 10일 오후 2시부터 4시까지 열립니다.

어휘 specialize in ~가 전문이다 exclusively 오로지 period home 특정 시대 양식에 충실한 저택 property 부동산, 건물 stunning 놀라울 정도로 아름다운 well-positioned 위치가 좋은 sought-after 많은 사람들이 찾는, 인기 있는 bustling 부산한 take off (갑자기) 성공하다, 인기를 얻다 within walking distance 걸어서 닿을 만한 곳에, 아주 가까이에 sizable 상당히 큰 to the rear 뒤쪽으로 manicure (잔디 등을) 다듬다, 손질하다 be comprised of ~로 구성되다 upstairs 위층에, 2층에 master bedroom 큰방, 주 침실 fixture (욕조·싱크대 등) 붙박이 세간 remodel 개조하다, 리모델링하다 intricate 정교한, 복잡한 woodwork 목재 세공 banister 난간 cast iron 주철 fireplace 벽난로 retain 보유하다 old-fashioned 구식의 amenities 편의 시설 premises 건물, 경내 potential 장차 ~가 될 real estate agent 부동산 중개인 deal with ~을 취급하다 open house 오픈 하우스 (기관, 집 등을 돌아볼 수 있게 공개하는 행사[날])

153.

번역 잉글우드 부동산에 대해 명시된 것은?
(A) 사무실이 패터슨 로에 위치한다.
(B) 주거 건물만 취급한다.
(C) 9월 10일에 오픈 하우스 행사를 열 것이다.
(D) 40년 동안 영업을 해 왔다.

해설 Not/true

첫 문장에서 '잉글우드 부동산은 지난 30년간 특정 시대 주택만을 전문으로 취급해 왔습니다(Englewood Realty has been specializing exclusively in period homes for the past thirty years)'라고 밝히면서 매물로 나온 한 집을 소개하고 있으므로 (B)가 정답이다.

Paraphrasing

지문의 specializing exclusively in period homes → 정답의 deals solely with residential properties

154.

번역 집에 관해 명시된 것은?
(A) 판매 가격이 내려갔다.
(B) 1층에 방이 5개 있다.
(C) 처음으로 시장에 나왔다.
(D) 지난 일 년 사이에 보수 공사를 했다.

해설 Not/true

네 번째 단락에서 '현재 주인들이 집을 전면 수리했기 때문에 집 곳곳의 붙박이 세간과 카펫들은 12개월이 채 안 됐습니다(All fixtures and carpets throughout the home are less than twelve months old, as the current owners have completely remodeled the home)'라고 말한 것으로 보아 공사한 지 12개월이 안 됐음을 알 수 있으므로 (D)가 정답이다.

Paraphrasing

지문의 remodeled → 정답의 renovated

155.

번역 바스케스 씨는 누구일 것 같은가?
(A) 건물 검사관
(B) 부동산 중개인
(C) 집주인
(D) 장래 구매자

해설 추론

마지막 단락에서 '제리 바스케스 씨에 의해 주택 경내에 대한 완벽한 검사가 이루어졌으며, 크게 수선이 필요한 사항은 없습니다(A complete inspection of the premises has been carried out by Jerry Vasquez, and there are no major repairs needed)'라고 말했으므로 (A)가 정답이다.

Paraphrasing

지문의 the premises → 정답의 building

156-157 이메일

수신: 바티스타 영업부 〈allsales@batistaincorporated.com〉
발신: 셜리 실바 〈silvas@batistaincorporated.com〉
날짜: 4월 8일
주제: 수수료 조정
첨부: salesdeptcomm.doc

영업 직원들께,

156바티스타 사(社)는 6월 1일부터 모든 영업 사원을 대상으로 새로운 수수료 정책을 시행할 예정입니다. 모든 판매에 10퍼센트의 고정 비율을 적용하는 것이 아니라 5퍼센트에서 18퍼센트에 이르는 보상금으로 수수료를 다르게 받게 될 것입니다. 여러분 대부분에게 이 정책은 전반적으로 더 높은 수입을 올리는 결과가 될 것입니다. 자세한 내용은 첨부했으니 확인해 보세요.

이는 데이번포트 컨설팅과의 합병에 이어 취해진 변화 중 일부입니다. 6월 1일부터 우리는 바티스타 사라고 불리지 않습니다. 대신 DB 솔루션즈로 알려질 것입니다. 이를 반영해서 새로운 제복을 마련하려고 하니, **157총무부의 이샤니 라발 씨에게 어떤 사이즈를 원하는지 알려 줘서 준비할 수 있도록 해 주세요.**

고맙습니다.

셜리 실바
영업부 부장, 바티스타 사

어휘 roll out (여러 단계의 계획 하에) 시작하다 commission 커미션, (위탁 판매 대가로 받는) 수수료 salespeople 판매원, 영업 사원 flat rate 고정 요금[비율] tier 여러 층으로 배열하다 compensation 보상 result in (결과적으로) ~를 낳다 earnings 수입 merger 합병 uniform 제복 reflect 반영하다 administrative office 총무부 make arrangements 준비하다

156.

번역 이메일의 목적은 무엇인가?
(A) 지불 방식의 변화를 설명하려고
(B) 합병에 관한 의견을 구하려고
(C) 새 영업 사원들을 모집하려고
(D) 잘못에 대해 사과하려고

해설 주제/목적
첫 번째 단락에서 '바티스타 사(社)는 6월 1일부터 모든 영업 사원을 대상으로 새로운 수수료 정책을 시행할 예정입니다(Batista Incorporated will roll out a new commission structure for all salespeople starting from June 1)'라는 말로 시작해 정책 변경 내용을 설명했고, 두 번째 단락에서는 정책 변경의 배경을 설명했으므로 (A)가 정답이다.

Paraphrasing
지문의 a new commission structure
→ 정답의 a change in payment

157.

번역 라발 씨는 어떤 일을 담당하고 있는가?
(A) 새로운 사무실 배정
(B) 옷 준비
(C) 직원 식사 계획
(D) 가구 배달 준비

해설 세부사항
두 번째 단락에서 '새로운 제복을 마련해야(get new uniforms)' 한다면서 '총무부의 이샤니 라발 씨에게 어떤 사이즈를 원하는지 알려 줘서 준비할 수 있도록 해 주세요(please let Ishani Raval in the administrative office know what size you prefer so she can make the arrangements)'라고 했다. 라발 씨가 제복을 준비하고 있음을 알 수 있으므로 (B)가 정답이다.

Paraphrasing
지문의 new uniforms → 정답의 some clothing

158-160 양식

요나스 전자 소비자 패널

내년에 시장에 출시될 예정인 YE 사진 복사기를 위한 우리 세션에 참가하셨던 게 즐거웠기를 바랍니다. 여러분의 의견을 제공하기 위해 이 양식을 완성해 주십시오. **158양식을 제출하신 후에는 시험하신 프린터를 가지고 집으로 돌아가시면 됩니다.**

이름: 얼 힝클리   기간: 7월 14일 오후 2시-5시

각 범주를 1(나쁨)에서 5(훌륭함)까지로 평가한 다음 자신의 의견을 알려 주세요.

전반적인 외관: 5 날렵한 모양, 그리고 은색과 검은색 두 가지로 나온다는 사실이 마음에 듭니다.

설치: 5 설명서를 참고할 필요도 없이 프린터를 내 스마트폰에 연결하는 게 쉬웠습니다.

특색: 4 **159주머니 속에 들고 다닐 정도로 충분히 작기는 하지만, 무거운 무게 때문에, 대다수 사람들이 회사에서 기대하는 대로 그렇게 하려고 하지는 않을 것 같습니다.**

가격: 3 사진의 질에 비해 가격이 높아 보입니다. 저 같으면 그냥 예전 프린터에 사진을 인화하겠습니다.

기타 의견: 피드백 세션 자체의 경우, **160그룹 내에 인원이 너무 많아 토론이 그다지 생산적이지 않았습니다.** 그래서 충분한 시간이 있었음에도 불구하고 어떤 사람들은 너무 수줍음이 많아서 자신의 의견을 내놓지 못했습니다.

어휘 session (특정 활동의) 기간 hit the market 시장에 출시되다 feedback 의견, 반응, 피드백 sleek (모양이) 매끄러운, 날렵한 available 손에 넣을 수 있는, 구입할 수 있는 setup 설치, 설정 refer to ~을 참고하다 manual (기계 등의) 설명서 feature 특색 compact 소형의, 간편한 carry around 휴대하다, 들고 다니다 anticipate 기대하다, 예상하다

158.
번역 소비자 패널에 대해 명시된 것은?
(A) 기간이 2시간 소요되었다.
(B) 새로 출시된 제품을 검토하는 게 패널의 목적이다.
(C) 요나스 전자 본사에서 열렸다.
(D) 참가자들은 기기를 가지고 가도록 허락되었다.

해설 Not / true
첫 번째 단락의 '양식을 제출하신 후에는 시험하신 프린터를 가지고 집으로 돌아가시면 됩니다(After you submit the form, you may go home, taking the printer you tested with you)'라는 말에서 시험해 보고 그 기기를 가지고 가는 것임을 알 수 있으므로 (D)가 정답이다. (B)의 경우, 제일 처음에 '내년에 시장에 출시될 예정인 YE 사진 복사기'라고 했으므로 틀린 진술이다.

Paraphrasing
지문의 taking the printer ➜ 정답의 keep a device

159.
번역 제품에 대해 암시된 것은?
(A) YE 스마트폰과 함께 판매된다.
(B) 세 가지 색깔로 나온다.
(C) 휴대할 수 있게 하려는 의도이다.
(D) 사진 스캔 기능이 있다.

해설 추론
특색 란에서 '사람들 대다수가 회사에서 기대하는 대로 그렇게 하려고 하지는 않을 것 같습니다(I don't think most people would do this as you anticipated)'라고 말했는데, 여기서 '그렇게 하려고(do this)'는 바로 앞에서 말하는 '주머니 속에 들고 다니는(carry around in my pocket) 것을 가리킨다. 원래 의도는 들고 다니는 것이었음을 알 수 있으므로 (C)가 정답이다.

Paraphrasing
지문의 compact enough to carry around in my pocket ➜ 정답의 portable

160.
번역 그룹 모임에서 힝클리 씨가 가장 마음에 들지 않았던 것은 무엇인가?
(A) 참가비
(B) 인원 수
(C) 모임 시간
(D) 모임 지도자

해설 세부사항
기타 의견에서 '그룹 내에 인원이 너무 많아 토론이 그다지 생산적이지 않았습니다(the discussion wasn't very productive because there were too many people in the group)'라며 인원 수에 불만을 표시했으므로 (B)가 정답이다.

161-163 메모

발신: 리에미 사이토, 사무장
수신: 랜달 솔루션즈 직원들
날짜: 3월 2일
내용: 최근 소식

여러분 안녕하세요,

오그덴 테크와의 회의는 기대했던 것보다 훨씬 잘 되었습니다. **161**그곳 총 책임자인 산지브 나다르 씨가 세 개의 공석을 채우기 위해 우리 서비스를 이용하기로 합의했습니다. 이 기회를 이용해 주요 고객을 확실하게 지키도록 합시다. 이 직책에 맞는 적절한 후보자로 나다르 씨에게 좋은 인상을 줄 수 있다면, 오그덴 테크와의 지속적인 계약을 얻어낼 수 있을 겁니다. **162**그 회사는 로스앤젤레스에서 제2지사를 열 계획이어서, 5월 중순까지 80명의 새 직원이 필요할 것입니다.

이 문제는 다음 직원 회의 때 좀 더 얘기하도록 하겠습니다. **163**3월 6일에 모이기로 했던 거로 알고 있는데, 이틀 뒤로 미뤘으면 합니다. 그때면 오그덴 테크의 요구에 대해 좀 더 자세한 정보를 갖게 될 거 같아서요. 덧붙여, 바스케즈 씨가 다음 주에 휴가를 떠납니다. 그러니까, 이번 달에는 월 경과 보고서를 3월 15일이 아닌 3월 9일까지 제출해 주십시오.

열심히 일해 주셔서 감사합니다!

리에미 사이토

어휘 secure 안전하게 지키다 permanent 영속적인 assignmanet 임무 postpone 연기하다 by ~만큼 detailed 자세한 progress report 경과 보고

161.
번역 메모를 받는 사람들은 누구일 것 같은가?
(A) 취업 후보자들
(B) 기술 분야 연구자들
(C) 부서장들
(D) 인력 공급 담당자들

해설 추론
첫 번째 단락에서 오그덴 테크가 '세 개의 공석을 채우기 위해 우리 서비스를 이용하기로 합의했다(has agreed to use our services for filling three open job positions)'라고 했고, 80명의 충원 기회가 있을 것이라고 언급했다. 이메일을 주고받는 사람들이 인력 충원 서비스 사업에 관여하는 사람들임을 알 수 있으므로 (D)가 정답이다.

162.
번역 오그덴 테크에 대해 암시된 것은?
(A) 본사를 로스앤젤레스로 이전할 것이다.
(B) 랜달 솔루션즈의 오래된 고객이다.
(C) 재정적인 어려움에 직면해 있다.
(D) 노동 인력을 확장할 계획이다.

해설 추론
첫 번째 단락의 '그 회사는 로스앤젤레스에서 제2지사를 열 계획이어서, 5월 중순까지 80명의 새 직원이 필요할 것입니다(The company will open a second branch in Los Angeles, so they'll need about eighty new staff members by mid-May)'라는 말에서 지사 설립에 따른 충원 필요성 얘기가 나왔으므로 (D)가 정답이다.

Paraphrasing
지문의 need about eighty new staff members ➜ 정답의 expand its workforce

163.

번역 사이토 씨는 이 메모를 받은 사람들과 언제 만날 것인가?
(A) 3월 6일
(B) 3월 8일
(C) 3월 9일
(D) 3월 15일

해설 세부사항

사이토 씨가 다음 직원 회의 얘기를 꺼내면서 '3월 6일에 모이기로 했던 거로 알고 있는데, 이틀 뒤로 미뤘으면 합니다(I know we were supposed to meet on March 6, but I'd like to postpone it by two days)'라고 말했다. 6일에서 이틀 뒤면 8일이므로 (B)가 정답이다.

164-167 문자 메시지

니콜라스 카스트로 [2:04 P.M.]
그 팀 늦게까지 일하나요? **164**오늘 저녁 내가 야근 승인 해 주는 게 아직 필요한가요, 신제품 스마트폰 앱 시장 요약 보고서 마무리할 수 있게요?
이사벨라 라니어 [2:06 P.M.]
그건 이제 필요가 없습니다.
리우 캬오 [2:07 P.M.]
한 시간쯤 전에 최종안을 제출했어요.
니콜라스 카스트로 [2:08 P.M.]
쇼 씨가 그거에 대해 만족할 거예요. **165**그는 내일 저녁은 돼야 받아볼 거라고 예상하고 있었으니까요.
이사벨라 라니어 [2:09 P.M.]
네, 우리는 그가 목요일 캬오 씨와 만나기 전에 수치를 검토하려면 하루가 더 필요할 거라고 생각했어요.
니콜라스 카스트로 [2:09 P.M.]
166우리가 캬오 씨에게 투자 자금을 얻어낼 수 있을 거라고 생각해요?
에드가 코토브 [2:11 P.M.]
네. 우리 조사 결과 시장에 유사한 앱이 전혀 없는 것으로 나타났어요.
리우 캬오 [2:12 P.M.]
그리고 앱이 사용하기 매우 쉬워서, 우리 생각에 소비자들이 매우 좋아할 거 같아요.
이사벨라 라니어 [2:13 P.M.]
167목표 시장이 청소년들이어서, 소셜 미디어에서 인기를 끌 가능성이 아주 많아요.
니콜라스 카스트로 [2:14 P.M.]
167그게 우리가 광고에 들이는 비용을 아주 많이 절감시켜 주겠네요.
에드가 코토브 [2:16 P.M.]
나도 그렇게 생각했어요.
이사벨라 라니어 [2:17 P.M.]
일단 이 프로젝트가 자금 지원을 받게 될지 아닐지를 우리가 기다려 봐야 할 거라고 생각해요.

어휘 work late 야근하다 approve 승인하다 overtime work 초과근무, 야근 wrap up 마무리하다 hand in 제출하다 draft 초안 additional 추가적인 go over 검토하다, 조사하다 figure 수치 fund 자금, 자금을 대다 young adult 청소년 potential 가능성, 잠재력 save (돈, 시간 등을) 절감시켜 주다

164.

번역 오후 2시 6분에, 라니어 씨가 "그건 이제 필요가 없습니다"라고 쓴 의미는?
(A) 제품이 출시되지 않을 것이다.
(B) 회사 정책이 바뀌었다.
(C) 팀원들이 늦게까지 남아 있지 않을 것이다.
(D) 요약 보고서가 승인을 받을 필요가 없다.

해설 의도 파악

바로 앞에서 '오늘 저녁 내가 야근 승인 해 주는 게 아직 필요한가요(Do you still need me to approve overtime work for this evening)'라고 묻는 질문에 대한 대답이다. 즉 야근을 할 필요가 없다는 뜻이므로 (C)가 정답이다.

Paraphrasing
지문의 overtime work → 정답의 stay late

165.

번역 시장 요약 보고서에 대해 명시된 것은?
(A) 일찍 제출되었다.
(B) 쇼 씨가 만들었다.
(C) 마지막 순간에 배정되었다.
(D) 여러 제품을 위한 것이었다.

해설 Not / true

오후 2시 8분 카스트로 씨는 쇼 씨가 보고서에 만족할 거라며, '그는 내일 저녁은 돼야 받아볼 거라고 예상하고 있었으니까요(He wasn't expecting it until tomorrow evening)'라고 했다. 바로 이어 라니어 씨도 '수치를 검토하려면 하루가 더 필요할 거라고 생각했어요(he might want an additional day to go over the figures)'라고 말했다. 즉, 보고서가 예정보다 하루 일찍 제출되어 검토할 시간이 하루 더 생겼다는 뜻이므로 (A)가 정답이다.

166.

번역 캬오 씨는 누구일 것 같은가?
(A) 스마트폰 판매원
(B) 기업 투자자
(C) 컴퓨터 프로그래머
(D) 취업 지원자

해설 추론

오후 2시 9분, 카스트로 씨의 "우리가 캬오 씨에게 투자 자금을 얻어낼 수 있을 거라고 생각해요?(Do you think we'll get the investment funds from her?)'라는 질문에서, 캬오 씨가 투자 자금을 댈 수 있는 사람임을 알 수 있으므로 (B)가 정답이다.

167.

번역 스마트폰 앱에 대해 암시된 것은?
(A) 치열한 경쟁을 하게 될 것이다.
(B) 사회 복지사들을 위해 고안되었다.
(C) 현재 소셜 미디어에서 인기를 얻고 있다.
(D) 광고비가 적게 들 수도 있다.

해설 추론

앱이 소셜 미디어에서 인기를 끌 거라는 말에, 오후 2시 14분에 카스트로 씨가 '그게 우리가 광고에 들이는 비용을 아주 많이 절감시켜 주겠네요(That would save us a great deal of money on advertising)'라고 했고, 이어 다른 사람이 동의했다. 소셜 미디어에 많이 등장하면 따로 광고를 많이 할 필요가 없다는 의미이므로 (D)가 정답이다.

Paraphrasing

지문의 save us a great deal of money on advertising
→ 광고의 advertising costs might be low

168-171 광고

엘리슨 모터스
오스틴 드라이브 511번지 ▽ 18번 가 793번지 ▽ 스톤 대로 429번지

가치가 점점 떨어지는 차 때문에 높은 월 대출 상환금을 떠안고 있지 마십시오. 오늘 엘리슨 모터스에서 차를 계약해 장기적인 위험 없이 최신 모델 운전을 즐기세요. 엘리슨 모터스에서는 2년, 3년, 5년의 계약을 제공하기 때문에, 자신의 예산과 라이프스타일에 가장 맞는 계획을 선택할 수 있습니다. **168계약금 없이 새 차를 매장에서 바로 타고 나가서, 자동 이체로 설정되는 감당할 만한 월별 지불액만 내시면 됩니다.** 계약 기간이 끝나면 차를 돌려주고 새 차를 쇼핑하세요!

저희는 그동안 높은 신뢰도로 명성을 쌓았으며, 서비스도 최고 수준입니다. 사실, **169저희는 저희 회사와 아무 연관이 없는 〈비히클 인사이트〉 잡지에서 만점을 받았습니다.** 모든 차가 3년 미만 된 것이고, **170공장에서 직접 차들을 공급받기 때문에 가장 낮은 가격을 보장합니다.** 절약된 금액을 바로 고객에게 전할 수 있는 완벽한 시스템을 갖추고 있다는 뜻입니다.

엘리슨 모터스에서는, 자신의 결정에 확신을 가질 수 있습니다. 공식적인 계약이 효력을 발하기 전에 고객들이 2주간의 유예 기간을 갖게 되기 때문입니다. 저희는 미니밴에서 스포츠카에 이르기까지 굉장히 다양한 차량을 확보하고 있습니다. 차를 고르는 데 도움이 필요하다면, 저희 경험 있는 직원들이 조언을 해 줄 것입니다. **171피츠버그 내 여러 편리한 위치 중 하나로 오늘 엘리슨 모터스를 방문해 주세요.**

어휘 saddled with (빚, 부담, 과제 등을) 떠안은 loan payment 대출 상환금 lease (부동산, 차 등을) 임대[임차]하다; 임대차 계약 long-term 장기적인 fit (크기나 정도가) 맞다 budget 예산 drive off the lot (차를 구입해 차를 세워둔) 부지에서 타고 나가다 with no money down 계약금 없이 manageable 감당할 수 있는 set up 마련하다 by direct debit 자동 이체 term 기간 reliability 신뢰할 수 있음 top-notch 최고의 have an affiliation with ~와 관련[제휴 관계]가 있다 source 공급받다 fleet (특정 조직에 속한 전체) 차들 saving 절약, 절약한 돈 confident 확신하는 grace period 유예 기간 go into effect 효력을 발생하다

168.

번역 서비스의 어떤 장점이 언급되나?
(A) 고객들은 계약 기간 중에 차량을 바꿀 수 있다.
(B) 무료 운전 교습이 포함된다.
(C) 고객에게 보증금이 부과되지 않는다.
(D) 계약 기간이 연장될 수 있다.

해설 세부사항

첫 번째 단락에서 '계약금 없이 새 차를 매장에서 바로 타고 나가서, 감당할 만한 월별 지불액만 내시면 된다(You can drive off the lot in a brand-new car with no money down, making manageable monthly payments)'라고 했으므로 (C)가 정답이다.

Paraphrasing

지문의 with no money down
→ 정답의 No deposit is required

169.

번역 앨리슨 모터스에 대해 암시된 것은?
(A) 관련이 없는 측에게 호의적인 평을 받았다.
(B) 최근 피츠버그에 세 번째 지점을 열었다.
(C) 업계에서 최고의 안전 등급을 받았다.
(D) 신규 고객에게는 특별 할인을 해 준다.

해설 추론

두 번째 단락에서 '저희는 저희 회사와 아무 연관이 없는 〈비히클 인사이트〉 잡지에서 만점을 받았습니다(we received a perfect score on *Vehicle Insight* magazine, which has no affiliation with our company)'라고 했으므로 (A)가 정답이다.

Paraphrasing

지문의 received a perfect score
→ 정답의 favorably reviewed
지문의 has no affiliation with our company
→ 정답의 an independent party

170.

번역 광고에 따르면, 가격을 낮추기 위해서 회사가 무엇을 하는가?
(A) 거래 기록 업무를 자동화한다.
(B) 생산업자와 직접 연계해 일한다.
(C) 사용되고 난 차량을 판매한다.
(D) 단기간의 계약만 제공한다.

해설 세부사항

두 번째 단락에서 '공장에서 직접 차들을 공급받기 때문에 가장 낮은 가격을 보장합니다(we ensure the lowest possible prices by sourcing our fleet straight from the factory)'라고 말했다. 생산 공장과 직접 거래한다는 뜻이므로 (B)가 정답이다.

Paraphrasing

지문의 straight from the factory
→ 정답의 directly with manufacturers

171.

번역 [1], [2], [3], [4]로 표시된 곳 중에서 다음 문장이 가장 적합한 곳은?
"차를 고르는 데 도움이 필요하다면, 저희 경험 있는 직원들이 조언을 해 줄 것입니다."
(A) [1]
(B) [2]
(C) [3]
(D) [4]

해설 **문장 삽입**

[4] 바로 앞에서 렌터카 회사에 대한 모든 광고가 끝난다. 이어 '직원들이 차를 선택할 때 조언을 해 줄 것이라'는 삽입 문장이 [4]에 들어가고, 또 이어서 엘리슨 모터스를 직접 방문해 달라는 말이 나오는 게 자연스러우므로 (D)의 [4]가 정답이다.

172-175 기사

노르웍 은행이 사이퍼트 파이낸셜을 인수하다

2월 19일 – 어제 발행된 언론 보도자료에서, 사이퍼트 파이낸셜은 자사가 시애틀에 근거지를 두고 있는 노르웍 은행에 매각된다고 발표했다. **174-A**북서 지역에서 같은 종류로는 최대 규모인 이 거래에, 토론토 지역에서 운영하는 사이퍼트 사의 지사 네 곳은 물론 사이퍼트의 자산 3억 6천 6백만 달러가 포함될 것이다. 이 기업 인수는 **174-C**미국 국경을 넘어 캐나다까지 사업 영역을 확장한다는 노르웍의 장기적인 목표에 있어 중요한 한걸음으로 기록된다.

172노르웍의 기업 고문 변호사인 로버트 코스트너 씨는, 양측의 이사들이 적절한 준비가 가능한 빨리 취해지도록 하는 데 매우 적극적이라고 보고한다. "**173**1차 협상은 3월에 열립니다." 코스트너 씨가 설명했다. "최종 계약은 그 다음 달에 체결될 겁니다." **174-D**노르웍은 현재 현금과 투자 기금, 기타 주식으로 12억 달러를 보유하고 있고, 이번 인수가 이 회사의 입지를 굉장히 높여 줄 것으로 기대된다. "사이퍼트 사의 비즈니스 모델의 근간을 이루는 장점들이 현재의 우리 상황을 균형 있게 해 줍니다." 홍보 부장 세스 마브리 씨가 이렇게 말했다. "**175**투자 은행으로서의 사이퍼트의 평판이 노르웍에서 이미 제공되는 서비스에 완벽한 보완이 되어줄 것입니다. 게다가, 주택 담보 대출 시장에 관한 직원들의 전문 지식이 매우 유용할 것입니다."

사이퍼트 파이낸셜의 현 고객들은 합의가 완결된 후에도, **174-B**노르웍의 웹 기반 계정 시스템을 이용해 이체하고, 잔고를 확인하고, 기타 금융 거래를 할 수 있지만, 브랜드의 즉각적인 변화는 없을 것이다. 목표는 모든 계좌를 6월 말까지 모 브랜드 하에서 운영하는 것이다. 노르웍의 경영 팀은 7월에 자회사의 필요 사항을 재평가할 예정이며, 그때 가서 대대적인 감축 또는 충원 움직임이 요구될 수 있다.

어휘 **press release** 보도 자료 **issue** 발행하다 **purchase** 구입하다 **transaction** 거래 **transfer** 이전 **asset** 자산 **acquisition** 인수 **long-term** 장기적인 **border** 국경 **corporate** 기업의, 법인의 **board member** 이사회 임원 **highly** 매우 **motivated** 의욕에 찬 **ensure** 반드시 ~하게 하다 **arrangement** 준비 **negotiation** 협상 **investment fund** 투자 기금 **holding** 보유 주식 **strength** 장점 **underlie** 기반을 이루다 **observe** 논평하다, 말하다 **public relations** 홍보 **complement to** ~에 대한 보완, 더 좋아지게 만드는 요소 **finalize** (계약 등을) 완결 짓다 **make transfer** 이체하다 **account balance** 계좌 잔액 **financial transaction** 금융 거래 **downsize** (인원을) 줄이다 **recruitment** 직원 채용 **drive** (조직적인) 운동, 움직임

172.

번역 코스트너 씨는 누구인가?
(A) 홍보부 직원
(B) 이사
(C) 법률 전문가
(D) 회사 소유주

해설 **세부사항**

두 번째 단락, 코스트너 씨의 말을 인용하는 부분에서 '노르웍의 기업 고문 변호사인 로버트 코스트너 씨(Norwalk's corporate lawyer, Robert Costner)'라고 언급했다. 변호사를 법률 전문가라고 할 수 있으므로 (C)가 정답이다.

Paraphrasing

지문의 corporate lawyer → 정답의 A legal professional

173.

번역 합의는 언제 완료될 것으로 예상되는가?
(A) 3월
(B) 4월
(C) 6월
(D) 7월

해설 **세부사항**

두 번째 단락, 코스트너 씨의 말을 인용하는 부분에서 '1차 협상은 3월에 열립니다. 최종 계약은 그 다음 달에 체결될 겁니다(The first round of negotiations will be held in March. The final contract will be signed the following month)'라고 했다. 3월에 열려 4월에 체결될 것이므로 (B)가 정답이다.

174.

번역 노르웍 은행에 대해 명시되지 않은 것은?
(A) 현재 네 곳의 지사를 운영한다.
(B) 온라인 은행 서비스를 제공한다.
(C) 캐나다로 확장할 계획이다.
(D) 자산이 10억 달러가 넘는다.

해설 **Not/true**

첫 번째 단락에서 거래 규모를 설명하면서 '토론토 지역에서 운영하는 사이퍼트 사의 지사 네 곳은 물론 사이퍼트의 자산 3억 6천 6백만 달러가 포함될 것이다(will include the transfer of Seifert's $366 million in assets as well as its four branches operating in the Toronto area)'라고 말했다. 현재 지사 네 곳과 큰 자산을 보유하고 있는 쪽은 노르웍이 아니라 사이퍼트이므로 (A)가 틀린 진술이다.

Paraphrasing

지문의 Web-based account system
→ 보기의 an online banking service
지문의 moving the business beyond U.S. borders and into Canada
→ 보기의 has plans to expand into Canada
지문의 has $1.2 billion in cash, investment funds, and other holdings,
→ 보기의 assets exceed one billion dollars

175.

번역 [1], [2], [3], [4]로 표시된 곳 중에서 다음 문장이 가장 적합한 곳은?
"게다가, 주택 담보 대출 시장에 관한 직원들의 전문 지식이 매우 유용할 것입니다."
(A) [1]
(B) [2]
(C) [3]
(D) [4]

해설 문장 삽입

두 번째 단락에서 두 회사의 합병으로 인한 장점을 설명하고 있다. [3] 바로 앞에서 사이퍼트 사의 투자 은행으로서의 평판을 첫 번째 장점으로 언급했고, 바로 이어 삽입 문장에서 직원들의 전문 지식을 두 번째 장점으로 드는 것이 자연스러우므로 (C) [3]이 정답이다.

176-180 송장+이메일

트렌턴 도매

상호: ECC 연락 담당자: 데보라 캠프
전화 번호: 859-555-0174 이메일 주소: deborah@eccservices.net
발송 주소: 스트랫퍼드 공원 253번지, 렉싱턴, 켄터키 주 40507
청구 주소: 위와 같음   주문 번호: 751275
주문 날짜: 3월 9일   예상 배달 날짜: 3월 12일

참조 번호	상표/품목 설명	단위당 크기/가격	수량	합계
T340	스펜서/**176영구 염색제**(검은색)	**177**500 ml/14.49달러	20개	289.80달러
R490	스펜서/스타일링 젤	500 ml/17.99달러	30개	539.70달러
W761	스펜서/샴푸	500 ml/18.49달러	35개	647.15달러
*D288	스펜서/컨디셔너	500 ml/18.49달러	30개	554.70달러
179 C492	힛텍스/핫 오일 트리트먼트	500 ml/23.99달러	15개	359.85달러
*는 재고가 떨어진 품목을 가리킴. 이 품목은 위에 명시된 배달 날짜에 나머지 제품과 함께 보내지 않음. 대신, 다시 재고가 생기는 즉시 발송됨 (약 1주).		소계		2,391.20달러
		세금		143.47달러
		배송		35.00달러
		합계		2,569.67달러

수신: 트렌턴 도매점 〈inquiries@trentonwholesale.com〉
발신: 데보라 캠프 〈deborah@eccservices.net〉
날짜: 3월 14일
제목: 주문 번호 751275

관계자 분께:

최근 주문(주문번호 751275)과 관련해 제가 갖고 있는 두 가지 문제를 알려 드리고 싶습니다. 저는 전화로 주문을 했습니다. 그래서 **178스펜서 스타일링 젤, 품목 R490이 카탈로그에 매겨져 있는 금액보다 거의 1달러가 더 비싼 것을 보고 놀랐습니다. 180-D**저는 몇 주 전에 우편으로 이 카탈로그를 받았기 때문에, 오래 돼서 안 쓰는 거라고는 생각하지 않습니다. **180-A**트렌턴 도매가 최근에 다른 업체에 인수되었다는 건 알고 있습니다. 하지만 고객들에게 이 같은 변화는 고지해야 할 의무가 있다고 믿고 있습니다. **180-C**저는 10년 넘게 제 사업을 운영하고 있고 예고 없는 이런 식의 가격 인상은 본 적이 없습니다.

또한, **179**제가 주문한 핫 오일 트리트먼트를 반송하고 싶습니다. 제품이 효과가 있을 것으로 보이기는 하지만, 향이 마음에 들지 않아요. **180-B**트렌턴의 환불 정책에 준해 제 비용으로 개봉하지 않은 병들을 돌려 보내겠습니다.

데보라 캠프
주인, ECC

어휘 dye 염색제 out-of-stock (일시적으로) 재고가 없는 dispatch 보내다, 발송하다 available 손에 넣을 수 있는 issue 문제 quote 값을 매기다 outdated (오래 돼서) 구식인, 쓸모가 없는 without warning 예고도 없이 effective 효과적인 scent 향기 in accordance with ~에 준해서, (규칙)에 맞게 return policy 환불 정책

176.

번역 ECC는 어떤 종류의 가게일 것 같은가?
(A) 가구 청소 서비스
(B) 미장원
(C) 헬스 클럽
(D) 미술 작업실

해설 추론
염색제, 스타일링 젤, 샴푸, 컨디셔너, 핫 오일 트리트먼트 등을 수십 개씩 주문한 것으로 보아 미장원을 운영하는 것으로 추측할 수 있으므로 (B)가 정답이다.

177.

번역 캠프 씨가 주문한 상품의 공통점은 무엇인가?
(A) 크기
(B) 상표
(C) 단가
(D) 배달 날짜

해설 세부사항
모든 상품의 크기가 500ml로 동일하므로 (A)가 정답이다. (D)의 경우, 별표*가 붙은 품목은 재고가 확보되는 대로 따로 보낸다고 했으므로 D288 컨디셔너는 늦게 배송될 것이다.

178.

번역 R490 제품에 대해 언급된 것은?
(A) 오래된 조제법을 사용했다.
(B) 다른 품목들과 함께 도착하지 않았다.
(C) 가격이 예상했던 것보다 비쌌다.
(D) 불쾌한 향이 났다.

해설 Not/true
이메일에서 '스펜서 스타일링 젤, 품목 R490이 카탈로그에 매겨져 있는 금액보다 거의 1달러가 더 비싼 것을 보고 놀랐습니다(I was surprised to discover that the Spencer Styling Gel, item R490, was nearly a dollar more than what is quoted in the catalog)'라고 했다. 몇 주 전에 카탈로그를 받고 가격을 예상하고 있었던 것이므로 (C)가 정답이다. (A)의 경우 오래된(outdated) 것은 카탈로그이고, (B)의 경우 다른 종목과 함께 도착하지 않을 것은 D288 컨디셔너이고, (D)의 경우 불쾌한 향이 난 것은 핫 오일 트리트먼트이므로 모두 다 언급되지 않은 진술이다.

Paraphrasing
지문의 nearly a dollar more than what is quoted in the catalog → 정답의 price was higher than expected

179.

번역 켐프 씨는 어떤 품목을 반품하고 싶어 하는가?
(A) T340
(B) W761
(C) D288
(D) C492

해설 연계
이메일 두 번째 단락에서 '제가 주문한 핫 오일 트리트먼트를 반송하고 싶습니다(I would like to return the hot oil treatments I ordered)'라고 말했는데, 위의 송장에서 보면 핫 오일 트리트먼트의 참조 번호는 C492이므로 (D)가 정답이다.

180.

번역 이메일에서 명시되지 않은 것은?
(A) 트렌턴 도매는 소유주가 바뀌었다.
(B) 고객들은 반송할 때 운송비를 지불해야 한다.
(C) 켐프 씨의 가게는 최소 10년이 넘었다.
(D) 트렌턴 도매는 주문을 우편으로 받는다.

해설 Not / true
첫 번째 단락 '저는 몇 주 전에 우편물로 이 카탈로그를 받았기 때문에(I just got this catalog in the mail a few weeks ago)'라고 말한 데서 카탈로그를 우편으로 받은 걸 알 수 있지만, 주문을 우편으로 했다는 단서는 없으므로 (D)가 정답이다. (A)는 '트렌턴 도매가 최근에 다른 업체에 인수되었다는 건 알고 있습니다(I know that Trenton Wholesale was bought by another business recently)'에, (B)는 '트렌턴의 환불 정책에 준해 제 비용으로 개봉하지 않은 병들을 돌려 보내겠습니다(I'll send the unopened bottles back at my own expense, in accordance with your return policy)'에, (C)는 '저는 10년 넘게 제 사업을 운영하고 있고(I've been operating my business for over a decade)'에 나와 있다.

Paraphrasing

지문의 Trenton Wholesale was bought by another business
→ 보기의 Trenton Wholesale is under new ownership
지문의 for over a decade → at least ten years

181-185 이메일 + 메모

수신: 조슈아 웬젤 〈j_wenzell@odbsolutions.com〉
발신: 루스 호프만 〈r_hoffman@odbsolutions.com〉
날짜: 8월 23일
주제: 강의 일정

웬젤 씨께,

현재 저는 회사에서 하는 9월의 수요일 오후 강연 시리즈 일정표 작업을 하고 있습니다. 회의실이 개조 공사 중이던 여름철에는 우리가 이 주별 전문성 신장 교육 시리즈를 잠시 쉬었습니다. **181**공사가 8월 20일 마감일을 넘길까 봐 걱정했는데, 그렇게 되지 않아서 기쁩니다. **182**우리 직원들이 가장 흥미로워 할 주제를 찾기 위해서 직원 설문에서 얻은 반응을 평가하고 있습니다. 지금까지는, 네 명의 연사 중 셋이 확답을 했습니다. 네 번째 연사인 마리아 누젠트 씨는 잠정적으로만 일정이 잡힌 상태입니다.

185누젠트 씨가 포틀랜드 어워드에 지명이 되면 우리 강연 현장을 방문할 수 없게 됩니다. 이 때문에 일정이 겹치기 때문이죠. 그럴 경우, 누젠트 씨를 다른 사람과 교체하지는 않을 겁니다. 모든 것이 확정되면 직원들에게 메모를 보내겠습니다.

루스 호프만

수신: ODB 솔루션즈 전 직원
발신: 루스 호프만
날짜: 8월 30일
내용: 읽어 주세요

ODB 솔루션즈 오후 강의 시리즈에 참가할 수많은 재능 있는 전문가들을 우리 손님으로 환영하게 되어 기쁩니다. **184**이들 개인은 자신의 분야에서 최고 위치에 있으며, 다른 사람들을 고무하고 동기부여 할 수 있는 능력이 있습니다. 모든 직원들은 전문성 신장을 위해 이들 좋은 기회에 참석해 주기를 요청합니다. **183**각 강연은 오후 1-3시에 있으며, 9월의 일정표는 다음과 같습니다.

- 9월 9일, 수요일: 레미지오 비안치 씨, "시간 관리 조언"
- 9월 16일, 수요일: 헨리 암스트롱 씨, "숨겨진 고객 요구"
- 9월 23일, 수요일: 쿠니미 이토 씨, "효력 있는 테크 솔루션"

강의를 듣기 위해 사전에 신청할 필요는 없지만, 좌석은 선착순으로 이용 가능하다는 점에 주의해 주세요. 인원이 너무 많을 경우, 일부는 뒤쪽에 서야 할 수도 있습니다. 여러분 모두 참석을 고려해 주시기 바랍니다.

어휘 remodel 개조하다, 리모델링하다 evaluate 평가하다 questionnaire 설문지 confirm 확인하다, 확정하다 tentatively 잠정적으로 be nominated for ~후보로 지명되다 scheduling conflict 일정이 겹침 replace 교체하다, 다른 것으로 대신하다 professional 전문직 종사자, 전문가 capacity 능력 inspire 고무하다 motivate 동기를 부여하다 invite (정식으로) 요청하다 professional development 전문성 신장 교육(매니저, 또는 전문직 종사자들이 지식과 기술을 습득하기 위해 받는 교육 및 훈련) talk 연설, 강연 work (제대로) 작동하다, 효과가 있다 register 신청하다 in advance 미리 session (교육, 회의, 강의 등의) 기간 on a first-come, first-served basis 선착순으로 overcrowding 과밀 in attendance 참석한

181.

번역 호프만 씨는 무엇에 기뻐하는가?
(A) 강의가 긍정적인 평가를 들어서
(B) 팀의 촉박한 마감 시한이 연장돼서
(C) 개조 공사가 제때에 끝나서
(D) 회의 일정이 승인돼서

해설 세부사항
이메일에서 '공사가 8월 20일 마감일을 넘길까 봐 걱정했는데, 그렇게 되지 않아서 기쁩니다(I was concerned that the work would run past the August 20 deadline, but I was pleased that didn't happen)'라고 말했으므로 (C)가 정답이다.

143

182.
번역 호프만 씨는 자신이 무엇을 했다고 말하는가?
(A) 연사들에게 지불금을 보냈다.
(B) 발표 자료를 프린트했다.
(C) 웹 사이트에 일정표를 게시했다.
(D) 조사 결과를 분석했다.

해설 세부사항
이메일에서 '우리 직원들에게 가장 흥미로울 주제를 찾기 위해서 직원 설문에서 얻은 반응을 평가하고 있습니다(I've evaluated the feedback from our employee questionnaire to find the topics that would be most interesting to our staff)'라고 했으므로 (D)가 정답이다.

Paraphrasing
지문의 evaluated the feedback from our employee questionnaire → 정답의 Analyzed some survey results

183.
번역 메모의 목적은 무엇인가
(A) 생산 일정을 조절하려고
(B) 직원들에게 발표에 관해 알리려고
(C) 새로운 팀원들을 환영하려고
(D) 직원들에게 강연을 해 달라고 요청하려고

해설 주제/목적
강의 발표자들의 특성을 소개한 후, '각 강연은 오후 1-3시에 있으며, 9월의 일정표는 다음과 같습니다(Each talk will take place from 1–3 p.m., and the schedule for September will be as follows)'라고 발표에 대해 알리고 있으므로 (B)가 정답이다. (B)가 정답이다.

184.
번역 메모에서, 첫 번째 단락 세 번째 줄의 "capacity"와 의미상 가장 가까운 것은?
(A) 기능
(B) 능력
(C) 용량
(D) 활기

해설 동의어
해당 문장은 '이들 개인은 자신의 분야에서 최고 위치에 있으며, 다른 사람들을 고무하고 동기부여 할 수 있는 능력이 있습니다(These individuals are at the top of their fields, and they have the capacity to inspire and motivate others)'라고 해석되고 여기서 capacity는 '능력'을 뜻한다. ability와 의미상 가까우므로 (B)가 정답이다.

185.
번역 누젠트 씨에 대해 암시된 것은?
(A) 시리즈에서 첫 번째로 발표를 할 것이다.
(B) 발표가 다른 날로 옮겨질 것이다.
(C) 수상자 후보로 지명되었다.
(D) 발표가 레미지오 비안치의 발표로 대체되었다.

해설 연계
이메일에서 '누젠트 씨가 포틀랜드 어워드에 지명이 되면 우리 강연 현장을 방문할 수 없게 됩니다. 이 때문에 일정이 겹치기 때문이죠(If she is nominated for the Portland Award, she won't be able to visit our site, as this creates a scheduling conflict)'라고 말했다. 그런데 메모의 발표 일정표를 보면 누젠트가 빠져 있다. 누젠트가 어워드에 지명되어 발표에 참석하지 못한 것으로 추론할 수 있으므로 (C)가 정답이다.

186-190 일정표+이메일

스프링 헤이븐 건강과 미용 박람회: 2월 3-4일, 컨벤션 센터
190총 만 명의 방문객 예상됨! 화장품 샘플, 메이크업 지도, 요리법 시범, 직접 사용해 보는 운동 장비 등의 일일 부스

2월 3일, 목요일
오전 10시-정오 / 스프링 헤이븐 병원에서 후원하는 무료 검진. 혈압, 콜레스테롤 수치, 신체 질량 지수를 의료 전문가에게 검사 받으세요.

오후 1시-4시 / 그랜트슨 퍼니처가 제공하는 '수면 습관 개선에 관한 조언.'
189-1킹사이즈 메트리스와 침대 틀 경품이 포함됩니다.

2월 4일, 금요일
오전 9시-정오 / 셀라던 스파에서 제공하는 어깨와 목 마사지. 10분간의 무료 마사지로 근육의 긴장을 사라지게 하세요. 공간이 제한되어 있기 때문에, **186행사 최소한 24시간 전에 회사의 웹 사이트에서 신청을 해야 합니다.**

189오후 2시-4시 / 에드워즈 안과에서 제공하는 '건강한 시력의 비결.' 나이가 들면서 시력을 유지해 나가기 위한 생활방식 변화에 관해 배우세요.

1월 5일에 최종 수정됨

수신: 질 리빙스턴 <j.livingston@grantsonfurniture.com>
발신: 페르난도 모라 <moraf@springhavenhbe.com>
날짜: 1월 17일
주제: 스프링 헤이븐 건강과 미용 박람회

187리빙스턴 씨께,

187요구하신 일정 변경에 관해 좋은 소식이 있습니다. 189에드워즈 안과 대표에게 얘기를 했더니, 기꺼이 그랜트슨 퍼니처와 시간대를 바꿔 주겠다고 했습니다. 그들은 액티비티를 위해 추가 시간을 갖게 된 것을 환영하고 있기 때문에, 처리가 아주 잘 된 겁니다. 최종 일정을 가지고 오늘 오후에 웹 사이트를 수정하려고 합니다. 또한, 올해 입장객 수와 관련해 말씀드리자면, **188저희 소셜 미디어 페이지 상의 수많은 확정 참가자 수로 미루어 작년보다 훨씬 많은 방문객이 올 것으로 보입니다.** 이번 주 말까지 모든 전시 참가 사에 최종 참가자 수치를 보내겠습니다.

페르난도 모라
행사 진행자, 스프링 헤이븐 건강과 미용 박람회

수신: 마르셀 바움 <m_baum@ruby-cosmetics.com>
발신: **190루시 서포크** <l_suffolk@ruby-cosmetics.com>
날짜: 1월 20일
주제: 다가오는 박람회

마르셀 씨께,

올해 스프링 헤이븐 건강과 미용 박람회에서 회사 부스 일에 협조할 수 있도록 동의해 주셔서 감사합니다. 행사 진행자에게 방금 이메일을 받았는데, **190원래 예상됐던 것보다 총 2000명 가량 더 많은 사람들이 참가할 것 같다고 합니다.** 모든 사람에게 하나씩 줄 수 있도록 충분한 샘플을 준비하려고 합니다. 이것으로도 충분하지 않을 수 있지만, 짧은 시간을 고려할 때 제가 할 수 있는 최선입니다.

루시

어휘 health screening 검진 get A (목적어)+과거분사 A를 ~되게 하다(수동) body mass index 신체 질량 지수(BMI) medical professional 의료 전문가, 전문 의료진 drawing 추첨, 제비뽑기 tension 긴장, (근육이) 팽팽하게 늘어난 상태 melt away 차츰 사라지다 complimentary 무료의 sign up 등록하다, 가입하다 prior to ~에 앞서 vision 시력 eyesight 시력 age 나이를 먹다 representative (단체를 대신하는) 대표 willing to 부정사 기꺼이 ~하는 switch 변경하다 time slot 시간대 appreciate 감사하다, 환영하다 work out (일이 성공적으로) 되어 가다 attendance 참석자 수 confirmed 확인된, 확정된 updated 최신의, 변경된 exhibitor 전시회 출품자, 참가자 time frame (어떤 일에 쓸 수 있는) 시간, 기간

186.

번역 셀라돈 스파의 액티비티에 대해 언급된 것은?
(A) 가장 인기 있는 행사이다.
(B) 참가자는 회비를 내야 한다.
(C) 4시간 걸릴 것이다.
(D) 사전 신청을 해야 한다.

해설 Not/true
일정표의 2월 4일 오전 행사에서, 셀라돈 스파의 마사지 행사를 소개하면서 '행사 최소한 24시간 전에 회사의 웹 사이트에서 신청을 해야 합니다(You must sign up on the company's Web site at least 24 hours prior to the event)'라고 했다. 사전 신청이 필수이므로 (D)가 정답이다. 오전 9시부터 정오까지 3시간 동안 진행되는, 10분간의 무료 마사지(complimentary ten-minute massage)이므로 (B)와 (C)는 언급되지 않은 진술이다.

Paraphrasing
지문의 must sign up on the company's Web site at least 24 hours prior to the event
→ 정답의 requires advance registration

187.

번역 리빙스턴 씨에 대해 명시된 것은?
(A) 행사에 참가하지 못할 것이다.
(B) 일정표 변경을 요청했다.
(C) 온라인 상의 세부사항을 수정해야 한다.
(D) 작년 박람회 때 부스를 열었다.

해설 Not/true
리빙스턴 씨에게 보내는 첫 번째 이메일이 '요구하신 일정 변경에 관해 좋은 소식이 있습니다(I have great news about the schedule change that you asked for)'라는 말로 시작된다. 일정표 변경을 이미 요청했음을 알 수 있으므로 (B)가 정답이다.

(C)의 경우 웹 사이트 상의 정보 수정(update our Web site this afternoon with the latest schedule) 얘기가, (D)의 경우 작년의 방문객(even more visitors than last year) 얘기가 나오지만, 모두 리빙스턴 씨와는 관계가 없는 진술이다.

188.

번역 첫 번째 이메일에서, 첫 번째 단락 여섯 번째 줄의 "tells"와 의미상 가장 가까운 것은?
(A) ~와 구분시키다
(B) ~에 대해 연설하다
(C) ~에게 정보를 주다
(D) ~을 찾다

해설 동의어
해당 문장은 '저희 소셜 미디어 페이지 상의 수많은 확정 참가자 수로 미루어 작년보다 훨씬 많은 방문객이 올 것으로 보입니다'라고 해석된다. 여기서 tells는 '~라는 것을 알려주다'라는 의미로 쓰였으므로 (C)가 정답이다.

189.

번역 상품 추첨은 언제 열릴 것 같은가?
(A) 목요일 아침
(B) 목요일 오후
(C) 금요일 아침
(D) 금요일 오후

해설 연계
'1월 5일에 최종 수정된(Updated January 5)' 일정표에서 보면, 그랜트슨 퍼니처가 제공하는 행사에 '킹사이즈 메트리스와 침대 틀 경품이 포함됩니다(Includes a drawing for a king-size mattress and bed frame)'라고 했고, 행사 시간은 목요일 오후로 되어 있다. 그런데, 첫 번째 이메일에 '에드워즈 안과 대표에게 얘기를 했더니, 기꺼이 그랜트슨 퍼니처와 시간대를 바꿔 주겠다고 말했습니다(I spoke to a representative at Edwards Eye Clinic, and he said that they would be willing to switch time slots with Grantson Furniture)'라는 내용이 나온다. 다시 일정표를 확인해 보면 에드워즈 안과 행사는 원래 금요일 오후로 되어 있다. 따라서 (D)가 정답이다.

190.

번역 서포크 씨는 얼마나 많은 샘플을 준비할 것 같은가?
(A) 2,000개
(B) 4,000개
(C) 10,000개
(D) 12,000개

해설 연계
일정표 맨 위에 '총 만 명의 방문객 예상됨(Ten thousand total visitors expected)'이라고 씌어 있다. 그런데 두 번째 이메일에서는 '원래 예상됐던 것보다 총 2000명 가량 더 많은 사람들이 참가할 것 같다고 합니다(about 2,000 more people in total will be attending than originally expected)'라며 샘플 준비에 관해 걱정하고 있다. 만 명에서 2,000명이 추가되어 샘플을 12,000개 준비해야 하므로 (D)가 정답이다.

191-195 광고+이메일+사용 후기

패리아스 커피 메이커: 완벽한 커피를 맛보세요!

모든 패리아스 커피 메이커는 각기 다른 맛의 캡슐을 사용해 필요에 따라 다양한 커피와 차를 만들어 냅니다. 이제 원하시는 고급 커피를 집에서 마실 수 있습니다!

패리아스 쁘띠뜨: 작은 주방 전용으로 디자인된, 저희 기계의 소형 버전 / 99.99달러
패리아스 셀렉트: 광물질 침전물을 줄이기 위해 자동 청소 사이클 기능 포함 / 129.99달러
패리아스 비아: 패리아스 비아(미리 끓임)는 기계에 미리 준비해 두었다가 스마트폰으로 시동할 수 있음. / 149.99달러
패리아스 모닝: 195두 개의 캡슐로 별개 컵에서 동시에 커피를 내림. 바쁜 가족들에게 아주 좋음. / 169.99달러

모든 기계의 입수 가능한 색상: 미드나잇 블랙(#101), 전통 은색(#117), 복고 빨간색(#119), 191크림빛 진주색(#134)

수신: 데보라 시몬스 〈simmonsd@crowndeptstore.com〉
발신: 193잭 헤레라 〈j.herrera@fariasappliances.com〉
날짜: 8월 8일
주제: 패리아스 커피 메이커

194시몬스 씨께,

194당신은 매장 책임자로서 저희 공급과 관련된 모든 변화를 알고 계셔야 할 것입니다. 191당장 오늘부터, 저희는 모든 패리아스 가전제품에 대해 134번 컬러 제품의 생산을 중단합니다. 공급 계약에 따르면 저희는 고객들에게 지속적인 지원을 해 줘야 합니다. 192영업부장 미셸 비크리 씨가 8월 15일에 당신의 매장을 방문하라고 제게 요청했습니다. 패리아스 비아 사용 시범을 보이기 위해서인데요, 이 제품은 일부 고객들이 사용자 설명서를 읽음에도 불구하고 사용하기 어렵다고 느끼고 있습니다. 사실, 이 업무는 레이먼드 페리 씨에게 할당되었지만, 193저도 함께 가서 당신이 제품들을 눈길을 끌게 전시해서 진열할 수 있도록 도울 수 있게 되어 기쁩니다. 그 밖에 그 매장에서 필요한 것이 있다면, 알려 주십시오.

잭 헤레라
사우스웨스트 제품 지원부, 패리아스

---

www.crowndeptstore.com/customerfeedback

사용자 이름: joe77   게시일: 8월 31일

의견: 저는 크라운 백화점에서 항상 받고 있는 고객 서비스가 마음에 듭니다. 최근에는 커피 메이커를 사러 그곳에 갔는데요. 모든 영업사원들이 바빴습니다. 194하지만 매장 책임자가 제가 기다리는 것을 알아채고는, 저를 도와 주었습니다. 그분의 조언이 제가 어떤 모델을 살지 결정하는 데 도움이 되었습니다. 195결국 패리아스 모닝 커피 메이커를 골랐는데, 마음에 들어요! 저는 이 제품과 당신의 매장을 다른 사람들에게 추천할 겁니다.

어휘 brew (커피, 차를) 끓이다, (끓여 낸) 커피 individual 각각의, 1인용의 flavor 맛, 향 pod 1회용 커피 캡슐 on demand 요청 시, 필요하면 compact 소형의, 조밀한 exclusively 독점적으로, 오로지 feature 특징으로 하다, 포함하다 mineral 광물질 buildup 축적, 침전물 preload 사전에 설치하다 [장착하다] simultaneously 동시에 classic 전형적인,

고전적인 retro 복고풍의 creamy 크림색의 stay informed (상황 등을) 잘 알고 있다 effective (~부터) 효력을 발휘하는 discontinue (생산을) 중단하다 appliances 가전 제품 ongoing 지속적인 demonstration (사용 방법 등을 시범으로 보여주는) 설명 arrange 배열하다, 정돈하다 eye-catching 눈길을 끄는 sales representative 영업사원 end up -ing 결국 ~하게 되다

191.

번역 패리아스는 어떤 색깔의 커피 메이커를 더 이상 만들지 않는가?
(A) 미드나잇 블랙
(B) 전통 은색
(C) 복고 빨간색
(D) 크림빛 진주색

해설 연계
이메일에서 '당장 오늘부터, 저희는 모든 패리아스 가전제품에 대해 134번 컬러 제품의 생산을 중단합니다(Effective immediately, we have discontinued color #134 for all Farias appliances)'라고 말했는데, 광고의 마지막 줄에서 보면 134번 컬러가 크림빛 진주색으로 되어 있다. 따라서 (D)가 정답이다.

192.

번역 이메일에서, 첫 번째 단락 네 번째 줄의 "asked"와 의미상 가장 가까운 것은?
(A) 요청했다
(B) 조사했다
(C) 질문했다
(D) 요구했다

해설 동의어
해당 문장은 '영업부장 미셸 비크리 씨가 8월 15일에 당신의 가게를 방문하라고 제게 요청했습니다'라고 해석된다. 여기서 ask는 '요청하다, 부탁하다'라는 의미로 쓰였으므로 '(~하라고) 요청하다, 청하다'를 뜻하는 invite와 같은 의미이다. 따라서 (A)가 정답이다.

193.

번역 헤레라 씨는 무엇을 하겠다고 제안하는가?
(A) 사용 설명서를 보내겠다고
(B) 시범 설명을 해 주겠다고
(C) 단절된 제품을 환불해 주겠다고
(D) 진열을 해 주겠다고

해설 세부사항
이메일에서 '저도 함께 가서 당신이 제품들을 눈길을 끌게 전시해서 진열할 수 있도록 도울 수 있게 되어 기쁩니다(I'm happy to come along as well to help you arrange the products in an eye-catching display)'라고 말했으므로 (D)가 정답이다.

Paraphrasing
지문의 arrange the products in an eye-catching display → 정답의 Set up a display

194.

번역 시몬스 씨에 대해 명시된 것은?
(A) 최근에 계약을 갱신했다.
(B) 후기 쓴 사람이 결정을 하도록 도와 주었다.
(C) 세일즈 팀의 팀장이다.
(D) 헤레라 씨에게 조언을 요청했다.

해설 연계
사용 후기를 쓴 사람이 '매장 책임자가 제가 기다리는 것을 알아채고는, 저를 도와 주었습니다. 그분의 조언이 제가 어떤 모델을 살지 결정하는 데 도움이 되었습니다(the store manager noticed I was waiting, so she assisted me. Her advice helped me to decide which model to buy)'라고 했다. 그리고 패리아스에서 시몬스 씨에게 보내는 이메일에서는 '당신은 매장 책임자로서 저희 공급과 관련된 모든 변화를 알고 계셔야 할 것입니다(As the store manager, ~)'라고 말했다. 즉, 후기 쓴 사람은 매장 책임자의 도움을 받았고, 그 매장 책임자는 바로 시몬스 씨이므로 (B)가 정답이다.

195.

번역 후기 쓴 사람이 구입한 제품에 대해 사실인 것은?
(A) 스마트폰으로 가동시킬 수 있다.
(B) 한 번에 한 잔 이상을 만들 수 있다.
(C) 스스로 청소하는 특별 기능을 가지고 있다.
(D) 패리아스에서 판매하는 것 중 가장 작은 모델이다.

해설 Not/true
후기에서 '결국 패리아스 모닝 커피 메이커를 골랐는데(I ended up purchasing a Farias Morning coffee maker)'라고 말했는데, 광고에서 보면 패리아스 모닝 커피 메이커가 '두 개의 캡슐로 별개 컵에서 동시에 커피를 내림(Brews two pods simultaneously in separate cups)'이라고 상품 설명이 되어 있다. 따라서 (B)가 정답이다.

196-200 기사+이메일+지도

5월 14일 – '전국 식품 상'을 두 차례 수상한 엣지웨이가 소비자를 위한 또 다른 아이디어를 가지고 다시 돌아왔다. **196**이 회사는 미스티 브루 출시를 발표했는데, 물과 섞여 인스턴트 아이스 커피를 만드는 농축 커피 믹스이다. 전국 커피 체인점에서 아이스 음료가 점차 인기를 얻자, 엣지웨이의 CEO 샌드라 잭슨 씨는 회사 연구팀이 이 추세에 맞게 무언가를 개발하기를 원했다. **197**얼마 안 있어 그들은 이 인기 있는 음료를 신속하고 편리한 형태로 사람들의 가정에 가져다 줄 수 있는 방법을 생각해 냈다. **198**독특하고 독창적인 상품으로 명성이 있는 엣지웨이가 요즘 소비자들의 요구에 부응하는 고급 식품과 음료를 계속 출시하는 것이 놀라운 일이 아니다.

엣지웨이는 잡지와 소셜 미디어를 통해 집중적으로 광고하는 것은 물론, 고객들에게 음료를 무료로 시음하게 함으로써 더운 여름철을 기회로 이용할 계획이다. 출시 과정의 일환으로, 이 회사에서는 **199**전국적으로 슈퍼마켓에 미스티 브루 샘플을 나눠주기 위해 단기적으로 수백 명 인력을 고용했다.

수신: 토니 오거스타 〈augustat@bensengrocery.com〉
발신: **199, 200**리안 쿠퍼 〈r_cooper@edgeway.net〉
날짜: 5월 27일
주제: 업소 방문

오거스타 씨께,

199엣지웨이가 신제품 미스티 브루 음료 무료 샘플을 배분할 수 있도록 자리를 제공하기로 합의해 주셔서 감사합니다. 이 일을 수행하기 위해서 6월 2일과 3일에 제가 벤센 식품을 방문하겠습니다. 매장에서 물을 사용할 필요는 없을 것 같습니다. 하지만 물과 믹스를 차갑게 하는 데 사용될 미니 냉장고가 있기 때문에, 전원 콘센트 접근이 필요할 겁니다. 가장 좋은 위치가 스낵 및 음료 복도 근처일 거라고 원래 생각하셨는데요. 하지만, **200**저는 시리얼 같은 아침 식사거리 근처가 사실 더 좋을 것 같습니다. 저희 제품이 주로 아침에 이용되기 때문입니다. 또한, 너무 북적거릴 거라는 생각이 들어서 계산대에 너무 가까운 것도 원하지 않습니다.

6월 2일에 직접 만나 뵙기를 기대합니다!

라이언 쿠퍼

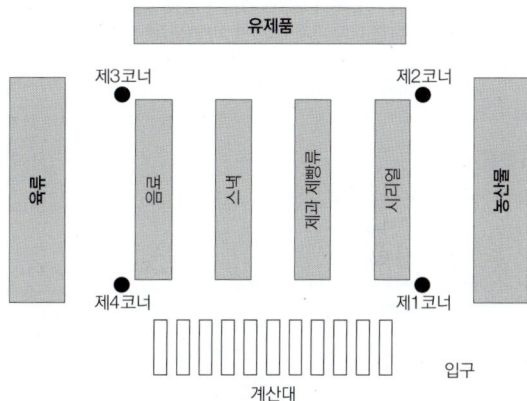

어휘 launch 출시 concentrated 농축된 combine 결합시키다 work out 생각해 내다 reputation 평판, 명성 meet the needs 수요를 충족시키다 take advantage of ~을 (기회로) 이용하다 on a short-term basis 단기적으로 give out 나눠 주다 distribute 분배하다, 나눠 주다 carry out 수행하다 power outlet 전원 콘센트 chill 차게 식히다 placement 배치, 위치 aisle 통로 checkout 계산대

196.

번역 기사를 쓴 이유는 무엇인가?
(A) 음료의 맛을 평가하기 위해
(B) 수상자를 발표하기 위해
(C) 신제품을 소개하기 위해
(D) 소비자 보고서를 설명하기 위해

해설 **주제/목적**
기사 첫 번째 단락에서 '이 회사는 미스티 브루 출시를 발표했는데, 물과 섞여 인스턴트 아이스 커피를 만드는 농축 커피 믹스이다(The company has announced the launch of Misty Brew, a concentrated coffee mix that can be combined with water to make instant iced coffee)'라는 말로 신제품 출시를 알린 후 개발 배경을 설명했고, 두 번째 단락에서는 신제품 홍보 방식을 얘기했다. 따라서 (C)가 정답이다.

197.

번역 기사에서, 첫 번째 단락 열세 번째 줄의 "worked out"과 의미상 가장 가까운 것은?
(A) 평가했다
(B) 고안해 냈다
(C) 개요를 설명했다
(D) 운동했다

해설 **동의어**
해당 문장은 '얼마 안 있어 그들은 이 인기 있는 음료를 신속하고 편리한 형태로 사람들의 가정에 가져다 줄 수 있는 방법을 생각해 냈다'라고 해석된다 여기서 worked out은 '생각해 내다'라는 뜻으로 쓰였으므로 '고안하다'를 뜻하는 devised와 의미상 비슷하다. 따라서 (B)가 정답이다.

198.

번역 엣지웨이에 대해 명시된 것은?
(A) 독창적인 아이디어로 잘 알려져 있다.
(B) 국내 최대의 식품 회사이다.
(C) 최근에 새로운 CEO를 고용했다.
(D) 음료만 판매한다.

해설 **Not/true**
기사 첫 번째 단락에서 '독특하면서 독창적인 상품으로 명성이 있는 엣지웨이가 요즘 소비자들의 요구에 부응하는 고급 식품과 음료를 계속 출시하는 것이 놀라운 일이 아니다(With its reputation for unique and innovative products, ~ that meet the needs of today's consumers)'라고 말했으므로 (A)가 정답이다. 수상 경력이 있고 독창적인 기업이라고 했을 뿐 규모에 대한 언급은 없으므로 (B)는 답이 아니다.

Paraphrasing
지문의 its reputation for unique and innovative goods
→ 정답의 known for its creative ideas

199.

번역 쿠퍼 씨에 대해 암시된 것은?
(A) 상점을 세 차례 방문할 것이다.
(B) 그는 임시 고용인이다.
(C) 수도꼭지가 근처에 있어야 한다.
(D) 전에 벤센 식품에서 일했다.

해설 **연계**
쿠퍼 씨가 이메일에서 '엣지웨이가 신제품 미스티 브루 음료 무료 샘플을 배분할 수 있도록 자리를 제공하기로 합의해 주셔서 감사합니다. 이 일을 수행하기 위해서 6월 2일과 3일에 제가 벤센 식품을 방문하겠습니다(Thank you for agreeing to provide a space for Edgeway to distribute free samples of our new Misty Brew drink. I will visit Bensen Grocery~)'라고 했는데, 기사의 마지막 문장에 보면 엣지웨이가 '샘플을 나눠 주기 위해 단기적으로 수백 명 인력을 고용했다'라고 나와 있다. 쿠퍼 씨가 그 단기 고용 인력임을 알 수 있으므로 (B)가 정답이다.

200.

번역 쿠퍼 씨는 어디에 배치되기를 원할 것 같은가?
(A) 제1코너
(B) 제2코너
(C) 제3코너
(D) 제4코너

해설 **추론**
쿠퍼 씨가 원하는 조건으로 '시리얼 같은 아침 식사거리 근처(near breakfast foods, such as cereal)'를 들었고 '계산대에 너무 가까운 것도 원하지 않습니다(I don't want to be too close to the checkout area)'라고 했으므로 (B)가 정답이다.